THE QUAKERS

THE QUAKERS

HUGH BARBOUR
and
J. WILLIAM FROST

Denominations in America, Number 3

Greenwood Press
New York • Westport, Connecticut • London

BX
7731.2
.B37
1988

Library of Congress Cataloging-in-Publication Data

Barbour, Hugh.
    The Quakers / Hugh Barbour and J. William Frost.
        p.   cm. — (Denominations in America, ISSN 0193–6883 ; no. 3)
    Bibliography: p.
    Includes index.
    ISBN 0–313–22816–7 (lib. bdg. : alk. paper)
    1. Society of Friends.   2. Society of Friends—United States.
3. Quakers—United States—Biography.   I. Frost, J. William (Jerry
William)   II. Title.   III. Series.
BX7731.2.B37   1988
289.6′73—dc19   88–10240

British Library Cataloguing in Publication Data is available.

Library of Congress Catalog Card Number: 88–10240
ISBN: 0–313–22816–7
ISSN: 0193–6883

First published in 1988

Greenwood Press, Inc.
88 Post Road West, Westport, Connecticut 06881

Printed in the United States of America

∞

The paper used in this book complies with the
Permanent Paper Standard issued by the National
Information Standards Organization (Z39.48–1984).

10   9   8   7   6   5   4   3   2   1

For Thomas and Mary Ellen Frost
For Ian Barbour
In memory of Freeland Barbour

CONTENTS

ILLUSTRATIONS

SERIES FOREWORD

The Greenwood Press series of denominational studies follows a distinguished precedent. These current volumes improve on earlier works by including more churches than before and by looking at all of them in a wider cultural context. The prototype for this series appeared almost a century ago. Between 1893 and 1897 twenty-four scholars collaborated in publishing thirteen volumes known popularly as the American Church History Series. Those scholars found twenty religious groups to be worthy of separate treatment, either as major sections of a volume or as whole books in themselves. Scholars in this current series have found that outline to be unrealistic, with regional subgroups no longer warranting separate status and others having declined to marginality. Twenty organizations in the earlier series survive as nine in this collection, and two churches and an interdenominational bureau have been omitted. The old series also excluded some important churches of that time; others have gained great strength since then. So today a new list of denominations, rectifying imbalance and recognizing modern significance, features many groups not included a century ago. The solid core of the old series remains in this new one, and in the present case a wider range of topics makes the study of denominational life in America more inclusive.

Some recent denominational histories have improved with greater attention to primary sources and more rigorous scholarly standards. But they have too frequently pursued themes for internal consumption alone. Volumes in the Greenwood Press series strive to surmount such parochialism while remaining grounded in the specific materials of concrete ecclesiastical traditions. They avoid placing a single denomination above others in its distinctive truth claims, ethical norms, and liturgical patterns. Instead, they set the history of each church in the larger religious and social context that shaped the emergence of notable denominational features. In this way the authors in this series help us understand the interaction that has occurred between different churches and the broader aspects of American culture.

Each of the historical studies in this current series has a strong biographical focus, using the real-life experiences of men and women in church life to highlight significant elements of an unfolding sequence. The first part of every volume singles out important watershed issues that affected a denomination's outlook and discusses the roles of those who influenced the flow of events. The second part consists of biographical sketches, featuring those persons and many others who contributed to the vitality of their religious heritage. This format enables authors to emphasize the distinctive features of their chosen subject and at the same time to recognize the sharp particularities of individual attributes in the cumulative richness that their denomination possesses.

This book by J. William Frost and Hugh Barbour, professors at Swarthmore and Earlham colleges, respectively, provides a remarkable synthesis of information related to the Society of Friends. Its focus is on the North American continent, as are all in this series, but it does not imply that the people otherwise known as Quakers are primarily an American phenomenon. This study acknowledges that England was the site of the group's formative years, and Great Britain has remained an important center of what now constitutes a global religious network. By concentrating on the American segment of this intercontinental story the authors expound Quaker experience in Pennsylvania and other seaboard colonies. After covering relatively familiar materials with great attention to detailed accuracy and balanced judgments, the book really comes into its own. Frost and Barbour go beyond customary narratives of denominational controversies and increased parochialism to show that nineteenth- and twentieth-century Quakers have remained a dynamic, energetic, and creative people. Part of the story relates geographical expansion throughout the Middle West and to the Pacific Coast. Another part describes Quaker response to larger cultural questions such as peace and war, social justice, and intellectual changes prompted by new developments in the sciences and humanities. The authors survey the entire life span of their church, from inception to contemporary times, and bring us up to date on a group that is both quietistic in personal devotions and passionately committed to the broader issues of community welfare.

HENRY WARNER BOWDEN

PREFACE

This book on Quakers in America, a survey of the movement from 1650 to 1987, is written for college students, scholars, and others seeking to understand the origins and evolution of the Society of Friends. Like the other volumes in this series, Part Two provides biographies of those people whose lives and actions particularly shaped American Quakerism. We have omitted equally important Friends in Europe, Asia, and Africa as well as all those still alive in 1988. We include also maps showing the growth of American Quakerism to 1890 and a chart of Yearly Meeting membership mainly since that date (also a date chart for clarity).

After initial chapters dealing with the genesis and early events and outlooks of Friends in seventeenth-century England, this book turns to colonial America and later mainly to the United States. British Quakers since 1700 are mentioned only for their impact on American Friends. The last comprehensive book on American Quaker history was printed in 1942. Since then more than a hundred scholars have explored many facets of Quaker life. This book covers all major branches of American Quakerism and is the first attempt to synthesize their twentieth-century trends and their relation to developments in the wider American culture. Friends have confronted more openly than most churches the new problems raised by war, slavery, revolution, migration, and social injustice and have felt free to share in worship experiences and doctrines of non-Quaker evangelicals and liberals. They do not always know how much they absorbed at each stage from non-Quakers. We first summarize the life of the Quaker community and then look more widely at the times and cultures in which they lived.

This book has been a collaborative work, but most chapters on English and midwestern Friends were drafted by Hugh Barbour and those on colonial and northeastern America by J. William Frost. We acknowledge gratefully those who helped us: The Rowntree Trust and Woodbrooke College in England gave Barbour a grant and hospitality for autumn 1982 to review recent work on seventeenth-century England, and Earlham College gave him two Faculty Development Grants for recent summers. A leave from Swarthmore College gave Frost time for research and writing. The staffs of Earlham College Library and of Friends Historical Library at Swarthmore College provided valuable assistance. Jane Thorson typed many versions of one-half of the manuscript. Claire Shetter, Pat O'Donnell, and Nancy Speers checked numerous details. Eleanor Stabler Clarke, Wilmer Cooper, Earle Edwards, Albert Fowler, Thomas Hamm, Mary Hoxie Jones, Jack Kirk, Jack Sutters, Steven Thiermann, Elizabeth Gray Vining, Richard Wood, and many Earlham and Swarthmore students read one or more chapters and by their own research gave us insights. Earlham students who worked on the maps were Laura Hoeckel, Tom Page, Rich Neff, Melinda Morton, Matt Wilson, and Patrick Lacey. Most of all, our wives have been patient for long years.

Part One
THE QUAKERS: A HISTORY OF FRIENDS IN AMERICA

1
INTRODUCTION: THE
SOCIETY OF FRIENDS

A benevolent old man in a broad-brim black hat, beaming out from a box of oats, is the best-known icon of a Quaker. Most educated Americans know other images: William Penn* shakes hands with the Indians; a plain-dressed couple helps a runaway slave to freedom across the Ohio River; Gary Cooper refuses to fight in the Civil War (in the movie *Friendly Persuasion*); Elizabeth Fry* preaches to inmates at Newgate prison; Edward Hicks* paints *The Peaceable Kingdom*. Since Quakers are linked to Pennsylvania as Puritans are to Massachusetts, car license plates of the "Quaker state" (it's a motor oil too) pun that "you've got a Friend in Pennsylvania." The name Quaker is misfitted to a whiskey, an exterminating company, football teams, and a string band. After sixty-nine such entries in the Philadelphia telephone book, the last one is "Quakers—see Friends, Religious Society of," the subject of this book.

The Quaker reality is today diverse, though rooted in a unifying tradition and inner life: silent worship in a 300-year-old meetinghouse; a revival meeting in a cathedral-like midwestern Quaker church; a hundred thousand African Friends in Kenyan villages; thirty Quaker boarding schools and fifteen colleges in ten nations; and Friends Service Committees deeply involved in the crises of American, English, Canadian, and South African society. Quakers are at home in twenty-five languages, but outside Africa and Hispanic America most think in English. George Fox* established their gathering place in London in the 1650s. By now they have spread to forty-six countries on six continents, but nearly half of all Quakers live in the United States, and their evolution since 1700 centered here. Most literate Americans know east coast Quakers rather than the two-thirds of the 120,000 American Friends who live west of the Appalachians.

Quakers recorded unusually directly their individual religious experiences: the

---

Quakers whose names are asterisked (*) (when first mentioned and in the index) are those whose biography is included in Part Two.

heart of the Quaker movement has been the "meeting for worship." For 300 years Friends have sat in outward silence as each person would pray, meditate, or "listen to the Light of God" within himself or herself and within the group. Until recently, their only "ministry" rose out of such "listening," when any member of the group felt led inwardly to offer a specific message, prayer, or song. Individuals who "appeared in ministry" often and helpfully were "recorded" and invited to sit on the "facing bench" at the front of the meetinghouse, along with the men or women "Elders" who provided guidance and counsel for the Meeting community.

Quaker group life rises out of a religious process. Traditionally, Friends have regarded each ethical standard as "Truth" and have shared positive "Testimonies" of living in honesty, equality, simplicity, and peace. The congregation as a "meeting for business" hopes, in a decision about their responsibilities or their personal life, to share a common "leading," avoiding both individualism and majority rule. Until about 1850, Quakers used distinctively plain meetinghouses, homes, and clothing to cut down human pride and distractions.

The Quaker movement broke early with the traditions of most Christians, in rejecting creeds, sacraments, and priesthood. Their stands reflected a negative experience with church institutions, notably in seventeenth-century England. National or regional gatherings of Friends gave them enough unity and uniformity. Members who felt led to visit other Meetings, and to speak or give counsel and support there, were given a "traveling minute" stating the home Meeting's endorsement of their trip. Meetings undertook financial support for travelers, as well as for the widows, orphans, bankrupt, and poor within and around Meetings.

Friends checked their own inward "leadings" against the Bible and the consensus of "weighty Friends" in the past and of those present in their Meeting. On ethical norms, a "discipline" process evolved to restrain or "disown" members who erred or seemed misled or a discredit to "truth." With no fixed authority more ultimate than the Spirit, however, Friends at different periods accepted as "truth" many norms of their immediate culture and era. Major Quaker groups therefore moved apart and emphasized in various places and times different doctrines and practices from their Quaker heritage.

QUAKERISM IN ENGLAND

The Society of Friends formed as a culmination to and reaction against the Protestant Reformation. Martin Luther and sixteenth-century Calvinism shaped Quaker beliefs in the seventeenth-century: that humans are "justified" by God's grace, not human merit; that all believers share a mutual priesthood; and that God's word both in the Scriptures and by the Spirit in human hearts demands primacy over human ideas and desires. Quaker life was also shaped by European Anabaptists and English Baptists, who rejected the Reformers' beliefs in predestination, infant baptism, and nationwide churches and who saw the essence of Christianity as obedience to God's demands for purity of heart, honesty, simple dress, and separation from the state and war-making.

Much of Quakerism can best be understood as growing out of Puritanism. Between 1530 and 1630 the national Church of England had been turned from Catholic to Anglo-Catholic by Henry VIII and then back to Catholicism and to Anglicanism again by his successors. The Bible in English, Puritan ethics, and Calvinist theology gave conviction to most of the active laity and clergy. In the 1630s King Charles I refused to reform the established Church and harried the Puritans, many of whom left to set up a new and godly Commonwealth in New England. The rest prepared to make England itself over on a similar pattern, once the years of deadlock ended in the defeat of King Charles I in Civil Wars in 1642–49. Amid immense social upheaval, the English reexamined their beliefs about religious authority, the roles of sacraments and clergy, the Scriptures, the power of the Spirit, and their hopes for the millennium. Early Quakers knew and used the ideas of radical Puritans.

George Fox's preaching in the North of England in 1652 began a regional Awakening among unchurched moorlanders. They drew upon the religious and social discontent, as the victorious alliance of radical and conservative Puritans under Oliver Cromwell could not agree on or achieve a God-ordained pattern of justice and religious and political liberty. The Quakers renewed the Puritans' struggle against evil and their confidence in sharing God's worldwide victory but now saw the center of "the Lamb's War" as within human hearts. Simple worship and new ways of honesty and equality in personal life created strong Quaker groups, who believed they were called as "the Camp of the Lord" to be the vanguard of the Spirit's conquest of the world. In twos and threes Quakers traveled throughout England and to Europe and New England to confront evil and gather the "convinced," the "Children of Light," into meetings, despite fierce opposition.

With the restoration of the English monarchy in 1660 came twenty years of severe persecution over worship itself that threw at least a tenth of the 50,000 Friends into prison. Internal tensions about Quaker organization forced Friends to change. Robert Barclay sought to clearly define Quaker beliefs. William Penn expressed a new Quaker universalism as he dealt with lawyers, judges, and court officials and tried to persuade Parliaments to endorse toleration. After 1670 Friends' emphasis began to shift from conquest to survival. Although the Meetings of Friends in England and America still grew, and their early sense of the world mission of "Truth" remained, it became clear that "the Children of Light" would not replace the Church of England. The Camp of the Lord became the Society of Friends.

After toleration came in 1689 English Quakers learned also to see themselves as one of the Nonconformist sects and sought and achieved peace, quiet, order, and prosperity. Quakers intermarried often and stressed family life. They formed stable urban communities, regulated by Monthly and Yearly Meetings. The wealth of Quaker merchants and bankers did not lead to relaxation of "plainness.'' Their business and scientific acumen earned admiration and their customs of dress, speech, and marriage seemed eccentric but not threatening. Silent worship, traveling ''ministers,'' extemporaneous (but not brief) preaching, reports to and from Yearly Meeting sessions, Epistles to the American Meetings, and after 1690 the traditional Christian doctrines on sin and Christ's death characterized eighteenth-century English Quakers.

IN THE AMERICAN COLONIES

In the 1650s twenty traveling Quaker prophets carried their message throughout the English New World settlements. In areas of Maryland, Virginia, and Carolina where there were few clergy or churches, Quaker meetings gathered a substantial minority of the population. Authorities from New England to Virginia persecuted Quakers who attacked their communities' religious and political ideals. The most violent confrontations took place in Massachusetts, where the Puritans executed four Quaker ministers. In this second milieu, most converts to Quakerism lived in outlying villages of the puritan colonies: Cape Cod, Rhode Island, Maine, and Long Island. When George Fox visited America from 1671 to 1673 he helped standardize the practices of the Meetings and Yearly Meetings.

When Friends set up West New Jersey in 1675 and Pennsylvania in 1681, a third kind of Quaker community arose, as English, Irish, and Welsh Friends came to these new colonies. William Penn's ''Holy Experiment'' repeated there the English Quaker ways of life and worship and pattern of Meetings, but Quaker settlers had to learn how to deal with legal, social, and religious power. Political clashes with Penn and the English government and religious hatreds stemming from the schism over George Keith kept the Delaware Valley Quakers in turmoil until the end of the seventeenth century. England's ''Glorious Revolution'' of 1688 and the resurgence of the Church of England in the colonies put American Friends on the defensive. The tendering of oaths of office in Maryland and the Carolinas ended Quaker political power there. New Jersey became a Crown colony where Friends experienced no persecution and kept their right to sit in the Assembly. Where Quakers lost political power their communities became tighter knit within themselves. In New England the Puritans eased restrictions on Friends to gain their support against Anglican power.

Pennsylvania remained the most prominent Quaker colony. Quakers kept their political power despite efforts of the Proprietors, Crown, and Church of England. After 1720 the Quakers learned to compromise their differences for stability. They intended Pennsylvania as a refuge of religious liberty for all, yet expected their distinctive beliefs against arms and oaths would become the consensus of everyone. Quaker leaders and politicians identified their concerns with the colony's and claimed credit for the peace and prosperity of the region.

Eighteenth-century Friends, unlike those in the 1650s, described their spiritual life in the language of moderate rationalism or of quietistic purity. Quietism stressed the complete subordination of self-will in the meeting for worship and in daily life. English and American Quakers traveled to knit their transatlantic community. Adult and young Friends were to be sheltered in the discovered Truth and to continue what had been established, not to strike out on their own. Yearly Meeting books of Discipline provided regulations for spiritual life, Meeting procedures, and conduct: speech, dress, furniture, marriage, wills, taxes, and especially the "guarded education" of children. These "Testimonies" structured a Quaker's life from birth until death. The spontaneity, exuberance, creativity, and individualism of early Quakerism were now subordinated to steady habits.

The harmony of Quaker life dissipated after 1750 under stresses caused by slavery, war, wealth, and efforts at reform. John Woolman* and others who tried to rethink Friends' role in society and resist the norms of most colonial Americans made creative innovations modifying inherited Testimonies. Friends decided that slavery was an immoral institution. They expanded the meaning of the Peace Testimony, grappled with the conflict between holding government power and obedience to God, and debated war taxes. Quakers worked to reconcile Indians and whites and to civilize Indians in English ways. Faced with a loss of religious depth that seemed due to accommodation to "the world," Meetings enforced a stricter definition of Quaker life. Through and after the Revolutionary era, they purged dissenting members over pacifism or intermarriage: internal purity outweighed numerical growth. Friends in the North and South united to oppose the slave trade and then slave-owning, freeing their own slaves. (In 1796 Philadelphia Friends finally allowed blacks to become full members). The 1770s brought special trauma for Philadelphia Friends. Their political power came to an ignominious end in a war for independence that Quakers opposed. By 1783 they were slowly making peace and "lobbying" with new American governments, but American Quakers now refused to hold office. Compared with their character in 1750 the Religious Society of Friends—the name they adopted as official—was now far more self-contained, withdrawn, and consistent, in a word sectarian. Outsiders saw Friends as one of many religious denominations, dominant in no state but tolerated in all despite suspicion of their pacifism and in the South of their antislavery stance. Quakers entered the new nation still numerically strong, with self-chosen new roles as keepers of the nation's conscience and dedicated to doing good for others.

IN NINETEENTH-CENTURY AMERICA

The migration that brought Friends to America continued after their first settlements on the east coast. After 1750 many moved into upper New York and New England, into western Pennsylvania and Virginia, and south to the piedmont hills of the Carolinas. After the Revolution some went west into Canada and Tennessee. Large wagon trains went into the "free soil" of eastern and southwestern Ohio and Indiana; later Quaker generations settled in Iowa and Kansas and finally in Oregon and California. Southern Quakers had felt divinely led to move to the Ohio Valley as they became alienated from slave culture; otherwise the primary push to move was economic: midwest and prairie farmland was richer and cheaper than New England's and Pennsylvania's. Quakers moved and settled as cohesive groups; migrants kept affiliations with home Meetings until new Monthly and Yearly Meetings were formed. Quaker primary and secondary schools were linked to each Meeting. By 1835 Indiana's 30,000 members were the largest Yearly Meeting, although Philadelphia remained the American Quaker cultural center.

Quakers, like other church communities, found after 1820 that their unity in worship and theology had evaporated. Sharp clashes on evangelical doctrines, the authority of Elders and the Discipline, and antislavery tactics led to the "Hicksite"–"Orthodox" separation in 1827–28. Quietist majorities in both groups were thus fractured by a division that reached down from Yearly Meetings into local communities. Among the theologically "Orthodox" a second split named for John Wilbur* of Rhode Island reflected quietist unease at the activist programs of Bible study and evangelical tract and mission work by Quakers. An English Quaker banker, Joseph John Gurney*, on a long American visit, encouraged these active "Gurneyite" programs. "Wilburite" conservatives in New England, Philadelphia, Ohio, and Indiana kept their isolation from the wider culture and in dress, in their schools, and at home kept many Quaker customs into the twentieth century. The three main bodies of American Quakerism, though maintaining Meeting schools and service programs, were thus paralyzed by schisms and conflicts from 1827 until after the Civil War, although individuals like Lucretia Mott* and John Greenleaf Whittier* made major national contributions to women's rights and to end slavery.

From the Revolution to the Civil War, Quakers debated effective ways to abolish slavery. They formed or joined manumission and colonization societies, petitioned Congress, and opened schools for blacks. Levi Coffin* in Indiana and Thomas Garrett* in Delaware earned fame helping fugitive slaves escape by "the Underground Railroad," although some Quakers disapproved of their work. A minority of Friends were radical abolitionists, but most Meetings warned members against cooperating with non-Quakers who did not use Quaker methods against evil. The Civil War challenged Friends to rethink their roles in society.

"Orthodox" Friends, whether following Gurney or Wilbur, had identified Quakerism with evangelical doctrine by 1827 but were wary of the "new methods" of revivalism and the "holiness" doctrines of complete and sudden perfection taught by evangelists among non-Friends. In response to quietism, and amid a sense of the breakdown of the Quaker Discipline during the Civil War, however, a Sunday-school movement and revivals broke out in midwestern "Gurneyite" Quaker Meetings from 1867, with a peak in 1877, which brought revival methods and "holiness" doctrines into evangelical Quakerism along with a new concern for foreign missions. Ohio Friend David Updegraff and others learned from Presbyterians, Baptists, and Methodists that revivals won many commitments by hymns, altar-calls, and "protracted" or "general meetings."

When Ohio evangelicals rejected the universality of the Inward Light and baptized adult converts, a conference of "Orthodox" Quakers in 1887 at Richmond, Indiana, drew up a Declaration of Faith opposing their teachings, although accepting new patterns of pastoral ministry and "programed worship."

THE TWENTIETH CENTURY

The "Orthodox" Friends gathering at Richmond agreed to form a joint board for foreign missions and by 1902 a Five Years Meeting including most "Gurneyites" under a uniform Discipline. The representatives at Richmond in 1887 from London, Philadelphia, and the Ohio "Gurneyites," however, could not persuade their Yearly Meetings to enter these programs. Western and midwestern evangelical Quakers now became more socially conservative as they faced ideas and temptations of urban and suburban life. Most evangelical Yearly Meetings had by 1900 turned one of their secondary academies into a college. In the twentieth-century, Quaker schools and colleges became seedbeds of new Quakers but foci of tension between pastors and professors and the businessmen among their trustees.

By 1900, however, many Friends in England and America had rejected both evangelicalism and quietism to become liberals. Learning from modern science, and the historical disciplines applied to religion and the Bible, many Quakers set aside credal theology and stressed religious experience and the symbolic nature of language. Under the inspiration of Rufus Jones*, who drew upon the European mystics and American transcendentalists, the liberal transformation of beliefs brought into Quaker membership educated and professional men and women in college towns and eastern cities. The liberals stressed the importance of creating a social order that would reflect the ethical teachings of Jesus. Some repudiated laissez-faire capitalism; many worked for temperance, a humane economic order, and civil rights for labor unions, blacks, and women. Liberalism made easier the reunification among Hicksite and Orthodox Yearly Meetings on the east coast in the 1950s.

The Peace Testimony has emerged in this century of world wars as the best-known belief of Friends wherever they live. The creation of the American Friends Service Committee and British programs in World War I marked the institutionalization of pacifism and service, as Friends sought to protect conscientious objectors and engage in constructive social action. In the seventy years since 1917 these committees have engaged in famine relief, peace education, social reconstruction, and international reconciliation, as well as organizing under government auspices the alternative service work of conscientious objectors in World War II.

The American Friends Service Committee, the Friends Forward Movement of 1920–22, the Friends Committee on National Legislation, and even the national offices of the "Hicksite" Friends General Conference and the "Orthodox" Friends United Meeting (Five Years Meeting, renamed) have all in different ways raised issues about how Quaker central organizations are or should be related to local Meetings. Some very liberal "unprogramed" Meetings and, on the opposite wing, the ardent revivalists who gather as the Evangelical Friends Alliance avoid subjection to central offices. Doctrinal issues also alienated some Quaker evangelicals from central Friends mission boards, as well as from Service Committees. Yet just when it has seemed that American Friends must divide even in spirit into four national communities, concern for Quaker unity produced the All Friends Conferences, Friends World Committee for Consultation, and the Faith and Life movement. Actual reunion took place between four pairs of once-split eastern Yearly Meetings. Quaker schools, international centers, and retirement centers serve to bring together for mutual learning Friends of various outlooks and non-Quakers.

In all eras, European and American Friends have broadened each others' understandings. A new kind of Quaker interaction has been between North American Friends and the Quakers and congregations of their former mission fields, the large, newly independent Yearly Meetings in East Africa, Asia, and Latin America. What do the old Quaker Testimonies mean in such diverse cultures? The richness of the Quaker tradition is not fully represented by the Friends of any one past period or present branch or nation. Quakers have always believed they were called to a peculiar relation to the whole human world. An understanding of the forces that created, changed, and preserved the Society of Friends in its 300-year history can aid today's Quakers in their search for spiritual nurture and social relevance.

2
THE RELIGIOUS SETTING OF
THE EARLY FRIENDS

The Quaker movement began in England in the 1650s as an intensely transforming religious awakening of individuals, many small groups, and a few whole regions. The striking changes Quakerism made in their ethical life included a new vision of human society: yet then and throughout Quaker history the wider English and American society shaped their religious experience and Friends' ideas. The setting in English religious life of the first Friends needs to be presented here in some detail both for readers unfamiliar with England and its colonies in 1650 and for scholars aware of conflicting claims about Quaker origins.

THE PURITAN UNDERSTANDING OF HISTORY

The puritan movement had dominated English faith for three generations and established the English and New England Commonwealths, when Quakers arose to extend, fulfill, and challenge it. The name *Puritans* is narrowly used for the English Calvinists who meant to turn the Church of England into a federation of uniform parishes and presbyteries. The wider puritan movement was a cluster of diverse religious groups committed to purifying every aspect of English life. The early Quakers can be understood only in the setting of the Puritan view of cosmic history. Calvin had felt his calling to be to glorify God through human community life. His ideal was expanded through the Puritans and Quakers into the English and American dream of "building the Kingdom of God on earth." George Fox*, the first leader of the Friends or "the Children of Light," saw them as the fruit of the renewal of the conquest of the world by the Spirit or Light of Christ, the climax of God's plan for world history that had begun with Paul the Apostle, had halted for a thousand years of Catholic apostasy, and had begun again as incomplete renewal in the Protestant Reformation and Puritan Revolution.[1]

Both Friends and Puritans saw themselves as parts of the people and Church they meant to transform. The ideal of a national Christian culture, and its practical basis in the parish system, pervaded every European nation throughout Puritan times. This ideal had begun after the collapse of the Roman Empire in Western Europe around A.D. 410, when only the clergy could tame, train, and civilize the invading Goths, Vandals, Franks, and Northmen, who became the ruling tenth of the population in Latin lands. Beyond the old "limits" of the Roman Empire newly Christian kings, who conquered the Saxons and Czechs or tried to unify the Germans, Danes, Norsemen, Swedes, or Poles, imposed on their peoples a virtual "platoon baptism" as a symbol of submission. They left it to the clergy and monks to educate and make Christian the culture of their masses of illiterate, nominally Christian subjects. Puritans and Quakers knew that this "universal pastorate" of the papacy from 400 through 1400 had bred paternalism and greedy bishops; only a few Friends knew the writings of the great Catholic mystics, inward in their relationship to God but usually centered on the sacraments.[2] As children and adults, Puritans in their home village or town had sat in the same pews in the same parish churches as had all their grandparents and ancestors, while the forms of worship had been changed twice from Catholic prayer books to Anglican and back and then to the puritan sermons and free prayer between 1560 and 1650. The puritan dream was to remake England through its common worship.

The Puritans were nevertheless pulled by three conflicting visions of the nature of Christian life: Luther's, based solely on trusting faith; the Anabaptists, centering on purity and martyrdom; and Calvin's, focusing on God's glory and power in the world and in history. Puritans knew their debt to Martin Luther for attacking Catholic corruption in 1517, for his vernacular prayers and Bible in German, and most for his message that salvation depends only on faith in Christ as God's word. Martin Luther's Church reforms in Saxony in the 1520s, despite the aid of the princes and the printing press, would not have withstood Catholic power but for the depth of Luther's own radically inward religious experience of God. He called human actions good only when they arose out of spontaneous love and gratitude to God. Otherwise even "good deeds" are "do-gooding" efforts to earn God's favor. Puritans and Friends learned from Luther to see self-made righteousness as the ultimate sin. Friends learned that every Christian can minister God's love to other humans.[3] The Puritan pastors learned from Luther that anxious parishioners needed to be told that God accepted them even as sinners and that in essence the Church is the whole people on its knees. To reform the Church, Luther went to the princes; the Puritans in 1640 and Friends in 1659 went to Parliament.

THE ANABAPTIST MODEL

The cautious reforms of Luther had seemed to many earnest Christians to be shameful compromises. In Switzerland, Germany, and Italy preachers and groups arose who proclaimed that the Church was called by Christ to uncompromising love, austerity, and nonviolence. They were named Anabaptists because for many of them their total personal commitment implied that baptism must be the immersion of adult believers. At least three streams met in the movement: biblical, spiritualist, and apocalyptic. The biblical protest echoed earlier movements such as the fifteenth-century Hussites and twelfth-century Waldensians. On the edges of the slower reform programs directed by magistrates and chief pastors in the Swiss cities, young enthusiasts, both clergy and laymen, started a wildfire village movement in 1527, obeying literally the Sermon on the Mount's teachings on war, oaths, and the perils of wealth. They were persecuted for denying that the wider Swiss society was Christian. A few groups were able to escape to estates or forests in Moravia to form a sect of "Hutterites" withdrawn from society; they shared all property communally.[4]

In Bavaria, in the Rhine cities, and in the Tyrol wandering preachers like Hans Denck drew less on the Gospels and more on the teaching of medieval mystics that only inner experience of God's purifying Word and purgation by suffering, "the bitter catharsis of inner cleansing," could save people.[5] Thus salvation came by God's grace without denying human freedom. Denck, Franck, and others claimed direct guidance by God's Spirit; their followers are now called spiritual Anabaptists.

Many of these same preachers, notably Thomas Müntzer and Balthasar Hubmaier, had taken part in the fierce Peasants' Revolt of 1524–25, which both Catholics and Protestants put down ruthlessly. The survivors' intense apocalyptic hopes thereafter centered on God's direct judgment upon the wicked rulers, predicted for 1528. By August 1527 all of the German apocalyptic Anabaptist leaders were arrested, tried, and executed as both heretics and revolutionaries. In 1535 the north German cathedral city of Münster accepted apocalyptic leaders from Holland and Strassburg. Under siege from the bishop's army they claimed to receive divine commands justifying armed resistance, communism of property, and polygamy. Münster's story was still used to blacken the name of Anabaptists a century after the city fell. Meanwhile, however, Menno Simons had built up in Holland the Mennonites on purely biblical Anabaptist roots: the ethic of the Sermon on the Mount, nonviolence, and simplicity of life and worship. Scholars then and now have debated about Anabaptist influences on Quakerism.[6] Dutch and English weavers, theologians, and refugees constantly exchanged ideas. Certainly, when Friends first visited Holland after 1656 they found much in common with the Waterlander Mennonites. Their rejection of moral compromise, oaths, and titles had also influenced the early Friends through the English Baptists, most of whom had blended these ideals, however, with Puritan approval of "holy war" and a coming "rule of the Saints."

CALVIN

Friends and Puritans learned to hear the call to the Christian community to be the instrument of God's power from John Calvin, although he rejected millenarian hopes and confidence in human holiness. At a key turning point in Calvin's life, at the University of Paris in 1533, he gave up his hopes for a career as a lawyer or a churchman to serve God's glory by reforming the Church. Calvin's *Institutes* and Bible commentaries taught Puritans and Quakers to see sin as self-will. Calvin left to the providence of God the future of his life and of all reformed Christianity in France and Europe. So Predestination was a liberating doctrine for him and for all of the Elect: since their ultimate salvation was totally in God's hands, they were free to forget themselves and to fulfill God's plans for human society. With a lawyer's logic Calvin insisted on working out Predestination's implications for those not the Elect. Quakers and radical Puritans disagreed about hell for infants; yet they, too, saw their "calling" and daily work through Calvin's eyes. In 1537 Calvin had been called to reorganize Geneva. He made it a model city copied in Scotland and in the Reformed cities of France and Holland: John Knox as a refugee in Geneva wrote home about "that pure Flock of late assembled in the maist godlie reformed Churche and Citie of the World."[7]

ENGLISH PROTESTANTISM

English traditions shaped the Quaker pioneers more than did those of continental Europe. An English tradition of prophetic protest against wealthy clergy and unjust landlords began in the fourteenth century, after the Black Death and peasants' revolts, when Wyclif's "Lollards" were themselves fed by older Franciscan ideals. Their millenarian hopes included a new "age of the Spirit" to supersede Catholic Christendom.

England, like France and Spain, had also a centuries-old tradition of national resistance to Rome's authority over local churches. Kings of France and Spain, eager to control the Church's wealth, lands, and castles and to appoint the bishops who ruled them worked out practical agreements with the popes that gave them what they wanted. The parallel efforts of German and English princes achieved much less. Henry VIII, to divorce his Queen Catherine and beget himself a male heir, felt forced to carry out his threats and divorce the Church of England from Roman controls. He had to turn for support to the scholarly "Lutherans" at Cambridge. Among them was Thomas Cranmer, who when he became Henry's new Archbishop of Canterbury, asked that an English Bible be provided for every parish church. Cranmer also began drafting what became the classic *Book of Common Prayer* of the Church of England. Henry's son the short-lived Edward VI helped Bishop Latimer's group of "Commonwealthsmen" to protect tenant farmers and set up an educated, preaching clergy like the later Puritans.

Queen Mary Tudor, devoutly Catholic daughter of Henry VIII and Catherine of Aragon, needed to confirm her own legitimacy by undoing the steps by which Henry had rejected Catherine and Rome. Latimer and Cranmer were burned at the stake along with "5 bishops, 21 divines, 8 gentlemen, 84 artificers, 100 husbandmen, servants and labourers, 26 wives, [etc.].[8] Mary died after only five years. She was important for Puritans and Quakers because under her persecution they merged Anabaptist ideals of heroic resistance to rulers with the national Protestant tradition. Brought up as Puritans, Friends and Protestant Americans learned through the "Book of Martyrs" of the Elizabethan John Foxe to see as their own heritage the struggles of the early Christians martyred by Roman emperors and the Protestants killed by Mary Tudor.[9] For them the Roman Church was Antichrist, the "Scarlet Woman" who is "Babylon" or Rome in the biblical Book of Revelation.

THE CHURCH OF ENGLAND

Anglicanism was finally stabilized under Mary's sister and successor Queen Elizabeth. Her Crown and the honor of her mother Anne Boleyn demanded that she and her country be Protestant, but her aim was a Church of England broad enough to include and satisfy nearly everyone. She came to the throne in 1558 and kept to her policy for forty-five years. Mary's exiles trooped back from Geneva, Frankfurt, Basel, and other Rhineland cities, eager to remake England and totally purify the Church. These early "Puritans" took over many key parish pulpits and professorships at Cambridge. Elizabeth let them restore the English Bible and Book of Common Prayer and draft a largely Calvinist creed of "39 Articles." She meant to burn no one, although Catholic plots to kill her were crushed: her Scottish cousin Mary Stuart died as a result. Elizabeth chose quiet middle-roaders for her bishops. Her Parliaments loyally voted funds to guard England against Spain and Catholicism, but she frustrated every move they made to transform the Church. Her bishops removed only the noisiest Puritans from Cambridge and some pulpits and mainly ignored those who in their own parishes more quietly replaced the Prayer Book by free prayers, and candlelit draped altars by Communion tables or who wore Geneva gowns instead of white surplices and scarlet stoles.

The religious life of most devout English homes quietly became Puritan: lay Elders, daily Bible reading, family prayers, and printed sermons spread everywhere, even if the religious apathy of "merrie England" still seemed supreme. To help their parishioners, Puritan preachers became expert pastoral counselors, wrote detailed guide books for "cases of conscience" in business and politics, and at home kept spiritual diaries (soon published) that inspired Quakers later to do the same. They tried to support big families on their share of "tithes," originally taxes meant for the Church, a major part of which had been diverted to lay gentry. Puritan theology was Calvinist but now stressed the pastor's concerns, who preached God's love to the Elect far more than the damnation of the Reprobate. He urged any Christian "pilgrims" who doubted if they were of the Elect to look for reassurance at God's work already in their own hearts and lives and at their habits changed by God's power. They could already be "visible saints," "professing" or converted Christians. William Ames convinced most

Puritans that God had covenanted with his Elect to uphold their morality as well as their salvation and had prepared their hearts for both.[10] Quakers later rejected the Puritan ethic because it compromised with sin too much, but they learned from wise Puritans the psychological pitfalls to growth in faith.

Elizabeth's death in 1603 ended a long waiting period for Puritans. Mary Stuart had been driven out of Scotland by her Protestant people. Her son James had been left as a boy to rule and be schooled in Scotland among the Presbyterians. Now that he became king of England the Puritans went to welcome him but found that he preferred bossing bishops to being bossed by presbyters. King James I allowed a better "Authorized Version" of the English Bible but otherwise forced the Puritans to return to their parishes, to wait for another generation for a chance to remake England. Puritans, Anglicans, and Catholics had all assumed that all Englishmen should belong to one national Church. A few working-class groups in London and a few trained pastors like Robert Browne and Robert Barrowe had wanted every congregation to be free to begin "Reformation without Tarying for Anie."[11] To get this liberty, John Smyth's flock from Lincolnshire had escaped together to Holland. There Smyth and some followers learned adult baptism from the Mennonites. Others found their children learning Dutch speech and customs, which drove them to charter a leaky boat to Virginia. These "pilgrim" separatists landed instead on Cape Cod and Plymouth Rock. Most Puritans had not yet given up faith in God's plan for England.

Even in 1620 only a few poetic saints like John Donne and Lancelot Andrewes had acquired a positive love for the liturgies and compromises of Queen Elizabeth. But the death of King James in 1625, a year after George Fox's birth, enthroned his son Charles I, who felt God's authority behind his own kingship and churchmanship. His authoritarian Archbishop of Canterbury, William Laud, required all pastors to restore their altars, candles, surplices, and rituals or lose their pulpits. The frustrated Puritans' dedication to God's plan for history led 20,000 lay folk and more clergy proportionately than anywhere in Europe to migrate to Massachusetts Bay, giving up their personal callings, homes, and wealth to build a "New England" as the pilot model of a godly commonwealth, for which the old England was still not ready.

THE PURITAN REVOLUTION IN ENGLAND

The Civil War of the 1640s was the central event in the experience of every pioneer Quaker. Puritans' confidence that God guided history had been shaken by the Turkish conquest of the Balkans and Hungary and by the ghastly Thirty Years War as Catholic Habsburgs tried to overrun Germany, where Protestantism was saved only by the Swedes. Cardinal Richelieu attacked the Protestants of France.

Between 1640 and 1650 God seemed finally to vindicate the Puritan faith. King Charles' effort to raise taxes without Parliament and to impose the Prayer Book upon the Scots aligned them against him with the Puritans, the lawyers, the merchants, and the tenants rioting against greedy landlords.[12] These groups, backed by London mobs, abolished the bishops. For the next twenty years the Church of England parishes had neither bishops nor fixed liturgies, and its leading "priests" were Puritans.

Civil War broke out in 1642 and saw drawn battles and some victories for the king's Royalist gentry before the volunteer regiments of Puritan "Ironsides," fighting by and for their faith, won the key fights for Parliament. Their leader Oliver Cromwell became eventually the regent or protector for the Puritan Commonwealth including England, Ireland, and Scotland, but the Puritans were no longer united.

THE "SEPARATISTS" AND BAPTISTS

The separatists and Baptists were the source of most early Friends individually and of many Quaker ideas. They had multiplied in the English towns during the Civil War. Many Puritan soldiers had been working men; their camp worship took radical forms: unplanned, Bible-centered, lay-led forms, independent of clergy and parishes. The Scots and the conservative Puritans meant to tie the national Church parishes into a hierarchy of Presbyterian synods. When the Scottish and English divines met at Westminster, the Westminster Confession and Catechism reflected their views. New England "Congregationalists," many gentry, and Cromwell's army officers, the "Independents," wanted a looser federation of more self-governing but uniform parishes. But within the army and in many towns, many working-class groups called themselves separatists because they totally rejected the parish network of "the Church of England" in every form. Their worship was, like that of other Puritans, centered on Scriptures, free prayers, and sermons. They allowed other ministers and laymen present to comment on the pastor's text and sometimes held round-robin biblical expositions called "prophesyings." Like most separatist groups since Queen Elizabeth's day, they met to worship in halls and homes and frightened more conservative Puritans by choosing ministers from their own working-class members: untrained "mechanick preachers" who were craftsmen, "shooe-makers, . . . boxe-makers, coach-men and felt-makers and bottle-ale sellers."[13] Men such as John Bunyan the tinker, stressed the openness of God's free grace to every person. No theologians, they talked of the Elect but did not believe in Predestination. Many English separatists stressed the commitment of adults, who must form "gathered churches"; they had read Dutch Mennonites' books. Many "General Baptists" practiced immersion. Except for individualists like Roger Williams, however, they were not truly Anabaptists, since they shared the common Puritan dream of creating the Kingdom of God and Rule of the Saints in England. Few were pacifists: separatists and Baptists provided the best of Cromwell's soldiers and even officers.

In 1647 the king was captured; each Puritan group felt, as did the Friends when they arose soon after, that its cause was the climax that God had ordained within the panorama of sacred events from the Book of Acts to Revelation.[14]

King Charles refused every proposal for a constitutional monarchy, escaped, and found support from the Scots and conservative Puritans for a "second Civil War." The king was again defeated, tried, and executed; Europe was shocked.

RADICAL RELIGIOUS AND POLITICAL GROUPS

Radical groups emerged, and the links between Quaker ideas and each of these groups has been argued with zeal. The Levellers' political ideas were held by many later Quakers. Led by John Lilburne and William Walwyn, the Levellers spoke for "the hobnailed boots" of "the poorest hee in England" but worked for political more than for basic social or economic changes, using a series of platforms called "the Agreement of the People." They demanded annual Parliaments that would hold ultimate authority as in a republic, extending the franchise to all heads of households, rich or poor (women and servants were not included).[15] They proposed major changes to simplify and localize English laws (making trials independent of expensive Latin-speaking lawyers to let each man plead his own case near home). They asked rental rights instead of medieval duties for tenants.[16] Cromwell only partially accepted demands by Levellers in his own army, but in 1653 he called together representatives of various church groups into a convention to draft a new constitution for England. His opening address made clear that he and they saw this "Nominated Parliament" as a "Parliament of Saints" to rule for God. They drafted as laws many Leveller proposals but became deadlocked over whether to abolish the parish churches and went home. Cromwell turned to ruling through the reformed Council of State and conventionally elected Parliaments and began five years of futile effort to persuade the radical, independent, and conservative Puritans and the Anglicans to tolerate one another.

The most radical "saints" reread Daniel 7 about four beasts from the sea, symbolizing ancient evil empires culminating in Rome (surviving, they said, in the Roman and Anglican bishops and even Cromwell). They proclaimed themselves "the Fifth Monarchy men" to replace Rome by "the Kingdom of the Saints of the Most High," which Daniel had predicted would follow[17] Cromwell squelched them. Thus the Quakers arose to renew apocalyptic hopes, just as the period ended when prophecy and dreaming had been spread throughout the whole Puritan movement.

The social revolution, which arose through the political and religious revolt against Charles I, has been the subject of a flood of excellent recent history writing, notably by English socialists who often identify Quakers with these revolutionaries.[18] London apprentices rioted, as did country tenants cheated by landlords out of drained fenland or enclosed pastures. Yet the only overall challenge to the private owning of land came from Gerard Winstanley and the "Diggers" before and around him, who together dug gardens on common lands in Berkshire and Bucks. Their writings mixed natural rights and pantheism but did not keep the Diggers from being driven off as squatters by troopers on horseback. Personal links between the Diggers and early Friends have been proved to have existed only after both groups were established on different paths.[19]

England's drifting population of vagabonds was regarded by historians as a "Threepenny Opera" underworld of beggars and thieves, until recent Marxists enfranchised them as an underclass.[20] Into it have lately been coopted the very individualistic "Ranters" largely because they too rejected official authority. Not a religious sect, the Ranters felt the presence of God in the natural world, not only in "openings" or providential events but in their own human bodies and essence. Ranters also rejected moral law for the sake of spiritual freedom: they have lately been called a "counterculture" like the "Hippies" of the 1960s.[21] Many acted in psychotic ways, but some were charismatic personalities. Clearly, they were Antinomians: Ranters claimed to be morally liberated from outward "legalism" by the Spirit of God within them and thus to be justified in shouting, cursing, drunken behavior, and nudity. Their angry egotism shocked the pious, but they were not mere rebels. Quakers who gave ultimate authority to inner impulses were called Ranters; Fox insisted that the Spirit "led" men to good, not evil, but Ranters said that all impulses of the Elect were from God and all acts were pure: tobacco, liquor, and women were good gifts from God. In using them they felt liberated from sin. Abiezer Coppe experienced a humbling of his pride in front of a poor beggar as did Saint Francis. Some Ranters like Jacob Bauthumley felt mystically united in spirit with God and made divine claims like Ludowick Muggleton. Results could be tragic: William Franklin claimed to be Christ reincarnate; under trial and imprisonment he renounced his claim. Mary Gadbury, who had left her faithless husband to follow him, was in despair.[22] Yet Calvinists in general had found that God's salvation of the Elect is undeserved, that his power is beyond human ideas of good and evil. Dedicated, sensitive Puritans like John Cotton also put God's will above moral respectability.

The Spiritual Puritans were a much wider group of individualists. Although Calvin had said that only by the work of the Spirit could the Bible "hit home" to change the hearts of the Elect, most Puritans denied that the Spirit worked apart from Scripture even for daily guidance. Yet the separatists and Baptists claimed to preach by the power of the Spirit rather than by an Oxford education. Some of Cromwell's best chaplains like Hugh Peters and university scholars like William Dell whom the Quakers later read eagerly agreed. John Bunyan looked for God's message and purposes in inward "openings" in which he was shown the meaning of specific Bible verses.[23]

Other Englishmen approached the Spirit more abstractly. Cambridge included shy scholars who drew from Plato and the Renaissance a contrast of spirit and matter, identifying the highest human reason and morality with the spirit. These "Cambridge Platonists" learned from Jewish Kabbala to look for spiritual meanings behind obscure texts. Theosophists, Alchemists, Rosicrucians, faith healers, and foretellers of the future worked on the edges of such intellectually adventurous circles.[24] Some radical Puritans and Quakers knew them well. The families of Thomas Simmonds and Giles Calvert, later printers of many Quaker books, reprinted in the 1640s the most ethically focused of the works of Jakob Boehme, a Silesian lay mystic of the sixteenth century.[25] Similarly, they printed some stiflingly nebulous spiritual tracts by Hendrick Niclas of sixteenth-century Holland, whose communes of "Familist" followers had been active in parts of southern England in the 1580s but had since died out.[26] "The Family of Love" had been accused of practising sexual freedom, nudity, and community of property.

The intensity and variety of the religious communities in England in the decades 1640–60, and especially the earnest search to understand the relationship of religious experience and morality, set the stage for early Quakerism. For some whom Fox won, Quakerism represented not so much new ideas as a touchstone, a way to test experiences they had already known. Most had personally run through the series of religious communities from Anglican to Puritan to separatist or Baptist. George Fox, to judge by his use of phrases like "unity with the Creation" and "the Everlasting Gospel," had been close to both Ranters and readers of Boehme:[27] in Puritan England some radical ideas were so widespread that their origin can never be proved. England was living through a ferment of ideas, when no hope seemed impossible.

NOTES

1. The names were biblical: (Luke 16:8, Jn. 12:26, Eph.5:8–9). Fox, in a fragment preserved in *The Journal of George Fox*, ed. John L. Nickalls (London: 1952, 1975), 709, said that "Friends" was used of some Midlands separatist groups before Fox joined them.

2. William Penn, Isaac Penington, and Robert Barclay, all convinced of Quakerism after 1657, knew early Christian theology and some Catholic mystics' works but were almost the only Quakers who quoted mystics before the eighteenth century. (See also comments below on Boehme.) Neither "negative" nor "love mysticism" were typical of early Quakers.

3. Penn cited Luther occasionally; Robert Barclay did so often: nine times in the *Apology for the True Christian Divinity* (1678); other early Friends hardly ever did.

4. For original sources see George H. Williams, *Spiritual and Anabaptist Writers*, Library of Christian Classics, vol. 25 (Philadelphia: 1957); Frank Friesen and Walter Klaassen, eds., *Sixteenth Century Anabaptism: Defenses, Confessions, Refutations* (Waterloo, Ont.: 1982); and the great *Quellen zur Geschichte der Täufer*, 13 vols., ed. Georg Baring, Manfred Krebs, Grete Mecenseffy, et al. (Guetersloh, Ger.: 1951–72). Good surveys include George H. Williams, *The Radical Reformation* (London: 1962). Of Anabaptist groups, the Mennonites, Amish, and Hutterites survive.

5. Werner O. Packull, *Mysticism and the Early South German–Austrian Anabaptist Movement, 1525–1521* (Scottsdale, Pa.: 1977), 178–79. As Packull showed, the German Anabaptists' stress on humans' *inner* response to God is also a medieval outlook.

6. Early Quaker–Baptist links are explored by Michael Mullett in *Radical Religious Movements in Early Modern Europe* (London: 1980).

7. John Knox, *Historie of the Reformation of . . . Scotland* (Edinburgh: 1732), 204.

8. *Foxe's Book of Martyrs*, ed. Marie G. King (Old Tappan, N.J.: Revell, 1968), 329. Since there were fewer victims and lower in class status than the Protestant martyrs in France, Italy, or Austria, most of the high-ranking English Protestants probably escaped to the Rhine cities. Christina H. Garrett, *The Marian Exiles* (Cambridge, 1938; London 1966).

9. A folio copy of Foxe's *Acts and Monuments* (1563) was chained in the Mancetter church where George Fox read it while an apprentice.

10. See Edmund Morgan, *Visible Saints* (New York: 1963); Norman Pettit, *The Heart Prepared: Grace and Conversion in Puritan Life* (New Haven: 1966). On compulsory tithes and their impropriation by lay "rectors" of previously monastic benefices, see Christopher Hill, *Economic Problems of the Church* (Oxford: 1956). Friends, like others before them, refused to pay Tithes to parish clergy but not to impropriators; their motives centered on religion more than on social injustice.

11. The title of Barrowe's "Brownist" or "separatist" tract of 1582.

12. See Brian Manning, *The English People and the English Revolution* (London: 1976).

13. See William York Tindall, *John Bunyan, Mechanick Preacher* (New York: 1934); Marshall Knappen, *Tudor Puritanism* (Chicago: 1939); William Haller, *The Rise of Puritanism* (New York: 1939). Michael Mullett, in *Radical Religious Movements*, 18–22, noted that oral aspects of religion typical of such popular preaching were characteristics of merchant city culture by contrast to the sacramental or theological faith of cathedral or university towns.

14. See William Penn, *Rise and Progress of the People Called Quakers*, used as preface to George Fox's *Journal* (1684). Other versions of Penn's "sacred history" are in *Truth Exalted* (1668) and the preface to his *Christian Quaker* (1674). In early exuberant days of the Reformation even Luther and Calvin had expected to live to see the completion of "sacred history" in the millennium. See Keith V. Thomas, *Religion and the Decline of Magic* (London: 1971), and Geoffrey F. Nuttall, "James Nayler: A Fresh Approach," *Journal of the Friends Historical Society* (hereafter *JFHS*), Supplement 26 (London: 1954); B. H. Ball, *The English Connection: The Puritan Roots of Seventh Day Adventism* (Cambridge: 1981).

15. Pauline Gregg, *Free-Born John: A Biography of John Lilburne* (London: 1961); on Walwyn, see W. Schenk, *The Concern for Social Justice in the Puritan Revolution* (London: 1948).

16. Richard H. Tawney, *Agrarian Problem in the 16th Century* (London: 1912).

17. See B. S. Capp, *The Fifth Monarchy Men: A Study in Seventeenth-Century English Millenarianism* (London: 1972); P. G. Rogers, *The Fifth Monarchy Men* (London: 1960); Louise Fargo Brown, *The Political Activities of the Baptists and Fifth Monarchy Men* (Washington, D.C.: 1912); On Simpson, Paul Hobson, and Henry Danvers, see Rich. L. Greaves, *Saints and Rebels: Seven Nonconformists in Stuart England* (Macon, Ga.: 1985).

18. Eduard Bernstein, *Cromwell and Communism* (London: 1930), was the pioneer book in this direction; see Christopher Hill, *Puritanism and Revolution* (New York: 1958), and *Intellectual Origins of the English Revolution* (Oxford: 1965). See also his *World Turned Upside Down* (Stanford, Calif.: 1972), particularly full of creative material on early Quakers. Other major works are Manning, *The English People and the English Revolution*; Leo F. Solt, *Saints in Arms: Puritanism and Democracy in Cromwell's Army* (Stanford, Calif.: 1959); Michael Walzer, *The Revolution of the Saints* (Cambridge, Mass.: 1965).

19. George H. Sabine, ed., *The Works of Gerrard Winstanley* (Ithaca, N.Y.: 1941), remains the definitive work, underlying Christopher Hill's Pelican Classic edition of *Winstanley: The Law of Freedom, and Other Writings* (Harmondsworth: 1973), whose limits have been well corrected in his "Religion of Gerrard Winstanley," *Past and Present*, Supplement 5 (1978). Keith Thomas and Professor Aylmer told of newfound Digger writings in *Past and Present* 40 (July 1968): 3–15, and 42 (February 1969): 57–68. Winthrop Hudson's discovery of the Quaker affiliation of Winstanley in his old age is given undue weight in "Gerrard Winstanley and the Early Quakers," *Church History* 12, 180–93. The detailed data was updated by David C. Taylor, *Gerrard Winstanley in Elmbridge* (Elmbridge, 1982), and James Alsop, "Gerrald Winstanley's Later Life," *Past and Present* 82 (February 1979): 73–81.

20. Hill, *The World Turned*, Ch. 3; idem, *Puritanism and Revolution*.

21. G. F. S. Ellens, "The Ranters Ranting: Reflections on a Ranting Counter Culture," *Church History* 40 (March 1971): 91–107. By contrast, Christopher Hill in *The World Turned*, Ch. 9, and A. L. Morton, in *The World of the Ranters* (London: 1970), 71, felt that "the Ranters, and they alone at this date, spoke for and to the most wretched and submerged elements of the population, and slum dwellers of London."

22. Tracts about Franklin were explored by the late Allen B. Hole, Jr.

23. See the definitive study by Geoffrey F. Nuttall, *The Holy Spirit in Puritan Faith and Experience* (Oxford: 1946); also the writings of William Dell, John Everard, and John Saltmarsh reprinted by Theodor Sippell in *Werdendes Quaekertum* (Stuttgart: 1937). On Muggleton see Douglas G. Greene, "Muggletonians and Quakers: . . . the Interaction of 17th Century Dissent," *Albion* 15, no. 2 (Summer 1983) 107–22. Kevin Lewis, "Vita: Lodowicke Muggleton," *Harvard Magazine* (July–August 1983), 36–37. Many groups calling themselves Seekers were expecting an apocalyptic outpouring of the Spirit, but Penn put undue stress on the Seekers as a separate community, which has misled many Friends.

24. See Thomas, *Religion and the Decline of Magic*; Gerald R. Cragg, *The Cambridge Platonists* (New York: 1968); and C. A. Patrides, *The Cambridge Platonists* (London: 1969). See also Ch. 6 in this volume.

25. On the printer Giles Calvert, the only study is the 1937 Columbia University M.A. thesis of Althea Terry, and on his in-laws Matthew and Thomas Simmonds, the notes of Geoffrey F. Nuttall, "Unity with the Creation: George Fox and the Hermetic Philosophy," *Friends Quarterly* (Jan. 1947) 134–43. Those printers reprinted seven short, mainly practical Boehme tracts in 1644–50. Seven more, including the theosophical *Signatura Rerum* and *Aurora*, and four reprints came out in the 1650s and seven more in 1661. On Everard's use of Boehme see Sippell. All of these sources seem too late to have influenced George Fox's youth. But William Erbury, a radical Puritan pastor often called a Ranter, whose daughter Nayler healed, quoted Boehme and may have influenced Friends.

26. See Alistair Hamilton, *The Family of Love* (Cambridge: 1981). The Familists were found in Emden, Antwerp, and Cologne in 1540–70 and in the Isle of Ely and south of London in the 1570s, when Christopher Vittels translated Niclas' tracts into English. See John W. Martin, "Elizabethan Familists and English Separatism," *Journal of British Studies* 20, no. 1 (Fall 1980): 53–73; and his "Family of Love in the Diocese of Ely," *Studies in Church History, Vol. IX: Schism, Heresy, and Religious Protest* (Cambridge: 1972), 213–22. Five of Niclas's tracts were printed in 1649 and five more in the 1650s. At his death Fox owned Niclas' *Mirror*, but only *Prophecy of the Spirit of Love* (1649) has been tied to a Friend earlier. Niclas's and Muggleton's claims were for unique

inspiration. Friends, who claimed that everyone can be led by God, were thus closer to Ranters than to the cults of such prophets.

27. See Nuttall, *James Nayler*, 3–9; on "Unity with the Creation," see pp. 134–143; Hugh Doncaster, "That State in Which Adam Was," *JFHS* 41 (1948): 13–24.

3
THE LAMB'S WAR AND THE AWAKENING OF THE NORTH OF ENGLAND

To describe the eruption of the Quakers into history, we turn from the religious ferment of all England in the 1640s to individual people and places, each in various ways unique, although shaped by the national currents of thought and faith. The five stages of our narrative of Quaker beginnings in the 1650s will be laid out so as to correspond roughly to five basic ways to interpret early Quakerism: they focus on George Fox the "founder"; the regional birth of the movement; its radical extension of Puritanism; the nation's response to the movement and vice versa; and the fusing of personal experience and social ethic into "the Lamb's War" as a cosmic world-view. Each overall historical interpretation is true but incomplete; yet each fits well one of the two-year periods of Quakerism's first decade.

THE LIFE OF GEORGE FOX TO 1651

To begin with Fox's life suggests the theory that Quakerism's essence is the teaching and disciples of Fox, that his experience and personality defined the movement. In fact, many early Friends went through similar religious experiences independently and for a period brought as strong a message as Fox. By the time of Fox's death Penn could write: "Thou, dear George, excellest them all."[1] The impact of his personality is reflected in letters of adoration from early followers (which troubled him) and in the journals of those he shook or healed.[2] Wry and rugged in his common sense, warm in his friendships, but firm and even stiff when his inward experience or beliefs were involved—which was usually the case—Fox has fascinated other great men but earned no good biography, perhaps because his *Journal* preempted other accounts.[3]

Fox was born in 1624 at Fenny Drayton, Leicestershire, a Midland village near the old Roman Road to Lichfield and Wales. A Puritan father, the Puritan local squire Purefoy, and a hard-working Puritan pastor Stephens who gave much time to talking with him all left Fox deeply ambivalent about wanting to please moral men and yet to be independent of authority. At a local primary school he evidently learned to read English but not to spell it well and no Latin. His intense firsthand experience kept even Fox himself from admitting what he learned from his reading, which throughout his life was evidently wide and careful but not scholarly.[4] In nearby Mancetter he was apprenticed to a cobbler and shepherd, learned to handle money and men, read his own Bible constantly, and while driving his master's sheep to market visited separatist prayer groups and Puritan pastors such as Walter Cradock of Coventry.[5]

Like many others in that chaotic decade of war, famine, and depression, he wandered restlessly before he was twenty: north to Mansfield in Nottinghamshire, where a cluster of separated ex-Baptists already called themselves "Friends," and south to London to visit a Baptist uncle Pickering. Perhaps he also knew Ranters or Familists, from whom he may have learned unusual beliefs about the inward nature of heaven, the Last Judgment, the sacraments, and Christ's "heavenly body" within believers.[6] He argued theology everywhere, but his *Journal*, written thirty years later, remembered mainly his wrestling with "temptations" and despair in each place. He was very sensitive to guilt in himself and hypocrisy in others; he ran from the presence of "professing" Christians and morally careless people but often, too, from his weaver father, "righteous Christer." Yet he feared seeming disobedient by being on his own. Evidently, he did not understand or trust his own conflicting motives. Of his friendships in these years, only Elizabeth Hooton's survived for decades.

In 1646–47 a series of religious "openings" came to him, moments of insight while alone that convinced him of the truth of some ideas that were already common among separatists and Baptists: that "being bred at Oxford or Cambridge was not enough to fit and qualify men to be ministers of Christ." More personally: "Christ was tempted by the same Devil and had overcome him" and so "there is one, even Christ Jesus, that can speak to thy condition." Fox began to preach among the Mansfield separatists, but he still frequently felt "temptations" and despair. Finally, a moment came when he found that "the natures of those things that were hurtful without, were within, in the hearts and minds: . . . the natures of dogs, swine, vipers, of Sodom and Egypt." He was seeing within himself the same evils he had tried to escape outwardly. He "cried, 'why should I be thus, seeing I was never addicted to commit those evils.' " He had never actually committed violent, lustful, or homosexual acts, but he suddenly knew himself kin to all tempted humans. He saw within himself "that there was an ocean of darkness and death, but an infinite ocean of light and love, which flowed over the ocean of darkness."[7]

Thereafter Fox found "the Lord's power" breaking out within himself and groups he addressed. He began preaching to many separatist congregations, "turning people to the witness of God within them," although they were "children of darkness." By proclaiming that "Christ is come to teach his people himself," Fox combined a call to inward experience with the apocalyptic urgency of the radical Puritans. He spent the winter of 1650–51 in Derby jail, charged with blasphemy for claiming to be purified and infallibly led, having "come up in spirit through the flaming sword into the paradise of God." There he refused a captaincy in Cromwell's army, since he "lived in the virtue of that life and power that took away the occasion of all wars."[8] He said the Quakers' struggle and victory are within, with "spiritual not carnal" weapons, as Paul had said (II Cor. *10:* 4). Released from Derby in 1651, Fox visited at home and then went north preaching through the Yorkshire hills, drawing to him as companions other separatists—Thomas Aldam, James Nayler, William Dewsbury, and Richard Farnworth—with whose help he began a religious revival in villages of the northeastern moors. A few Puritan pastors welcomed them, and lace was burned in repentance in the public square at Malton-in-the-Moor. Aldam and six others, however, were arrested and held in York Castle dungeon for more than two years.[9]

THE RELIGIOUS AWAKENING OF THE ENGLISH NORTHWEST: 1652–53

A similar campaign the next summer achieved such dramatic results that "the Lake District" is still "the 1652 country" to Quaker pilgrims. As had happened on a smaller scale on the Yorkshire moors, there were mass meetings, fiery emotions, and the winning of local separatist leaders: more than half the first generation of Quaker leaders came from this area.[10] Early Quakerism itself can be seen as a regional religious Awakening with parallels in the American frontier and Great Awakenings, Wesley's mass meetings of miners, and the ferment in the twelfth-century Italian hills that produced the Waldensians and Franciscans. All of these regions were isolated but self–aware, Christian in tradition but neglected by the Church, catching fire from centers of quieter religious reform.

In May 1652 Fox had come northwest through the Yorkshire hills. Traveling behind Pendle Hill, he felt an inward call to climb it and, as in Isaiah *40:*9, to "sound forth the day of the Lord; . . . and the Lord let me see in what places he had a great people to be gathered." Fox went to Sedbergh market during the Whitsun Fair, to Brigflatts, and to other farmsteads and spoke to a gathering of a thousand separatists on Firbank Fell. Thus began a mass movement in villages near Kendal and the manor house of Swarthmoor, home of the Puritan judge Thomas Fell, who gave hospitality to traveling preachers and who came home from his court circuit to find that his wife, Margaret, and their seven daughters had become ardent disciples of Fox. For Margaret Fell herself the turning point came at the Sunday service in Ulverston parish church under a Puritan pastor the judge had chosen:

[Fox] came not in till people were gathered, . . . and opened us a book we had never read in, . . . the Light of Christ in our consciences, and . . . declared of it that it was our teacher; . . . and Christ and the Apostles' words was not ours, but theirs that spoke them: "You will say, 'Christ saith this and the Apostles say this'; but what canst thou say? . . . What thou speakest, is it inwardly from God?'' And I sat down in my pew and wept while [pastor] Lampitt preached.[11]

The nickname "Quaker" reflected the physical shaking aroused by inner struggles of individuals facing their inner motives "under the Light" in the Quaker meetings. Margaret Fell's trembling fit in front of her husband while Farnworth was speaking in Swarthmoor Hall and an ecstatic letter to Fox from all of the Swarthmoor women added to the judge's pain on his return and underscores for us his tolerance. These women and even some of their servants were all later to be travelers and leaders in the new movement.[12]

During the summer of 1652 and again the next year Fox, Nayler, and the newly convinced separatist leaders Francis Howgill, Edward Burrough, Camm, Hubberthorne, and younger men, each of whom had just been through his own purging experience, went out from Swarthmoor Hall. Groups met in homes or on crags, reported Puritan Francis Higginson:

sometimes a hundred or two hundred in a swarm, . . . and continue all night long. They have no singing of psalms, . . . no reading or exposition of holy Scripture, no administration of sacraments. . . . Their speaker for the most part uses the posture of standing, or sitting with his hat on, his countenance severe, his face downward, his eyes fixed mostly towards the earth, his hands and fingers expanded, continually striking gently on his breast, . . . his voice . . . low, his sentences incoherent. . . . Some stand in the market place . . . and cry "Repent, repent, woe, woe, the judge of the world has come." They exhort people to mind the Light within, to hearken to the voice and follow the guide within them, to dwell within. . . . The priests of the world [they say] do deceive them, . . . they speak of living under the cross, and against pride in apparel and covetousness.[13]

In the English Northwest Fox and Nayler were at first violently beaten or stoned and called Puritans. Anger was proportional to the excitement the Quaker preachers aroused. Pastor Higginson in his youth had come back from Massachusetts to study theology at Leyden and then chose Kirkby Stephen as a dark back-country parish in which to offer his life. When Fox and Nayler were tried at Lancaster, Puritan Judges Fell and West released them over Higginson's angry protest. But Nayler and Howgill were jailed all winter at Appleby, and in 1653 Fox was in Carlisle castle charged with blasphemy again. Cromwell's radical "Parliament of Saints" had him set free.

In 1652–53 the Quaker movement gathered at least a tenth of the people of the English Northwest: of these, a quarter, about 10,000, became permanent Friends.[14] The moorland shepherds and farmers of Cumberland, Westmorland, and Furness felt they were disinherited by the Church. The great dukes who took over the monasteries' huge estates in 1536 were absentees hated by all their tenants.[15] Local squires were respected, but some were Catholics and most were Royalist in the Civil War. Parishes were huge and pastors often drunk or absent.

A few Puritan preachers tried to overcome centuries of pagan folk customs and biblical ignorance. Quakers harvested a fertile field.

THE QUAKER CAMPAIGN THROUGHOUT ENGLAND: 1654–55

In the third summer of the Awakening, pairs of north-country farmers or women, recently "convinced" of their need of the Quaker Light, set out to carry a prophetic call to all parts of England. They called themselves "the Camp of the Lord in England" (later Friends named them "First Publishers of Truth" or "the valiant sixty"). Like the biblical Apostles they traveled light as to clothing and baggage. They felt called to each day's work by the Spirit whose breaking out seemed the climax to world history:

Now is the Lord appearing in this day of his mighty power, . . . and exalting Jesus Christ to be King of Kings, to lead his Army he hath raised up in the North of England, and is marching towards the South, in the mighty power of the living Word of God, which is sharp as a two edged sword to cut down the high and low, rich and poor, priests and people, and all powers of the land.[16]

Fox and Nayler still preached in northern England; most Quaker teams went south, where they were dunked by the students at Oxford and Cambridge and jailed wherever Puritans were strong. Eighteen-year-old James Parnell became the first famous Quaker martyr: he preached in Essex and was imprisoned in Colchester Castle, where he fell from a ladder, cold, sick, and fasting, and died of his injuries. Fox and Margaret Fell set up patterns to guide Quaker apostles: on the road they would write regularly to Swarthmoor Hall, and those in jail and their families were supported from a central fund set up at Kendal.[17] Fox called "General Meetings" of these Quaker traveling "ministers" to report on and plan work in various parts of Britain. On the Welsh border, a Quaker regional Awakening happened again. Among Baptists response was warm but not dramatic. Informal friendships and contacts with ex-"Ironsides," printers, and wool traders opened the way in London and Bristol for preaching in public halls by Burrough and Howgill, Audland and Camm, and later for Nayler and Fox. Friends remembered with awe the huge crowds that gathered in the rented hall of the "Bull and Mouth" tavern in London or an orchard in Bristol:

John Audland, who very much trembled, . . . stood up, full of dread and shining brightness on his countenance, lifted up his voice as a trumpet, and said "I proclaim spiritual war with the inhabitants of the earth, who are in separation from God." . . . some fell on the ground, others crying out under the sense of the opening of their [spiritual] states. . . . Oh, the tears, sighs and groans, tremblings and mournings, . . . in the sense of our spiritual wants and necessities. . . . We were forced to meet without doors, and that in frost and snow, when several thousands have been assembled together.[18]

Here one can stop to look at early Friends from yet a third historical viewpoint. The Mission to the South of England in 1654–56 also showed Quakers as the radical extension of Puritanism. The same social historians who now recognize Royalists, Puritan conservatives, and radicals as corresponding to the upper, middle, and lower social classes in England, often claim the early Quakers as a working-class protest movement. Early Quakers protested against the titles and formal greetings expected by the gentry and attacked wealth and power based on status; they exalted the lowly and meek. The early Friends, who acclaimed Jesus' Apostles as fellow workingmen, were largely tenant farmers and hand-craftsmen. In the Northwest most Friends owned their own homes even when renting fields or pastures. In Essex, Norfolk, and around Bristol weavers became Quakers: English and Dutch weavers had been prominent in sects and protest movements since Lollard times. In large farm areas like Buckingham, Friends convinced mainly sensitive educated folk who were already dissatisfied as Puritans: Isaac and Mary Penington, young Penn, and Thomas Ellwood. In London and other cities rich merchants as well as poor craftsmen were won. Although Quakers were from all classes, Friends perhaps had a higher proportion of working-class leaders than any other group.[19] In Scotland and Ireland, soldiers or officers in Cromwell's garrisons became Friends, to the consternation of their superiors. Among the ninety-five Quaker ex-soldiers, Dewsbury, Nayler, Edmundson, and most others came from the North; some settled around London. George Bishop of Bristol had headed a branch of Cromwell's secret service. Hardly any former Royalists joined Friends.[20]

In ethics and worship more than in economics the Quakers represented the "left wing" or ultimate extension of the Protestant Reformation, which made the daily life of Christians more radical and internal than even the Catholic definition of the "seven deadly sins" as inner attitudes: pride and anger, rather than mere actions like killing. Yet Confession and penances had given an external and impersonal character to Catholic ethics. In protest Luther, although he knew the need for outward self-discipline for the sake of being free to serve human needs, looked more at the inward self-righteousness that corrupts every action. Calvin, although concerned with service and biblical commandments in God's world, saw Election as conversion of human wills. Quakers made ethics totally inward but stressed active obedience. True worship, for Puritans, came only from the "prepared heart" of the converted "saint." This attitude was carried farther by Friends in their silent worship, avoiding as far as possible all merely human words.[21] As Protestantism moved from Lutherans and Anglicans through Calvinists and Puritans to Baptists and Anabaptists, clergy and the sacraments, crucial for Catholics, thus also became more marginal and more deeply rooted in believers' faith, until Quakers totally rejected them. Many Friends had made just this pilgrimage from Church to church.

The early Friends took more Puritan practices for granted than they realized. Even Quakers' central message about the guiding and judging Light of Christ in the heart was an intensification of radical Puritan teachings about pride,

conversion, and the Spirit.[22] Friends and Baptists agreed that a true Church is
the self-winnowed community of "saints." Quakers accepted Baptist ideas about
worshipping only under leadings from God, rejecting holy days and places,
titles, wedding rings, pagan names for months and weekdays, and other medieval
superstitions. In dress and speech, on titles and luxuries, Baptists and Quakers
spoke as Puritans with working-class accents. Yet they did break at some points
with even the closest forebears. They rejected water in Baptism and wine in
Communion and, above all, the supreme authority of Scripture text.[23] Their
Peace Testimony clashed with Baptists and other godly radicals who fought holy
wars.

THE ALIENATION OF QUAKERS FROM PURITANS
IN 1656–57

England as a whole was turning conservative. The failure of the Puritan armies
to make England a dedicated nation had become clear to many. Cromwell's later
Parliaments were elected by the old elite electorate and led by conservative
Puritans. Cromwell's law to curb the Quakers' interruption of other churches'
worship was popular with both radical and conservative Puritans. When in December 1655 Fox's symbolic Quaker mission to "Land's End" in Cornwall
landed him and his party in the "Doomsdale" dungeon in Launceston, other
Quakers characteristically converged on the point of conflict but were imprisoned
too: among those at Exeter were Nayler and a group of his disciples.

The alienation of Quakers from Puritans can thus be linked to some historians'
view that Quakerism was a turning inward or back from radical Puritanism.
Socialists see the Civil War as a social revolution that failed when Cromwell
"betrayed" and defeated the Levellers and "Fifth Monarchy men," and they
see Quakers as diverting the hopes for a rule of working-class English saints.
Other groups were drawn from the disillusioned: many hill-country peasants and
"clubmen" had turned angrily to protect their flocks against both the Royalist
and Ironside soldiers. The "Seekers" despaired of the Church and the sacraments
in all current forms. Thus in 1652 Dewsbury, Nayler, and Hubberthorne had
come to Fox in part out of discouragement over their hopes for achieving a new
Kingdom of God by arms. When John Lilburne returned from fifteen months of
imprisonment in the Island of Jersey, in Cromwell's last years, he turned to
Quakerism instead of to new Leveller campaigns. Even Gerrard Winstanley may
have become a Friend.

In a more complex way Isaac Penington, son of a Puritan Lord Mayor of
London, seems to have gone through a period of breakdown or retirement about
1650, when he was willing to leave the dark future entirely in the hands of God
who "destroyeth the perfect and the wicked." As a Cambridge graduate, "one
who hath been deeply affected with wisdom, true wisdom, heavenly wisdom,
inward wisdom, and vehemently pursuing it from the womb," he had been "at
length wholly stripped of all his riches in this kind." He was a mystic before

he became a Quaker just in those years 1656–58. Then he learned that God is good and judges evil. When challenged by crude Friends he reexamined himself:

In my waiting, in my spiritual exercises, . . . I met with the very strength of hell. The cruel oppressor roared upon me, and made me feel the bitterness of his captivity. . . . Some may desire to know what I have at last met with. I answer, I have met with the Seed. . . . I have met with my God, I have met with my Saviour: and he has not been present with me without his salvation, but I have felt the healings drop upon my soul from under his wings. I have met with the true knowledge, the knowledge of life, the living knowledge.[24]

The turn inward was also Penington's discovery of joy in God.

Friends in 1656–58 did not show a "failure of nerve"; they were not pessimistic about the future. When English crowds turned hostile, Fox urged older Friends to visit the Quaker groups gathered earlier. Younger ones went on wider missions to Holland, France, and colonies in America. Veterans Howgill and Burrough each felt God called them to go together to preach in Ireland: English–Irish hatred there led to Friends convincing mainly a few Protestants in Cromwell's garrisons in the eastern counties between Belfast and Cork. John Perrot and John Luffe set out to convert the pope, Mary Fisher* reached the sultan at Adrianople, and George Robinson the Arabs of Palestine, though with few successes. Katherine Evans and Sarah Cheever, trying to reach Jerusalem, spent two years in the Inquisition's jail at Malta.

The disgrace of James Nayler in 1656 did cut off Friends from Puritans and political hopes. Some of Nayler's disciples, while jailed in Exeter, had attacked Fox as a spiritual leader. Fox's anger prevented reconciliation, as Nayler refused to judge their claimed "leadings" from the Spirit. In October, when Nayler's group were released from prison, they felt a divine command to lead Nayler on a horse into the city of Bristol, to throw their garments in the muddy road and sing "holy, holy" in repetition of Jesus' Palm Sunday ride into Jerusalem. They meant to salute and proclaim the Spirit of God within Nayler, but to Puritans everywhere and to the citizens and most Quakers of Bristol, the ride implied that Nayler was equal with Jesus, which was blasphemy. Nayler was tried before Parliament itself, whose conservative leaders wanted a case over which to challenge Cromwell's policy of toleration. They wanted to execute Nayler, but no English law required death for blasphemy. Instead, he was brutally whipped, branded, and imprisoned for three years. Neither Cromwell nor Parliament won much joy from this compromise. In Bridewell Prison in London, Nayler asked Friends to forgive the hurt he had caused their reputation, waited for Fox to be reconciled to him, and meanwhile wrote sensitive tracts on violence and evil, among them his "dying words":

There is a spirit which I feel, that delights to do no evil, nor to revenge any wrong, but delights to endure all things, in hope to enjoy its own in the end: its hope is to outlive all wrath and contention, and to weary out all exaltation and cruelty, or whatever is of a nature contrary to itself. . . . As it bears no evil in itself, so it conceives none in thoughts to any other. If it be betrayed it bears it; for its ground and spring is the mercies and forgiveness of God.[25]

RETHINKING "THE LAMB'S WAR": 1658–59

Even when thrown back, Friends announced and lived by a radical, inward ethical challenge. A fifth approach to interpreting early Friends builds on this, using a phrase that Nayler took as his title for a tract printed anonymous while he was in jail: *the Lamb's War*, meaning God's victory over evil within human hearts and history, through Christ who is the Lamb in the Book of Revelation. The phrase, used by many Friends, united the inner and outer sides of Quaker experience and movement until 1674.

The period 1658–59 was the time of crisis for Puritanism and for England. In 1658 Oliver Cromwell died, hoping to stabilize his achievements by passing his power to his oldest surviving son. Richard Cromwell lacked his father's wisdom and also Oliver's support by the army he had led. A triangular struggle began between Richard, the army leaders, and the radical Puritans who briefly restored the "Rump" of the "Long Parliament," which had won the Civil War. In the end the most conservative generals gained power and restored the Stuart kings. Earlier in 1659 when the fruits of a century of Puritan hope and twenty years struggle were in the balance, the radical Puritans asked Friends to take part for the first time in that struggle.

Thus, 1659 was also the crisis time for Friends, who from the depths of their experience had to understand their new lives. Fox himself spent the autumn of 1659 in great "darkness of spirit" before advising Friends to decline to enlist as commissioners of the militia. Quakers asked themselves what God was doing "in all these overturnings," which seemed at first to promise greater justice or at least wider toleration. "The Lamb's War" had meant the conquest of the whole world by the Spirit, which worked most visibly through the Quaker movement. The number of Quakers may have doubled each year from 1650 to 1656. Even after that their growth remained spectacular, in places reached if not in membership: how long would it take to win all nations? No rolls were yet kept, but the Quaker movement grew steadily at least until 1672.[26] "The Lamb's War" had first overpowered each of them personally, driving them into painful human conflicts. Apart from a few tracts defending individual Friends' calls to travel as preachers, Friends began first in 1658–59 to write journals of their religious pilgrimages, trying to understand personal and national events together. The Quaker experience of sitting down "under the Light," to recognize and surrender all habits and ideas arising out of self-will or pride, had been harrowing. It often lasted for weeks or months, with tears and sleeplessness as well as quaking; language from war or conquest felt appropriate. Quaker preachers told their hearers that they had already been through the Day of Judgment (though others might suffer it physically after death) and entered a new heavenly life empowered by the same Spirit that had broken them. Their mental pilgrimages (apart from contrasting end results) were like those under a rigorous psychotherapy. So many Quaker autobiographies written in old age tell the same story that a modern reader wonders if their words became stereotyped; but the oldest are the least original in language: an example is letters to Fox written in July 1652 by Richard Hubberthorne, already a northwestern separatist leader, in the midst of his struggle of "convincement":

Dear heart, since I saw thee, the hand of the Lord hath been mightily exercised upon me, and his terrors hath been sharp within me, . . . terrible unto the brutish nature which could not endure the devouring fire. . . . All that which was my life and that which had fed and nourished it must all now perish together. . . . In the midst of his terrible judgments there was a mercy hid which I saw not. . . . All things which is pure and holy is hid from man, for he is separate from God.[27]

Margaret Fell warned new Friends to "let the Eternal Light search you, . . . for this . . . will rip you up and lay you open . . . naked and bare before the Lord. . . . Keep down your Minds that questions and stumbles at the power of God."[28]

The joy and peace of spirit that broke through to Friends newly "convinced" (i.e., convicted) came at first at long intervals and then more steadily, with an outbursting love for other Friends who had gone through the same experiences. Thereafter, a Quaker also expected that at every moment the Spirit or Light would give "leadings" to veto and prompt specific actions: this applied most to religious messages. The first "leading" to speak in a silent Quaker meeting and the first message to non-Quakers were key steps in a Quaker's pilgrimage. John Banks of Cumberland gave up schoolteaching while he went through inner confusion for six years. He came to inner peace.

[But then] as I was sitting in silence waiting upon the Lord in a meeting of Friends upon Pardshaw-Crag, a weighty exercise fell upon my spirit; and it opened in me, that I must go to the Steeple-House at Cockermouth, which was hard for me to give up to. But the Lord by his power made me to shake and tremble, and by it I was made willing to go. But . . . I would have known what I might do there; . . . And as I was going, it appeared to me, as if the priest had been before me; and it opened in me [that I must say] "If thou be a minister of Christ, stand to prove thy practice; and if it be the same the Apostles and ministers of Christ was . . . in doctrine and practice, I'll own thee; but if not I am sent of God this day to testify against thee."[29]

Fox also had strange "leadings" such as his impulse to preach barefoot through the Lichfield market square crying, "Woe to the bloody city of Lichfield" (which had been the scene of a massacre in the Civil War).[30] A modern scholar can ask if a subconscious memory was mistaken as a divine prompting (even if God might also work by such indirect means). Often the early Friends' trust that God drove them to speak was only strengthened when their message and the impulse to give it seemed totally independent of reason or the speaker's conscious will.

Quakers often echoed biblical phrases but perhaps they seemed the normal language of the Spirit. Friends were also willing to obey a lack of leading, when no words were given. Higginson noted with mirth that two Friends came to visit a Cumberland squire, stating they were "sent from God," but when he "demanded what that voice commanded them to say to him they answered it was not yet given to them." They still had not received a message next day and went home.[31]

In the tradition of the Hebrew prophets, some Friends also felt called to make symbolic gestures, such as going through the streets of a city naked or in sackcloth, as a warning against moral nakedness (cf. Is. *20*:2–3).[32] The shock that such an act aroused in every Puritan mind would make any Quaker's half-conscious impulse to do the same seem a "cross" to pride and self-will and drive him to yield to such impulses. The Puritans naturally called such "signs" Ranterism.

The Quaker mission was thus both a product of the inner "Lamb's War" that each Friend had been through and an extension of it across the world as a spiritual conquest of new peoples. At times "the Lamb's War" was a regional ingathering of masses of unchurched families, as in the English Northwest. At other times it was sharply focused on regions of proud resistance, as in Cornwall and New England. Public resistance to "convincement" after 1656 made Friends realize that aggressive preaching and shocking "signs" often aroused hostility without shaking hearts. Nayler and Penington reexamined "the Lamb's War" and its relation to Quaker behavior and how God deals with evil.

NOTES

1. William Penn, Preface to George Fox, *A Journal* (1694), J-2.

2. See John Banks, *A Journal of the Life . . . of . . . John Banks* (1712), 66–67. Fox, feeling divine power not only in himself but also in others, hated adoration.

3. Thomas Lower, who had married Mary, daughter of Margaret Fell, wrote at Fox's dictation the "Spence manuscript" of his *Journal* in 1674. George Fox, *A Journal* (1694), edited by Thomas Ellwood at Fox's request from the Spence manuscript and other documents, was abridged in many later editions. In 1911 Norman Penney published literatim the manuscript version (hereafter Fox, *Camb. Jnl*). *Fox, Journal*, ed. John L. Nickalls (Cambridge: 1952), included all of Fox's main autobiographical manuscripts. No certifiable portrait of Fox survives. William Penn and Robert Barclay exalted Fox's role and the authority of his inward guidance in reply to Friends who rejected Fox's leadership in the 1670s. Until 1656 James Nayler and others had shared Fox's roles as leader. Lewis Benson's *Catholic Quakerism* (Philadelphia: 1968) and articles in *Quaker Religious Thought* (hereafter *QRT*) and *New Foundation* publications are the latest to identify Quakerism wholly with Fox's teachings.

4. The scapegrace ex-Quaker Nathaniel Smith claimed in *The Quakers Spiritual Court Proclaimed* (1668) that, while jailed with him at Lancaster, Fox told him the world was flat.

5. See Joseph Pickvance, *George Fox and the Purefeys . . . in Fenny Drayton* (Lon-

don: 1976) and his taped London Yearly Meeting Lecture (1982) on Drayton, Mancetter, and Baddesley. See also Joan Allen on Hartshill.

6. Some of these beliefs were held by German Anabaptists such as Hans Denck and Melchior Hofmann, a few by Hendrik Niclas or Boehme, but no clear links have been shown.

7. Fox, *Journal* (1952), 8, 11, 12, 19. He recorded at least seven such early "openings," some, like John Bunyan's, simply insights into remembered Bible texts. Fox used the phrases interchangeably: "it was said to me," "it was shown to me," "the Lord showed me," "it was opened."

8. Fox, *Journal* (1952), for example, 27, 65. His first surviving letter is one he and Elizabeth Hooton wrote to the magistrate who jailed them. Another was to Justice Bennett, who used the nickname "Quakers" of him.

9. The first Quaker tract was probably *False Prophets and False Teachers Described* published in 1652–53 by the six Quaker prisoners at York, including Aldam, Mary Fisher*, and Elizabeth Hooton. Aldam's imprisonment broke his strength for Quaker preaching. On Quaker beginnings in Yorkshire see the accounts by individual Meetings in Norman Penney, ed., *The First Publishers of Truth* (London: 1907ff.), from manuscripts sent after Fox asked the Meetings for records of who first convinced them, the first local Friends, and those who first went out to preach.

10. See Hugh Barbour, *The Quakers in Puritan England* (New Haven: 1964), Appendix. The most detailed study of data on individual Friends is the work of Richard Vann, *The Social Development of English Quakerism* (Cambridge, Mass.: 1969), and Richard Vann and Richard Eversley, *Demography of Quakerism in England and Ireland* (in press). See also a debate between Vann and Judith Hurwitz: *Past and Present* 43 (May 1969): 71–91 and 48 (Aug. 1970) 156–64.

11. Combined from Margaret Fell's "Testimony" prefacing Fox's *Journal* and her narrative in Spence MSS III, 135. See Hugh Barbour, *Margaret Fell Speaking* (Wallingford, Pa.: 1976). See also her "Relation" introducing her collected [*Works*]: *A Brief Collection of Remarkable Passages* (1710).

12. See William C. Braithwaite's classic *The Beginnings of Quakerism* (London: 1912; Cambridge: 1955); hereafter *BBQ*; Isabel Ross, *Margaret Fell: Mother of Quakerism* (London: 1949; York: 1984). Documents in Penney, *First Publishers of Truth*; Hugh Barbour and Arthur Roberts, eds., *Early Quaker Writings* (Grand Rapids, Mich.: 1972); hereafter *EQW*.

13. Francis Higginson, *A Brief Relation of the Irreligion of the Northern Quakers* (1655), 11–13; cf. *EQW*, 70–72.

14. Barry Reay, *The Quakers and the English Revolution* (New York: 1985), 28–29, based on his Oxford Ph.D. thesis, "Early Quaker Activity and Reactions to It, 1654–64" (1979), but broader, thorough, more balanced.

15. See Barbour, *Quakers in Puritan England*, Chs. 2, 3. In the "Pilgrimage of Grace" in 1536 the whole North of England rose in protest against Henry VIII's policies: even monasteries and lesser gentry were unpopular with their tenants in the Northwest, although not elsewhere; see Madeline Hope Dodds and Ruth Dodds, *The Pilgrimage of Grace, 1536–37, and the Exeter Conspiracy, 1538* (Cambridge: 1915).

16. William Dewsbury, *A True Prophecy of the Mighty Day of the Lord* (1655). See *EQW*, 93ff.

17. See *Stephen Crisp's Testimony Concerning James Parnell* (1662); the Swarthmoor letters and Kendal accounts are a treasury for scholars.

18. Charles Marshall, in Preface to *The Memory of the Righteous Revived* (1689), the collected works of Camm and Audland.

19. See Vann, *Social Development*; Vann and Eversley, *Demography*; and the excellent local materials in Russell Mortimer, ed., *Minute Book of the Men's Meeting of the Society of Friends in Bristol, 1667–1686* (Bristol, Eng.: 1971); Michael Mullett, *Early Lancaster Friends* (Lancaster, Eng.: 1978); Pearson Thistlethwaite, *Yorkshire Quarterly Meeting (1665–1966)* (Harrogate, Eng.: 1979).

20. Reay, *Quakers*, 18–20, 38–43; W. Alan Cole, "The Quakers and Politics" (Ph.D. thesis, Cambridge University, 1955); J. W. Martin, "The Pre-Quaker Writings of George Bishop," *Quaker History* (hereafter *QH*) 74, no. 2 (Fall 1985): 20–27.

21. See Richard Bauman's impressive study of basic Quaker dynamics, *Let Your Words Be Few* (Cambridge: 1983).

22. See Nuttall, *Holy Spirit*, Ch. III.

23. Normative for Friends has been Robert Barclay, *Apology* (1678), Propositions XII and XIII. See Francis Hall, ed., *Quaker Worship in North America* (Richmond, Ind.: 1979); Alan Kolp, "Friends, Sacraments, and Sacramental Living," *QRT* 57 (1984): 36–51; Merle Strege, ed., *Baptism and Church* (Grand Rapids, Mich.: 1986), 99–114; H. Barbour, "Protestant Quakerism," *QRT*" (Autumn 1969): 2–33.

24. Isaac Penington, *Light or Darknesse, Displaying or Hiding Itself as It Pleaseth* (1650); "An Account of his Spiritual Travel," from Thomas Ellwood's Testimony prefacing Penington's *Works* (1681). See R. Melvin Keiser, "From Dark Christian to Fullness of Life: Isaac Penington's Journey from Puritanism to Quakerism," *Guilford Review* 23 (Spring 1986): 42–63; and especially, Andrew Brink, "The Quietism of Isaac Penington," *JEHS* (London) 51 (1965–67): 30–53.

25. James Nayler*, *A Collection of Sundry Books* (1716) *Works*, 696. William G. Bittle, *James Nayler, 1618–1660: The Quaker Indicted by Parliament* (York, Eng.: 1986), is a good study of Nayler's role in Parliamentary policy under Cromwell.

26. See Vann, *Social Development*, 93ff; Vann and Eversley, *Demography*. We may guess a total of 60,000–75,000 English Quakers by 1700 and, by then, 10,000 in America.

27. Swarthmore MSS 3, 1, quoted in *EQW* 157–85. See Geoffrey. F Nuttall's catalogue and indices, *Early Quaker Letters from the Swarthmore Manuscripts to 1660* (London: 1952). Parallel experiences are in the *Works* of John Burnyeat, Stephen Crisp, Francis Howgill, Camm, and Audland.

28. Fell, *Brief Collection*, 69, 95.

29. Banks, *Journal*, 9–10. Banks seems not to have noticed that the identical message was given against the same Puritan pastor, George Larkham of Cockermouth, in George Fox's *Great Mistery* in 1659, perhaps the same year. Which man first gave the message is not clear.

30. See Fox, *Journal* (1952), 71.

31. Higginson, *A Brief Relation of the Irreligion*, 7–8. The best discussion of these patterns is Bauman's *Let Your Words Be Few*.

32. Robert Barclay's "Sign" of this kind during his student days was discussed in his own tract A *Seasonable Warning to the Inhabitants of Aberdeen* (1672).

4
QUAKER WORSHIP AND ETHICS AND THEIR TRANSFORMATION, 1652–1662

The distinctive form of Quaker Worship is for a group to sit in an unadorned room in silence of mind and body "waiting upon God" until one or more members feel led by the Spirit to speak or pray. This Quaker way only gradually became distinct from those of Seekers and other separatists who met informally in homes with much silence and lay leadership. Early Quaker prophetic messages of judgment and confrontation were often given in a marketplace or during a puritan church service. For longer presentations, crowds of noisy but interested hearers were gathered on a moor or daily in a rented hall in an "appointed" or "threshing" meeting. Hearers who were "convinced" by these forms of mission were taken into smaller gatherings in private homes, where they shared their struggles of self-judgment under the Light with other seekers in daily or weekly "gathered meetings" with prayer and messages of guidance as well as silence and tears: "Upon a time [wrote Stephen Crisp] being weary of my own Thoughts in the Meeting of God's People, I thought none was like me, and it was but in vain to sit there with wandring mind. . . . I thought to go forth; and as I was going, the Lord Thundred through me, saying 'that which is weary must die.' So I turned to my seat and waited."[1] George Fox's "Epistles," clearly shaped by Paul's, were meant for such times: "Stand still in the Light, and submit to it, and the temptations and troubles will be hushed and gone: and then content comes from the Lord, and help contrary to your expectation. Then ye grow up in peace."[2] Ecstatic letters of affection between partners in Quaker mission journeys remain as signs of the love released by common struggle.

Ministry to those already gathered must not interrupt the Spirit:

Friends [wrote Fox], take heed of destroying that which ye have begotten. . . . Meetings you come into, when they are set silent, . . . are many times in their own. . . . It is a mighty thing to be in the work of the ministry of the Lord . . . for it is not as acustomary preaching, but to bring people to the end of all preaching; for [after] your once speaking to people, then people come into the thing ye speak of. . . . Take heed of many words, but what reacheth to life from the life received from God, that settles others in the life.[3]

Quaker worship after 1659 was thus transformed by no change in the central experiences but by stripping away the public "threshing" meetings and most of the anguish of the newly convinced. Fox began to write: "dwell deep"; other Friends: "center down." Robert Barclay, convinced at home in 1666, gave the best-known definition of it:

Many are the blessed experiences which I could relate of this silence and manner of worship, . . . for as [it] consisteth not in words, so neither in silence, as silence; but in a holy dependence of the mind upon God from which . . . silence naturally follows until words can be brought forth which are from God's Spirit. . . . And as everyone is thus gathered . . . inwardly in their spirits as well as outwardly, . . . though there be not a word spoken, yet is the true spiritual worship performed . . . and our hearts . . . overcome with the secret sense of God's power . . . without words . . . ministered from one vessel to another.[4]

Quakers denied dead ritual but felt their own worship was worth jail.

QUAKER ETHICS

Quaker actions have always expressed special "Testimonies" of truthfulness, simplicity, equality, and peace, but their essence began from the judgments and the leadings of the Light or Spirit of God as both were experienced in worship and in "the Lamb's War." The Light came to early Friends as an uncoverer of one's own motives and as "a cross to one's own will." Friends always had to look twice at unexpected impulses in case self-will or pleasure were their source; they were fierce with Ranters who claimed that God made all desires pure.[5] They also expected the light of Truth to be consistent and its leadings, though individualized, to be recognizably similar for all times and persons, including biblical prophets, apostles, and all Friends. What one Quaker felt as a leading was tested against guidance given to other Friends and the Bible and after 1656 submitted to the joint guidance given to a group by the Spirit as "the sense of the Meeting." Each of the norms that early Friends accepted were considered to be "Truth."[6] This standard applied to honesty in the marketplace but also to "plain language" as true grammar: Puritan Humphrey Bache said "how are you today" to a Quaker who then "asked . . . if I believed that thee & thou to one perticular Person was truth; I said yea; said he then: if I did not come into obedience to what I was convinced of to be Truth I must come under condemnation."[7] Bache became a Quaker.

Clearly, Quaker "Truth" began from moral axioms that seemed self-evident to a sensitive conscience in a puritan culture: the Gospel of Matthew was a series of commands Christ expected disciples to keep. A prime evil was waste, whether of wealth while the poor starved or of time while work was needed. A basic sin was the idolatry that prefers a self-made image of God to God's own reality. Luxury was putting oneself ahead of God.

Some unjust acts or untrue phrases were nevertheless easier to notice from one social class or region of England than from others. It was much harder for William Penn or Thomas Ellwood, raised at Oxford, to keep on their hats before their fathers and friends than for a north-country farmer from the wet moors who wore his hat even indoors. Saying "thee and thou" to a gentleman had the same impact that was once felt in America when a black man called a white woman by her first name. Some Yorkshire farmers still say "thee" among equals.[8] "Thee" had once been said to everyone, but for two centuries before Fox, gentlemen said "thee" only to God, lovers, children, and servants.

Bache's case shows a fourth special mark of the ethics of early Friends: they expected their actions, like their words, to challenge the conscience and conduct of their hearers by the contrast of the Quaker's and the hearer's behavior. To London merchants Fox wrote: "Act in the truth, . . . which lets everyone see all the deeds and actions they have done amiss: So the Witness of God within them ariseth a swift witness against them. . . . Then are ye a dread and a terror to the unjust. . . . Here your lives and words will preach."[9] An early Quaker who refused to bargain in the marketplace was as startling as someone who bids only once in an auction. Yet Quakers, like Puritans, assumed that private morality was most important as part of God's ongoing work in history to remake humanity and society (Americans would later say: "to build God's Kingdom"). This transformation must begin with an opening of every heart and conscience.

FIVE POINTS ABOUT EACH OF FOUR QUAKER "TESTIMONIES"

Note in each Testimony its truth element; second, the double roots in Bible and religious experience of this specific norm; third, its support in class or regional custom; fourth, the ways in which this Testimony served as a weapon in "the Lamb's War"; fifth, that each case will show how the Testimony became a uniform and united stand among Quakers and then a badge of loyalty that Friends upheld even when its truth and shock value were gone.

Fox, when he dictated his *Journal* later in his life, summarized the content of Quaker ethics: he was called "to turn people from darkness to the light that they might receive Christ Jesus"; to bring them away from all ceremonies and churches; to use "thee and thou"; to refuse to take off their hats to anyone; to "cry for justice" to judges; to warn against drink, sports, May-games, vanities, and cheating; and to reject oaths.[10] Modern Friends may group these "Testimonies" under four basic concerns, for honesty, equality, simplicity, and peace.

Honesty

We already noted honesty as it was applied in "plain language." Rejection of oaths was a more crucial application; an oath that "this time I'm telling the truth'' implies dishonesty at other times. Oaths were also used for cursing, using God's name for one's own purposes. The biblical basis was clear: Jesus said ''let your yea be yea and your nay be nay'' and forbade all swearing as evil (Matt. 5:33–37). Not only Fox but English Baptists quoted these verses daily. Like simple clothes they were part of the radical Puritan lifestyle. North-of-Englanders were particularly proud of taking every person at his or her word. The region was famous in border ballads for its loyalties. Men hated the endless oaths of allegiance demanded by each new ruler or government. There was a shock value too in the Quakers' standard: Friends in law courts regularly offered to pay the penalties of perjury for any untrue statement they made and yet let themselves be convicted of treason rather than swear an oath of allegiance. Only after fifty more years did courts accept Quakers' affirmations instead of oaths.

Quaker honesty in business meant asking and giving only what each article was worth. Later, this was called the fixed or single price, and Quakers have been credited with inventing the price tag. But in the Middle Ages the Catholic Church itself had tried to protect workmen against unfair wages and poor people against monopoly prices by fixing just prices and wages in Church courts. Churchmen saw charging high interest on loans to farmers in a year of crop failure as unneighborly conduct. When Calvinists took power, although bans on usury could seldom be applied as between merchants and bankers, they too tried to oversee business and to ensure justice for the glory of God and their godly community. Calvinists, Puritans, and Quakers did not accept laissez-faire, despite more opennes in allowing venture capital, until 150 years after Calvin, when their Commonwealths had failed, forcing individuals to run their lives without a united godly society.[11] When George Fox told justices of the peace in market towns to set fair wages and prices, he meant simply to make honest the old close-knit town communities he had known. Honesty might so terrify cheating merchants as to convert them: it was not meant to make a new economy. Fox noted that their honesty made Quakers respected, and once persecutions were over it often made them rich.[12]

Other honesty issues included Friends' rejection of pagan names for months and days of the week: Mars' Month and Woden's Day reflect pagan violence. Before the Quakers arose many Baptists had rejected these names in favor of clear names like Seventh Month for September (the Julian calendar then in use began the year in March). For both Quakers and Baptists, the Church was not a building but God's people, all of whom were Saints: so Friends spoke of Paul's Yard in London, meaning St. Paul's Churchyard. Friends were even more negative about personal titles: untrue personal relationships were implied by ''my Lord,'' ''my lady,'' or ''your humble servant.'' Titles were rarer among Puritans; in the North even an earl could be called ''Harry Hotspur.'' Around London, people as saintly as John Donne used flowery palaver. Titles also fed men's pride. For the same reasons, Friends refused to take off their hats to anyone but God and only in prayer.

Equality

Early Friends put less stress on equality in the abstract than do modern ones: Friends meant less to liberate classes than to obey Truth and the teachings of Jesus, who said "call no man Master." They came from regions and groups that praised a farmer's or a working man's independence, but they refused titles and gestures of honor to humble everyone equally rather than honoring everyone equally. They never "treated charwomen like duchesses," as did aristocratic Oscar Wilde. Before royalty they spoke about Friends' integrity, not equality.

Equality among early Quakers also applied to God's ability to speak through any receptive person. Thus the equality in ministry of all Friends, rich and poor, young and old, educated and unschooled, and especially women and men, was noticed by everyone in the 1650s. Baptists let any member pray or exhort in the worship services, but the ministers, although mostly unschooled craftsmen or merchants, were set apart from lay members. When the highly trained Puritan pastors were offended by these crude "mechanicks," the Baptists and Quakers pointed out that Jesus and his disciples were workingmen. Quakers showed no humility when speaking by the authority of the Spirit. When Puritans reminded Friends that Saint Paul had said women shouldn't speak in church meetings, Fox replied that Paul did not forbid God to speak through a woman. When Richard Baxter, the leading West-of-England Puritan pastor, wrote to James Nayler that even after his many years of study he did not know all the answers, Nayler replied that Quakers had told Nayler this already. Only the infallible Spirit gave Friends authority.[13] Quakers' attacks against paid pastors were so much sharper than those against rulers, aristocrats, or the rich that we must see them as based on honesty in worship and on God's initiative, not on social equality. The proof that Friends' concern was religious is that in the late 1650s more Friends were jailed over Tithes than for any other charge.

Equality of men and women was practiced among Friends more than it was proclaimed, except at the key point of ministry on which Margaret Fell's 1666 tract *Womens Speaking* was a pioneer.[14] Ministry had come to include tract writing. Englishwomen's role as heads of households, familiar when husbands were dead or away, became common for the wives of Quaker preachers. Chapter 6 discusses Quaker women's meetings for business; from both Quakers and Puritans the most revolutionary message was that all daily life was equally part of God's direct Call to each of his "saints."[15]

Quakers stood out also, however, for their faith in non-Christian cultures. Friends assumed that God's Spirit worked through Turks, Chinese, or American Indians, as well as through the Englishmen who knew that the Spirit's proper name was Christ. Fox wrote to the Emperor of China, reminding him of "a Power above all Powers, . . . Creator, and Former and Maker of all things, . . . who would have all to know him and worship him in the Light . . . which Jesus Christ hath enlightened you withal, that doth let you see your evil thoughts."[16]

Penn later made this equality apply politically in Pennsylvania's treatment of the Indians. Earlier universality had not softened "the Lamb's War." Margaret Fell wrote two friendly tracts for the Jews of Amsterdam and their famous chief Rabbi Manasseh ben-Israel. She used biblical verses entirely from the Old Testament and recalled the Jews to the Light and Covenant that Isaiah and Jeremiah proclaimed. Yet she called Jews as sternly as Christians to repent, to give up outward legalism under the Torah, and in effect to become Quakers.[17] The Quaker "Testimony" of equality began as a spirit-centered radicalism that was retained only by John Woolman and a few others. It was for most Friends transformed by the Restoration era into a more secular concern, shallower but broader, regarding the poor. This made Quakers into examples and occasionally leaders for later political movements.

Quaker Simplicity

Simplicity, too, had roots in both the Bible and puritanism, which had attacked pride (though not inequality) in wealth or costume. North and West-of-England farmers did not distinguish social classes by costumes as did Londoners. They were not ascetics and knew the goodness of "the creation." Friends like Puritans stressed a "moral athlete's" life, "traveling light" as pilgrims on earth, and as suspicious as an athlete of all indulgence. Friends like Penn turned their attack more directly against injustice and inequality:

The sweat and tedious labour of the husbandman, early and late, cold and hot, wet and dry [is] converted into the pleasure, ease and pastime of a small number of men; severity [is] laid upon nineteen parts of the land to feed the inordinate lusts and delicious appetites of the twentieth. . . . [Later, more compactly] The very trimming of the vain world would clothe all the naked one.[18]

Early Quakers and radical Puritans refused to wear silver buckles or buttons or to waste cloth, food, or drink for pride or pleasure.

It is thus ironic that in the period 1660–85 when persecution was transforming the inner meaning of all Quaker norms, Quaker dress and speech ceased to shake the pride of people Friends met, or even of Quakers themselves, and so ceased being an actual Testimony. Quaker dress was not yet fixed in cut but cuffless and brown, black, or gray. Quakers so opposed love of fashion that Quaker plain dress became old-fashioned and unique. The Quaker practice was left "high and dry" by changes in English custom. When everyone said "you" to all classes, the Quaker "Truth" of "thee and thou" was a quaint habit. Under persecution, loyalty to the Quaker community made Friends maintain all of the "Testimonies" openly and uniformly. Booklets survive in which, for instance, all women members of Kendal Meeting signed to affirm that they had not and would never pay tithes to a parish pastor. Any Quakers whose behavior was felt to disguise or disgrace "Truth" was "disowned." Sensitive consciences broke new ways for Friends just in those areas in which "Truth" had not established a consensus under Fox.

Peace

The Quaker Testimony that was the most creative and to modern Friends the most interesting was peace. It was the most slowly formulated. Biblical and Puritan roots and Quaker ideas of Truth and "the Lamb's War" were all again involved. We can also record, better than with the other issues, the evolution of Friends' peace concerns from individual conscience to collective Testimony and to national policy.

George Fox's *Journal* describes a challenge in Derby jail in 1651, when he was offered freedom if he would captain a company in the army that Cromwell was raising for his final battle with the Royalists at Worcester. Fox's refusal was rooted in "the Lamb's War": the Bible showed that wars come from inner desires and lusts; the true struggle against evil is therefore within men. Fox was still following God's Light within him, he felt, not an abstract pacifist principle. Private conscience held back other Quakers from arms: Thomas Lurting became convinced while serving as a sailor on a warship that he could not kill men and was duly mustered out at the end of the battle. Some men became Quakers while soldiers in Cromwell's garrisons and were expelled from the army only if they would not obey their officers. There was clearly no uniform Testimony yet about peacetime service. There was none against police restraint. Quaker tracts reminded Cromwell and his army of the high ideals for which they first had fought.

Deeper insight than refusal to bear arms underlay James Nayler's 1657 tract, *The Lamb's War*, describing nonviolent love and patient suffering as God's way of conquering. Violence, said Nayler, was natural enough, the human result of anger that came from hurt pride. Anyone who confronted Quaker truths would be angry. Violence was the Devil's distraction by which men are turned from facing real evils within to destroying the outward "creation," parts of the physical world that God had made good. Intolerance and persecution were other defenses ("projections," we now say) to avoid inner truth. Early Quakers thus took for granted that they would meet violence and persecution in "the world," even though they would not use outward weapons. Their own suffering could also help further to purge their own pride.

There was no North-of-England tradition opposing warfare. Early Friends naturally quoted Jesus about loving enemies and turning the other cheek, putting up Peter's sword, and refusing to fight against Pilate. The Anabaptists after Münster had rejected war but the English Baptists had not, being also radical Puritans hoping for the "rule of the saints." Since Friends had needed to find their own way to Peace, they did not cite the Bible against arms as legalistically as (following the Baptists) they did against oaths. Instead of standing upon individual Bible texts, Nayler summed up the message of the Sermon on the Mount as a whole. Friends also seldom accepted pacifism so unquestioningly as to use pacifism as a shock tactic to convince non-Quakers, although attackers might be shaken by nonresistance. Francis Rous convinced a highwayman who started to rob him, but Arend Sonmans was killed by another.

A consistent Peace Testimony of the whole Quaker movement was first affirmed in 1659–60, when the Puritan Commonwealth was going under. After Cromwell died the radical Puritans in Parliament called on Quakers to enroll as commissioners of the militia to keep local forces out of Royalist hands. Half a dozen Quakers actually did so.[19] The Commonwealth fell in any case. When the conservative Puritans restored the old king's son, King Charles II, at Breda in Holland, offered Puritans freedom to run their own parishes, and Baptists toleration outside the Church of England. Charles was shrewd and easygoing and probably meant the promises he had made. The Restoration Parliament and the Cavalier Parliament that followed, however, turned out to have a heavy majority of Royalist country gentry, ardent Anglicans. In 1661 they restored the Episcopal bishops and Prayer Books in the Church of England and went on the next year to require all clergy to follow these or lose their pulpits. Seventeen hundred and sixty of the Puritan pastors left the parish churches rather than obey. Most of the Puritans suffered in silence, but a gang of "Fifth Monarchists" tried to take over London in a midnight riot. Quakers too were suspected of plotting a new Civil War. Suddenly, Friends realized how vital it was to be able to point out that they had not borne arms even in 1659. In 1660 and 1661 Quakers made statements to the king, Parliament, and England at large, stating that since they had always rejected violence they could be counted on to do so even under Cavalier persecution: "The Spirit of God by which we are guided is not changeable; the Spirit of Christ, which leads us into all Truth, will never move us to fight and war against men with outward weapons."[20] The consistency of the Spirit was a new emphasis in Quaker messages, although Friends had moved toward it in their concern for uniform group Testimonies on issues like tithes. So the standardizing that made Quaker speech and dress no longer a prophetic challenge made the "Peace Testimony" more challenging. The need to balance the absoluteness and the universality of the Light became the point around which Quaker theological doctrines were transformed.

NOTES

1. Stephen Crisp, *Journal of the Life of Stephen Crisp* (1694), 18–19.

2. George Fox, *Epistles* No. 10 (1652), from Markey MS. See John Banks, *A Journal of the Life . . . of . . . John Banks* (1712), 6–7.

3. George Fox, *Journal*, ed. Norman Penney (Cambridge: 1911), 1, 311–23.

4. Robert Barclay, *Apology* (1678), Proposition XI, ix, vi.

5. Fox showed anger at Ranters' amorality often in his *Journal* (e.g., ed. John L. Nickalls [Cambridge: 1952], 47, 79–81, 181–83, 212); at times (cf. p. 113) he could not distinguish between Ranters and Calvinist antinomians. See also Geoffrey Nuttall, *James Nayler* (London: 1954), a masterly study.

6. See James Childress, "Answering That of God in Every Man," *Quaker Religious Thought* (Thereafter *QRT*) 15, no. 3 (1974): 2–4.

7. Humphrey Bache, *A Few Words in True Love Written to the Old Long Sitting Parliament* (1659), 9.

8. American Quakers who say "is thee going?" also preserve old rural English with Norse verb forms and are closer to early moorland Quaker language than English Friends who ask "art thou going?"

9. George Fox, *The Line of Righteousness Stretched Forth Over All Merchants* (London: 1661), 3, 4, 5.

10. Fox, *Journal* (1952), 34–38. Other early summaries are in Edward Burrough, *A Message for Instruction* and *The Testimony of the Lord Concerning London* (both 1657); Barclay, *Apology*, Proposition XV; William Penn, Jr., *No Cross, No Crown* (London: 1669, expanded 1682) and other works. See also Howard H. Brinton, *Friends for 300 Years* (New York: 1952), Ch. 7.

11. See Richard H. Tawney, *Religion and the Rise of Capitalism* (London: 1926), replying to Max Weber's *Protestant Ethic and the Spirit of Capitalism* (London: 1930), whose "protestant" examples are mostly from the 1750s, all post-1675.

12. Fox, *Journal* (1952), 169–70.

13. Richard Baxter, *The Quakers Catechism* (1655), 9–10, replied to by [James Nayler], *An Answer to . . . Baxter* (1655), 9–11.

14. See bibliography in Hugh Barbour, "Quaker Prophetesses," in J. William Frost and John M. Moore, eds., *Seeking the Light* (Wallingford and Haverford, Penn., 1986) 41–60; Mary Maples Dunn, "Women of Light," in Carol Ruth Berkin and Mary Beth Norton, eds., *Women of America: A History* (Boston: 1979) 114–138; and Elaine C. Huber, "A Woman Must Not Speak," in Rosemary Reuther, ed., *Women of Spirit* (New York 1979), 153–182.

15. See Haller; Knappen; Hill; and J. William Frost, "Secularization in Colonial Pennsylvania," in *Seeking the Light*, ed. Frost and Moore, 105–28.

16. George Fox, *Gospel Truth Demonstrated in a Collection of Doctrinal Books* (1706), 207–08. The rare original (1660) never reached China.

17. Margaret Fell, *To Manasseth-ben-Israel* (1656); *A Loving Salutation to the Seed of God Among the Jews* (1657). See Isabel Ross, *Margaret Fell* (London: 1949), Ch. 7.

18. Penn, *No Cross, No Crown*, 1, Ch. 18, 10; and his *Some Fruits of Solitude* (1693), no. 67 (no. 68 in later editions).

19. See Alan Cole, "The Quakers and Politics, 1652–1660" (Ph.D. thesis, Cambridge University, 1955); Barry Reay, *The Quakers and the English Revolution* (New York: 1985), Ch. 5.

20. *Declaration* of Eleventh Month (Jan.) 21, 1660–61, in Fox, *A Journal* (1694), 234.

5
THE MISSION TO AMERICA

The missionary impulse that drove early Friends to travel to Lutheran, Calvinist, Roman Catholic, and even Muslim countries rested upon the belief that Quakers had revived true Christianity and that all who did not respond to the Inward Light followed false religions. Although a few Protestant mystics and pietists in Holland and the Germanies received the Quaker message sympathetically, in general Friends made converts only when there were substantial numbers of English people. Since seventeenth-century English people were in the process of settling an empire—colonizing in Ireland, the West Indies, and the mainland of North America—Quakers journeyed to these areas and found adherents as well as formidable opponents.

Friends experienced some persecution everywhere, but the most dramatic confrontations—that ultimately created four martyrs—were in New England. The Puritans who migrated to Massachusetts wanted to create a godly commonwealth that rested upon close cooperation between minister and magistrate, religious uniformity, and an intense personal piety. The Puritans expected individual conversion and tried to confine this experience within the limits of a narrowly defined system of theology. Those who disagreed with the New England way were free to move elsewhere, and if gentle persuasion did not suffice, the colony was willing to employ more drastic measures.

Although since its settlement in 1629 Massachusetts Bay had been torn by controversy, its leaders had concluded that the success of their "Errand into the Wilderness" required the maintenance of true religion.[1] Otherwise, God would punish the colony as he had disciplined the ancient Israelites who had forsaken their Covenant. The determination to preserve what they defined as the one true religion had, even before Quakers began, resulted in the series of refugees. Roger Williams, who served as a minister in Salem and later in Plymouth, was a well-educated man who agreed with most of the doctrines of the Congregationalists but questioned whether, in the 1630s after centuries of apostasy, anyone could know the exact form the Church should follow. Williams feared that religious intolerance would threaten and harm suffering servants of Christ as much as heretics, suggested that the state should legislate morality but not right belief, and advocated separation of church and state. Williams' ideas clearly threatened the foundation of the biblical Commonwealths in Massachusetts and Connecticut, and he was forced to seek refuge with the Indians, from whom he bought land in what is now Providence, Rhode Island.[2]

Anne Hutchinson, the wife of a Boston merchant, threatened to upset the close balance between reason and revelation, Church authority and individual conversion, by her emphasis upon the unmediated experience of God. She criticized the Puritans' emphasis upon preparation for grace, which she called a "works righteousness." Her expositions of the ministers' sermons in weekday gatherings in her home earned her a substantial following in Boston, but—after a trial in a civil court and expulsion from the Church—Hutchinson fled to Portsmouth, Rhode Island, in 1637, and her followers, including Mary Dyer, settled Newport. When the first Quaker missionaries reached Rhode Island twenty years later, they found an area populated by men and women who supported Williams's commitment to religious freedom and who had been prepared by Anne Hutchinson to accept a belief in the efficacy of the Inward Light of Christ. The Puritan authorities had gained experience in dealing with heresies, particularly those spread by women.[3]

In the battle for the religious loyalties of New Englanders in the 1650s the Puritans found themselves in a defensive position, made worse by their own insecurity. During the first decade of settlement, the history of Massachusetts Bay seemed a series of God-ordained triumphs over heretics, Indians, and royal authority. The success of the alliance of Congregational Church and magisterial authority, ensured by giving the franchise only to adult male Church members, pointed the way for England's Puritans. The English Civil War against Charles I ended by spawning sectarians and, to the disgust of Massachusetts' clergy, even the English Congregationalists became defenders of a limited religious toleration. By the late 1640s, the religious policies of Massachusetts and Connecticut seemed to radical Puritans less like a new wave than a backwater, and the response of the authorities in church and state was to tighten laws against dissent and in support of the established Congregational Church.

Throughout the 1650s Quakers remained confident that they were to inaugurate the reign of Christ on earth. Their missionaries humbly waited on God, but they approached Massachusetts as God's emissaries. They judged the New England Puritans' rejection of Quakers as signs of the reign of Antichrist. Quaker ministers were not interested in polite discourse, civility, and compromise but in overthrowing the New England church system. They would obey no law that would interfere with their obedience to the Light Within, and they would defend their tactics with appeals to the experience of the Light of God and the rights of Englishmen. Denouncing Puritan ministers as "hireling" ambassadors of Satan, the Friends insisted on free speech and open debate as a means of proselytizing, and they would meet openly or in secret with sympathizers. Believing that God directed them and that disobedience to his will was sin, the Friends accepted persecution as a witness to their faith.[4]

Neither Puritan nor Quaker could admit to the validity of the others' religious insights without calling into question their own knowledge of God's will. Their conflict began, continued, and ended with no questioning of this fundamental issue. In the seventeenth century, for these two groups religious experience was too important to be relativized. The vitriolic debate between them became tragic because the Puritan oligarchy had both the will and the power to inflict physical punishment and even death.

Even before Quakers visited New England, the Puritan authorities knew them by reputation as religious fanatics and disturbers of government. So when Mary Fisher and Ann Austin appeared on a ship in Boston in 1656, the authorities wasted no time seizing both women immediately, imprisoning them without trial, burning their Quaker tracts, and, after a five weeks imprisonment, requiring the ship's captain to return them to Barbados. Two days later eight more Quaker missionaries arrived and met the same harsh treatment. The General Court passed a law levying fines on ship captains who brought Friends to Boston, on Friends who came, on those in the colony who defended Friends, and on those who possessed any Quaker literature. The ostensible grounds for these penalties were not the Quakers' religious dissent per se but their seditious qualities: failure to take oaths, to obey laws, to doff their hats to magistrates, and to serve in the militia. Clearly, reasoned the Puritans, Quaker beliefs would undermine all government.

To early Friends, suffering served as a way of showing their faith, of identifying with the apostles of the early church, of attracting new converts, and of witnessing to their unquestioning obedience to the demands of God.[5] When Friends could not obtain passage to Boston because of the Massachusetts law, Quaker Robert Fowler built his own small boat, the *Woodhouse*, and with eleven missionaries (six of whom had already been expelled from Massachusetts) set sail from England for New England using as navigational aids "neither latitude nor longitude" and relying upon the Inward Light as "Leader, Guide, and Rule."[6] Nine of the Friends went to the Puritan stronghold seeking converts and openly denouncing the laws, the Puritan Church, and the ministry. The authorities responded by tightening laws, but their brandings, ear-croppings, fines, prison, and whippings proved ineffective. Between 1656 and 1659 thirty-three Quakers entered the Bay Colony. The persecution created sympathy. Although local magistrates hesitated to impose the full stringency of the law, they banished some Salem converts and, on one occasion, tried to sell the children of one Quaker couple into indentured servitude.

In desperation and in spite of opposition among the inhabitants, the General Court decided to invoke the death penalty against the missionaries who visited the colony for the third time. The effect of the new law was described by Marmaduke Stephenson. Stephenson, a resident of Yorkshire in England, was plowing his fields in 1655 when the "Word of the Lord came to me in a still small Voice . . . saying to me, in the Secret of my Heart and Conscience, 'I have Ordained Thee a prophet unto the Nations.' " The call of God conferred ordination, and soon after, Stephenson felt led to visit Barbados. While there, he learned of the New England law enacting the death penalty. As he pondered the news, "immediately came the Word of the Lord unto me, saying, 'Thou knowest not but that thou mayest go thither.' " He went, was arrested and banished, returned, was again arrested and sent away; soon he was back for a third time.[7] Stephenson was joined in Boston by William Robinson and Mary Dyer, Quakers on their third visit and well aware of the threatened death penalty.

Stephenson, Robinson, and Dyer were sentenced to death in August 1659. The men were not allowed to speak before their executions for fear they might corrupt the population; the authorities had drums beaten to make sure no communication occurred. After witnessing the hangings of the two men, Mary Dyer mounted the platform and had her feet and arms tied and the hood put on at the gallows. Then, as she awaited death, she received a reprieve and was again banished. She soon returned, and although offered her freedom if she would not visit Massachusetts, she refused. Stating that she did not come to Boston for "self-ends," she defied the Puritans: "Do you think you can restrain those whom you call 'cursed Quakers' from coming among you, by anything you can do to them! God hath a Seed here among you for whom we have suffered and yet suffer and the Lord of the harvest will send more laborers to gather this seed."[8] This time there was no last-minute stay of execution. William Leddra was executed the next year.

The Puritans hanged four Quakers, but the hangings did not stop the missionaries from coming. The jails filled and the publicity did not help New England's reputation, particularly when the magistrates denied the appeal of William Leddra to be tried under the laws of England before executing him. In 1660 Charles II returned to London in triumph, and he was no sympathizer with the Puritans who had executed his father and triumphed in the civil war. Charles issued an order to Massachusetts Bay forbidding putting Quakers to death. Samuel Shattuck, a Friend under penalty of death should he return to New England, delivered "the King's Missive," which brought the end to hangings and the release of twenty-seven Friends from prison.

New England Puritans still despised Quakers, and in 1661 the General Assembly, cognizant of what was happening to Friends in England under the Restoration Parliaments, passed a "Cart and Whip" act that allowed for the arrest and imprisonment of Friends and their transportation in a cart from one town to the next until the borders of Rhode Island were reached—with whippings being carried out at each locality. The fines, whippings, and imprisonment did not deter Elizabeth Hooton* and other visitors, and gradually the Puritans learned to accept the presence of Friends.[9] Most persecution was directed at visiting Quakers, not at the converts within the colony. The Puritans realized that the existence of small Quaker Meetings in Salem, Kittery, or Sandwith did not jeopardize their errand into the wilderness.[10] In retrospect, any persecution appears unnecessary—even counterproductive, for Friends made only a few converts in the heartland of Puritanism—Massachusetts, New Haven, and Connecticut. They had their successes in the peripheral areas, in Cape Cod, Nantucket, Maine, and Rhode Island.

RHODE ISLAND

Ultimately, the main significance of the Quaker invasion of Massachusetts Bay lay in its effect on the evolution of New England Puritans who grudgingly accepted toleration. Of less drama but greater importance to the history of Quakerism was the establishment of meetings on Aquidneck Island in Rhode Island, which became the center of the new movement in the northern colonies. Unlike the Quakers in Massachusetts, who were forced to exist on the fringes of town, Rhode Island's Quakers fit into the general society with comparatively little difficulty and almost immediately enjoyed high social status and soon obtained political power.

In 1657 the Rhode Island authorities rejected the Puritans' plea to persecute Friends and to refuse them sanctuary, suggesting in return that toleration was more likely than harshness to preserve civil and religious peace. Sometime between 1656, when the first Quaker itinerants appeared in Rhode Island, and 1660 prominent settlers from Newport and Portsmouth joined the Friends. What prompted these families to become Quakers? Their conversions may have been a partial response to the chaotic nature of religious observances on the island. Roger Williams was too much a religious seeker and individualist to mold the settlers into one church. Anne Hutchinson showed no inclination to lead and organize those who had followed her into exile. There was no tax support for religion, the magistrates had no religious authority, and there were neither Congregational nor Anglican churches clergy anywhere in the colony. Quakers shared many beliefs with spiritualists, Hutchinsonians, and some Baptists.[11] All of these groups opposed infant baptism and university education as a qualification for the ministry. In 1647, long before Friends appeared, the Rhode Island Assembly passed a law allowing for an affirmation for those who scrupled taking oaths.[12] Quakerism offered spiritual nurture, moral stringency, a lay ministry, a sense of belonging to a religious body, and the confirmation of already held beliefs on the efficacy of the Holy Spirit or Inward Light for salvation. Rhode Islanders wanted to have toleration but not spiritual anarchy. In the absence of a state church and with turbulence of political strife both within the colony and against its Puritan neighbors, the settlers of Aquidneck island found in Quakerism a congenial faith and a source of stability. The rapid growth of the meetings around the Newport–Portsmouth area, where perhaps a majority of the people became Friends, helped discipline and unify the colony.

By the 1670s Quakers had emerged as a religious–political force controlling the General Assembly and having one of their members elected governor. Under

Quaker leadership, the colony enacted a provision allowing for conscientious objection from militia duty. When George Fox visited America in 1671–73, he was greeted as a celebrity in Newport, and he clearly rejoiced in the economic, social, and political prestige of Friends. The Quakers' spiritual confidence and rise to political prominence disgusted Roger Williams, who had opposed Puritan arrogance and saw Quaker assurance as equally dogmatic. Williams issued a challenge for a debate with Fox. The message did not get delivered until Fox had left Newport, but other traveling ministers accepted the challenge, and for five days Williams and Friends debated theological and political issues. As an attempt to rebuild the Baptist political party, Williams's debate was a failure.[13] However, Friends were temporarily eclipsed when King Philip's War broke out in 1675. Friends were voted out of office, and the religious exemption from military service was repealed.

The General Meeting held by Fox in 1671 was institutionalized as the New England Yearly Meeting. It was composed of two Monthly Meetings in Plymouth Colony, two in Massachusetts and the very large Monthly Meeting in Newport, which included all of Rhode Island and—until 1695—the Long Island Monthly Meeting. Observers throughout the end of the seventeenth century and through the first part of the eighteenth century testified to the continuing growth and strength of Quakerism in New England. In 1772 the Yearly Meeting had thirteen Monthly Meetings and forty-seven Particular or individual congregations.[14] The attendance at the Yearly Meeting was occasionally said to rival that of Philadelphia in numbers. Rhode Island Friends continued to be politically active in the eighteenth century, and there were several Quaker governors and always Quakers in the Assembly. But because of the religious diversity of the population—which increased in the eighteenth century after the founding of Congregational and Anglican churches—Rhode Islanders never thought of themselves as living in a "Quaker" colony.[15] Friends in politics had positions on most issues that did not differ from their fellow settlers, and they made no attempt to make the Quaker peace Testimony the policy of the colony.

NEW YORK AND THE SOUTH

The New England Puritans' fear and persecution of Friends before 1680 were not atypical. The authorities in New Amsterdam, Maryland, and Virginia also assumed that Friends would destroy civil government and resorted to force in attempts to keep traveling ministers away. As in Massachusetts, persecution brought converts, but most growth appeared in those areas where established churches were weakest and where settlers of vaguely puritanical or separatist inclinations were already living.

The Dutch in New Amsterdam promised religious toleration, and Long Island was settled by many English people who had been exposed to and then migrated away from Massachusetts and Connecticut. Among those settlers were many religious seekers. Five of the ministers of the *Woodhouse* came to New Amsterdam in 1657. Initially, the preaching of the two women members of the group scandalized Governor Peter Stuyvesant, who had them thrown in jail and sent them on to Rhode Island eight days later. After the men of the *Woodhouse* began proselytizing on Long Island, Stuyvesant arrested them, but sympathizers had already appeared. Soon Meetings formed in Gravesend and Flushing; when Stuyvesant continued persecution of Friends, the inhabitants of Flushing sent him an eloquent defense of religious freedom. John Bowne, a leader of the Flushing Meeting, journeyed to Holland and appealed to the directors of the West Indies Company, who controlled the colony. They rebuked Stuyvesant and ended the harassment.[16]

The English conquest of "New York" in 1664 brought a guarantee of religious liberty to all former Dutch inhabitants, which included the Quakers. Although there were incidents over tithes and militias and, on one occasion, the jailing of a minister, Quaker Meetings were generally left in peace. In 1695 the New York Yearly Meeting was set off from New England; it consisted of two Quarterly Meetings at Westbury, Long Island, and Shrewsbury, New Jersey, and a total of four Monthly Meetings. In the eighteenth century as the island of Nantucket became crowded, Quaker settlers from there joined with other Friends from Long Island migrating up the Hudson River Valley and founding Meetings in the Oblong section of what is now Dutchess County near Poughkeepsie. By the 1770s the New York Yearly Meeting had four Monthly Meetings and twenty Particular Meetings.

As was the case in New England and New York, the honor of introducing Quakerism to the South belongs to a woman. Elizabeth Harris traveled in Maryland, and perhaps Virginia as well, either in 1655 or 1656. London Friends sent books to Virginia in 1656. By 1657 there were converts in Maryland in the Annapolis vicinity and on Kent Island, that is, on both the Western and Eastern Shore. The first members included persons of substance in their communities; several were radical Puritans who had seized power in Maryland from Lord Baltimore in the 1650s. When persecution occurred in 1658 against Friends and forty-three men and one woman suffered, the causes were as political as religious and involved maneuverings for power between pro- and antiproprietary factions. The ostensible issues were Friends' refusal to take oaths or to serve in the militia. As elsewhere, the magistrates there attempted to stop the visits of traveling Friends, but nearly sixty came before 1662.[17]

The Restoration brought an end to most political persecution, and the Proprietor sought to encourage migration by extending religious liberty. Friends remained free to proselytize and to hold meetings. Some Quakers living on the eastern shore of Virginia, repelled by persecution and attracted by Maryland's toleration, settled in Baltimore and Talbot counties in the 1660s.

The visits of George Fox, John Burnyeat, and William Edmundson stimulated the growth and organization of the Meetings. At a General Meeting held by Fox and Edmundson, an estimated 1,000 people attended, including many converts, and prepared the way for a general expansion of the movement before 1700. As in Rhode Island, there also the lack of an established church, a shortage of ordained clergy, and the puritanical inclination of many English settlers fostered the growth of Quakerism. Although never attracting a majority of Marylanders, Friends served as a stabilizing element in the colony and before 1688 attained positions of authority in the government. The West River Yearly Meeting, later termed the Maryland Yearly Meeting, first met in 1672. By 1700 there were four Monthly Meetings, which, by the time of the Revolution, contained twenty Particular Meetings.

Stephen B. Weeks, a leading historian of Southern Quakerism, argued that imposing colony-defined borders on Quakerism in Virginia and North Carolina was misleading because the movements in both areas were ''one'' in origins, in struggles, in their protest against slavery, and in decline during the nineteenth century. The Church of England remained firmly established in the Old Dominion, and the colony had laws requiring uniformity in worship. In 1657 Josiah Coale and Thomas Thurston, who had already visited in New England, went to Virginia. In 1660 the Assembly mentioned Quakers, specifically insisting that they were irreligious and seditious, and levied fines and/or imprisoned Quakers, whom they deported ''not to return again.''[18]

The Virginia magistrates did not actually execute any Quakers, although they incarcerated minister George Wilson in a ''nasty, stinking prison'' until he died. Most Virginia Quakers lived on the borders close to either Maryland or North Carolina and far away from the colony's political centers at Jamestown and later Williamsburg. Although persecution for failure to join the militia or to pay tithes long remained a feature of life in Virginia, Quakers had gained a measure of acceptance before Fox's visit in 1672. As in Maryland, traveling ministers strengthened the ties of Virginia Quakers with the London Yearly Meeting, converted many individuals, and met many prominent officials. In 1772 the Virginia Yearly Meeting was composed of five Monthly Meetings and twenty-six Particular Meetings.[19]

Unlike Virginia, which was very slow in accepting religious toleration, the Proprietors of the Carolinas promised toleration in an effort to attract settlers. When Fox and Edmundson visited North Carolina in 1672, even the governor welcomed them. Their visit marked the effective beginning of Quakers in North Carolina, who had become organized before Edmundson returned in 1676. The earliest records of a Monthly Meeting are in 1680.[20] The North Carolina Yearly Meeting dates from 1698, and at that time there were three Monthly Meetings, one at Pasquotank and two in Perquimans County. In 1772 there were seven Monthly Meetings composed of twenty-three Particular Meetings.

QUAKERS IN THE WILDERNESS

The first Quakers in America were convinced after they had settled in the wilderness. The Society of Friends became an intercontinental religion because its ministers attracted the unchurched, and its worship filled the spiritual needs of those who were nominal members or unhappy with other churches. The process of being uprooted from England, migrating to America, and settling disrupted the texture of life and made the colonists uneasy with the primitiveness of their lives. Outside of a relatively small area of New England and Virginia, the European population was widely scattered, and there were few churches, clergy, and schoolmasters; minimal governmental authority; and much freedom. Customs that were a part of growing up in a village or town in Europe were no longer automatic, perhaps not even necessary. The settlers, many of whom even in the South were vaguely puritanical, wanted to escape from the heavy hands of ecclesiastical authority and political power, but they feared anarchy and moral decay. The English saw in "savage" Indians what would happen to themselves if they cut their ties with learning and succumbed to the attractions of the wilderness. In 1670, to be civilized meant to be a Christian, and a church provided an intellectual, moral, and social system through which one could understand what life was all about. Quakerism appealed to those who saw the need to be religious but found unsatisfactory whatever beliefs they had brought from England.

The religion of Friends was easily adapted to wilderness conditions. There was no necessity of an educated priesthood, no tithes, no physical sacraments of baptism or communion, no hymns, no elaborate structures. The worship was held in a meetinghouse, and usually, the structure was just a dwelling. The new faith promised that isolation and the loss of civilization did not affect one's relation to God. All carried within them "that of God," the Inward Light of Christ that would bring salvation and morality. The meeting for worship, which began with silence, required no great number of attenders. Quakerism permitted men and women to participate in the business of the Meeting and allowed these laypersons to control all activities.

Quakerism was well adapted to those caught in a perplexing environment who wanted certainty. In worship the settlers found confirmation of the belief that God was in all. They also believed that the Holy Spirit led them to the distinctive testimonies of Friends on language, dress, and Scripture. The intercontinental nature of Friends also brought a sense of significance. The Quakers in Maine or Maryland knew that their Meeting was important enough that ministers would leave England, sail to America, and experience the incredible hardships of seventeenth-century travel to bring the gospel.

George Fox preached to many unconverted during his journey in America, but he saw his primary role as bringing a sense of order to procedures. Since the procedures that Meetings followed had been worked out previously in England, all that American Friends needed to learn was how to carry on the concerns of the group. The small membership in a local meeting for worship joined with Friends from a larger area to create a meeting for business. This organization ensured that Friends associated with other Quakers to build a religious community that transcended a small area.

In essence, the small and wide-scattered groups of colonial Friends formed a community whose distinctive patterns of dress, speech, and worship set them apart from their neighbors. Undoubtedly, many joined Friends by default. There was no other church in the vicinity, and it was better to hear any minister than be isolated, better to attend any service than be damned. But within the Meeting, Quakerism molded attenders and members creating a distinctive style of life. Even before the settlement of the Delaware River Valley, Quakerism had become an important religious movement in North America.

NOTES

1. Perry Miller, *Errand into the Wilderness* (Cambridge, Mass.: 1956), 48–98.

2. Edmund Morgan, *Roger Williams: The Church and the State* (New York: 1967); Edmund Morgan, *The Puritan Dilemma: The Story of John Winthrop* (Boston: 1950), 115–33.

3. Morgan, *Puritan Dilemma*, 134–56; Kai Erikson, *Wayward Puritans: A Study in the Sociology of Deviance* (New York: 1966), 71–106; Emery Battis, *Saints and Sectaries: Anne Hutchinson and the Antinomian Controversy in Massachusetts Bay* (Chapel Hill, N.C.: 1962); David Hall, ed. *The Antinomian Controversy, 1636–1638* (Middletown, Conn., 1968).

4. George Bishop, *New England Judged* (London: 1703); Erikson, *Wayward Puritans*, 107–36; and Arthur Worrall, *Quakers in the Colonial Northeast* (Hanover, N.H.: 1980), 1–58, are general accounts of the Quaker invasion of Massachusetts. See also Mary Hoxie Jones, *The Standard of the Lord Lifted Up* (n.p.: 1961).

5. William Wayne Spurrier, "Persecution of the Quakers in England, 1650–1714" (Ph.D. diss., University of North Carolina, 1976), contains a discussion of changing Quaker attitudes toward persecution.

6. Rufus Jones, *Quakers in the American Colonies* (New York: 1911; reprinted 1966), 50.

7. Quoted in Ibid., 82–83.

8. Ibid., 84.

9. There were nineteen traveling visitors from England before 1660; forty-six between 1661 and 1684. G. J. Willauer, Jr., "First Publishers of Truth in New England: A Composite List," *Quaker History* (hereafter *QH*) 65 (1976): 39–44.

10. Jonathan Chu, *Neighbors, Friends, or Madmen: The Puritan Adjustment to Quakerism in Seventeenth-Century Massachusetts Bay* (Westport, Conn.: 1985).

11. David Lovejoy, *Religious Enthusiasm in the New World: Heresy to Revolution* (Cambridge, Mass.: 1985), is an excellent account of the radical religion in colonial America and includes a chapter on Massachusetts Bay, Rhode Island, and the Quakers.

12. *Records of the Colony of Rhode Island and Providence Plantations*, ed. John R. Bartlett (Providence, R.I.: 1856), I, 111, 150, 282, 396, 441; II, 111–12, 142.

13. Worrall, *Quakers in the Colonial Northeast*, 31–42. In 1676 Williams's account of the debate was published in *George Fox Digg'd out of his Burrowes*. Perhaps enjoying the pun, Friends replied in *A New-England Fire-brand Quenched* (1678).

14. An Account of all the Yearly, Quarterly, Monthly, and Particular Meetings of Friends in America, 1772, MS, Quaker Collection, Haverford College, Haverford Pa.

15. Sydney V. James, *Colonial Rhode Island: A History* (New York: 1975), 188, 217–19.

16. Jones, *Quakers*, 215–62; Worrall, *Quakers in the Colonial Northeast*, 20, 21, 64–86.

17. Kenneth Carroll, *Quakerism on the Eastern Shore* (Baltimore: 1970); David Jordan, " 'God's Candle' within Government: Quakers and Politics in Early Maryland," *William and Mary Quarterly*, 3d ser., 39, no. 4 (October 1982): 628–54; Bliss Forbush, *A History of Baltimore Yearly Meeting of Friends* (Sandy Spring, Md.: 1972), 7–39.

18. Jones, *Quakers*, 265–302; Kenneth Carroll, "Quakerism on the Eastern Shore of Virginia," *Virginia Magazine of History and Biography* 74 (1966): 170–74.

19. Virginia had more than sixty meetinghouses between 1655 and 1775, because there was great internal migration within the state and settlers moved south from Pennsylvania. Forbush, *History*, 30.

20. Ibid.; Stephen Weeks, *Southern Quakers and Slavery* (Baltimore: 1896), 8–69; Francis Anscombe, *I Have Called You Friends: The Story of Quakerism in North Carolina* (Boston: 1959), 56–70: Howard Beeth, "Outside Agitators in Southern History: The Society of Friends, 1656–1800" (Ph.D. diss., University of Houston, 1984) is a recent interpretation of the impact of Quakers on the South.

6

ENGLAND, 1660–1689: PERSECUTION, THEOLOGY, AND THE UNIVERSALIZING OF TRUTH

Early Quaker theology and political thought, like Quaker worship and ethics, took two forms: the "Lamb's War" radicalism of the 1650s and a more universalistic, tolerant view in the 1670s after a decade of harsh persecution had shown that the Spirit in Friends would survive but not conquer the world. Under pressure Quakers became clearer in doctrine and more creative in politics, as they tested the universality of truth, whereas ethical discipline within the Society of Friends became more rigid through struggles over unity and consistency in moral truth.

THEOLOGY AND DOCTRINE

For Fox and early Friends doctrines were weapons in "the Lamb's War." Debate flourished because puritan pastors challenged the Quakers on doctrinal rather than ethical issues. Since Friends believed their moral warnings were prophetic messages from God, they had to defend their doctrines as divinely inspired too; nor could Quakers leave any challenge unanswered lest silence might imply defeat.[1] Often they argued with a pastor in his church and then felt driven by interruptions to finish the debate in print. They published their defenses in law courts, like two of Friends' first three tracts: Fox's and James Nayler's *Saul's Errand to Damascus* and Thomas Aldam's *Brief Discovery* (both 1653). The Puritan Commonwealth saw the greatest outburst of print before modern times, including sermons, newsheets, and thousands of tracts. Friends published more per head than any other group: before 1660, 540 books and tracts, of which 165 were theological debates; 3,759 before 1700, including 797 debating doctrines. Fox's and later William Penn's* were the most numerous, but there were 650 early Quaker authors, including 82 women (though only 8 percent of the women's tracts were doctrinal).[2] Their opponents included the best-trained spiritual leaders of their time: Puritans Richard Baxter and John Owen, Baptists

Roger Williams and John Bunyan, and mystic Henry More. Both sides used the standard format of medieval university debates, taking up an opponent's argument sentence by sentence with an answer or taunt and ridicule for each. Even Fox's 550-page *Great Mistery* replied one by one to fifty anti-Quaker tracts. Puritan anti-Quaker tracts were orderly in choosing topics, making Quaker answers seem orderly. Since the Spirit was Friends' only authority, they rarely quoted each other, but no Quaker could easily admit another Friend had erred. Thus their tracts defended each others' doctrines, however casually some had been first thought through.

The issues debated remained much the same in 1700 as in 1652, not always much clarified by all the printed pages.[3] The commonest issue was the Quaker claim that every person could be saved by God's Light within them, without requiring Scripture or knowledge of Jesus. Puritans said this was merely a "natural light," the human conscience, universal, but not enough to change hearts and save sinners. Quakers agreed with Puritans that human minds and human motives are twisted, but whereas Calvinists fell back on biblical revelation, every Friend had faced self-judgment as a purging of his or her motives and desires and trusted the redeeming power of "waiting on the Light of Truth." Friends did not challenge the inspiration of the Bible, which records experiences of God and should be used to test the validity of "leadings." A Quaker's own experiences also validated passages in the Bible; she or he denied only its supposed key role in salvation. Samuel Fisher's 750-page tome *Rusticus ad Academicos* also undercut biblical literalism by noting variants in Bible manuscripts and the late, uncertain use of Hebrew vowel points.[4] He ignored a key Puritan challenge about the unique role in salvation of Jesus' life and death.

Early Friends assumed that Jesus' death made available for humans God's forgiveness, canceling the moral debt for past sins. But the Quakers depended for present and future living on purification by God's Spirit, which ends sinning as well as guilt. Fox linked the "blood of Christ" with each person's purification through Christ's Spirit. Atonement through the Cross was interpreted as an eternal principle that demanded the setting of "the Cross to our own wills" over each act of daily life: every impulse that came from self-will must be denied. Fox and early Friends affirmed that Christ was the Spirit that they knew within them and that in Jesus of Nazareth this Spirit took a human body "prepared" by God. They were not clear how the "Word–God" or Christ–Spirit was related to the human mind or will of Jesus; Friends understood the incarnation as Jesus' "Spirit-possession," because of their own experience in which the human mind and will seemed to be simply set aside, not transformed or made new. Ironically, many Friends now accuse Calvinists of making too much of human depravity, but in Fox's day the situation was reversed.

Yet Friends claimed that human perfection was possible through total openness and obedience to the Light. Friends accused Luther and the Puritans, who said that humility demands that we deny that humans can be perfect, of "pleading for sin" since God accepts us as we are. Richard Baxter said that "Christ's

Kingdom is an hospital; he has no subjects in it but diseased ones''; Fox replied that "it is not a hospital, for he heals them."[5] No Friend (except perhaps Fox and Nayler in the earliest days) claimed to be living in perfection, but Friends did claim infallibility for the Light whose leadings moment by moment made perfection possible. Puritans accused Friends of pride and self-deception; Quakers accused Puritans of denying God's power. Lest Friends claim power to save themselves, Samuel Fisher, William Penn, and Robert Barclay* (but not Fox) distinguished between the Light by which God shines into each person to show the Truth and the Seed that is each person's ability to respond to the Light. Like Fox, they said the Seed in hardened people is buried "under hard earth" until plowed up by Quaker preaching; it can become "seared" beyond hope. But in a newly tolerant spirit they also said the Light itself may be given in different "measure" to different people.[6]

Quakers thus endlessly assaulted salaried or professional pastors whose role was to reassure still imperfect people of God's grace and salvation: they demanded only prophetic ministry coming from God's voice within. No kind of true worship could start from one's own will; prepared sermons and prayers and even Psalm singing were imitations.

Quakers also rejected the outward sacraments, taking to the limit the Catholic contrast of the outward form or symbol and the "substance" or power of God within the water, bread, or wine. Baptism, said Friends, was by and in the Spirit, and they had experienced it in their harrowing "convincement." The "body of Christ" was the Light, as Christ's "real presence," or was the Quaker body, "the Children of Light." The "blood" was the purifying Spirit that gave life.[7]

Several Friends had by 1662 already written systematic presentations of Quaker doctrine before William Penn, George Keith*, and Robert Barclay, who brought Quakers into a more creative dialogue with non-Quakers. James Nayler, Edward Burrough, and Francis Howgill were farmers before 1652 but had read widely and had been separatist preachers. Isaac Penington amassed a library while studying at Cambridge. Samuel Fisher went through Oxford and held parish and Baptist pulpits before joining Friends. Each wrote thorough books covering many doctrines.[8]

William Penn began as an eager young radical, self-confident and ready for at least a verbal fight.[9] He had stood on the quarter-deck beside his father the admiral and James, Duke of York, at the start of a war with Holland, his mother's homeland. He had also survived smallpox, had gone to a good classical grammar school, and had been sent to Oxford, from which he was expelled in 1662 in part for attending Puritan prayer meetings. The admiral sent him off to learn courtly manners and French at a Huguenot academy, from which he returned as a "Renaissance man" to enter law school in London. When Penn went the next year to manage his father's estate in Ireland, he went through a heart-searching time and then met again a Quaker, Thomas Loe, who had visited the Penns in his boyhood. He found himself in jail along with the Cork Quaker group and pled their case to the Governor-General of Ireland. The admiral heard, called

Penn home, and disowned him. Penn stuck to his Quakerism, wrote some fiery tracts (one against the Dutch), and beside young George Whitehead took the role of defender of Quaker doctrines against a trio of Puritan pastors. He found himself a prisoner in the Tower of London for denying the Trinity. Penn had repeated Fox's claim that the word *Trinity* was not in the Bible and had borrowed arguments from Unitarians whom he respected for their moral earnestness. To be freed from the Tower, Penn had to show that he did not deny Christ's divinity but only his distinctness from God the Father. Penn was still fighting "the Lamb's War" and wrote in the Tower a first short version of his book against luxury, court extravagance, pride, and worldly living, *No Cross, No Crown*: "If you will daily bear the holy Cross of Christ, and . . . listen to the light . . . and square your thoughts, words and deeds thereby . . . in this present evil world, then may you look for . . . the coming of Christ? . . . Why will you die? Remember that 'No Cross, No Crown.' "[10]

A year later Penn and William Meade were arrested for addressing a Quaker meeting outside their padlocked meeting-house in Gracechurch Street, London. Their trial at the Old Bailey is famous because the judge's sentencing of the jury for refusing to jail Penn was reversed on appeal. Penn, however, now began to write tracts on toleration appealing to non-Quakers because the universal Light had already given "a measure of Truth" to everyone. Everyone would see that persecution of upright Quakers was wrong. In 1674 five Baptists led by Thomas Hicks arranged to debate Penn and four other Quakers at their Barbican Hall and the Quakers' Wheeler-Street meeting-house. Three thousand Londoners attended until the gallery began to collapse under the load. When Penn wrote about the debate, he dug to the roots of the Quaker teaching that the Light was present within everyone.[11]

Fox and early Friends had said the Light judged within each person. Penn's new universalism, the social and political aspects of which we will discuss later, assumed that truth, even moral truth, is universal, and everyone already knows enough for their salvation. Quakers believed that since salvation came by obeying step by step, as more Light was given, it would finally lead everyone to Quakerism. Penn now said that people like Socrates were already saved. Even the knowledge of the unique coming of the Light in Jesus Christ and of his death, while true, was not essential. Moral commitment, not doctrine, was universal.

George Keith, a quick-tempered Scot with the best philosophical mind among Quaker leaders, took up the Quaker affirmation that knowledge given by the Light is revelation but distinguished sharply between humans' physical and spiritual senses and the kinds of knowledge each gives. His ideas made him a friend of Anne, Countess Conway, quietly a Quaker philosopher, and Cambridge Platonists around Henry More.[12]

Among the guests that were invited to provide the consolation of philosophy for the countess' migraines was Keith's fellow student at Aberdeen, Robert Barclay, laird of Ury, from whose debates over Quaker doctrines with classmates had come a set of *Propositions*.[13] Barclay expanded these theses into a Latin volume to persuade non-Quakers; he then printed it for Friends in English as *An Apology for the True Christian Divinity*. Barclay began by discussing human knowledge of God, following the sequence of doctrines in Aquinas, Calvin, and the Westminster Confession. He came to the issue as a man weary of church feuds and hungry to know God's will, whereas Calvin had begun from the blindness caused by sin. Barclay, like Keith, discussed knowledge in relation to the dualism of spirit and matter rather than the duality of Gods' will and human wills, like Fox. (At this point Barclay, not Fox, is the theological source of Quaker mysticism.[14]) He spoke of God's acts; he was still too much a Quaker to think of God merely as *being* Spirit, love, or pure essence. But his moving and personal descriptions of God's working within individuals and the Quaker group in silent worship, the heart of his book, made it a classic for both Friends and non-Friends that echoed the universal experiences of God's presence.

Barclay's book defended, too, the universal and saving nature of the Light; he started from the Quaker view that a person was given more Light only when he followed the truths he already knew and developed that view into a doctrine that perfection in obeying is possible at each stage of growth. There was thus no single landmark point at which salvation is possessed or assured. When in his later chapters he gave clear, compact summaries of Quaker views on the Bible and sacraments, society and the state, he gave credit to people who conscientiously still used sacraments or bore arms on their way (he said) to the fuller Light of Quakerism. Thus the universalism of Penn and Barclay is to be distinguished from other ideas common in their culture, which they, too, sometimes shared: from *latitudinarianism*, which makes a minimum list of beliefs enough for salvation (Friends never doubted or emphasized the existence of God or future rewards and punishments); from *relativism*, which makes religion true or false only in relation to the person and his culture; and from *universalism* in the later American sense that assumes God's love will eventually save everyone. Barclay assumed that Quaker worship and belief were true.

PERSECUTION UNDER THE CONVENTICLE ACTS

During the Restoration era persecution of all non-Anglican worship formed the setting of the change from theological warfare to Quaker universalism and persuasion. Under Puritan rule in 1651–59 many Friends had been jailed for offenses like interrupting a pastor in his pulpit. Both Margaret Fell and Isaac Penington interpreted persecution as a natural human response to Quaker attacks on pride in the Lamb's War: "The Lord knows what bitter fights we have had with the enemy in our own hearts before we could leave our [former] principles, paths and practices of darkness. . . . Then we meet with a new fight abroad in the world, the same principle and power fighting against us as did first in ourselves."[15] The inner conflict was also cosmic; when Quakers were jailed in Cornwall or Boston, other Friends felt called in conscience to converge upon the battlefield. Unlike the Bostonians, the rulers of the English Commonwealth seldom attacked Quakers unless they interrupted other groups. (Confronting Cromwell, his tolerance only bothered them.[16]) Local English Justices jailed Quakers over specific acts of blasphemy, "contempt of court" and "disturbance of the peace," or refusal of tithes or oaths. James Parnell died in jail, and John Camm and James Nayler died soon after release.

In 1661 and after 1664, however, Friends worship itself was banned. Friends (especially traveling ministers) were jailed after every meeting for worship. For eighteen years, up to 3,400 at a time were in prison, a total of 8,600 in Charles II's first five years. Friends in London, Yorkshire, Bristol, Somerset, Lancashire, Cheshire, and Berkshire suffered the most.[17] About 500 Quaker prisoners died, including many leaders: Edward Burrough, Francis Howgill, Richard Hubberthorne, and William Dewsbury. A first fury of arrests came under a "Quaker Act" when the Friends and "Fifth Monarchists" were thought to be planning rebellion.[18] The legal basis of long-term persecution was directed against all Puritans by the Clarendon Code named for Charles II's chancellor but which in fact was the work of the Anglican Cavaliers in Parliament. The Act of Uniformity drove from parish pulpits 1,700 pastors who would not use daily the Prayer Book rituals. The Corporation Act excluded all non-Anglicans from the City Councils of any chartered town. For Friends and Baptists the hardest law was the Conventicle Act of 1664, which made attending any worship outside the Church of England an offense punishable by prison or deportation. A lull in persecution in 1668–69 gave Friends time to reorganize. When the Conventicle Act was renewed in 1670, Parliament supplemented the jailings by huge fines, part of which were paid to informers who reported where Quakers met. Isaac Penington lost his home and library. Quaker farmers lost their furniture, animals, and tools seized by sheriffs in lieu of fines. Friends were fined more than £48,250 between 1670 and 1685, when £10 was a good annual wage and £5 bought an Atlantic passage.[19]

Non-Quaker bystanders felt shame and pity.[20] Quakers' minds were more changed, however, when events that seemed God's judgment on king and Parliament led to no result: the devastating plague in 1665, the fire of London in 1666, and the burning by the Dutch of a large part of the English fleet, anchored empty in the Medway harbor in 1666. As a result of these disasters Clarendon fell, but power went to a rakish boyhood friend of King Charles, the Duke of Buckingham. The immorality of the Restoration court remained shameless.[21] The king in 1672 issued the Declaration of Indulgence suspending the Conventicle Act; Parliament overrode him. Quakers looked in vain for England to repent.

QUAKER MEETING ORGANIZATION

Meetings were thus organized in response to persecution. Practical needs of traveling preachers had earlier led Fox to call "General Meetings" of itinerants to plan their work. The "Kendal Fund" supported their families or prison and travel expenses. Margaret Fell tactfully asked all Quaker groups to contribute. By 1658 Fox was calling regional Meetings of Quaker "ministers" in southern England; those who were in London met every Monday in the Second-Days Morning Meeting to make sure the needs of each local worship group were met. It came to be an elite body of London leaders, taking over the previously informal work of men like Amor Stoddart and of the "Two Weeks Meeting" of Elders. One of their tasks was to arrange for the printing of Quaker writings, so as to present the Friends' message to the world and make Quaker tracts available to Meetings around England. They raised funds from local Meetings, took manuscripts to the printers, and in the process had to choose and sometimes edit manuscripts sent to them. Inevitably, they were accused of censorship by authors who had felt divinely led to write the rejected manuscripts, even by Fox on one occasion. A central fund or "stock" in London gradually replaced the one in Kendal.

Practical needs of local worshipping Quaker groups, which we can now call Meetings, were first met by the "General Meetings of Elders." One at Balby in the Yorkshire hills in 1656 asked all local Meetings to set up ways to cover the burials and marriages of their members and the needs of widows, orphans, and "the poor." Quakers refused to be buried in parish churchyards or to be married by pastors: marriage to non-Quakers threatened to divide homes under persecution.

The Balby meeting said they did not mean to make their suggestions "a rule or form to walk by." A formal list of Meeting members was an eighteenth-century addition, but each Meeting had to decide whom they must support in need, prison, or old age or bury in their burial grounds (simply, without gravestones). To oversee and record weddings could be vital for the legal status and property rights of children. Until the nineteenth century, English registries of births, deaths, and marriages were kept by church parishes.[22]

When the Conventicle Act threw traveling Quaker leaders into prison, Fox in 1668 insisted that each local meeting for worship or a group of small ones must meet as a Monthly Meeting for business. He wisely trusted all decisions to the shared "sense of the Meeting," rather than to leaders' authority after Nayler's "fall." A "Clerk" in each Meeting recorded decisions and prepared a list of business agenda. When answers offered by one Friend were rejected by another, the Clerk also had to sense which one the Spirit was moving or suggest a complex new answer that would integrate elements of Truth in each person's ideas. The process drew on the group's knowing a common responsibility.

After 1669 Fox traveled to convince Friends to set up separate Women's Meetings for business alongside the men's. London women had already met for ten years in what was called "the Box Meeting," to provide food and clothing for poor Friends and prisoners. Margaret Fell spent much of the 1660s in prison; her daughter Sarah showed that she could run the family estate and in 1675 wrote an Epistle on how to lead a Women's Business Meeting.[23] At best the

Women's Meetings usually had to work with much smaller funds than the Men's Meetings or go to the men for money. But in Meetings where "weighty" Quaker men had not been challenged the new pattern felt like interference.

THE AUTHORITY OF FRIENDS' MEETINGS OVER INDIVIDUALS

Quaker Meeting structures had always reflected in part their need to be right and united in response to persecutors. Nayler's fall brought Friends to face the need to balance the individuality of "leadings" with the religious experience shared by the group. Friends believed that the Spirit's leadings would always be moral and consistent with truths it had presented to other people and lead them into unity. Nayler's failure to restrain his disciples was seen to be weakness, not love, since the uniformity of Truth should lead to mutual restraint.

During the next fifteen years three groups splintered away from the main body of Friends to follow John Perrot, returning from jail in Rome; William Rogers and the Pennymans of Bristol and London; and John Wilkinson and John Story in the Northwest. These leaders in each case seemed "tender" in spirit but felt inwardly led to reject Fox's "leadings" even in prayer and his pattern for Women's Meetings. When they asked why Quakers must all worship together at fixed hours, Friends thought they hoped to avoid the watching sheriffs' men.[24] Even a regional meeting called by Margaret Fell failed to reunite them with other Friends. Penn and Barclay wrote harsh tracts to make clear that God gave authority to Meetings as a whole and to spiritually experienced "weighty Friends" like Fox.[25] Penn and Barclay used some arguments strangely like those of Catholics: surely, God would grant his Church some reliable authority. Such clashes forced Quakers under persecution to ask how far private "leadings" could rightly diverge.

After 1673, therefore, central Friends Meetings that had served practical purposes tried to overcome division by giving guidance for the spiritual life of all Friends. A monthly "Meeting for Sufferings" in London, receiving representatives and reports from local Meetings, sent petitions to Parliament and money to prisoners and fine-bankrupted Friends. But the sessions of the London Yearly Meeting from 1679 also sent Queries and Advices to the local Meetings, where they were copied into the Minute books and replies were sent back.[26] Local, Monthly, and Quarterly Meetings now watched over the behavior as well as the needs of individuals. Quakers never formally excommunicated members or "handed them over to Satan" as other churches did, but lest disreputable behavior give Quakerism a bad name, Meetings began as early as Nayler's ride to disown evil actions and then disown the person unless he or she condemned those acts. Steps that seemed to individuals authoritarian seemed to Meetings justified by their cosmic responsibility. Nevertheless, the pressure of persecution and the organizing steps by which Friends met it might have turned them into a pure but self-isolated sect, as John Woolman wished a century later (and the Mennonites and Amish achieved). This did not happen, partially because of the universalism of Penn and Barclay in politics as well as faith.

QUAKER THOUGHT ON GOVERNMENT
AND TOLERATION

Friends' concern for justice led to no concrete platforms before 1659, in part out of fear of replacing God's leading with human ideas. In the same spirit Quakers attacked intolerance as human resistance to God's message. One early Friend wrote to King Charles:

Observe the hand of the Lord in thy coming . . . into power. . . . Thou wilt find it is because [Cromwell and Parliament] unto whom God gave such power over you were not faithful: . . . talking for liberty they brought forth oppression. . . . I exhort and warn thee in the name and fear of the Lord to take heed that thou bind not the consciences of any. . . . For the Lord God hath brought forth a people in these nations, . . . and if thou oppressest this people, the Lord will surely take away thy power.[27]

Quakers demanded the right like Old Testament prophets to interrupt false worship; early Friends approved and sometimes sought governmental restraint of evil actions and approved policemen, although never control of worship. True worship could not lead to immorality and so needed no curbs. This was as theocratic a perspective as any in New England. In 1659, when the Commonwealth was in the melting pot, Fox, George Bishop, Edward Burrough, Edward Billing*, and Thomas Lawson each gave Parliament lists of proposed new laws for all England.[28] Some echoed the Leveller platforms: a wider electorate, annual Parliaments, better poor-houses, localized law courts, and laws in English for trials fairer to the poor. As Quakers they added abolition of oaths, parish churches, and persecution. In 1659 Friends nominated suitable justices.

Penington drew on Baptist arguments in his wider toleration appeal: "Conscience is of God, and . . . God would not have the true conscientiousness in any of His crushed."[29] Such a basing of toleration upon human conscientiousness, rather than on God's Truth revealed within consciences, led to William Penn's transformation of Quaker ideas on toleration and eventually on government. In *The Great Case of Conscience*, just after his Old Bailey trial in 1670, he used every argument that would appeal to a persecutor: the Quakers' reputation for morality, English law and historical precedent, the danger of making worship hypocritical, and the economic and political disruption persecution caused. He made no theocratic claims. Penn, like Milton, assumed that religion could persuade men by reason or even by self-interest and used economic arguments increasingly as time went on. In 1679: "By sacrificing Men's Property [he said], look what number they cut off from . . . the Government, . . . provoking them to be dangerous. It tends to the utter Ruin of Thousands of Traders . . . and Husbandmen."[30]

Penn, earlier a radical, had become a reformer hoping to persuade English consciences a step at a time. Penn accepted all kinds of allies, most of whom would never be convinced to be Quakers, toward his first step: toleration. Mild Anglicans formed the Whig Party pledged to toleration. Penn helped in their election to Parliament. From 1678 to 1680 Whigs dominated an England aware that Catholics were plotting to take over England and its Church. Penn's Catholic friend the Duke of York became King James II when his brother Charles II, after beating the Whigs, died in 1685. Penn was one of the few who believed James honestly wanted toleration. The Whigs threw James out in a bloodless revolution and called as rulers his Protestant daughter Mary and her Dutch husband, William. Few in England found much further difficulty in passing a Toleration Act suspending the Conventicle Act in 1689. This did not repeal laws requiring tithes, over which Friends still went to jail, nor the Test act that continued for 150 years to exclude from Parliament and the universities all Puritans and Quakers. They had to accept permanent minority status in England as denominations of "dissenters," ending hopes that Saints would rule.

Penn's universalism produced nothing more in England than an alliance for toleration and an end to "the Lamb's War." In America two new colonies and their governments gave Friends the chance to apply in statecraft Penn's combination of prophetic morality and universalism about Truth. Later times would notice the difference between his social ideals and the individualism that Locke and the Whigs called liberalism and would call Penn a pioneer Protestant reformer. Yet it was vital that after 1660 the Quakers and Puritans, by their morality and nonviolence under persecution, had earned the trust and respect of all English people. The Quaker Peace Testimony also prepared the way for multiparty government. If those who lose an election lose their lives when their rivals control the courts and police, violent revolution becomes their ultimate resort. Respect for law leads to peace only when laws are just. But in England the party out of office came to call itself "His/Her Majesty's Loyal Opposition" and to concentrate on persuading the nation to choose better policies. The trust that could allow an opposition to win elections needed the nonviolence of all religious and political dissenters but at first was only sure regarding the Friends.

NOTES

1. Thus Thomas Underhill's *Hell Broken Loose or a History of the Quakers* (1659–60) drew gentle Howgill into *The Mouth of the Pit Stopped* (1659–60).

2. See Appendix by David Runyon and Hugh Barbour in *Early Quaker Writings*, ed. Hugh Barbour and Arthur O. Roberts (Grand Rapids, Mich.: 1973); hereafter *EQW*; Hugh Barbour, "Quaker Prophetesses and Mothers in Israel," in *Seeking the Light*, 41–60; and Barbour, "[Penn] The Young Controversialist," in *The World of William Penn*, ed. Richard S. Dunn and Mary Maples Dunn (Philadelphia: 1986), 15–36.

3. Good summaries of early Quaker theology are Maurice Creasey's published Ph.D. thesis *Early Quaker Christology, with Special Reference to the Teaching and Significance of Isaac Penington, 1616–1679*; (Leeds, Eng.: 1956); Melvin B. Endy, Jr., *William Penn*

and Early Quakerism (Princeton, N.J.: 1973); and J. William Frost "The Dry Bones of Quaker Theology," in his *The Quaker Family in Colonial America* (New York: 1973). Good interpretations of the underlying experience are Richard Bauman, *Let Your Words Be Few* and Howard Brinton, *Friends for 300 Years*. See also Dorland C. Bales's "Barclay's Apology in Context," Ph.D. thesis (University of Chicago: 1982).

4. Christopher Hill, delighted to hail any opponent of biblical authority, has a lively chapter on Samuel Fisher in *The World Turned Upside Down* (London: 1972).

5. Richard Baxter, *Quakers Catechism*, 24; George Fox, *Great Mistery of the Great Whore Unfolded* (1659), 30.

6. See Robert Barclay, *Apology*, Proposition V-VI (xxiv); William Penn, *The Invalidity of John Faldo's Vindication* (1673); Samuel Fisher, *Rusticus ad Academicos* (1660), "Epistle to the Reader." Fox saw the Seed as Christ himself reborn in each Quaker. Penington seems to have equated Seed and Christ–Spirit in an autobiographical fragment, "I have met with the Seed," included in Edward Burrough's "Memorial" introducing Penington's *Works* (1681).

7. See Maurice Creasey, "Quakers and the Sacraments." See also *Quaker Religious Thought* (hereafter, *QRT*), 5, no. 1 (Summer 1963): 2–25 and *QRT* 14, no. 4 (Spring 1973). Fox also said Christ's "eternal body" was the "spiritual substance" of Light.

8. James Nayler, *Love to the Lost* (1656); Edward Burrough, *A Declaration to All the World of Our Faith* (1657); and idem, *A Standard Lifted Up* (1659), were the earliest. Samuel Fisher's huge *Rusticus ad Academicos* (1659), Francis Howgill's *Glory of the True Church Discovered* (1662), Isaac Penington's *Way of Life and Death* (1658), and Penington's *The Scattered Sheep Sought* (1659) all predate the Conventicle Act and Penn's or Barclay's syntheses. See also Penington's more inward *Naked Truth* (1672).

9. For a general Penn bibliography see his entry in Part Two. On his debates see Hugh Barbour, "Young Controversialist" in *The World of William Penn* and "William Penn," Model of Protestant Liberalism," *Church History* 48, 2 no. (June 1979): 156–73; on his theology see Endy, *William Penn and Early Quakerism*.

10. The title came from Thomas Loe's last words; in the much expanded and gentler 1682 edition Penn made this Chapter XVIII, section 11.

11. William Penn, *Spirit of Truth Vindicated* (1672); idem *The Christian Quaker* (1674).

12. For a Keith bibliography see his entry in Part Two and Ch. 7; on Anne Conway see her *Principles of the Most Ancient and Modern Philosophy* (The Hague: 1982); Marjorie H. Nicholson, *Conway Letters: The Correspondence of Anne, Viscountess Conway, Henry More, and Their Friends, 1642–1684* (New Haven: 1930); and especially, the seven articles in *Guilford Review* 23 (Spring 1986).

13. For a bibliography on Barclay see his entry in Part Two.

14. Barclay drew on Platonism to answer Descartes and pressed his spirit–matter dualism much farther in his book *The Possibility and Necessity of Immediate and Inward Revelation* (1682). Here, and on Barclay's "Calvinist Idea of sin," Endy has well corrected Rufus Jones.

15. Isaac Penington, *Concerning Persecution* (1661), 12.

16. See letters of Francis Howgill and John Camm to Margaret Fell, 1654, A. R. Barclay MS #20, *London Friends House Library* and Anthony Pearson, Swarthmore MS #3: 34.

17. See William Wayne Spurrier, "The Persecution of the Quakers in England, 1650–1714" (Ph.D. Thesis, University of North Carolina, 1976): his figures (pp. 113–16) are

based on Joseph Besse's *Collection of the Sufferings of the People Called Quakers* (1753). See also Gerald R. Cragg, *Puritanism in the Period of the Great Persecution* (Cambridge: 1957);

18. Barry Reay, *Quakers and the English Revolution* also shows how Quakers, by inspiring fears that parish churches would be abolished, aided the Monarchists in over-throwing the Commonwealth.

19. Besse's figures via Spurrier, "Persecution," 111–12.

20. See Samuel Pepys' *Diary* for 7 August 1664. See Also Cragg, *Puritanism*; Harry Grant Plumb, *Restoration Puritanism* (Chapel Hill, N.C.: 1943); Michael Watts, *The Dissenters* (Oxford: 1978); C. Hill, *Experience of Defeat* (New York: 1984).

21. See Winifred, Lady Burghclere, *George Villiers, 2nd Duke of Buckingham* (Port Washington, N.Y.: 1903–71), 187–98.

22. On all aspects of Meeting organization, see Arnold Lloyd, *Quaker Social History* (London: 1948); and Richard Vann, *Social Development*, Chs. 3, 4.

23. Milton Speizman and Jane C. Kronick published her Epistle from the Lancaster Women's Meeting in *Signs* 1 (Autumn 1975): 235ff.

24. Kenneth Carroll, *John Perrot: Early Quaker Schismatic* (London: 1971).

25. William Penn, *The Spirit of Alexander the Coppersmith* (1673); idem *Judas and the Jews* (1673); Robert Barclay, *The Anarchy of the Ranters* (1674).

26. See L. Hugh Doncaster, *Quaker Organisation and Business Meetings* (London: 1958).

27. George Fox, "the Younger" [not the Quaker founder], *A Noble Salutation . . . unto Thee Charles Stuart* (London: 1660), 9, 15, 17.

28. George Fox, *To the Parliament: . . . 59 Particulars* (1659); Thomas Lawson, *Appeal to the Parliament Concerning the Poor* (1660); Edward Billing, *A Mite of Affection Manifested in 31 Proposals* (1659). Later he applied many of these ideas in the "Concessions and Agreements" of West New Jersey.

29. Isaac Penington, *Concerning Persecution* (1661). On the history of arguments for toleration and their underlying assumptions see Michael Freund, *Die Idee der Toleranz im England der groszen Revolution* (Halle: 1927); Johannes Kuhn, *Toleranz und Offenbarung* (Leipzig: 1923); and W. K. Jordan, *Devel't of Relig. Toler'n in England* (Cambridge, Mass.: 1932–40).

30. William Penn, *Address to Protestants*, in *Works* (1678), I, 797–99 and *Works* (1728) I, 797–99. Penn used every basis of argument all his life, but his emphasis shifted: in *The Perswasive to Moderation* (1685) he used only pragmatic arguments. In 1685 Penn defended with wit a tract for toleration by the duke of Bucks.

7
THE QUAKER COLONIES

When George Fox returned to England from America in 1673, one of the first Friends to greet him was young William Penn. There is no evidence that Fox dreamed of a massive Quaker emigration from England to the New World, but he was enthusiastic about the spread of the religion in America, and a substantial number of the most influential Quakers including Robert Barclay*, George Keith*, and William Penn*, became involved with the New World in the next decade. The reasons that prompted other Englishmen to migrate also influenced Friends. England seemed overcrowded and land poor, and opportunities for land and trade appeared much better in America. Instability in government seemed chronic, and plague and war were constant dangers. Friends believed in religious liberty and wanted freedom from persecution. They experienced sporadic persecution and a variety of petty harassments from local and national authorities. Living in the midst of what they regarded as a population generally hostile and immoral, Friends saw in the New World the promise of a genuine Quaker community. Those who disliked local authorities, those who wanted an adventure, those who desired to convert Indians, and those who wished to better their economic status or to leave adequate property to their children saw opportunities in America.

In 1674 John Fenwick and Edward Billing bought from John Lord Berkeley for £1000 the land and the power to govern one-half of New Jersey. The transaction was of dubious legality, for Berkeley's title to the land was suspect, and only the Crown had the right to transfer government. Also, Fenwick was acting as an agent for Billing, who was in debt and faced bankruptcy. Penn and Fenwick may have arranged the land sale in West Jersey to save Friends from having to disown Billing or pay his debts. There were difficulties in paying the £1000, Fenwick and Billing quarreled, and Friends intervened to mediate the dispute. William Penn's involvement with colonization dates from his arbitration of the

West Jersey dispute. He gained six years' experience in colonizing before he received his charter for Pennsylvania.[1]

In 1675, in an attempt to restructure the enterprise and end the quarrel between Billings and Fenwick, thirteen Proprietors (twelve of whom were Friends) bought out Billing, leaving Fenwick one section of land. Before an orderly settlement could be organized by the new Proprietors, Fenwick left England with 150 settlers and founded a town at what is now Salem, New Jersey. The other Proprietors, none of whom came to America, sent ships to found Burlington in 1677. West New Jersey was founded as a Quaker enterprise with that mixture of religious and economic motives typical in the seventeenth century.

Before Pennsylvania was founded, West Jersey had an Assembly, 1,400 immigrants, and a very liberal constitution: *The Concessions and Agreements of West Jersey*. Edward Billing, a former Leveller turned Quaker, probably wrote the *Concessions*, and it expresses the views typical of radicals of the late 1650s. The *Concessions* guaranteed trial by jury, no taxation without consent, and full freedom of conscience and vested virtually all powers in the Assembly.[2] Unfortunately, there remained a question whether the Proprietors or settlers of West Jersey had a right to establish any government, since Berkeley's power to sell the rights to govern was not established. The resulting insecurity and disputes, along with an attempt by Fenwick to gain royal support for his claims, made Quaker control of West Jersey's government problematic.

In the meantime, the heirs of Sir John Carteret, who was owner of the eastern half of New Jersey, sold his share to a group of Proprietors, of whom a majority were Quakers including Penn. To raise money, the East Jersey Proprietors incorporated Scottish owners, and the character of West and East Jersey differed sharply. West Jersey remained predominantly Quaker, and East Jersey, which had few Quaker settlements, attracted a wide diversity of population including Dutch, Puritan dissidents from New Haven who founded Newark in 1665, and Presbyterian settlers from Scotland. East Jersey's commercial and political ties were to New York, but West Jersey, which bordered the Delaware River, oriented its trade and religious activities toward Philadelphia.

THE FOUNDING OF PENNSYLVANIA

William Penn's aristocratic connections with the king and the duke of York eventually brought him a grant of land. Why Charles II decided in 1681 to give the Charter for a new land, which he named Pennsylvania in honor of Admiral Penn, to his Quaker courtier cannot be precisely documented. The ostensible reason was a debt of £16,000 owed to Sir William Penn, the admiral, for victualing the fleet, but the Stuart monarchs were habitually in debt and generally did not worry about paying off their subjects. Charles may have seen the political power of the growing Quaker movement and decided that a refuge would drain away some of the most troublesome members of his kingdom. The land was vacant (to him, Indians didn't count), and a charter for an area that was worth little would please Penn and his aristocratic supporters, pay a debt, and add a colony at no expense to the Crown.[3]

The blending of incompatible emphases that characterized Penn's ideas on toleration and theology reappeared in his plans for Pennsylvania. Only now the divergencies were compounded by Penn's roles as owner of the land, Lord Proprietor (and, therefore, the source of governmental authority), speculator in need of a profit from his estates and investments, advertiser seeking settlers, adviser to an absolutist king, and weighty Quaker minister.

Penn hoped that his colony would become a "Holy Experiment" or experience. He believed that God had inclined the king to give him the land and that his and the settlers' responsibilities were to wait on insight from the Lord on how to establish and whether to migrate to Pennsylvania. Pennsylvania was to be a meeting in the wilderness. If he and the colonists followed the Light, God would bring peace, prosperity, and piety. Philadelphia, the name Penn picked for his capital city, derived from a Greek connotation as a place of brotherly love in Palestine and in the book of Revelation. There Philadelphia was the town that became a new Jerusalem as its inhabitants followed the will of God. In Penn's initial vision Pennsylvania would inaugurate a new order where peace among settlers and between Christians and Indians would flourish, and its success would prefigure the return of Christ at the end of the world.[4]

Pennsylvania was also a place to make money. Penn wished to repay his debts from his new estate, and he advertised in England, Scotland, Ireland, and the Low Countries promising good soil, a healthful climate, and friendly natives. Hard work and a favorable government would result in a competent standard of living. Penn did not promise wealth and warned idle people not to migrate. He wanted orderly development of the land, but he also sold large tracts to his wealthy Friends who saw the colony as a speculative money-making venture.

Penn took his responsibilities as governor seriously. Before settlement could begin, an orderly plan of government had to be devised, and at least twenty versions of a constitution or Frame of Government were drawn up. Even so, when he published the Frame in 1682, he carefully limited the function and good that any constitution could bring:

any government is free to the people under it, whatever be the frame, where the laws rule and the people are a party to those laws, and more than this is tyranny, oligarchy, or confusion. . . . Governments, like clocks, go from the motion men give them, and as governments are made and moved by men, so by them they are ruled too. . . . Let men be good and the government cannot be bad: if it be ill, they will cure it. But if men be bad, let the government be never so good, they will endeavor to warp and spoil it to their turn.[5]

The Frame and the first laws, written by Penn and modified and confirmed by the settlers, provided for liberty of conscience and no established church but restricted officeholding to those who believed in God and Christ. All inhabitants were guaranteed trials by jury, and Penn attempted to reduce the punishment for serious crimes, make jails into workhouses, and provide for a simplified jurisprudence. The laws established a group of arbitrators or peacemakers to settle disputes among people without invoking the formalities of law. To preserve order and to discourage licentiousness, Penn drew up a stringent moral code that forbade gambling, racing, card playing, and games; outlawed drinking toasts and oaths; and levied fines for various moral offenses. The Quaker customs of plain style of dating and marriage without ministers were made standard practices. There was no provision for militia or defense, even though the Charter gave Penn responsibilities as captain-general for all of the colony's forces.

The laws made few allowances for those who did not believe in the distinctive customs of Friends. The outsiders who came were expected to conform to Quaker usages, possibly because the settlers saw their habits as not peculiar to Friends but important for all Christians. The colony did attract some Presbyterians and German pietists, but—as far as we can tell—most of the early settlers were or became Friends. The only regular organized worship before 1692 was in the Meetings.

The Friends who emigrated from England, Ireland, and Wales left for a variety of reasons: economic opportunity, religious freedom, wanderlust, quest for adventure, desire to help create a Christian Commonwealth, escape from unhappy political or domestic situations. The London Yearly Meeting warned Friends against migration simply to escape persecution or to attain wealth. According to the Meeting, any Friends debating leaving had to seek the Lord's direction, as in any major decision, and should leave only after being clear in his or her own mind of following the Inward Light. The migration from England depopulated some Meetings, weakened others, and may have drained many of the most talented and ambitious Friends away. At any rate, the numerical growth of English Friends, which was constant before 1680, began to cease. Although the changing character of late seventeenth-century English Quakerism should not be ascribed to migration only, there is no question that the efforts involved in colonization helped transform the Friends. Henceforth, English Quakers became concerned with keeping unity within a far-flung transatlantic community while preserving in England the heritage of the First Publishers.

The migration to Pennsylvania and West Jersey was part of a general populating of new lands that occurred in seventeenth-century England, but the characteristics of that migration depended on the nature of those leaving. In Virginia and the South much of the migration was by single men, most of whom came as indentured servants. In Pennsylvania and West Jersey the migration was by family, and in some cases, a community of Friends existing in England determined to move together. Penn sold nearly one-half of the total land sales to sixty-nine wealthy men, few of whom migrated. The new colony was composed mostly of "middling" people—yeomen, artisans, small merchants. Many came from the West of England and the London areas, and there were substantial groups from Wales and Ireland. The migration began in 1682, and by the end of the

next year after the arrival of nearly forty ships there were perhaps 4,000 inhabitants in Pennsylvania and 5,000 in the Delaware Valley, nearly two-thirds of
them Friends. By 1684, 800 Friends attended first-day and midweek meetings
for worship in Philadelphia.[6]

The adaptability of the organization established by George Fox is shown by
the ease with which structures and procedures developed in England were transferred to the Middle Colonies. Prospective settlers obtained certificates listing
members of the family or, if single, clearness for marriage. These certificates
were presented to the newly self-constituted Monthly Meetings. Friends gathered
to worship in a home or homelike structure called a meetinghouse. Several of
these Particular Meetings joined to form the Monthly Meeting where all business
was transacted in a gathering that occurred once a month. All Monthly Meetings
in a given area—which could be as large as a county—joined to form a Quarterly
Meeting, so named because it met for business and worship sessions four times
a year. By 1710 there were sixteen Monthly Meetings, sixty-five Particular
Meetings, and three Quarterly Meetings in Pennsylvania. In New Jersey there
were also three Quarterly Meetings and by 1745 twenty-nine Monthly Meetings.

Above the Quarterly Meeting was the Yearly Meeting. There were in colonial
America autonomous Yearly Meetings for New England, New York, Pennsylvania and New Jersey, Maryland, Virginia, and North Carolina. The Philadelphia
Yearly Meeting, as it came to be called, encompassed what was essentially the
Delaware River Valley—West New Jersey, Pennsylvania, Delaware, and parts
of the Eastern Shore of Maryland. This annual gathering met on alternative years
at Burlington and Philadelphia until 1745 when it was decided to meet only in
Philadelphia. After 1685 the Philadelphia Yearly Meeting recognized itself as a
separate body, began corresponding with the London Yearly Meeting on a formal
basis, and eventually began sending Epistles to all other Yearly Meetings.

These Epistles combined religious exhortation with practical advice to sister
Meetings on a wide variety of moral issues. When combined with Epistles from
the London Meeting for Sufferings, Second Day Morning Meeting, and weighty
Friends in England and America, the constant letter writing served as a method
of preserving harmony. In theory all Yearly Meetings were equal, but in practice
the London Yearly Meeting had the most prestige and provided answers to
questions asked by Americans. Philadelphia provided a somewhat analogous role
in the colonies, but its influence was not as great as London's. Since London
Quakers had access to members of Parliament and the Crown, American Friends
grew accustomed to having them represent their interests to the authorities regulating colonial affairs.

William Penn hoped that demonstrating benevolent intentions, respecting their
customs, and dealing justly with the Indians would ensure peace. Before first
journeying to Pennsylvania, he instructed his commissioners to deal fairly, although at the same time he suggested making shrewd bargains over land before
the Indians gained an inflated sense of its value. Theoretically, by virtue of the
royal Charter Penn already owned all land, but he treated the Indians as owners

and dealt with them to clear title. Although there is no surviving evidence of a general treaty of Penn with the Indians, he met with the Lenni Lenape or Delaware Indians in 1682–83 and again in 1701, and for the next hundred years both Indians and settlers commemorated the tradition of respect for each other shown in Penn's initial dealings.[7]

At first Penn seemed to be as successful in conciliating the settlers as the Indians. In 1682 Penn met with the settlers to make modifications in the Frame and laws; helped plan and lay out his capital city of Philadelphia with wide roads, public plazas, and spacious plots using a grid design that would become standard in American cities; participated in Quaker meetings; and sold lands. By surveyor's errors and perhaps because Penn had worried about access to the sea, his Charter had been drawn up granting him lands that had already been given to Lord Baltimore. The two men proved unable to compromise their differences, and Penn decided to return to England to press his case. He left America in 1684 planning to come back shortly, but because of events in England he did not return until 1700. In his sixteen-year absence dissatisfaction, factionalism, and animosity grew. The early history of Pennsylvania might have been more harmonious if Penn had been present to deal with problems firsthand and to use his considerable skills as a weighty Friend and able diplomat on the settlers.

Within the Meeting, Quakers seemed to have found unity, but outside there was discontent with each other and with Penn. Part of the difference was contrasting views of political responsibility. The Frame had envisaged a Council of 72 as the main initiator of legislation and a large Assembly of between 200 and 500 that could consent to or reject, but not initiate or amend, proposed laws. The numbers involved meant that the Assembly was almost a direct democracy, as in ancient Athens. The settlers, not willing to spend much time on politics when they had to build homes and farms, proposed scaling down the Council to 18 and the Assembly to 36, but the functions of the two bodies remained unchanged. The result was a twenty-year struggle in which the Assembly attempted to gain the right of legislation and to reduce the power of the Council and Proprietor.

A second issue concerned finance. Penn sold the land but required the annual payment of a fee called a quitrent. The settlers objected to paying these rents at first because they said they were too poor and had no cash currency, but perhaps it was because they resented restriction on their free titles and did not want to pay rents at all. Penn, already living beyond his income, bore the major expenses of obtaining the Charter, organizing the colony, and providing the initial government, but he expected the colonists to pay the expenses of the proprietary government. The settlers viewed Penn as having established a profit-making venture and saw no reason why he should not pay for the government. The resulting impasse led to animosity on both sides.

Penn moved easily among aristocrats and Friends in England, but he had not learned how to govern people from afar. Quakers had a tradition of disobeying the laws in England that went against their religion, and in Pennsylvania there were few of the informal restraints of rank and place so characteristic of life in the Old World. Penn's choices of deputy-governors who ruled in his absence were bad, and the colonists proved adept at taking advantage of their ineptness. The Proprietor also faced increasing pressure from royal officials, who disapproved of all private colonies, to enforce the laws against smuggling and piracy and to support the Church of England. As long as Charles II or James II remained king, Penn was safe from royal officials, but the Glorious Revolution of 1688 deposed James II, who went into exile. Penn, an adviser and supporter of James II, was suspected of treason against William and Mary and had to go into hiding. The Crown seized his right to govern the colony from 1691 to 1693. Penn eventually proved his innocence and regained the colony, but for the rest of the decade he was caught between forceful royal officials and restive settlers.

Quakers in Pennsylvania needed to learn how to exercise power in a responsible manner quickly for they had almost no prior experience in governing England. They had to decide what was principled opposition and what was sheer obstructionism. What responsibilities could a Quaker magistrate exercise in enforcing the law, in determining the death penalty for murder, or in tendering an oath to a non-Friend? How should those who favored Penn deal with Friends who refused to pay taxes? Should Quakers provide money to use in the war with Louis XIV that followed the expulsion of James II? The debate in the Quaker community became a virulent controversy during the Keithian schism of 1692–94.

THE KEITHIAN CONTROVERSY

The Society of Friends has always existed somewhat uneasily within the pale of orthodox Christianity. The denial of baptism, the eucharist, a paid ministry, formal creeds, and all liturgical observances made many seventeenth-century Englishmen deny that Friends were part of the Christian Church. Friends always asserted that they were Christians, closer to the practice of the primitive church than their critics. While affirming both the essential sameness and the distinctiveness of God, the Holy Spirit, and Jesus, Friends refused to employ the term *Trinity* as unscriptural. An essential theological issue for American Friends as posed by George Keith was what constituted the relationship between the Light Within and Jesus of Nazareth who lived, died, rose, ascended into heaven, and continues as a physical being. The tendency of Friends, both the theologically astute and the majority, was to spiritualize religion, to make anything physical or fleshly nonessential. The question then became whether the bodily resurrection—of Jesus or of the faithful—was purely spiritual?

The Quaker who became distressed at this spiritualizing of all religion was the Scottish theologian George Keith. Keith, who was converted to Friends in 1664, associated with Robert Barclay, George Fox, and William Penn in missionary journeys and defenses of the faith. Keith and Barclay, the best systematic theologians produced by Friends, affirmed the immediacy of the experience of the Light and, at the same time, attempted to keep Friends sound on what they regarded as the fundamentals of Christianity.[8]

Keith migrated to New Jersey in 1685 as surveyor-general, and he laid out the dividing line between East and West Jersey, but in 1689 he moved to Philadelphia where he taught Latin school, engaged in religious controversies with New England Puritans, and made missionary journeys. In his publications he continued to define the boundaries of the faith, and his wide-ranging intellect and sharp vision were occasionally directed against his less acute fellow ministers. Keith also sought reforms within the Society of Friends.

The exact issues that caused the dispute to begin cannot now be isolated. "Sense of the Meeting" procedures work well when there is love within the community and an agreement to seek unity. Neither Keith nor his opponents in the Philadelphia Monthly Meeting showed charity or love in dealing with each other, and the decisions by the Meeting of Ministers to rebuke both sides only inflamed the participants. What may have begun as a dispute over theology became a battle of technique. Keith and his supporters appealed to the Quarterly Meeting, after the Philadelphia Monthly Meeting rebuked him, and then to the Yearly Meeting of Ministers and the Philadelphia Yearly Meeting. Unable to persuade the majority of Friends in Philadelphia to support him, Keith separated from the local Meeting and published an inflammatory account of the causes of the dispute. For Quakers elsewhere, the issue then became not Keith's theology but his publishing a libelous account and insisting that the ministers were guilty of "damnable heresies."

The only printer in Pennsylvania, a supporter of Keith, offered to publish accounts from both sides, but Friends did not wish to encourage an open airing of the issues, preferring to solve disputes within the Meeting. The opponents of Keith included many of the most prominent Friends in government and ministers. The Quaker magistrates claimed that Keith was undermining their civic authority and attacking their government and so had him arrested and seized the printer's type for publishing without a license. After a bitter session the Philadelphia Yearly Meeting pronounced Keith out of unity, not because of his beliefs but because of his manner of proceeding. Although tried and convicted (the printer was acquitted), Keith was released from further proceedings by a new royal governor. Both sides appealed to the London Friends for vindication.

Although beginning as a purely theological dispute, the schism had political implications. The followers of Keith tended to be his fellow Scots as well as those outside of the emerging American Quaker aristocracy. Keith became increasingly bitter at the close relationship between the Meeting and the government and raised fundamental questions about whether Quakers should be involved in enforcing laws, catching pirates, and compromising with evil. Perhaps influenced by some German pietist followers, Keith published the first American book against slavery.

London Quakers who were trying to convince the English government that they were sufficiently orthodox to qualify under the Act of Toleration were appalled by the schism. They were unhappy with Keith's publishing and dismayed at what looked like official persecution by the Pennsylvania magistrates. After long hearings, the London Friends rebuked both sides. Keith refused to apologize and began attacking English Friends by sermons and tracts, and these attacks brought his disownment. Keith organized groups of so-called Christian Quakers in both Philadelphia and London, but he became convinced eventually that heresy was endemic to Friends, and so he repudiated them and joined the Church of England.

The Keithian controversy was of fundamental importance for the history of Friends in the Delaware Valley. In spite of their censure of Keith, the issues he raised would haunt Friends for the next century: could Quakers participate in government without jeopardizing their faith, should slavery be allowed, how did the Inward Light relate to the historic creeds of the Church, what was the role of theology and the educated person within the Meeting? The Keithian controversy marked the end of a united Quaker community in the Delaware Valley; his followers either returned to the Meeting or joined Baptists, Anglicans, or Mennonites. Religious diversity became a fact of life in the Delaware Valley.

NOTES

1. John Pomfret, *Colonial New Jersey* (New York: 1973), 22–48.
2. Caroline Robbins, "Laws and Government Proposed for West New Jersey and Pennsylvania," *Pennsylvania Magazine of History and Biography* (hereafter *PMHB*) 105 (October 1981): 373–92; Hugh Barbour, "From the Lamb's War to the Quaker Magistrates," *Quaker History* (hereafter *QH*) 55 (1966): 14–17.
3. Mary Maples Dunn and Richard Dunn, ed., *Papers of William Penn* (Philadelphia: 1982), II, 81–238.
4. J. William Frost, "William Penn's Holy Experiment: Promise and Myth," *PMHB* 107 (1981): 419–52.
5. Frederick B. Tolles and E. Gordon Alderfer, ed., *The Witness of William Penn* (New York: 1957), 111.
6. Edwin Bronner, *William Penn's Holy Experiment* (New York: 1962), and Gary Nash, *Quakers and Politics: Pennsylvania, 1681–1726* (Princeton, N.J.: 1968), are the standard histories of early Pennsylvania. See also Edwin Bronner, "Quakers in Colonial America: The Middle Colonies" (MS, Quaker Collection, Haverford College, Haverford, Pa), Chs. 3, 4.
7. Dunn and Dunn, *Papers of William Penn*, II, 439–506; Marshall J. Becker, "Lenape Land Sale, Treaties, and Wampum Belts," *PMHB* 108 (1984): 351–56.
8. Ethyn Williams Kirby, *George Keith* (New York: 1942), is a good biography. The documents of the Keithian controversy are reprinted in J. W. Frost, ed., *The Keithian Controversy in Early Pennsylvania* (Norwood, Pa.: 1980); a recent interpretation is Jon Butler, "Gospel Order Improved: The Keithian Schism and the Exercise of Authority in Pennsylvania," *William and Mary Quarterly*, 3d ser. 31 (1974): 431–45.

8
A TOLERATED SOCIETY OF FRIENDS

ENGLISH QUAKERS

The Glorious Revolution of 1688 deposing James II and bringing in William and Mary as monarchs was followed by laws making orthodox Protestant dissent legal and spelling out the rights of Nonconformists. With a few modifications, the Restoration settlement in religion endured until the nineteenth century. Dissenters could worship and hold property but could not attend universities or sit in Parliament, and the Church of England remained established and supported by the tithes of all subjects.

The Quakers' attitude to the tithe indicates their adjustment to eighteenth-century society. Before 1680 Friends regularly denounced tithes and were prepared to go to jail rather than compromise. By the 1730s the Testimony against tithes was more waffling, and in normal cases, Friends accepted a modus vivendi with local authorities in which the distraint for the value of the tithe caused neither Quaker nor clergy much trouble. Occasionally, the arrangement broke down, often because of the opposition of the local minister or magistrate, and the Quaker would have to face a costly suit before the Exchequer or Ecclesiastical Court. Those Friends who feared the expense and vexation of appearing before these courts were likely to pay the tithe, rather than maintain what many regarded as a trifling principle.

Friends sought through Parliament relief from court proceedings over the tithe but could obtain no satisfaction.[1] They never campaigned against the tithe itself or the inability to attend the universities, serve as sheriff or in Parliament, or participate in juries.

The laws exempting Quakers and other dissenters from the penalties for nonconformity had to be renewed periodically. Many high church Anglicans opposed granting Friends any privileges, since Quakers remained the most anticlerical and antisacramental of the dissenters. After toleration, London Friends adopted a defensive posture, attempting to work with their sympathizers in the House of Lords or Commons and at Court to secure reenactment of laws easing their sufferings. Prominent weighty Friends in the Meeting for Sufferings lobbied with Parliament in an attempt to remove existing disabilities, but compromise rather than defiance and placidity rather than outrage characterized Friends' approach to the religious and social ills in England. Not civil disobedience but working within the system was the approach favored by London Friends.[2]

Early Friends kept accounts of their sufferings to present to the authorities in London in seeking redress. When prominent ministers including James Parnell, Edward Burrough, and Richard Hubberthorne died as a result of persecution, Friends attempted to keep alive their Testimonies and memory by publishing an edition of their complete writings. When all their tracts were joined in a volume also containing a biography or spiritual autobiography and an account by other Friends of the person's characteristics, the resulting book might have several hundred pages. By the 1690s Friends had committed substantial time and money to the publication of the collected works of prominent deceased ministers.

The need to preserve past records occupied an increasing share of the Meetings' activities. Monthly Meetings kept carefully written minutes; the Meeting for Sufferings gathered and saved thousands of pages of accounts of sufferings of Friends. Joseph Besse's edition of a two-volume set of extracts of the sufferings was published in 1733. John Whiting in 1708 issued the *Catalogue* listing Friends' publications. The Swarthmore Manuscripts, the letters of George Fox,* and libraries of books were all kept. In the 1650s Quakers repudiated Church tradition as a rationale for policies. By 1700 Quaker traditions had become decisive in the formulating of policies, and Meetings made certain that they knew their history. The result of devoting so much attention to the past was a decline in numbers of original Quaker writings.[3] Obviously, if Friends were going to read thousands of pages of Fox, Burrough, Robert Barclay,* and Isaac Penington, they would have little time to peruse more recent authors.

Quaker tracts produced in the eighteenth century did not vary from earlier writings in variety, but the proportion of each type varied considerably—particularly as the century progressed. The shrill prophetic denunciation of immorality and calls to repent that had dominated the 1650s became much rarer and were replaced by devotional readings. These spiritually elevating books contained little systematic theology. The controversial religious literature produced by Friends sought to defend the reputation of the Society of Friends against clergymen or outsiders (like Charles Leslie and David Hume who attacked directly or sniped at Quakerism), to present the Meeting in a nonthreatening way to outsiders, and to confirm the faithful in the distinctive Testimonies of the faith.

Eighteenth-century British Friends continued to follow the religious paths blazed by early Friends. The years of persecution, of opponents' misrepresentation of tenets, of schism, of organization, and then of colonization had taken a toll of the creative energies of those who remained. The death of George Fox

in 1691 and of Robert Barclay a few weeks later and William Penn's* preoc-
cupation with political and colonial affairs removed the three most creative men
from Quaker affairs. George Whitehead (1635–1722/3), converted in the 1650s,
became the unofficial spokesman of London Quakers. He suffered imprisonment
during the Restoration, traveled widely in the ministry but never came to America, and wrote extensively upon Quaker topics. Whitehead ably defended Friends
against the polemics of George Keith*, Francis Bugg, and Charles Leslie after
1690 and represented Friends to the court. Theologically astute and politically
adept, Whitehead remained a conservative trying to keep alive a past religious
fervor rather than a radical expanding the religious and social consciousness of
Friends. Whitehead was a steadying influence, but under his leadership the
excitement of being a Quaker seemed to disappear. Friends drew in upon themselves, becoming increasingly sectarian, safe, sound, orthodox, and dull.

Friends kept no membership registers, and estimates of the number of Quakers
in England in 1690 vary from 40,000 to 60,000. By 1715 Friends had 696
congregations in England and Wales. Richard Vann's calculations of the membership of Friends in Buckingham, Norwich, and Norfolk counties from 1690
until 1740 showed that there was little growth or decline but substantial population
shifts as Friends moved to towns.[4] In part, this town migration merely reflects
changes in England, but the percentage of Friends involved argues that there
may have been additional incentives—such as tithe persecutions—to leave the
land as well as the attraction of dwelling among coreligionists. There remained
small enclaves of Friends in Scotland and Ireland and many rural Friends, particularly in the northern counties of Yorkshire, Lancashire, and Westmoreland.
The country Friends remained suspicious of the compromises that the leaders in
London felt obliged to make in matters such as the affirmation.[5] Bristol, Norwich,
and, above all, London became the center of Quaker decision making. By 1700
there may have been 10,000 or 12,000 Quakers in London; the Devonshire
House Monthly Meeting alone had 2,000 members, and there were five other
Monthly Meetings in the metropolis.[6] London was where the Meeting for Sufferings and the Morning Meeting and Yearly Meeting met. The most important
Quaker printers and many prominent ministers and elders lived there. Negotiations with the Cabinet or members of Parliament took place in the capital city.
The men who constituted the Meeting for Sufferings rarely had titles or aristocratic connections like William Penn; instead, they tended to be prosperous
merchants who had the leisure to spend upon the time-consuming tasks required
of weighty Friends.

During the Restoration it had been exhilarating to be a Friend—awaiting the
eschaton, making converts, enduring schisms, working for religious toleration,
escaping or enduring persecution. After the defection of George Keith, far more
disruptive in America than in England, London Friends closed ranks, keeping
their differences within the confines of the Meeting. Until the end of the eighteenth century, there were no major controversies to inflame passions. The impres-

sion derived from reading the minutes of all levels of organization is the importance of committees and routine. Every May the Yearly Meeting gathered in London, listened to reports, worshipped, composed Epistles, and adjourned.

Because Quakers in Georgian England looked, talked, and worshipped differently from all other church people, they were on the defensive. So they produced a constant supply of tracts defending their distinctive ways, although they were read chiefly by those already convinced. The Meeting for Sufferings and the Yearly Meeting addressed the general body politic only on issues of importance to Friends, except on ceremonial occasions like addresses to the throne on the accession of a new king.

INDUSTRY AND SCIENCE

The lack of originality of English Friends in religious matters was compensated for by their stunning achievements in science and industry. The hypothesis that those barred from real political power and subjected to various kinds of discrimination in a nation will channel their creative efforts elsewhere is borne out by eighteenth-century British Quakers. The Meetings' requirements for honesty and fairness and trading within one's capital reassured outsiders that Friends were trustworthy. Their plain living, dependable work habits, and inventiveness made many Quakers prosper.[7] Since the children of Quaker business families married the offspring of other Quakers, the capital accumulated by one generation was passed on to others of similar proclivities. By the mideighteenth century Quakers had become almost a clan of extended kinfolk bound together by patterns of commerce and religion.

Three generations of Abraham Darby (1677–1791) at Coalbrookdale revolutionized the manufacture of iron. Abraham Darby I patented a method of casting ironware in sand so that new shapes of pots could be made, and then he successfully marketed them. Abraham Darby II was the first to use coal, changed into coke, in the production of iron; Abraham Darby III pioneered in the use of the iron for structural work. In 1779 he built the first iron bridge; his Severn bridge was an engineering and aesthetic triumph that still survives. The Darbys also cast the iron for use in the first iron ships and steam engines and showed the usefulness of iron for railroads.[8] In addition, the Darbys followed paternalistic policies designed to provide decent wages and adequate housing for their employees. The Darbys along with other Quaker families—the Reynolds, Lloyds, Champions, and Rawlinsons—dominated the British iron industry throughout the eighteenth century, and their technical innovations facilitated the coming of the industrial revolution to England.

The Darbys' achievements were not isolated events. The Champion family also made improvements in the refining of brass, lead, and zinc; Benjamin Huntsman found a way to manufacture the fine steel for which Sheffield has become famous. William Cookworthy discovered the Cornish deposits of China clay and, through his experiments, helped create an English industry in fine china and porcelain. Joseph Fry's investigations resulted in improvements in the manufacture of chocolates and medicines. Quakers created new processes in precision clock and instrument making, bathing machines, and type face for printing. Quaker merchants helped design and finance early English canals and railroads.[9] The commitment of these successful business and scientific Quakers to the Meeting is striking. Many served as ministers and elders and devoted copious amounts of time to the tasks of the Meeting.

Quaker dynasties also emerged in commerce. The Gurney family of Norwich after 1683 became involved in the woolen trade. Five generations of Gurneys pursued the business of collecting yarn, manufacturing cloth, and financing the putting-out system. The Pease and Backhouse families also made fortunes in the woolen industry. The Barclays and Hanburys accumulated fortunes through trade with colonial America. Quakers became involved in virtually the entire spectrum of English artisan, manufacturing, and commercial activities including pharmaceutical supplies, tinplating, smelting of lead, mining of copper and lead, and brewing of beer.[10]

The fortunes the Quakers made in iron and commerce needed to be reinvested. Since Friends proved reliable, other people gave them monies for safekeeping and prudent investment. The eighteenth century saw the rise of a series of Quaker banks: Freame and Barclay, Hoare's, Backhouse's, Gurney's, Lloyd's, Pim's. Even after two centuries of mergers, two of the largest English banks, Barclays and Lloyds, retain the names of their Quaker founders.

Early Friends had been too preoccupied with religious matters to make major contributions to science. Thomas Tompion (1638–1713) and George Graham (1673–1751) became notable as makers of precision instruments, clocks, watches, and part of the apparatus used at the Royal Observatory in Greenwich. Several Quakers became interested in agricultural reform and natural history. Robert Ransome (1753–1830) improved the design and the steel used in plows, and he is sometimes given the credit for the first use of interchangeable parts. Peter Collinson (1693–1768) was a naturalist who collected plants from all over the world and also arranged for the first publication of Benjamin Franklin's experiments with electricity. John Dalton (1766–1844), a schoolmaster, became the most important Quaker scientist for his discovery of the law of chemical combinations and calculations of the atomic weights of various elements.

Quakers also made notable contributions to the practice of medicine. Since Friends were barred from English universities, Quaker doctors had to attend the University of Edinburgh. John Fothergill, (1712–80), member of the Meeting for Sufferings and a founder of Ackworth School, attended Edinburgh before beginning practice in London. Fothergill made extensive clinical observations of diseases, helped inoculate people for smallpox with live vaccine, and helped found the London Medical Society. Fothergill and his associate John Coakley Lettsom (1744–1815) supported plans for humanitarian relief and civic improvements and corresponded with Friends in America about the necessity of changes in the conditions of prisons.[11] Lettsom and other Quakers conducted the experiments necessary to prove that Jenner's use of cowpox was a safe way to inoculate against smallpox.

NEW ENGLAND AND THE SOUTH AFTER 1688

The Glorious Revolution of 1688 deposing James II and bringing in William and Mary as monarchs was followed by laws making orthodox Protestant dissent legal and spelling out the rights of Nonconformists. The results of the Revolution in America were more mixed, and there were substantial contrasts between the treatment of Friends in Maryland and the Carolinas, New England, New Jersey, and Pennsylvania.

In the colonies Friends and their opponents knew of James II's support for easing the legal restrictions on Quakers and of his close relationship to William Penn and Robert Barclay. Therefore, the Glorious Revolution meant an immediate loss of political influence as settlers in Massachusetts, New York, and Maryland who staged revolutions against purported agents of James regarded Friends with suspicion. William Penn and Lord Baltimore lost control of their colonies as royal governors came to Maryland and briefly to Pennsylvania. The Glorious Revolution also marked the end of a long period of weakness and turmoil and the beginning of a resurgence in the Church of England and the culmination of a struggle against all proprietary governments—two movements that threatened the well being of Friends in the colonies. Maryland was a royal colony from 1692 to 1715; New Jersey became a royal colony in 1702, North Carolina in 1691, and South Carolina in 1726. The Church of England became established in both Carolinas, Maryland, and New York. Opponents of Friends attempted to make Pennsylvania a royal colony and to establish the Church of England in both New Jersey and Pennsylvania.

The threat of the resurgence of royalism and Anglicanism to Quaker political power and religious freedom is illustrated by events in Maryland. Long before Fox's visit to Maryland in 1672, the Society of Friends had achieved rapid growth and respectability and had exercised a stabilizing influence in the area far beyond their numbers. Before 1688 Friends were elected to the Assembly; served as sheriffs, county magistrates, and justices; and became members of the Provincial Court and the Governor's Council. Esteemed by their neighbors as good citizens and dependable representatives, Friends also worked to secure their rights to affirm, avoid militia service, and enjoy full political rights. The Maryland revolutionaries of 1688 were anti-Proprietor, anti-Catholic, and anti-Quaker. They insisted that all elected officials take oaths, not affirmations. Having reduced Quaker political power in the Assembly by this measure, they then attempted to create an established church. Friends appealed to the Meeting for Sufferings in London, which persuaded the Crown to veto statutes in 1696 and 1699 as deleterious to dissenters, but in 1700 a revised statute became law. From then until the American Revolution Maryland Quakers were subjected to tithes and fines for failure to perform military service and were barred from political offices because of required oaths. Maryland had been founded as a haven for Catholics, and its 1649 law on toleration is deservedly famous, but after 1688 religious liberty disappeared as neither Catholics nor Quakers could hold political office. Friends at least still had the right to worship in public, a privilege Catholics no longer enjoyed.[12]

Essentially the same process of restriction of religious liberties and Quaker rights occurred in the Carolinas. There was a large Quaker settlement in North Carolina and a few Friends lived in Charleston. As in Maryland, because they were good citizens, Friends exercised political power in excess of their numbers and had considerable success in bringing harmony to the turbulent settlers. After North Carolina became a royal colony, Anglicans and royal officials succeeded after a political struggle in establishing the Church of England in 1704. The authorities subjected Friends to militia duty and the tithe, while excluding them from political power.

Before 1684 the clergy of the established Congregational Churches in Massachusetts and Connecticut begrudged toleration to Anglicans and especially to Quakers. Whatever the calamity—Indian war, witchcraft, drought—some Puritans saw it as resulting from God's punishment for being too gentle to Friends. Still, Edmund Andros and the Dominion of New England (1684–88) forced upon the Puritans a limited toleration, and there was no reversal of the policy after New England's revolution and the new Charter. Massachusetts remained a Charter colony but now had a Crown-appointed governor. The Congregational Church remained established, but Quaker ministers were no longer jailed, whipped, or fined. Quakers continued to debate religious liberty with Puritans, but the issues were not survival and punishment but payment of tithes, militia service, and laws requiring towns to support an orthodox Congregational minister. In towns on the southern border of Massachusetts near Rhode Island (in what had previously been Plymouth Colony), Baptists and Quakers constituted either a substantial minority or actual majority of the people, and they resisted taxes for a Puritan cleric's salary. Elsewhere Quakers disliked having to pay fines for refusing to serve in the militia and opposed going to magistrates for certificates allowing their tithes to be paid to the church in which they were members. Quakers disliked forced taxation for any religious body, even their own. The London Meeting for Sufferings supported the New England Quakers' complaints about continuing legal disabilities, but onerous laws remained on the books.[13]

THE MIDDLE COLONIES

The Quakers' loss of political control in New Jersey bears only a superficial resemblance to similar events in Maryland and North Carolina. When East and West Jersey were reunited as the royal colony of New Jersey in 1702, Quakers and most other inhabitants welcomed the change. The weaknesses in the Proprietors' title to government was made evident in 1684 when the English Ministry incorporated both Jerseys into the Dominion of New England. In both East and West Jersey there was constant insecurity and occasional riots. In this context the settlers responded favorably to the Crown's offer to buy the rights of government from the Proprietors, a proposal that included guarantees of the rights of the Assembly and of continued Quaker participation in government.

Compared to its two neighboring colonies, New Jersey remained obscure and noncontroversial for the next seventy years. After 1702 the Quakers in the colony were neither as powerful as in Pennsylvania nor as sectarian as in the South. Friends served in the Assembly and on the Council and in a wide variety of local offices, and they dominated the area from Burlington to the Delaware Bay. The former West Jersey remained oriented to Pennsylvania and an integral part of the dominant Quaker culture. Ambitious young men like Samuel Jennings, John Kinsey, and John Smith moved from West Jersey to Philadelphia in search of fortune and political power. The unity that the Society of Friends and Philadelphia commerce imposed upon the Delaware River Valley was more crucial than the political divisions into Pennsylvania, New Jersey, and Delaware. Burlington experienced a slow growth of population and commerce in the eighteenth century but remained a subsidiary town to Philadelphia and had almost no trade with East Jersey and New York. Most West Jersey Quakers remained farmers, and long after the American Revolution, the area remained culturally distinct from East Jersey. West Jersey remained a place marked by quiet resolution of disputes, conservatism, and outward placidity.[14]

Such attributes do not describe the characteristics of Pennsylvania after 1700. Eighteenth-century Pennsylvania remained an anomaly because only there did Quakers begin with political power and retain it until the eve of the American Revolution. In England Friends exercised no political authority, and most Delaware Valley Anglicans and royal officials thought that Pennsylvania should become a royal colony with an established church. Whether they disliked Friends for theological reasons or saw them as impeding their hopes for advancement and profit, after 1700 there was a vocal Anglican minority who aimed to subvert the existing proprietary government through the intervention of the Crown.

William Penn finally returned to Pennsylvanian in 1699 in an attempt to bring order to his troubled colony. With Penn present, matters seemed to run smoother. The Assembly passed bills against smuggling and pirates, and Penn granted a new Frame of Government in 1701 that reduced the powers of the governor and Council and recognized the strength of the Pennsylvania Assembly. Not all problems were solved, and in spite of Penn's wishes, the division between Pennsylvania and Delaware became permanent.[15] A pending attack upon all proprietary colonies in Parliament forced Penn's return to England in 1701. He never saw America again.

Penn's new Frame of Government required reenacting all of the colony's previous laws, which, with additions, made nearly ninety statutes. The laws were submitted to England for royal approbation. In 1705 the Crown vetoed nearly half of the colony's laws, complaining that they were pro-Quaker, different from English law, unreasonable, too strict (as on crime and adultery), or too tolerant (on religion). The English government argued that the rights enjoyed by Quakers in the mother country were sufficient and should not be expanded. Religious toleration was allowable but going beyond toleration to religious liberty—the nonpreferential treatment of all Christians—was ill advised. The Pennsylvania Assembly tried again, modifying some laws to meet objections, camouflaging minor changes with new rhetoric, preserving the stringency of moral legislation, and preserving the right of affirmations. Since neither Penn nor the Assembly would accept the Ministry's restricted version of their rights, the result was a series of laws and vetoes that ended with the Quakers finally emerging as victorious in 1726.[16]

Another source of instability in Pennsylvania after 1700 was the unwillingness of the Quaker colonists to provide Penn with adequate revenue to support the government and to agree with him on the division line between the governor's and the Assembly's power. Penn was in debt and in desperate need of money. He spent 1707 in debtor's prison, and the settlers made few efforts to help.

Pennsylvania sometimes verged on anarchy, and William Penn became a frustrated and embittered man. In debt, unable to control the colony, and finding it impossible to obtain sufficient revenue to support the government, Penn approached the Crown and began negotiations to sell the right of government, a process similar to what had occurred in New Jersey. While discussions as to how to preserve the rights enshrined in the Frames of Government continued, Penn suffered a stroke that left him incapacitated and unable to complete the transaction. William Penn survived for six years after his stroke in 1712 with impaired mental faculties. Although Pennsylvania's settlers did not follow him as a political leader and landowner, they respected his abilities to protect their liberties, to procure peace with Indians, and to serve as a living example of the ideals of the Quaker faith.

By the end of the first quarter of the eighteenth century, the political and ecclesiastical battles in Pennsylvania quieted. Pennsylvania Anglicans learned that they could not count on the support of English authorities in driving the Quakers from political power and came to accept the reality of religious pluralism with no established church, no tithe, and no official support. The English government stopped trying to undermine proprietary government and showed less disposition to interfere with internal affairs either in Pennsylvania or the rest of colonial America.

The animosities dividing the Quaker community between conservative and popular parties also ceased. The sons of William Penn were non-Quakers and derived most of their support from Anglicans and various officials. Perhaps in response to the rapid influx of immigrants, the Quakers seemed to draw closer together. By most outward signs—numbers of members, new meetinghouses, geographic expansion—the Society of Friends was growing, even though its percentage of the total population of the Delaware River Valley steadily shrank.

Early Pennsylvania had been characterized by general equality of status. By the 1720s social inequality was apparent, and in both New Jersey and Pennsylvania, the members of a few prominent families could be seen in the legislature, courts, counting houses, and meetinghouses. John Kinsey symbolized the links between politics, wealth, and religion. Moving from West Jersey to Philadelphia, Kinsey in 1731 became a member of the Assembly. By 1739 he was speaker of the Assembly, and in 1739 he became attorney general and deputy trustee of the Loan Office. He also served as clerk of Philadelphia Yearly Meeting from 1730 to 1749, during a period in which election day fell just after the Yearly Meeting and Quakers were accused of using their annual gathering for political purposes. Kinsey's appointment in 1743 as chief justice of the Provincial Court by Thomas Penn showed that Quaker political leaders in the Assembly had learned how to compromise and work with the Proprietor.

The new era of harmony rested upon a lack of divisive issues.[17] England was at peace, the Society of Friends was united, Pennsylvania was prospering, religious enthusiasm among Protestant denominations was muted, and only the amount of paper money to be issued divided conservatives from moderates. The constitutional issues of allotment of power and taxation seemed settled by the 1701 Frame and later compromises, and Penn's sons acquiesced in the Assembly's domination of the government.

Nearly two-thirds of the members of the Assembly were Quakers and belonged to a faction called the Quaker Party. That party's domination of elections was based upon its appeal to the general electorate, since Friends alone could not elect a majority of the representatives.[18] The Quaker Party wrapped itself in the mantle of William Penn; offered freedom, peace, and low taxes; and claimed credit for the general prosperity. The Assembly offered to most citizens the right to be left alone. The Quaker Party offered to immigrants easy naturalization processes, loans to purchase lands, and ample currency in the form of paper money to keep commerce thriving. Quakers boasted that their policy of respect for Indians' rights brought peace and meant that there would be no taxes for military endeavors and no militia service. Quakers also claimed credit for the success of religious liberty, and the Council and Assembly protected the rights of religious minorities.

The supporters of the Proprietary Party—the opposing faction—had major liabilities to overcome and never succeeded in winning an election. Thomas Penn was landlord of an immense domain, and he desired orderly settlement in order to stop squatting, to sell the lands expensively, and to clear title in orderly fashion from the Indians. Immigrants wanted to settle on vacant lands—whether or not surveyed—to have their squatting claims upheld, and still to get the land cheap. They did not want to pay quitrents. Quaker Assembly members were sympathetic to all of their desires. If the proprietary faction complained about the defenseless state of the colony, the Quakers responded that conciliation was cheaper than war, and no one wanted compulsory militia service. Since the Penns and their supporters tended to be Anglicans, the Quaker politicians charged that they aimed at establishing the Church of England in Pennsylvania and levying Church rates.

Also, the supporters of the Proprietor and Thomas Penn himself tended to look and act like aristocrats. Quaker politicians were more astute. They dressed nicely but plainly, associated with the electors but never campaigned, encouraged talented young men, and ran the Assembly on practices borrowed from the Meeting—seeking compromise, not dominance, considering the wishes of all, and creating consensus. The result was that Pennsylvania became virtually a one-party state, and Quakers mobilized popular support.[19]

NOTES

1. J. William Frost, "The Affirmation Controversy and Religious Liberty," in *The World of William Penn*, ed. Richard S. Dunn and Mary M. Dunn (Philadelphia: 1986), 303–22.

2. Norman C. Hunt, *Two Early Political Associations: The Quakers and the Dissenting Deputies in the Age of Sir Robert Walpole* (Oxford: 1961).

3. Isaac Sharp, "Joseph Smith," *Journal of the Friends Historical Society* (London) (hereafter *JFHS*) 11 (1914): 9.

4. Richard Vann, *The Social Development of English Quakerism, 1655–1755* (Cambridge, Mass.: 1969), 162–67; John Punshon, *Portrait in Grey: A Short History of the Quakers* (London: 1984), 103.

5. Nicholas J. Morgan, "Lancashire Quakers and the Oath, 1660–1722," *JFHS* 54 (1980): 235–54.

6. William Beck and T. Frederick Bell, *The London Friends' Meetings* (London: 1869), 172.

7. Isabel Grubb, *Quakerism and Industry Before 1800* (London: 1930).

8. Barrie S. Trinder, *The Darbys of Coalbrookdale* (Chichester, Eng.: 1981).

9. Arthur Raistrick, *Quakers in Science and Industry before 1800* (London: 1830); Humphrey Lloyd, *The Quaker Lloyds and the Industrial Revolution* (London: 1975).

10. Jacob Price, "The Great Quaker Business Families of Eighteenth-Century London: The Rise and Fall of a Sectarian Patriciate," *The World of William Penn*, ed. Richard S. Dunn and Mary M. Dunn (Philadelphia: 1986), 363–400.

11. Hingston Fox, *Dr. John Fothergill and His Friends* (London: 1919); Betsy C. Corner and Christopher Booth, eds., *Chain of Friendship: Selected Letters of Dr. John Fothergill of London, 1735–1786* (Cambridge, Mass.: 1971).

12. David W. Jordan, " 'God's Candle' within Government: Quakers and Politics in Early Maryland," *William and Mary Quarterly*, 3d ser., 39, no. 4 (1982): 628–54.

13. Arthur Worrall, *Quakers in the Colonial Northeast* (Hanover, N.H.: 1980), 103–6, 111–27, 131–35; William McLoughlin, *New England Dissent, 1630–1833: The Baptists and the Separation of Church and State* (Cambridge, Mass.: 1971), I, 165–199.

14. John Pomfret, *Colonial New Jersey* (New York: 1973), 77–122.

15. Gary Nash, *Quakers and Politics: Pennsylvania, 1681–1726* (Princeton, N.J.: 1968), 69–76, 81–84, 236; John Munroe, *Colonial Delaware* (New York: 1978), Chs. 4, 5.

16. J. William Frost, "Religious Liberty in Early Pennsylvania," *Pennsylvania Magazine of History and Biography* (hereafter *PMHB*) 105 (October, 1981), 434–48.

17. Alan W. Tully, *William Penn's Legacy* (Baltimore: 1977); Jack D. Marietta, *The Reformation of American Quakerism, 1748–1783* (Philadelphia: 1984), 131–42.

18. Hermann Wellenreuther, "Quest for Harmony in a Turbulent World: The Principle of 'Love and Unity' in Colonial Pennsylvania Politics," *PMHB* 107 (October, 1983), 537–76.

19. Alan W. Tully, "Ethnicity, Religion, and Politics in Early America," *PMHB* 107 (October, 1983), 491–536; idem, "Quaker Party and Proprietary Policies: The Dynamics of Politics in Pre-Revolutionary Pennsylvania, 1730–1775," in *Power and Status: Officeholding in Colonial America*, ed. Bruce C. Daniels (Middletown, Conn.: 1986), 75–195.

9
A SPIRITUAL EXISTENCE

THE EIGHTEENTH-CENTURY CONTEXT

At first sight the stance of Friends in 1725 appears to bear little relationship with the spontaneous outbursts that created and sustained Quakers in the 1650s. Denouncing injustice, going naked for a sign, calling for political transformation, interrupting church services, pronouncing judgment on society, welcoming the imminent millennium, were either absent or little emphasized after 1700. Far from identifying with the poor and outcast, Quakers viewed these groups as social problems to be helped by workhouses and relief. Friends had become respectable artisans, farmers, and merchants with only a smattering of the poor or gentry.

The transformation in relations with the external world was paralleled by changes within the Meeting. Early Friends used a minimum of organization, which was designed to ease the sufferings of those imprisoned and to coordinate the work of the traveling ministers. By 1725 virtually every part of Quaker procedures had been standardized and written down in books of "Christian and Brotherly Advices," and a Friend's life from birth until death took place under a maze of regulations. Exuberance gave way to steady habits.

The causes of these changes lie in the heritage bequeathed by the first generation, the evolution of the outside society faced by Friends, and the Meetings' creative response to new conditions. The early eighteenth century was not a time of regression or decline from the religion of the First Publishers of Truth. In all religious movements, the high drama of the foundation eventually gives way to coalescing, definition, and preservation of the traditions.

From the beginnings of the movement, Friends had insisted that the governance of the Light led to strict moral behavior. Quakers were just as "puritanical" as other religious radicals and had insisted upon due order within meetings for worship and Christian behavior in the outside world. Precise standards for behavior had grown naturally out of the climate of opinion in revolutionary England. The difference between early and eighteenth-century Friends in plain style was, therefore, one of degree not kind. Those who were attracted to Friends sought an austere style of life. In time the austerity had been organized and set down in codes for correct dress, house furnishings, and conduct. What had been assumed to be in 1655 a natural function of following the Light was in 1725 the Truth received by the forefathers; in the latter case, just to make sure, the rules were written down.

The most far-reaching change that had occurred had less to do with Friends than with the external society—the disappearance of converts gained either through the "public threshings" and/or debates and the silent gatherings for worship in sympathizers' houses. Friends did not stop trying to convert English people; they continued to travel in the ministry and to visit areas where there were few members and to proclaim the value of the Inward Light of Christ, which they remained committed to following. They did not lose confidence in their direct experience of God. Rather, the change came because of a diminished sense of attractiveness of what Friends proclaimed to the serious and/or religiously inclined English men and women. When seventeenth-century Quakers preached boldly, their audience had been conditioned to expect assurance and prophecy. Quakers, after all, spoke no more fervently than other radical Puritans and separatists, and what all said was similar in form and, often, in substance. In the early eighteenth century neither Quakers nor anyone else preached in such a manner. In their "Augustan Age" the English prided themselves on order, rationality, and dignity and rejected "enthusiasm" and fanaticism. Rather than defining themselves as sole possessors of *all* Truth and damning most of Christendom as apostates, Quakers were seen and saw themselves as part of Dissent or Nonconformity. The general society showed neither hostility nor sympathy but only apathy or amused condescension to Friends' Testimonies. The English were learning how to tolerate, and Friends were becoming accustomed to being tolerated. Increasingly, Friends defined themselves as a "peaceable" or "peculiar people" (I Peter 2:9), elected by God to follow distinctive customs.

To outsiders many of the insights of the First Publishers seemed not the mark of God's direction but the hallucination of enthusiasts, peculiar customs in a pejorative sense. Englishmen looked back on the days of the Commonwealth as remote history, and they wanted stability in government, respect for the Church of England's liturgy and dogma, and reasonableness and moderation in all religious matters. Just as Friends remained within, even while they attempted to change, the climate of opinion in the 1650s, they followed—unknowingly—the ideals of the eighteenth century and sought to bring their Testimonies into harmony with what other religious people were doing.

When the number of converts to Quakerism decreased, the strategy Friends used to survive drew upon existing strengths: the prestige of George Fox and the martyrs for the faith, an agreed-upon set of structures and procedures within the Meeting, a unified theology that joined Friends to Christian Protestant orthodoxy while preserving distinct emphases, an intense fellowship among members, and the overwhelming importance that many adherents attached to the preservation of the new faith. Because the external world treated Quaker beliefs and customs coldly, the new Quakerism erected barriers between members and the external world. If outsiders did not see the wisdom of joining Friends, the Meeting would concentrate its attention upon those already within the fold and ensure that a rising generation of Quaker children retained their commitments to the faith. The twin emphases dominating early eighteenth-century Quakerism became the Discipline—the rules governing procedures within and outside the meeting—and the family.

The eighteenth-century history of Friends contains little of the excitement or the dramatic events that punctuated earlier decades. Now the Meeting could change quietly because the issues that seventeenth-century Friends fought each other and outsiders about had been settled—at least within the Quaker community. Friends had come to agree on what the Inward Light was and how it was experienced, the responsibilities of ministers, the necessity of organization, and the roles for women within the Meeting. Virtually everything that characterized eighteenth-century Quakerism had been present, at least in embryonic form, from the beginnings of the movement.

Early Friends tried to live by the Scripture and saw themselves as following literally the precepts of Jesus. Since the Bible was legalistic, so were Friends. But in the seventeenth century such legalism was balanced by bitter debates, large-scale conversions, martyrdoms, and colonization. As all of these things came to an end, good men and women taking their religious commitments seriously, and with no sense of humor about themselves or opponents, had to face the implications of the traditional Testimonies. As Quakers attempted to clarify their responsibilities, they began to make the freedom to follow an exuberant experience of the Light into the duty to abide by the rules of the Society of Friends. The emphases could be redirected, but the heritage of the founders became the legitimatizing feature of Friends' practices.

RATIONALISM AND QUIETISM

If an outsider asked an eighteenth-century Friend how her beliefs differed from those of early Quakers, the answer most likely would have been, "in no way." If pressed to be more specific on what she believed, the Quakeress might have presented the observer a copy of Robert Barclay's* catechism or *Apology*. She would have been mostly correct, because on all of those issues on which Barclay had taken a stand, Quakers still agreed with him. But there were differences, although the general Quaker antipathy to systematic theology, fear of schism, and an unwillingness to probe too deeply into the mysteries of the faith kept them hidden. In retrospect, we can find two distinct emphases on beliefs— quietism and rationalism—present in Barclay and early Friends' writings, but not in the form used in the eighteenth century.

All Friends agreed on the centrality of the experience of the Inward Light of Christ. Salvation depended upon the unity of the believer with the Light, and Christian living meant following the direction of the inward monitor. Inward grace was experienced in the conscience but was not part of it; that is, the Light was not a purely natural phenomenon—it was a gift of God. In the eighteenth century Friends reached no consensus over the relationship of the Inward Light of God to the natural light of reason, or whether use of one's intellectual faculties would contaminate knowledge gained through the operation of the Seed. Were reason and religious feelings compatible and harmonious or in dire opposition— in short, could a Quaker think about religion or only "feel" his or her way to Truth? The first alternative was a kind of Quaker latitudinarianism; the second is often called quietism. Both interpretations had their roots in the affirmations of early Friends. Fox had declaimed against the reliance upon "head knowledge" by Puritan preachers who made university education more crucial than the suf- ficiency of the Holy Spirit. Barclay showed that silence in the meeting for worship was essential for stilling one's own will so that God could be perceived. But early Friends also saw reason as a gift of God and did not distrust its usefulness in daily life. God in his creation of the world had left his marks on the natural world, and humans could discern them, giving them a capacity to understand Him. Fox had approved education in "whatsever thinges was civill & useful in the creation," and early Friends included men skilled in languages, mathematics, natural sciences, and divinity.[1] When early Friends confronted opponents, they did not disdain reasoning with them, and the controversies required intellectual tools. Barclay insisted that although Quakers derived their Truth from the Inward Light, these conclusions were compatible with and not contrary to the deductions of reason.[2]

William Penn, in his search for toleration, sought for fundamentals of faith on which all rational people could agree and rejoiced in the potential of natural religion to bring harmony. Penn and the latitudinarian Quakers had emphasized the harmony of the Inward Light and reason and the similarity between the life of Christian virtue and that of moderation. Penn's *Some Fruits of Solitude* (1693) shows the emphasis upon ethics so characteristic of early eighteenth-century rational Quakers:

It were happy if we studied nature more in natural things, and acted according to nature, whose rules are few, plain, and most reasonable.

If thou rise with an appetite, thou art sure never to sit down without one.

All excess is ill, but drunkenness is of the worst sort.[3]

In the early eighteenth century the preeminent spokesman for moderate Quak- erism was Alexander Arscott, a Bristol schoolmaster who served as clerk of the London Yearly Meeting four times and whose death sayings became part of *Piety Promoted*. Between 1730 and 1734 Arscott wrote a three-part defense of Christianity and attack upon deism that was reprinted in Philadelphia.[4] Even in the first part, ostensibly a defense of Christian revelation using only Scripture, Arscott's reliance upon reasonable religion that produces ethical lives is apparent. The rationalist Friends did not deny revelation or the atonement or divinity of Christ, and they could be very critical of deism. Their credo is best summarized in the preface to Thomas Beaven's *Essay Concerning the Restoration of Primitive Christianity*:

> For tho' none of the *real* Injunctions of *Religion* and *Piety* are, or ever can be contrary to *right Reason*, yet the *common Reason* of Man stands in Need of Light and Help from *Heaven*, for attaining the *true* Knowledge and Practice of *Religion* and *Piety*; as the great *Lock[e]* acknowledgeth. . . . Which *Light* and *Help* . . . is, so far from being destructive or repugnant to *Reason*, that 'tis the *divine Spirit*, which *enlightens* and *influences* the *noble* Faculty of *Reason*, to the highest Pitch of Knowledge and Certainty in heavenly Things, and gives it the greatest Repose, Delight and Satisfaction: Nevertheless Reason and the Spirit of God remain always, two several Powers and Principles in Man, of different and distinct Natures.[5]

Beaven's "reason" was inspired by both the Cambridge Platonists and seventeenth-century rationalists like John Locke. Other defenders of a latitudinarian Quakerism were John Bockett, Richard Claridge, Benjamin Coale, James Logan, and on occasion Thomas Story.

Rational Quakerism was a compromise position that, like the ethical life it valued, did nothing to extremes. It combined reason and revelation, Scripture and nature, and refused to choose between them. Arscott, for example, can in one section be extremely rationalistic and in another very quietistic. His Quakerism suited the mood and needs of eighteenth-century British Quakerism— respectful of tradition, requiring ethical behavior, firmly Christian, and acceptably genteel. It fit the needs of those Quakers making improvements in commerce and industry. Since rational Quakerism complemented the theological endeavors occurring among dissenters and in the Church of England in the same period, Arscott allowed Friends to be different but not strange.

More prevalent in the colonies and rural provinces was quietism. Even rationalistic Quakers became quietistic in the meeting for worship. Organized religious devotion took place at the meeting for worship. The meetinghouse was perfectly plain; no stained glass, no ornamentation, and no organ music detracted the person from silently waiting upon God. The benches were hard and might or might not have backs; usually, there was a raised platform or gallery at the front with a bench where the ministers and elders could sit facing the congregation. In keeping with what may have been an earlier practice of the English parish churches, men and women sat apart. Except that ministers and elders sat in the gallery, no distinction was made in seating arrangements. Quakers were expected to enter quietly and sit down, filling the seats at the front first.

Friends were supposed to approach the meetinghouse seriously. Frivolous matters were not to be discussed either just before or after worship. New England's Discipline warned against levity in riding a horse away after the meeting.

The congregation entered, sat down, and waited in silence. Men kept their hats on, except when someone prayed. The meeting ended when a Friend (normally a clerk or an elder) shook hands with the person seated next to him. The best description of a Quaker Meeting was written by Peter Kalm, the Swedish traveler, who attended Bank Meeting House in Philadelphia, December 7, 1750:

Here we sat and waited very quietly from ten o'clock to a quarter after eleven. . . . Finally, one of the two . . . old men in the front pew rose, removed his hat, turned hither and yon, and began to speak. . . . In their preaching the Quakers have a peculiar mode of expression, which is half singing, with a strange cadence and accent, and ending each cadence, as it were, with a half or . . . a full sob. Each cadence consists of two, three, or four syllables, but sometimes more, according to the demand of the words and means; e.g. *my friends/* /put in your mind/ /we/ /do nothing/ /good of ourselves/ /without God's/ /help and assistance/ /etc.[6]

This sermon took half an hour. Thomas Clarkson in the first decade of the nineteenth century provided a description of several of the preachers he heard. The ministers spoke in an odd tone of voice that Clarkson called ''unpleasant'' and likened to the noise made by street vendors. The speakers began very softly and slowly, but their speech became louder and faster as the discourse progressed. As fuller involvement came, the minister spoke ''beyond the quickness of ordinary delivery,'' and some were ''much affected, and even agitated by their subject.'' The changes of speed in delivery resulted, Clarkson thought, from the minister's caution in outrunning his gift. When he began to talk, he knew neither where his opening would lead him nor what he was going to say. As insight grew, the speed of delivery increased.[7] This singing style of preaching became more prevalent as the eighteenth century progressed, and by the middle of the nineteenth century many Quakers did not esteem a minister who did not sing his sermons.

Eighteenth-century Quaker worship services began with a period of silence that allowed the attenders to still their wills in order to experience the Inward Light. In theory, worship occurred during periods of quietness or during the prayers and sermons of the ministers; quiet times were not seen as preparation for speaking or vice versa. Ministers, who could be adult men or women, socially prominent or poor, attempted to foster a common experience arrived at individually of the presence of God. Those who spoke claimed to be guided by the Holy Spirit, and they insisted that intellectual preparation was inappropriate.

Published sermons, taken down in shorthand by nonmembers, and comments about messages in meeting by Friends show considerable variety of topic, a knowledge of minutiae of Scripture and an amazing ability to quote texts on any subject, and a strongly practical orientation. Subjects might include an explication of a biblical text, preparation for death, education of the young, the need for constant prayer, defenses of distinctively Quaker tenets, the need for love and unity among members, cautions about business practices, and the necessity of going beyond habit to genuine religious experience. Many of the sermons could have been delivered in services of other religious denominations, and when a particularly distinguished traveling minister visited, many non-Friends came to listen. Neither published sermons nor the comments of outsiders indicate that either sex dominated worship by frequency of appearance. Brevity was not a requisite either. The meeting for worship generally lasted for two hours, and although it would have been unusual for a minister to speak for the entire time, an extemporaneous discourse of from thirty minutes to an hour was not uncommon. Most of the speaking was done by men and women who were recorded "ministers." In urban areas like London and Philadelphia where each meeting for worship had several ministers who were members, Friends made certain by advance planning that ministers would cover all of the locations and not all congregate at the same service.[8]

Quietism dominated the practice of the ministry. A minister was a spokesperson for God and was forbidden to speak out of his or her own will. The divine origins of messages became apparent in the practices of prophecying, telling visions, and speaking to individual states. All of these practices could be justified by biblical citations. Also, the first Friends had used the biblical practices to justify their visions, denunciations, forecasting of events, and judgment of opposers. Although the rapturous, enthusiastic element had been an essential ingredient in pre-Restoration Quakerism, after 1700 such outbursts were looked at with suspicion. The distrust of individual ecstasies continued throughout the colonial period. Committees cut out some of Thomas Chalkley's rapturous poetry and muted John Woolman's visions.[9] But although Quaker committees downplayed such frank supernaturalism, the phenomena of visions, dreams, and omens remained part of Quaker lay peoples' world-view. So a Quaker minister might tell and interpret a dream, find in an earthquake or epidemic a sign, or describe the immorality or lackluster attitudes of the populace as an indication of coming judgment. Some ministers saw in the French revolution a time of troubles that would usher in the reign of the Antichrist or the fall of the papacy. In the midst of an exegesis of a verse from the Gospels, the minister might suddenly stop and begin speaking about a person's problem.[10] That individual and his problem might not be known to the minister who claimed to have felt an impulse to speak to someone in the Meeting contemplating suicide or marriage to a non-Quaker, overindulging in strong drink, or attempting to trade beyond what was prudent. Such speaking to conditions—when it proved applicable—proved to many Friends the close involvement of the deity with the ministers' discourse.

THOMAS CHALKLEY

In the absence of many published sermons, historians rely upon spiritual autobiographies or journals as the best source of information about ministers.[11] Journal keeping arose out of two sources—short narratives of spiritual experiences and notes kept by ministers of their journeys. Although the journals are very circumspect about many details of family life and daily affairs, they provide a myriad of details about the way devout Friends viewed their religious pilgrimage. Thomas Chalkley, born in Southwark (London) in 1675, later migrated to America and became the most prominent American minister in the first half of the eighteenth century. His journal was the first autobiography by an American Friend published on both sides of the Atlantic, and it rapidly became a minor Quaker classic. An analysis of Chalkley's *Journal* will show the life patterns of many Quaker ministers and also shed light upon the distinctive culture of early Pennsylvania.

Chalkley was religiously precocious as a child. His parents were devout Friends who sent him to a Quaker school. Chalkley early internalized Quaker strictures against idleness, being willing to rebuke his playmates for frivolous activities. As a young man, he described himself as inconstantly religious—feeling a glimmering of the divine presence but then succumbing to a love of music, card playing, and sports. Like many Quakers, Chalkley could not date the precise time when he was converted—religious life was a gradual process of growth in understanding the experience of the Light and its increasing demands on conduct.[12] For Chalkley, growth in grace was a process lasting throughout his life. Constant attendance at meetings, visible adherence to Quaker habits of speech and dress, and reliability in business as an apprentice and then as an adult grain merchant in London contributed to Chalkley's reputation.

For many eighteenth-century Quaker ministers, the decision to speak in meetings was so traumatic that they could describe the events in vivid detail. Often they began to feel pressures from within their consciences to speak but were equally fearful of acting in their own wills. Chalkley was unusually young when he began to preach—around twenty. As an apprentice he had given pious admonitions to others, and his preaching seems to have grown out of such counsels. Even as a young man Chalkley spoke well and frequently in meetings, but—unlike most seventeenth-century Quaker preachers—he constantly questioned the acceptability of his preaching to God. Quietists remained confident of the complete Truth of the Quaker religion and the divine impetus behind their communication, but the exuberant confidence that had characterized Fox and Burrough remained absent. Quietists constantly worried about their motives and questioned the purity of their messages. Being a minister was an onerous responsibility, and those who presumed to speak for God fluctuated between periods of spiritual exultation and confidence in their messages and times of what they termed barrenness or leanness when God seemed remote and silence the only correct response.

From 1695 on Chalkley began to travel in the ministry, sometimes as a concomitant to his business but more often leaving it behind. Although he was not a good voyager, being often seasick, and had difficulties riding horseback because of his heaviness, for the rest of his life Chalkley at least once a year would engage in the traveling ministry. He experienced Indian wars, shortages of food and water at sea, violent storms, illness, and taunts from opposers in order to bring the message of the Gospel particularly to Friends but also to many others who were religiously inclined. Between 1691 and 1800 ministers made 130 trips from Europe to America and the colonists made 89 journeys to England to preach the Gospel.[13] Such statistics do not include the many more trips made by Friends who frequently traveled but rarely crossed the oceans.

Chalkley and other ministers "felt" a "leading" to travel in the "service of Truth." They presented that "concern" to the Monthly Meeting, which either provided him or her with a certificate and informed a Quarterly Meeting of the individual's inclination or suggested remaining "quiet" for additional guidance. After "weightily" deliberating, the Monthly, Quarterly, or Yearly Meeting would find "unity" with the "concern" and provide a minister with a certificate of "clearness."[14] As the minister traveled and preached, he would carry the certificate with him, and it would be signed by clerks of the various Particular Meetings where he visited. The host Meeting provided hospitality and arranged a special gathering for the visitor to attend. On such occasions, the visiting Friend could deliver a stirring sermon, but at other times, the Friend might find he had nothing to say and would sit in silence. The impact of a minister upon a location depended upon the length of his stay, what he said in private to his hosts and in public to the Meeting, and the receptivity of the community to his message. Theoretically, the minister could have a major influence, but visiting Friends were rarely in any locality—except maybe Philadelphia or London—for long enough to inspect closely what Friends were doing or to provide adequate oversight for a deviant Meeting. What traveling ministers could do best was to remind Friends that they belonged to a transatlantic community. For Quakers in North Carolina or Maine to meet and converse with a Thomas Chalkley, Samuel Fothergill, or Catharine Phillips was to gain a sense of the significance of all areas in the Society of Friends.

At age twenty-four Chalkley decided upon marriage, and his account in the *Journal* conforms to correct Quaker practice. Martha Betterton was a "religious young woman" whom Chalkley "entirely loved for that piety, virtue, and modesty, which I beheld in her." A young Quaker man was not to seek the consent of the maiden first; his initial task was to acquaint his and her parents of his intentions and to gain their consent. Only then was he to approach the young lady. Chalkley did not dwell upon Martha's good qualities, but she needed to be capable of managing business enterprises and his estates while he was traveling in the ministry and tolerant of his long absences.

Soon after marriage, Thomas and Martha Chalkley decided to migrate to Pennsylvania and received the permission of their parents and the Meeting to move. Chalkley did not indicate his reasons for leaving, except that he saw it as a "duty." In 1701 they settled in Philadelphia where Chalkley purchased a lot and followed his calling at those times when he did not travel. Chalkley's initial economic success in the New World paralleled that of other Friends. Philadelphia rapidly became a major seaport, shipping the produce of farms of New Jersey, Delaware, and Pennsylvania to the West Indies and serving as an entrepot for goods being brought from England. Quaker merchants like Chalkley had relatives and acquaintances in major places of trade and were advantageously situated to profit from the rise of commerce. As the earliest settlers in much of the Delaware River Valley, Friends had located on extremely fertile soil. The growth of the wheat export trade in the eighteenth century caused Quaker farmers to prosper and to add a cash crop to a mode of life generally aimed at self-sufficiency.

Thomas Chalkley as merchant, farmer, and land buyer profited from the prosperity of the area. Chalkley was a minister before he was a businessman, and he was not willing to forgo his journeys. During the 1720s disasters occurred—his ships sank, debts mounted, and illness followed. Because there was a danger of bankruptcy and the Meeting cautioned against imprudent speculation, some Friends criticized Chalkley in a manner he thought unjustified. Eventually, by serving as a ship's captain (and preaching when he was in port) and then buying his own vessel, Chalkley repaid his debts and regained prosperity. His initial successes, comparative poverty, and final prosperity made Chalkley a perceptive observer of Quaker economic practices and the resulting tensions between religion and wealth.

Quakers, like other Christians who read Bible stories as prefiguring their own lives, saw Jehovah bringing plenty and famine to Israelites. Health, prosperity, and success were rewards from the Lord; illness, failure, and troubles were not accidental occurrences. So when Quaker merchants in London, Newport, and Philadelphia prospered, they naturally saw their virtues commended. Quakerism fostered certain attitudes that were conducive to economic success.[15] Friends disliked ostentacious displays of wealth, distrusted idleness, and denounced gambling and drunkenness. The Meeting insisted that Quakers be scrupulously honest in honoring contracts, paying their debts, and remitting their taxes. If there were a dispute between members over business, the Meeting appointed arbitrators to settle the matter, and disobeying the arbitrator's decision was a disownable offense.

Chalkley's attitudes toward business show a desire to cultivate the "inward plantation of religion" and the "outward plantation" of affairs: "The farmer, the tradesman, and the merchant, do not understand by our Lord's doctrine, that they must neglect their calling, or grow idle in their business, but must certainly work, and be industrious in their callings."[16]

Chalkley took pride in his and the colonists' success, but he feared the creeping in of luxuries and an overreliance on worldly matters such successes brought. Yet Chalkley's own flirtation with economic disaster at a time when there was no corresponding deviation from the faith made him qualify the "riches = God's favor = virtue" equation. Chalkley could not accept that those who were making large amounts of money were better people than the poor. When, in 1741, he became ill on the island of Tortola while on a missionary journey, Friends wrote down the words of his last sermon. Quoting the Apostle Paul, Chalkley announced in a halting, broken delivery: "I have fought a good fight, I have finished my course, I have kept the faith, henceforth there is laid up for me a crown of righteousness.''[17]

Chalkley represents a kind of middle-of-the-road early eighteenth-century Quakerism: concern about kind treatment of slaves but no moral outrage against slavery; worry about excessive emphasis upon wealth but no fundamental critique of the way Quakers made money; respect for Indians but no undue interest in them; advocacy of pacifism but little worry about whether Quaker political power jeopardized it; preference for simplicity in life-style but acceptance of hierarchical social structure, with plainness being conditioned by wealth; pride in the distinctive pattern of religious liberty in the Delaware River Valley but only the faintest foreboding that it was in danger. Circumstances that were to a large extent unanticipated by him and beyond Friends' control made his positions seem inadequate within a decade of his death.

NOTES

1. George Fox, *The Journal of George Fox* (Cambridge and Philadelphia: 1911), I, 119; J. William Frost, *The Quaker Family in Colonial America* (New York: 1973), 93.

2. Robert Barclay, *An Apology for the True Christian Divinity* (London: 1678), Proposition 2, pg. IV, and Propositions 5 and 6, pg. XVI.

3. Frederick B. Tolles and E. Gordon Alderfer, eds., *The Witness of William Penn* (New York: 1962), 169, 173, 188.

4. Alexander Arscott, *Some Considerations Relating to the Present State of the Christian Religion* (London: 1731–34).

5. Thomas Beaven, *An Essay Concerning the Restoration of Primitive Christianity* (London: 1723), V.

6. *Bulletin of the Friends Historical Society* (hereafter *BFHA*) 31 (1942), 28–29.

7. Thomas Clarkson, *Portraiture of Quakerism* (London: 1807), II, 281–83.

8. Frost, *Quaker Family*, 35–40.

9. Henry Cadbury, *George Fox's Book of Miracles* (Cambridge: 1948); Phillips P. Moulton, *The Journal and Major Essays of John Woolman* (New York: 1971), 24, 46, 64, 65; George Willauer, Jr., "Editorial Practices in Eighteenth-Century Philadelphia: The Journal of Thomas Chalkley in Manuscript and Print," *Pennsylvania Magazine of History and Biography* no. 107 (hereafter *PMHB*), April 1983, 217–34.

10. *Records and Recollections of James Jenkins*, ed. J. William Frost (Lewistown, N.Y.: 1984), 252–54, 263–65.

11. Howard Brinton, *Quaker Journals* (Wallingford, Pa.: 1972), is the best analysis of Quaker journalists' religion.

12. Thomas Chalkley, *A Collection of the Works of Thomas Chalkley* (London: 1791), 1–8.

13. Frost, *Quaker Family*, 225.

14. The words in quotation marks are illustrative of the jargon Friends employed in discussing religious matters.

15. Frederick Tolles, *Meeting House and Counting House* (Chapel Hill, N.C.: 1948), Chs. 1, 3, 4, contains excellent discussions of Quaker attitudes toward business.

16. Chalkley, *A Collection of the Works*, 100.

17. Ibid., 331.

10
A DISCIPLINED CHRISTIAN LIFE

Quakerism began as a spontaneous outpouring of religious fervor but survived because people found its institutions conducive to experiencing the Inward Light and developing Christian character. This chapter discusses the methods Friends used to create a distinctive manner of living, shows why Friends came to codify correct behavior norms in books they called "Disciplines," how they applied the rules in the "Disciplines," and why members accepted the Meetings' power to regulate their conduct. The rules served as a hedge against the world for adults and as an "enclosed garden" in which children could develop Quaker habits.

Friends early began preserving documents. George Fox's* identification of Friends with the early Church involved an imitation of the Book of Acts and the Epistles of Paul, John, and Peter. Because the early Church issued pastoral Epistles, Friends would do the same. There could be no parish register of baptisms, deaths, and marriages, so Friends would keep their own lists, which would be a legal record. The parish had provided cemeteries on consecrated grounds; Quakers who refused baptism could not gain admission to such cemeteries. So Friends would buy their own burial grounds. The Society of Friends, like the Church of England, would structure the crucial rites of passage of birth, marriage, and death.

In the seventeenth century the English government operated without a written constitution, but Parliament still had well-defined procedures and traditions. As long as Parliament was a continuing institution there seemed to be no compelling reason to write down what all members knew. The same situation characterized early Friends, even though persecution after 1660 disrupted the continuity of leadership and Meetings. The expansion of the Society of Friends into the New World created a situation in which there were many newcomers and few leaders close by to ensure continuity. So it is not surprising that the first attempts to go beyond the informal procedures took place in America.

When Fox visited Newport in 1672, someone wrote down and preserved his suggestions on providing proper marriage procedures, recording births and deaths, and ensuring morality; Rhode Islanders also preserved a copy of what Fox had told Meetings in Barbados.[1] The New Englanders seem to have preserved these and other letters of early Friends because they contained spiritually edifying and practical Advices. In 1703 Friends in the Delaware River Valley decided to draw up a compilation "relating to good Order and Discipline."[2] This Discipline, presented to the Philadelphia Yearly Meeting for approval in 1704, was made more orderly and lengthened in 1719 and again in 1747 and 1762. New England drew up a Discipline in 1708; New York may have used the Philadelphia Disciplines for a while. London codified its rules in 1737, made several variations in the eighteenth century, and published a version in 1785. Soon after, the various Yearly Meetings in America published their Disciplines, beginning a practice that continues to this day.

The manuscript Disciplines, owned by the Monthly Meetings, had blank pages where decisions arrived at after the initial compilations could be entered. Subjects discussed included Advices, apprentices, arbitrations, appeals, burials, books, disownment, education, elders, gravestones, Monthly Meetings, ministers, oaths, overseers, Queries, and wills. By the mideighteenth century the various Meetings throughout America owned copies of the Disciplines of the London and Philadelphia Yearly Meetings.[3]

The contents of the Disciplines were very similar no matter where the Yearly Meeting was located, partially because Friends wanted to preserve a unity in practice. Yet Meetings added sections reflecting local problems. For example, in the early eighteenth century the city Meetings in London faced the problem of providing charity for the many poor Friends of the country who moved to the metropolis. The problem was twofold: how to tell whether the individual was a Friend and how to determine which Meeting should provide relief. London Friends did not believe that they should be forced to give aid when they had not been consulted on the advisability of the move. The result was a series of decisions that required the country Friend to bring a certificate conveying the permission of the rural Meeting, defined for the first time just what made a birthright Friend, and stipulated that the Meeting of origin was responsible for relief for the first few years after migration. These decisions were formalized in London's first written Discipline of 1737.[4] Poor relief was a primary factor forcing English Friends to write down their Discipline. American Meetings did not face similar problems of poverty for many years, and they did not define what made a birthright member or deal with the qualifications for charity until years later. But Meetings in the New World included sections on selling alcohol to Indians and treatment of slaves, subjects of no immediate concern to the English.

Today the early Disciplines appear cold and legalistic, a series of laws imprisoning the members and Meetings in a straitjacket. Yet eighteenth-century Friends insisted that the Disciplines contained "Christian and Brotherly Advices," which they interpreted in the spirit of love and charity. Clearly, the manner of enforcement depended upon the nature of the local Meeting and the characteristics of the ministers and elders. Reading over minutes gives the impression that often Friends used the Advices as pious admonitions to encourage Christian living; on occasion, however, as in the 1750s, the Discipline appears as a series of harsh regulations used to weed out those deemed too lax.

Eighteenth-century Quakers became a people who lived by rules. To follow rules, they had to know what was expected of them. English Friends in the 1680s and Americans in the next century used Queries, a series of questions read in Monthly Meetings on at least a quarterly basis. After hearing the Queries, the members had to respond either orally or in writing to the Quarterly and then the Yearly Meeting on whether the Queries were observed. A summary of the 1743 Philadelphia questions shows the range of disciplinary concerns:

1. Are Friends careful to attend Meetings at the time appointed and to refrain from sleeping or chewing tobacco in Meetings?

2. Do Friends stay clear of excess in "drinking Drams"?

3. Do young Friends keep company for marriage with non-Friends or marry without parental consent?

4. Are Friends clear from tattling, tale bearing, and meddling?

5. Do Friends stay free from music houses, dancing, and gambling?

6. Are Friends careful "to train up their Children in the Nurture and Fear of the Lord, and to restrain them from vice and Evil Company, and keep them to plainness of Speech and Apparel"?

7. Are the poor taken care of, are their children put to school and then apprenticed out to Friends, and do Friends apprentice their children only to Friends?

8. Are Friends cautious not to launch into business beyond what they can do?

9. Are Friends careful not to remove without a certificate?

10. Are Friends on guard not to deprive the king of his duties?

11. Do Friends stay clear of the importing or buying of Negroes?

12. Are Friends prudent in settling their affairs and in leaving wills?[5]

The overseers had responsibility for enforcing the rules in a fair and consistent manner. Their tasks included watching out for possible infractions, warning individuals before the misdeeds became too serious, visiting miscreants on behalf of the Meeting. The overseers provided supervision for the entire Quaker community and also took care of the property of the Meeting. They often served as delegates to the Quarterly and Yearly Meetings, distributed poor relief, attended weddings to make certain that all behaved with proper decorum, and kept minutes. Overseers tended to share functions with elders, men and women who watched over the ministry in order to nurture the spiritual life of the Meeting. The elders and ministers joined in special gatherings where they answered special Queries designed to provide the same kind of examination of spiritual awareness that the Monthly Meetings' Queries did for Discipline. In meetings for worship, elders and ministers sat together on the "facing bench" overlooking the rest of the congregation, an architectural testimony to their importance. Overseers and elders tended to be older and to come from more settled and prosperous families. They tended to be on the most committees and to spend much time on arbitrations and other tasks for the Meeting. Along with the ministers, the elders and overseers tended to dominate the Meeting, and little could be done without their consent. If in theory all members were equal, then in practice there was an oligarchy of the devout.

The men's and women's Monthly Meetings had the responsibility for enforcing the rules of Discipline, but only the men's could disown, that is, decide that the person was no longer a Quaker. Theoretically, official Monthly Meeting involvement occurred only after private conversation between a supposed miscreant and a weighty member.

If the offense were serious—marriage by a priest or to a non-Quaker, drunkenness, fighting, fornication—the matter came directly to the Monthly Meeting. The Women's Meeting investigated all charges relating to women; the men's for men.[6] Usually, the Meeting selected a committee to visit the person. If he or she admitted a mistake, the committee required an acknowledgment in writing that the Meeting accepted, judging the sincerity of penitence by his or her sorrow for past transgression and future good behavior. If the written apology were not explicit or contrite enough, the Meeting might require amplifications.

If the offender refused to change his or her ways or to acknowledge errors, the Meeting could make one last try to reclaim the person, or it could proceed at once to disownment. A committee drew up a paper stating the reasons for the disownment; the Meeting accepted the paper, had it read publicly or posted, and presented a copy to the person. If at any subsequent time, the person repented, he or she could seek readmission. In the meantime the person was still able to attend meetings for worship, but was barred from meetings for business, could not contribute funds, and was cut off from other tangible benefits of belonging to Friends.

If a person thought the Monthly Meeting had not followed proper procedures or had reached mistaken conclusions, he or she could appeal the decision first to the Quarterly and ultimately to the Yearly Meeting. There a committee would listen to representatives from the Monthly Meeting and also the appellant. Occasionally, the representatives from the Yearly or Quarterly Meeting would reverse a previous decision. There was no appeal from one Yearly Meeting to another because all Yearly Meetings were equal and autonomous.

Meetings for business were select; that is, only Friends in good standing could attend. Quaker business was not a secular proceeding; rather, it was a different kind of worship that began with a period of silence and in which decisions were made under the direction of the Inward Light. There was a crucial difference in the way the Light operated in the meeting for business. Quietistic theory belittled exercise of the intellect and reason. A meeting for business was conducted making constant use of reason. The clerk appointed committees to investigate possible wrongdoing; members talked to evil-doers and reported their findings to the Meeting. In adjudicating issues, the members might "feel" a sense of rightness, but they also examined evidence. The final decision, the "sense of the Meeting," was not the sum total of the evidence, but a corporate coming together after seeking the Lord's will. In practice, the direction of the Inward Light was used as a rationale to justify the theory and practice of all Quaker business meetings, and individual decisions could be freely debated. If an individual guilty of a violation of Quaker practices believed in the divine origin of Quaker beliefs and the importance of salvation, he had no real alternative other than to submit to the Meeting's scrutiny and make public apology. For others the practice of endogamous marriage meant that family members were Friends, and defiance of Quaker norms would mean isolation from relatives and most neighbors, since Friends in America tended to settle in enclaves.

Membership in a Friends Meeting produced tangible benefits; for the poor, reduced or free tuition at Quaker schools, relief if one became destitute or if a calamity occurred, social acquaintance with prosperous Friends who might take one's child as an apprentice or servant and provide employment, a place for burial in a Meeting's graveyard. Rich Friends in Pennsylvania and West Jersey also obtained entrée to politics and to the elite group that established the tone of the society at large. Merchants wanted to appear reliable and respectable, and being a Quaker helped a person appear reputable. Quaker artisans and farmers cultivated their image as honest men willing to give a full measure of value. Quakers also tended to prefer to do business with their coreligionists whom they thought were likely to be cautious and honest.

If in 1700 a New Jersey or English Quaker left the Meeting, where should the person go to worship? The Church of England with its liturgy and heritage of persecuting was anathema to even nominal Quakers. Anglicans, Presbyterians, and Lutherans needed church buildings and paid ministers, and there was a dire shortage of all ordained clergy in the Delaware River Valley and in those areas of North Carolina and New York where Friends settled. Quakers in old and New England had revolted against Puritanism because of its laxity and formalism, not its moral conservatism. Throughout the eighteenth century the devout church-goers of most Protestant denominations in America expected the church to exercise oversight and discipline of members. Quakers differed from other dissenters not in kind but in degree and in what they defined as morally objectionable.

In the early eighteenth century the Quaker Testimonies against theft, murder, and adultery constituted a small percentage of the total number of cases brought to the Meeting. Since in new settlements there were bound to be frictions over land boundaries, contracts, and rights, the Monthly Meeting frequently appointed committees to serve as arbitrators. Quakers were forbidden to enter a lawsuit against other Quakers (but not against outsiders), so the Monthly Meeting's attempt to keep harmony among members appropriated some of the functions of government.

Eventually, most of the Monthly Meeting time would be taken up with carrying out the Testimonies on marriage, approving those couples who wished to wed with the approval of the Meeting, and censoring those individuals who violated the Meeting's ban on marriage to a nonmember or having the ceremony done by priest, clergyman, or magistrate.

MARRIAGE

Quakers formulated their ideals about correct courtship and marriage in the seventeenth century when men discussed marriage in a context of legal contracts, financial settlements, and family allowances. Early Quakers opposed these crass considerations but did not escape the pervasive cultural emphasis upon familial control of the selection process and the fear of unrestrained individual choices by immature young persons.

Friends wanted marriage for love, but love was defined as stemming from a spiritual harmony between the persons and resting upon similarities in religious feelings, outward temperament, and class. Friends spoke out against marriages of rich and poor, steady and frivolous, old and young, and Quaker and non-Quaker, but only the latter constituted a disownable offense.

Two kinds of parents—the physical ones from birth and the spiritual parents in the Meeting—played an essential role in the process of selecting a mate. In theory, Quaker courtship began when a young man made a decision to marry. He then began to look around for an eligible maiden and might ask his parents or weighty members of the Meeting for advice. After selecting a potential partner, he approached her parents for permission to court. If they refused, the matter stopped there. If they consented—and the minutes are not specific whether at this stage anyone ought to have consulted the young woman—he could begin to court her.

The Meeting was very clear that no young woman was to be forced to wed without her willing consent. Parents were not to refuse a young man's request to court without good reasons (perhaps involving the young woman's disinclination). After consent was given to court, it was not easily withdrawn and other young men were not to push their proposals until she said either yes or no. Romantic love might develop as an adjunct during the courtship, and certainly a spiritual love was a necessary requisite for marriage. The unity among male and female that the Meeting sought was a solidly grounded esteem based upon an appreciation of all of the qualities of the other person. Some quietist Friends insisted that the Lord not only told them when to wed, but whom, and one early minister claimed that he had married "contrary to my will."[7] The few surviving early Quaker love letters reflect the accepted beliefs and stress the unity established by the Light.

After deciding to marry, the young people approached the Women's and the Men's Meetings for permission. Both Meetings appointed a committee to make sure that the parties were clear from other entanglements (i.e., had not been courting or promised to marry someone else) and had parental consent. The approval of parents was essential, no matter what the age of the applicants. If the parents refused, they had to satisfy the Meeting that their reasons for opposition were not based on money alone. If boy and girl were Friends in good standing and everything else was in order, at its next session the Monthly Meeting granted approval and scheduled a special meeting for marriage. The investigation of couples preparatory to wedding and working with those who had violated some facet of the Discipline on marriage became in the eighteenth century the most time-consuming task of the Monthly Meeting. The necessity of waiting for at least two Monthly Meetings and then calling a special Meeting meant that the whole process was a slow affair in which all parties had time to consider the matter.

The wedding ceremony was a normal meeting for worship in which God performed the role of a clergyman linking the couple together. The bride and groom sat in the front and, after a period of silence that might be broken by prayers and preaching from the guests, said their vows. At the conclusion the bride and groom signed a certificate drawn up by the Meeting that summarized the contents of the vows and that was witnessed by those in attendance. The certificate served as a legal document attesting to the marriage. After the ceremony, the couple and their invited guests would have some kind of celebratory meal.

During the early eighteenth century the Meetings were often not rigorous in disowning violators. As long as Friends had sufficient confidence in the attractiveness of their principles, they would make extraordinary efforts to reclaim errant individuals.[8] Many who were married to outsiders, or by a priest, if no other offenses were involved, could retain membership if they signed a certificate condemning their violations. Some who married outsiders claimed ignorance of the strict Quaker policy; other non-Quaker spouses either were converted or attended Meetings regularly enough to escape scrutiny.

Whether the procedures as outlined in the Quaker Disciplines governing courtship and marriage ever really defined normal practice is difficult to establish.[9] Many journals, early letters, and published writings support the formal procedures, but this may be because there were various ways of escaping potential stress points. Quaker children, for example, seem to have grown up with a large number of acquaintances. Quaker boys and girls sometimes attended school together; entire families came to Monthly, Quarterly, and Yearly Meetings as well as weddings and funerals. Adolescent boys and girls in colonial Pennsylvania had considerable freedom playing games, skating, and taking walks together. Girls walking to market with their mothers might encounter young men. Investigation of the diaries of upper-class Philadelphia Quaker women has disclosed a pattern of frequent visiting by relatives and friends.[10] Young women accompanied their mothers on these visits, and occasionally, a young man might stop in for conversation and tea.

Whatever the theory, there were lots of opportunities for Quaker children and young adults to see each other on an informal basis and to learn each other's characteristics. When a Quaker youth decided to marry, he already knew a good deal about the pool of prospects. Since in many areas orthodox Protestants did not want to socialize with Friends and Friends wanted isolation, Quaker young people had few occasions to meet outsiders. As long as Friends could maintain their isolation, as long as the religious theory of spiritual unity remained dominant, as long as the parental and Meeting's authority remained predominant, and as long as the Meeting was not too stringent upon enforcement, the Quaker marriage testimonies served to weld people to the Meeting and to bring in outsiders. All of these conditions held for many places in colonial America through the 1720s. But each would be challenged before the Revolution.

The marriage testimony was a tribute to the importance Quakers attached to the family. In a mixed marriage, the family would be divided in allegiance, and observance of the "peculiar" customs of speech and dress might lapse. Quakerism required a strict observance within the home as well as without. The Quaker practice of endogamous marriage rested upon the assumption of Quaker Truth and the world's error. So marriage to a Presbyterian or Anglican was an offense comparable to other moral failures. Quaker exclusiveness meant that they could assume that dissenters should be tolerated because coercion by the state in religious matters was wrong. But among "Children of Light" to allow members' errors to go unpunished would be license for flagrant sin to flourish. The Quakers' Testimonies against hireling ministers and marriage to unbelievers were not incidentals, accidents of historical development. These beliefs were fundamental Truths delivered by Jesus Christ and confirmed by the Holy Spirit's testimony to early and present-day Friends. Quakers preferred to ensure the continuing survival of the faith by discouraging challenges, and the most effective manner of stopping questions was to foster isolation. The Quaker practice of moral oversight erected a "hedge," cutting off outside influences.

Eighteenth-century Quakers used two forms of isolation. In populated areas where Friends were a pronounced minority, as in most of England and Ireland, they created their own institutions to curtail external interactions, particularly personal and informal relationships. In America, Quakers settled in enclaves and many rural Quaker Meetings continued to exist with few alternative institutions. But Philadelphia soon became an ethnically and religious diverse city, and Friends were a minority there as early as 1700. The Quakers' strategy here was a mixture of withdrawal and domination. Friends sought to control the government to preserve their rights as founders of the city and colony. A Quaker majority in the Assembly would ensure that no legislation could pass hostile to their Testimonies on tithes, oaths, peace, and clergy. Because of their continuing social, political, and economic power and prestige, Philadelphia Quakers throughout the eighteenth century continued to preserve their exclusiveness by attempting to influence the entire culture.

CHILDHOOD

Those who attempted to dominate and control the realms of government and business were adult men. But what for men was permissible contact with the temptations of worldly affairs was viewed as dangerous for weaker vessels, that is, women and children. Even in Philadelphia there were many outsiders practicing dissolute customs—like saying "you" to a single person and playing cards—and sin remained attractive to children and youth. The solution was the creation of a life where the child would be secluded from evil influences and grow up accustomed to Quaker practices. The movement for withdrawal in order to create an enclosed garden for children coincided with the establishment of religious toleration in England, the decline in the number of converts, and the greater emphasis on plainness and enforcing the Discipline at the end of the seventeenth century.[11]

Quakers repudiated the traditional Christian doctrines of original sin and the need of a sacrament of baptism to cover the taint and serve as a symbol of the Church's care for the child. Babies, said Friends, were born innocent and children retained their innocence until they reached an age of reason. Eventually, all humans would knowingly commit sin, and then their fall and surrender to the dominion of sin would occur. Even after the child had willingly sinned, he or she could experience occasional glimmerings of divine love. Such insights into Truth, while not guaranteeing salvation, showed that God's care extended to children.

The symbol of innocence denoted both goodness and frailty. Exposure to evil might corrupt innocence, so parents had to make sure that external forces did not overwhelm the natural goodness. Their home was to be a Christian environment. For parents the first requisite was to be good Christians, because children learned first by watching, and emulation was a much more potent force than exhortation. A parent who could not control himself or herself would not be able to control the child, and it was important to mold the child while young.

Quaker parents had to learn how to adjust correction to the temperament of the child. If they were too harsh or if they were too mild, the child would be lost. Friends did not caution parents so much on the method of discipline as on the manner in which it was imposed. Anger begat anger; love begat love. The object of all parental concern was to make the child "tender" so that he or she could experience the grace of God.[12]

The Disciplines encompassed the whole pattern of growing up under the term "education." Quaker education was not only or even predominately book learning, and it was not confined to a school. Quaker education, as defined by the Christian and Brotherly Advices, meant the acquiring of the traits of virtuous lives—learning to dress and speak plainly, to control one's temper, to accept moderation in outward desires, and to act with a becoming sobriety of manners. Such education took place in a secluded environment, first in the home and later in a Meeting-controlled school with a Quaker teacher and Quaker classmates.

Birthright membership developed naturally from the Quaker conceptions of seclusion from evil and the innocence of children. The child was born a Quaker, educated as a Quaker, adopted Quaker habits, and eventually would confirm the Quaker heritage by experiencing and continuing in the Light. What is remarkable is that birthright membership came about before 1700 with virtually no discussion of the implications of the custom. Friends did not debate whether ensuring that all Quakers had experienced the Inward Light was more important than that their children have a birthright.[13]

DEATH

Concern with death, present from the beginnings of Quakerism, became more intense after 1690. A devout Quaker should live every day as if it were the last. Death was the climax to life; the period just before the end was supposed to reveal either the righteous prevailing and triumphant or the wicked filled with fear and repenting. The dying person, neither fully part of this world nor yet joined to the next, could speak to those around with an authority possessed by no ordinary person. An entire household gathered in the death chamber to hear the final words of exhortation. Many visitors, including young children, would gather around the dying individual who, in her closest relationship to God, would preach to them. The Monthly Meeting commissioned someone to write a memorial to the deceased that was read in the Meeting and then forwarded to the Yearly Meeting.

In 1701 John Tomkins compiled a collection of the dying sayings and deathbed scenes of young and old Friends under the title *Piety Promoted*. The first *Piety Promoted* was so successful that Tomkins issued *Piety Promoted, The Second Part* the next year. By 1775 several compilers had produced nine parts. There were thirty-nine editions or reprints of the various parts before 1800. The last American edition appeared in 1854. *Piety Promoted*, with its brief autobiographies and emphasis upon the sanctity of the faithful, was the most popular form of English Quaker literary expression throughout the eighteenth century. The vignettes in *Piety Promoted* used morbidity, tears, and sorrow to foster emulation of the suffering, dying Friends' piety. Complete resignation was expected from the survivors and also from the dying person, who was not to desire life or death but should welcome whatever the Lord brought. If death came, he or she accepted it as a deliverance from this world of tribulation. If health returned, God had rewarded the person's submissiveness. Friends' assurance of knowing the will of God carried over into the experience of dying. On occasion, the dying person or a visitor experienced a foretaste of future existence. He might announce that his sins had been forgiven and claim to be dying in harmony with Friends and at peace with God.

NOTES

1. George Fox at Barbados, 9 May 1672; Disciplines, Ancient Epistles, Minutes, and Advices, Archives of New England Yearly Meeting, Rhode Island Historical Society, Providence, R.I. The content of Fox's letters and preaching in New England resemble in tone and content what he was advocating in England.

2. Edwin Bronner, "Quaker Discipline and Order, 1680–1720, Philadelphia Yearly Meeting and London Yearly Meeting," in *World of William Penn*, ed. Richard S. and Mary M. Dunn (Philadelphia: 1986), 323–36.

3. For general treatments of the Discipline in America see J. William Frost, *The Quaker Family in Colonial America* (New York: 1973), 48–63, and Jack D. Marietta, *Reformation of American Quakerism, 1748–1783* (Philadelphia: 1984), 3–31.

4. For different interpretations see Arnold Lloyd, *Quaker Social History, 1669–1738* (London: 1950), 44, 160.

5. Philadelphia Yearly Meeting, Christian and Brotherly Advices (1743), 121–22. Minutes, I, 34.

6. Bucks Quarterly Meeting's minutes show that the women carried out virtually all functions of oversight of women. Marietta argued that this was the normal practice, evidence of the power that women exercised, in *Reformation*, 29–30.

7. Thomas Holme to Margaret Fell, 8 mo. 1654, Swarthmore MSS (Friends House, London), I, 195; David Ferris, *Memoirs of the Life of David Ferris* (Philadelphia: 1825), 56–62.

8. Marietta, *Reformation*, Ch. 1, charts the changes in enforcement of the marriage and other disciplinary actions.

9. Barry Levy argued that romantic love, affection, and a child-centered approach characterized Quaker families in the later seventeenth and eighteenth centuries. Barry Levy, "The Light in the Valley: The Chester and Welsh Tract Quaker Communities and the Delaware Valley, 1681–1750" (Ph.D. diss., University of Pennsylvania, 1976); idem, "The Birth of the 'Modern Family' in Early America: Quaker and Anglican Families in the Delaware Valley, Pennsylvania, 1681–1750," in *Friends and Neighbors: Group Life in America's First Plural Society*, ed. Michael Zuckerman (Philadelphia: 1982), 26–64.

10. Nancy Tomes, "The Quaker Connection: Visiting Patterns among Women in the Philadelphia Society of Friends, 1750–1800," in *Friends and Neighbors: Group Life in America's First Plural Society*, ed. Michael Zuckerman (Philadelphia: 1982), 174–95.

11. London Yearly Meeting, *Epistles from the Yearly Meeting* (London: 1760), 47–48.

12. Frost, *Quaker Family*, 65–92.

13. Richard Vann, *The Social Development of English Quakerism 1655–1755* (Cambridge, Mass.: 1969), 122–57; Frost, *Quaker Family*, 67–69.

11
CRISIS AND REFORMATION

John Woolman* (1720–1772) is the most celebrated eighteenth-century Quaker, and his fame rests upon his *Journal*. From almost the date of its publication in 1773, people recognized the special qualities of this spiritual autobiography. The *Journal* has continued in print into the present, and it has been used as devotional material by persons who have no appreciation of Quakerism or awareness of the eighteenth-century context. The author creates a sense of quietist worship and awe from his initial sentence: "I have often felt a motion of love to leave some hints of my experience of the goodness of God: and now, in the thirty-sixth year of my age, I begin this work."[1]

Reading the *Journal* as a religious classic takes away its historical context. Woolman took the traditional forms of Quaker journal writing and thrust into them his passionate response to evil and great inward turmoil over compromise. To understand him we should confront the dilemmas that burst upon the Meetings' awareness in the 1750s: slavery, Indians, war, wealth, and purity of Discipline.

SLAVERY

The Society of Friends is significant in world history for becoming the first religious group publicly to denounce slavery and the first to require all members to free blacks held in bondage. The theoretical framework supporting slavery had been ingrained in Western civilization for so long that becoming an abolitionist required a major intellectual revolution.[2] Seventeenth-century Friends initially encountered chattel slavery in their missionary journeys to the West Indies. Black slavery there was particularly vicious, since planters growing sugar found it more profitable to import new slaves from Africa than to provide adequate food and care for those they already possessed.[3] Some Englishmen in the islands proved susceptible to the preaching of Friends, and Quaker Meetings appeared in Barbados as early as 1655.

Many Englishmen encountered slavery in the West Indies, but only a few traveling Friends, none of them planters, seemed disturbed by the institution. George Fox* never condemned slavery per se, but he cautioned masters about humane treatment and insisted upon the necessity of religious instructions. Fox may not have understood the implications of West Indian slavery, for he spoke of it using a familial language more appropriate for children and servants and compared the bondage to a Hebrew servitude that terminated after a period of time in a jubilee year.[4] The honor of first questioning slavery belongs to the Irish Quaker minister William Edmundson.* Edmundson arrived in New England in the aftermath of King Philip's War and learned that Rhode Island Friends opposed selling the Indian captives into slavery. In a letter to New England Friends, he queried: "And many of you count it unlawful to make slaves of Indians, and if so, then why the blacks."[5]

The next focus on slavery came from Friends in the Delaware River Valley. In 1688 a few Dutch pietist Quakers from Germantown petitioned their Monthly Meeting, noting that in Europe "there are many oppressed for conscience sake; and here there are those oppressed which are of a black colour."[6] If Pennsylvania was a free land, how could the settlers justify servitude? The petition may have reached the Philadelphia Yearly Meeting, but it was not mentioned in the minutes. Even so, a series of seventeenth-century Pennsylvania Quakers pressed the issue in memorials to the Yearly Meeting.

These early Quaker abolitionists thought that slavery and the peace Testimony were incompatible. Slavery rested upon force in the capture of the blacks in Africa, in the middle passage to America, and in continual labor with no hope of freedom. Friends could not accept the "just war" rationale for slavery: that Africans taken captive in a just war deserved death but were spared and should be thankful for perpetual bondage. Quakers rejected the notion of just war and saw no reasons why captivity justified slavery for blacks in Africa more than for Quakers and other whites in Europe seized by Turks or Mediterranean pirates. Finally, the colonists were well aware that blacks did not like slavery and could revolt. An armed insurrection by blacks might require so much force to quell that it would be indistinguishable from a war.[7] The fear of a slave revolt was reinforced by racial antipathy. Quakers did not wish to build a multiracial society in the Delaware River Valley and feared that having large numbers of blacks who would not be integrated into the religious and political systems would destroy liberty.

In 1696 the Philadelphia Yearly Meeting issued its first official statement on slavery. The recommendation suggested that Friends not encourage the importing of slaves. Such temporizing hindered neither the slave trade nor slavery. Friends in Chester County remained dissatisfied and through their Quarterly Meeting frequently placed slavery again on the agenda. Evidently no sense of the meeting could be reached, because Philadelphia wrote to the London Yearly Meeting asking to know their opinion and the views of other Friends. The 1719 Discipline summarized the position of Friends who were told neither to buy nor sell Indian slaves nor to import black slaves.[8]

Friends in the Assembly seemed to have an effective way of hindering the growth of slavery. They passed two laws in 1711 and 1712, the first a prohibition of slave importation and the second a duty of £20 on each slave imported into Pennsylvania. Such gradual measures might have stopped the foreign slave trade if the Crown had not interposed and vetoed the statutes. In 1729 the Assembly passed a revised tax of £2, but this law was designed to raise money and not to outlaw the trade.[9] In Newport and Philadelphia wealthy Friends had migrated from the West Indies and still had relatives there. The Redwood and Hazard families of Rhode Island owned slave plantations. Thomas Richardson, clerk of the New England Yearly Meeting from 1728 to 1760, participated in the slave trade, as did Philadelphians James Logan, Jonathan Dickinson, and Isaac Norris. Although few Quakers participated directly in the slave trade, many Friends throughout the colonies continued to buy slaves in the first half of the eighteenth century.

The Meetings' continued mild and ineffective stance on antislave trade irritated William Burling of Long Island, John Hepburn of New Jersey, William Southeby of Pennsylvania, and James Farmer, a visiting minister from England. Southeby and Farmer's preaching against the slave trade and Friends' inactivity brought disciplinary proceedings in an attempt to silence them. Burling remained a Friend in good standing and little is known about Hepburn. Hepburn's 1713 tract showed how sophisticated the antislavery argument had become. Seeing the cause of slavery as greed, attacking a belief that human beings could be considered property, mourning the discrepancy between profession and activity, Hepburn denounced slavery on a basis of Quaker beliefs, scriptural exegesis, personal knowledge of the cruelties involved, and natural rights.[10] The arguments and images marshaled by the early antislave trade and antislavery Friends would reappear in abolitionist literature until the Civil War. When Hepburn employed them in 1713, there was no response.

The persistent undercurrent of opposition to slavery emerged again in 1729 when the Chester Quarterly Meeting asked the Philadelphia Yearly Meeting that since Friends had previously agreed not to import slaves, should they also refuse to buy them after someone else imported them? In 1730 the Yearly Meeting asked each Quarterly Meeting to formulate an answer, a clear indication of divided opinion on an important issue. The rural Quarterly Meetings favored the revision, but the two Quarterly Meetings with the most wealth and merchants—Philadelphia and Burlington—opposed. Not until 1743 did the Yearly Meeting change the Queries to read that Friends were not to import slaves "nor to buy them after Imported."[11] The answers of all Quarterly Meetings during the next decades showed overwhelming compliance with the Query.

The transformation of antislave-trade feeling into abolitionist sentiment is shown in the wills of deceased rural Friends. Virtually all Friends of Shrewsbury and Rahway, New Jersey, who owned slaves provided for their freedom in wills by the 1730s, but during this period, Chesterfield and Burlington, New Jersey, Friends did not free slaves.[12] Elihu Coleman, a Nantucket Friend, published in 1733 the first officially sanctioned pamphlet against slavery. In Pennsylvania two recent immigrants, Ralph Sandiford and Benjamin Lay, whose first encounter with slavery had been in the West Indies, found that antislavery sentiments in Meetings brought no response. Knowing they could not get permission from the overseers of the press to publish, they did so anyway. Their pamphlets are moving evocations of the moral outrage, internal trauma, and prophetic zeal occasioned by slavery.[13] Both men were declared to be out of unity for publishing attacks upon Quaker hypocrisy. Lay was not deterred, particularly after the death of Sandiford whom he thought of as a martyr. A hunchback, Lay had developed a particular sympathy for the downtrodden. At the Yearly Meeting in 1738, Lay appeared in a concealing cloak. In the quiet of the meeting, Lay stood up and denounced slavery, then throwing off the cloak to show a military uniform, declared:

Oh all you negro masters who are contentedly holding your fellow creatures in a state of slavery during life, well knowing the cruel sufferings those innocent captives undergo in their state of bondage . . . , you might as well throw off the plain coat as I do. . . . It would be as justifiable in the sight of the Almighty. . . . if you should thrust a sword through their hearts as I do through this book.[14]

Lay drew out and thrust his sword into a hollowed out book in which he had previously hidden a bladder filled with red berry juice. The "blood" spattered out on the surrounding people.

The rising tide of antislavery sentiment among reformers could not be indefinitely postponed by the conservative prosperous Quakers who ran the Assembly and the Meeting. Landowners did not need to rely upon slaves to provide labor. The 1740s and early 1750s saw the high mark of German immigrants, most of whom came as indentured servants willing to provide work for a period of years to pay the cost of their transportation.[15] The wealthy Philadelphia merchants seem to have opted to purchase indentured servants rather than slaves. Even though slavery increased in Pennsylvania as a whole, the number of slaves held by Friends declined. Those Friends who continued to purchase and use slaves were concentrated in the artisan class.[16] In a political culture characterized by deference and in a religious society where a spiritual elite held dominance, the economic needs of artisans could not long delay actions.

Quaker beliefs eased and hampered the Yearly Meeting's change of position on slavery. Revelation was progressive, so there could be new knowledge and a growth of understanding of the demands of Truth. Antislavery could be seen as a continuation of the peace testimony against possessing war prize goods, the need for humility in controlling others, and the desire for simplicity in standard of living. But the decision to change had to come from the entire body of Friends;

no one's influence was crucial. In 1750 the death of John Kinsey changed the context. Kinsey's influence in bringing harmony in the political and religious realms had required compromise, but his reputation and methods fell into disrepute when it was discovered that he had embezzled £3,000 from the colony's loan office. Kinsey's offices of speaker of the Assembly and clerk of Philadelphia Yearly Meeting would never again be held by the same person. The new clerk of the Yearly Meeting was Israel Pemberton, Jr.*, an astute, wealthy merchant who had long advocated reform.[17] The influence of the Pemberton brothers helped persuade the Philadelphia Monthly and Quarterly Meetings to adopt an anti-slavery position. The clerk of the Yearly Meeting also appointed new members to be overseers of the press.

In 1746 John Woolman had written a treatise on slavery that he had circulated in manuscript. His father Samuel, on his deathbed, suggested to his son that the manuscript be submitted to the overseers. During the sessions of Philadelphia Yearly Meeting in 1753, the overseers of the press reported that Woolman's manuscript would soon be printed. If there were any doubt of the new policy, the Epistle of the Philadelphia Yearly Meeting in 1754—probably written by Anthony Benezet and issued in 5,000 copies—declared unequivocally the un-righteousness of slaveholding. The next step, taken in 1758 in the midst of the French and Indian War, was to appoint a Yearly Meeting committee, for which Woolman pled and on which he served, to visit individual Meetings and those Friends who still held slaves. In 1758 the Yearly Meeting decided that those Friends who held political office in the Assembly or bought or sold slaves would be visited by committees, forbidden to attend meetings for business, and not allowed to contribute money—a sort of limbo status that kept the pressure on the Friend by keeping him under the scrutiny of the Meeting. Note that the reformers in 1758 gained only partial victory. Holding slaves was wrong but not yet a disownable offense. The discipline would be invoked only for the slave trade.[18]

PEACE

Friends' definition of religious liberty included the right not to bear arms and to keep Pennsylvania demilitarized. The colony created no militia and no fortifications and relied upon conciliation and fair treatment of neighboring Indians to preserve the peace. The location of the colony far up the Delaware River seemed a sufficient protection against a European power. Non-Quaker residents of Delaware and Pennsylvania could not expect Friends to pick up a sword on their behalf. During England's long wars with France from 1690 to 1713 there was a persistent pressure on the Pennsylvania Assembly to create a militia and to vote a tax to meet the Crown's demands. On one occasion a bill to establish a militia was introduced, but it never became law; several times the Assembly appropriated money, but always with a proviso that it not be spent directly on war materials. Voting to provide relief to the Indians or for foodstuffs provided a compromise solution. When the Assembly voted £2,000 "for the Queen's use" in 1711, it appointed a committee to make sure how the money was spent—a clear infringement on executive privilege. The money had not been spent by the end of the war. After 1700 the Assembly refused to authorize a militia, insisting that those who wanted to form one could do so under the governor's authority. When non-Quakers tried to form a voluntary militia, few would show up, and the Assembly provided no support.[19]

Political and religious opponents of Friends charged that the Quaker definition of religious liberty made them unfit to govern and discriminated against non-pacifists. A few Quakers, like James Logan, sympathized with the outsiders and suggested that Friends should either resign the government or accept the legitimacy of defensive war. Perhaps knowing that their pacifist principles were unpopular in Whitehall, the Assembly generally justified its half-hearted compliance with royal requests in pragmatic rather than theological language. The contrast to Pennsylvania's actions was in New Jersey, where Friends were exempted from serving, but the colony had a militia, and all settlers had to pay taxes used to buy war supplies.

The long peace following the Treaty of Utrecht in 1713 allowed the issue of Quaker noncompliance in war to be eclipsed, even though neither the Crown, the governors of Pennsylvania, nor the non-Quaker nonpacifist settlers were happy with the situation. England and Spain fought between 1739 and 1742, and England and France fought in King George's War of 1740–48. The main impact of the wars in America came in a British-led expedition to capture Cartagena, for which all colonies were asked to contribute men and money, and a New England expedition that took Fort Louisbourg. Initially, Pennsylvania's Assembly voted neither money nor men, although it had no objection to volunteers. After Governor Thomas attempted to enlist indentured servants, promising them their freedom, the Assembly strongly condemned his actions as an attack upon the rights of property. Thomas and the Assembly, presided over by Quaker John Kinsey, engaged in a debate over the theological and practical implications of the peace testimony. Eventually, they compromised so that no indentured servants could enlist without their master's permission, and £3,000 was voted for the king's use. After Louisbourg fell in 1745, the Assembly voted £4,000 to be used "in the purchase of Bread, Beef, Pork, Flour, Wheat, or other Grain."[20] Years later Benjamin Franklin wrote that the governor interpreted "other grains" to include gunpowder, but there is no contemporary evidence that Friends knew this would happen.

By the late 1740s the imperial rivalry between England and France over control of the Mississippi Valley began to affect events in western Pennsylvania. The French established a series of forts along the Great Lakes, the Illinois River, and the Mississippi River. The area linking the two systems of forts lay in western Virginia and Pennsylvania at the beginning of the Ohio River. In 1754 Virginia sent Washington and 150 soldiers to drive out the French. Instead, the French with Indian allies ambushed and captured them at unfinished Fort Necessity. Even though England and France were ostensibly at peace, the British decided to send an army under the command of General Edward Braddock to drive out the French. This decision was supported by certain imperialist-minded British Friends, and Pennsylvania furnished some foodstuffs for the army. Braddock's expedition sailed to Virginia (using some Quaker-owned ships that normally were employed in the tobacco trade) and proceeded to cut a road through the wilderness. When the army was within a few miles of the new French Fort Duquesne, a French-Indian ambush led to the death of Braddock and the rout of the British, who retreated all the way to the safety of Philadelphia, leaving the border area unguarded. To the surprise of Friends, some of the formerly friendly Delaware Indians joined the French and proceeded to ravage the exposed settlements of Germans and Scots–Irish on the frontier.

The initial response of Philadelphia Friends was shock and disbelief. Why had God in his providence allowed violence to occur in his Holy Experiment? What had Friends done to deserve such punishment? What could be done to rebuild trust with the Indians? What should the response of Friends be to the war? For the Quaker majority in the Assembly the first task was to protect the frontier. The Assembly voted £50,000 to defend the settlements and passed a law authorizing a militia, even though the first clause granted a comprehensive exemption from serving for all those conscientiously opposed. Ever since George Keith, a few Friends had opposed voting funds for military-related purposes, but most had acquiesced in the argument that Friends had traditionally paid taxes to higher authority that did not share their values. In 1755 there was no request from a higher authority for funds. The Assembly had voted the war tax, authorized the militia on its own initiative, and entrusted the money to its commissioners for waging war.[21] Not even the Proprietor was responsible, for his instructions were more concerned with resisting paying any taxes on his lands than in providing for defense.

The war crisis of 1755 divided Friends and ended the religious–political harmony that had characterized Pennsylvania. Supporters of Thomas Penn, the absentee Proprietor, took advantage of the crisis to try to force Friends from the legislature and to regain power—even at the cost of not providing for defense at a time of emergency. Politically active friends, like Isaac Norris II who was speaker of the Assembly, opposed the Proprietor's assault and defended the tax and defensive measures as justifiable considering the circumstances. Many weighty Friends, including John Woolman and Israel Pemberton, Jr., saw assemblymen putting their trust in carnal weapons rather than reforming sins or relying upon the deliverance of God.

Before 1755 Friends on both sides of the Atlantic had interpreted Paul's advice to "be subject to the governing authorities" as requiring payment of taxes whether used for war or peaceful purposes.[22] Now a few Friends refused to pay the war tax, creating a situation in which other Quakers serving in the Assembly or as magistrates passed and enforced laws that might result in fines, distraints, or imprisonment. Neither the Philadelphia nor London Yearly Meeting endorsed tax refusal, but in 1755 twenty-one prominent Friends, including Woolman, issued a declaration supporting tax resistance.

The crisis of 1755 allowed those who had long sought to reform the Society of Friends and Pennsylvania to gain a temporary ascendency over the politicians and the compromisers. American Friends put pressure upon members in the Assembly to withdraw so they would not be implicated in war measures. The war also served as an opportunity for supporters of the proprietary to lobby against Quaker political power. William Smith, Anglican clergyman and provost of the newly founded College of Philadelphia wrote pamphlets accusing the Quakers of sacrificing the people on the frontier to pacifism. Ignoring the war tax, the militia, and the incompetence of the British army, Smith argued that an effective defense required getting rid of the Quakers by tendering them an oath.[23] Recognizing the gravity of the situation, members of the London Meeting for Sufferings reached an understanding with the British government whereby Pennsylvania Friends would not have a majority in the Assembly in wartime.

Even before news of the agreement reached Pennsylvania, the Yearly Meeting had brought pressure on a sufficient number of Quaker assemblymen that ten either resigned or declined to run for office again. Although in a short time, many Quakers would again enter the Pennsylvania Assembly, never after 1756 would many devout Friends serve, and there would not be a Quaker majority. A few Friends like Isaac Norris II braved the opposition of the Meeting and continued to serve, but leadership of the "Quaker Party" passed from Friends to Benjamin Franklin. The Quaker Party still stood for religious liberty, the power of the Assembly, and the legacy of William Penn, but it was now a party and not Quaker.

INDIAN RIGHTS

Quakers who had been deeply involved in politics but were now out of office sought to determine why the Delawares (Lenni Lenape) had turned hostile. In their search the French tended to disappear as a causal factor. Friends also did not focus on the whites' relentless westward migration but instead emphasized the illegalities or shady dealings in the process. They complained about the settlers, mostly Germans and Scots–Irish squatting on Indian lands, and about the fraud and drunkenness used by the fur traders. Most attention focused on the Proprietors' purchase of lands from the Delawares in 1737, which has become known as the Walking Purchase.

In 1686 William Penn concluded a purchase agreement with the Delawares for a tract in northeastern Pennsylvania of the size that a man could walk around in a day and a half. The Indians lost title but were left in possession of the lands in the Lehigh Valley. In 1737, when the tract was surveyed, the walkers, who were the fastest runners available, traveled a cleared path and covered more than twice the assumed area. When the Delawares protested the injustice, the government used the Iroquois, who claimed suzerainty over the Delawares, to force submission. Both before and after 1737 the Proprietors purchased lands lived on by the Delawares from the Iroquois, who lived in New York. The most detailed examination of Pennsylvania's Indian policies has found a strong probability of outright fraud by James Logan or the Proprietors, who destroyed or altered deeds of William Penn that reserved lands for the Delawares.[24]

The Walking Purchase and the Proprietors' misdeeds not only provided an intelligible reason for the war but could serve as a political weapon to use against Thomas Penn. In addition, the Quakers made contact with Teedyuscung, a chief of the Delawares, who made public the Indians' complaints about fraud and the Iroquois. With the outbreak of war pacifism seemed somehow irrelevant, but in an effort to rebuild their political and humanitarian reputation a few Quaker leaders, notably Israel Pemberton, Jr.,* with the support of Mennonites and other sectarians, created The Friendly Association for Regaining and Preserving Peace with the Indians by Pacific Measures. The Friendly Association attempted to regain the confidence of the Delaware Indians by presenting gifts and serving as an intermediary between the Delaware Indians, the colonial governments, and the British authorities. By representing the Indians the Quakers risked the wrath of frontiersmen who wanted the Delawares killed, not coddled. Neither the Proprietors nor the British government cared for an investigation of misdeeds; they wanted the Indians subdued and the French defeated.

The Friendly Association also marks the beginning of a continuing official concern by the Society of Friends for the welfare of the Indians. Teedyuscung asked for a model town to be built and missionaries provided to instruct the Indians in a new way of life. Although the initial missionary effort was a failure, even the British approved of the cooperation between the Assembly and the Association in creating a policy for the licensing of traders and establishing of stores where the Indians could obtain reasonable prices for their furs. After a few years the Association proved irrelevant to the problems of the Indians and was disbanded. There were difficulties in stocking the stores, interest in the Indians lessened after peace was established in Pennsylvania following General Forbes's conquest of Fort Duquesne in 1757, and the Indians did not prove receptive to later efforts to "civilize" them.[25]

The Friendly Association shows a change in Quaker attitudes toward reform. In both England and America Quakers had been content with the complex structures of Quakerism to deal with the problems of the world. Except for the meeting structures and schools, Quakers formed no voluntary associations and created no external institutions. But the 1750s marked a decisive change. In Pennsylvania Friends joined with others to create and sustain the Pennsylvania Hospital in 1751, the first private hospital in the colonies. In the eighteenth century a hospital was not a scientific institution but a charity facility to care for the poor and, in this case, the insane. The Quakers soon constituted an absolute majority of the Board of Governors and succeeded in obtaining the Assembly's financial support.

With their increasing concern for the poor, blacks, and Indians, the Society of Friends in Pennsylvania was slowly beginning to turn away from its concentration upon politics as the mechanism to shape the general society.

INTERNAL REFORM

Indian rights, withdrawal from government, pacifism, and antislavery were all reforms associated with the events of the 1750s. The long war and subsequent events also strengthened the prestige of those who had long been striving to purify the Society of Friends internally. They viewed the early settlers as a "city upon a hill" and a beacon of hope for the world. Now the reformers watched with misgivings the rising importance of commerce and outward display of wealth, most noticeable among Philadelphia and Newport merchants, but not uncommon even among country folk. As increasing numbers of outsiders settled among them even in rural areas, it became increasingly difficult to sustain a homogeneous Quaker culture—particularly among youth. By their involvement in politics and commerce at both the colonywide and local levels, Quakers had close contacts with and were influenced by those who did not share their perspectives on music, novels, dress, and speech.

By midcentury a group of Philadelphia merchants, Quaker Grandees, had emerged who were oriented toward English society.[26] They built elegant Georgian townhouses and country estates, dressed in the plain style but in the finest fabrics, enjoyed having their portraits painted, decorated their homes with elegant Queen Anne and Georgian furniture, and read English periodicals like *The Gentleman's Magazine*. The cultural sophistication and civic consciousness of these people showed in numerous civic improvements and organizations. They supported the Library Company of Philadelphia, the Pennsylvania Hospital, and later the American Philosophical Society.[27] Quaker Grandees found in Franklin a young man of promise and they provided him patronage and support, making him clerk of the Assembly, an important politician, and even their colonial agent in England. They shared Franklin's interest in fire protection, inventions, self-help organizations, and science—even if, with the exception of Logan, they did not share his brilliance. The prosperity and confidence of the leaders of the city and colony were shown in a splendid new statehouse, now called Independence Hall, whose bell celebrated William Penn's Frame of Government in its motto "Proclaim Liberty throughout All the Land."

The reformers viewed the genteel pattern of life in Philadelphia and Newport with misgivings and attempted to turn back the clock. They wanted to restore primitive Quakerism by revitalizing the Society of Friends. In 1739 George Whitefield's itinerant preaching throughout the colonies had sparked a revival termed the Great Awakening, particularly among Congregationalists and Presbyterians. At the same time the efforts of Count Zinzendorf among the Moravians and Henry M. Muhlenberg among the Lutherans had fostered denominational consciousness and a quickening of religious fervor. Friends disapproved of the enthusiastic zeal of certain of the revivalist preachers and disliked the controversies and schisms within the German and Presbyterian churches, but they appreciated the new emphasis upon spiritual awakening, moral strictness, and inward piety.[28]

The Quaker reformers in England and America did not attack wealth but its fruits. They created no new doctrine and no new methods of worship. With little understanding of the complexities of the Puritan revolution or the tremendous variety in practice and beliefs among early Friends, the reformers—John Griffith, John Churchman,* Samuel Fothergill, Sophia Hume, Catharine Phillips, Israel and John Pemberton*—seized upon the Discipline as the critical element in Quaker life. They sought to make Quakers distinctive in child rearing, education, speech, and dress—to cut off the influences of the outside world and to foster the clear mandates of Gospel living.[29]

The reformers tried to persuade Quakers to withdraw from political office, to support those who refused to pay taxes, to work with those who still owned slaves, and to disown those who violated the Discipline. Their instrument of reform was the visiting committee. Since early in the eighteenth century Yearly Meeting Epistles had advocated visiting committees. These committees of ministers and other weighty Friends would meet at home with each family in the Meeting for a time of admonition, encouragement, and worship. Knowing that a visiting committee would be sitting in the parlor soon might make a housewife careful of buying too ornamental a teapot or chest. What began in Philadelphia in 1755 and spread to London in 1760 was the appointment of visiting committees composed of reformers. Traveling ministers informed Meetings in New York, New England, Maryland, and North Carolina that they should use inspection visits and, on occasion, undertook the visitations themselves. The committees sought to standardize the behavior and the application of rules everywhere. They rebuked Meetings that looked away from offenses or allowed too easy apologies for offenses or neglected any of the Testimonies.

The result of the visiting committees was a revival of strictness in Discipline that occurred in the Philadelphia Yearly Meeting in the 1750s, London in the 1760s, and New England in the 1770s. With Meetings increasing their scrutiny and showing less toleration of mistakes and little charity in accepting acknowledgments, there was a predictable and sudden increase in disownments. The statistics for the Philadelphia Monthly Meeting illustrate events throughout its Yearly Meeting. Before 1700 there were few cases of discipline and fewer disownments, but the numbers of cases—though not of disownments—rose steadily through the next decades. Then from 1750 to 1754 the number of cases doubled and shot up again from 1755 to 1759. Between 1756 and 1775 the Philadelphia Monthly Meeting dealt with 1,175 disciplinary cases involving 885 persons with 473 being disowned. Twenty-nine percent of the members in 1760 were dealt with and 16 percent disowned. One-third of all disciplinary cases involved marriage regulations and three-quarters of them involved Friends who were guilty of marrying a non-Quaker.[30]

The revival of Discipline shows the strengths and weaknesses of mideighteenth-century Quakerism. The reformers believed that only a unified family could preserve the Testimonies and raise a new generation of believers. But they were not willing to attempt to convert non-Quaker husbands or wives instead of disowning members.

The reformers succeeded in making the Society of Friends oppose two powerful eighteenth-century themes. One was the increased tolerance and acceptance among the various Protestant denominations in England and America. By mid-century many Protestants came to realize that the crucial issues were not variations among denominations but the difference between those who were religious and those who were apathetic or irreligious. For example, Friends learned to co-operate with Presbyterians and Lutherans in petitioning the Assembly against theaters. By the 1750s Friends saw themselves as only one among a variety of Protestant religious bodies, and in the Middle Colonies virtually everyone accepted the value of toleration and the necessity of the separation of religious bodies from the state. So when the Quaker reformers attempted to tell parents and children that marriage to a Presbyterian would be a religious disaster, many members remained skeptical.

Equally, if not more important, fostering marriage out of unity was a new attitude to marriage arising in Western civilization. Poets and novelists first popularized it; now it became a primary force—romantic love. For many the crucial ingredient between a boy and girl before marriage was love, not a rational, controlled feeling subordinated to religious unity and parental power, but an irrational, passionate impulse impossible to obliterate and dangerous to deny. Romantic love was subversive of all authoritarian control of youth either by parents or by the Meetings. It could best be prevented by control of the environment and strict seclusion, but that was becoming difficult to achieve in the diverse populations in the Middle Colonies. Marriage out of unity became a method of revolt, of affirming a personal right of choice. If only those who were young had succumbed to romantic love, the Meetings' task would have been easier, but the new attitudes permeated all ages and all classes. The only solution the reformers found was to practice seclusion in a totally controlled environment offered in a boarding school set in the countryside. In America this movement to create boarding schools came during and after, but not before, the Revolution.

The reformers gained a purified Society of Friends—much more strict, much more divorced from the world, much more consistent. In other words, Friends were becoming sectarian. Only sects can afford to defy the world's wisdom consistently because they want purity rather than numbers—to be a remnant who were right, even if unpopular. Sympathizing with Indian rights, condemning slavery, and maintaining pacifism were the positive results of the revival movement. A harsh doctrinal narrow-minded legalism also came that sacrificed individual feelings for the shibboleths of the seventeenth century. The ultimate price of purity would be a total loss of political power. The Society of Friends began its long tradition of doing good works for other people, but its preservation as a religious body seemed to require being hesitant to accept new members.

In the 1750s the reformers remained a minority within American Quakerism. They gained control of neither the Philadelphia nor the London Yearly Meeting, although they started both Meetings on reform activities.

WOOLMAN

Despite the popularity of John Woolman's *Journal*, the most important source for information about him, and in spite of extensive research, there remain many unanswered questions about Woolman's significance to his contemporaries.[31] For example, his importance in the antislavery awakening is well known, but the Burlington Quarterly Meeting—to which Woolman belonged—lagged far behind some other New Jersey Meetings in freeing slaves and conformed only after the Yearly Meeting made manumissions mandatory. If Woolman before his death could not sway members of the Burlington and Chesterfield Monthly Meetings to free their slaves, to assume that he was instrumental in the evolution of the Testimony of the entire Yearly Meeting remains open to question.[32] The *Journal* and his other writings stress reform and withdrawal from government but shed little light on Woolman's attitude to the revival of the strict marriage discipline in the 1750s.

Like other Quaker journalists, Woolman provides few details of his daily life unless they have religious significance and ignores his secular activities and opinions. Certainly, he was no typical Quaker—a saint is unique—and all that we have been able to discover indicates a congruence between the persona in the *Journal* and the man his countrymen knew. We may never have the depth of information to create a rounded portrait of John Woolman, but what he wanted us to know about his spiritual struggles, slavery, Indians, business, and travels was clearly delineated.

Woolman's parents were pious Friends who farmed near Burlington, New Jersey. At age twelve "my father being abroad, my mother reproved me from some misconduct, to which I made an undutiful reply; and the next First Day as I was with my father returning from meeting, he told me he understood I had behaved amiss to my mother, and advised me to be more careful in the future." Woolman never afterwards spoke "unhandsomely to either of my Parents, however foolish in some other things." Even so, by age sixteen Woolman enjoyed what he called "wanton company." For the next few years he vacillated between experiencing God's judgment and mercy and "giving way to youthful vanities."[33]

Woolman attended a local Quaker school, read the books in his father's library, and attained "schooling pretty well for a planter," and he served an apprenticeship as a combination bookkeeper and shopkeeper.[34] When his customers were in debt, he suggested buying cheaper goods and in 1756 stopped selling buttons, trimmings, "cloaths," and linens. Having experienced qualms about the worldly entanglements in running a store, Woolman determined to become a tailor. Tailoring was a low-status occupation where he would not make much money and could be free to travel in the ministry. In later life he combined tailoring with farming and kept a school. As a teacher he insisted on small classes so that he could adjust the learning to the temperament of each child. He wrote a primer making use of rhymes, stories, and pious apothegms in an attempt to make learning easier.[35] Woolman gave no prizes for good work and allowed no competitions, because such activities taught the children to strive to excel rather than to seek moderation.

He began writing a journal in 1756, revising it several times, and its present form shows his mature perspectives. Some time between ages sixteen and twenty-one he outgrew his tame adolescent rebellion. In 1741 "being under a strong exercise of spirit, I stood up, and said some words in a meeting, but not keeping close to the divine opening, I said more than was required of me; and being sensible of my error, I was afflicted in mind some weeks."[36] Six weeks later he again spoke in a meeting at which time he found "peace." In 1743 the Meeting recognized him as a minister, and he began his traveling ministry in 1746 with a trip to Virginia, which sparked his interest in slavery. He married Sarah Ellis in 1749; she figures only incidentally in the *Journal* but seems to have shared his quest for religious purity. Somewhere he also learned to write a marvelously evocative restrained prose.

The language of the *Journal* combines traditional Christian terms, Quaker jargon, and evangelical, quietist, and rationalist influences. Only in the mid-eighteenth century was such a merger of theological emphases possible. The description of Woolman's religious awakening portrays in evangelical terms God coming in judgment "in my soul, like a consuming fire." Later he felt "the love of God, through Jesus Christ, to redeem" and "to succor" through tribulations. The distinctive evangelical emphases are muted. There is no discussion of the virgin birth, the divinity of Christ, or the efficacy of the atonement, but in a vision, while close to death from pleurisy, he identified himself with the suffering of all humanity. Quietism appears in Woolman's stress upon "singleness of heart," "clearness," "purity," and "resignation." Whether in beginning a series of family visits or pondering a trip to Barbados, Woolman was "often bowed in spirit before the Lord, with inward breathings to him that I might be rightly directed." Quietism merged with rationalism in picturing God as an "Inward Principle," the "divine wisdom," and "invisible incomprehensible Being" of whom "no language" can be "equal" to convey a "clear idea." A person's "harmony" with God shows in "universal love" and "right order."[37] Woolman described a vision that occurred on May 13, 1757:

sleeping a short time I awoke; it was yet dark, and no appearance of day or moonshine, and as I opened my eyes I saw a light in my chamber at the apparent distance of five feet, about nine inches in diameter, of a clear, easy brightness, and near its center the

most radiant. As I lay still looking upon it without any surprise, words were spoken to
my inward ear, which filled my whole inward man. They were not the effect of thought,
nor any conclusion in relation to the appearance, but as the language of the Holy One
spoken in my mind. The words were, 'Certain evidence of Divine Truth.'[38]

The Light has an obvious Quaker connotation; the fear that a "thought" or
"conclusion" could influence the words is quietistic; the content of the revelation
"certain evidence" is rationalistic. Christianity has to be proven true by the
evidence of a completely supernatural occurrence. Many eighteenth-century apol-
ogists for Christianity rested the proof of the Bible on miracles; Woolman, also
seeking certainty, cited a vision and a voice.

Rationalists looked to nature for information about God and morality. So also
did Woolman use nature as a source of ethics. To abuse nature in either its
human forms or as the "least creature" is contrary to the love of God. The
earth, helped by moderate labor, will produce the necessities for life. An inordinate desire for material goods leads to oppression. Woolman is more ascetic
than either Penn or Chalkley and more critical of Friends' opulence. "The least
degree of luxury . . . hath some connection with evil," he wrote, and "hath some
connection with unnecessary labor."[39]

Although certainly a reformer who welcomed the laying aside of politics,
Woolman's vision of religious unity was very inclusive. He endorsed "no narrowness respecting sects and opinion" and found the external varieties of religion
unimportant since "the sincere upright-hearted people in every Society, who
truly love God, were accepted by him." His library included books from Anglicans, Congregationalists, Moravians, and Roman Catholics.[40]

The sensitivity shown in dealing with animals and other religious groups also
characterized Woolman's approach to slavery. The *Journal* documents his gradual awakening to the evils in that institution and his increasing demands upon
himself in response to it. As a young man, Woolman was told by his first employer
to write a bill of sale for a Negro woman. Although uneasy, he did it but found
no peace in the action. When next requested to draw up a bill of sale, he declined.
By refusing to write wills for men who wanted to bestow slaves as part of their
property, Woolman became involved in the grass-roots antislavery movement.
Quaker antislavery was built upon the denunciation of a series of reformers and
also on the decisions of those individuals who owned slaves to set them free.
Both kinds of actions prepared the way for the Yearly Meeting's policies in 1755
and 1758. In missionary journeys to the South and to Rhode Island, in Meetings
in the Middle Colonies, and as a member of a committee of the Philadelphia
Yearly Meeting to visit owners, Woolman bore his quiet testimony against
slavery.

The special quality in Woolman that makes him so appealing is illustrated by
two incidents that occurred on his journey to the Indians in the Pennsylvania's
Wyoming Valley in 1761 at a time of great tension. On the way Woolman met
a fur trader, and they discussed the practice of selling rum. Such a practice,

Woolman reflected, is a "great evil" because of its effects on the Indians who are "thereby deprived of the use of reason and their spirits violently agitated, quarrels often arise." Also, when drunk, the warriors sold for low prices or more rum their "skins and furs, gotten through much fatigue and hard travels in hunting" and afterwards suffered for "want of necessities of life" and became angry, ready for war. Most colonial Americans stopped their analysis of the rum trade at this point with a denunciation of the traders. Woolman proceeded further asking why the frontier dwellers engaged in the Indian trade? Because of poverty. Why were they poor? Because the exorbitant rents charged upon lands close to the city had forced them to the frontier. Those high rents resulted because a few engrossed large quantities of land to support their desire for luxuries. So the responsibility for abusing the Indians had to be shared by the wealthy land speculators and the fur traders.[41]

Woolman's purpose in visiting the Indians was to show compassion and to affirm the unity between his religious impulses and theirs. Soon after his arrival in the village of Wyalusing, Woolman's mission of peace and love was interrupted by news that war had broken out between other Indians and the English. There were supposedly hostile natives in the area. A short time later the following incident occurred:

Our pilots took us to the house of a very ancient man, and soon after we had put in our baggage, there came a man from another Indian house some distance off. And I, perceiving there was a man near the door I went out; and he having a tomahawk wrapped under his match-coat out of sight, as I approached him he took it in his hand. I, however, went forward, and speaking to him in a friendly way perceived he understood some English. My companion joining me, we had some talk with him. . . . Though his taking his hatchet in his hand at the instant I drew near to him had a disagreeable appearance, I believe he had no other intent than to be in readiness in case any violence were offered to him.[42]

Few people in any age would be so inclined to see good in others.

In 1772 Woolman traveled to England in the ministry and while there caught smallpox and died. Only after the publication of his *Journal* in 1774 did he become famous as a moral exemplar for the emerging antislavery movement in England and America.

NOTES

1. John Woolman, *Journal and Major Essays of John Woolman*, ed. Phillips Moulton (New York: 1971), 23. All quotations from John Woolman's *Journal* are from this edition.
2. David B. Davis, *The Problem of Slavery in Western Culture* (Ithaca, N.Y.: 1965), 351–64.
3. The standard guide to the Quaker response to slavery from the 1670s until the Civil War is Thomas Drake, *Quakers and Slavery in America* (New Haven, Conn.: 1950).
4. George Fox, "Gospel Family Order," in *Quaker Origins of Antislavery*, by J. William Frost (Norwood, Pa.: 1980), 35–55.

5. J. William Frost, ed., *Quaker Origins of Antislavery* (Norwood, Pa.: 1980), 56–67.

6. Ibid., 69.

7. Ibid., 3–4, 70–72; "An Exhortation to Friends Concerning Buying or Keeping of Negroes" in *The Keithian Controversy in Early Pennsylvania*, ed. J. William Frost (Norwood, Pa.: 1980), 213–18.

8. Frost, *Quaker Origins*, 73–76.

9. Donald Wax, "Quaker Merchants and the Slave Trade in Colonial Pennsylvania," *Pennsylvania Magazine of History and Biography* (hereafter *PMHB*) 86 (1962): 143–59; "Negro Imports into Pennsylvania, 1720–1766," *Pennsylvania History* 32 (1965): 254–87; "Negro Import Duties in Colonial Pennsylvania," *PMHB* 97 (1973): 22–44.

10. John Hepburn, *American Defense of the Christian Golden Rule* (1715) in *Quaker Origins of Antislavery*, J. William Frost, ed. (Norwood, Pa.: 1980), 82–122.

11. Ibid., 131–33.

12. Jean Soderlund, *Quakers and Slavery: A Divided Spirit* (Princeton, N.J.: 1985), 112–47.

13. Ralph Sandiford, *A Brief Examination of the Practice of the Times* (Philadelphia: 1729); Benjamin Lay, *All Slavekeepers . . . Apostates* (Philadelphia: 1737); Elihu Coleman, *A Testimony Against that Unchristian Practice of Making Slaves of Men* (1733).

14. Roberts Vaux, *Memoirs of the Lives of Benjamin Lay and Ralph Sandiford* (Philadelphia: 1815), 26–27.

15. Marianne Wokeck, "The Flow and Composition of German Immigration to Philadelphia, 1727–1775," *PMHB* 105 (1981): 259–61; Jack Marietta, *Reformation of American Quakerism* (Philadelphia: 1984), 115–16; Gary Nash, "Slaves and Slaveholders in Colonial Philadelphia," *William and Mary Quarterly*, 3d ser., 33 (1973): 244–45.

16. Soderlund, "Conscience, Interest, and Power," 165–81.

17. Marietta, *Reformation*, 42–45.

18. The best description of the entire reform movement is in Marietta, *Reformation*, 32–128. Sydney V. James, *A People among Peoples: Quaker Benevolence in Eighteenth-Century America* (Cambridge, Mass.: 1963), 128–92, provides considerable evidence for an alternative view.

19. Peter Brock, *Pioneers of the Peaceable Kingdom* (Princeton, N.J.: 1960), 63–140; J. William Frost, "Religious Liberty in Early Pennsylvania," *PMHB* 105 (October 1981): 441–45; Robert Davidson, *War Comes to Quaker Pennsylvania, 1682–1756* (New York: 1957).

20. Hermann Wellenreuther, "The Political Dilemma of the Quakers in Pennsylvania, 1681–1748," *PMHB* 94 (1970): 156–72; idem, *Glaube und Politik in Pennsylvania, 1681–1776* (Koln: 1972).

21. Jack Marietta, "Conscience, the Quaker Community, and the French and Indian War," *PMHB* 95 (1971): 3–27; Marietta, *Reformation*, 150–55.

22. Romans 13:1; Marietta, *Reformation*, 315.

23. William Smith, *A Brief State of the Province of Pennsylvania* (London: 1755).

24. Francis Jennings, "Miquon's Passing: Indian–European Relations in Colonial Pennsylvania" (Ph.D. diss., University of Pennsylvania, 1965), 110–111, 155–56.

25. Theodore Thayer, *Israel Pemberton: King of the Quakers* (Philadelphia: 1943), 97–149; James, *A People among Peoples*, 178–92.

26. Frederick B. Tolles, *Meeting House and Counting House* (Chapel Hill, N.C.: 1948), 45–62, 109–43.

27. Ibid.

28. Frederick B. Tolles, *Quakers and the Atlantic Culture* (New York: 1960), 91–113.

29. Marietta, *Reformation*, 3–72.

30. Ibid., 3–31.

31. Edwin Cady, *John Woolman* (New York: 1968), is the best introduction to Woolman's thought.

32. Soderlund, "Conscience, Interest, and Power," 218, 241–57; Drake, *Quakers and Slavery*, 51.

33. Woolman, *Journal*, 25–27.

34. Ibid., 29.

35. John Woolman, *A First Book for Children* (Philadelphia: 1774).

36. Woolman, *Journal*, 31.

37. Ibid., 27, 28–29, 155.

38. Ibid., 58.

39. Ibid., 28, 54, 183; John Woolman, *A Plea for the Poor* in *Journal and Major Essays of John Woolman*, ed. Phillips Moulton (New York: 1971), 239, 246.

40. Woolman, *Journal*, 28. Frederick B. Tolles, "John Woolman's List of Books Lent," *Bulletin of the Friends Historical Society* (hereafter *BFHA*) 21 (1942): 72–81; Walter Altman, "John Woolman's Reading" (Ph.D. diss., Florida State University, 1967).

41. Woolman, *Journal*, 125.

42. Ibid., 129–30.

12
THE AMERICAN REVOLUTIONS

THE WAR

The expulsion of the French from North America in the peace treaty of 1763 did not restore harmony to the Quaker communities of the Middle Colonies. The British badly mishandled relations with the midwestern Indians by occupying French forts, cutting off supplies of guns and ammunition that the natives had used for hunting, and not restraining westward settlements. The Indians had not recognized a light French control over them as sovereignty, and they now resisted being incorporated into the British Empire. The French had been defeated, but the Indians were not conquered. Indian resentments boiled over into a war, called by the English "Pontiac's Rebellion," which meant renewed attacks on the Pennsylvania frontier.

Settlers in the exposed country in what is near present-day Harrisburg, mostly Scots–Irish and Germans, blamed Pennsylvania's Quaker-dominated Assembly for failing to protect them. A substantial number of these frontiersmen, called Paxton Boys, wanted revenge on the hostile Indians. Since finding warring Indians was both difficult and dangerous, the Paxton settlers instead massacred friendly Conestogas, particularly venting their wrath upon the Christianized peaceful natives converted by the Moravians. After two ugly massacres by the Paxtons who did not spare women and children, the government supported by Friends determined to bring other threatened friendly Indians to Philadelphia and then to send them to New Jersey or New York for safety. The other colonists refused to accept the praying Indians in their borders.

The Paxton settlers in February 1764 began to march on Philadelphia, threatening to kill both the Indians and their Quaker supporters. When the Paxton mob approached Germantown, nearly 200 young Quaker males armed themselves, used a meetinghouse as barracks, and prepared to defend the Indians. A delegation of Assembly leaders, led by Franklin, met with leaders of the Paxton settlers, promised a redress of grievances, and persuaded the mob to disperse.[1] The Meeting condemned the action by the young men and sought apologies for their actions, but ultimately no one was disowned.

No sooner was the Paxton crisis ended when the political crisis over repeal of the Charter began. The Quaker Party, now led by Benjamin Franklin and Joseph Galloway but retaining Friends' support, insisted that the Penn family in England sought power and wealth at the expense of the welfare of the colony. The impasse over taxation of proprietary estates at the height of the crisis of 1755, which exposed the Assembly to calumny, seemed to show that Thomas Penn did not support the 1701 Frame of Government. The Assembly's leaders decided to obtain from the Crown a repeal of the Charter, a guarantee of the privileges in the Charter by the king, and a royal governor.[2] The move to make Pennsylvania a royal colony divided the populace, with Germans and Scots–Irish opposed and many of the Quakers supporting the Assembly.[3]

The Paxton fight and the battle over the Charter polarized politics, and the rhetoric of both issues involved religion. Quakers had for years identified the frontier dwellers as Presbyterians and had linked them to the persecuting Puritans of old and New England of the 1650s. They saw Presbyterians as intolerant and seditious and feared their becoming a majority in Pennsylvania. Friends did not publish their fears in tracts, but the non-Quaker supporters of Franklin and the Quaker Party did. In response the Philadelphia Presbyterians, although they had no great love for the frontiersmen, took up their pens on behalf of their faith and fellow believers. The political rhetoric of the 1760s was reminiscent of the religious warfare of the 1650s. The Paxton and Charter struggles showed the beginnings of a political division between eastern conservatives and western radical Presbyterians in Pennsylvania, a division that would climax in 1776.

After Franklin arrived in England in 1764 as agent for the Pennsylvania Assembly to seek repeal of the Charter, he soon learned that his mission was doomed by English political realities. Besides, royal government did not look so advantageous close up in London where the Ministry was tightening up control over all colonies. Franklin shelved the attempt to repeal the Charter and began lobbying to prevent Parliament from passing the Stamp Act.

The Peace of Paris in 1763 left England with Canada, an Indian problem, and an enormous war debt. Since the debts had resulted partially from driving the French from North America, the English told the colonies to help pay it. Pontiac's Rebellion had supposedly shown the need for an army to protect against Indians, and armies were also useful as a way of controlling colonists. The English also believed that the British ratepayer was bearing the cost of the empire and that the colonists were undertaxed. So the Ministry decided to tighten enforcement of the Acts of Trade to stop smuggling and to raise a revenue from a Stamp Act. The colonies protested, but the law passed in 1765.

If to the English their actions were prudent and necessary, to virtually all American colonists they were a dangerous innovation, an usurpation of their right to "no taxation without representation." In 1765, and as late as 1774, few in America wanted independence.[4] The colonists sought restitution of their rights as Englishmen. Also the colonists had many Whig supporters in Great Britain who distrusted the motives of the government and saw the Americans as engaged in a defense of freedom as important to Britons as to the colonists.

Quakers on both sides of the Atlantic opposed the Stamp Act. American Friends protested vigorously, supported the boycott of British goods as a means of peaceful pressure, and applauded when the Pennsylvania Assembly announced that only colonists could tax colonists. Perhaps because of Quaker merchants' control and involvement in the anti-Stamp Act movement, the Pennsylvania boycott was effective, and unlike the case in Massachusetts and Rhode Island, here there were no outbreaks of violence. English Quakers lauded the Americans' actions, and played a major role in the successful campaign for repeal.[5]

When Parliament passed the Townshend Duties in 1767, American Friends maintained their policy of peacefully upholding constitutional rights. A delegation of Philadelphia merchants—four of the ten signers were Friends—petitioned English traders to intercede against the new taxes. After Parliament refused to repeal the duties, a Committee of Twenty-Three (including eleven Friends) demanded nonimportation. English Friends in the Meeting for Sufferings, believing their government's position to be both unwise and unconstitutional, supported the colonists but, at the same time, advised Friends to remember that they were peaceful subjects of the king. Eight members of the Philadelphia committee to enforce nonimportation were Quakers. As the mechanism for enforcement became an extralegal body exercising power over citizens, Friends had reservations about their participation and, in 1769, withdrew from the committee. The Philadelphia Meeting for Sufferings suggested that Friends in Maryland and New York refrain from actively supporting economic measures, if those measures might lead to violence.[6]

The repeal of all Townshend duties except that on tea in 1771 brought general rejoicing. Like other Americans, Friends supported a continuing of the boycott on tea, but the Philadelphia Yearly Meeting insisted that the traditional Testimony against defrauding the king of his customs be maintained. Drinking smuggled tea was against Quaker religious principles, and paying the duty on English tea was against their political precepts. Answers to Queries in Rhode Island showed that some members violated the prohibition and drank smuggled tea.

The Tea Act of 1773 upset whatever equilibrium prevailed between England and America after 1770. Ironically, the two ships carrying the tea to Boston were owned by Quakers! Philadelphia Quakers became somewhat suspect to the radicals in Philadelphia because the East India tea was to be distributed through the firms of James and Drinker and Thomas and Isaac Wharton—firms whose owners were Quakers. In addition, Friends officially abstained from participating in the mass meetings and threats of violence that forced the tea consignees to resign and stopped the tea from being landed. Letters show that rich Friends thought the Tea Act unconstitutional, but they were equally opposed to the Boston Tea Party and suggested that the Bostonians reimburse the British for destroyed property.[7] The wealthy Philadelphia Quakers' involvement with the tea trade made the radicals suspicious of their motivation.

The Coercive or Intolerable Acts and the strong response of the patriots prompted the Philadelphia Meeting for Sufferings again to advise Friends to withdraw from politics. Friends should not approve measures that might destroy the heritage of religious freedom and privileges conferred upon Pennsylvania by the Charter. Particularly dangerous was any attempt to subvert the authority of the Crown. Individual Quakers—including some in good standing—served on the Committee of Correspondence and as delegates to the First Continental Congress, which met in 1774. Seeing the Plan of Union proposed by Joseph Galloway, a Quaker, as a constitutional method to preserve the empire, Quaker privileges, and peace, Friends strongly approved. The Congress's call for a total boycott, defeat of Galloway's plan, and denial of all authority of Parliament over the colonies appalled Friends, who concluded that the patriots were no longer interested in reconciliation. Patriotism and religion now seemed at odds.[8]

The First Continental Congress recommended that all merchants sign an association or agreement to refrain from importing or buying British goods. Public meetings elected committees to enforce the boycott, and initially the Philadelphia Committee contained a few Friends. The committees began to enforce the boycott and to rely on mass meetings to enforce their will on the population. Although receiving no official sanction from the Assembly, the committees were exercising a power of coercion normally reserved to a government. Although the radical colonists disavowed any intention of seeking independence, Friends feared that the momentum of the committees and the protest might lead to violence and an undermining of legitimate authority. Although Friends accepted the boycott, some withdrew from all political activities; others still attempted to influence the committees to proceed cautiously; a few rejected the caution advised by the Yearly Meeting and wholeheartedly supported the emerging patriot cause.[9]

George III and the English government greeted the resolves of the Continental Congress and the association as calls for war. Philadelphia Friends, as advised by John Fothergill, quietly petitioned the king for what they hoped would be conciliatory measures. The king rejected their suggestions. Friends were caught in the middle as both English and Americans began preparations for war.[10]

In order that their rationale be understood as strict neutrality between contending groups, in January 1775 the Philadelphia Meeting for Sufferings published a declaration "against every usurpation of power and authority, in opposition to the laws and government, and against all combinations, insurrections, conspiracies and illegal assemblies."[11] The document received wide publicity, being circulated by Friends to other pacifist churches such as the Moravians and Mennonites and reprinted in newspapers in Virginia, Boston, and England. Other Yearly Meetings in the North and South followed the lead of the Philadelphia Friends. Proclaiming neutrality between contending factions combined with a belief in supporting the existing government as God given struck many patriots as pro-English.

A final attempt at reconciliation occurred in England in the winter of 1775; Quaker merchant David Barclay and Fothergill served as intermediaries for Franklin and Lord Howe.[12] The positions of the two sides could not be compromised. English Quakers opposed the new anti-American laws passed by Parliament and decried the impending civil war. In April 1775 General Gage's attempt to use his army to seize Samuel Adams, John Hancock, and the patriots' military stores resulted in the battles of Lexington and Concord. An army of New Englanders then formed outside of Boston and fought the British at the battle of Bunker Hill.

The Second Continental Congress, meeting in Philadelphia, now recommended that each colony form an army. The Pennsylvania and New Jersey Assemblies authorized a militia, although guaranteeing some rights of conscientious objectors. A few patriotic Quakers formed themselves into a company called the "Quaker Blues." Even before the fighting began in April, the Philadelphia Yearly Meeting moved to disown members actively involved in revolutionary politics. By the end of 1775 in Pennsylvania alone Meetings dealt with 163 members, disowning 65; 144 cases were for military actions, 6 for holding public office, and 13 for both offenses.[13] Ex-Quakers ultimately proved good soldiers, providing the Americans with two colonels and three generals, of whom the most famous was Rhode Island's Nathanael Greene.

In January 1776 ex-Quaker Thomas Paine had published *Common Sense*, making the issue of independence openly discussable (it had been shunned as a treasonable activity). The Philadelphia Meeting for Sufferings, appalled at the fighting and opposed to independence, issued "The Ancient Testimony and Principles of the People Called Quakers renewed with respect to the King and Government."[14] Friends declared their "abhorrence of all such Writing and measures" designed to break up the "happy connection" until now enjoyed with Great Britain. This declaration, naturally enough, brought the wrath of the patriots down upon Friends everywhere. Quakers in New England, New York, Maryland, and North Carolina did not occupy strategic positions in society and had not been involved either in politics or revolutionary agitation, except for insisting on their right to be pacifists. Now Tom Paine and Samuel Adams charged Quakers everywhere with betraying the American cause.[15]

Political alignments in Pennsylvania followed religious lines. Presbyterians favored independence; Lutheran and Reformed were divided but most reluctantly endorsed independence; Anglicans were divided; most Quakers, Moravians, Mennonites, and German Brethren were opposed. If offered a choice between the status quo of 1763 and independence, the old arrangement with Britain would have been preferred by an overwhelming majority. What the radicals had tried to do in early 1776 was to show that the old option was dead, and the alternatives were tyranny or independence.[16] In 1775 several Assemblies, including Pennsylvania's, had instructed their delegates to the Continental Congress to oppose independence. The struggle in 1776 was over rescinding those instructions, and the crucial event was the elections for the Pennsylvania Assembly occurring on

May 1. By a narrow margin the conservative party opposed to independence won. Fifteen days later, the Continental Congress issued a mandate that governments deriving their authority from the Crown (i.e., Pennsylvania's Charter) were not sufficient to the exigencies of the time. That language prompted the radicals to stage a peaceful coup d'etat by subverting the authority of the Assembly, denying the authority of the Charter, and calling a convention to draw up a new constitution.

The new revolutionary government established under the Pennsylvania Constitution of 1776 marked the end of the traditional political leaders. Presbyterians, German Lutherans, and Reformed replaced the once-dominant Quakers and Anglicans. The persecution of Friends in Pennsylvania after 1776, far worse than that which occurred anywhere else in America, came because the new Pennsylvania government was insecure in both its legitimacy and authority. After July 4, 1776, the official position of Friends was that members had refrained from participating in any way in the revolutions in the English government in 1660 and 1688, and they would follow the same practice now. Quakers remained neutral between both contending factions because the setting up and tearing down of governments was the exclusive prerogative of God. The patriots saw Quakers as a political denomination ostensibly neutral, actually loyalist, and prepared to resume their positions of power if the British should win. Loyalty to the king in January had been suspect; after July it became treason.

American Quakers defined their task as implementing the peace testimony. All good Friends agreed that fighting was wrong. But did accepting "continental" paper money entail an approval of the patriots' position, since these bills of credit were issued as a method of financing the war? Should Friends affirm allegiance to the revolutionary state? In September 1776 representatives of most America. Yearly Meetings gathered at the Philadelphia Yearly Meeting and formed a committee to provide guidelines for uniformity of conduct. The approved pattern of behavior is as follows:

1. Strict neutrality. Friends would not favor or support the English or the American governments.

2. Noninvolvement. Friends would refrain from voting and would accept no political office and do no service for either side. Taking an affirmation of fidelity to a warring power became a disownable offense. Since the British did not tender abjuration statements to Friends, the issue was only with the American states. The refusal of Quakers to take loyalty pledges disenfranchised them throughout the Revolutionary period.

3. Peace. If drafted, a Quaker would not serve. If provision were made (as it was in all colonies) to hire a substitute, pay a certain sum in lieu of service, or be fined for not serving, Quakers would not comply since a payment recognized that the state had a valid claim on the person and the money would be used to finance a war.

4. War taxes. No taxes levied for the carrying on of the war should be paid. Some Quakers continued to pay levies for road repairs and taxes for carrying on normal governmental functions, believing they were upholding the biblical injunction to sup-

port existing authority. North Carolina and New England Friends accepted the Revolutionary government as de facto and paid local and even some war taxes. A few New Jersey and Pennsylvania Friends took a more uncompromising position, refusing to pay any taxes to governments with uncertain powers and no legitimacy. Ever since the French and Indian War, Friends had been debating war taxation, and there was more variation in practice on this issue than others.

5. Sufferings. Friends who suffered expected to be persecuted for their positions and were to record all pecuniary losses as well as imprisonment.[17] The New England Yearly Meeting established a Meeting for Sufferings in 1775, Maryland in 1776.

The Quaker position was not easy either for individual Friends or for the Revolutionary governments. When the states thought they had made adequate provision for noncombatants or for taking an affirmation rather than an oath and Quakers did not cooperate, hostility resulted. The legislatures decided to fine those who refused either to fight or to provide a substitute. Several states required noncombatants to pay double or triple taxation. When the British or American armies wanted to buy or requisition supplies, Quakers refused to sell. If an army then seized the materials, Quakers declined to receive any compensation.

How much Friends suffered because of the war depended upon the security of the Revolutionary regime and the proximity of the armies. New York Quakers suffered because the British occupied the City and parts of long Island, but the Americans controlled upstate. Quakers in Dutchess County, caught in between, were victimized by marauders more interested in plunder than politics. New Jersey Friends also remained divided between American and British forces. Except in Newport and Aquidneck Island, which the British occupied, New England's Friends escaped being at the scene of military activities. Nantucket Quakers were in a particularly vulnerable position, because they were dependent upon whaling for commerce and the mainland for supplies. Eventually, Quaker William Rotch appealed and received permission from both British and American authorities for Nantucket's ships to sail.[18]

Pennsylvania and West New Jersey Friends experienced the most animosity. In 1777 the publication of the spurious Spanktown Yearly Meeting documents purporting to prove that Quakers cooperated with the British occasioned hostility throughout the colonies. Fearing the loss of Philadelphia to the British and determined to end Quaker treason, the Congress and Pennsylvania Council arrested eleven prominent Philadelphia Friends and exiled them to Virginia, although neither body claimed authority for this action and no trial occurred.[19] The exiled Friends were allowed to return home a year later.

Friends who were drafted but refused to serve experienced a variety of treatment. Some militia officers took a sympathetic attitude, but others inflicted physical punishment and prison sentences. New England treated Friends most generously, but the South was more rigorous, partially because authorities were not so well acquainted with Quaker scruples.[20] Friends kept an active lobby intervening with state legislators, who generally allowed conscientious objectors to return home just to be rid of them. The Meetings provided certificates of membership to those in good standing but refused to allow their privileges to be jeopardized by outsiders shirking military service. In Pennsylvania the state barred teachers and merchants who refused to take oaths of loyalty from carrying on their occupations.

In all of the colonies, most of the sufferings recorded came from fines and distraints. In Pennsylvania Friends claimed to have lost £38,500; in New Jersey, £16,029; in Virginia, £11,221; in North Carolina, £9,888; and in New England, £11,397. Some Meetings distinguished between sufferings incurred for unpaid taxes and those levied as fines and distraints. In New England, about one-third of the total listed was for taxes; in Delaware, one-half; in New Jersey, of the specified sufferings of nearly £12,000, only £488 was for taxes. Although the Meetings made certain that the populace knew of their sufferings, Friends did not object to their disabilities.[21] If their religious beliefs were as important as they claimed, devout members should be prepared to endure ill consequences.

During the occupation of Boston in 1775, New England Quakers began a program of relief designed at first to care for members but soon expanded to care for all. Friends provided goods and shelter in all theaters of the war and, most remarkably, Friends in England and Ireland made significant donations. Most of the aid went to Quakers, but not all. After battles in vicinities where Friends dwelt, they aided the wounded from both sides.

The American Revolution, our first civil war, split families. Some Quakers did not accept the Meetings' official position because they saw the war as just. Consequently, they paid taxes, took affirmations of loyalty, joined the military, and often accused other Quakers of being Tories. The Meetings treated deviations harshly, particularly those for military service. The number of Quaker males disowned for war-related offenses constituted one-third of those of age to be eligible for military service in New Jersey; 19.0 percent in Pennsylvania, 6.5 percent in New York, 5.0 percent in New England, 10.0 percent in Maryland, and 5.0 percent in Virginia. Including North Carolina, Delaware, and Georgia with the above states, there were 2,350 dealings and 1,724 disownments, most of which occurred during the early years of the war and involved the bearing of arms.[22]

In 1781 a few disowned and patriotic Quakers in Philadelphia, led by Samuel Wetherill, Jr., and including Betsy Ross, established the Society of Free Quakers. Repudiating the Discipline, tests for membership, established dogmas, and disownments, the Free Quakers attempted to have a meeting for worship without authoritarian beliefs and practices. They corresponded with a few sympathizers in Rhode Island and the South, but the new church—which never had more than a hundred members—endured only until the 1830s. A few other disowned Friends after the war acknowledged their offenses and were received back into membership.

The Free Quakers and many patriots insisted that the neutralist position followed by Philadelphia Yearly Meeting brought unnecessary opprobrium upon

Friends. They argued that if all members had accepted the practices of Quakers outside the Middle Colonies who paid taxes and used Continental currency, Friends could have been genuinely neutral and preserved the peace Testimony. Those who made policies in the Meeting for Sufferings—the Pembertons, Fishers, Henry Drinker—were called crypto-loyalists and unrepresentative of rural Quakers. There was some truth in the Free Quakers' charges, but it is difficult to accept their argument in its entirety. Unfortunately, the nature of the records perserved does not enable us to see how decisions in the Yearly Meeting or Meeting for Sufferings were made and by whom. The overwhelming majority of those disowned in all states were for direct military service, and there was no sentiment among weighty Friends to jettison or weaken the peace testimony. The basic weakness in the Free Quakers' argument is that it ignores the reform movement that had been going on within the Society of Friends since the 1750s.

John Churchman, Anthony Benezet, and John Woolman had advocated divorcing the Meeting from politics. Until the 1770s those who believed in the heritage of the "Holy Experiment" and the value of political action could neutralize these reformers. The Revolutionary crisis allowed the reformers to take control. These men and women were not pro-British, but they used the Revolutionary War to purify the Society of Friends. Unwilling to compromise with what they saw as evil, they joined with the Philadelphia merchant aristocracy to make American Quakers into a sect. Consistency, internal purity, withdrawal from politics, and rejection of the American ways of love, marriage, and war characterized Friends. In 1776 Friends also repudiated their responsibility for the religious and moral tone of Pennsylvania. The reformers sacrificed power and numerical growth in order to embrace religious suffering.[23]

FREEDOM

Even while the war dragged on Quakers quietly continued their own peaceful revolution against slavery. The Philadelphia Yearly Meeting's decisions in 1754 and 1758 marked a major step forward by condemning both the slave trade and slavery itself. The only offense bringing a disciplinary response was selling or buying a black, even though committees visited Friends who already owned slaves. But with the imprimatur of the largest and most influential Yearly Meeting in America, traveling ministers from and those visiting Philadelphia picked up the Testimony and spread the message. Within a few years Friends in London, New York, New England, Maryland, Virginia, and North Carolina showed the unity of Quakers by condemning the slave trade. If John Woolman symbolized the initial awakening of antislavery, the man who epitomized the next phase of opposition was Anthony Benezet.*

Benezet (1713–84) made the parochial Quaker antislavery impulse interact with and add impetus to a more general revulsion against slavery emerging in England and France. His many reform activities also show the emergence of a humanitarian–philanthropic spirit among Friends. Anthony Benezet was the child of French Huguenots who settled in England to escape religious persecution. Before the family migrated to Pennsylvania in 1731, Anthony was converted at age fourteen to Quakerism. After a brief career as a manufacturer, Benezet became a teacher. But while teaching was his vocation, good works was his avocation.[24]

Like Woolman, Benezet wrote a popular primer and also read widely in both religious and secular sources. He became the best read American Quaker of his day, but he was restricted to teaching in the English schools because he lacked knowledge of classical languages. In 1755 he opened the first advanced Quaker school for girls and later taught several years in the first Quaker school for blacks.

Benezet was never a minister but became an elder in the Philadelphia Monthly Meeting, an overseer of the press, a member of the Meeting for Sufferings, and an eloquent penman for Friends for thirty years, writing a history of Quakers, a defense of pacifism during the Revolution, and many Epistles. He also popularized the devotional writings of the French quietists. In his spiritual emphases, concern for a simple life, and desire for religious reform, he resembled his close friend John Woolman. When the British expelled the Acadians from Nova Scotia and dumped them on Philadelphia with no provisions, Benezet badgered the Assembly and wealthy individuals until he obtained supplies. Like Woolman, he worried about the widespread consumption of intoxicating liquors and wrote one of the earliest American temperance tracts.

The cause to which Benezet devoted most energy was antislavery. Unlike Woolman who couched his arguments within the narrow language of quietistic purity, self-denial, and asceticism, Benezet used a wide variety of arguments drawn from history, natural rights, evangelical religion, and sentimentality. His investigation of the effects of the slave trade upon traditional African cultures culminated in 1762 in the first English-language history of West Africa; he expanded, modified, and published the book ten years later as *Some Historical Account of Guinea*.

When, after 1765, the American colonists charged the English with trying to enslave them, Benezet reminded both sides what slavery really was and showed how incompatible it was with their beliefs in natural liberties and the rights of Englishmen. Picturing the noble black and idealizing the family ties in Africa, Benezet drew on the heightened emphasis upon feelings and sympathy in late eighteenth-century romanticism to emphasize the barbarities in and sufferings caused by the slave trade.

Benezet attacked all of the standard arguments used against emancipation. Using his educational experiences with black children as a source, he insisted that their intellectual and moral capacities were equal with whites. If blacks appeared inferior, any differences were due to environment. Slaves had supported masters for years. So the master who emancipated his slaves should be responsible that the freedmen did not become public charges. If white and black could not live together at present as equals, whites should set aside lands in the American

West for the blacks. Slavery impoverished both races and oppression left its deleterious scars on the characters of whites and blacks.

After 1770 Benezet's arguments against the slave trade generated enthusiasm from both Northerners and Southerners. Benezet did not realize that some patriots were using his arguments to discredit the British by blaming the slave trade on them, hoping to increase the value of their own slaves through stopping additional imports. He was bitterly disappointed when most Americans dropped the anti-slavery cause as the Revolution approached. But his pamphlets and letters helped make the antislavery movement international. Granville Sharp, Thomas Clarkson, John Wesley, and the Abbé Raynal in France corresponded with Benezet. He sent copies of his tracts to American politicians and to be distributed to every member of Parliament, Anglican bishops, and the royalty of England, France, and Portugal. In 1775 he formed the first antislavery society in America, an organization designed to protect free Negroes unlawfully held in bondage. When the Pennsylvania Assembly in 1780 decided to end slavery gradually, Benezet—now an old man—served the cause by marshaling information and collecting petitions.

Benezet disliked the eulogistic testimonies Friends issued as memorials, but when pressed as to his preference for an epitaph, said, "they may say Anthony Benezet was a poor creature, and through divine favor, was enabled to know it."[25]

The antislave trade and antislavery exertions by Woolman, Benezet, and others first bore fruit in New England. In rural New England and on Nantucket Island since the early eighteenth century there had been a few antislavery Friends. But their attempts to broaden their Yearly Meeting's Testimony had been rebuffed from city dwellers in Newport. Woolman's visit in 1760 prompted the New England Yearly Meeting to bring its Testimony in line with Philadelphia's. Antislavery Quakers in New England soon began agitating for additional measures, querying whether consistency did not demand making the Testimony against holding as well as buying and selling slaves. In 1769 the South Kingston Monthly Meeting raised the issue formally; a Yearly Meeting committee visited all Monthly Meetings during the next year and reported that all slaves should be freed except the very young and old. Between 1772 and 1776 Friends in New England ceased to own slaves and disowned those who resisted—even if they were prominent like Governor Stephen Hopkins.[26]

The Philadelphia Yearly Meeting began catching up with New England in 1772. First the Yearly Meeting took a survey of all members who owned slaves. Then in 1773 and 1774 it made owning slaves a disownable offense. The Meetings created manumission books to record copies of the transaction so that the newly freed men and women could never be reenslaved. Local Meetings appointed committees to visit recalcitrant slaveowners. An example of the pressure that these committees could bring is shown by the account of Clark T. Moorman of North Carolina.

Moorman, who owned one or two blacks, had long resisted the efforts of Friends for manumission. Eventually, the Meeting resolved to disown him, but one member pled for one last attempt. Moorman heard of their planned visit and instructed his wife to refuse Friends admission to their house. But she invited them in and to supper. When Moorman found the committee, he resolved to defy them. But all during supper and during a period of silence following, no one mentioned slavery. Finally the committee left, and Moorman went to bed and had a dream

in which it clearly appeared to him that himself with some friends was taken up to heaven, to the Pearl Gate, which was opened for their entrance by a little *Black Boy*, and while friends were entering, he made several attempts to go in, but the little Black Boy always presented himself in the way, so that Friends entered, the Gate was shut, and he was left on the outside.[27]

Moorman awoke and told his wife that the next day he was going to emancipate his slaves.

Philadelphia Friends showed reluctance to disown over slavery, perhaps because that action would not help the blacks. The Meetings agreed in some cases to long apprenticeships or indentures whereby the slave would not be freed until age thirty. By 1783 the Philadelphia Yearly Meeting could memorialize the state and national legislatures confident that Quakers had by gradual measures ended slavery and set an example for the nation.[28]

In Maryland slavery was more deeply entrenched than in the North. By the late 1760s members of the Third Haven Monthly Meeting on the Eastern Shore began freeing slaves. In 1772 the Maryland Yearly Meeting established committees to meet with slaveholders. Since the active members of these committees had freed their slaves, their words and example carried weight. In 1776 the committee visited fifty-eight Quakers who owned 955 slaves and persuaded thirteen of them to free 77 slaves. Quakers on both sides of the Chesapeake continued to free their slaves, with the largest number freed by an individual being Samuel Snowden's 84. In 1778 the Yearly Meeting began disowning those who refused to free blacks, and this process had generally been completed by 1780.[29]

Quakers in the Middle Colonies and to a lesser extent in Rhode Island and Maryland had sufficient numbers and prestige that they could shape public opinion. This was not the case in either Virginia or North Carolina. The southwestward migration from Pennsylvania brought Quakers into these colonies who had strong ties with the Philadelphia Yearly Meeting. The Virginia Yearly Meeting in 1766 and North Carolina in 1768 inserted strong condemnations of the slave trade in their Disciplines and strengthened their Testimony on the eve of the Revolution. Both colonies had laws against manumissions except under extraordinary circumstances, and these laws made the movement against slavery more complex than in the North.

The North Carolina Friends began freeing their slaves between 1775 and 1777, but the state reenslaved them and passed another antimanumission law in 1777. Quakers hired a lawyer who proved to the satisfaction of the courts that the reenslavement of the freed Negroes was an ex post facto use of the new law and illegal. But the legislature overruled the court and kept the blacks in slavery. Repeated attempts to persuade the legislature to change the law failed, so in 1808 the North Carolina Friends decided that the only legal way of freeing people was to give title to them to the Yearly Meeting. Those blacks who wanted to remain in the state were nominally still slaves, but most migrated to the Middle West, Pennsylvania, or Africa. The North Carolina Yearly Meeting "owned" slaves until the Civil War.[30]

Virginia had a law restricting manumissions until 1782. Consequently, when the Virginia Yearly Meeting recommended freeing slaves in 1773, most members delayed while Friends lobbied to get the law changed. Most emancipations in Virginia occurred after 1782. Robert Pleasants, a wealthy Virginia planter, led by example the movement for freeing blacks. He liberated eighty slaves at a cost of £3,000 and corresponded with leading Southerners like Patrick Henry, attempting to persuade them of the moral, religious, and economic benefits of emancipation.[31]

In 1828 an English Friend estimated that North Carolina Friends had freed their slaves at a cost of £50,000.[32] Whether or not that figure is accurate, the actions of Maryland, Virginia, and North Carolina Friends in freeing their slaves were extraordinary. Elsewhere in the South a few Methodists and Baptists preached emancipation, but their religious organizations soon made their peace with the "peculiar institution." Friends in North and South proved that they did not stop freedom at the color line.

NOTES

1. David Sloan, " 'A Time of Sifting and Winnowing': The Paxton Riots and Quaker Non-Violence in Pennsylvania," *Quaker History* (hereafter *QH*) 66 (1977): 3–22; George Franz, "Paxton: A Study of Community Structure and Mobility in Colonial Pennsylvania Backcountry" (Ph.D. diss., Rutgers University, 1974).

2. James H. Hutson, *Pennsylvania Politics, 1746–1770* (Princeton, N.J.: 1972); William Hanna, *Benjamin Franklin and Pennsylvania Politics* (Stamford, Calif.: 1964).

3. Alan W. Tully, "Ethnicity, Religion, and Politics in Early America," *Pennsylvania Magazine of History and Biography* (hereafter *PMHB*) 107 (1983): 491–536.

4. The best treatments of the coming of the Revolution to Pennsylvania are Richard Ryerson, *The Revolution Is Now Begun: The Radical Committees of Philadelphia, 1765–1776* (Philadelphia: 1978) and David Hawke, *In the Midst of a Revolution* (Philadelphia: 1961).

5. Arthur J. Mekeel, *The Relation of the Quakers to the American Revolution* (Washington, D.C.: 1975), 17–25.

6. Ibid., 34–48.

7. Ibid., 65–78; Jack D. Marietta, *The Reformation of American Quakerism*, 216–18.

8. Mekeel, *Relation*, 84–88.

9. Mekeel, *Relation*, 89–92; Ryerson, *Revolution*, 89–115.

10. Ryerson, *Revolution*, 113–22.

11. *Testimony of the People Called Quakers* (Philadelphia: 1775); Philadelphia Meeting for Sufferings, I, 430, 440–42. Marietta, *Reformation*, 223–25, argued that this declaration was "impolitic," tying Friends to the Galloway faction and tainting them with loyalism.

12. Mekeel, *Relation*, 122–23.

13. Ibid., 132.

14. *The Ancient Testimony* (Philadelphia: 1776); Philadelphia Meeting for Sufferings, Minutes, II, 53–59.

15. Thomas Paine, *Common Sense . . . To Which Is Added an Appendix: Together with an Address to the People Called Quakers* (Philadelphia: 1776).

16. Carl Becker, *History of Political Parties in the Province of New York, 1760–1776* (Ph.D. diss., Univ. of Wisconsin, 1909; reprint, Madison, Wisc.: 1960), 22, 239–256. David Hawke, *Paine* (New York: 1974).

17. Philadelphia Yearly Meeting, Minutes, III, 349–62; Marietta, *Reformation*, 261–71.

18. Mekeel, *Relation*, 142–44, 228–30; William Rotch, *Memorandum Written by William Rotch in the Eightieth Year of His Age* (New York: 1916).

19. Thomas Gilpin, *Exiles in Virginia* (Philadelphia: 1848); Elizabeth Vining, *Virginia Exiles* (Philadelphia, 1955).

20. Peter Brock, *Pioneers of the Peaceable Kingdom* (Princeton, N.J.: 1968), 197–202.

21. Mekeel, *Relation*, 202, 212, 236, 252, 262, 273.

22. Ibid., 200, 212–13, 236, 253, 262, 274.

23. Charles Wetherill, *History of the Religious Society of Friends Called by Some the Free Quakers* (Philadelphia: 1894).

24. Nancy Slocum Hornick, "Anthony Benezet: Eighteenth Century Social Critic, Educator and Abolitionist" (Ph.D. diss., University of Maryland, 1974), 131; George S. Brookes, ed., *Friend Anthony Benezet* (Philadelphia: 1937), reprints many of the letters.

25. Roberts Vaux, *Memoirs of the Life of Anthony Benezet* (Philadelphia: 1817), 136.

26. Arthur Worrall, *Quakers in the Colonial Northeast* (Hanover, N.H.: 1980), 156–65.

27. Philip J. Schwarz, "Clark T. Moorman: Quaker Emancipator," *QH* 69 (1980): 33–34.

28. J. William Frost, ed., *Quaker Origins of Antislavery* (Norwood, Pa.: 1980), 171–250; Jean Soderlund, "Conscience, Interest, and Power: The Development of Quaker Opposition to Slavery in the Delaware Valley" (Ph.D. diss., Temple University, 1981), Chs. 1–3.

29. Kenneth Carroll, "Maryland Quakers and Slavery," *QH* 72 (1983): 27–42; Thomas Drake, *Quakers and Slavery in America* (New Haven, Conn.: 1950) 81–82.

30. Stephen Weeks, *Southern Quakers and Slavery* (Baltimore 1896), 206–25; Howard

Beeth, "Outside Agitators in Southern History: The Society of Friends, 1656–1800" (Ph.D. diss., University of Houston, 1984), 462–465, 513–516.

31. Weeks, *Southern Quakers*, 199–206; Drake, *Quakers and Slavery*, 83.

32. Drake, *Quakers and Slavery*, 84.

13
QUAKER MIGRANTS TO CAROLINA AND THE MIDWEST; EASTERN PHILANTHROPISTS

Early Friends and Puritans lived and traveled as "pilgrims and strangers" on earth (I Peter 2:11) while founding many new Bethels or (Jeru-)salems. Under persecution, eighteenth-century Quakers and dissenters had moved within England from farms into villages that became cities like Birmingham. In the American colonies those who became Friends in New England and the South had been recent settlers; even the Friends founding New Jersey and Pennsylvania did not all stay put. The familiar image is misleading, that eastern towns centered on stable Quaker Meetings (or New England churches) where families continued for centuries. In almost every family some stayed while others migrated; those who left often moved several times. The isolation of Kentucky's log cabins may also blind us to how often a group of couples with their children moved as a wagon train together to a new village that a few of their men had scouted, cleared, and prepared with cabins for them.[1] Another half-truth is that the frontier was settled by misfits from eastern towns and immigrants directly from Europe, who could never "go home again." In the eighteenth century this was true of most Scots, Ulstermen, German Lutherans, or sectarians but not of the Friends. Daniel Boone, a birthright Quaker, had indeed become estranged from his Bucks County Meeting and explored by himself. But most settlers merely came from large families in East Coast communities where the best land was subject to church taxes or fully bought up. Migrants wanted new farms but kept in touch with eastern cousins. Meetings or churches on the East Coast helped the new congregations and sent out traveling Quaker "ministers," Presbyterian pastors, or Methodist circuit riders. Friends encouraged the founding of new Meetings. Home Meetings gave certificates of membership to emigrants only after careful reassurance that they would not be cut off from Quaker schools and worship. Most communities began with "allowed" Meetings in private homes. Until a new Monthly Meeting (and in time a new Quarterly and Yearly Meeting) was "set off" by the parent group, migrants' certificates were deposited in the

Meeting nearest the new settlement, often many miles east of their new homes. Friends transplanted names: New Garden, London Grove, Sandy Spring, and Hopewell were carried from Pennsylvania and Maryland into North Carolina, Ohio, Indiana, and Iowa; also English town names like Chester and Richmond were transplanted. Their children later moved in the same way to Kansas or Oregon; pioneers with packhorses cleared new land; their families followed in covered wagons.

THREE STAGES

By 1760 there were 50,000 to 60,000 Quakers in the seacoast colonies, about half around Philadelphia and in Maryland.[2] Many had moved west within Pennsylvania and Virginia. Menallen Meeting beyond the Susquehanna and Hopewell beyond the Potomac, begun in 1733 and 1735, became anchors of Western Quarterly Meeting, set up by Philadelphia Yearly Meeting in 1758. They were transferred in 1789 to Maryland and thereafter called Baltimore Yearly Meeting.[3] Germanic Quakers moved up the Shenandoah Valley; later the area was strongly Hicksite. Overcrowding and church taxes on Nantucket and throughout New England drove many Friends to the "Nine Partners" area above Poughkeepsie on the Hudson. But more went southwest to North Carolina's Piedmont. There, New Garden Meeting, founded in 1754, had by 1781—when it was used as a hospital for both sides in the Battle of Guilford Court House—acquired forty-one Nantucket families, forty-five from Pennsylvania and thirty-five from Virginia. Of the twenty-nine certificates brought to establish Bush River Meeting, South Carolina, in 1770, fourteen were from Pennsylvania. Southernmost was Wrightsborough, Georgia, from 1773. By 1800 there were fourteen Piedmont Meetings and seven near Bush River. The Guilford area overshadowed the ten earlier Quaker settlements near Albemarle Sound, becoming the new center of North Carolina Yearly Meeting.[4]

The Appalachians and hostile Indian tribes kept colonists from moving west easily until after the Revolution, but Friends families joined a second stage migration of mixed religious and ethnic groups southwest into eastern Tennessee, where the New Hope and Lost Creek Meetings began in the 1780s and Friendsville Academy near Marysville survived until the 1970s; from the Delaware Valley west to the Redstone area on the Monongahela south of Pittsburgh; and from the Hudson northwest into the Genesee tract, to form among the New York "finger lakes" what became Scipio Quarterly Meeting that had 4,000 Friends by 1827.

This second phase of migration, in the 1790s, merged into a third, the key expansion for Friends, into the Ohio Valley after 1800 (see maps). The Revolutionary War's end, the Northwest Ordinance of 1787, and the defeat of the Ohio Indians in 1794–95 opened up the Middle West where slavery was forbidden and whole farming towns could settle together on flat land. Six thousand North

Carolina Quakers moved west in twenty-five years.[5] Ten thousand to 12,000 came from the whole South, 5,000 from the Delaware Valley.

FIVE WAYS WEST CONVERGED ON OHIO AND INDIANA

Around 1800, some upstate New York Friends moved along the lakes, like many Congregationalists and Presbyterians, to the "Western Reserve" around Cleveland. Others moved across the Niagara River into Ontario. A little Meeting at Catawissa, Pennsylvania, moved as a unit to land near Toronto in 1800–1806. The Meetings in Ontario and Maritime Canada were reinforced by "loyalist" Quaker New Yorkers and Pennsylvanians, who chose British over "patriot" rule after the Revolution. In 1808 Philadelphia Yearly Meeting authorized a Canadian Half Year's Meeting, with three Monthly Meetings: Yonge Street near Toronto, Adolphustown near Kingston, and Pelham near Niagara.[6]

A second migrant group came from central Pennsylvania, joined by Friends from the Shenandoah and farther south, along the "Cumberland Trail" (soon to become the "National Road"), from the Potomac to the Monongahela and by keel-boat down the Ohio. By 1806, 800 Quaker families had moved west through the new Quarterly Meeting centered at Redstone and Westland, Pennsylvania, to valleys running from the west into the northern loop of the Ohio River.[7] From 1800 onward, Mount Pleasant, Short Creek, and Concord, Ohio, northwest of Wheeling, had become a new center for Virginia Quakers and the meeting-place of Ohio Yearly Meeting, "set off" by Baltimore in 1813. Fifty miles north, Salem and Damascus, Ohio, became a center for Pennsylvanian (and later for evangelical) Friends: the west edge of this cluster was Kendal, later Massillon, Ohio, founded as a model town by a New England Quaker whaler, Thomas Rotch.[8] A cluster of Meetings along the Zane Trace west of Wheeling near Barnesville later became the center for "Conservative" Friends.

A third main migrant group was the Virginia and Carolina Friends who came over the Blue Ridge and down the Kanawha River to the Ohio, landing on Quaker Bottom and around Chillicothe, Ohio, where Ohio's Westland would become a Hicksite center. But many went down the Ohio to join a fourth stream, which came out of North Carolina through the Cumberland Gap from Tennessee and over the Boone Trail to Cincinnati. They went up the Great and Little Miami Rivers to Waynesville, Ohio, and to Clinton County around Wilmington, Ohio, settling north of the deep ravines on the rich glacial soils.[9] There the Land Office had surveyed half-mile-square homesteads that dispersed Quaker communities more than in the thickly settled East. Friends spread northwestward to Richmond and Newport (Fountain City), Indiana, being among the first Indiana settlers north of the Ohio bottomlands. By 1821 Indiana Yearly Meeting had 20,000 members and had spread northwest to Muncie and Marion, Indiana.[10] To Indiana by then a fifth migrant stream of southern Friends had come down the Tennessee and Cumberland Rivers and up the White or Wabash Rivers to the area from

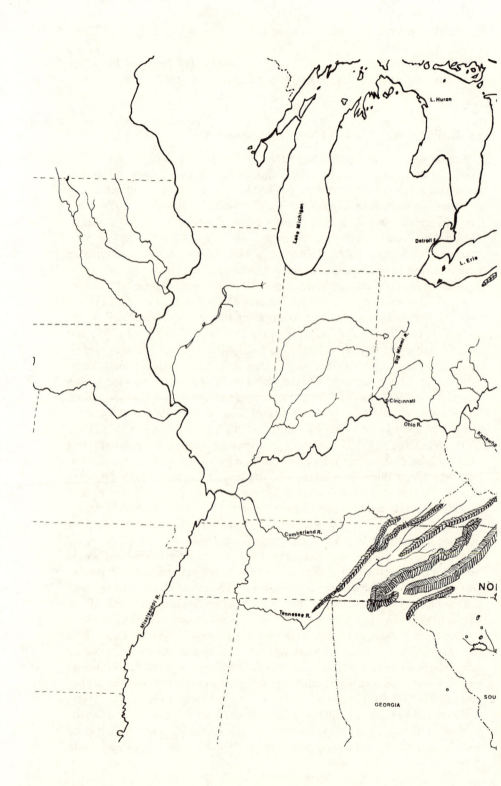

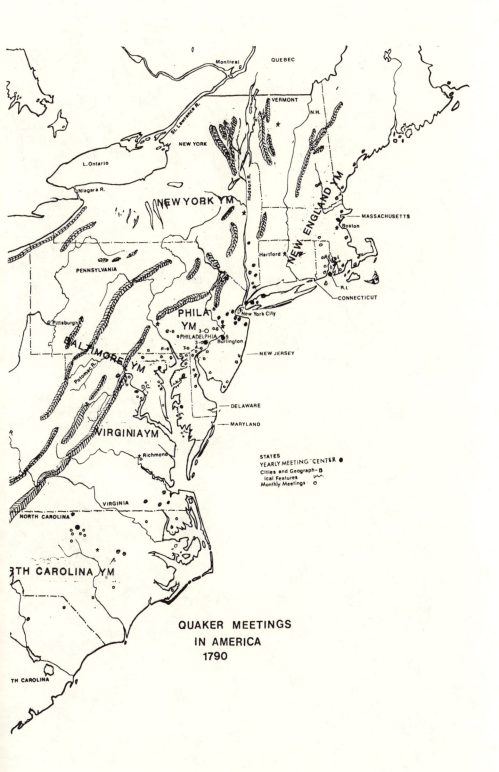

QUAKER MEETINGS
IN AMERICA
1790

STATES
YEARLY MEETING CENTER ●
Cities and Geograph- ▣
ical Features ⌐
Monthly Meetings o

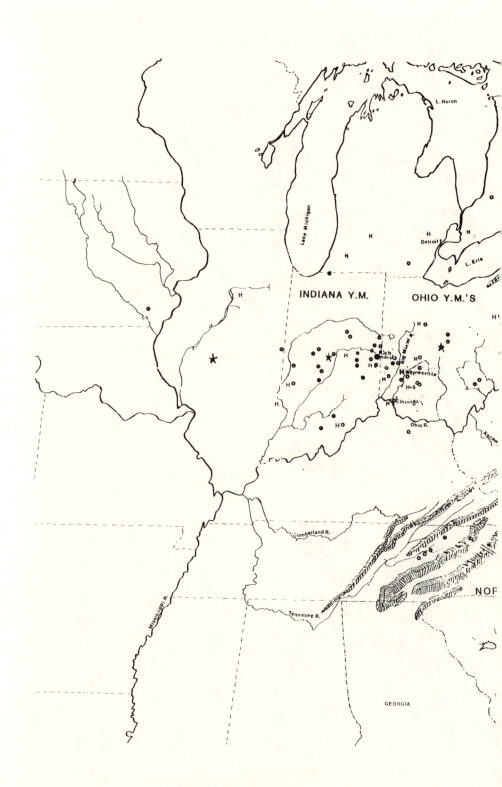

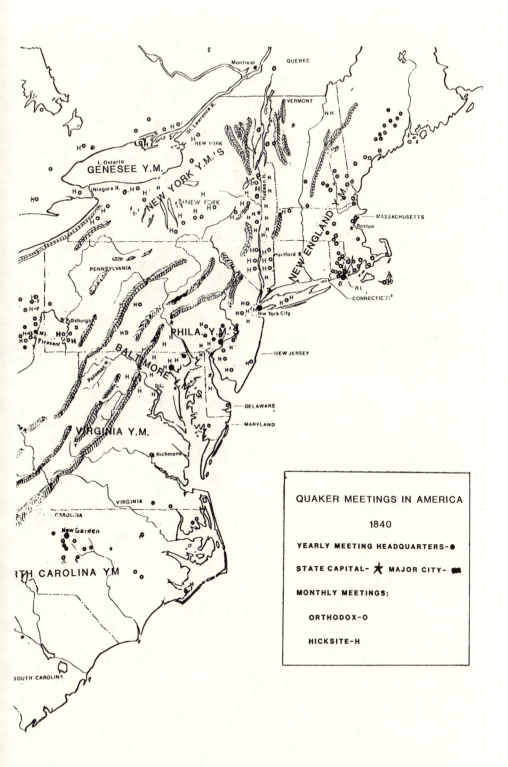

QUEBEC

Montreal

VERMONT

N.H.

L. Ontario

GENESEE Y.M.

St. Lawrence R.

NEW YORK

Niagara R.

NEW YORK Y.M.'S

NEW YORK

Hudson R.

NEW ENGLAND Y.M.

MASSACHUSETTS

Boston

PENNSYLVANIA

Hartford

CONNECTICUT

R.I.

Pittsburgh

Pleasant

New York City

PHILA. Y.M.'S

BALTIMORE Y.M.'S

Potomac R.

NEW JERSEY

D.C.

DELAWARE

MARYLAND

VIRGINIA Y.M.

Richmond

VIRGINIA

CAROLINA

New Garden

NORTH CAROLINA YM

SOUTH CAROLINA

QUAKER MEETINGS IN AMERICA

1840

YEARLY MEETING HEADQUARTERS- ●

STATE CAPITAL- ★ MAJOR CITY- ▰

MONTHLY MEETINGS:

ORTHODOX-O

HICKSITE-H

159

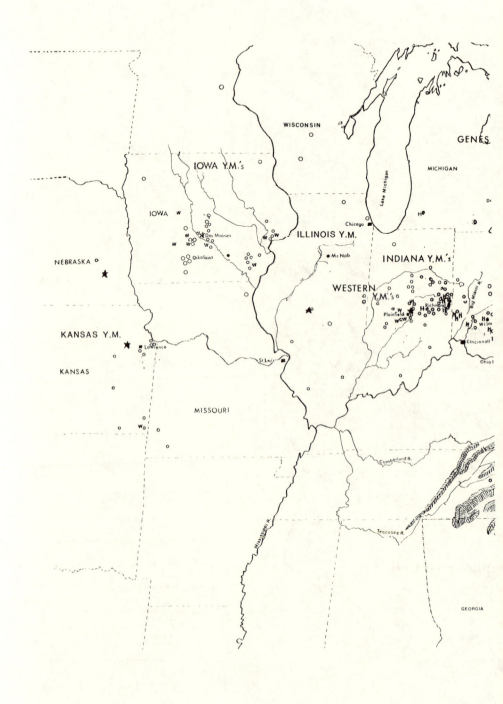

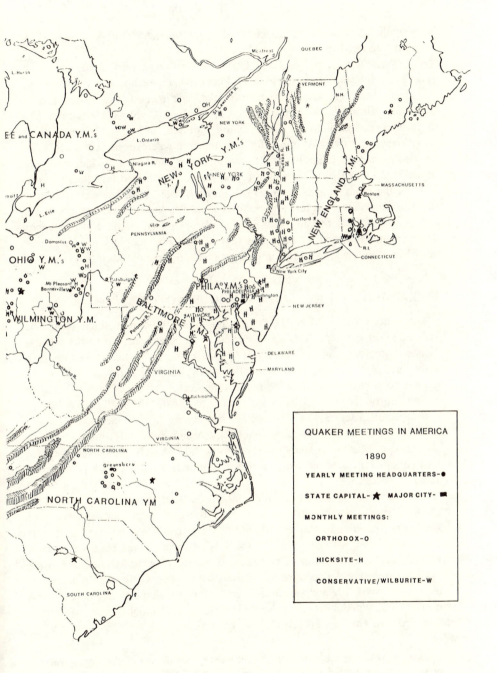

QUEBEC

L. Huron

Montreal

VERMONT

L. Ontario

St. Lawrence R.

NH

EE and CANADA Y.M.'s

OH

NEW YORK

NEW YORK Y.M.'s

Niagara R.

NEW YORK

MASSACHUSETTS

Boston

L. Erie

Detroit

Hudson R.

NEW ENGLAND Y.M.'s

R.I.

Hartford

CONNECTICUT

Damascus

PENNSYLVANIA

OHIO Y.M.'s

New York City

Mt Pleasant
Barnesville

Pittsburgh

PHILA° Y.M.'s

PHILADELPHIA

WILMINGTON Y.M.

BALTIMORE
Y.M.

Wilmington

NEW JERSEY

Potomac R.

BALTIMORE

DELAWARE

VIRGINIA

MARYLAND

Kanawha R.

Richmond

VIRGINIA

NORTH CAROLINA

Greensboro

NORTH CAROLINA YM

SOUTH CAROLINA

QUAKER MEETINGS IN AMERICA

1890

YEARLY MEETING HEADQUARTERS- ●

STATE CAPITAL- ★   MAJOR CITY- ■

MONTHLY MEETINGS:

ORTHODOX-O

HICKSITE-H

CONSERVATIVE/WILBURITE-W

Indianapolis and Plainfield to Kokomo, the heart of what would become in 1858 Western Yearly Meeting.

The continuity of the stages of Quaker migration is seen in the career of Thomas Beals. Born in Chester County, Pennsylvania, he moved with his parents to western Maryland in 1738, where he matured, married, and moved first to Hopewell, Virginia, and then to Cane Creek, North Carolina. He became one of the first settlers of New Garden, North Carolina, and, as a "recorded minister," traveled to visit meetings for worship from wherever he settled. In 1778 he tried to make a religious visit to the Shawnee and Delaware Indians living beyond the Ohio River, preaching to the troops who turned him back, and in 1792 to the Ohio Indians during Little Turtle's war. With his sons and their families, Beals resettled three more times in the Virginia–Tennessee mountains and moved in 1801 to Salt Creek, Ohio, where in 1802 he died in the woods "from a hurt received by his horse running under a stooping tree" and was buried in a hollowed treetrunk in the first Quaker grave in Ohio.[11]

ECONOMIC, FAMILY, AND RELIGIOUS MOTIVES

Many motives merged in these migrations. Land in Ohio or Indiana could be claimed under the Land Acts for fifty cents to $5.00 an acre, but hard work and meager living conditions preoccupied Quaker pioneers. Although half the men and a third of the women who moved out of Virginia Meetings were unmarried, many who married soon after had rejoined fiancé(e)s. Married migrants' median age was thirty, the unmarrieds' below twenty-five. After 1750, 70 percent moved with children, keeping families together and hoping to give each son a farm.[12] A Hoosier Quaker gave his quarter-section to one son "for $1 and love" as he moved on to Marion. A study of New Jersey and Pennsylvania Quaker families (not emigrants) found an average of 5.69 children per family; 15 percent had 10 to 14 children.[13]

The main noneconomic issue for southern Quakers was slavery. In all of the southern states, notably in Carolina, Friends found neighbors, and laws the neighbors passed and enforced, forbidding them to educate, evangelize, or free their own slaves without posting ruinous bond money. Free blacks had to be moved out of the state or made nominally the property of the Meeting; they were often kidnapped back into slavery.[14] Slavery determined where, even if not when, a Quaker moved: when other Southerners migrated with their slaves to Alabama or the Mississippi delta, Friends went to free territory. Borden Stanton of Georgia recorded how Quakers probed motives for leaving.

For several years Friends had some distant view of moving out of that oppressive part of the land, but did not know where until . . . 1799, when we had an acceptable visit from some traveling Friends of the western part of Pa. [who asked if] it would not be agreeable to best wisdom for us unitedly to remove north-west of the Ohio River, to a place where there were no slaves held. . . . It seemed as if they were messengers sent to call us out . . . from Egyptian darkness, [but] being well settled in the outward, . . . I strove against the thoughts of moving.[15]

Traveling Quaker ministers like Beals, William Hobson*, Joseph Dew of North Carolina, and Timothy Rogers of Vermont, after visits to new lands themselves, led groups of migrants. Friends did not lose touch with the places they had left. Levi Coffin* followed his father and brother to Newport, Indiana; taught school a year; rode with a friend across the Wabash onto Sangamon Prairie, where for six days they saw no human being; and returned to North Carolina to marry his fiancée before settling in Newport, but he made many later visits south to organize the "Underground Railroad" for escaping slaves.

Southern Quakerism was drained by emigration: 11 Virginia Meetings and 83 of the 136 in North Carolina were laid down, 9 being in Guildford County. South Carolina's Cane Creek Meeting moved as a body to Caesar's Creek, Ohio, and Bush River followed. North Carolina issued certificates for 16 families moving to Pennsylvania, 294 to Ohio, and 784 directly to Indiana. Wrightsborough, Georgia, sent 50 families to Ohio in 1804–5 and was discontinued. In 1844 Virginia Yearly Meeting as a whole had so few members that it was merged with Baltimore YM.[16]

Friends first moved to Iowa in 1835 along the "National Road" through Richmond, Indiana, to St. Louis, as part of the national westward migration after the Black Hawk War. Northern Illinois and Iowa were settled by New Englanders, but Hoosier Friends moved up the Des Moines, Iowa, Cedar, and Skunk rivers of southeastern Iowa, where a fifth Quaker Salem (after Massachusetts, North Carolina, Ohio, and Indiana) became their center. Later, central Iowa opened for settlement: Oskaloosa became the Quaker focus, with Indianola and Bear Creek to its west, Bangor and Honey Creek in "the big woods" to the north, and What Cheer and West Branch near Iowa City northeastward. Robert Lindsey from England was taken by Joseph Hoag of Salem to visit all of these Meetings. The new Iowa Yearly Meeting was "set off" by Indiana in 1863, five years after Western Yearly Meeting was created out of all Meetings northwest from Indianapolis.[17]

By this time railroads made Quaker migrating and visiting simpler. Kansas Quakerism began from the covered wagon treks or Indian work of Iowa Friends, but Quakers went to Oregon and California by the Union Pacific and the Santa Fe, which also freed Quaker preachers to cover many towns per month. Their moves and ministry are discussed in later chapters.

BELIEFS AND WORSHIP

As midwestern Friends moved to the South and Midwest, their doctrines changed, but Quaker speech and dress and the "guarded education" of Quaker day schools survived for a generation. When the Philadelphia Friends split over Hicks in 1827, more Indiana Friends took the side of the evangelical Elders than that of the small quietist Meetings from which many of them had come. Migrant Friends came less often from large urban Meetings than from quietist rural ones. Some continued living in isolated Quaker villages: Mount Pleasant and Waynesville, Ohio; Spiceland, Indiana; West Branch, Iowa. Families living half a mile from the next farm found Bible study a necessary part of home worship. But Friends there mixed with non-Friends on the road and in stores more than had been necessary in rural eastern Pennsylvania. Midwestern non-Quaker neighbors were less often shut off by pride than members of the "First Church" of a New England town; everyone felt free to visit the nearest Baptist, Methodist, or Disciples Church. Religion was active, and immorality centered on drinking, swearing, and cheating. From the 1750s to the Civil War, Friends were more often disowned for fornication and drunkenness than for any other cause except marriage with non-Quakers.[18] Evangelical Christianity thus commended itself to midwestern Friends by its moral strength even more than by its doctrines of sin or Christ's atonement and conversion. In that era, non-Friends accepted dogmas as diverse as the Mormons', the Universalists', or the Shakers', if they led to stable lives and communities.[19]

The urgency of American revivalism was at first directed against unchurched immigrants; it changed Quaker worship only after 1860. Yet in response to the national ferment of "the Second Awakening" after 1800 two Quakers gathered new communes of more than 200 members each, with basically Quaker beliefs: Jemima Wilkinson's "Society of the Public Universal Friend" built two successive "Jerusalems" on the New York "finger lakes"; outside Toronto, David Willson gathered at Sharon "the Children of Peace," whose Temple still stands.[20] Ann Lee who founded the Shakers had been raised by Friends.

PHILANTHROPY IN PHILADELPHIA

The lives of Friends who stayed in eastern cities changed under quite different cultural forces. Prospering in Philadelphia killed the itch to migrate. Philadelphia Friends felt the shock of being excluded both from political power and from social acceptance during and after the Revolution. They regained status by their continued integrity and success in business and trade and minimized the "peculiarities" that cut them off from non-Friends.[21] They also copied, joined, or founded enterprises for the welfare of society as a whole. Leaders of the evangelical movement in the urban churches of England and America had founded by 1820 an impressive array of voluntary societies to support foreign and home missions, translate and distribute Bibles and tracts, and set up day schools and Sunday schools for poor children. Such societies set a pattern for England and America where social welfare and social change still are entrusted to volunteer groups, usually religious in motive but not church run, indeed often interchurch. Equivalent programs in continental Europe are usually begun and run by the state or the state church.

Evangelical reformers attacked an immense range of issues but stopped short of questioning the fundamental social structures of property or class structure. Jonathan Edwards had taught the preceding generation to see the highest form of love as *Benevolence*: affirming other creatures in their individual being. Motives of upper-middle-class humanitarians thus combined religious zeal, altruism, compassion, sentimentality, a sense of social responsibility picked up from a nobility obliged to help their dependents, and fear. During and after the French Revolution England watched industries create a large class of urban poor who could not vote, had no voice in Parliament, and appeared irreligious and ready for revolution. American immigrants, who soon could vote, seemed to conservatives likely to overwhelm democratic institutions. Even before the influx of "shanty Irish," whose drinking, brawling and sabbath breaking drew evangelicals into anti-Catholic "Know-Nothing" campaigns in the 1850s, earlier immigrants' regrettable lack of industry, frugality, cleanliness, and morals moved both Quakers and evangelicals to take concern for "fallen women," the sick, and the poor. Early nineteenth-century English and American Quakers led in care for the insane, prison reform, antislavery laws, and Lancastrian Schools that used older children to teach younger ones.

Quaker involvement with the insane began in Pennsylvania Hospital, founded in 1751 to provide care for the sick poor and those who were "disordered in their senses." Benjamin Rush, who joined the staff in 1783, insisted that a hospital was not a jail: patients should be treated with compassion and housed in physical comfort. In 1796 a separate wing was built for housing one hundred insane patients, the first recognition in America that the mentally ill required special medical institutions. A book of accounts of patients by Samuel Coates, a Friend who served as member, secretary, and then president of the Hospital's Board of Managers for forty years, shows his belief that the patients had lost neither their humanity nor their ability to receive and understand the Inward Light. He saw the fleeting nature of human accomplishments: problems of daily life caused mental illness.[22]

In England, Quaker concern began with their own insane. William Tuke, a tea merchant of York, who helped to found The Mount and Ackworth schools, worried over a Quaker patient's death. He persuaded the local Friends to establish "the Retreat" in 1796. When unable to find a doctor, Tuke as a layman moved into the asylum to supervise treatment. His patients followed occupations and amusements designed to stimulate their capacity for self-control: they wore their best clothes for tea parties, with good food.[23] Thomas Scattergood from America visited the Retreat while on a six-year visit to Europe. In 1811, when Pennsylvania Hospital was overcrowded, he made and Philadelphia Yearly Meeting accepted a proposal to create an institution like the York Retreat. In 1817 the Friends Hospital was the first private asylum in the United States, with aesthetic buildings and grounds and a farm for work that was part of the therapy. Patients and staff ate together and lived in the same buildings. Doctors did use strong medicines, blisters, and bleeding but no chains. The atmosphere was religious: until 1834 all patients were Quakers. Twenty-five of the sixty-six patients in the first three years were discharged as cured or much improved, in an era when insanity was considered incurable.[24]

Thomas Eddy, a New York Quaker merchant, was president of the New York Lunatic Asylum begun for paupers in 1808 and soon overcrowded. He led in the building in 1821 of the Bloomingdale Asylum modeled on Tuke's ideas, in a seventy-seven-acre rural Manhattan setting. The Pennsylvania Hospital for the Insane, a private nonsectarian institution to serve all classes and churches, took as superintendent Thomas Kirkbride*, earlier resident physician at Friends Hospital and Pennsylvania Hospital. He popularized the moral treatment, making his asylum comfortable for patients and supporting it by rich patients' fees and by donations.[25]

Quaker work in prisons began much earlier than the famous pioneering of Elizabeth Fry. Friends had known prisons personally in the seventeenth century and proposed reforms to Cromwell's successors. England had relied upon whipping, deportation, and executions; there were 170 capital crimes in the law books as late as 1770. Jails housed prisoners awaiting trial, housing together children and adults, minor offenders and professional criminals. Jailers supported themselves by selling food and liquor to prisoners unless families brought meals. William Penn intended capital punishment to be only for murder, although treason and piracy were later added in Pennsylvania to satisfy the Crown. The only death sentence in seventeenth-century Quaker New Jersey was on a servant convicted of buggery with a cow and after public protest was commuted.[26] But prisons in Pennsylvania did not differ much from those in England. In 1786 Pennsylvania passed a new penal code that announced that the purpose of imprisonment was not just punishment but reformation. In 1787 the mainly Quaker Philadelphia Society for Alleviating Miseries of Public Prisoners made plans: the new jail on Walnut Street would be a penitentiary where criminals in individual cells would repent of their misdeeds and evil habits. Manual tasks would develop work habits; visits by members of the Prison Society would provide better moral uplift than socializing with fellow criminals. The Walnut Street jail became overcrowded, and Roberts Vaux* and other Prison Society visitors persuaded the Pennsylvania legislators to build in 1830 a model institution, the Eastern State Penitentiary. Under a Quaker warden it became world famous. Ohio built a penitentiary in Columbus.[27] In New York, where Thomas Eddy also tried to reform the penal code, John Griscom founded a Society for the Reformation of Juvenile Delinquents and in 1825 persuaded New York to open a pioneer House of Refuge for juveniles. Roberts Vaux in turn copied it in Pennsylvania. In England, Elizabeth Fry, who began work with women prisoners in the 1830s, was among the first to protest that solitary confinement, though healthier at night, was by day more than most prisoners were strong enough to bear.[28]

English Quakers' concern for educating the poor was matched in America mainly regarding blacks and Indians. In both countries Quaker children mainly remained in purely Quaker day and boarding schools, though for them the 1790s saw the opening of Moses Brown School in Rhode Island, Nine Partners above New York, and Westtown outside Philadelphia. At some points, Friends copied evangelical philanthropists: the Friends Tract Association, founded in 1817, had by 1830 distributed 332,000 pamphlets. In America around 1820 only ironmaster Josiah White, among Quaker industrialists, and the Drinker and Wharton merchant clans had come close to the prominence of the Quaker Barclays, Gurneys, Frys, Lloyds, and Darbys in the English business world. Only George Logan as a pacifist in the U.S. Senate had entered federal politics in an era that increasingly saw national policy made in Boston, Washington, and New York rather than Philadelphia.[29] But eastern urban Friends had daily shared with evangelical non-Quakers social programs and religious ideals, as well as meeting as equals in business and society. In the Separation of 1827 many would clash with quietists and rural or poorer Friends.

NOTES

1. On causes and patterns of migration see Larry Dale Gragg, "Migration in Early America: the Virginia Quaker Experience" (Ph.D. thesis, University of Missouri, 1982), statistics based on William Wade Hinshaw, *Encyclopedia of America Quaker Genealogy*, 6 vols. (Ann Arbor, Mich.: 1946). On the role of New England's Church taxes in driving Friends to emigrate, see Arthur Worrall, *Colonial Northeast*, Ch. 7.

2. See James Harris Norton, "Quakers West of the Alleghenies and in Ohio to 1861" (Ph.D. thesis, Western Reserve University, 1965).

3. See Forbush, *Baltimore* (Baltimore: 1972), Ch. 5.

4. See Weeks, *Southern Quakers and Slavery*, 97–104; Seth B. Hinshaw, *The Carolina Quaker Experience* (1984), Ch. 2; William Medlin, *Quaker Families of South Carolina* and *Georgia* (Columbia, S.C.: 1982). JoAnne McCormick showed in "The Quakers of Colonial South Carolina, 1670–1807" (Ph.D. thesis, University of South Carolina, 1984), that despite the strong leadership of Mary Fisher,* Bayly Crosse and her granddaughter Sophia Hume, the Meetings at Charleston and Wateree, South Carolina, were dead by 1782.

5. Figure from Timothy Nicholson cited by Seth B. and Mary E. Hinshaw in *Carolina Quakers* (Greensboro, N.C.: 1972), 28. See Drake; Weeks *Southern Quakers*; Hinshaw, *Encyclopedia*; Seth and Mary Hinshaw, *Carolina Quaker*, Ch. 13.

6. Arthur G. Dorland, *The Quakers in Canada* (Toronto: 1968), Chs. 3, 4.

7. See Norton, "Quakers West," 18, 50.

8. See David L. Johns, "Thomas Rotch" (Paper given at the Conference of Quaker Historians and Archivists, Canton, Ohio, June 24, 1986, from his Malone College thesis).

9. See E. Leonard Brown's geography doctoral thesis, "Quaker Migration to the Miami Country" (Michigan State University, 1974), 83–89.

10. See Errol T. Elliott, *Quakers on the American Frontier* (Richmond, Ind.: 1969); hereafter *QAF*; R. P. Ratcliff, ed., *Our Special Heritage: Sesquicentennial History of Indiana Yearly Meeting: 1821–1971* (New Castle, Ind.: 1978).

11. Daniel Scott, *A History of the Early Settlement of Highland County, Ohio* (Hillsboro, Ohio: 1890, 1983), 45. See also Norton, "Quakers West," Appendix 1.

12. See Gragg, "Migration," tables, pp. 6–16.

168 THE QUAKERS

13. John Harvey's deed for the Barbours' present home; statistics in J. William Frost, *Quaker Family*, 70, 206.

14. Hiram Hilty, *Towards Freedom for All: North Carolina Quakers and Slavery* (Richmond, Ind.: 1984).

15. *Friends Miscellany*, xxii, 216–19, quoted in Rufus Jones, *Later Periods of Quakerism* (London: 1921), I, 406–8.

16. See Medlin, *Quaker Families*, 33; Weeks, *Southern Quakers*, 271–72.

17. See Louis T. Jones, *The Quakers of Iowa* (Iowa City: 1914), 145, 183, 192 ff. See also Myron D. Goldsmith, "William Hobson and the Founding of Quakerism in the Pacific Northwest" (Ph.D. thesis, Boston University, 1962).

18. For Pennsylvania see Jack Marietta, *Reformation*, 6–7; for Indiana, Timothy Terrell, Thomas Hamm, and Frances Fuson have manuscript data. In 1809–80 more Richmond, Indiana, Friends were disowned for "marrying contrary to Discipline" than were married by the Meeting. Hamm also noted an account of the Indiana split in the Hicksite Yearly Meeting minutes.

19. See Whitney Cross, *The Burned-Over District: . . . Western New York, 1800–1850* (Ithaca, N.Y.: 1950); Alice Felt Tyler, *Freedom's Ferment* (Minneapolis: 1944). Most Quakers voted Whig, but David Bowen, "Quaker Orthodoxy and Jacksonian Democracy" (B.A. thesis, Swarthmore College, 1968), has tried to tie up Hicksite with Jacksonian views.

20. See Dorland, *Quakers in Canada*, 104–11. Thomas M.F. Gerry, "Amongst the Assemblies We Hope No More: David Willson's Writings on His Separation from the Quakers," *Journal of Canadian Studies* 20, no. 2 (Summer 1985): 102–117, stressed Willson's emphasis on the Light's universality, against "Orthodox" Friends. Wilkinson was more millenarian.

21. Due to the health and stability of the Quaker's homes, they were noted for longer lives and marriages than other citizens, especially outside Philadelphia: see Susan Edith Klepp, "Philadelphia in Transition: a Demographic History . . . 1720–1830" (Ph.D. thesis, University of Pennsylvania, 1980).

22. Nancy Tomes, "The Domesticated Madman: Changing Concepts of Insanity at Pennsylvania Hospital, 1780–1830," *Pennsylvania Magazine of History and Biography* (hereafter *PMHB*) 106 (1982): 271–86.

23. William K. Sessions and Margaret Sessions, *The Tukes of York* (York, Pa.: 1971).

24. Kim Van Atta, *Account of Friends Hospital* (Philadelphia: 1976), 7–28.

25. Samuel L. Knapp, *The Life of Thomas Eddy*. (Philadelphia: 1834); Nancy Tomes, *Thomas Story Kirkbride* (New York: 1984).

26. *The Burlington Court Book: A Record of Quaker Jurisprudence in West New Jersey, 1680–1709* (Washington, D.C.: 1944), 142–43, for 1692.

27. Negley K. Teeters, *They Were in Prison: A History of the Pennsylvania Prison Society* (Philadelphia: 1937), 1–217; Jacqueline Thibaut, "To Pave the Way to Penitence: Prisoners and Discipline in 18th Century Pennsylvania," *PMHB* 106 (1982): 187–222; Michael Meranz, "The Penitential Ideal in 19th Century Philadelphia," *PMHB* 107, no. 4 (1984): 419–50.

28. John H. Griscom, *Memoir of John Griscom, LL.D.* (New York: 1859).

29. J. William Frost, "Years of Crisis and Separation," in *Friends in the Delaware Valley*, ed. John Moore (Haverford, Pa.: 1981), 62, 60; E. Digby Balzell, *Puritan Boston and Quaker Philadelphia* (Boston: 1979), 196.

14
SEPARATIONS

The search for continuity in the Society of Friends is a fascinating as well as frustrating task. In no other denomination can one generation's emphases be so completely transformed by the next, while both continue to define themselves as remaining faithful to the essence of the faith and in an unbroken tradition of continuing revelation. None of the theological issues confronting Friends in the early nineteenth century was new, and most had been debated at length during the formative years before 1690 when the acceptable perimeters of belief were delineated. Yet disagreement came on fundamentals: what was the Inward Light and how was it connected with Jesus of Nazareth, what was the relationship of intellect and reason to the operation of the Inward Light, what authority did Scripture possess and what power did it convey, how much uniformity in belief was to be required, and who guaranteed the transmission of the authentic faith? Not ethics or ritual but the relation of belief to contrasting experiences of either radical inner obedience or self-surrender to the atonement came increasingly to be seen as decisive and eventually became divisive.

The first indication of the theological controversies that would convulse Quakerism in the nineteenth century came in Ireland. Abraham Shackleton, a schoolmaster and elder in Ballitore, became disturbed at what he saw as Friends' overemphasis upon legalistic Discipline, disownment, Advices, and visiting committees. His first sign of open disagreement came in 1797 when, as a clerk of the Carlow Monthly Meeting of Ministers and Elders, he refused to read the revised Queries because they applied the word *Holy* to the Bible. Shackleton had doubts whether God had commanded the wars in the Old Testament. Early Friends, he claimed, had emphasized the primacy of the experience of the Light of God and had used Scriptures in a secondary role. In 1799 Shackleton was removed as an Elder, and he was disowned in 1801. He was suspected also of sympathy with the French Revolution. Several influential Irish Friends shared

Shackleton's religious sentiments and, when the main body of Friends proved unsympathetic to their position, withdrew.[1]

The same subjects that had perplexed the so-called Irish New Lights resurfaced in the Hannah Barnard* controversy. Hannah Barnard (c. 1754–1825) resembled Anne Hutchinson in many ways. Both women were eloquent, intelligent, courageous, and perceptive—willing to discuss openly the implications of their beliefs. Hannah Barnard, who lived in Hudson, New York, became convinced about age eighteen. She soon became a minister and traveled extensively; in 1797 she received a certificate to visit England. In England during her ministry she made no secret of her pro-French, republican, and democratic manners—insisting, for example, that masters and servants sit together during her family visits. She was an outspoken American woman at a time when many English resented former colonists. Eventually, Barnard went to Ireland where she discussed her beliefs with both the main body of Friends and the New Lights. When some time later Barnard asked the London Yearly Meeting of Ministers and Elders for a certificate so that she could travel in Europe, an Irish minister charged her with being unsound on "important points of doctrine."[2] The Yearly Meeting denied her a certificate and suggested that she return home. When she declined, the Ministers and Elders referred her case to the Devonshire House Monthly Meeting.

In 1801 the London Yearly Meeting undertook a full investigation as to whether Hannah Barnard's beliefs were those of Friends. The issues were the same as for the Irish New Lights—wars in the Old Testament, the miracle stories, the virgin birth. Barnard did not deny the truthfulness of the "historical" accounts contained in the Bible. She could not affirm that the events happened, however, because the Lord had not "revealed" such occurrences to her, although she believed in the power of God to do such wonders. She emphasized the necessity of experiencing the indwelling Christ as the essence of Quakerism, not beliefs in the Trinity or the holy Bible.

Joseph Gurney Bevan denounced Barnard's positions as derogatory to Scripture and to the faith of early Friends. There was nothing in her confession of faith, he declared, that could not have been said by a Unitarian. Bevan defended as essential beliefs God's authorization of the holy wars in the Old Testament, all the miraculous occurrences in either Testament, and the virgin birth. The Yearly Meeting pronounced against Hannah Barnard, and she returned home to be disowned by her Monthly Meeting. In 1801 the London Yearly Meeting in essence had pronounced that Friends believed in the Trinity, in the inerrancy of Scripture, and in the importance of doctrinal orthodoxy. Traveling ministers—Stephen Grellet,* Thomas Shillitoe,* David Sands—would carry the new evangelicalism, concern for doctrinal purity, and fear of Unitarianism and rationalism to America.

The London Yearly Meeting now consisted largely of quietists and evangelicals. Those sympathetic to Hannah Barnard and the Irish New Lights left or were disowned. William Matthews, Edmund Rack, and Henry Portsmouth saw difficulties in the practice of Discipline.[3] They had difficulty in believing that paying tithes and marriage out of unity were so sinful as to merit disownment. When the Meeting disowned these men, there was no major schism because the issues remained at an abstract intellectual level. The moderates wanted a balance of reason, quietism, and evangelicalism. Both quietists and evangelicals, however, saw an attack upon the Truth of Christianity as dangerous. When a few of the same issues that had faced the London Yearly Meeting in 1801 appeared in the Philadelphia Yearly Meeting in the 1820s, English Friends prepared to counter apostasty.

In the early nineteenth century Quakers on both sides of the Atlantic in significant numbers modified or repudiated quietism.[4] In England and America the French Revolution symbolized the excesses to which a worship of reason and attack upon revelation could lead. No longer seen as a perfect guarantor of Truth, quietism seemed inadequate to buttress the faith against the challenges of the enlightenment or an increasingly negative rationalistic religion.

The decline of quietism and rationalism in relation to rising evangelicalism appeared in both England and America. In 1770 the largest church bodies in America were Presbyterian–Congregationalist, Anglican, and Quaker. By 1850 the Methodists and Baptists had numerical dominance, and the Presbyterians continued their growth only by espousing the revival techniques associated with the Second Great Awakening. The rapid increase of immigration, the loss of political power and prestige, and the undynamic quality of traditional Quaker worship stimulated prominent Philadelphia Friends to rethink the implications of their faith.

We cannot now determine whether those American Friends (later termed "Orthodox") became evangelical because English Friends had first embraced these doctrines, because of the pervasive effects of evangelical doctrines in American society, or because they were in search of a method of revitalizing Quakerism and the successful theology at hand was evangelicalism. Quaker evangelicals in England and America belonged to Bible societies, created tract societies, endorsed missionary work, and supported a variety of reform groups advocating temperance, prison reform, peace, and antislavery. Evangelical religion among Quakers is notable for an intense activism. Theology and Church government were the immediate causes of the schism among American Friends, but geography, economic status, and kinship influenced the patterns of division. The Orthodox within the city of Philadelphia comprised a socially cohesive, business oriented, small community.[5] Those in the country who joined them had close contacts with Orthodox leaders, family connections being very important. Hicksites in the city were likely to be recent immigrants from rural areas or families with old wealth like the Biddles and Whartons who resented the commercialism of the rising entrepreneurs. There was a high correlation between evangelical emphasis, residence in a city, ownership of stock, upward mobility, and participation in commercial enterprises. Evangelicals tended to favor close cooperation with other religious groups in a great enterprise to make America a Christian civilization.

Historians attempting to explain why evangelicalism appealed to conservative merchant classes have developed several intriguing hypotheses. One interpretation stresses the ambivalence of Americans wanting wealth yet desirous of a much simpler life than commercialism represented.[6] Those who were prospering in the rapid expansion of Philadelphia desired, unconsciously perhaps, a religion that would enable them to escape from guilt. Supposedly, quietism with its demand for purity and "centering down" was less attractive than evangelicalism with its emphasis upon benevolent activities, conversion, and correct belief.

An alternative explanation views the Quaker merchants as struggling under the dislocation of rapid economic transformation and searching for a means of stability. Evangelical doctrines that stressed the authority of Scripture, historical revelation, and agreement upon the fundamentals of Christianity offered a much more easily attainable certainty than had traditional quietism. Evangelicalism also offered a method of controlling the excesses of American democracy, for the network of benevolent voluntary associations, which would Christianize the workers and the immigrants, would also guarantee the future of American democracy by producing the educated moral citizenry necessary for the functioning of society.[7]

One difficulty with accepting these explanations is that they ignore why people said they were acting as they did. We can establish a correlation between evangelical doctrines and new wealth, but we cannot prove that evangelicals were more insecure and more worried about America than liberals or quietists. Sufficient numbers of Quaker country dwellers became Orthodox and enough city merchants became Hicksites to make any psychological interpretation suspect. A more plausible hypothesis is that evangelicalism was used by part of the leadership of the Philadelphia Yearly Meeting in an attempt to revitalize the Society of Friends. In London an older traditional quietist leadership gradually died off, and although there were serious conflicts, there was no major separation. Urban Philadelphia Friends who became Orthodox were more likely than were the Hicksites to have visited England and to have entertained English Friends in their homes. Since Philadelphia Quakers, even while claiming equality of Yearly Meetings, stood very much in awe of English respectability, the traveling English ministers' fear of heresy and advocacy of evangelical doctrines had a powerful influence. City Friends may have felt the growing numerical insignificance of Quakers more than country dwellers.

Evangelicalism flourished when there was an enemy to identify, and the danger in the 1820s came from free thinkers, rationalists, and Unitarians. In Massachusetts the old Puritan doctrines had gradually been undermined by rational religion. When the evangelical Congregationalists discovered the danger and sought to regain control of the churches, the Unitarians, aided by court decisions on who could vote on parish-property matters, took control of most of the important Congregational Churches around Boston. The battles between Unitarians and evangelicals occurred simultaneously with developing controversies in the Philadelphia Yearly Meeting. Those Quakers who formed the Orthodox party thought they were fighting the same battle for Christianity going on in Boston.

The evangelicals accused their opponents of undervaluing Jesus Christ. The authoritative source of knowledge about Jesus was the Bible, which proclaimed that Christ shed his blood as a sacrifice to satisfy the justice of God and thereby save humankind. No one could be saved without the blood of Christ, and the image of the suffering Jesus on the cross was central for Orthodox piety. Christ was equal with God, a person in the Trinity, born of the Virgin and without sin. The virgin birth, Scriptural inerrancy, the Trinity, a physical resurrection, and heaven and hell became important to evangelicals mainly as guarantees of the atonement. Orthodox Friends did not stress an emotional conversion experience but did insist that certain revelation, obtained only in the Holy Scriptures, was authenticated by the experience of the Holy Spirit.[8]

In opposition to the evangelicals were those Friends whom their opponents later called "Hicksites" but who, like the "Orthodox," thought of themselves simply as Friends. The Orthodox are more easily identifiable because they had a common program: stamp out infidelity in the Meeting. The Hicksite party was formed in opposition to that of the Orthodox, and it made little attempt to formulate its views in a systematic fashion.

The largest faction among Hicksites was the traditional quietists who accepted the Truth of Scripture, the divinity of Christ, and the resurrection. But the symbol they emphasized above all else was the indwelling Christ. Truth in religion could be guaranteed by no external focus like the Bible, and theology was "head learning" of no great significance. Ministers preached under the direct leading of the Spirit, and the authenticity of their beliefs was confirmed by their lives and by the response within the believers. The outward blood of Christ had once been shed, but people were now saved by the inward bearing of His cross. Bringing the Light of Christ to bear upon a corrupt will was a long, difficult process and resulted not in a creed or belief but a sanctified life. Justification and sanctification occurred together continuously through a Christian's witness. If all Hicksites had been quietists, there probably would have been no division, since there was a quietist majority also among the Orthodox.

Within the membership of those who became Hicksites were some—their numbers cannot be determined with any accuracy, but they were a distinct minority—who also wanted to revitalize Friends but whose motivating impulses were formed by a more critical or rational approach to traditional Quakerism and Christian doctrines. Like the quietists, these members disliked creeds, but their opposition was based upon a newly emerging view of Church history. The most distinguished Church historian of the eighteenth century was the German Protestant Johan Mosheim, who viewed the development of doctrine as understandable in terms of prevailing philosophical systems and political and social needs of the times. Mosheim attempted to treat the various "heresies" of the early Church sympathetically and not to assume that a mysterious hidden revelation guaranteed the truth of the decisions of church councils. A Friend reading Mosheim's description of the developments of trinitarian doctrine could easily come to assume that the final formulation was a historical accident and not to be taken as equivalent in authority to the Scripture.[9] Some of Elias Hicks's* emphases sound like Mosheim added to quietism. The Quakers who edited *The Berean*, a periodical first published in 1825 in Wilmington by David Ferris and James Gibbons, clearly had read Mosheim and absorbed some of his historical relativism.[10]

A second source for Quaker *liberalism* (the term in the 1820s described those criticizing evangelical doctrines on the basis of reason) came from rational Christianity and Scottish Common Sense philosophy. What these movements sought was a clear, reasonable, and benevolent deity who would appeal to human intellect. Mystery or emotion had little role in religion and only encouraged priestcraft, superstition, and despotism. Presbyterians were particularly suspect, and the liberals accused them of using a benevolent empire of reform to create a religious establishment.

All of the symbols most precious to the evangelicals seemed suspect to the liberals. Early Quakers had opposed the term *Trinity* as unscriptural; liberal Quakers thought the whole concept was absurd. God, a benevolent father, did not need a substitutionary atonement to achieve his justice. In fact, just to attempt to conceive of an eternal being dividing into three persons and then deciding to sacrifice one part to another made no sense. Liberals used a variety of methods of interpreting the Bible. Like Origen and the early Church fathers, these Friends allegorized the creation story in Genesis, parts of the Bible that made no sense unless interpreted figuratively and much that was usually called history. Miracles proved the Bible was true, but how miracles occurred was not important, only the "fact" that they had happened.[11] Inward revelation—the term *inner light* now began to replace the Inward Light of Christ—served as a scientific guarantee of the Truth of not only Quakerism but also Christianity. If for evangelicals the blood of Christ was the prime symbol, for liberals it was freedom: freedom from dogma, from hierarchy, from superstition. Most of the literature of the Orthodox–Hicksite separation was written by evangelicals or liberals who forgot who their opponents actually were as they waged battles against imaginary and pernicious evil men.

Elias Hicks (1748–1830) appears almost incidental against the backdrop of intellectual and social division in the Society of Friends, but the controversies surrounding him brought on the schism and determined the way the two new groups would develop. The character of Hicks's thought is best described as that of an extreme quietist or spiritualist tinged with rationalism. Formal theology he saw as "head learning" designed to foster pride and destroy godliness. During his travels as a minister, Hicks preached against outward knowledge of evangelical doctrines. When called to account, he claimed immediate inspiration and insisted that he was in unity with the Meetings where he spoke. If Orthodox accounts can be believed—neither Hicksite nor Orthodox were objective—Hicks on one occasion compared the "virtue" of the outward blood of Christ with the blood of a chicken.[12] As early as 1808 an English Quaker traveling with Hicks found his communications unsound, but many American Friends found Hicks an inspiring preacher, and during his travels throughout America he attracted large crowds and kept the full support of his Monthly, Quarterly, and Yearly Meetings in New York.

Orthodox Friends were at a distinct disadvantage in the struggle over silencing Elias Hicks. Hicks, who was seventy-six in 1824, had spent most of his adult life in the service of Friends, and his quietist posture and eloquence reminded listeners, particularly in rural communities, of the kind of Quakerism with which they had grown up. His strictures on worldliness, against commercialism, and in favor of a strong antislavery position, including a boycott of materials produced by slave labor, found a sympathetic audience outside the cities. Because Hicks insisted on the need for harmony and for the autonomy of the Light, his opponents seemed to many to be advocating thought control and denying freedom of worship when they claimed only to be defending Christianity. The liberals linked their cause with Elias Hicks and the Green Street Monthly Meeting and represented the contest as between an emergent priest class, supported by visiting ministers from aristocratic England, against the efficacy of the Inward Light, holy living, and the autonomy of local Meetings.

The Orthodox experienced frustration in dealing with what seemed a fundamental challenge to the faith. Elias Hicks appeared maddeningly evasive when the normally reliable disciplinary procedures failed to work. When elders and ministers attempted to declare the fundamentals of Christianity, they encountered opposition from country Friends both in the Meeting for Sufferings and the Yearly Meeting. Worse, they found themselves pilloried as pseudo-Presbyterians and aristocrats. In an age when rural–urban tensions were high and elitism was decried as un-American, these devout Philadelphia Quakers, whose prosperity was a blessing from God and a tribute to their hard work, were being defied by less educated, less affluent, less sophisticated farmers. Unable to silence Hicks or even gain an acknowledgment of error from him, and hampered by his sympathizers even within the city, the Orthodox decided to employ the agencies at their disposal: the support of English Friends, predominance in the Meeting for Sufferings and Meeting of Ministers and Elders, and the clerkship of the Yearly Meeting.

From 1819, when Jonathan Evans, a former clerk of the Yearly Meeting and elder of the Philadelphia Monthly Meeting, first publicly manifested his disapproval of Elias Hicks, the controversy grew rapidly.[13] Visiting ministers from England like William Forster, Anna Braithwaite, and Elizabeth Robson disagreed with Hicks and openly preached against him. A controversy in a religious journal from 1820 to 1823 between a Presbyterian minister and Benjamin Ferris, a Wilmington Friend, brought the charge that Quakers denied the essence of Christianity with a reply enunciating a liberal version of what Friends required.[14] The tone of the Quaker response irritated the evangelical members of the Meeting for Sufferings who proceeded to compile a list of extracts from the writings of early Friends to prove that Quakers were Orthodox Christians. The extracts were strongly evangelical and the supporters of Hicks and Ferris objected to the publication of any such "creed" with the imprimatur of the Meeting for Sufferings. The maneuverings and charges of both sides, which climaxed in a debate in the Yearly Meeting, showed the depth of distrust and animosity.[15]

In the city of Philadelphia all Monthly Meetings except the Green Street Meeting opposed Hicks, who continued to travel in the ministry and came to visit in 1822 and again in 1826. When Hicks attended different Meetings and spoke, opponents testified against him and disruptions occurred. The elders insisted that Hicks did not believe that Jesus Christ was the only begotten Son of God and attempted to forbid him from preaching. The Philadelphia elders now shifted from using the Discipline for morals to using it for theology. The Friends of Green Street, incensed that several of its elders cooperated in this venture, attempted to discipline one elder who sided with the Orthodox and to replace others. On appeal, the Philadelphia Quarterly Meeting overruled the Green Street Monthly Meeting and reinstated the elders, denying that local Meetings had the authority to replace elders who had done no wrong. When the Green Street Meeting defied the Quarterly Meeting, the Orthodox moved to lay down the Meeting; in response, the Green Street Meeting attempted to secede from the Philadelphia Quarterly Meeting and to join the Abington Quarterly Meeting. The Mt. Holly Meeting in New Jersey transferred to the Bucks Quarterly Meeting in an attempt to leave the Orthodox-dominated Burlington Quarterly Meeting.[16] The issue now became constitutional: did effective power rest with a Monthly Meeting or a Quarterly Meeting? That question would be dealt with in the 1827 Yearly Meeting.

Since the 1760s in both England and America, the Yearly Meetings had appointed committees to visit local Meetings and persuade the members to achieve uniformity in disciplinary practices. In 1827, in spite of the opposition of some Friends, the Ministers and Elders Meeting decided to ask the Yearly Meeting for a visiting committee to investigate the doctrine of members.[17] The Hicksites saw the evangelicals as aiming at silencing and disowning all of those who opposed them.

Samuel Bettle, clerk of the Philadelphia Yearly Meeting, testifying in court after the schism, declared that he was accustomed to recognizing to speak and to considering only the advice of reliable Friends, that is, the Orthodox.[18] In an attempt to safeguard their interests, the anti-evangelicals appointed double the normal number of representatives to the 1827 Yearly Meeting. Country Friends decided that protection of their freedom required the elevation of the assistant clerk, John Comly,* to the clerkship. The disunity manifested in Monthly, Quarterly, and Yearly Meetings was so distressing to Comly that early in 1827 he began discussing with certain members whether in the event of continued bickering a peaceful solution might be a temporary withdrawal.

The Yearly Meetings' sessions opened with a deadlock over continuing Bettle or nominating Comly as clerk, but after a protracted dispute Bettle continued to serve since he had previously been clerk. Sympathizers of Comly began holding special sessions in the evening at the Green Street Meeting to debate appropriate action. When, in the last session, without general approval, the clerk appointed a special committee composed of evangelicals to visit each Meeting to test the soundness of the membership, separation became inevitable.

If relationships between Friends were unedifying before the Yearly Meeting, that bickering came to seem almost harmonious in the events that followed. Both groups called themselves the Philadelphia Yearly Meeting and claimed to be the only authentic Quakers; each accused the other of assorted despicable practices. The Orthodox position was that the Hicksites were neither Quakers nor Christians, and since originally all Quakers had been Christians, all property should belong to them as legitimate heirs of the first Friends. Compromise and division of property with heretics would betray Christianity, and the separatists should be disowned as soon as possible. Marriage between an Orthodox and a Hicksite was joining a Christian and an infidel. The Hicksite position was that property should be divided, probably on numerical lines, a position that had many advantages for the more numerous Hicksites.

In virtually all Meetings there were scenes in which either Hicksite or Orthodox took control, and although both sides proclaimed peace and love, they acted with passion and cunning. Personal vituperation, disownments, court trials, divisions of Meetings, expulsion of Hicksite pupils from Orthodox schools, and an outpouring of tracts kept the animosity burning for years.

A trial in New Jersey over a trust fund showed a breakdown in communication between both sides. The Orthodox thought the division was over theology and insisted upon discussing beliefs; the Hicksites thought the division was over Church government and, while refusing any discussions of theology, talked about the rights of members.[19]

Only in the city of Philadelphia did the Orthodox have a clear-cut majority. Elsewhere the Hicksites were dominant and they claimed that twenty-eight of the original Monthly Meetings remained Hicksite whereas only three became Orthodox. Burlington, Haddonfield, and Westtown had strong Orthodox constituencies. A convenient approximation is that Hicksites had 70 percent and the Orthodox 30 percent of the members.[20] Orthodox Friends kept control of the Arch Street meeting-house, Westtown School, and Friends Asylum.

Within a year both Philadelphia groups had reorganized and during the same month held separate Yearly Meetings. Both Yearly Meetings attempted to keep communications with the London Yearly Meeting and sent Epistles expecting to have them answered. London remained strongly evangelical, and English ministers had helped precipitate the schism by their stringent views. The predictable result was that London communicated only with evangelical Yearly Meetings and refused to recognize the Hicksites as Quakers. Orthodox relations with Presbyterians and Methodists also improved, since evangelicals in many donominations sympathized with the battle against infidelity. Naturally, the Hicksites found sympathy among Unitarians and Transcendentalists.

As if the separation in Philadelphia were not serious enough, both sides attempted to gain vindication from other Yearly Meetings and so managed to precipitate divisions in Baltimore, New York, Ohio, and Indiana. The history of the schisms in the New York and the Baltimore Yearly Meetings lends some credence to the hypothesis that urban–rural tensions helped determine who chose which side. Most of the pro-Orthodox Friends in these two Yearly Meetings lived in New York City and Baltimore.[21] Many had been prosperous merchants and had been involved in reform activities. The Hicksites had a majority of three-quarters or more in both Yearly Meetings. Hicks was from Long Island and was widely known. The leader of the opposing faction, Thomas Shillitoe from England, could not gain the support of the Meeting for Sufferings in New York. Recognizing that the walkout at the Philadelphia Yearly Meeting had occasioned the Hicksites to lose property, their sympathizers in Baltimore and New York determined not to withdraw. Instead, they recognized the credentials of Elias Hicks and of traveling ministers from the Philadelphia Yearly Meeting, Hicksite. Outnumbered, the Orthodox left the Meeting in protest. Both sides organized competing Yearly Meetings. In New York the Hicksites claimed 12,352 adherents, the Orthodox claimed 5,913, and there were 857 neutral; as they were in Philadelphia, the Hicksites were strongest in the oldest rural Meetings.[22]

Why the Hicksites were a larger proportion of the Baltimore Yearly Meeting than of any other (roughly four to one) while North Carolina and the dwindling Virginia Yearly Meeting stayed linked to the Philadelphia "Orthodox" is not clear, but the Meetings on both sides of Chesapeake Bay were older and more isolated than any others in America. After 1828 all of the old meeting-houses remained in Hicksite hands except for the sharing of Hopewell in the Shenandoah Valley; outside of Baltimore City most Meetings in the Baltimore Orthodox Yearly Meeting were in southern Pennsylvania.[23]

In New England, North Carolina, Virginia, and Ohio the rural–urban hypothesis does not work. North Carolina Friends remained overwhelmingly rural and very Orthodox in sympathy. There were so few Hicksites that the Yearly Meeting's recognition of only Orthodox ministers occasioned no division. The same is true for the New England Friends, although keeping peace there was easier because of an earlier withdrawal of the "New Light" Friends from New Bedford who became Unitarians.

In Ohio, in 1828, the presence of visiting ministers, Elias Hicks and Amos Peaslee for the Hicksites and Thomas Shillitoe and Isaac and Anna Braithwaite from England, precipitated the bitter separation. After the division in Philadelphia, partisan ministers from both sides traveled to other Yearly Meetings seeking vindication by having their certificates accepted and endorsed. They also brought Epistles from their Yearly Meetings. Hicks had visited Ohio Meetings in 1819 to general satisfaction. His return in 1828 divided the Meetings.

The separations in Ohio began at the Monthly and Quarterly Meeting levels. By the time for the 1828 Ohio Yearly Meeting in Mt. Pleasant, the competing Meetings had authorized two sets of delegates. As in Philadelphia, the clerk in Ohio was Orthodox, and so the Hicksites decided he must be replaced. Not to be overcome, the Orthodox determined to control the Yearly Meeting by using door keepers who allowed only their partisans to enter the meeting-house. The Hicksite men appeared en masse before the doors and shoved their way inside. The Meeting opened with a dispute over clerks, continued in chaos, and disintegrated into a riot. Both sides came to the Yearly Meeting fully organized into rival Quarterly Meetings (except for Redstone), and with many Monthly Meetings already divided, following a clash between the Concord Meeting and its overseers from the Short Creek Quarterly Meeting. Only forty-six meetings remained undivided, thirty-eight of them Orthodox. The Orthodox emerged with eighty-five Monthly Meetings (later adding ten more) and about 10,000 members; the Hicksites had fifty-six meetings (of which only twenty survived to the Civil War) and 6,000 members.[24]

The Orthodox were strongest at the northern area of the Yearly Meeting around Salem, where Pennsylvania settlers were concentrated, and in the Barnesville area. Virginians and Marylanders who settled around Mt. Pleasant and the Deerfield community west on the Muskingum became Hicksite.[25]

In the Indiana Yearly Meeting the split was quieter; the oldest Meetings such as Waynesville Meeting in Miami Valley mostly remained Hicksite, but the Orthodox, who were centered in Richmond, outnumbered them nearly ten to one and took over most of the schools. In the West, in Illinois, the Clear Creek Meeting at McNabb was planted in 1830 by Hicksites from the Redstone–Westland–Short Creek area of the Ohio Yearly Meeting. Around it grew the Illinois Yearly Meeting (Hicksite).[26]

REORGANIZATION

After the initial controversy had subsided, a main Orthodox principle became preventing a repetition of the Hicksite schism. The first requisite was a clear statement of what Friends believed, and a general gathering of representatives from the Orthodox Yearly Meetings took place in Baltimore. The fruit of the Meeting was *The Testimony of the Society of Friends in the Continent of North America* (1831), a tract of thirty pages, sponsored by eight Orthodox Yearly Meetings. This was followed by the reprinting of works of early Quakers.[27]

The second phase of the Orthodox revitalization was the elimination of any ambiguity in Discipline that had been cited by the Hicksites as justification. The result was a much more tightly centralized and hierarchical structure with power explicitly vested in the Yearly Meeting and the Meeting for Sufferings. In revisions of the Discipline in 1832 and 1834 the Philadelphia Yearly Meeting adopted new procedures for laying down Meetings, disowning or disciplining ministers and members even if the Monthly Meeting to which they belonged did nothing, and restricting the freedom of ministers to travel and visit.

The power to disown over matters of belief was made explicit. Any member could be disciplined and disowned for "printing, selling, or distributing books or papers which tend to the denial or laying waste a belief in the divinity, mediation, and atonement of our Lord and Savior Jesus Christ, the immediate influence of the Holy Spirit, or the authenticity and divine inspiration of the Holy Scriptures."[28] Anyone who denied the propitiatory sacrifice of Christ "without us" was guilty of blasphemy. Believing that the schism came because of widespread ignorance of Scripture, in 1829 a group of prominent Friends, including members from several Yearly Meetings, issued an appeal for a Bible Association of Friends in America whose main function was to print and distribute Bibles at little or no cost to Friends schools and families. The headquarters was in Philadelphia and with its auxiliary branches (by 1831 there were twenty-one) distributed Bibles throughout America. The society estimated that during the first five years of existence it printed and distributed nearly 10,000 Bibles and 8,000 New Testaments.[29]

If the Orthodox assumed that belief in the inerrancy of the Bible and stipulations in the Discipline would guarantee harmony, they were disappointed. The Philadelphia Yearly Meeting (Orthodox) never separated again, but the differences between evangelical and quietist members severely strained unity—particularly after divisions among the Orthodox Yearly Meetings in New England (1838) and in Ohio (1854). Samuel Bettle, who had been clerk at the time of the Hicksite controversy, had concluded that that division was a tragedy and not worth the bitterness it had engendered. He wanted at all cost to avoid a repetition, even at the cost of consistency. In 1855 the Philadelphia Meeting suspended communication with New England Yearly Meeting (Gurneyite) giving no reason for the action. Finally, in 1857 the Philadelphia Meeting decided to have no correspondence with anyone. Isolation might preserve a semblance of unity.

The two factions in the Philadelphia Yearly Meeting (Orthodox) endured. Quietists' strength in the city was centered at the Arch Street Monthly Meeting and the Tract Society. Their publication was *The Friend*. Gurneyite members attended the Twelfth Street Meeting and supported Haverford College. Their publication was *The Friends Review*, begun in 1847. Official Yearly Meeting sessions brought both groups together for worship and for cooperation on a limited range of traditional activities, Westtown School, and the Indian Committee. In the evening Wilburites went home, and the evangelicals met at Twelfth Street to discuss their distinctive concerns. Thomas Pym Cope, who stopped attending all meetings for business because he did not like the acrimony, exemplified the response of many Quakers.[30]

If in the 1830s the Orthodox had a quietist majority and an evangelical minority, the Philadelphia Hicksites had a quietist majority and a liberal minority. But the Hicksites had an easier time of staying together because they believed in decentralized authority and were unwilling to disown over matters of doctrine. They did not, however, endorse subjectivism. They believed that "God alone is the sovereign Lord of Conscience," but their Discipline required disownment for denying the divinity of Christ or the "authenticity" of Scripture.[31] The Yearly Meeting made only slight changes in the Discipline. To emphasize its subordinate position, the Meeting for Sufferings, when reestablished, was called the Representative Meeting and its power over publications diluted. Monthly Meetings received the right to change elders. Friends disowned by the Orthodox could be admitted to Philadelphia Hicksite Meetings on their own request.[32]

The liberal faction saw the division as an opportunity to reconsider certain disciplinary practices, but the quietist majority resisted basic changes of any kind, feeling that preservation of Quaker traditions was the surest method of proving continuity between George Fox and the nineteenth century. The Hicksite Philadelphia Yearly Meeting warned against taking part in non-Quaker activities in 1838 and against participation in political strife in 1840.

A reform movement associated with the Hicksites, though drawing members and ideas from others, was the Progressive or Congregational Friends of Longwood.[33] Established in the 1840s for religious, social, and educational changes, Longwood Friends advocated a religion of humanity that stressed the inherent goodness and perfectibility of humankind. They identified with what they saw as the spirit of Fox and Woolman, and, like Emerson, preached an inner light that linked humanity to nature and God. Longwood Friends disliked dogma and their real commitment was to reform. Their causes exemplify antebellum crusades: Garrison-type abolitionism, temperance, women's rights, opposition to capital punishment, prison reform, homestead legislation, pacifism, Indian rights, economic regulation, and practical and coeducational schooling.

Edward Hicks, famous for paintings of the *Peaceable Kingdom*, was a quietist Hicksite who saw in the liberalism of the Motts and the Progressive Friends the destruction of traditional Quakerism. Hicks, who had strongly opposed the Orthodox, before his death in 1849 saw what he called the essential similarity between the quietists in the two Yearly Meetings. In 1846 at the time of the death of Jonathan Evans, the elder who so strongly opposed Elias Hicks, Edward Hicks wrote: "should I ever be permitted to enter the abodes of the ransomed and redeemed of the Lord, I shall hope to see the angelic spirit of dear Jonathan Evans and Elias Hicks, clothed in white raiment, with palms of victory in their hands, united forever."[34]

In retrospect, the schism did immense and irreparable harm to all Yearly Meetings and diluted the impact of Friends upon American society. Virtually all Quakers continued to press for Indian rights, temperance, pacifism, and legal equality for blacks in South and North. The Meetings' methods for changing people were love of neighbor, moral example, and appeals to reason. Against the rising tide of animosity between regions, Friends pleaded for moderation, gradual reform, and respect. Unfortunately, everyone could see that Quakers did not practice toward each other what they advocated for everyone else.

A second result of the division was the removal of countervailing tendencies within segments of a divided Quakerism. A system of carefully balanced emphases—Inward Light and Scripture, quietism and evangelism, individual initiative and group authority—built up over 150 years disappeared as Orthodox and Hicksites engaged in selective exegesis of biblical and Quaker sources. The results were simplified versions of the faith in which neither body could resist additional controversies. Some Hicksites flirted with Unitarianism, transcendentalism, and spiritualism, while some Orthodox espoused a narrow revivalism and others canonized an ossified quietism.

A positive but unintended aftermath of the separation was the dawn of toleration within the Society of Friends. During the seventeenth century Friends fought for religious freedom in England, but toleration of error stopped at the boundaries of the Meeting. Such confidence or rigidity could be easily maintained if virtually all members, or all influential ministers and elders, agreed on what constituted the Truth. In the 1820s the Philadelphia Friends made the traumatic discovery that the eighteenth-century consensus had vanished and could not be refashioned. Ministerial authority, disownment, tract writing, vituperation, and schism only brought to light additional disagreements. Ever so slowly, and most begrudgingly, Friends learned to live with, respect, and even love individuals within their Meetings with whom they had profound differences. Such tolerance of diversity brought the birth of modern Quakerism.

NOTES

1. Rufus Jones, *Later Periods of Quakerism* (London: 1921), I, 293-311; William Rathbone, *A Narrative of Events That Have Lately Taken Place in Ireland among the Society Called Quakers* (London: 1804).

2. J. William Frost, ed., *Records and Recollections of James Jenkins* (New York: 1984), 339–80.

3. Ibid., xl, 181.

4. Elizabeth Isichei, *Victorian Quakers* (London: 1970), 1–52 is the standard source on English Friends in this period.

5. Robert Doherty, *The Hicksite Separation* (New Brunswick, N.J.: 1967), 33–66; H. Larry Ingle, *Quakers in Conflict: The Hicksite Reformation* (Knoxville, Tenn. 1986), is the best survey of events leading to the separation.

6. Marvin Myers, *The Jacksonian Persuasion* (Stanford; Calif.: 1957).

7. Lois Banner, "Religious Benevolence as Social Control," *Journal of American History* 60 (1973): 23–41; David Bowen, "Quaker Orthodoxy and Jacksonian Democracy" (M.A. thesis, Swarthmore College, 1968).

8. *The Friend* 1 (1827): 38, 344.

9. There were several English editions of Johan Mosheim, *An Ecclesiastical History,*

Ancient and Modern. The Philadelphia edition of 1812 contained a refutation of the discussion of Friends signed by a clerk of the Philadelphia Yearly Meeting.

10. *The Berean* (Wilmington: 1826), I, 13.

11. Ibid., 27–28, 298; *The Friend* 1 (1827): 344; 2 (1828): 382–83.

12. Bliss Forbush, *Elias Hicks, Quaker Liberal* (New York: 1956); *The Friend* 1 (1827): 204, 341; Elizabeth Robson quoted in Edwin B. Bronner, *The Other Branch: London Yearly Meeting and the Hicksites* (London: 1975), 7.

13. William Bacon Evans, *Jonathan Evans and His Time* (Boston: 1959), contains the best detailed description of the 1827 Yearly Meeting.

14. *Letters of Paul and Amicus, Originally Published in the Christian Repository* (Wilmington: 1823).

15. Forbush, *Elias Hicks*, 218–20.

16. *The Friend* 1 (1827): 174, 182–83; Samuel Janney, *History of the Religious Society of Friends* (Philadelphia: 1867), IV, 236–45, 273–74.

17. Philadelphia Yearly Meeting of Ministers and Elders, Minutes, 1827, 161; Philadelphia Yearly Meeting, Minutes, 1827, 412–29.

18. Jeremiah Foster, ed., *An Authentic Report of the Testimony in a Cause at Issue* (Philadelphia: 1831), I, 36, 82.

19. Ibid., I, 21–22, 34–35, 50, 61.

20. *The Berean*, (1828) I, 176–77 claimed a division of 15,699 to 4, 256; in court the Hicksite census claimed 18,485, Orthodox 7,344, neutral 429. Thomas Evans in six quarters found 1,979 more Orthodox and 1,332 fewer Hicksites. The Hicksite figures showed that the division in Philadelphia was approximately equal; the Orthodox claimed a majority of 2,926 to 1,461 adults. Two-thirds of the ministers and elders became Orthodox. Janney, *History*, IV, 287; Foster, *Authentic Report*, II, 495; *The Friend* 2 (1828): 141–43; *The Berean*, I, 145–46.

21. Bliss Forbush, *History of Baltimore Yearly Meeting of Friends* (1972), 66; Anne Thomas, *The Story of Baltimore Yearly Meeting from 1672–1938* (Baltimore: c. 1938), 52.

22. Jones, *Later Periods*, 477.

23. Forbush, *History*, Ch. 9; Kenneth Carroll, in *Quakerism on the Eastern Shore* (Baltimore: 1970), hardly mentioned the Hicksite Separation.

24. Jones, *Later Periods*, 477–81; James H. Norton, "Quakers West of the Alleghenies and in Ohio to 1861" (Ph.D. diss., Western Reserve University, 1965), Ch. 6.

25. Norton, "Quakers West," 157, 161ff.

26. Marion Lundy Dobert and Helen Jean Nelson, *The Friends at Clear Creek: 1830–1930* (Dekalb, Ill.: 1975).

27. In 1837 William and Thomas Evans began issuing the fourteen volumes of *The Friends Library: Comprising Journals, Doctrinal Treatises, and Other Writings*. The Hicksites created a ten-volume *Friends Miscellany* beginning in 1831, published the *Works* of George Fox in eight volumes, and reprinted William Penn's *The Sandy Foundation Shaken*.

28. Philadelphia Yearly Meeting (Orthodox) *Rules of Discipline* (Philadelphia: 1834), 25.

29. Edwin B. Bronner, *Sharing the Scriptures: The Bible Association of Friends in America* (Philadelphia: 1979).

30. Thomas Pym Cope, *Philadelphia Merchant: The Diary of Thomas P. Cope, 1800–1851*, ed. Eliza Cope Harrison (South Bend, Ind.: 1978), 402, 417, 420–21, 430.

31. Philadelphia Yearly Meeting (Hicksite), Minutes, 1827, 4; idem, *Rules of Discipline* (1831), 23.

32. Philadelphia Yearly Meeting (Hicksite), Minutes, (1829) 47, 50–51; (1836) 159; idem, *Rules of Discipline*, (1831), 26.

33. Albert J. Wahl, "The Congregational of Progressive Friends in the Pre-Civil War Reform Movement" (Ed.D. diss., Temple University, 1951).

34. *Memoirs of Edward Hicks* (Philadelphia: 1851), 138.

15

THE MIDCONTINENT IN THE MIDCENTURY, 1828–1867: GURNEYITES, CONSERVATIVES, AND SLAVERY

In 1822 Elisha Bates* of Mount Pleasant, Ohio, printed a detailed list of the sixteen Monthly Meetings in Ohio Yearly Meeting and the twenty-eight in the newly made Indiana Yearly Meeting. He did not estimate membership, perhaps because of constant new settlement. After the Hicksite separation the Discipline book and silent worship remained the same in Meetings of both Quaker branches.[1] Once the logs and the Meetings were split Quaker farm life in Ohio and Indiana did not change dramatically until the coming of canals, the railroads, and the Civil War.

For the evangelicals, doctrinal Truth, and for the Hicksites, freedom from the authority of the elders remained the key issues of difference. Orthodox leaders used strictly their power to "elder" and "disown" Friends on issues of doctrine, whereas the Hicksites maintained traditional Quaker patterns of ethics and plain dress and speech. Ethically uncompromising Friends have often disagreed over the central leaders' authority to discipline individualists. John Woolman's* "Reformers" had "disowned" Friends over ethics. In the nineteenth century the Hicksites, with similar ethics, opposed powerful elders and insisted on the autonomy of each local Meeting. The Orthodox insisted that Yearly Meetings could override Monthly Meetings' decisions: many wanted a uniform Book of Discipline for all American Friends.[2]

Elisha Bates was clerk of the Ohio Yearly Meeting for five years before and after the Hicksite split and wrote a book much read and reprinted among the Orthodox, *The Doctrines of Friends* (1825). Like Joseph John Gurney's* *Observations*, it kept the traditional Quaker emphases on the primacy of the inward Spirit over the Scriptures, on silent worship without sacraments, and the universality of grace; but Bates in very uncompromising language also stressed sin, atonement, the divinity of Christ, the authority of sacred Scriptures, miracles, and the Devil. By 1828, Ohio's year of decision, Bates was particularly stern in disowning "infidels."

Indiana Friends were less bitter. In 1836 Joseph John Gurney left Philadelphia less than a week after he had landed from England to hurry westward in a hired coach along the newly cleared but unpaved National Road to attend the Ohio and Indiana Orthodox Yearly Meetings. In Richmond he addressed 3,000 Friends camped with covered wagons by the Yearly Meeting-house. He found there Stephen Grellet* from Philadelphia. Gurney was impressed by the Hoosiers, and they feasted him royally. He ignored the Hicksites and went west sixty miles to put straight the Duck Creek Meeting on the doctrine of physical Resurrection.[3]

THE HICKSITES

Even in Ohio and Indiana the Hicksites lived in isolated Quaker communities detached from the pressures of society. Some opposed railroads and canals, which most Orthodox Quakers hailed as signs of progress but which made farm life more worldly and city centered.[4] The Hicksite Meetings slowly withered throughout the century. Their Ohio Yearly Meeting ceased to meet in the 1940s, and the Indiana Hicksites shrank to five active Meetings until they were revived by the upsurge of twentieth-century college-town Meetings. By contrast, the Indiana Orthodox held their own, even after "setting off" the Iowa and Western Yearly Meetings in 1858 and 1863. In 1845 the London *Friend* estimated Indiana at 30,000 out of the 81,000 Orthodox (and 23,000 Hicksites) in America.[5]

A key contrast of Orthodox and Hicksites in Ohio and Indiana, as in Philadelphia, was in their attitudes to organizing committees for service and outreach. The meager handwritten minute books of the midwestern Hicksite Yearly Meetings focus on memorials for deceased members and curt summaries of replies to Queries on "the State of the Society."[6] They list from two to a dozen visitors annually from eastern Hicksite Yearly Meetings, evidently vital to their survival. From 1833 there was also a committee to start schools for freed "colored" families settled in Brown and Highland counties near the Ohio River. From 1857 to 1864 Indiana Hicksites also ran schools for blacks in Dublin and Richmond, Indiana, and Alum Creek, Ohio. But the Ohio and Indiana Indian Committees complained that "no way has opened, as the [Indian school] establishment is in the hands of our [Orthodox] oppressors," until they found they could share Baltimore's Indian projects.[7]

THE ORTHODOX YEARLY MEETINGS

The Orthodox Friends early circulated their minutes in print. These minutes also contained lists of representatives and visitors, memorials, and Yearly Meeting Epistles, but most of the space and concern went to detailed reports of committee activities. Many of these reports were duplicated by smaller, corresponding Quarterly and Monthly Meeting Committees. Ohio and Indiana Yearly Meetings and later Western and Iowa Yearly Meetings reported on elementary day schools, First-Day (Sunday) Schools, boarding schools for Friends, and various vocational schools for Friends and other groups. Both Ohio and Indiana tried unsuccessfully to start asylums like those in Philadelphia. The longest reports often came from committees on tract and Bible distribution, on work with Indians, and from a "colored" or "African Committee." By 1835 only nineteen Indiana Orthodox Quaker families lacked Bibles, after distributions in all Quaker schools and First-Day Schools. By 1860 the Indiana Central Book and Tract Committee, which had for thirty years sent copies of each tract to 3,000 members, had sent 122,000 tracts, totaling a million pages, to non-Friends and Quaker books to all of the county libraries.[8]

THE WILBURITE SEPARATION

Endless committee meetings and the appeals for funds for their projects became sore points in a conflict that arose within the Orthodox Quaker ranks between the activists, or "Gurneyites," and those calling themselves "Conservative," (often labeled "Wilburites"). At first the latter were much like rural Hicksites in outlook if not in doctrine. In New England an open break had already come by 1845 between John Wilbur's* mainly rural Rhode Island supporters and the more urban elders of the Yearly Meeting. The issue was Wilbur's effort to follow Joseph John Gurney around a circuit of New England Meetings to warn them that Gurney's encouragement of Bible study and Sunday School programs conflicted with the heart of quietist Quaker worship: dependence solely on God. When Wilbur's home Meeting at South Kingston, Rhode Island, refused to discipline him, the Yearly Meeting tried to dissolve it and then the Quarterly Meeting, which persisted in supporting him. The result was a split where, as with the Hicksites, each New England Yearly Meeting denied that the other was legitimate. Tactless actions on each side seem to have been decisive, not doctrines, but the key issue was human initiative in organizing many committees.

When the two Yearly Meetings sent Epistles and visitors to Philadelphia Orthodox Yearly Meeting, it, too, faced a crisis. The clerk was the same Samuel Bettle around whom the Hicksite split had broken. In fear of another similar disaster he agreed, after a crisis in 1857, to a policy whereby Philadelphia Yearly Meeting would not formally send Epistles to any other Yearly Meeting, although in practice Epistles and visitors from London and many other Meetings were welcomed. Within Philadelphia city, the Arch Street Meeting, where Yearly Meeting sessions were held, remained quietist and "conservative" in outlook while Twelfth Street Meeting (later the home of the American Friends Service Committee) was "Gurneyite" in outlook, actively supporting Quaker schools and colleges as well as Indian and antislavery work.

Although no charges of doctrinal heresy were raised against Wilburites in either New England or Philadelphia, when the conflict spread into Ohio Yearly Meeting, it became clearer that the religious issues that were at stake were those that had caused conflicts in Christian circles outside Quakerism. The context was the new approach to evangelical theology in midwestern evangelistic revivals.

THE DEVELOPMENT OF EVANGELICAL QUAKERISM

Three important issues are often confused: evangelical doctrine, evangelistic methods, and the experience of sudden, permanent, infused holiness as a "Baptism by the Spirit." The previous chapter and those that follow show how these underlay, respectively, the "Orthodox" attack on Hicks, the "Gurneyite" split from "Wilburite" conservatives, and the later break of the Evangelical Friends Alliance from the milder evangelicalism of the Five Years and Friends United Meeting. In the first third of the nineteenth century "Orthodox" Friends fought only for Evangelical experience and biblical doctrine, which emphasize God's forgiveness of every human who will receive it through Jesus' atoning death. Evangelicals were prepared for this doctrine by experiencing humans' helplessness to save themselves. Although George Fox* and early Friends affirmed the atonement, it was not their main witness, nor was the doctrine held to be valid without holiness of life reached by the detailed inner testing and purging experience of "the Lamb's War," and was continued by lifelong openness to the Light's Leadings. But the Bible and salvation by Christ's death were the central concerns for "Orthodox" American Friends in the 1820s. Gurney urged Bible study on such topics but sought no changes in Quaker worship or ethics.

In the Midwest, however, Friends also came into contact with evangelistic revivalists who taught "new methods" of revivalism and new attitudes toward strong emotions and sudden conversion experiences. Such "new methods" had developed among non-Friends in the 1830s during a new peak in American evangelism. Many of its new features lasted through two further peak periods of revivalism in 1858 and 1878.[9] A revival in Rome, New York, in 1830 was headed by Charles Grandison Finney, a small-town lawyer until he became converted. As a Presbyterian preacher his rhetoric and organizing skills made him famous from New York to the frontier, though suspect in New England and Philadelphia. His *Lectures on Revivals* became a famous handbook of what Finney himself called the "new methods" for bringing people to commit themselves to Christ: the gathering of supporting pastors from many denominations, long revival meetings on many successive nights to build up emotional readiness, the use of intense hymns and music to help conversion, and, centrally, Finney's stress on conversion as an act of decision or commitment. He used altar calls and pledge cards, prepared "mourners' benches" or kneeling rails for individuals hoping to be converted, and set aside quiet rooms where the revivalist's helpers could talk and pray for hours with those who had just made acts of life commitment and needed to pray or think through their future.[10]

Finney's tactics were not copied by Friends for half a century. But the doctrinal clash his stress on conversion as decision caused in Calvinist churches was the same aroused among Friends between John Wilbur and aggressive committee organizers. Conversion, for Saint Paul and Augustine, Luther, David Brainerd, and Jonathan Edwards, always came at God's initiative and only by God's act of grace. Human initiative, for each of these men, had stood in their way. Fox and Robert Barclay* had tried to get all humans to surrender their wills permanently but meant to be led by God in all prayer and in all speaking and action. The Quaker pioneers had in varying degrees spoken of new emotional power and new beliefs in their converted lives, but each had first to leave his or her own salvation in God's hands. Finney's new stress on decision gave humans the initiative. Most midwestern Christians approved: they were activists in religion. Wilbur's crisis among Friends paralleled the Presbyterian "New School"–"Old School" split in the same years.

The continuing tension over activism, in committees and later over revivals, persisted for thirty years among midwestern Quakers. The specific breaking points came in different times and places. The little Baltimore Orthodox Yearly Meeting tried in 1849 and 1851 to call all Orthodox Friends together to reunite the Gurney and Wilbur factions but finally failed. In the Ohio Orthodox Yearly Meeting, the mildly conservative clerk, Benjamin Hoyle tried to postpone every disputed issue. But in 1854 the sessions were attended by Eliza Kirkbride Gurney, widow of Joseph John, and by Wilbur's close friend Thomas Gould, each determined to force the issue. Friends divided over the choice of a clerk (as in Philadelphia in 1827) and the question of whose "Traveling Minute" to recognize. The "Gurneyite" party tried to push their proposed new clerk Jonathan Binns to the front of the Meeting until the table and gallery in the Mount Pleasant meeting-house splintered. The division of the Yearly Meeting left the "Wilburite" Conservatives for the moment with the Mount Pleasant Boarding School and a majority of the members and meeting-houses except in the northern area around Salem and Damascus. They had twenty-four Monthly Meetings and 4,000 members; "Gurneyites" had twenty Meetings and 3,000 members.[11] Between 1868 and 1875 the Gurneyites challenged the ownership of the school in court and gained control, only to see the building burn down and be replaced by the Conservatives' Olney School at Barnesville.[12]

QUAKER SCHOOLS

Schools were important to all branches of midwestern Friends, but also shed light on the three Quaker branches' attitudes to wider society. Systematic public education in America began after 1830, and only in 1851 in Indiana. The District Schools founded in midwestern towns had been preceded by Quaker schools, some in private homes but about half directly supervised by Monthly Meetings.

After 1828 Midwestern Hicksites seem to have produced few new schools and to have kept only a few Meetings' elementary schools. The Yearly Meeting minutes from 1828 to the Civil War report with uniform words and disinterest that "schools are generally encouraged," but "there are none under our care."

Indiana Hicksites opened academies at Waynesville, Ohio, and Richmond, Indiana.

The Hicksite split in the Midwest seems to have given both Ohio and Indiana Orthodox Friends a strong urge to keep accurate and centralized school records. Yearly Meetings noted large numbers of children taught by Quakers in other kinds of schools, and often the numbers of Quaker teachers, but especially prized the "guarded education" in purely Quaker primary day schools. Among most midwestern Friends the number of schools and the proportion of Quaker children who attended them grew steadily only until the 1850s, when Indiana Yearly Meeting alone averaged 115 Monthly Meeting schools and 3,790 children. Half of the children did not go to schools run by their Meeting, but half of the remainder were taught at home or by Quaker teachers. Western and Iowa Yearly Meetings, as soon as they were "set off" from Indiana in 1858 and 1863, took over the schools their Meetings already ran, adding more until about 1870.[13] By contrast, New England Friends sent 90 percent of their children to public schools, even though they ran the famous Moses Brown and Oak Grove boarding schools. North Carolina Quaker schools nearly gave up during the Civil War.[14] After the 1854 split Ohio Gurneyites were too heavily involved in wider society to insist on separate schools. Wilburite conservatives, who avoided active involvement in service programs outside the Quaker world, were more concerned for maintaining their children's loyalty by Quaker schools and maintained their support more uniformly than other Friends.

After the Civil War Quakers everywhere became less distinct, and their children accepted the local public primary schools, often still taught by Friends. Midwest and New England Quakers' concern shifted dramatically to Sunday schools. Secondary schools became the other Quaker focus: ten of them arose in North Carolina, eleven each in Iowa and Kansas, and seven in Indiana, including the Iowa and Indiana White's Institutes to train Indians and whites in manual skills.[15] These secondary schools taught the Bible and science thoroughly, were accurate in reading and mathematics, and offered a limited, pruned curriculum of the classics and literature. Quaker dress and daily Bible reading or worship were also required.[16] Corporal and other punishments were used more gently than in non-Quaker schools. Women teachers, though respected, drew half the pay of men. Perhaps Quakers' inability to afford separate boys' and girls' secondary schools was one factor in their early use of coeducation, with boys and girls in separate classes, halls, and dining tables. Gender equality in subject matter, if not social interaction, always marked Quaker schools. Ackworth in England (1779), Moses Brown in Rhode Island (1784, 1819), and Nine Partners in Poughkeepsie and Westtown outside of Philadelphia (1799) were "co-ed" early. At York, England, Bootham School for boys and The Mount for girls began only in the 1830s. Carolina developed New Garden; Ohio, Indiana, and Iowa Orthodox Friends began plans for their own coeducational boarding schools. By the 1850s the prestige of Haverford led the Indiana and North

Carolina Yearly Meetings to elevate their boarding schools (1847, 1839) into Earlham and Guilford Colleges.

Links between the Quaker splits and branches and their philosophies of education still need study. Most of the old Quaker secondary and boarding schools, apart from Sandy Spring in Maryland and Alexandria, Virginia, became Orthodox in the separation of 1828 and pushed Hicksites to create Friends Central School to parallel Friends Select and Swarthmore College (1867) and George School (1891) to match Haverford and Westtown. It is not surprising that Iowa Orthodox Friends, more Gurneyite and acculturated than those farther east, developed fewer primary schools and concentrated largely on academies and a massive Sunday school program for all ages. In 1869 Indiana Yearly Meeting and in 1872 Iowa and Western Orthodox Yearly Meetings issued a new form of questionnaire to local Meetings that no longer bothered to ask how many Quaker students attended Quaker schools, asking instead about Sunday schools.

SUNDAY SCHOOLS

Midwestern Friends renewed their concern for First-Day Schools, usually called Scripture Schools, from about 1860. But this may also show an effort to achieve recommitment to Christian faith in general to replace waning commitment to Quakerism. Charles F. Coffin*, who succeeded his father as clerk of Indiana Yearly Meeting in 1858, advocated interdenominational Union Sunday schools. The American Sunday School Union among Protestants dated from 1824. Joseph John Gurney had urged Friends to form Scripture schools on all of his American travels in 1837–41. The nationwide revival in 1858 and the trauma of the Civil War may have prodded Friends to take stock. Indiana Yearly Meeting set up a First-Day Scripture School Committee in 1858, Western Yearly Meeting did so in 1861, and Iowa did so as soon as the Yearly Meeting was set up in 1863. In each case it was reported that all but a handful of the Monthly Meetings had Sunday Schools, whose attendance (including adults) was larger than its total of school-age children; only 10 percent of Friends' children failed to attend. Statistics remained almost constant throughout the 1860s. Western Yearly Meeting's first published statistical report in 1862 noted fifty-nine Scripture Schools enrolling 3,934 pupils, with an average attendance of 3,252, when the Yearly Meeting had only 3,146 children under twenty-one.[17]

NATIVE AMERICAN INDIANS

Friends met and worked with, rather than for, the Indians in the eras of William Penn* and John Woolman; in the multisided clashes of the 1750s they also became used to mediating at treaties between Indians and non-Quaker whites. Keeping their special friendships with the Delawares, Quakers also built bonds with the Senecas and Shawnees and were present at the treaties of Newtown in

1791, Sandusky in 1793, and Canandaigua in 1794. Philadelphia and Baltimore Yearly Meetings in 1795 set up committees ''for the civilization and real welfare of the Indians'' in line with the government policy of settling the Senecas in agricultural villages. Three young Friends in 1798 set up their homes on a model farm at Tunesassa, New York, among the Senecas. For better or worse, Seneca life became acculturated to whites, economically if not in religion. Later the Philadelphia Hicksites established a women's manual training school and the Orthodox a boarding school at Tunesassa. Friends failed to keep Presidents Jackson and Van Buren from moving most of the Seneca westward, along with Cherokees and other tribes in the South, when white companies coveted the land, but persuaded Congress to restore one New York reservation. Baltimore Yearly Meeting had worked with the Delawares and Shawnees and, after a disruption during the War of 1812, with the Wyandottes and Miamis in Ohio, notably through a school at Wapakoneta partially staffed and funded by Indiana Friends. When those tribes, too, were evicted in 1831, Friends renewed contact with them in Kansas and reopened their school in 1837.[18] Except at treaties, Friends worked individually with Indians, often far from their home Meetings.

LIBERAL AND RADICAL ATTITUDES TOWARD SLAVERY

Differing strategies concerning slavery emerged in various Quaker groups. Ohio Gurneyites, a few Hicksites, and the Indiana Orthodox all took leading roles. Throughout the century, all three groups kept ''Committees on People of Colour,'' funding, staffing, and maintaining schools for freed black settlers in areas close to Quaker communities. Most Friends lobbied Congress and their state legislatures, notably in North Carolina, to forbid slave trade from overseas, to permit owners to manumit slaves and to educate and convert those still enslaved.[19] When most such efforts failed, Quakers divided over approaches to freeing blacks, although we lack statistics on numbers of Friends from each branch in each form of program.

Although Friends have worked since the 1650s to change society as much as the life-style of individuals, the early nineteenth century saw a contrast of two Quaker—indeed, two American—ways of working to end slavery, paralleling the two approaches to ethics among Friends we noticed with Fox and Penn. These two we can nickname radical and liberal, not always matched by radical, liberal, and conservative theologies. *Radicals in ethics* tend to polarize good and evil, to reject compromise. They may see good and evil in terms of social structures and oppression, but if they are also religious, they may see evil motives as the root of the evil system, not the products of it. They will work to change human motives, for instance by education, but are more likely to try to persuade good people to isolate themselves out of society into pure groups. This kind of ''sectarian separatism'' is natural for radical Christians like Woolman, for whom the root of social evil is human self-will. When such radicals are quietist like Hicks, they may try to silence ''the old Adam'' within themselves and other people. Yet if like Fox they find a new power working within them strong enough to transform their own lives and will, they may try to share this new life and experience with other people and radically remake society. (Social *conservatives*, who also see human hearts as evil, may see seemingly oppressive social structures as products of human wisdom that restrain cruel people from doing worse. But Quakers, whose hopes are based on what God can do within humans, offer few good examples except Herbert Hoover).

The experience of the *liberal* or *reformer* in ethics begins from the universal and gradual nature of the powers that govern the world and change evil into good. He or she may see justice not as breaking oppression but as redressing imbalance. Penn thought that human self-centeredness can be overcome by truths that all people can share and by an awareness of common humanity. He saw good as well as evil in all men and women and appealed to the good in each to achieve reforms step by step. English and American liberals also trust human creativity and each person's ability to learn for herself or himself.

Over slavery, then, the quietist Elias Hicks was a radical: he distrusted equally self-will and slaveowners. He was also a separatist, seeing the Society of Friends as a pure community against the corrupt world. His *Observations on the Slavery of the Africans* (1811) included a scathing attack against slave raiders who

by fraud, force or purchase from those who had stolen them prisoners in war . . . became possessed of . . . Africans born free. . . . Does the Highway robber that meets his fellow citizen on the way, and robs him of all his property [but] then leaves him at liberty . . . commit as high an act of felony as he that . . . takes a man [into] the state of a slave for life?[20]

To the anger of Philadelphia merchants, Hicks accused as accomplices anyone who bought slave-grown produce, since Quakers had always disowned those who profited by "prize goods" seized in war. Many rural "Hicksites" after 1828 were radical about slavery. Even Lucretia Mott*, who was liberal in theology and reached out to people of all churches and races, was radical against compromise on slavery and about women's rights. But theologically, Hicks as a quietist was as wary of his own motives as of those of others and urged Friends to "labor to be still, . . . to still our bodies, . . . to have our minds still, . . . till unruly passions . . . are brought down into submission to the divine will."[21]

Some "Orthodox" Quakers of 1828 were socially conservative, but many were liberal reformers, active in service programs, hospitals, prisons, and even against slavery. The best model may be Joseph John Gurney, whose theological books in 1824 and 1825 had given much encouragement to the "Orthodox" Friends. Gurney put aside banking for the years 1837–41 to travel in America. After visiting the Indiana Yearly Meeting he went to the Carolinas to see slave conditions firsthand. Then he chartered a brig to visit the British West Indian islands, where the slaves had been freed five years before. He published at his own expense an open letter to Henry Clay describing how plantation owners profited by the harder work of the free blacks and how much stabler freedmens' marriages and homes were without slavery. He closed with detailed calculations of how Carolina plantation owners could profit by freeing their own slaves.[22]

Gurney visited Congress in Washington, talked to Henry Clay, Daniel Webster, and Carolina Senator John Calhoun and held a prayer meeting in the Capitol attended by President Van Buren and John Quincy Adams. More than Hicks, Gurney reached out in his own way beyond Friends to all Americans in seeking reform. His liberal methods, based on sympathy and persuasion, were typical also of his sister Elizabeth Fry's work for women prisoners and other reform work by Philadelphia "Orthodox" Friends. In practice Gurney and Fry also worked closely with non-Quaker evangelicals like William Wilberforce, whom Elizabeth Fry invited to dinner and to visit the prison ships on which men and women were being deported to Australia. Wilberforce in Parliament worked with the Gurneys on prisons and slavery.

Joseph John Gurney's theology appealed to the authority of the Bible and to humans' need for the atonement of Christ and may seem conservative and alien to his reforms. But he knew common human needs and injustices. Gurney defended silent worship, Quaker speech, dress, and pacifism like an old-line Friend, but his little book *On . . . Love to God* became a Quaker classic for its sensitivity to Jesus' suffering:

Jesus selects for himself . . . a life of poverty. His birth-place is a stable; his early home a Galilean village, . . . his reputed father a mechanic. . . . But . . . who shall tell the sufferings which he endured? The greater advances we make toward divine purity, the more acute becomes our sympathy with the sufferings of others, our distress because of the sinfulness of the world. . . . Our blessed Lord, though clothed in humanity, was perfectly pure. How tender & acute therefore must have been his sympathy with an afflicted generation.[23]

Gurney's liberalism and conservative theology interacted in a new way when he tried to show that atonement was a universal experience of all humankind, not limited to those who center it in Christ.[24]

The contrast of liberal and radical approaches to slavery was not limited to the Quakers. The period from 1758 to 1820 may be called the era of national hope, at least in the North. It is hard to find clear non-Quaker protests before Woolman's in 1750. But Samuel Hopkins, the "New Light" pastor of Providence, Rhode Island, was already preaching against slavery in that slave-traders' port in the 1750s. In 1787 the Rhode Island legislature passed the first law against the slave trade, apart from one passed in early Pennsylvania but vetoed in England. It was the easiest aspect of slavery to ban. In 1807 the U.S. Congress forbade the importing of slaves (though not the selling of those born locally), and England did the same that year. Slave ownership itself was harder to end. New York banned it in 1799; the New England states had just done the same, although there was also a federal law in 1793 protecting the rights of owners of fugitive slaves. An important event in this period was the invention of the cotton gin, which made large-scale slavery profitable on southern plantations. But America was hopeful and not yet deeply divided.

From 1820 to 1837 Americans wrestled over antislavery methods. Public feeling was growing but took two diverse routes. Gradualists favored the American Colonization Society, which shipped freed blacks back to Africa; the state of Liberia was founded for this purpose. At its peak there were 1,015 chapters of the Colonization Society, 250 of them in the South. It was especially popular in North Carolina, where slaveowners did not like having freed blacks around, tempting their slaves to run away. It had therefore become legally almost impossible for Quakers and others to free their own slaves. However, when a shipload of free blacks on the *Julius Pringle* put into Philadelphia harbor and decided to go ashore and settle, the anger of Philadelphia Friends who shipped them on to Liberia seemed to Southerners to show they were no different in their prejudices. A black Quaker sea captain, Paul Cuffee* from Cape Cod, who had his own ship and black crew, made several voyages to Liberia with black settlers.[25] Two other ideas that the gradualists shared with Gurney, which Hicks rejected, were that slaveowners should be reimbursed for their investment in the freed slaves and that periods of apprenticeship for the freed blacks' education would be a reassurance that they would not riot or need poor relief. As late as 1837 Gurney was still speaking persuasively for all of these gradualist ideas. As late as 1843 Philadelphia "Orthodox" Yearly Meeting wrote the *History of the Quaker Anti-Slavery Testimony* so as to repeat their stand without offending anyone.

Abolitionists, of whom Benjamin Lay and Elias Hicks were early Quaker examples, began to emerge in the 1830s. The most famous was William Lloyd Garrison, a New England non-Friend who edited his own magazine, the *Public Liberator*. Garrison's direct successor in editing another paper, *The Genius of Universal Emancipation*, was the Quaker Benjamin Lundy of Ohio. John Greenleaf Whittier*, the Quaker poet of abolitionism and of quietist worship, was also first persuaded by Garrison to be a journalist. The American Anti-Slavery Society was founded in 1833 by groups of such people, mostly in Philadelphia, New York, and New England. Lucretia Coffin Mott* helped to found both the Philadelphia Anti-Slavery Society and the Female Anti-Slavery Society. Her membership in the national group bothered some men so much that they pulled out to form an all-male American and Foreign Anti-Slavery Society led by Quakers like J. G. Birney, who helped to found the Liberty and Republican Parties. There were individual Quaker women like the sisters Sarah and Angelina Grimke*, who like Lucretia Mott became important both for abolitionism and for the women's rights movement, following the Seneca Falls Convention of 1848.

From 1837 to 1850 was a time of crisis. Southerners had already become afraid and angry with the northern abolitionists, since the violent slave revolt of Nat Turner in Virginia in 1831. Congress still accepted the petition of Caln

Quarterly Meeting of rural Pennsylvania Friends in 1835, and in 1836 those of Farmington Monthly and New York Yearly Meetings, but that year the Senate voted to accept no more antislavery petitions. In 1837 at Alton in the southern tip of Illinois a non-Quaker abolitionist Elijah Lovejoy was lynched by a mob as he stood guard to keep them from smashing his press for a third time. In 1838 Friends took the lead in building Pennsylvania Hall as a meeting-place for antislavery and peace groups. A mob set it on fire the week it was opened. Whittier rescued his papers for his magazine *The Pennsylvania Freeman* and published on schedule:

Atrocious Outrage! Burning of Pennsylvania Hall

Pennsylvania Hall is in ashes! The beautiful temple consecrated to Liberty has been offered a smoking sacrifice to the Demon of Slavery. . . . All day yesterday a body of ill-disposed persons lingered around the Hall. The crowd increased towards evening. . . . The mayor addressed the crowd, who answered with cheers but refused to disperse.[He had promised that no troops would be called out]. About 8 o'clock the work of destruction commenced. . . . The doors were broken open with axes. . . . Soon the cry of fire was heard, and flames appeared from the building. . . . The engines of the fire men were not permitted to play upon the Hall. The flames soon rose above the roof, casting a baleful light upon the crowd of 15,000.[26]

Behind all of these tensions was the struggle of the Texans against Mexico and the U.S.–Mexican War. The northern states bitterly opposed the war, lest it would give slaveholding states control of the Senate. Antislavery champion Daniel Webster met with his longtime rival Henry Clay to work out the Compromise of 1850, admitting new states in a balance of slave and free, with a tougher Fugitive Slave Law to pacify the slaveowners. Whittier wrote a scathing satire, "Ichabod," against Webster. The compromise was politically wise but solved no basic issues. Between 1838 and 1840 the national Methodists and Presbyterians and soon after the Baptists split apart, eventually forming northern and southern denominations of each church.

Friends went through their own split over slavery before the Civil War, but it did not last long and was not bitter. Friends made the Philadelphia–Baltimore area, Mount Pleasant, Ohio, and the area northwest of Cincinnati the three main channels for blacks escaping illegally from southern slavery by "the Underground Railroad." Both Hicksite and Orthodox Quakers took part: Isaac Hopper, Lucretia Mott, Elisha Bates, and Charles Osborn had also edited journals or written tracts on abolition. Levi Coffin drew to him in Newport (now Fountain City), Indiana, both Osborn and Arnold Buffum of New York. These men, with Walter Edgerton, formed a group of activists as strong as those in New York and Philadelphia.[27] But his "gradualist" cousin Elijah Coffin, clerk of Indiana Yearly Meeting, removed them from all committee posts. Levi Coffin and his friends formed in protest the "Indiana Yearly Meeting of Anti-Slavery Friends," a split not over differences in doctrine but over approaches to ending slavery. Levi

Coffin was one of many hundreds (the biggest part blacks, who stayed nameless and daily risked death or being kidnapped into slavery) to help fugitive slaves escape to Canada. Levi Coffin was well supported by his own town and by his knowledge of southern Quakers and of slavery laws. He enjoyed outfoxing pursuing slave hunters or slaveowners: three escape routes from the Ohio River crossing points converged on his Newport home: 2,000 fugitives received meals or lodging there without any being captured. But this "railroad" was the first reason for which Friends had felt a duty to break an unjust law *secretly* (as the risk was not to Quakers' but to the slaves' lives). Contrary to Quaker tradition, Levi Coffin used his meeting-house for joint abolitionist meetings with non-Quakers. Most Friends were also staunch Whigs, hoping to avoid secession or Civil War. When Henry Clay was campaigning in Richmond against the "Pol-kat" Democrats in 1842, Hiram Mendenhall took him a petition urging that Clay could at least liberate his own slaves in Lexington. Clay was angry; Elijah Coffin apologized, taking Clay in his carriage to worship at the Indiana Yearly Meeting session.

In 1843 the Indiana Yearly Meeting of Anti-Slavery Friends began with twelve Monthly and four Quarterly Meetings and 2,000 members, including some in Iowa and Ohio. The 25,000 in the main Yearly Meeting, however, were also against slavery; when the *Dred Scott* case made them realize that they agreed on the immorality of hunting fugitive slaves and the need to hide them, the two sides quietly came back together. Neither apologized or demanded an apology.[28]

Slavery had not been ended. In Kansas, the "free-soilers" from Iowa and slaveowners from Missouri began guerrilla warfare. John Brown, who had taken part, began the military training for his band of raiders upon Harper's Ferry on the Quaker Coppocs's farm in Iowa.

THE CIVIL WAR

Since slavery was a central issue, the Civil War challenged the Quaker "Peace Testimony" as no war had done since Fox's time. In the South, Friends were doubly suspect for opposing both war and slavery. English and Yankee Quakers, concerned for southern Friends, got passes to carry relief through the lines to specific Meetings and families. Some east coast Quakers, and many in the South, accepted imprisonment and threats of death rather than bear arms. Job Throck-morton and Seth Loflin died of their mistreatment by Confederate sergeants.[29] Some young southern Friends camped out for years as "bushwhackers" in the woods, and Delphina Mendenhall arranged legal or Underground Railroad trips for blacks north through the battle lines.

In Indiana as a whole, an exhaustive study of regimental and Meeting records and graveyards shows that out of about 4,500 Quaker men of military age, 2,170 Quakers pled their conscience and tradition against serving, but 1,198 served in the Union ranks, about 24 percent compared with 62 percent of all Indiana men. Of them, 236 Friends died during the war. Some recruited each other; five companies had each more than 20 Quakers, and 69 Friends were officers. Most had enlisted; only 22 waited to be drafted, and 20 asked for noncombatant service.[30] Many young Friends let kindly draft officers parole them or exempt them for farm work or teaching; but statistics also ignore the soldiers whose Quaker backgrounds went unlisted. The Quaker Testimony was explicit even against voluntary payment of a fine or of the cost of a substitute for a draftee, although Lincoln or Secretary Stanton offered to use the fees for a Freedmen's fund or hospitals. East coast Meetings opposed both options. New England Friends had foreseen "the time when our faith is practically tried" and could rightly claim that "the exceptions to faithfulness are . . . but few." They could state that "it is not for us to enter into deadly strife, or to promote in others the spirit which tends to unsheath the sword," and at the same time sincerely mourn Lincoln's death and like him turn to face "effects of the awful strife . . . calling for our tender sympathy and the open hand of help."[31]

If Friends as loyal to Quaker ideals as Whittier, Bright, and Lucretia Mott could not help wishing for a Union victory that would end slavery, lesser Friends found choices even harder. The Western Yearly Meeting's visitation committee reported in 1861 that "we learn with . . . deep regret that some of our dear young Friends in different places have engaged in this sanguinary conflict."[32] Some Yearly Meetings printed and distributed stern warnings on the Peace Testimony by their Meeting for Sufferings and from the London and Ireland Yearly Meetings. In Western and Iowa Yearly Meetings throughout the war the concern was stated only in a brief note in summaries of "the State of the Society": "Friends maintain a testimony against Priests' & Ministers' wages, against Slavery, Oaths, bearing arms and all Military services, . . . except that . . . all [Monthly Meeting] reports mention a few cases of . . . bearing arms . . . [and] care taken" by disciplinary eldering.[33]

As the Union armies advanced, Friends could find creative outlet for their torn consciences by working for some of the 3 million freed blacks left, often uprooted, on southern soil. In 1862 Philadelphia Quakers formed a new Women's Aid Society, which later worked with the National Freedmen's Relief Association, raising $130,000 in seventeen months and eventually $349,000 for work in camps round Vicksburg and at Helena, Arkansas, where Southland Academy cradled the only black Quaker Meeting. The New England Friends created a Washington Mission for Freedmen, raising $4,264 in 1867 before shifting their concern over to Tennessee. In the Midwest, Freedmen's work was an almost reflex extension of work for two decades by their "Committees on People of Colour." Friends became involved in extensive plans to provide food, blankets, and shelter for nearby Freedmen. The Western Yearly Meeting's figures for blacks "in our limits" rose steadily from 446 families and 2,289 individuals with eleven schools in 1861 to 576 and 3,242 in 1864. By 1865 they employed 8 Quaker relief workers and 3 teachers in Clarksville, Indiana, and in 1866 opened nine new schools in Columbus, Mississippi; they later expanded to Macon, Mississippi. Indiana matched Western's effort: Levi Coffin, after visits to Cairo and Vicksburg while the siege was still continuing, was sent twice to England and raised $87,750 for Freedmen's Aid.[34] Southern Friends had of necessity remained more conservative in both theology and ethics: Allen Jay* and Nereus Mendenhall* gave a decade of hard work to rebuilding North Carolina Meetings and schools.

Among northern Friends the eventual chief religious result of the Civil War trauma was a turn toward the "Holiness" forms of revivalism in the Middle West, discussed in the next chapter. But this may have been linked to the breakdown of the Discipline and sense of shared guilt throughout the North over young Friends who had enlisted. Indiana, Iowa, and Western Orthodox Yearly Meetings, an area intensely partisan against slavery, received in 1865 a flood of more than 30 visiting Friends, twice the usual number. After the war mid-western Friends found it hard to disown their younger members who had served; 148 were disowned by Indiana or Western Orthodox or Hicksite Meetings; 220 more "condemned their conduct" (not always in deep shame) and were restored to membership, but 596 Hoosier Quakers who served were kept as members without any act of Discipline.[35] In 1865 Western Yearly Meeting minuted "deep solicitude and Christian sympathy that they may be restored to the fellowship of the church." In 1866 Iowa too minuted "fervent charity towards one another in relation to that which is past." The issue was sharpest in 1867: thereafter, the concern of both the Iowa and Western Yearly Meetings was deposited in Peace Committees that reported annually on conferences held and tracts distributed.

Hicksites, with their tradition of localized discipline, seem to have found it even harder. In 1867's Ohio Hicksite Yearly Meeting, a "Committee to propose some uniform course of action in regard to the violations of our Testimony against war" would "not admit of a general disownment," proposing Monthly Meeting Committees "to labor with such members" as "desire to retain [the] right of membership."

Scholars and local traditions agree that the Meetings' unwillingness to disown members who had fought went with equal reluctance to disown automatically members who married non-Friends. The Miami (Ohio) Monthly Meeting alone had recorded 68 disownments for "marrying out" in 1804–28. Midwestern Friends were called lax by those who knew the much stricter Discipline of Philadelphia after the Reformation of 1755, but many Meetings were already relaxing their standards before the Civil War. Whitewater disowned three times as many as it gained from 1830 to 1850 (two-fifths for "marrying out") and reversed this ratio by 1860.[36] Like other Yearly Meetings, Western changed its Book of Discipline: "When a Friend shall marry a person not a member of our religious society, . . . if he express a wish to remain a member, and evince his attachment to the Society by his practice of attending our religious meetings, . . . he shall be retained." Already in 1859 the New York Yearly Meeting had also relaxed its Discipline about dress and speech.[37] From the American Civil War onwards, Quakers have never dared to expect unanimity about conscientious objection to bearing arms or any of the once uniform ethical "Testimonies." Burdened by the breakdown of the Discipline, doctrinal orthodoxy and the Holiness revivals seemed to many Friends a better way of restoring the purity that they knew earlier Quakers had preached.

NOTES

1. In 1834 the Indiana Yearly Meeting (Hicksite) modified its Book of Discipline and issued 300 copies of the new one, but the changes were not major. Yet the new Western and Iowa Yearly Meetings (Orthodox) made many detailed changes in the 1860s, the years of the Holiness revival.

2. James H. Norton, "Quakers West," 140, dates this from 1817. Bridget Bower found that whereas the Philadelphia and Ohio Orthodox Monthly Meetings disowned Hicksites by name, their Hicksite counterparts never disowned individual "Orthodox" Friends: ("Gospel Order among Quietist Quakers in the 19th Century to 1860: A Comparison of Hicksite and Wilburite Understandings of the Discipline" [M.A. thesis, Earlham School of Religion (hereafter ESR), 1986]).

3. See Joseph John Gurney, A *Journey in North America* (Norwich, Eng.: 1841) Benjamin Seebohm, ed., Memoirs of Grellet (Philadelphia: 1860), II, 445; Minutes of Indiana Yearly Meeting. See also entries for Grellet and Gurney in this volume.

4. David Bower, "Quaker Orthodoxy and Jacksonian Democracy," 110, 99, 96.

5. Cited in Seth Hinshaw, *Carolina Quaker Experience*, 149.

6. The Indiana Hicksite minutes (though printed from 1857) averaged less than ten pages annually from 1828 to the Civil War. The Ohio Hicksite minutes, printed from 1832, were even shorter. By contrast, the Miami Monthly Meeting minutes (later Hicksite), listing individual migrating Quaker families, ran 730 pages in the first forty years, 1803–42.

7. The Indiana Yearly Meeting (Hicksite) minutes for 1829 to 1836 and Ohio for 1832 professed inability to help Indians. Minutes of Indiana in 1837 to 1879 and Ohio in 1834 report work with eastern Hicksites' Committees.

8. John William Buys, "Quakers in Indiana in the Nineteenth Century" (Ph.D. thesis, University of Florida, 1973), 56ff., 76–78.

9. See Timothy Smith, *Revivalism and Social Reform* (Nashville: 1957); William G. McLoughlin, *Modern Revivalism: Charles Grandison Finney to Billy Graham* (New York: 1959); idem, *Revivals, Awakenings, and Reform* (Chicago: 1978); and Melvin Easterday Dieter, *The Holiness Revival of the Nineteenth Century* (Chicago: 1978).

10. See Charles G. Finney, *Lectures on Revivals* (New York: 1836): See also Alice Felt Tyler, *Freedom's Ferment* (Minneapolis: 1944); Whitney Cross, *The Burned-Over District: Western New York, 1800–1860* (Ithaca, N.Y.: 1950).

11. Norton, "Quakers West," 255; William R. Taber, *Eye of Faith: A History of Ohio Yearly Meeting, Conservative* (Barnesville, Ohio: 1985); Charles P. Morlan, ed., *A Brief History of Ohio Yearly Meeting of the Religious Society of Friends (Conservative)* (Barnesville, Ohio: 1959).

12. See William R. Taber, *Be Gentle, Be Plain: A History of Olney* (Barnesville, Ohio: 1976).

13. Data from Indiana and Western Yearly Meeting Minutes, 1840–1870.

14. Statistics from *Meetings of Friends in New England* (New Bedford, Mass.: 1849)

and New England Yearly Meeting Minutes; see also Zora Klain, *Educational Activities of New England Quakers* (Philadelphia: 1928), 22 ff.; George Selleck, *Quakers in Boston* (Cambridge, Mass.: 1976). On North Carolina, see Zora Klain, *Quaker Contributions to Education in North Carolina* (Philadelphia: 1925).

15. Rufus Jones, *Later Periods*, 706–709, listed eighty-four English schools and fifty-seven in America, mostly secondary, founded by ninteenth-century Friends. See also Ibid. chapter 17; Errol Elliott, *QAF* ch. 9; Ethel Hittle McDaniel, *The Contribution of the Society of Friends to Education in Indiana* (Indianapolis: 1939); John W. Parker and Ruth Ann Parker, *Josiah White's Institute* (Dublin, Ind.: 1983). Studying the later history of these schools, Elbert Russell reported in "Friends Secondary Schools" in *The Quaker* 1, no. 15 (November 12, 1929): 171–74, that of fifty-six American Quaker secondary schools founded before 1920, only nineteen predated the Civil War. Twenty-four, including ten of the fourteen Hicksite schools, were founded in 1861–1887. Nineteen later schools (only four pre-Civil War schools) had since closed under public school competition. See also Elbert Russell, *History of Quakerism* (New York: 1942; Richmond, Ind.: 1979) 258–61, 400–407, chapter 33.

16. See Helen B. Hole, *Things Civil and Useful* (Richmond, Ind.: 1980), an expert's study of Quaker education in both continents and all centuries.

17. Western Yearly Meeting Minutes, 1860–62. All data are from Yearly Meeting Minute books.

18. Diane Rothenberg, "Friends Like These: An Ethnohistorical Analysis of the Interaction between Allegheny Senecas and Quakers, 1798–1823" (Ph.D. thesis, City University of New York, 1976); Rayner Kelsey, *Friends and the Indians, 1655–1917* (Philadelphia: 1917); Indiana Yearly Meeting Minutes.

19. See Hilty, *Towards Freedom*; Rufus Jones, *Later Periods*, 679ff. Woolman and Moses Brown supported Rhode Island's pioneer bill ending slavery in 1784. Whittier and Benjamin Lundy worked on Massachusetts and Ohio Laws.

20. Elias Hicks, *Observations on . . . Slavery* (New York: 1811).

21. Sermon by Elias Hicks at Friends' Meeting, Key's Alley, Philadelphia, December 12, 1826, from *The Quaker*, ed. Marcus T.C. Gould (Philadelphia: 1830) 1:105ff in Hugh Barbour, *Slavery and Theology: Writings of Seven Quaker Reformers, 1800–1870* (Dublin, Ind.: 1985).

22. Joseph John Gurney, *A Winter in the West Indies, Described in Familiar Letters to Henry Clay of Kentucky* (London: 1846).

23. Joseph John Gurney, *Essay on the Habitual Exercise of Love to God* (London: 1834).

24. Gurney discussed atonement ideas among the Indians in *Observations on the Religious Peculiarities of . . . Friends* (London: 1829); he added this section in 1829 to later editions of his (1824) work.

25. See Weeks; Drake; Anna Cox Brinton, *Quaker Profiles* (Wallingford, Pa.: 1964).

26. *Pennsylvania Freeman*, " 18th of 5th Mo." [1838]. See Elizabeth Gray Vining, *Mr. Whittier* (New York: 1974), 63. Whittier's best poems, apart from those on Quaker worship, are his satires on slavery, for example, "Hunters of Men" (1834) in *Poems by John G. Whittier* (1838), 32.

27. Levi Cottin, *Reminiscences* (Cincinnati: 1876), the great arsenal of Underground Railroad stories. See also Ruth Anna Ketring, *Charles Osborn and the Anti-Slavery Movement* (Columbus, Ohio: 1937); Larry Gara, *The Liberty Line: The Legend of the Underground Railroad* (Lexington, Ky.: 1961).

28. See *The Minutes of Indiana Yearly Meeting of Anti-Slavery Friends, 1843–57* (Newport, Ind.: 1859); Walter Edgerton, *History of the Separation in Indiana Yearly Meeting* (Cincinnati: 1856), 171–75; 1842 files of *Richmond Palladium*.

29. Jones, *Later Periods*, 741–53; Hilty, *Towards Freedom*.

30. Jacquelyn W. Nelson, "The Military Response of the Society of Friends in Indiana to the Civil War," *Indiana Magazine of History* 81 (June, 1985): 101–130; idem. "Military and Civilian Support of the Civil War by the Society of Friends in Indiana." *Quaker History* 26 No. 1 (Spring 1987) 50–61.

31. *New England Yearly Meeting Minutes, 1863, 1861, 1864, 1862, 1865*. New England reported in 1863 that twenty out of forty-three men who had enlisted had been disowned and seven more were "under notice." See Jones, *Later Periods*, 729ff, reporting that only ten in New York had volunteered by 1863, most of whom were disowned. By 1864 eight New Yorkers and one-hundred Philadelphia Friends had been drafted, about twice as many paid commutation.

32. *Western Yearly Meeting Minutes, 1861*, 8.

33. *Western Yearly Meeting Minutes, 1862*, 11; cf. minutes through 1865 for Western and Iowa Yearly Meetings.

34. Levi Coffin, *Reminiscences*, Chs. 19–20; *Western Yearly Meeting Minutes, 1867* 32. On Southland see Rufus Jones, *Second Period*, 597–617. See also Thomas C. Kennedy, "The Last Days at Southland" in *The Southern Friend* 8, no. 1 (Spring 1986): 3–19.

35. See Nelson, "Military Response," 109–110. The detailed data in the Ph.D. thesis on which this is based (Ball State University, 1984) show that many Meetings with unusually high ratios of men enlisted and not disciplined were also starters of revivals in 1867–77 and after: Walnut Ridge, Back Creek, Hinkles Creek, Spiceland, Westfield.

36. See Thomas D. Hamm, *The Transformation of American Quakerism: Orthodox Friends, 1800–1907* (Bloomington, Ind.: 1988), Ch. 2, based on his Ph.D. thesis (Indiana University, 1986) with the same title.

37. Ibid., Ch. 3.

16
WEST AND MIDWEST, 1867–1902: REVIVALS, HOLINESS, MISSIONS, AND PASTORS

The transformation of evangelical Quaker worship by sermons and hymns after the Civil War makes "the great revival" of 1867–77 a subject of intense argument and research.[1] The less noticed interaction of patterns of revivalism and pastoral ministry with the experience and doctrines of holiness shaped much of western and midwestern Quakerism.

THE NATIONAL HOLINESS REVIVALS OF 1858 AND 1867

New patterns had developed out of Charles Finney's "new methods" thirty years before among non-Quakers. In New York in 1835 Sarah Lankford and her sister Phoebe Palmer, wife of a homeopathic doctor, had begun a series of noonday home prayer meetings to seek total self-dedication and holiness, supported by some clergy but led by lay persons. In 1839 they had persuaded the Reverend Timothy Merritt of Boston to edit a journal, *The Guide to Christian Perfection*. Phoebe Palmer's own autobiographical *Way of Holiness, with Notes by the Way* (1845), became a best-seller. Professor Thomas Upham of Bowdoin and several Methodist Bishops joined the movement. By 1858 (the year after a banking crisis) these women had become the center of an intense national "Lay Awakening" mainly in cities. Their ideas drew on those taught at Oberlin, founded in 1836 after Lane Seminary split over abolitionism. Oberlin President Asa Mahan and Theology Professor Charles G. Finney began to publish Holiness doctrines.[2]

In 1867 other pastors began a series of summer "Bible conferences" like camp meetings at places such as Vineland, New Jersey; Manheim, Pennsylvania; and Round Lake, New York. These meetings were interchurch, though led by Methodists such as John S. Inskip. Their organizers took as their title The National Camp Meeting Association for the Promotion of Holiness. Ohio Quaker David Updegraff* led some of their sessions at Mountain Lake, New Jersey.

Philadelphia Friend Hannah Whitall Smith* found religious power in 1867 through a Holiness meeting near her temporary country home in Millville, New Jersey, and wrote the movement's best-seller *The Christian's Secret of a Happy Life* in 1875.[3]

The Holiness movement went forward in both wider and narrower forms than the revivals of 1858 and 1867. In the late 1870s the mass meetings of the great evangelist Dwight L. Moody drew support from Holiness churches and pre-millenarian sects and at the same time from among students, doctors like Wilfred Grenfell, and scientists such as Henry Drummond. They began summer student conferences, the Student YMCA, and the Student Volunteer Movement for foreign missions. The Quaker doctor Henry Hodgkin was among thousands who learned in these groups to feel that their gifts could not be as fully used anywhere else as in the newly open lands of Asia and Africa. The cordial responses of some English Friends who visited Iowa and Ohio Quaker revivals in 1866–87 may partially have been due to the rapport between Moody and educated British Christians. Over an equally wide front, most of American Protestantism was in eager ferment in the 1870s. On a narrower front, though, the end results were fundamentalism and pentecostalism. Early in the twentieth century denominational splits opened, and new "Holiness" Church denominations arose such as the Wesleyan Methodists, the Free Methodists, the Churches of God, and the Nazarenes with whom evangelical Friends now exchange members, pastors, hymn books, and beliefs.

THE QUAKER RENEWAL OF THE 1860S

Before 1867 these events had affected individual Friends more than Meetings as a whole. New England's evangelical "Gurneyite" revivalists stirred Meetings in the Midwest more than at home. Yet all Friends felt a renewal movement throughout the 1860s. Concern revived for home worship and Quaker schools, for growth in numbers of Sunday schools, and for work for black freedmen. Quakers in North Carolina, helped by Allen Jay* and the Baltimore Association, were preoccupied with rebuilding their Meetings and membership after wartime injuries. The 1860s were the turning point in Carolina Quaker history. Friends channeled the religious renewal to expand their network of schools from four to forty, besides thirty more for black freedmen and five for Cherokee Indians. Jay was a powerful preacher, despite his cleft palate, and trained his schoolteachers to act as missionaries: "no Methodist bishop ever had a more loyal set of workers."[4] A solid core of older evangelical leaders in Ohio, Indiana, and Iowa shared in sober organizational work to renew midwestern Quakerism after the Civil War. William and Timothy Nicholson, Barnabas Hobbs*, and Benjamin Trueblood* took only a reluctant part when revivals later broke out. Each showed his sense of calling also as head of a Quaker college or in state school and prison programs.[5]

FRIENDS' "GREAT REVIVAL OF 1867"

Revivals and Holiness aroused new tensions among midwestern Quakers like those conflicts that had led to the "Gurneyite–Conservative" division of 1854. Both kinds of "Orthodox" Friends had rejected the Hicksites' theology, not Quaker ways of worship. The "new methods" that alienated the "Wilburite" conservatives had merely consisted of Gurney's Bible and Tract societies and directed Bible study. The revival meetings and forms of preaching, hymn singing, "mourners' benches," and appeals for decision that Finney called "new methods" were not found in any Quaker Meetings before the Civil War. They entered Quakerism in 1867 in local revivals in Walnut Ridge, Indiana, and Bear Creek, Iowa. Two young eastern Iowa Friends claimed:

We made a brief stay at Bear Creek and held one public meeting, where the power of the Lord was wonderfully manifested. Many hearts were reached and all broken up, which was followed by sighs and sobs and prayers, confessions and great joy for sins pardoned. . . . But alas some of the dear old Friends mistook this outbreak of the power of God for excitement and wild fire and tried to close the meeting, but we kept cool and held the strings.[6]

At Bear Creek no one but the young leaders planned or even expected a revival; the setting was an ordinary meeting for worship. At Walnut Ridge, Quakers who had attended a Methodist prayer meeting held a special meeting among Friends and then a joint revival in the Gilboa Methodist Church and a series of intense meetings for worship in the Quaker meeting-house. There were "agonized crying, [and] instantaneous conversions," but "in the meeting-house the mourners bench was not used, and no one sang."[7] The next spring Nathan and Esther Frame*, who had been Iowa Methodists until her church refused to let women preach, began four decades of revival ministry among Friends and non-Quakers by revisiting Walnut Ridge.[8]

The transition from spontaneous to planned revival meetings had been prepared among other Quakers. From 1,000 to 3,000 young Friends had taken part in an intensely moving special evening session at the Indiana Yearly Meeting in 1860 led by the young clerk Charles Coffin; his wife, Rhoda; two Maine brothers now settled near Wilmington, Ohio, Robert and John Henry Douglas*; and David B. Updegraff, farmer, businessman, and Haverford alumnus of Mount Pleasant, Ohio. "Several hundred testimonies, prayers, confessions, yearnings . . . were heard" until after 1:30 a.m.[9] Sybil Jones* of Maine, aunt of Rufus Jones, spoke words of exhortation, rather than the sing-song chant used in quietist Quaker ministry. Continuing to meet at intervals, these men and women formed a permanent group of revival leaders.

After 1867 Midwestern Friends began to hold frequent "general meetings"; so did North Carolina Friends from 1870. In Chicago in 1868, and Kansas in 1869, these meetings began as Friends' public lectures and worship for non-

Quakers, but in most places they were transformed into "union revivals" for a whole community. Quaker preachers frequently planned revivals jointly with other denominations. Luke Woodard reported one from Fountain City, and the New Providence (Iowa) Friends held another as early as 1865. Esther Frame and John Henry Douglas did so throughout their ministry.[10] Along with providing new styles of music, the revivalists used sequences of emotional hymns, named unconverted attenders to be prayed for, and made urgent appeals for surrender or decision. These patterns, carried by visiting preachers into Iowa and North Carolina, became normal in midwestern meetings, to the bitter irritation of some older Friends. In 1867 the Indiana Yearly Meeting's Committee on General Meetings recommended that such special events be left in the hands of the Quarterly Meetings. The next year they reported that 6,000 had attended such a revival held by Northern and Wabash Quarters. Reports came in of 2 General Meetings in 1869, 4 in 1871, 6 in 1872, and 8 in 1873. By 1882 nearly every Monthly Meeting reported, to what was now called the Committee on Ministry, their own revival meetings: 2,700 were held and 4,000 people converted, 750 of whom applied for membership. Equally high figures continued through the 1880s, totaling 22,420 converted in eight years and 9,158 membership applications.[11] South of Toledo, Ohio, Indiana Friends' newly opened Van Wert Quarter grew by revivals in the 1880s from no members to 1,000. Ohio, Iowa, and Western Yearly Meetings asked their standing Committees on General Meetings or Home Missions Committees to organize revivals. Iowa's committee announced 9,367 converted in 1884–90, besides 1,442 sanctified, 2,335 renewals, and 13,144 blessed, in a Yearly Meeting that just then reached its peak of 12,000 members. Yet many new or old members were reported as inactive.[12] By 1871 two young New Vienna, Ohio, Quakers, Daniel Hill and John M. Hussey, were getting out a weekly journal, *The Christian Worker*, to report Quaker "protracted meetings" throughout the Midwest. It debated with the Philadelphia "Gurneyite" *Friends Review* under Henry Hartshorne.[13]

CONVERSION, MILLENNIALISM AND EXPERIENCES OF INSTANT, TOTAL HOLINESS

Revival experience made a bridge to new doctrines for many Quakers. Some Quaker preachers had already begun to stress intense and sudden conversion experiences rather than early Friends' lifelong struggle to purify their hearts "under the Cross" in obedience to the Light. Elizabeth Comstock* in Michigan complained that the Apostles had converted 3,000 in one day, Friends not so many in a lifetime. Sudden conversion in this context meant a human act of commitment, but a revival was also an attack on egos that resisted. Some revivalists used aggressive coercion (and male dominance) in breaking sinners' pride:

Sermons were never the end of [Updegraff's] preaching, but always *SOULS*. . . . From the moment he made the call or gave the invitation . . . he was *burning with zeal for* . . .

individual souls: . . . ready to do anything that would help a person . . . *take the initial step,* . . . to hold up the hand or to rise. "Now sister, pray" [said Updegraff to a woman]. She scarcely does so much as open her mouth. He puts words into it. The simplest kinds of words. Then, "A little louder, sister. Pray aloud if it kills you. For whoever shall *call* on the name of the Lord shall be saved." . . . She breaks out in tears and weeps. Then his own eye moistens, his voice trembles, he weeps with her, thanks God for a baptism of tears, and again urges her to pray. Now the victory comes. Her tongue is unloosed, her face is wreathed with smiles. Her soul leaps out into victory. She sings or shouts, or takes him by the hand, grateful for an emancipation.[14]

Yet it would be a mistake to stress only the dominance of the preacher over the convert. Clearly, some inner victory beyond simple acceptance of God's forgiveness often took place that appeared to justify such methods. Early Friends' inner struggles with self-will reflected also the intensity of inner conflict between Friends' human motives or urges and the social values they had identified with God.[15] But early Friends, like the Holiness revivalists, often felt the Spirit also to be in conflict with the current culture's immorality and victorious over it. "The world" as well as "the flesh" were of the Devil.

One sign of such a polarization may be the strong "Adventism" or "premillennialism," already widespread in the 1870s among Holiness revivalists, most of whom believed in the return soon of Christ as judge from heaven. Methodist preachers (and George Fox) were postmillennial: the outpouring already of the Holy Spirit and belief that perfection was possible now made Jesus' return out of heaven seem to them needless until after the millennium. But from the 1880s onward many revivalists insisted that the present age is becoming darker, not lighter, toward its end, when Christ will condemn it. Although some revivalists came from displaced social elites, others were just plain people from rural backgrounds who were shocked by urban mores.[16]

Yet revivalists were carried by a sense of being given inner power. Updegraff, John Henry Douglas, and by 1877 most other Quaker evangelicals moved on like non-Quaker revivalists from preaching conversion to a doctrine and experience of instantaneous and total holiness.

Holiness and *perfection* are good biblical words from Leviticus and Matthew's Gospel, but they have been given various meanings. Perfection was sought by monks, George Fox, and John Wesley and was claimed by John Humphrey Noyes's Oneida Community. In the codes of Leviticus, Holiness meant purifying rituals and ethical purity. Anabaptists and many separatist sects had insisted that perfect moral obedience was the criterion of a Christian. Saint Francis and the medieval monks above all sought perfect humility. This contrasts in turn with the perfect surrender to the will and glory of God, which made early Calvinists powerful in history and glorified the conversion of later Calvinists like Jonathan Edwards. For John Wesley, on the other hand, any true Holiness came by the power to love that God infuses into people, although their love depends, too, on God's love shown in Christ's death for humans. As Wesley wrote on perfection, he meant that pure, wholehearted love can be the motive of every act a person does. In applying knowledge, he said, sanctified Christians can still make mistakes out of ignorance. After Wesley, Methodists preached constantly on Holiness. Some—but not Wesley—felt power to do all acts in perfect love.[17]

Early Quakers' way of perfection shared much with the Calvinist and Anabaptist patterns and even with monks' humility but belongs in a class by itself. George Fox described early experiences of purity when he "was come up in spirit through the flaming sword into the paradise of God, . . . [when] all the creation gave another smell unto me than before." Whereas Anabaptists had stressed perfect outward obedience to the commands of the Sermon on the Mount, Fox had preached perfection as a constant, total openness and obedience to the Spirit within each person. For Fox, inward obedience assumed God's initiative.

Phoebe Palmer and Finney also preached perfectionism but stressed not God's initiative but human surrender of the will that allows God's sanctifying work. Updegraff's friend Quaker Dougan Clark wrote:

Beginning [with] a fixed belief that holiness is attainable, . . . the next step which the seeking enquiring soul will . . . take is an act of unalterable consecration to God, . . . entire surrender to Christ. Consecration is our own act. Sanctification is God's act. . . . A complete submission [is] necessary to everyone who would receive . . . the priceless blessing of a clean heart. . . . *How do I know when God has sanctified me wholly?* The first evidence is consciousness . . . that [I have] really surrendered all to Christ. (Emphasis original.)[18]

Holiness preachers knew that the power to love is dependent on being forgiven. But unlike Luther, whose sanctification was an inward, unplanned work of God's grace, the fellow revivalists of Finney came to it by acts of sacrifice, "laying on the altar" their own ambitions: Phoebe Palmer surrendered her own life and also her daughter's.[19]

Preachers of Holiness in the 1830s had experienced a sudden moment of grace, a "second blessing" or "baptism of the Holy Spirit," with the sort of renewal earlier evangelicals had found in conversion. It included overwhelming power to love, as a gift from God. Yet Midwest Methodists and Baptists argued and split over this new doctrine. Both Phoebe Palmer and David Updegraff had experiences of sanctification that were "instant" and "complete," words distinguishing the "Holiness movement" from Wesley's own teaching and Fox's. They identified their "baptism by the Spirit" with the baptism of Jesus and ordinary conversion with John's baptism of repentance. They denied that the Spirit dwelt in anyone who had not shared their "second blessing."[20] Most Quaker revivalists after 1867 could remember the date of their sanctification. In 1860 David Updegraff had "made public confession of sins and need of a savior" in a Methodist revival and that evening in his own home "was converted through and through, *and I knew it.* I was free as a bird. Justified by faith, I had peace with God.[21]

[But in 1869] came waywardness, neglect and disobedience. . . . to be sure I was only a business man, and utterly averse to the idea of being a minister. . . . I felt within me a quenchless protest against the formalism all about me . . . It had never occurred to me that I had not received the Holy Ghost. . . . But . . . a brother who had heard . . . John S. Inskip . . . told us of their . . . preaching of consecration and holiness. It was only a spark of God's fire that was needed to kindle into a flame the sacrifice that was placed upon his altar. As I went upon my knees . . . with the resolute purpose of "presenting my body a living sacrifice to God," . . . the misapprehensions, suspicions, sneers and revilings of carnal professors were all pictured before me. . . . Denominational standing, family, business, reputation, friends, . . . were quickly and irrevocably committed . . . to my Almighty Savior. And I had no sooner reckoned myself "dead unto sin and alive unto God" than the Holy Ghost fell upon me. . . . Instantly I felt the melting and refining fire of God permeate my whole being.[22]

QUAKER FOREIGN MISSIONS

The holiness experience of a special baptism of the spirit and sense of being set apart needs to be studied in relation to the special lifelong calling felt by some Friends toward foreign missions. Being called to mission had been part of the world vision of most evangelicals before 1800. Before 1860 Friends' personal experiences of being called, as was true among early Quakers, came for specific short-term projects: Sybil and Eli Jones* from China Lake, Maine, preached mainly to Quakers but like Gurney and Grellet felt moved to explore the state of freed slaves, this time those resettled from America in Liberia and Sierra Leone. On a later trip they found in Palestine and "convinced" a Swiss missionary, Theophilus Waldmeier, who headed the Quaker schools the Joneses began for Christian Arabs in Brummana, Lebanon, and Ramallah, Palestine.

Just as for revivals, interaction with non-Quaker evangelicals shaped other nineteenth-century Quaker foreign mission efforts. London evangelical Friends knew the Asian work of Baptist William Carey and Anglican Henry Martyn. Joseph Bevan Braithwaite was friend and business agent for David Livingstone. Quaker schoolteacher Hannah Kilham had felt called to Gambia and Sierra Leone in West Africa as early as 1823. Former naval captain Daniel Wheeler, becoming a Friend in 1832, felt called to sail around the South Pacific to explore sites of present and potential missions. Later, British Quakers began missions in India, China, and Madagascar.[23] But before the Civil War American Friends worked for non-Quakers mostly through their own programs for prisoners, the mentally ill, slave and free blacks, and native American Indians.

The previous chapter described the work of Philadelphia, Baltimore, Ohio, and Indiana Friends with the Oneidas, Senecas, Delawares, and Shawnees, whom they followed with their schools from New York State, Pennsylvania, and Ohio to Kansas and Oklahoma. When in 1869 war-weary President Grant asked Friends to administer the federal Indian agencies in Kansas and Nebraska, Enoch Hoag, Lawrie Tatum, and other Iowa Orthodox Friends undertook to try to pacify and adapt to white culture the Kiowas, Cheyennes, and Comanches, while Hicksite Friends took up the Nebraska superintendency. Threats to cut off food subsidies and even to call in federal troops failed to keep young Kiowas from raiding into

Texas. President Hayes canceled the Quakers' commission in 1879, but Friends went on working together in the Associated Executive Committee of Friends on Indian Affairs, formed in 1869. Four Indian Quaker Churches survive in Oklahoma.[24]

Quaker missions overseas, by contrast, began usually from a sense of special calling felt by specific Friends in touch with non-Quaker evangelicals. In 1871 Samuel Purdie, a New York Quaker teaching in North Carolina, loosely supported by an Indiana Friends committee set up the year before, crossed the U.S. border into Mexico "not to preach [Quaker] peculiarities but to preach the gospel and began a periodical and a chapel.[25] In 1881 Evi Sharpless, hearing of English Friends' visits to Jamaica, found support in Iowa to begin a Jamaican mission and schools. In 1885 Esther Butler* of Ohio accepted the call of a Methodist doctor to come to Nanking as a nurse and stayed to found an orphanage and a hospital. In entering China the Ohio Yearly Meeting blended the world-conquering outlooks of biblical Israel and of the American "open-door policy" in China: "At the time of Esther Butler's going, our church seemed to awaken to the great possibilities of its future . . . and realizing that the ports of every nation were open to receive the Gospel, the church would be without excuse if it did not enter in and possess the land.[26]

J. Walter and Emma Malone* of Cleveland started in the local Quaker Church a program of Sunday school classes. Among those inspired by the Malones were the young Ohio Quakers Esther Baird and Delia Fistler, who felt called to work in India. They served under Methodists until their own school and mission program could develop in Bundelkhand. The Malones went on in the 1890s to set up in their private home a Bible College modeled on Moody's and found themselves training and encouraging evangelists for America but also missionaries for overseas.[27] In 1892 a concern that sent the Kansas Quaker Weesners and Perry Hadleys and the Iowa Replogles to work for Alaskan Indians was taken over by California and Oregon Friends.[28] Unlike the revivals, these were small undertakings of one to three families feeling a personal call, but each of these Quaker missions became in the twentieth century a self-governing Yearly Meeting, whose interaction with American Friends is told in Chapter 21. Earlier, each had a separate American supporting committee. In 1877 Stanley Pumphrey from England had suggested a joint Quaker Mission Board to Ohio and Indiana Yearly Meetings. In 1888 Mahala Jay, who had already played a leading role as secretary of Indiana committees, called a Quaker women's missionary conference at Indianapolis, leading after 1894 to the unified American Friends Board of World Missions.

In 1902 the Ohio mission committees also began to support what would become a much bigger project and later the biggest Yearly Meeting in the world, when Edgar Hole, Willis Hotchkiss, and Arthur Chilson* began the Friends Africa Industrial Mission at Kaimosi, Kenya. Their working background and lack of theological education made them able to begin with practical needs. The area that Friends chose, northeast of Lake Victoria, was pointed out to them as mainly neglected by other Protestants with whom they worked in comity.[29]

PASTORAL MEETINGS AND PROGRAMMED WORSHIP

A more massive change resulting from the revivals of 1867–77 was the rise of the pastoral system among Friends. Often this has been interpreted as due to the dissatisfaction of local rural Meetings with the stereotyped, singsong ministry of older quietist Friends and the lack of any kind of ministry in many Meetings. But a different hunger was felt by those who joined Meetings after revivals, with no previous Quaker background, for whom Quaker elders felt the need for a teaching program.[30] As important was the change the pastoral system made in the relation of the preacher to his or her hearers, even for those who had earlier been "recorded" as "ministers" and enshrined on "facing benches" in front of their home Meetings. The inward call to become a minister took new meaning when it meant bringing crowds to conversion or sanctification.

An open crisis came over salaries for pastors. It aligned at once Philadelphia Gurneyites like Hartshorne of the *Friends Review*, who pointed to the old Quaker rejection of "Hireling ministers," against most Midwestern Friends, who protested that at best, Quaker pastors were underpaid (as late as 1912 the Iowa average, apart from three city churches, was $382 a year).[31] Argument continues whether the first Quaker pastor was in Iowa in 1871–74 or was Luke Woodard who in 1873 moved two miles from New Garden, Indiana, to serve as minister in Fountain City. The first North Carolina pastors began only after 1889.[32] More significantly, the midwestern Yearly Meetings by 1885 had turned their Committees on General Meetings or on evangelistic work into Committees on the Ministry and were regularly putting about $100 per pastor into their salaries. "The aggressive principle of the gospel requires the cash," said Benjamin Trueblood.[33]

Such central funding was linked to the appointment of a general superintendent, first for the "Evangelistic, Pastoral and Church Extension Work," and soon for the Yearly Meeting itself. This role was foreshadowed by superintendents for schools and Indian work and Allen Jay's work under the Baltimore Association in the 1870s. The first administrative head over Friends was John Henry Douglas* in Iowa, formally superintendent in 1886 but already active for a decade before in finding pastors and persuading Meetings to hire them. Douglas had led Ohio, Iowa, and Oregon interchurch revivals in the 1870s.

"Pastorization" of Meetings was thus a late fruit of the revivals and no direct result of evangelical doctrines. By 1900 only 62 percent of Friends were members of Yearly Meetings allowing pastors, and even of them, in Indiana, for instance, the date by which half the Meetings had pastors was 1897. North Carolina was slower.[34] As hotly disputed by conservative Friends as paying pastors was the expectation that "a minister or other individual assumes the prerogative of governing or leading the exercise of the Meeting by calling on this or that person for . . . prayer, exhortation, singing, or in giving their experience to the congregation, . . . thus virtually denying the headship of Christ in his Church.''[35] Despite suggestions and financial guidance from a superintendent and the Committee on Ministry, local Meetings had free choice in picking pastors. Many who first come to town as evangelists were non-Friends from Nazarene or Holiness Methodist backgrounds; nor did formal educational standards limit Quaker pastors, as they did in main-line denominations.

Like Gurney and Grellet earlier, English evangelical Friends strengthened American Gurneyites even when they wielded less influence at home. Elizabeth Comstock* moved, as a widow, from England to Canada and in Michigan led the temperance movement. In 1850 Robert Lindsey with Benjamin Seebohm traveled in Iowa and in 1859–60, with Sarah Lindsey, went by Panama to a year's visit in California and Oregon. In 1875–79 Stanley Pumphrey strengthened evangelicals in 440 American Meetings, and Walter Robson encouraged the Douglases and Updegraff in Iowa.[36]

NEW CONSERVATIVE SPLITS

The pressure of all of these changes made 1877 a year of crisis in "Orthodox" Quakerism. David Updegraff persuaded Ohio Yearly Meeting to reject formally any doctrine of the Inner Light that taught the presence of Christ or the Spirit in persons who had not been converted and sanctified. In Western Yearly Meeting, responses to a revival at Plainfield, Indiana, split the Meeting: ninety-nine Friends walked out of the Yearly Meeting Sessions, led by Robert Hodson, who said "he felt he and his party had no longer any rights or privileges among us."[37] They formed a new Conservative Yearly Meeting continuing in silent worship; their Meetings gradually died out. Kansas had a similar split in 1879. In North Carolina Conservative Friends did not secede until the 1902 Uniform Discipline.[38]

Canadian Orthodox Friends, who might have avoided a Hicksite separation in 1828, but for the influences of Henry Tuke's very orthodox book *Principles of Religion* and visits by English Friends George Withy, William Forster, Elizabeth Robson, and Thomas Shillitoe, had been part of New York Yearly Meeting until they formed their own Meeting in 1867. (In 1834 Canadian Hicksites had been joined with those in upstate New York to form Genesee Yearly Meeting). When the Canadian Orthodox proposed to adopt a new Discipline in 1877, they were visited by twenty-two Friends of all theologies, notably Robert W. Douglas and Luke Woodard of Indiana. In Norwich, Ontario, Monthly Meeting Gurneyites and Conservatives split in 1877, and Canada Yearly Meeting and many Monthly Meetings followed bitterly in 1881.[39]

The longest and most painful clash came in Iowa. There had already been a small split in 1851 due to the settling of Ohio "Wilburite" Friends in Red Cedar (they later founded Scattergood School). The Bear Creek Monthly and Quarterly Meetings split in 1877 following a revival, when one Friend reported:

I did not believe what the leaders told us, that if we would go to the mourners' bench and let them pray for us, we would be converted. Every bench wherever I sat was a mourners' bench. I knew I needed Christ. . . . To do as they urged us . . . would bring condemnation and not the peace I longed for. It was too cheap for me. One elderly woman, before departing, standing in front of the "mourners' bench," declared that the Society of Friends was now dead, that this action had killed it.[40]

The little Iowa Conservative Yearly Meeting later merged with the older Wilburite group and picked up also a unique Monthly Meeting of Norwegian Friends at Stavanger, descended from sailors who had been convinced of Quakerism while held prisoners in a Scottish port. The Iowa Yearly Meeting clerk, Joel Bean*, and his Philadelphian wife, Hannah, determined to stay with the main body of their Yearly Meeting. But they had visited Hawaii and California in 1861 and England in 1872 and had taught for two years at the Friends School in Rhode Island and knew Quakerism widely. In 1882 they migrated to San Jose, California, to escape Iowa conflicts. But Joel Bean wrote a letter on "The Issue" to *The British Friend* and was persuaded to travel eastward across American Quakerism with a British Quaker who disliked revivals. Since the San Jose Meeting belonged to Honey Creek Quarter in Iowa, the latter withdrew Bean's rights as a minister and forced the splitting of the San Jose Friends. The Beans' group became College Park, worshipping in silence, the seed out of which later grew the Pacific Yearly Meeting.[41] Bean's account in *The British Friend* began London Quakers' turn from support only of Gurneyites toward sympathy for Wilburites and Hicksites.[42]

Conservatism and revivalism divided Kansas Friends almost from the start. A few Friends went to Kansas during the inrush of Northerners and Southerners, which made it a bloody battleground for and against slavery before and during the Civil War. William Hobson, visiting northeastern Kansas in 1863, found thriving Meetings. A Yearly Meeting began at Lawrence in 1872, with twelve Monthly Meetings, twenty-five Sunday schools, and 2,620 members. But revivals like that in 1874 in Cottonwood Quarter left some Friends angry. They formed a Conservative Meeting, Spring River, where Cyrus Harvey edited *The Western Friend*.[43]

WATER BAPTISM

Adult baptism also caused keen discussion among midwestern "Orthodox" Quakers in the 1880s. In 1882 David Updegraff suddenly felt a divine leading to undergo immersion, when visiting the church of a Baptist pastor friend, and in the five following years he persuaded some hundreds of Ohio Friends to follow him into water baptism. At his memorial service his friend Dougan Clark, theologian and Bible professor at Earlham, felt led to be baptized also. When Elisha Bates of Ohio had been baptized after 1835, Sarah Smiley of Philadelphia in 1872, and Helen Balkwill in England in 1879, all had left Friends. Now the encouragement of adult baptism by the Ohio Friends who followed Updegraff produced an unsuccessful effort in the Yearly Meeting of 1885 to renew the traditional Quaker rejection of sacraments. Ohio Yearly Meeting agreed instead to tolerate differences; but the same year Indiana and other Yearly Meetings reaffirmed that water baptism was a needless "outward form."[44]

Second, baptism was one of the issues that led many Quakers to plan a uniform Discipline for all Friends, to overrule their diversities. Evangelical Yearly Meetings had been redrafting their Books of Discipline so as to reinterpret the meaning of ministry. Ohio's 1876 Discipline cut seven pages from the 1859 edition's discussion of plainness and called it simplicity. The sections on doctrine were built up instead.[45] Disownment penalties were removed from intermarriage and many ethical offenses, although alcohol, Masonic secret societies, dancing, and card playing were explicity condemned. Updegraff and his friend Inskip had in 1851 led a campaign for "promiscuous seating" of men and women together. Separation of the sexes during worship faded among Friends.

THE RICHMOND CONFERENCE AND DECLARATION OF 1887

Baptism and Discipline needed a new consensus among all Friends. Moving fairly fast, a group of Philadelphia and Indiana Quakers met in 1886 and called for a conference of delegates from all Yearly Meetings in Richmond, Indiana, for 1887. To Richmond came ninety-nine Friends from twelve "Orthodox" Yearly Meetings: Hicksites and Wilburites were not expected and did not come, but informally, the Philadelphia Yearly Meeting sent a solid group from its activist, "Gurneyite" faction. Updegraff was among those from Ohio; Esther Frame and Robert and John Henry Douglas were among the Indiana and Iowa representatives. Present also were others less revivalistic: Hoosiers Timothy and William Nicholson, six English and three Irish Friends, educators Benjamin Trueblood and Barnabas Hobbs, James Wood from New York, and Henry Hartshorne from Philadelphia.

Discussion on many issues was carefully recorded.[46] Early in the week it became clear that various Friends hoped for a normative statement of faith for Friends: a committee was chosen to discuss this; one member, Joseph Bevan Braithwaite* of England, was asked to draw up a document. Like his mother, Anna Braithwaite, he had traveled in America before and in England had sympathized with the ardent evangelical group around Isaac Crewdson's *Beacon* in 1835. He brought to Richmond statements used by London Yearly Meeting, from which he drew up a draft that the committee and the Richmond Conference carefully discussed but changed very little. This became the Richmond Declaration of Faith: solid evangelical theology with little stress on distinctively Quaker elements. Central emphasis was put upon the Bible, Christ, and the atonement, although it made fully clear the Quaker rejection of the outward sacraments. Although it presented the Quaker tradition on silent worship, it did not condemn pastors or mission boards. God's demand for holiness was stated in general terms, which did not rule out the gradual and purging process that earlier Quakers had gone through: the Declaration said of the Holy Spirit, that

dwelling in the hearts of believers, He opens their understandings that they may understand the Scriptures, and becomes, to the humbled and surrendered heart, the Guide, Comforter, Support and Sanctifier. . . . The essential qualification for the Lord's service is bestowed upon His children through the reception and baptism of the Holy Ghost. . . . We own no principle of spiritual light, life or holiness inherent by nature in the mind or heart of man, but the influence of the Holy Spirit of God bestowed on mankind, in various measures and degrees, through Jesus Christ our Lord.[p. 29]

Thus of the key disputes the revivalist leaders had raised, the conference overruled them only on the sacraments, and it seemed to many of them at the time a reconciling document.[47]

The baptized Ohio Friends went home protesting (in phrases that liberals would echo later) against the intolerant imposing of a Quaker creed. More unexpectedly, London and Dublin Yearly Meetings were already feeling the challenge of liberal thought about the Bible and theology and declined to adopt the Declaration formally. When the remaining "Gurneyite" Yearly Meetings (except Ohio and Philadelphia) met again in 1897 they found in Fox's *Journal* a letter written in 1671 to the Governor of Barbados by the group who sailed to America with Fox, to clear Friends from charges of heresy, and gave it equal status as a statement of faith.

The Richmond gathering of Evangelical Friends set precedents that satisfied most Friends. Those who had wanted to see an authoritative national group meet triennially had been overruled, but consultations every five years in Richmond or Indianapolis led to the forming in 1902 of a Five Years Meeting with delegated powers. (See Chapter 18.) The *Book of Discipline of the Five Years Meeting*, adopted in 1902, was accepted as the "Uniform Discipline" the Richmond Conference had hoped for. The American Friends Board of Missions, formed in 1894, was made the Five Years Meeting's organ. In 1904 it began to coordinate staffing and financial support for the work Yearly Meetings had begun in Jamaica, Cuba, Palestine, and Kenya. The Quaker projects in India, China, and Alaska continued to be the special projects of Yearly Meeting Boards that reflected more fully a Holiness theology.

By 1902 most of the leading evangelical Quakers had died. Younger revivalist leaders felt threatened by a rising tide of liberal thinking among eastern Quakers. They counterattacked against evolution and biblical criticism. Their theology was premillennial, linked to distrust of social reform and of intellectuals, with a scorn of Quaker history and "the kind of holiness somebody had two hundred years ago."[48]

NOTES

1. Thomas Hamm, *The Transformation of American Quakerism: Orthodox Friends, 1800–1907* (Bloomington, Ind.: 1988); hereafter Hamm, *TAQ*, is notable for scope and documentation. Whereas Hamm underlined the contrast between the evangelical Quaker "Renewal" of 1850–67 and the Holiness-centered revivalists of 1867–1910, Mark D. Minear in his alert *Richmond, 1887* (Richmond. Ind.: 1987) stressed the continuity of the two movements. So did J. Brent Bill, *David B. Updegraff: Quaker Holiness Preacher* (Richmond, Ind.: 1983), and B. Eugene Fisher, "A Study of Toleration among Midwest Quakers, 1850–1900" (M.A. thesis, ESR, 1972). More balanced are Lawrence E. Barker's M.A. thesis "The Development of the Pastoral Pattern in Indiana Yearly Meeting of the Religious Society of Friends" (ESR, 1963) and William P. Taber, Jr.'s *Eye of Faith* (Barnesville, Ohio: 1959). Richard E. Wood, "Evangelical Quakers in the Mississippi Valley" (Ph.D. thesis, University of Minnesota, 1984), was first to explore this topic.

2. Timothy Smith, *Revivalism and Social Reform* (Nashville: 1957), is the most complete study. William G. McLoughlin, *Revivals, Awakenings, and Reform* (Chicago: 1978) is broad; Melvin Easterday Dieter, *Holiness Revival* (Chicago: 1978), is oriented to "Holiness Church" denominations, as is Charles Edwin Jones, *Perfectionist Persuasion: The Holiness Movement and American Methodism, 1867–1936* (Metuchen, N.J.: 1974); but Jones's bibliography *A Guide to the Study of the Holiness Movement* (Metuchen, N.J.: 1974) includes the works of both Douglas brothers, Updegraff, and Hannah Whitall Smith.

3. See works listed in the entry for Hannah Whitall Smith in Part Two.

4. John Timothy Terrell, "Building up the Waste Places: Revivals and Reconstructionist Quakers in North Carolina" (B.A. Honors thesis, University of North Carolina, 1983) 47. See Allen Jay *Autobiography of Allen Jay: Born 1831. Died 1910* (Philadelphia: 1910), 196, Chs. 19–21. See also Zora Klain, *Quaker Contributions . . . North Carolina* (Philadelphia: 1925); S. B. Hinshaw and M. E. Hinshaw, *Carolina Quakers* (Greensboro, N.C.: 1972) and local Meeting histories of the North Carolina Friends Historical Society. On Nereus Mendenhall in North Carolina see Errol T. Elliott, *Quaker Profiles from the American West* (Richmond, Ind.: 1972), 1–24; but Hamm believes Mendenhall withdrew to teach at Haverford, rather than endure the Holiness revivals in North Carolina.

5. Minear, *Richmond, 1887*; Hamm, *TAQ*, Ch. 3; Elliott, *Quaker Profiles*.

6. Louis T. Jones, *The Quakers of Iowa* (Iowa City: 1914), 164, quoting Stacy Bevan. The other revivalist was John S. Bond. Also quoted in Darius B. Cook, *History of Quaker Divide* (Dexter, Iowa: 1914), 6.

7. Daniel Clark's letter to the *American Friend* 1 (12th month, 1867) 302, as summarized in Hamm, *TAQ* 77. See also Barker, "The Development of the Pastoral Pattern," 35.

8. *Reminiscences of Nathan T. Frame and Esther G. Frame* (Cleveland: 1907), 56ff.

9. Luke Woodard, who was present, named Lindley Hoag and Rebecca T. Updegraff, as the leaders: *Sketches of a Life of 75* (Richmond, Ind.: 1907). Most accounts draw on Mary Coffin Johnson, ed. *Rhoda Coffin: her Reminiscences* (New York: 1910), 79–80, and *Friends Review* 14, (10th Month 20th Day, 1860): 104.

10. Jones, *Quakers of Iowa*, 101, said John Henry Douglas in 1887 was swamped with invitations to preach at union revival meetings.

11. Barker, "The Development of the Pastoral Pattern," 36–44. See Indiana and Iowa Yearly Meeting Minutes; Hamm, *TAQ*, Ch. 3; Seth Hinshaw, *Carolina Quaker Experience* (Greensboro, N.C.: 1984) Ch. 17.

12. Jones, *Quakers of Iowa*, 386.

13. The first issue, February 15, 1871 has a report on a "General Meeting." See also Minear, *Richmond, 1887*.

14. Dougan Clark and Joseph H. Smith, *David B. Updegraff and His Work* (Cincinnati: 1895), 70 (partially in Bill, *David B. Updegraff*, 20). See also the scandal into which Logan Pearsal Smith stumbled. Some women preachers used similar tactics; Nathan Frame reported that "one night after the sermon, when the house was thronged, . . . there was a man standing in the doorway. . . . Esther [Frame] went to him and pressed him to give his heart to the Lord, but he refused, . . . 'No, I will not.' Then Esther lifted her voice in vocal prayer and said, 'Lord, bring him down! Lord, bring him down!' and he began to reel and . . . fell prostrate on the floor . . . and he was soon converted" (*Reminiscences*, 139).

15. See William James, *The Varieties of Religious Experience* (New York: 1903), Chs. 5, 6; Anton Boisen, *Religion in Crisis and Custom* (New York: 1955). Freud's human image assumes permanent conflict of id, ego, and superego but regards conversion as a hysterical phenomenon.

16. See Hamm, *TAQ*, Ch. 3.

17. John Wesley, *Christian Perfection*, in *John Wesley*, ed. Albert Outler (New York: 1964), 252–71. See also Dougan Clark, *Offices of the Holy Spirit* (London: 1878), 104f.

18. See Clark, *Offices*, 119, 150, 106. Italics original.

19. See ibid., Ch. 3.

20. Phoebe Palmer, *The Way of Holiness* (New York: 1845), 33.

21. Clark and Smith, *David B. Updegraff*, 19, 20.

22. See his "Personal Testimony," in David B. Updegraff, *Old Corn* (Boston: 1892), 375–78. For Luke Woodard's more guilt-burdened conversion, call to the ministry, and consecration, largely centered on accepting where he should work as a revivalist, after fearing he would be called to Africa, see his *Sketches of a Life*, 5–9.

23. For early British Friends mission work see *Memoirs of the Life and Gospel Labours of the Late Daniel Wheeler* (London: 1842), and John Ormerod Greenwood, *Quaker Encounters* (York: 1977), II, Chs. 6–10; (1978), III, Chs. 1–3.

24. Kansas Yearly Meeting Minutes, 1879ff.; Lawrie Tatum, *Our Red Brothers* (Philadelphia: 1899, 1970); Thomas C. Battey, *Life and Adventure of a Quaker among the Indians* (Boston: 1875); Rayner W. Kelsey, *Friends and the Indians* (Philadelphia: 1917); Ruthanna Sims, *As Long as the Sun Gives Light* (Richmond, Ind.: 1970); Clyde Milner II, *With Good Intentions: Quaker Work among the Pawnees, Otoes, and Omahas in the 1870's* (New York: 1976).

25. Christina Jones, *American Friends in World Missions* (Elgin, Ill. 1946), 107.

26. *History of Ohio Friends Missions*, published by the Friends Missionary Board of the Ohio Yearly Meeting (Damascus, Ohio: c. 1898), 5. Similarly, Friends' work in Cuba included Banes where "work was begun in Feb. 1903, by Chas. Haworth and wife. This is a new settlement built largely by the United Fruit Company and is quite American in appearance. . . . Our mission premises are located in the best part of the company's town." (*Friends Work in Cuba*, Tract by the Women's Foreign Missionary Union of Friends (Westfield, Ind.: nd.), 3.

27. See Byron Lindley Osborne, *The Malone Story* (Newton, Kan.: 1970) and biography of Walter Malone in Part II.

28. Arthur O. Roberts, *Tomorrow Is Growing Old* (Newberg, Oreg.: 1978), Chs. 1–5.

29. See Rose Adede, "The Impact of Quaker Missionaries in Kenya: The Work of Emory and Deborah Rees" (M.A. thesis, ESR, 1986).

30. See Barker, "The Development of the Pastoral Pattern," 53, 60–64; Minear, *Richmond, 1887*, 90–95; Hamm, *TAQ*, Ch. 6; Wood, "Evangelical Quakers."

31. Jones, *Quakers in Iowa*, 312.

32. Woodard, *Sketches*, 77; Jones, *Quakers in Iowa*, 104–5.

33. Benjamin Trueblood, "Ministers' Wages," *The Christian Worker* 2 (October 1872): 186, quoted in Minear, *Richmond, 1887* (Richmond: 1987), 91. See also Barker, "The Development of the Pastoral Pattern," 44ff.; Jones, *Quakers in Iowa*, 114, 286; Western Yearly Meeting Minutes.

34. David LeShana *Quakers in California* (Newberg, Oreg.: 1969), 166, quoting John Wilhelm Rowntree; Richard Ratcliff, *Our Special Heritage: . . . Indiana Yearly Meeting of Friends* (New Castle, Ind.: 1970), 94–146.

35. *Testimony for Truth*, issued by the Meeting for Sufferings of Western Yearly Meeting, 1878, quoted in Barker, "The Development of the Pastoral Pattern," 54. They also noted changes in "the use of hymn books" and "the manner of receiving persons into membership."

36. On the Lindseys, see Jones, *Quakers in Iowa*, 56–58; LeShana, *Quakers in California*, 69–78; Walter R. Williams, *The Rich Heritage of American Quakerism* (Grand Rapids, Mich.: 1962), 201.

37. Walter Robson, quoted in Edwin Bronner, *An English View of American Quakerism* (Philadelphia: 1970), 67.

38. Seth Hinshaw, *Carolina Quaker Experience*, 217–22.

39. Arthur Dorland, *Quakers in Canada* (Toronto: 1968), Chs. 9 and 13.

40. Ella Newlin's typed manuscript, 1935, quoted by Herbert C. Standing in "Historical Notes Concerning the Conservative Friends at Bear Creek" (1977). See also Darius B. Cook, *Memoirs of Quaker Divide* (Dexter, Iowa: 1914); Jones, *Quakers in Iowa*, Part II, Ch. 4.

41. See excellent account in LeShana, *Quakers in California*, Chs. 5, 7. Further details are in Hamm, *TAQ*, Chs. 5, 6; Howard H. Brinton, "The Revival Movement in Iowa: A Letter from Joel Bean to Rufus M. Jones," *Quaker History* 50 (Fall 1961): 107–9.

42. See Edwin Bronner, *"The Other Branch": London Yearly Meeting and the Hicksites, 1827–1912* (London: 1975).

43. See Myron D. Goldsmith, "Hobson," 172, see chapter 13, note 17; Errol Elliott, *Quakers on the American Frontier* (Richmond, Ind.: 1969), 147; Kansas Yearly Meeting Minutes, 1872, 1873; Hamm, *TAQ*, Ch. 5.

44. See Fisher "A Study of Toleration"; Minear, *Richmond, 1887*, 85–89; Hamm, *TAQ*, Ch. 6.

45. The 1891 Western Yearly Meeting Discipline insisted that "no one should be recorded as a minister whose doctrinal views are not clearly in accord with the Affirmative of the Questions" on God, Christ, and the Spirit that they printed.

46. The committee for printing of *Proceedings, including Declaration of Christian Doctrine, of the General Conference of Friends, held in Richmond, Ind., U.S.A., 1887*, was Allen and Mahalah Jay and Thomas N. White. Their book included a stenographic report on the discussions.

47. See Minear, *Richmond, 1887*; Fisher, "A Study of Toleration."

48. Dougan Clark, "The Society of Friends and Holiness," in *The Christian Worker*, January 14, 1886, quoted also by Hamm, *TAQ*.

17
THE LIBERAL
TRANSFORMATION

Between the Civil War and 1900 eastern Quakers changed at a glacial pace while urbanization, industrialization, and immigration revolutionized the world around them. Philadelphia Friends in 1880 remained divided over the issues of the 1830s. Orthodox Friends, who united in refusing to associate with the heretic Hicksites, were composed of two disputing factions—Wilburites and Gurney-ites—and only just managed to stay together in the Arch Street Yearly Meeting. The Wilburites, or quietists, distrusted higher education, opposed any change in dress or Discipline, disliked religious activities like First Day Schools or Bible societies, and idealized the virtues of a fast-disappearing rural way of living. The Gurneyites disagreed on each of the above, supporting learning and Haverford College, gradually dropping the distinctive Quaker language and dress, participating in a large variety of charitable and philanthropic activities, and attempting, unsuccessfully, to make minor modifications in the Discipline.[1] By 1900 the Philadelphia Orthodox numbered only 4,460, about one-third the size of the Hicksites, and were concentrated in urban areas where they resembled more an extended family or clan rather than a denomination.

The Hicksites had an easier task of accepting change since they had long claimed to stand for diversity and equality among members. Almost from the time of the separation the Hicksites embraced notions of the unimportance of creeds, the symbolic nature of religious language, and the priority of experience. In 1894 a revision of the Hicksite Discipline essentially ended disownment for mixed marriages or any other cause, merged Men's and Women's Meetings for business, and broke the equation between simplicity and the plain style of dress and language.[2] The Hicksites, recognizing that Swarthmore College could not continue as a satisfactory boarding school and college at the same time, in 1893 established George School in Bucks County as their equivalent to Westtown. As early as 1866 the Hicksite Yearly Meeting endorsed an attempt to establish contacts with all other Friends. By 1900 the Hicksite Yearly Meeting sessions had become a forum for education and worship, and large standing committees set the policies on most issues. In 1900 all Hicksite Yearly Meetings in America joined to create the Friends General Conference, a consultative and educational body that met every other year. The 12,000 Philadelphia Yearly Meeting Hicksites comprised over half of the total membership of the General Conference.

To insiders the differences between the Arch Street Wilburites, the Twelfth Street Gurneyites, and the Race Street Hicksites appeared immense. To outsiders all three groups seemed the same. Members of both Yearly Meetings generally voted Republican at the national level and sought for honest government at the local level, though very few were willing to become actively involved in municipal politics. They favored temperance, supported Indian rights, and accepted their role as the bridge between black and white Americans. Both Yearly Meetings supported schools for the blacks, tended to ignore immigrants, and sponsored paternalistic charities for the urban poor.[3]

Any differences in wealth and status between members of the two Yearly Meetings had long since disappeared. Friends remained concentrated overwhelmingly in middle and upper classes with few members who were blue collar, immigrant, or black. Although a small number of Friends appeared in the *Social Register*, they tended to be nominal members. The movement of Quakers away from agriculture and into the white-collar professions—law, teaching, management—was well under way before 1900. There were still a few Quakers with great wealth. Joseph Wharton's fortune came from organizing the American lead and zinc industry before he helped found Bethlehem Steel. The Strawbridge and Clothier department store proved that Hicksite and Orthodox could unite in making money by retailing merchandise that did not conform to Quaker simplicity. Quakers managed the Provident Bank and Life Insurance Company in a conservative and profitable style. Friends continued to play a significant role in medicine, helping to found the Women's Medical College (the first in the nation for women) and to serve as trustees of the Pennsylvania Hospital and Friends Hospital.[4]

The most striking evidence of similarity between the two Yearly Meetings was in the steep decline in numbers of members. Between 1827 and 1900 the Hicksites lost 38 percent and the Orthodox 40 percent of their members so that there were only 16,000 Friends out of a total Philadelphia population of 1.3 million. Even worse, many of the 16,000 were only nominal members. Philip Benjamin's analysis of city Quakers found that 54 percent could be classified as nominal; that is, they were not ministers, elders, or overseers and rarely served on committees or appeared in the minutes in any capacity. The conservative Arch Street Meeting had the highest percentage of weighty and practicing Friends, and the progressive Race Street Meeting had the highest percentage (63 percent) of nominal members. Attendance at Quaker schools and endogamous marriage in unity provided the highest correlation with continuing activity in the Meeting.[5]

In the late nineteenth century the Hicksite Meetings in Ohio and both Philadelphia Meetings did not grow. Meetings in New York, New England, Maryland, and North Carolina had small increases. The London Yearly Meeting's membership rose nearly 25 percent between 1871 and 1900. Evangelical Meetings in Ohio, Indiana, and the Far West enjoyed spectacular success during the same periods. Clearly, the Hicksites changed their Discipline in 1894 because of numerical decline. With nearly 40 percent of their marriages being between members and outsiders by the 1860s, the Hicksites either had to modify policy or become extinct. Still, the changes did not change the downward trend.

What factors made Philadelphia's Yearly Meetings fail to grow? One factor was clearly demographic. Nearly 40 percent of the women in the two organizations remained single.[6] The requirement for endogamous marriage that the Orthodox kept until after World War I meant that some women had to choose between their faith and being married. More women than men remained active in the Meetings, and Quaker schools and charity organizations provided a way to earn a living or engage in worthwhile activity. A few may have chosen not to marry because of academic interests. Bryn Mawr was organized in 1885 and Swarthmore was chartered in 1864 as a coeducational institution, and many late nineteenth-century women college graduates did not marry.

A second factor retarding growth was the opposition and bitterness within the Quaker community. Schisms and controversy did not weaken midwestern Friends and other denominations in this period but these churches vigorously proselytized through revivals and Sunday schools. Philadelphia Friends refused to seek outsiders and recommended caution in welcoming them to membership. The conservatism of Philadelphia Friends who had constantly to prove to each other that they were really Quakers also contributed. London and midwestern Friends dropped distinctive customs of dress and speech. Arch Street Friends kept the Gurneyites from innovating, and all the silent Meeting attenders opposed holding revivals.

By 1900 Philadelphia Quakers appeared to most outsiders as quaint survivals of the colonial period whose customs and beliefs were irrelevant to the wider society. The meetings either had to change or face extinction. The change was liberalism.

CHALLENGES TO FAITH

At the beginning of the nineteenth century in England and in America large numbers of Friends embraced evangelicalism. At the end of the century a similar transformation occurred, only now evangelicalism was dropped. The rise of liberalism after 1890 would end quietist and evangelical dominance in the London and the Philadelphia Yearly Meeting (Orthodox) and would allow a close relationship and eventual reunification to take place among the two Philadelphia, the two New York, and the two Maryland Yearly Meetings. Liberalism, like evangelicalism, originated outside the Society of Friends and could be adopted because its tenets were compatible with existing Quaker emphases.

There were four sources of Quaker liberalism: the traditions of Friends, an American religious heritage originating in New England transcendentalism, European intellectual developments, and a creative response to the challenges presented by developments in science and history. We now can see that liberalism's credo complemented or even duplicated several elements in Quaker history: that the source of authority in religion came from experience, that creeds camouflaged as often as they elucidated and were secondary, and that religious commitment should culminate in service to the distressed. Liberals built their faith upon the fatherhood of God, the example of Jesus as a guide for ethics, and the kinship of all peoples.[7] At times William Penn*, John Woolman*, John Greenleaf Whittier*, and Lucretia Mott*, by focusing upon contact with God in the meeting for worship, had espoused a religion like that of the liberals, but they had done so in a far different context. All had almost unconsciously exempted the Bible, the Inward Light, and the traditions of the Meeting from critical historical scrutiny.

Literary critics, historians, and theologians in the nineteenth century revolutionized the study of the Bible. The Germans, in particular, pioneered the use of philology, archeology, and history to show the variety of sources and different times of composition of the books in the Bible. Knowledge of the cultures surrounding ancient Israel allowed scholars to demonstrate how Canaanite, Babylonian, Persian, and Greek ideas had been incorporated into Judaism and Christianity. In short, religion could not be divorced from a cultural context.[8] In the Bible religious practices and interpretations evolved according to circumstances, and to assume a continuity in tradition or that the "right" invariably triumphed was naive. Prooftexting without considering the entire perspective of the Deuteronomistic historian or of First, Second,—was there a Third?—Isaiah or of the Q source containing teachings of Jesus behind the synoptic Gospels would distort the Scriptures. Biblical Truths were plural and not static and evolved as the Hebrews reached higher stages of maturity.

A second reinterpretation of the Bible came from the geologists, paleontologists, and Charles Darwin. By 1860 scholars found it increasingly difficult to accept Genesis' chronology for creation without stretching the language (redefining the "days" in Genesis I) or ignoring the fossil evidence.[9] The textual critics put the Bible in history; Darwin put humankind in history. He marshaled sufficient evidence to convince scientists that the ancestry of humans came through the natural world and not by a special creation that divorced them from the rest of the animal kingdom. Many Victorians experienced trauma in learning that being made a little lower than the angels now meant having cousins in the ape family.

Darwin representing science and textual criticsm representing history posed serious challenges for those who believed that all Truth was united and that honest intellectual endeavor would always confirm the Truths of the Christian religion. The response of the devout to the new thought ranged from denying the conclusions of the scholars to be valid if they disagreed with the Bible (called *fundamentalism* in the twentieth century), insisting upon the separate spheres of religion and science, and attempting to reconcile the Bible and scholarship in a higher unity. The last two methods had at their disposal an interpretation of religion stemming from Kant in Germany, Coleridge in England, and Emerson and Bushnell in America that embraced philosophical idealism and repudiated materialism, biblicism, and evangelicalism.[10] Long before Darwin, men like Emerson insisted that the ground of authority in religion was not the Bible or creed but experience. The Bible contained the early Hebrews' and Christians' science, poetry, history, and mythology as well as a witness to the evolution of their faith. Scriptures remained useful as a guide for the spiritual life of the religious community and contained Truths about human existence. Viewing the Bible as a human as well as a divinely inspired book allowed for richness in understanding God's revelation and human response.

The essential outlines of liberal theology were well established long before Quakers (and most Americans) learned them. Orthodox Friends in England and America repudiated the ideas on first contact, but even before the schism some Hicksites had been sympathetic. The main change after 1890 would come to the Gurneyites, who, because they had accepted the value of a college education, were more susceptible than the Wilburites. All of the nineteenth-century Quaker colleges except Swarthmore were founded and attended by Gurneyites. Colleges required professors and that meant training some Quaker youths to be competent in science, history, and classical languages. England had no Quaker colleges, but it had excellent boarding schools that needed teachers. Quaker liberalism began in the academy and was propagated by educators who wanted to train their pupils in a way that would preserve faith without repudiating science.

LIBERALISM IN ENGLAND

The leading English Victorian Quakers were evangelicals. After 1827 the London Yearly Meeting recognized only the Gurneyite Meetings in America while repudiating first the Hicksites and later the Wilburites and Conservatives. Even so, London's blend of Quakerism and evangelical doctrines did not prevent internal tensions. Some members wanted the Meetings to repudiate the doctrine of the Inward Light and to adopt hymns and sacraments.

Ministers from Great Britain who traveled in the western United States after 1870 found Gurneyite Quakers singing hymns, holding revivals, giving testimonials, and paying ministers. Some responded sympathetically, talking about changing conditions and the numerical successes; others had more difficulty in understanding the disorder in western gatherings in contrast with the silent meetings among the Hicksites. Occasionally, a minister might even suggest adopting revival techniques in Great Britain. English Friends already used Bible readings, hymn singing, and leaders in a combination adult Sunday school–home missionary endeavor they conducted among workers and lower-middle-class artisans in factory towns. When these men and women sought to become members, they introduced a different class as well as changed perspective into the Meetings.

Recruitment from the children and adults attending the Mission Schools stopped the numerical decline of the London Yearly Meeting.[11] Still, English Quakerism remained in the control of a small number of wealthy and interrelated familes. When the evangelicals encountered conservative opposition within the Meeting, they simply bypassed it and created their own voluntary association.

Liberalism originated in the London Yearly Meeting as a movement of a younger generation whose fathers and mothers had often led the evangelicals. For example, J. Bevan Braithwaite* (1818–1905), a lawyer, scholar, and traveling minister, was a principal author of the Richmond Declaration of Faith. His son William Charles Braithwaite became a leader of the liberals, friend of Rufus Jones, and author of an impressive two-volume history of the origins of Quakers. Edward Grubb, A. Neave Brayshaw, John Wilhelm Rowntree, John W. Graham, and Thomas Hodgkin all came from prominent Quaker families. Undoubtedly the respectability in family as well as the ability of these men facilitated the introduction of liberalism into English Quakerism.[12]

James Rendel Harris (1852–1941), a Cambridge graduate, symbolized the transatlantic character as well as the major theological and social concerns of the liberals. He engaged in relief work in Armenia. He became one of the foremost New Testament scholars of his time, discovering a Syriac version of the *Apology of Aristides* and the *Odes of Solomon*, teaching at Johns Hopkins University and Haverford College before returning to Clare College, Cambridge, as a reader in palaeography. He turned down the chair of ancient Christian literature at the University of Leyden to become the first director of studies at Woodbrooke. Like his fellow liberals, Harris was not a stuffy scholar, being described as a "Puck turned Saint and now and then Puck gets so much the upper hand."[13]

The first public questioning of evangelical emphasis in the 1870s brought little response, but the liberals received widespread support in two events during the 1890s. J. Bevan Braithwaite attempted to gain the London Yearly Meeting's endorsement of the Richmond Declaration of Faith in 1887. The effort failed, ostensibly because Friends did not wish to adopt a creed. The second indication of dissatisfaction with evangelicalism occurred at a summer conference held in Manchester in 1895 to consider the relationship of Quakerism to modern thought. More than 1,300 Friends attended and spent four days listening to liberal speakers discuss theology, science, the Bible, and practical ethics.[14]

The response to the Manchester Conference led to the creation of an annual summer school. George Cadbury, head of Cadbury chocolate and an industrialist who pioneered in providing social services for his employees, offered his house and estate in Birmingham and an endowment to create a center for Friends to study religious and social topics. Woodbrooke opened in 1903 as a college for adults, a place for scholarship, a retreat, and a center for training leaders.[15] Since evangelicals had earlier moved outside the structures of the Meeting to sponsor missionaries, liberals now ignored the London Yearly Meeting in holding summer schools, creating Woodbrooke, and founding a journal, *Present-Day Papers*.

English liberalism was not a response to institutional weakness nor numerical decline; rather, it was an educated younger generation's response to new intellectual and social conditions.

The changed theological climate after 1890 allowed a reassessment of London's policy of recognizing only Gurneyite Meetings. When the policy had been instituted, it was assumed that the Hicksites, like other schismatic groups, would soon die out. Traveling ministers first began to question the wisdom of nonrecognition. They found it difficult to distinguish the Philadelphia Hicksites who came to hear them from the Orthodox. Still, the official Hicksite overture for contact in 1866 was ignored. After the midwestern Friends adopted new forms of worship, the silent-meeting Hicksites looked better to Londoners. Contact with Swarthmore College faculty, marriages between English and Philadelphia Hicksite families, cooperation in peace activities, increasing social contacts among members of the two Philadelphia Meetings, and recognition that English Friends had helped precipitate the original division caused the London Yearly Meeting in 1908 to send out an Epistle to "all who bear the name of Friends."[16] The Hicksites responded. The Philadelphia Yearly Meeting Orthodox issued a similar Epistle in 1897 and in 1906 acknowledged receipt of London's annual Epistle. Isolation had ended.

RUFUS JONES

In England liberalism appears as a contribution of a generation. In America it appears as the elongated shadow of one man—Rufus Jones.* Jones (1863–1948), a child of Gurneyite farmers, grew up in the secluded atmosphere of South China, Maine, where Quakers seemed an extended family. Sybil and Eli Jones,* his aunt and uncle, were influential traveling Quaker ministers who founded a school in Ramallah, Palestine, and who had many acquaintances in England and America. Rufus attended schools in Maine among relatives; later he went to Moses Brown boarding school in Rhode Island among cousins and received the B.A. and M.A. at Haverford where he found more cousins. At Moses Brown his science teacher introduced him to Darwin's theory of evolution, and his professors at Haverford set him to work upon mysticism and Emerson. There he discovered affinities between Quakerism and mystical religion. After spending a year teaching in a Quaker school after graduation, he journeyed to Europe meeting relatives and prominent Friends in England and studying philosophy in Germany.[17]

In 1893 Jones came to Haverford as instructor in philosophy and editor of the *American Friend*. He edited the magazine for twenty years, and it gave him an excellent forum for influencing Friends. After a second trip to Europe in 1897, where he found a shared viewpoint with English liberals and planned with John Wilhelm Rowntree a series of books on the history of Friends, he spent a year studying philosophy at Harvard. He returned to Haverford College in 1898 as professor of philosophy and taught there for the next forty years.

Jones's impact upon Friends was facilitated because he was and was not a Philadelphia Quaker. He kept his membership in the New England Yearly Meeting, which became part of the Five Years Meeting. Yet his positions as editor and faculty member allowed him to participate in the Philadelphia Yearly Meeting Orthodox, even if some Arch Street conservatives refused for years to invite him to sit in the ministers' gallery. Jones wrote with the speed of a journalist and the precision of a scholar. Editorials, story books for children, devotional literature, book reviews, history, philosophy, sermons, autobiography, biography, introductions for other authors' books, editions of Quaker writings—in all there were fifty-four books and a bibliography of his writings contained thousands of entries.[18]

In addition to being a writer of vivid prose, Jones excelled as an orator. Speaking in a down-east Maine twang and using anecdotes to illustrate difficult topics, Jones communicated his ideas to evangelicals, conservatives, liberals, scholars, and the barely educated. He also had a gift for friendship. He liked to talk to students, work on committees, tell stories, and listen. He was as effective in working with his farmer neighbors in Maine as with John D. Rockefeller, Jr. A good administrator, an effective fundraiser, a superb diplomat, a respected scholar—Jones combined the personal and professional skills necessary to persuade and influence. Above all, Jones's effectiveness came from his religious qualities. He didn't just talk about mysticism, he lived it and shared his deepest convictions and experiences. The public saw in him a man touched by God, and this quality disarmed mere theological disagreements.

Jones in his initial encounter with Philadelphia Quakers saw an ossification of forms cutting them off from their own heritage and the wider world. He believed that both quietists and evangelicals distorted the vital testimony of early Friends. Quietists followed a false dualism expressed in Robert Barclay's* *Apology* and dominant in the eighteenth century that divided existence into discrete physical and spiritual realms and required passive waiting to seek an imaginary purity. The evangelicals had enshrined a set of static dogmas that violated the essence of the Bible and the religious impulses of early Friends. Jones saw his role as emancipating modern Quakers from these relics of the past and restoring the creative and dynamic impulses to Quakerism. Friends had originally been and should again become a part of a general movement of spirituality, a prophetic and mystical Christianity.

Jones's research into original sources was not just to compile dry facts but to free modern Friends from recent errors. He wrote five of the seven Rowntree Series of Quaker histories that portrayed the spiritual forebearers of Friends, the characteristics of the First Publishers, the later influences of quietism, evangelicalism, and schism.[19] He later wrote studies of George Fox,* the English Commonwealth, and the mystics of the fourteenth century. History remained part of Jones's religious vision in which events had a moral dimension, showing the steps by which humanity had learned to encounter the divine. He qualified in later life but never repudiated his belief in an evolutionary cycle that brought progress.

Like other liberals, Jones was less interested in creeds than in the deeper significance of traditional formulations. For example, the doctrine of virgin birth expressed the incarnation. The atonement was a means of communication of the nature of God to humans. The Trinitarian formula showed how early Christians experienced the unity of God as Father, Son, and Holy Ghost. More important than the preexistence of Jesus was that "on the highest level that has been reached since the race began, God as Spirit has broken through into visibility and has shown His true nature in life and action."[20]

Quakerism was a spiritual religion, a way of life in which people learned to cooperate with God. Quakers needed no special sacraments because all of life was sacramental—a place where God and humans learned to touch. Such encounters were what Jones labeled affirmative mysticsm—a spiritual sense of the goodness of the universe and the kinship of humanity with ultimate reality. Jones did not deny either the transcendence of God or the power of evil but stressed the immanence of God and the goodness of people. These affirmations were not made lightly. In 1899 his wife, Sarah, died of tuberculosis, and four years later his son Lowell died of a reaction to inoculation for diphtheria. Jones had chronic ill health and, at the onset of World War I, experienced a crippling depression. His optimism rested upon his mystical experiences.

For Jones, Quaker mysticism differed from the negative mysticism of the Middle Ages that sought the loss of self in individual contemplation of the divine. He distinguished between a "positive" type—ethical, loving, encounter—and "negative" kind of Vedanta, Neoplatonic, or Dionysian, where God is timeless, changeless, formless, imageless. Quaker mysticism took place in a group—the meeting for worship—and did not require a suspension of the intellect. It culminated in moral activity.

Because God was involved in the world and could not be confined to creeds, Jones saw no reason to adopt a narrow definition of correct Quakerism. He could preach in a pastoral Meeting, ponder in advance what he might say in a silent Meeting, participate in a communion service when he was with non-Friends, meditate with Buddhists, and serve as guest minister for Unitarians and Baptists. He regarded the divisions among American Quakers as a scandal and sought to foster contacts among all groups of Quakers. As editor of the *American Friend* and a representative from the New England Yearly Meeting, he helped organize the Five Years Meeting, lectured at Meetings of Friends General Conference, attempted to break down the isolation of the Philadelphia Yearly Meeting (Orthodox) and to merge it with the Hicksite Yearly Meeting, and participated in summer schools of English Friends.

In 1916 English Friends determined to hold a conference with all varieties of Quakers to seek ways of preventing war. The conference could not be held until 1920.[21] Jones played a role in its organization, attended and spoke at it, and

served as a presiding clerk at a successor Friends World Conference held in
1937 at Swarthmore and Haverford colleges. The liberals' vision of Quaker unity
was institutionalized in the Friends World Committee for Consultation, which
exists to foster intervisitation among Friends throughout the world.[22]

As a major figure among Protestant liberals, Jones became a frequent speaker
at college chapel services. In 1929 and 1932 he participated in general evaluations
of the missionary enterprise of American churches. He was active in the National
and World Council of Churches. Through his writings and speeches, Jones
exerted more impact on other denominations than any previous Quaker.

NOTES

1. Philip Benjamin, *Philadelphia Quakers in the Industrial Age, 1865–1920* (Ann
Arbor, Mich.: 1971), 14–19. The Wilburites outside of Philadelphia remained rural. In
the Philadelphia Yearly Meeting they were recent migrants to the city who created in
Arch Street the feeling of a rival Meeting.

2. *Rules of Discipline and Advices of the Yearly Meeting of the Religious Society of
Friends* (Philadelphia: 1894).

3. Benjamin, *Philadelphia Quakers*, 75–125.

4. Ibid., 49–67, 160–64.

5. Ibid., 218.

6. Ibid., 159.

7. William R. Hutchinson, *Modernist Impulse in American Protestantism* (Cambridge, Mass: 1976) 2–9; Paul Carter, *The Spiritual Crisis of the Gilded Age* (Dekalb,
Ill.: 1971).

8. James Turner, *Without God, Without Creed* (Baltimore: 1985), 141–67.

9. Herbert Hovenkamp, *Science and Religion in America, 1800–1860* (Philadelphia:
1978), 119–45.

10. Sydney E. Ahlstrom, *A Religious History of the American People* (New Haven:
1972), 583–614, 775–84.

11. Elizabeth Isichei, *Victorian Quakers* (London: 1970), 269–279.

12. Roger Wilson, "Friends in the Nineteenth Century," *The Friends Quarterly*,
October 1984, 353–63. The whole issue is devoted to the centenary of the publication
of *A Reasonable Faith* (1884) by Francis Frith, William Pollard, and W. E. Turner.

13. Elizabeth Gray Vining, *Friend of Life: A Biography of Rufus Jones* (Philadelphia:
1958), 70. A sketch of Harris's life and scholarship by H. G. Wood is in Robert Davis,
ed., *Woodbrooke, 1903–1953* (London: 1953), 19–30.

14. Isichei, *Victorian Quakers*, 33–43; Roger Wilson, "The Road to Manchester,
1895," in *Seeking the Light: Essays in Quaker History*, J. William Frost and John M.
Moore, (Philadelphia: 1986), 5, 145–162.

15. Davis, ed., *Woodbrooke*, 13–18.

16. Edwin Bronner, " 'The Other Branch,' London Yearly Meeting and the Hicksites,
1827–1912," *Journal of the Friends Historical Society* (London), Supplement 34 (1975):
55–59.

17. There are two biographies of Jones: Vining, *Friend of Life*, and David Hinshaw,
Rufus Jones, Master Quaker (New York: 1951). Jones wrote three autobiographical
volumes, *A Small Town Boy* (New York: 1941), *The Trail of Life in College* (New York:

1929), and *The Trail of Life in the Middle Years* (New York: 1937). Additional citations can be found in *Dictionary of American Biography*, Supplement Four, 1946–50 (New York: 1974), 441–43, entry by Edwin Bronner.

18. Nixon O. Rush, *A Bibliography of the Published Writings of Rufus M. Jones* (Waterville, Maine: 1944), contains forty-eight pages of entries.

19. Rufus M. Jones, *Spiritual Reformers of the 16th and 17th Centuries* (London: 1914), idem, *The Later Periods of Quakerism*, 2 vols. (London: 1921); idem, with Isaac Sharpless and Amelia M. Gummere, *Quakers in the American Colonies* (London: 1923): idem, *Studies in Mystical Religion* (London: 1936).

20. Harry Emerson Fosdick, ed., *Rufus Jones Speaks to Our Time* (New York: 1951), 10.

21. E. R. Orr, *Quakers in Peace and War, 1920–1967* (Sussex, Eng.: 1974), 23.

22. Herbert Hadley is currently writing a history of the Friends World Committee for Consultation.

18
SUBURBAN AND COLLEGE FRIENDS: WEST AND MIDWEST, 1902–1960

The alienation Friends had felt after the Revolution from the national and military ideals of Americans faded in the mid-century. Friends had not idealized frontier expansion as did Mormon "Zion" mytholology, nor did they, like Methodists, try to convert the crude Jacksonian Kentucky and Tennessee frontiersmen, but the antislavery crusade gave religious meaning to Friends' migrations from the Carolinas to the Ohio Valley and on into Iowa and "bloody Kansas." Friends carried their tight community life wherever they resettled, but in the Civil War they shared with northern Protestants the traumatic clash of peace and antislavery ideals and their concern for black freedmen after the war. City Quakers worked with non-Quakers in philanthropy. Although the urban lay Holiness Awakening of 1858 had not involved Friends, after 1867 they shared the rural outreach of the Holiness movement in small-town "union revivals." By 1902 Friends were probably less alienated from American religious and cultural ideals than ever in their history. In 1902 American "manifest destiny" was at its peak; Friends reflected it in their mission moves into Cuba and into newly opened doors in China, East Africa, Guatemala, and Jamaica, although they mainly ignored the Spanish-American War and Chinese "Boxer" Rebellion.[1]

CITY VALUES AND SUBURBAN LIFE

The dominant fact in America in 1902, however, was the rise of the non-Protestant cities. The influx of Catholic Italians and Poles and Russian Jews, like the earlier Irish and later Mexican and Puerto Rican migrations, created "cities within cities" with life-styles contrasting with the Protestant patterns into which the German and Scandinavian immigrants had fit. Meanwhile, cities were turning farmland into suburbs or into large farms using machinery small farms could not afford and raising regional crops for a national market. All of the rural churches felt the cultural shocks:

the farm-to-city movement became a torrent [wrote Timothy Smith, the historian of the Nazarenes]: . . . Dixieland Negroes now moved in large numbers upon Detroit, Chicago, Indianapolis, New York and Philadelphia, creating grievous tensions. Meanwhile, mass education and the allurements of city life quickened the pace by which young people threw off parental restraints and discarded old values. The daily newspaper, the popular magazine, the moving picture theater, and the automobile, radio, airplane and television each in turn increased the passion for movement, [and] spread novel ideas.[2]

The revival meetings that had spread from frontier to cities and out to small towns now became annual events in suburban churches with an increasingly conservative aim, to bring young people into "old-time" faith and morality. Threats seeming to stem from the new sciences produced a "warfare of science and religion." Fundamentalist doctrines on the verbal inerrancy of Scripture, the physical virgin birth, resurrection, and miracles of Christ became bulwarks to protect faith in God's atoning love. Holiness had earlier focused wholly on love and self-surrender. It now became defined negatively, as purity from pollution by the theaters, saloons, dress customs, card playing, and smoking habits of the cities. Friends had long disowned each other for drunkenness; the "guarded education" of Friends schools excluded cards and novels, music and dancing. But Quakers now worked politically for Prohibition and attacked the introduction of saloons into "Quaker towns" like Newberg, Oregon, and Whittier, California. Friends became state and national executives of the Anti-Saloon League and Women's Christian Temperance Union.[3]

In the 1830s the Free and Wesleyan Methodists, Disciples, and Cumberland Presbyterians, identified with midwestern farms and small town life, had already broken with centralized church authorities. They often denied any desire for denominational structures. In the 1890s churches committed to Holiness began to "come out" and split from the "worldly" denominations centered in eastern cities where the lay Holiness revival had begun in 1858. To them were now added a kaleidoscope of Churches of God, Assemblies of God, and, eventually, Nazarene and Pentecostal churches centered on instant, total "second-blessing" Holiness experience. Some Holiness preachers added dispensationalist premillennialism or faith healing. Some moved from Vermont to Boston suburbs or from Iowa and Tennessee to new towns in Texas, Colorado, and California; but as western towns also became worldly the movement's heartland became again midwestern suburbs and small towns.[4]

A key center was often a Bible college or institute for preachers, modeled on Moody's in Chicago. Many such schools were rural, serving small-town churches: Asbury in Kentucky, Taylor University in Indiana, Peniel in Texas (later merged with Bethany Nazarene College, Oklahoma), Vennard (earlier Central Holiness University) in Oskaloosa, Iowa, and Friends Bible College of Haviland, Kansas. Others were urban or suburban: Azusa (California), Cascade (Oregon), God's Bible School (Cincinnati), Gordon College (near Boston), and Walter and Emma Malone's Cleveland Bible College. Each school reached out to all of the Holiness churches. Many Quakers were among their founders, teachers, and students. More Quaker pastors today are graduates of such schools than of broader liberal arts colleges. Quaker revivalists changed membership easily: Seth Rees went on to head the Independent Holiness Church in Texas and Oklahoma. Oregon Quaker pastor Lewis I. Hadley became a Nazarene leader in Whittier, Edgar P. Ellyson a Nazarene superintendent, after heading a Bible college at Marshalltown, Iowa, and teaching at Peniel. In the present decade David LeShana left George Fox College's presidency and joined the Free Methodists to head their Seattle Pacific University.

Through the sixty years covered in this chapter, many traditional programs continued in local Meetings. Christian Endeavor programs involved dozens of young people in every town, usually on an interchurch basis. In the 1920s they were replaced by Young Friends and parallel denominational groups. The peace and temperance societies that once flourished in local Meetings had mostly been dropped by 1940, as the leaders became involved in Yearly Meetings, national committees, or interchurch associations. Regional Quaker Women's Missionary Societies not only funded but guided most foreign and home mission work in the last third of the nineteenth century. The First National Gathering of Friends Women, 1888, began triennial meetings of the Friends Women's Foreign Missionary Union, after 1948 called *United Society of Friends Women*. It meets independently of the Friends United Meeting but supports that group's missions. In 1950 *Quaker Men*, too, became a national organization, also active in towns, at Yearly Meetings, and in fund raising.

RURAL FRIENDS

Those rural midwestern Yearly Meetings that did not share these regional developments showed only quieter changes. Most Hicksite Monthly Meetings in Ohio and Indiana were so individualistic and relatively isolated that they achieved little new and in Ohio slowly withered. While the rural Hicksites were dying out, the Iowa and Ohio Conservative Yearly Meetings were tightly enough knit and deeply enough rooted in farming families that with minimal additions of new members they survived. They continued plain dress and plain language until the midtwentieth century. They remain Christ-centered in doctrine, though Ohio Friends experienced a charismatic or "tongues" movement. Their religious activities have centered at their secondary boarding schools, Olney at Barnesville, Ohio, and Scattergood at West Branch, Iowa, whose community spirit, shared work, and teaching have drawn many students from other branches of Quakerism. In North Carolina the traditionalists only reluctantly formed a Conservative Yearly Meeting in 1902, in protest against the Five Years Meeting Uniform Discipline.[5]

The Orthodox Yearly Meetings with strong rural roots accepted revivals, gospel hymns, Holiness, and the pastoral system but mostly entered the twentieth century as united communities. Revivalism came to North Carolina only in the

Chart of Membership Figures for Yearly Meetings in United States and Canada

Yearly Meeting:	Year Est'd-Split or reunited	1845 memb.	1872 memb.	1892 memb.	1902 memb.	1912 memb.
Alaska (EFA)	1970					
Baltimore (FUM)	1672-1827	562	c 600	1,012	1,217	1,211
Baltimore (FGC)	1672-1827	c 2,100	c 4,000	c 3,200	c 2,995	c 2,673
Baltimore (Jt: FG, FU)	1968					
Canada (Cons.)	1881					
Canada (FU)	1867		1,641			1,060
Canada (FG)=Genesee	1834				c 534	c 230
Canada (Jt: FU, FG, C)	1955					
Central (indep. from Ind. & Western) 1926						
Central Alaska	1969					
Evang. Fds Church-ER (EFA)	1813-1854 (ex-Ohio)		2,858	4,733		
Illinois (FGC)	1875				c 506	c 728
Indiana (FUM)	1821-1828	c 28,000	17,200	22,015	20,224	20,585
Intermountain (independent)	1975					
Iowa (Cons.)	1863-1877					
Iowa (FUM)	1863-1877		8,599	11,291	11,073	9,903
Lake Erie (FGC)	1939					
Mid-America (EFA)	1872 (ex-Kansas)			9,347	11,002	11,697
Missouri Valley (independent)	1955					
Nebraska (FUM)	1908-1957				1,791	2,099
New England (Cons.)	1661-1845					
New England (FUM)	1661-1845	8,021	4,618	4,020	4,462	4,109
New England (Jt: FU, FG, C)	1945					
New York (FUM)	1695-1828	c 6,000	4,403	3,895	3,545	3,582
New York (FGC)	1695-1828	c 12,500			c 1,752	c 908
New York (Jt: FU, FGC)	1955					
North Carolina (Cons.)	1698-1904					
North Carolina (FUM)	1698-1904	c 4,500	4,936	5,905	5,194	7,053
Northern (FGC)	1975 (from Illinois)					
North Pacific (FGC)	1973 (from Pacific)					
Northwest (EFA)	1893 (ex-Oregon)				1,000	2,338
Ohio (Cons.)	1813-1828	18,800 (w. Orthodox)				
Ohio (Hicksite)	1813-1828	c 5,000			c 217	c 80
Ohio Valley (FGC)	1821-1828 (ex-Ind.) c 1,500				c 907	c 720
Pacific (FGC)	1947					
Philadelphia (FGC)	1681-1827	c 16,000			11,270	10,694
Philadelphia (independent)	1681-1827	8,686	c 5,500	4,513		4,400
Philadelphia (Jt)	1955					
Rocky Mountain (EFA)	1957 (from Nebraska)					
South Central (FGC)	1961					
Southeastern (FG, FU)	1962					
Southern Appalachian (FGC)	1970					
Virginia	1689 d. 1845	331	0			
Southwestern (EFA)	1895 (ex-California)				1,710	3,686
Western (FUM)	1858-1877 (from Indiana)	9,749	13,734	15,915	15,388	
Western (Cons.)	1858-1877					
Wilmington (FUM)	1892 (from Indiana)				6,273	6,355

Individual independent Mtgs.						
Hicksite=FGC totals:		c 35,000		c 22,000	c 18,181	c 16,033
Orthodox=5 Yrs. Mtg=FUM totals		c 53,414	c 51,905	76,142	79,861	89,192
Conservative & Phil. Orthodox totals		[8,686]	c 11,500			
Evangelical Friends Alliance totals				[4,733]		
Subtract Joint FUM/FGC Meetings						

TOTAL FRIENDS: USA & CANADA		c 97,100				

1922 memb.	1935 memb.	1952 memb.	1962 memb.	1972 memb.	1982 memb.	1982 No. Mtgs.	1902 No. Pastors
		1,727	c 1,500	2,467	2,860	11	
1,271	1,213	1,114					0
c 3,127	2,251	2,185	2,157				
				5,346	3,435	30	
	100	107					
992	729	450					
c 317	444	325					
			623	943	1,086	23	
		576	506	466	446	11	
					140	2	
5,948	5,607	6,161	7,207	7,874	8,612	86	
c 491	285	552	943	1,120	1,093	23	
17,743	15,944	13,886	13,847	11,513	9,123	88	44
					655	15	
	950	853	724	763	709	11	
9,122	7,477	7,052	6,146	5,242	5,315	44	65
			511	820	1,061	17	
	9,098	8,103		7,746	8,000	75	na
			81	200	100		
	2,390	1,775		1,314	1,204	6	na
	117						
3,867	3,506						5
		3,330	3,222	3,534	3,704	58	
3,552	3,565	4,098					
c 835	2,035	3,283					16
			6,763	6,774	5,480	60	
	500	500	250	311	375	7	
9,111	10,826	13,415	13,543	14,886	14,833	86	2
					400	10	
					425	8	
3,423	3,135	4,582	5,537	5,972	8,465	47	4
	1,260	990	860	796	763	11	
c 25	22	0					
c 519	680	556	650	793	863	16	
	75	756	2,309	2,023	1,453	35	
10,594	10,505	11,633					
4,493	4,732	5,220					
			17,657	15,817	13,532	99	
			1,437	1,557	1,583	26	
			211	316	383	11	
			278	432	445	10	
				200	115	6	
4,825	4,484	6,149	7,186	7,459	6,941	36	10
13,630	13,069	12,549	12,528	11,140	9,116	70	31
	200	50	50				
6,098	5,296	5,025	4,492	3,556	3,396	32	2
	603	938	1,081	200	755		
c 15,908	16,297	19,290	31,102	38,118	33,615	354	
86,812	77,597	68,816	70,608	71,707	62,633	554	179
	7,859	8,296	1,530	1,870	1,847	29	
[5,948]	[8,742]	[20,573]	24,249	23,149	26,660	234	
			− 7,386	− 17,029	− 14,150	− 181	
	93,894	98,623	121,184	117,815	110,605	990	

NOTES AND SOURCES FOR CHART OF YEARLY MEETING MEMBERSHIPS

Dates of Figures: chart figures are recorded as of date published; most represent previous year's members, include absent members, and exclude children. Membership data omitted when not in Yearly Meeting or other printed sources.

Abbreviations:

Cons. = Conservative or Wilburite Yearly Meetings, plus Central and Philadelphia Orthodox Yearly Meetings.

EFA = Holiness-based Yearly Meetings or later in Evangelical Friends Alliance.

FGC = Hicksite Yearly Meetings or later members of Friends General Conference.

FUM = Gurneyite Yearly Meetings in Five Years Meeting or Friends United Meeting.

indep. = 20th Century liberal Yearly Meetings or Monthly Meetings not in FGC.

Jt. = Yearly Meetings joining Hicksite, Gurneyite and/or Conservative Friends or linked to both FUM and FGC. Membership sometimes counted twice.

Data Sources:

1845: Friend (London) quoted in Seth Hinshaw, Carolina Quaker Experience (Greensboro; 1984) 145, plus estimates from T. Hamm orally.

1872: Friend (London), March 1, 1872, p. 47.

1892: Christian Worker, April 7, 1897, 211-13; Bliss Forbush, History of Baltimore Yearly Meeting (Sandy Springs, Md., 1972); U.S. Census Data.

1902; 1912; 1922: Minutes of Five Years Meeting, and of Phildelphia and Baltimore Yearly Meetings; figures for other FGC Yearly Meetings are estimates multiplying by four the members attending Sunday Schools (estimates are validated by data from Philadelphia and Baltimore).

Members in 1935; 1952; 1962; 1972; 1982; Meetings in 1982: Handbook of Religious Society of Friends (ed. FWCC) for these years. (for 1941 data see also E. Russell, History of Quakerism (New York; 1942) 526-7).

1902 Pastors: Minutes of Five Years Meeting.

1880s and to pastors gradually between 1892 and 1940. Women like Mary Mendenhall Hobbs and Mary Woody were as strong as their husbands in both teaching and worship: the Women's Yearly Meeting functioned independently until 1898.[6] By 1920 most North Carolina Friends lived in towns and their nine Quaker Academies and Blue Ridge Mission had closed. Quaker Meetings in northeastern Kansas predated the Indian Agency and were still largely rural, although Friends University in Wichita became their center.[7] After spreading into Texas towns they have lately renamed themselves the Mid-America Yearly Meeting. Few Friends came into Nebraska until after Indian work ended. The chance in 1899 to buy out a defunct college in Central City provided a base for the new Yearly Meeting organized in 1908.[8] In 1957 twenty-one new town and suburban churches centered around Denver led an exodus to form a Holiness-based Rocky Mountain Yearly Meeting.[9]

In 1892, after resisting pleas for a decade, Indiana Yearly Meeting set off as Wilmington Yearly Meeting their formerly revivalistic Quarterly Meetings south and east of Dayton, Ohio. The new Wilmington College reassured Indiana Friends.[10] Strong rural roots around Clinton County, Ohio, added to Wilmington Yearly Meeting's stability into the twentieth century. Indiana and Western Yearly Meetings kept unity, too, until the 1920s. All of these Meetings and Iowa and Kansas were losing rural members (see Chart of Membership Figures for Yearly Meetings, United States and Canada) despite revivals.[11] Leading Quakers of Indianapolis, Richmond, and Marion, Indiana, and Wilmington, Ohio, set up "First Friends Churches," but these city people felt remote from Back Creek, and from revivalistic urban churches.

URBAN EVANGELICAL YEARLY MEETINGS

Four Yearly Meetings followed their urban and suburban members, building city community churches to include neighbors and pastors coming from many Holiness and revivalist denominations. Ohio Yearly Meeting (Gurneyite), recognizing its new identity, has from 1971 called itself the Evangelical Friends Church, Eastern Region. Its mother Meetings along the upper Ohio shrank, but as the industrial complex of Canton, Cleveland, and Akron grew, so did their churches there as did those around Columbus. Throughout the northeastern states Quaker congregations and pastors who focus on doctrine, revivals, or Holiness have joined them. Their sharpest crisis came in 1906, when Levi Lupton and his missionary training school in Alliance, Ohio, set up a World Evangelization Company and African mission to rival the Malones', but Lupton's misuse of funds and his "speaking in tongues" (learned from the Azusa, California Pentecostalists) alienated Ohio Friends.[12] Lupton's disciple William M. Smith built better by founding the Union Bible School in Westfield, Indiana, to become the center of the largely rural Central Yearly Meeting, splitting from Indiana and Western Yearly Meetings to protest their "modernism" in 1924. They combine the heart-warming Holiness experience with a conservative life-style.[13]

THE WEST COAST

Oregon and the San Francisco Bay area had been visited by many Friends in the "gold rush" days.[14] The Lewellings settled in the Willamette Valley before 1847; William Hobson went to Oregon in 1870 by the new Union Pacific Railroad and searched throughout the region by stagecoach and riverboat for a place for a Quaker settlement. On a second trip in 1875 Hobson found the Chehalem Valley near Newberg. He brought 154 settlers from his Honey Creek, Iowa, home in 1882. Even by train such a trip took many days with stops every few miles: "a tourist car was held on the railroad siding and its prospective occupants were given several days in which to furnish their respective compartments. . . . They curtained off their rooms in the end of the car and had a place to eat and a place to sleep."[15] In Oregon there were already by 1879 spontaneous religious revivals. In 1890–91 John Henry Douglas came to plan others and encourage a pastoral system, to Hobson's annoyance. In 1893 Oregon was set up by Iowa as an independent Yearly Meeting, and already in 1885 the Friends Pacific Academy had opened, which in 1891 produced Pacific College, later renamed George Fox College.[16] In Idaho, although a few Friends had settled and worshipped in 1896, and came under Oregon's care in 1899, there were still only three Monthly Meetings in 1906.[17]

In Southern California, by contrast, Friends from the Midwest migrated not to farmlands but to instant suburbia, often with only padres, prospectors, or ranchers preceding them. Churches grew up with a culture that was never rural. The land boom of the 1880s boosted by the Santa Fe and Southern Pacific Railroads' cheap fares brought hundreds of thousands of settlers west. By 1882 the oldest Meeting had formed in Pasadena, followed by El Modena in Orange County and in the 1890s seven others in the Los Angeles area. In 1887 a Chicago Quaker couple, Aquila and Hannah Pickering, used a Land and Water Company to turn a ranch into the model town they named for the poet Whittier. By 1895 Whitter's name had extended to a college and a Quarterly Meeting. The same year Iowa approved the forming of California Yearly Meeting, renamed Southwest Yearly Meeting in 1985.[18] The Yearly Meeting met in Whittier, eventually growing to thirty-five Monthly Meetings. They oversaw missions in Alaska and later Guatemala. In Southern California every town borders on several others; a church can no longer escape to the outskirts when its neighborhood changes. Concern for their home communities led California Friends to work for Mexicans, Chinese, Japanese, and lately for Cambodian and Vietnamese subcongregations of their Meetings.

The Oregon Quakers lived in more varied social settings. The rural Quaker churches in Idaho with their struggling Greenleaf Academy and the "Quaker town" of Newberg with its college remained close-knit communities. The four suburban churches of Portland Quarterly Meeting and the four around Eugene in Salem Quarter, however, led the fight in 1922–26 for Holiness doctrines against the Five Years Meeting and in 1949 for the annexing of the Indiana-linked urban Quaker churches of the Puget Sound area.[19] In 1971 the same churches promoted their change of name to Northwest Yearly Meeting. The churches in each Quarter of Oregon Yearly Meeting were founded in two clusters: 1878–1914 and after 1944.[20] In between came the 1929 Depression and the crisis in the 1920s over the Five Years Meeting.

FIVE YEARS MEETING

Representatives of all of the "Gurneyite" Quakers exept Ohio and Philadelphia Yearly Meetings agreed to meet every five years after 1887, to coordinate their Yearly Meetings' overseas mission work under the American Friends Board of Foreign Missions, to try to centralize Sunday school resources under the Board of Education, and to merge the Philadelphia *Friends Review* with the Quaker revivalists' *Christian Worker* (by then in Chicago) into a new *American Friend* edited by Rufus Jones and later by Edgar Nicholson. After a decade of debate, a "Uniform Discipline," accepted by all Gurneyite Yearly Meetings except London and Philadelphia, helped to launch Five Years Meeting in 1902, with the Mission and Education Boards under it. By 1907 this body consented to amass inclusive statistics and to join the Federal Council of Churches; by 1912 it had created a central office, general secretary, and Board of Publications in Richmond, Indiana. In the same year, responding to liberal Friends' fear of a centralized dogmatic authority, it agreed that the 1887 Richmond Declaration and other doctrinal statements in the new Discipline "are not to be regarded as constituting a creed."

As World War I began in 1914, Five Years Meeting felt called to share in the cost of a list programs needed by men in the army and war victims, and in reconstruction. The 1915 International Conference of Men Friends set up the Committee of Seven, under Nicholson, to find ways to cut out excessive small central Boards and respond to "openings for church extension in the newer settlements as well in our large cities. . . . When the days of world reconstruction come the Society of Friends deserves to have a voice in keeping with its well known policies of Christian brotherhood."[21] Their report, duly adopted by Five Years Meeting, proposed combining committees into six national Boards for Foreign Missions, Peace, Prohibition, Indian Affairs, Home Mission and Extension Work, Publications, and Bible School and Young Friends. A major new step was to ask for a combined annual $2 million fund for the needs of all of the boards. Then Quaker schools and colleges added their needs: $3 million more.

By the spring of 1919, as General Secretary Walter C. Woodward later reported, "for the want of any system for raising money for our united benevolent work, the thing fell down," with less than half of even the first year's pledges paid. The Five Years Meeting had taken part in the Federal Council of Churches Quadrennial meetings in 1908, 1912, and 1916 in which a major joint postwar program evolved, the Interchurch World Movement, whose 1920 annual budget was $336,777,572! The Five Years Meeting Executive Committee agreed to take $4,500,000 as the Friends' share. They had set up the Friends Forward Movement, both to raise money and to send Clarence Pickett* to visit Quaker schools and colleges to discuss individuals' vocations. As Minister at Large they appointed Indiana Friend Levi Pennington*, on leave from Pacific (later George Fox) College. A newssheet reported lively activity toward a June 1920 deadline and another flurry in November. The pace then slowed after 1,470 promotion teams had reached 40,000 Friends.[22]

In that postwar era Friends shared great hopes for world peace and democracy. Yet America faced political conservatism, "Red scares," heresy trials at church colleges, and prosecution of those teaching evolution. Among Friends, criticism focused upon Five Years Meeting, whose new central office and budget undercut local programs. In the 1920s and 1930s many of the Five Years Meeting staff and pastors of city Friends churches such as Norval Webb, Levinus Painter, Glenn Reece, Clarence Pickett, George Selleck, and Furnas Trueblood studied the Bible under Moses Bailey and Alexander Purdy* at Hartford Theological Seminary and turned away from their fundamentalist origins. In May 1919 Homer Cox called a meeting of Oregon Quaker pastors and others to express "dissatisfaction in regard to the different Boards of the Five Years Meeting, especially the Board of Publication and the Bible School Board." Oregon Yearly Meeting adopted Cox's concern, adding that "it would be well to have inserted in the application blank for use of candidates for the [mission] field some question which would help the Board to ascertain whether or not the applicant had definitely sought and received the baptism with the Holy Ghost, which our branch of His church believes to be essential."[23] Throughout 1920 General Secretary Walter Woodward* received letters challenging the Five Years Meeting's "soundness." The Five Years Meeting session of 1922 received a resolution from the Kansas Yearly Meeting:

The "Essential Truths" . . . in our uniform discipline, "The Declaration of Faith" issued by the Richmond Conference in 1887, and George Fox's Letter to the Governor of Barbadoes, [are] the doctrinal basis upon which the Yearly Meeting established the Five Years Meeting. . . . All ministers, teachers, missionaries, and other persons holding official positions in the Five Years Meeting, should therefore substantially accord in their views with the teachings contained therein. . . . Central Boards should not assume to exercise the rights and privileges which belong alone to the Yearly Meetings. . . . The primary task of the Society of Friends is EVANGELIZATION AT HOME AND ABROAD. . . . We ask . . . to have the Boards of the Five Years Meeting so organized as to command the confidence of those who feel that the former executives and secretaries . . . overstepped their authority.[24]

The 1922 Five Years Meeting, in a moving session of reconciliation headed by Rufus Jones, responded by rescinding the statement that the "Richmond Declaration" was not a creed.[25] Yet the centralized mission and publication policies were not greatly changed. Oregon Yearly Meeting set up a watching committee and, when it reported disapproval, voted in 1926 to withdraw from Five Years Meeting, despite Levi Pennington's plea for patience. In 1937 Kansas also withdrew. With Oregon, and later with the Ohio Orthodox Friends and Rocky Mountain Yearly Meeting (neither had belonged to Five Years Meeting), these formed a loose association that became in 1961 the Evangelical Friends Alliance.[26]

The need for closer touch with member Yearly Meetings made Friends want the General Board meetings and sessions of Five Years Meeting to be more frequent. In 1955 they opened the new Friends Central Office building on Quaker Hill in Richmond, Indiana. Discussion led to decisions in 1960 to meet every three years and in 1966 to call the body the Friends United Meeting. A major simplification led to combining the boards into three Commissions for Wider (later, World) Ministries, Meeting Ministries, and General Services. The Friends United Meeting also included as members the new Yearly Meetings of the former mission areas overseas.

STRUGGLES IN THE QUAKER COLLEGES

Whereas the dramatic clashes in other denominations centered on seminaries and key pulpits, among Friends they were over colleges. The 1922 crisis showed that each represented a huge investment of time and resources by any Yearly Meeting with only 5,000 to 15,000 members. All Quaker colleges west of the Mississippi spent their first decades struggling merely to survive. This personal involvement made each of them a center for tension. Each tug-of-war involved at least five parties, often divided within themselves: the Yearly Meeting, the trustees, the president, the faculty and student body, and the town or business community. At Earlham, as at George Fox, Guilford, William Penn, and Wilmington, half or more of the trustees are named by Yearly Meetings that founded the college. Trustees supported President Kelly at Earlham against Elbert Russell's* liberal faculty and town group in 1915 but in part upheld Alexander Purdy against fundamentalist critics in 1920.[27] Earlham became a national rather than a regional college under Thomas Jones*, who drew D. Elton Trueblood and young pacifist idealists to the faculty after the war. But the town, Yearly Meeting, and trustees of William Penn College, Iowa, turned back a similar "Holy Experiment" under President Cecil Hinshaw in 1944–49. Nine faculty members and "three-quarters of the student body" resigned with Hinshaw.[28] The college regained accreditation in 1960. By contrast, Wilmington College's Yearly Meeting and faculty recovered control in 1959 from a president-elect eager to make it more secular and concerned for business enterprise, as Whittier College had been secularized in the 1920s.[29] Yet George Fox College was turned by its Yearly Meeting under Edward Mott in a decisively evangelical direction in 1941–49. Malone College also remained evangelical in its new setting in Canton, Ohio, after 1956. Guilford and Friends University have kept a balance of autonomy with involvement in Quaker Meeting life. The new experiments of Friends World

College and the outstanding academic achievements of Swarthmore and Haverford have drawn on their Quaker heritage, professors, and librarians more than on work by Yearly Meetings.[30]

THE COLLEGE MEETINGS

The West and Midwest in 1902–60 also produced a second form of Quakerism, almost wholly cut off from evangelical Friends and different even from the older eastern Quaker patterns. Meetings in non-Quaker college and university towns typically meet for worship in silence in private homes or rooms rented in public buildings. Its members think much; talk much; read much, especially in mystical classics and psychology; study social justice issues and Asian religions; and are seldom born Friends. They care much about religious experience, often being refugees from other churches' theology: some are ex-Catholics, ex-Jews, or ex-fundamentalists. Many were first drawn to Quakers by their concern for peace or by Quaker work camps or Civilian Public Service in World War II. They are diffident about official procedures, forming Monthly Meetings or joining a Yearly Meeting. Such informal Meetings are vital centers of life for many couples and families who gather for common meals, projects of social aid, protest, or common study. A history of these groups should record great books and pamphlets written in Boulder and Ann Arbor, carloads traveling to Washington, D.C., or to vigils at naval bases, and volunteers working in prisons. It would not occur to such Friends to spread Quakerism by sending a pastor to set up a church in a new suburb.[31]

Fifty years after the first such Meeting, Joel and Hannah Bean's College Park Association at San Jose, California, in the 1880s, their granddaughter Anna Brinton* called together a group of Friends from similar Meetings that became in 1947 Pacific Yearly Meeting. At colleges where Rufus Jones was read or heard other groups sprang up, often around a single Quaker family. Major universities in Toronto, Chicago, Minneapolis, Atlanta, and even places with evangelical Friends churches already active such as Pasadena and Cincinnati had strong "silent" Meetings" by the 1930s, owning buildings or sharing them with the American Friends Service Committee or other action groups. Those in New Haven and Hartford, Connecticut, and in Cambridge and the Amherst area, Massachusetts, played a major role in bringing together the Wilburite and Orthodox New England Yearly Meetings.[32]

By 1982 there were nearly one hundred of these "college Meetings" outside of the long-established Hicksite Yearly Meetings. Older lists called them Unaffiliated or Independent Friends. Most Yearly Meetings of Friends United Meeting picked up one or more of these new Meetings; the Iowa and North Carolina Conservative Yearly Meetings attracted a few. More joined and revitalized the Illinois and Indiana Hicksite Yearly Meetings, which had each declined to only three or four old Meetings still active. Thus in 1976 the Indiana Hicksites were reborn as Ohio Valley Yearly Meeting, and Illinois had grown enough to set off the Minnesota area as Northern Yearly Meeting. By 1960 five major new associations of unprogrammed midwestern Meetings were also already forming. The Lake Erie Association, stretching from Pittsburgh to Kalamazoo, became a Yearly Meeting in 1963, joining Friends General Conference. Southeastern, centered in Florida, worked from 1962 patiently for admission to both Friends United Meeting (FUM) and Friends General Conference (FGC). Southern Appalachian Yearly Meeting and Association, having joined the FGC, was rebuffed by FUM. Most Meetings of the loose Missouri Valley Conference gradually accepted membership in other Yearly Meetings; but Pacific and its offshoot North Pacific, South Central in the wide Texas area, and Intermountain in Colorado–New Mexico find it takes so much travel to maintain Yearly Meeting ties that they avoid national obligations. Many midwesterners find that the benefits of a Yearly Meeting can be better provided in an age of cars and airlines by a national gathering such as Friends General Conference. Once held biennially as an ocean week for Philadelphian families at Cape May, the taking over of their conference center in 1970 by Carl McIntyre's fundamentalists drove FGC to gather on campuses inland. Midwestern conferences in "the alternate years" soon equaled the biennial sessions, leading in the 1980s to an annual gathering of 1,500 Friends for a week of worship, study, and fellowship. Business sessions are minimal because, unlike among British and FUM Quakers, those in the FGC leave the programs needing time and money to the work of independent groups like the American Friends Service Committee (AFSC) and the Friends Committee on National Legislation (FCNL). In 1975, however, after twenty years of planning, the FGC joined the AFSC, Friends World Committee for Consultation (FWCC), and Philadelphia Yearly Meeting in moving their offices into a new Friends Center beside the Race Street meeting-house.

NOTES

1. Rufus Jones closed each issue of *The American Friend* with a column of "News and Events." many were on Quaker missions and colleges, but one paragraph weekly in 1898 was on Cuba and one weekly in 1900 on China; his editorials opposed war with Spain to annex an American empire. On religious aspects of American expansion across the continent and overseas see Sydney Ahlstrom, *Religious History of the American People* (New Haven: 1972), Chs. 27, 44; and Edwin Scott Gaustad, *Documentary History of Religion in America, Vol. 3: Since 1865* (Grand Rapids, Mich.: 1983), 32–54, 104–21.

2. Timothy L. Smith, *Called unto Holiness: The Story of the Nazarenes: The Formative Years* (Kansas City, Mo.:1962), 13.

3. Rural habits were accepted: Walter Robson at the Ohio Yearly Meeting in 1877 said "the floors would look cleaner if spittoons were used" (Edwin Bronner, ed., *English View* [Philadelphia: 1970] 50).

4. See Smith, *Called unto Holiness*, Chs. 3, 6; Ahlstrom, *Religious History*, Ch. 48.

5. Seth Hinshaw, *Carolina Experience* (Greensboro, N.C.: 1984) Ch. 19; Willard Heiss, *A Brief History of Western Yearly Meeting of Conservative Friends* (Indianapolis:

1963). See William Taber, *Be Gentle, Be Plain* (Barnesville, Ohio: 1976) and idem, *Eye of Faith* (Barnesville, Ohio: 1985) on Ohio conservatives and Herbert Standing's unpublished papers on Iowa conservative Friends.

6. Hinshaw, *Carolina Experience*, 196, 230, 234, 241ff.

7. Errol Elliott, *Quakers on the American Frontier* (Richmond, Ind.: 1969), Ch. 6; hereafter *QAF; Sheldon G. Jackson, Quaker Pioneers in the Cherokee Strip:* . . . *Alvin and Laura Coppock* (Azusa, Calif.: 1982).

8. Herbert Mott, *Nebraska Central College* (Central City, Neb: n.d.); Elliott, *QAF*, included his own boyhood memory of life in a covered wagon and sod house.

9. See Elliott, *QAF*, 284–85.

10. Ibid., 102–3, 223.

11. In Indiana the median date for the first setting up of the surviving rural Meetings was 1844; for town churches, 1881; and for those in places that became major cities, 1866; but twelve out of sixty-two rural Meetings did not become Monthly Meetings until after 1910. Thirty-three Meetings (all but two rural) were laid down or merged with larger Meetings and seventy-two more transient local Meetings. Data from Ratliff, *Our Special Heritage*, 94–105. On growth figures see Kenneth Ives's pamphlet, *Which Friends Groups are Growing, n Why?* (Chicago: 1977).

12. Pentecostalism also reshaped the life of Quaker A. J. Tomlinson who became a founder of the Church of God.

13. See Thomas Hamm, *The Transformation of American Quakerism* (Bloomington, Ind.: 1988), Ch. 7; hereafter *TAQ*. See also David Holden, *Friends Divided* (Richmond, Ind.: 1988), Ch. 13, on Central Yearly Meeting.

14. Iowa Monthly, Quarterly, and Yearly Meeting archives are in a vault at Friends Church, Oskaloosa, Iowa. California Meeting archives are at the Southwest Yearly Meeting office in East Whittier, California. See also David LeShana, *Quakers in California*; (Newberg, Oregon: 1969) Ralph K. Beebe, *A Garden of the Lord: A History of Oregon Yearly Meeting of Friends Church* (Newberg, Oreg.: 1968).

15. Theodore Hoover, *Mildred Crew Brooke: An Unfinished Manuscript* (Casa del Oro: 1940), quoted by LeShana, *Quakers in California*, 84.

16. See Myron Goldsmith, "Hobson," 118ff; LeShana, *Quakers in California*, 68–81; Errol T. Elliott, *Profiles* 131–49; Ralph K. Beebe, *A Garden of the Lord: A History of Oregon Yearly Meeting of Friends Church* (Newberg, Oregon: 1968).

17. See Beebe, *Garden*; Elliott, *QAF*, 171–72.

18. LeShana, *Quakers in California*, Ch. 7, 132–33; Yearly Meeting Minutes. On these missions see Ch. 21 in this volume. On Whittier see Charles W. Cooper, *Whittier: Independent College in California* (Los Angeles: 1967), with Jessamyn West's Preface; Charles Elliott, Jr., *Whittier College* (1986); and LeShana, *Quakers in California*, Ch. 7.

19. Donald McNichols, *Portrait of a Quaker: Levi Pennington* (Newberg, Oregon: 1980), 90–97, 89. See also the entry for Levi Pennington in Part Two.

20. Beebe, *Garden*, Appendix.

21. *Five Years Meeting Minutes, 1917*, 57, 64.

22. General Secretary's report of 1922 Five Years Meeting; Newssheet *The Caller*; and *Staff Correspondence* newsletters, 1920, all from Letters and Papers of Walter C. Woodward in Earlham College Archive.

23. Pennington family papers and Oregon Yearly Meeting Minutes, 1919, both quoted in McNichols, *Portrait of a Quaker*, 91, 92.

24. Five Years Meeting Minutes, 1922, 67–69.

25. In a similar crisis in the 1975 Friends United Meeting session, the consensus reached was that the 1922 decision that the Richmond Declaration was not "not a creed" had never been negated.

26. See Elliott, *QAF*, 341–42.

27. *Elbert Russell, Quaker: An Autobiography* (Jackson, Tenn.: 1956), 143–57; Opal Thornburg, *Earlham: The Story of the College, 1847–1962* (Richmond, Ind.: 1963), 262–66, 297–301. Purdy left in frustration.

28. *Des Moines Register*, April 27, 1947; April 1949; S. Arthur Watson, *William Penn College: A Product and a Producer* (Oskaloosa, Iowa: 1971). Statements by participants used by Susan Henry in term paper (Earlham College, November 1977), included: "For a black and white boy and girl to walk down town together was enough to set the town on fire."

29. Elmer Howard Brown, "A History of Wilmington Yearly Meeting" (M.A. thesis, Butler University, 1940); Wilmington Yearly Meeting Minutes; *Wilmington News-Journal* October 12, 1959; October 14, 1959; and campus *Quaker Quips*. See also Cooper, *Whittier*, 129–32, 246, 257–70, 323, 325ff; Herbert E. Harris, *The Quaker and the West: The First Sixty Years of Whittier College* (Whittier, Calif.: 1948).

30. See Floyd Souders and Norma Souders, *Friends University, 1898–1973* (Wichita, Kans.: 1974). On George Fox see Beebe, *Garden*, 129–48; McNichols, *Portrait of a Quaker*, Ch. 4. Arthur Roberts renamed the college.

31. See George Selleck, *The Quakers in Boston (Cambridge, Mass.: 1976); Isabel Bliss, "Unaffiliated Friends Meetings,"* in *American Quakers Today*, ed. Francis Hall (Philadelphia: 1966).

32. William Watson, "The Reunion of New England Friends of 1945" (Paper read at the Conference of Quaker Historians and Archivists at Providence, R.I., June 16, 1984): deposited at Haverford College.

19
CREATIVITY IN PEACEMAKING

In peacetime a commitment to pacifism is relatively easy, even respectable in the general society. Wars have made Friends unpopular and occasioned much soul searching among pacifists who have sought what William James called "a moral equivalent to war," a method of demonstrating by constructive action their search for a better way of solving disputes than killing as well as their worth to the countries they love but for which they refuse to fight.[1] The origins of Quaker pacifism lie in an individual's commitment to abide by the example and commands of Jesus, but the form of that obedience has changed markedly over the centuries. The evolution of Quaker thought and actions on war is this chapter's subject. It is a story that had a sudden and major change of plot during World War I.

Pacifist responses have taken various forms depending upon the nature of the war, the position of Friends in the general society, and the opportunities allowed by circumstances. For example, in New England just before King Philip's War, in Pennsylvania after 1755, and in England and America before the Revolution, Friends offered their services as mediators, attempting to foster negotiations between the conflicting parties in an attempt to avert or end bloodshed. More recently, Friends have offered their services as neutral facilitators of negotiations between Israel and Egypt in 1956 and in the civil war in Nigeria in the 1970s.[2] Today Quaker centers at the United Nations in New York and in Geneva, Washington, and London provide an institutional setting where diplomats can meet to discuss problems "off the record." Such Quaker efforts at mediation require privacy.

Relief activities, a second form of pacifist witness, is a very public activity whose operation depends upon wide-scale knowledge of the distress, private contributions, and permission or acquiescence from both the country from where the supplies originate and the officials in the recipient nation.

British Friends were well equipped to deal with the challenges of World War

I. They had gained expertise in over a century of foreign relief operations and had more recently become involved in the social work movement through agencies like Toynbee Hall and the Bedford Institute. The energy for good causes that had characterized the evangelicals did not disappear under liberalism; instead, it appeared in new form as Quakers worked to create the Kingdom of God on earth and to serve God by caring for the oppressed.

Friends in England (and America) were not expecting total war in 1914. The last major war the English had fought in western Europe was against Napoleon; even the Crimean War occurred three generations before. The Boer War was fought in remote South Africa and was waged more for imperial pride than national survival. Like other middle-class Englishmen, Friends rejoiced in the achievements of Western civilization that Europe was extending to the world as part of continuing progress. Peace agitation was fashionable and international law and arbitration seemed methods useful for settling disputes—particularly those among "civilized" nations—without fighting. The arms race with Germany was unsettling, but Friends hoped that the vital interests of the major powers could be protected by compromise and goodwill.

The entrance of Britain into war in August 1914 resulted in an outburst of patriotic fervor, and many rushed to join the armed forces. Since Friends interacted with and echoed the norms of the wider society, not surprisingly about one-third of their eligible young men also enlisted in the armed forces, though several served as noncombatants. There remained about 1,000 Quaker conscientious objectors of whom, after conscription was decreed, 753 applied for exemption and about one-fourth served prison sentences.

Friends also provided leadership and membership in various nonsectarian pacifist and humanitarian groups that emerged during the war: the No Conscription Fellowship, Save the Children Fund, League of Nations Union, Fellowship of Reconciliation, and the organization that later became the Women's International League for Peace and Freedom. These groups early began making plans for the postwar period, seeking to create the conditions under which another war could be prevented.

Friends continued an earlier tradition in which they banded together to do good without seeking the sanction of the Yearly Meeting. The Friends Ambulance Unit (FAU) came into existence during the first weeks of the war to provide medical care to soldiers and civilians wounded in the fighting in Flanders. The FAU purchased ambulances and staffed a field hospital in Dunkirk, two ambulance trains, and ambulance ships. Both Friends and outsiders joined the unit, but nurses and doctors came mostly from the Red Cross, the Belgians, or the British army. The Unit members accepted special uniforms and "acting officers rank" to work with the armies. Later the Unit worked mostly with civilian refugees. An offshoot, the Italian Ambulance Unit, served under fire at the front north of Trieste, with its own nurses, after Italy's entry into the war in 1915. The FAU provided a form of alternative service for many conscientious objectors, and the government approved of its work since these volunteers, at least indirectly, aided the war effort. The FAU remained a civilian body operating directly in the war zone. At the armistice it had 640 members abroad and 720 in England and ran twelve hospitals. Twenty men died or were killed in action.[3]

Since few envisaged a long war, Friends initially assumed that their relief efforts would approximate those of the Franco–Prussian War of 1870, a brief effort at caring for refugees. The first problem was to help Germans and Austrians caught in England when the war began. There had been close ties between the English and Germans and extensive trade before the war began, and the outbreak of war stranded 30,000 Germans in London alone. In spite of popular opposition to any kind of "Hun coddling," the Meeting for Sufferings established an Emergency Committee to find homes and work for the aliens. Throughout the war the Emergency Committee attempted to alleviate conditions in the internment camps set up by the British and to aid those who were victims of the war hysteria.[4]

The Friends War Victims Relief Committee, established by the Meeting for Sufferings soon after the German advance began, aided civilians and refugees in Belgium and France. The FAU prided itself on efficiency and practicality. The War Victims Relief Agency was more visionary, dedicated—as A. Ruth Fry its general secretary proclaimed—to a "real experiment in socialism, and in interdenominationalism, the most varied characters living together, united in their aim of helping their fellows."[5] Men and women worked together as equals, hierarchy was kept to the bare minimum required for efficiency in dealing with army and government officials, and all workers ate together and received the same subsistence allowance. No wages were paid. Relief workers experiencing the savagery of war began to rethink fundamental postulates concerning the functions of government and society, and many became socialists.

The scope of the relief effort in France—financed by English Friends, American Friends, and sympathizers in both countries—required a degree of organization and structure previously lacking in the Society of Friends. There were 270 workers in London and 1,078 English in the field; the committee in charge met daily for long hours, and specialization of function and delegation of authority became necessary. The committee had to obtain the English and French governments' permission for workers to enter the war zone. They had to find supplies, arrange for transport, insure that the workers in France had the necessary skills, establish priorities so that some of the many needs could be met, supervise workers in the field, and cooperate with other relief organizations—of which the Red Cross was the most important. Since all relief activities cost money, Friends had to establish a means for the general public to learn about what they were doing. All of these activities had to be carried through successfully in a nation suspicious of all pacifists.

The main center of Quaker relief activity in France was in the area between the river Marne and the trenches that had been seized by the Germans in their initial push to the West and then fought over by the two sides as the Germans pulled back. Here were refugees from the areas of France that the Germans still occupied and peasants whose lands and houses had been devastated during the battles. The first task was to care for the wounded and the destitute, providing food, clothing, and shelter. Later the workers would rebuild houses, provide prefabricated houses, and furnish seed for the next spring's planting. Friends created a maternity hospital, a regular hospital, and a home for the elderly. Although they sought to involve French local authorities in their work, Friends were personally involved in all stages of the relief effort. Success depended upon the cooperation of French local and national government officials, who provided supplies for some of the projects.[6]

Although the Friends War Victims Relief Committee (FWVC) proclaimed its leftist orientation, in practice its attitudes remained conservative. For example, the relief workers encountered what they saw as ingrained peasant opposition to modern techniques of mechanized farming and sought to overcome what they regarded as obstructionism. Yet the workers feared corrupting these same peasants into laziness if they fostered habits of dependency. So when the FWVC restocked farms with rabbits, chickens, goats, sheep, and so on, the people "were asked to contribute something of the cost."[7]

In England the peace testimony occasioned conflicts with government officials. The government approved of conscientious objectors working in the FAU but not on the Emergency Committee or in the FWVC. The Yearly Meeting and Meeting for Sufferings did not cease their public witnessing for peace, even when the chairman of the Friends Service Committee was tried, convicted, and jailed because he had signed his name to a Quaker peace pamphlet.[8] The government treated conscientious objectors harshly, imprisoning 279. The army sought to transport forty-one conscientious objectors to France because in a war zone the men could be shot for nonperformance of duty. Quakers visited the conscientious objectors in prison and debated whether to publicize the horrendous conditions they found as means of alleviating suffering or to advise the men to endure quietly as a witness to their beliefs, whatever the government did.[9]

THE CREATION OF THE AMERICAN FRIENDS SERVICE COMMITTEE

English Friends had nearly three years' experience in relief work before America entered the war. So Americans learned from the English and also had time to prepare in case the United States became involved. Friends established contacts with important government officials before the war was declared, seeking to protect the rights of conscientious objectors in the event of a draft. High-level contacts in the Wilson administration and succeeding administrations proved valuable. President Wilson, for example, had taught at Bryn Mawr College and had sympathy for pacifism and Friends. Herbert Hoover,* an engineer who earned an international reputation organizing food relief for the Belgians and later became secretary of commerce and president, was a Quaker who became the American government's "food czar" directing efforts to increase agricultural production during World War I. The unofficial Quaker motto "Speak Truth to

Power" had credibility because from 1917 until 1980 Quakers generally could gain access to high government officials, whether Democrats or Republicans, in the executive branch or in Congress.

American Friends' experience of total war forced a rethinking of the meaning and implications of the peace testimony. An individual's refusal to serve in the military preserved his Christian witness but did little to hinder the war effort, prevent another conflagration, or persuade others to pacifism. Somehow the antiwar testimony had to be broadened to involve those who questioned the utility of sitting on the sidelines while others fought "to end wars" and to "make the world safe for democracy."

Quakers also had to grapple with their close identification with the norms of the surrounding culture. Nineteenth-century evangelicals and liberals repudiated the emphasis upon sectarian isolationism, gradually abandoned distinctive customs of dress and speech, and emphasized the value of education. Friends cooperated with adherents of other denominations in organizations working to foster international peace. American Quakers in all areas joined in the wide range of progressive-era reforms including social work, temperance, women's suffrage, and participatory democracy.[10] As America went to war, Friends watched in dismay as their erstwhile allies deserted pacifism and embraced militant patriotism.

Members were surprised to discover the disunity within the Meetings. In March 1918 after America became a belligerent, 120 Philadelphia Hicksites published a broadside disassociating themselves from the antiwar position of the Meeting.

We do not agree with those who would utter sentimental platitudes while a mad dog is running amuck biting women and children, with those who would stand idly by quoting some isolated passage of Scripture while an insane man murdered him, ravished his wife, bayoneted his babies or crucified his friends.[11]

During the war, after intense student pressure, Swarthmore College had a Student Army Training Corps on the campus that drilled but had to march to nearby Chester to use real guns; the college refused its pacifist and socialist professor Jesse Holmes permission to use the meeting-house for a peace lecture. In 1918 after Haverford professor Henry Cadbury* wrote a critical letter to the *Public Ledger* approving a sympathetic reception of German peace feelers, the Haverford Alumni Association and Board (mostly Friends) pronounced the letter "treasonable," and he resigned under pressure.[12] More than two-thirds of the eligible Quaker young men served in combat positions. Disciplining or disowning the Quaker soldiers was not a realistic alternative because a substantial percentage of older members supported the war effort.[13] The corporate power of the Meeting to compel the behavior of members had slowly eroded during the last half of the nineteenth century and was no more.

The official policies of all American Yearly Meetings—Conservative, Orthodox, Hicksite—remained pacifist. Evidently, those members caught up in the war enthusiasm accepted the right of other Friends to reaffirm traditional standards. War was a primary impetus in bringing American Friends back together as they discovered that the peace testimony—however variously interpreted—was an aspect of their tradition they did not want to jettison. Our century of war has also strengthened ties between Quakers, the Brethren, and the Mennonites who have worked together to guard the rights of conscientious objectors and for social service.

The strong official proclamation of pacifism by the Meetings in the face of significant repudiation of it by individuals is a continuing feature of the Society of Friends. Outsiders continue to attribute to Friends a unity of opinion on war that does not, in fact, exist. The Meetings' traditions seem no more decisive in determining members' views on wars than class, education, geographic area, and occupation. Friends' leading role as spokespersons for pacifists rests upon the shared commitments of a few and not a sense of the Meeting of the whole body of Friends.

In April 1917 representatives from the Philadelphia Yearly Meeting (Orthodox), Friends General Conference (Hicksite), and Five Years Meeting (Gurneyite) began working together to create an independent organization whose services would parallel the English Friends Ambulance Unit and the FWVC. Its founders claimed that the new agency would demonstrate "by sacrificial service" the Friends "love for our country and our desire to serve her loyally" through work that would help both "our country and humanity."[14] The result was the creation of the American Friends Service Committee with Rufus Jones* as chairman.

From its inception the committee reflected diverse goals. It would bring Quakers together, reaffirm the peace witness by providing conscientious objectors an alternative to fighting, give to Friends at home a method of witnessing to their faith in wartime, and accomplish social reconstruction abroad.[15] The committee worked with government officials to secure the rights of conscientious objectors (COs) and visited those who were in prison, but its initial primary responsibility was relief activity, and those selected to go abroad were chosen for competence, not religious dedication.

Even before a settled program was agreed upon, a contingent of one hundred volunteers arrived at Haverford College to begin training. Meanwhile, representatives were sent to England and France to see whether the Americans could join the FWVC. President Wilson had centralized all American relief efforts under the direction of the Red Cross, a decision that aided Friends because the official in charge of the Red Cross activities in France had attended Haverford and was a friend of Rufus Jones. The Friends Reconstruction Unit functioned under the auspices of the Red Cross throughout the war. Red Cross sanction meant that Friends could enter the war zone and also brought financial support.

After a difficult negotiation with the War Department, the government agreed to furlough the men from the draft so they could go to France. By the end of 1917 there were 116 men and 20 women in France working with English Friends and also initiating their own projects. After some initial culture shock—midwestern farm boys encountered war-hardened English Quakers who were socialists, smoked, and drank wine—the English and American Quakers worked together successfully on reconstruction, agricultural reclamation, and medical work. Eventually, 60 Mennonites and a few Brethren joined the relief agency.

The Service Committee attempted to enlist the support of Friends throughout America. In activities that paralleled the government's attempts to increase food production and civilian involvement in the war effort, the Service Committee issued booklets for women that contained patterns for sewing and knitting and instructions on canning and drying food (all the food had to be donated to make this project cost efficient).[16] Friends could donate and collect garments to be sent overseas, and workers, mostly women, sorted the clothing. When the Red Cross launched a fund drive, the pledges of Philadelphia Quakers went to the Service Committee. Initially, the Service Committee set out to raise $100,000 and then changed its goal to $250,000. At the end of the first year Friends alone had raised nearly three times that amount. The first year's donations show the wide support: Mennonites, $91,205; Brethren, $3,046; Five Years Meeting, $107,239; Ohio Yearly Meeting, $3,336; Conservative Yearly Meetings, $8,850; Hicksite Yearly Meetings, $196,910 (Philedelphia gave 118,635 of this); Philadelphia Yearly Meeting Orthodox, $198,253.[17] Since the Orthodox had only 4,000 members, their generosity was impressive. Even with this outpouring of funds, the Service Committee needed support from Red Cross and the American government, for it spent $2 million in its first two years of existence. Volunteers and free labor kept the Service Committee operating; of every $100.00 expended, $96.50 went to the victims of war.[18]

POST WAR RELIEF

The war ended eighteen months after America entered, and one week later English Friends began providing relief in Germany. In November 1919 Herbert Hoover* requested the Service Committee to take charge of a program for feeding German children one hot meal a day, and the program began in Berlin in February. By July volunteers fed 632,000 children a day; by 1921 the number had increased to 1 million a day. Friends withdrew German relief in 1922, but the invasion of the Ruhr by France and Belgium in 1923 brought the collapse of the mark and the return of Friends.[19]

The feeding the children program was a joint endeavor of the U.S. government, the German government, and the Society of Friends. Most of the food (except flour and sugar) came from the United States; Germany provided free freight, insurance, and 20,000 (later 25,000) volunteers who did the work. The twenty-eight Service Committee representatives organized the operation.

In 1921 the Service Committee had forty-four Americans working in Germany, twenty-two in Poland, sixteen in Austria, fifteen in Serbia, three in France, and one in Russia. But the Russian program increased dramatically when there was a famine. In all relief operations, most financial support came from non-Quaker sources. For example, the Austrian feeding program received $100,000 from the American Red Cross, $50,000 from the American Relief Administration, and $500,000 from the Save the Children Fund. The balance between Quaker efforts and outside contributions can be shown by the 1921 budget, which listed $297,653 raised from Meetings and individuals and $1,343,337 from the American Relief Administration.[20]

The relief and reconstruction programs carried out by British and American Friends first in France and later in Central Europe and Russia involved dealings with governments and business arrangements on a scale unprecedented in Quaker history.[21] If Friends were going to continue this kind of work—and they took pride in their accomplishments—they needed to adopt the methods of modern bureaucracies and to adapt Quaker procedures to these techniques.

The London Yearly Meeting combined its missionary work and the FWVC into the Friends Council for International Service and then into the Friends Service Council in 1926. The American Friends Service Committee (AFSC) is an independent agency run by a Quaker board, some of whose members are nominated by Yearly Meetings. Friends accepted the need for a permanent organization in 1924 and divided the AFSC into four sections: Foreign Service, Interracial, Peace, and Home Service. Each section was controlled by a committee of twenty individuals who met bimonthly.[22] The first domestic relief operation occurred in 1922–1923.

The AFSC still concentrated most efforts on foreign work; in 1926, of total expenditures of $264,027, $228,231 went for foreign work.[23] Home service included support of relief workers in the hill country, work camps, schools, peace education, and programs designed to oppose racism. The foreign work was divided into relief activities, which were coordinated with British Friends, and support for newly established international centers in Europe. These centers located in Paris, Geneva, and Berlin served as gathering places for those sympathetic to the Quaker programs of peace and service.[24] There people could meet to discuss freely the prevalent religious, political, and social issues.

THE QUEST FOR A JUST PEACE

With minor modifications, the synthesis of religion and politics seen as necessary for creating peace that resulted in the creation of the AFSC endures to this day. In their efforts to follow Jesus, Friends have sought through famine relief, reconstruction projects, and aid to both sides in war to create goodwill and the conditions for peace. Internationally, they supported the League of Nations, the International Court, the United Nations, various attempts to create a world federation or world law, arms control, and disarmament. Domestically, the Peace Testimony has prompted Friends to press for social welfare programs and equal rights for racial minorities and against the draft and universal military training.

The AFSC's aims have shown continuity, but there has been a constant search for the best methods to achieve goals without sacrificing moral principles. A. J. Muste left the Congregational ministry and became a militant pacifist and Quaker fellow traveler during World War I. For the next fifty years through his writings, work with the Fellowship of Reconciliation, and political agitation, Muste helped middle-class Friends see the values of labor union strikes, passive disobedience, and absolute noncooperation with the state in military matters.[25] Friends influenced, associated with, and learned from Gandhi and the movement for Indian independence and Martin Luther King, Jr., and the black civil rights movement. Gandhi and King's combination of moral power, nonviolent activities, and political success provided a form of coercion compatible with democratic institutions and Quaker methods. The Cold War, the nuclear arms race, and the prevalence of conflicts since 1945 have prompted Friends to explore the possibilities of using conflict-resolution techniques, peacekeeping forces under United Nations auspices, and conversion of war industries to peacetime production.

From its foundation, making the Service Committee operate smoothly required individuals capable of integrating Quaker sense of the Meeting procedures with modern bureaucratic management. By 1940 the size and complexity of the organization were baffling. There were 31 Quakers who constituted the Board of Directors and set policy, an administrative staff of 43, a field staff of 38 working in Relief Centers in France and 6 at Refugees Centers, with an additional 38 serving refugees at various hostels in the United States. The AFSC operated twelve work camps in addition to the Philadelphia service groups; there were 119 full-time student Peace Volunteers engaged in peace education at various schools and colleges and 75 volunteers working in New York and the Philadelphia offices. Each major division had a standing committee that implemented projects: the Social and Industrial Committee alone had 135 members, Peace 120, Refugees 46, and Clothing 8.[26] The headquarters staff raised funds, wrote peace literature, selected and trained workers for the field, coordinated activities, made sure that supplies arrived on time, worked with COs, and presented their views to officials in Washington. Field workers ran work camps, managed international centers in Europe, helped refugees, provided medical care, and distributed food and clothing.

The membership of the various committees reads like a Who's Who of prominent Quakers. The impact on Philadelphia Orthodox and Hicksites was immense as a significant proportion of the local leadership was directly involved in Service Committee activities. In an effort to make the AFSC less Philadelphia centered, in 1939 regional offices, with responsibility for their own program and finances, were established. Add to this the influence on local Meetings of those who attended work camps, served on the various committees and boards as nominees from the twenty-nine American Yearly Meetings, and worked at headquarters or in the field. Then there were those who were attracted to Friends by the work of the AFSC for peace education, for the COs, or on behalf of sharecroppers, unemployed miners, or blacks.[27] The cooperative efforts of all American Friends in support of the modern peace testimony was a powerful force for unity among the various factions.

The Service Committee is most famous as a relief organization that provides food in times of famine, treats the civilian population suffering the ravages of war, and aids refugees escaping from economic and political oppression. A list of countries whose population has received aid reads like a history of twentieth-century wars: Spain and later France in the 1930s; Western Europe, Japan, and China in the 1940s; Kenya, the Congo, and the Middle East in the 1950s; Vietnam Latin America, and South Africa in the 1960s and 1970s.[28] Frequently, when famine strikes, the Service Committee is there, although in general, other natural disasters are left to bigger agencies like the Red Cross. Recognizing that emergency aid alone is rarely the cure of long-standing problems, the AFSC has attempted projects in America and abroad aimed at reshaping the social environment.

Work camps, supervised by volunteers or staff members of the AFSC, attracted youth who worked for a summer or short period on a relief project. Beginning in 1933, working with local residents, the campers built houses and community centers, initiated soil conservation measures, ran nursery schools, and laid pipes. After World War II, overseas volunteers taught farming techniques, provided medical care, and fostered home industries. Hundreds of young Friends gained firsthand experience in dealing with the problems of poverty in work camps. The AFSC's successes in using volunteers paved the way for the United States government's development of the Peace Corps in the 1960s. Even before World War II, the literature issued by the Committee stressed the importance of involving the people to be aided in making the significant decisions about their future direction. The goal has been to use Service Committee funds as seed money to start a project which the local population will then continue.

The AFSC began and has continued the support of conscientious objectors. Friends through the Peace Division have provided information on legal options for those debating whether to request CO status, provided legal counsel for those defining their right of conscience, and sent visitors to meet and encourage those in prison. During the 1930s the AFSC actively engaged in the broad-ranging peace movement with the Fellowship of Reconciliation, the War Resisters League, and the No Conscription Fellowship.[29] Friends took a major role in proselytizing for peace, and Peace Caravans composed of students and young adults visited communities and campuses. They also sponsored seminars where Friends and outsiders could gain a perspective on issues relating to peace.

Before World War II, as before World War I, representatives of the Service Committee and various Yearly Meetings held discussions in Washington to persuade administrative and legislative officials to write laws protecting the rights of pacifists. During the war the Committee, along with officials of other peace churches, Mennonites and the Church of the Brethren, accepted responsibility from the government for financially supporting and supervising Civilian Public Service Camps for those who sought alternative service. In the Stearns Amendment Congress insisted that the military have ultimate authority over the conduct of the camps and refused to allow any COs to go abroad to engage in relief activities. Instead, the government tried to isolate pacifists in camps where they were supposed to find significant nonmilitary work. Caught between the COs' desire to help people and the military's narrow definition of what was permitted, Friends had a difficult time in administering the camps. The COs, who received no pay or financial benefits from the government, chafed under a regime that was neither civilian nor military, and some left the camps, accepting prison as a preferable method of peace witness. Still, the 12,000 men from the Civilian Public Service did many worthwhile conservation projects, worked in mental hospitals, served as "guinea pigs" for medical research, and fought forest fires. The Civilian Public Service Camps provided an alternative to prison and helped to create a cadre of leaders who joined Friends and remained active in peace causes (often working for the AFSC) in the postwar period.[30] The frustrations of dealing with the military in wartime caused Friends to despair of working closely with the U.S. government. Although in specific relief projects the AFSC cooperated with the government, in general since 1945, the Service Committee has kept its distance from official policies. Neither the government nor Friends wished to repeat the Civilian Public Service experience, and in the Korean and Vietnamese wars COs were not segregated in camps.

In 1949 in an attempt to influence public discussion of major issues of foreign policy, the Service Committee began issuing policy papers. The first, *The United States and the Soviet Union*, contained a discussion of steps that could be taken to reduce tensions between the superpowers. A panel of experts—mostly Friends, including people associated with the Service Committee and the academic community—after wide-ranging discussion and research, formulated a policy statement that would be presented to the board. The board determined whether to amend or endorse the recommendations and publish the findings in a pamphlet or small book. The policies are the positions of the AFSC, not those of the constituent Yearly Meetings or all Friends. Since 1949 the Service Committee has issued policy statements on disarmament (1952), Vietnam (1966), the Middle East (1970, 1982), crime and the administration of justice (1973), and abortion and euthanasia (1970). These policy papers resemble the productions of the Brookings Institute and other "think tanks." Specifically Quaker or religious language is not used in an attempt to reach the widest possible audience.

The long war in Vietnam strengthened the commitment of Friends to the peace testimony and generally eased the discrepancy between the Meetings' proclamations and the members' actions. For once in American history, being a pacifist in wartime was almost popular. Quakers officially as well as individually questioned both the rationale for being in the war and the tactics used by the military, and few joined the armed services. Meetings petitioned the government, organized vigils and demonstrations, issued tracts, provided draft counseling, debated tax refusal, provided relief and medical supplies to the Vietnamese people, and gave sanctuary to those opposing the draft.

Americans searching for ways of legitimating their opposition to the war and refusal to fight found the Friends' peace testimony most attractive. The antiwar movement drew upon the questioning of American mores initiated by those struggling for civil rights and women's liberation. Friends had traditionally supported and continued to work in both of these causes and had approved of an emphasis upon simple living and truth telling. But when the antiwar feeling became joined with a pervasive countercultural revolt, Friends became apprehensive. They did not approve of vituperation, personal immorality, use of drugs, anti-intellectualism, and the violence that accompanied many antiwar protests. The predictable result was the disillusionment of those radicals who hoped to use the Meetings as a vehicle in creating a political–social revolution but who did not understand the Quakers' emphasis upon a disciplined, spiritual life.

The Service Committee was a response by Friends in World War I to a changing view of religious life. At the end of the nineteenth century, midwestern and far western Friends had accepted a pastoral system as a form of religious calling. Eastern and liberal Friends found in working for peace an analogous religious vocation. Many of the early leaders of the Service Committee—Clarence Pickett* E. Raymond Wilson*, Henry J. Cadbury*, Rufus Jones*—came out of an evangelical background. Today the Service Committee resists precise definition because it is a relief institution, an agency for social change, a defender of pacifists, an educational network, a meeting for worship, and a bureaucracy. The contradictions and possibilities are inherent in the American Friends Service Committee's original function of attempting to bring peace and goodwill to all peoples.

Pacifism has emerged in the twentieth century as the most distinctive belief of Quakers, that which sets them apart from other churches and American society. To be a pacifist in America is to be radical, no matter how middle class one feels. The Cold War, the arms race, apartheid, the pervasiveness of poverty, and the preponderance of oppressive regimes have forced Friends to seek, debate, and agonize over what it means to be peacemakers. Peace can no longer be defined simply as the absence of organized violence, and the peace testimony must be broadened from its Quaker and Anglo-American roots. In their 300-year history Friends have rarely produced first-rate theologians, but in virtually every generation those grappling with the implications of the peace testimony have been truly creative. The constant challenge is for Friends to be effective Christian witnesses for peace.

NOTES

1. William James, *The Moral Equivalent of War*, quoted in Clarence Pickett, *For More Than Bread* (Boston: 1953), 309.

2. Clarence Yarrow, *Quaker Experience in International Conciliation* (New Haven: 1978); Elmer Jackson, *Middle East Mission: The Story of a Major Bid for Peace in the Time of Nasser and Ben Gurion* (New York: 1983).

3. John Ormerod Greenwood, *Quaker Encounters: Friends and Relief* (York, Eng.:

1975), I, 185-93; John W. Graham, *Conscription and Conscience* (London: 1922), 344–52; Leigh Tucker, "English Quakers and World War I," 1914–1920 (Ph.D. diss., University of North Carolina, 1972).

4. Greenwood, *Quaker Encounters*, I, 195–197.

5. A. Ruth Fry, *A Quaker Adventure* (London 1927), 16.

6. Fry, *Quaker Adventure*, Part I, France; Part II, Holland and Belgium; Greenwood, *Quaker Encounters* I, 194–208.

7. Fry, *Quaker Adventure*, 41, 75-76, 107.

8. The Friends Service Committee of the London Yearly Meeting was created during World War I to deal with problems of military service. In addition to the chairman, the treasurer and secretary of the FSC were convicted. The specific charge was the failure of the Service Committee to submit pamphlets for censorship. Leigh Tucker, "English Friends and Censorship," *Quaker History* (hereafter *QH* 71 (1982): 115–24.

9. Graham, *Conscription*, 115–16; Thomas Kennedy, "Fighting about Peace: The No-Conscription Fellowship and the British Friends Service Committee," *QH* 69 (1980): 3–22; 70 (1981): 47–54; John Rae, *Conscience and Politics: The British Government and the Conscientious Objector to Military Service, 1816-1919* (London: 1970).

10. Philip Benjamin, *Philadelphia Quakers in the Industrial Age, 1865–1920*: (Ann Arbor, Mich: 1971), 180–191; Charles De Benedetti, *Origins of the Modern American Peace Movement, 1915–1929* (Millwood, NY: 1978).

11. Benjamin, *Philadephia Quakers*, 204–5; "Some Particular Advices for Friends and a Statement of Loyalty for Others" (Philadelphia: Third Month, 1918).

12. Margaret Bacon, *Let This Life Speak: The Legacy of Henry Joel Cadbury* (Philadelphia: 1987), 37–48.

13. American Friends Service Committee, *Bulletin*, no. 6 (1917?).

14. Young Friends had held joint Meetings before World War I, and in 1915 the Friends National Peace Conference at Winona Lake, Indiana, was attended by Friends from throughout America. Its National Committee met with the Peace Committees of Philadelphia Yearly Meeting—Hicksite and Orthodox.

15. Rufus Jones, *A Service of Love in Wartime* (New York: 1920), 6; American Friends Service Committee, *Bulletin*, no. 2 (1918): 1.

16. American Friends Service Committee *Bulletin*, no 4 (1917?); no. 5 (1917?).

17. Ibid., no. 17 (1918?): 5.

18. Ibid., no. 21 (1919?).

19. Ibid., Nos. 24 (1920); 33 (1920); 43 (1921); 52 (1922); 59 (1924); Fry, *Quaker Adventures*; Jones, *Service of Love*.

20. American Friends Service Committee, *Bulletin*, no. 43 (1921): 13–14.

21. Greenwood, *Quaker Encounters*, I, 219–25 (Germanies); Richenda Scott, *Quakers in Russia* (London: 1964), 146-227 (Russian campaigns); Mary Hoxie Jones, *Swords into Ploughshares: An Account of the American Friends Service Committee, 1917–1937* (New York: 1937).

22. American Friends Service Committee, *Bulletin*, no. 67 (1925–26): 2; Walter Kahoe, *Clarence Pickett* (Moylan, Pa.: 1966), 16.

23. American Friends Service Committee, *Bulletin*, no. 67 (1925–26): 15.

24. Frederick J. Tritton, *Carl Heath* (London: 1951).

25. Jo Ann Robinson, *Abraham Went Out: A Biography of A. J. Muste* (Philadelphia: 1981).

26. American Friends Service Committee, *Annual Report*, 1940.

27. Clarence Pickett, *For More Than Bread* (Boston: 1953), and Jones, *Swords into Plowshares*, provide descriptions of the various Service Committee projects in the period before World War II.

28. Roger Wilson, *Quaker Relief* (London: 1952), and A. Tegla Davis, *Friends Ambulance Unit* (London: 1947), concentrate on the service of English Friends in World War II. Howard E. Kershner, *Quaker Service in Modern War* (New York: 1950), is about work in Spain and France after the Spanish Civil War. Additional information is in Greenwood, *Quaker Encounters*, and Pickett, *For More Than Bread*.

29. Earle Charles Chatfield, *For Peace and Justice: Pacifism in America, 1914–1941* (Knoxville, Tenn.: 1971).

30. Larry Wittner, *Rebels against War* (New York: 1969), 70–84, Hobart Mitchell, *We Would Not Kill* (Richmond, Ind.: 1983), Alfred Hassler, *Diary of a Self-Made Convict* (Chicago: 1954), and James Peck, *We Who Would Not Kill* (New York: 1958), are accounts of those who refused to join Civilian Public Service Camps and were jailed.

20
SOCIAL SERVICE AND
SOCIAL CHANGE, 1902–1970

Quaker philanthropists in the nineteenth century supported a multitude of temperance programs, children's homes, schools for blacks, aid societies, and clothing workrooms for indigent women.[1] After the end of southern Reconstruction, the most important social and moral reform for all Friends was temperance. Virtually no one in Protestant circles could justify allowing liquor. For workers, drinking beer at lunch led to drowsiness, inefficiency, and accidents. Laborers who squandered their wages on whiskey reduced their families to destitution, and alcohol supposedly caused crime, insanity, prostitution, and political corruption. Support for total abstinence was characteristic of British as well as American Friends through the 1920s. The effort throughout a century to free Quakers from using alcohol or selling liquor led the Quaker tea-selling Fry, Rowntree, and Cadbury families into the English cocoa and chocolate business. American rural areas with many Quakers used the local option to "go dry." Today there is diversity in Quaker attitudes toward alcohol. Evangelical Friends usually insist on abstinence; liberals often allow moderate drinking, but many abstainers remain in eastern Meetings, some also preferring a vegetarian diet or natural foods.

Although many Quaker women who were first active for women's rights stopped attending worship, Lucretia Mott* and Anna Sharpless made voting rights for women a vital issue within Quaker Meetings. Friends like Sarah and Angelina Grimke* and Elizabeth Comstock* played key roles in the early nineteenth-century women's movement, as later did Susan B. Anthony and Abby Foster Kelly. Philadelphia Hicksites publicly supported women's suffrage in 1914; the Orthodox never took a stand. The tactics of Quaker Alice Paul's Congressional Union during World War I, which included picketing the White House, civil disobedience, and going to jail, were too radical for most Friends.

THE SOCIAL GOSPEL

New needs led Friends to begin programs that implied new attitudes to society. Cornelia Hancock* exemplified the change from concentrating upon blacks and education to living with the urban poor while she dealt with slum housing. At Wharton Center in Philadelphia, and Emily Greene Balch's* Denison House in Boston, Friends who had learned from Jane Addams and other settlement house pioneers also shaped programs for the poor. Friends in urban work were excited by the writings of slum pastors like Walter Rauschenbusch in Manhattan's "Hell's Kitchen," Washington Gladden in Columbus, Ohio, and Charles Kingsley in England that gave theological justification for "the social gospel." Quakers had long expressed their faith by aiding individuals, quoting Matthew 25:40: "inasmuch as you have done it unto the least of these my brethren, you have done it unto me." Now social gospellers began applying the Golden Rule to governmental policies, international relations, and corporate practices; economic structures and social institutions fostered injustice and must be changed in order to build the Kingdom of God here on earth. Since individual conversion did not solve corporate evils, social workers and social gospel thinkers read eagerly the proposals of Henry George and many kinds of Christian socialists.[2]

Friends accepted social gospel ideas later than reformers among the Methodists, Catholics, and Anglicans who in an "established Church" had for centuries assumed responsibility for all society. Since both Quaker evangelicals and liberals had rejected sectarian isolation and distinctive Quaker dress and speech, they now worked easily with members of other churches in organizations for women's suffrage, schools, temperance, peace, social work, and participatory democracy.[3] Yearly Meetings in England and America created standing committees where Friends discussed the treatment of immigrants and blacks, the cooperative movement, the future of capitalism and socialism, the regulation of business, and whether a strike or arbitration was the better way to solve industrial strife. The generation of young English and American east coast Friends who came of age after 1900 were well educated and cosmopolitan; they had grown up with innovations in commerce, industry, and technology and had mastered the skills necessary to run large-scale bureaucratic organizations. They questioned not only inherited theology but political conservatism and read and discussed ideas of Christian socialists and the pacifists in the labor movement. Their encounters with the poor and the inequalities of wealth made many reject laissez-faire economics. New members came to Quakerism out of adult education programs for factory workers or as a result of war experiences. Yet as in other denominations, those Friends who were most critical of capitalism and favored massive government intervention in the economy remained a minority.

The Peace Testimony changed after World War I. Traditional Quakers defended their witness against war as obedience to God's commandment and Jesus' example. Friends quoted the Epistle of James (4:1) that wars arose from the personal passions and sins of humans. Such Friends stressed the need of individual conversion or transformation as a condition for a new social order. During World War I the personal sins of the kaiser, the king of England, the czar, and the president seemed less responsible for the origin and duration of the war than national policies that grew out of the political, social, and economic life of their society. Just when Meetings stopped exercising corporate authority over individualistic members, Friends had to confront institutional power in national society.

The American Friends Service Committee (AFSC) became an institutional way of expressing pacifism. Quakers drew upon the emerging professionalism of the social sciences in interpreting war and pacifism. Entire societies went to war; thus to make peace required understanding business practices, wage systems, poverty, life-styles, schools, and journalism. Most Friends still agreed with John Bright* that free trade "is directly implied in our peace testimony."[4] Yet the root causes of war were increasingly seen in the 1920s as class conflict, racism, militarism, capitalism, imperialism, and nationalism. Friends could not withdraw from society and often drew on purely political theories to take responsible stands on international arbitration, the Treaty of Versailles, the League of Nations, and reparations.

Quakers still grounded their pacifism in religious commitment. Only personal conviction had supported conscientious objectors when war began: organized churches and the idealistic labor movement had surrendered to nationalism. For some Friends the Peace Testimony became their religion, integral to their faith unlike customs of dress and speech. Their experience of the Light required living in peace, taking literally the Sermon on the Mount, respecting the worth of every individual, and building the Kingdom of God on earth.

HENRY CADBURY AND TOM KELLY

If educated American Quakers had an unofficial spokesperson after Rufus Jones,* it was Jones's brother-in-law Henry J. Cadbury,* fiery worker for peace and cool-headed New Testament scholar. With dry wit he wrote Quaker history and tried to unite Friends. Although most educated readers warmed to Jones's devotional and historical books, Cadbury wrote as a scholars' scholar. He loved the Bible, was dispassionately accurate, and was tolerant even of those who distrusted modern biblical criticism, but many of his best insights could be understood only by New Testament specialists. Cadbury was unhappy with labels. Unlike Jones, he refused to call himself either a liberal or a mystic and was reticent about claiming religious experiences, insisting that the essence of a disciple was Christian living.[5] He used historical research to illuminate contemporary problems: loyalty oaths, black membership in the Society of Friends, the evolution of the Peace Testimony, or *The Peril of Modernizing Jesus*. Unlike Jones, who saw history as a way to communicate a vision of Quakerism, Cadbury preferred to be a detective of facts and used obscure manuscripts meticulously to recreate concrete events. Scholars, Bible translators, and Friends stood in awe of his intellectual acuity and loved his gentle sense of humor, but he resisted becoming a guru or starting a school of interpretation. Always a teacher, he quietly presented the evidence so that his listeners could see the implications for themselves. Yet through the same years he chaired the American Friends Service Committee. He helped to organize its relief in post–World War II Europe; when the AFSC received the 1947 Nobel Peace Prize, he accepted the award in a tailcoat borrowed from an AFSC relief shipment meant for bombed-out musicians.

Thomas R. Kelly* and Douglas Steere, writers as deeply mystical as Cadbury was prophetic, were asked by Rufus Jones to be his colleagues at Haverford. Each showed in different ways how mystics respond to crises in the world and society. Steere knew the need of Europeans for understanding as well as help. He led after World War II in starting the work-camp movement in Finland and later kept touch with Catholics at Vatican II and with many church people in South Africa.

Kelly's work overseas changed him more personally. He had been a well-loved teacher but did not achieve his goal of recognition as a philosopher. His resulting breakdown released in him an intense spiritual sensitivity that flowered during his visit in 1938 to the German Quakers living under the terror of Nazi rule. Unable to repeat the names of the victims or offer anything but empathy, he returned to Haverford "with the sound of weeping in one's ears, in order to say, . . . the last vestige of earthly security is gone. It has always been gone, and religion has always said so, but we haven't believed it."[6] Kelly then gave talks that were collected into a modern classic, *A Testament of Devotion*, after his sudden death in 1941:

Deep within us all there is an amazing inner sanctuary of the soul, a holy place, a Divine Center, a speaking voice, to which we may continuously return. . . . we are torn loose from earthly attachments and ambitions [in a] *contemptus mundi*. And we are quickened to a divine but painful concern for the world—*amor mundi*. He plucks the world out of our hearts, loosening the chains of attachment. And he hurls the world into our hearts, where we and He together carry it in infinitely tender love.[7]

THE SERVICE COMMITTEE AS AGENT FOR SOCIAL CHANGE

A series of crises in the American Friends Service Committee represented responses to the social gospel of Cadbury and Kelly. In 1922–23 its founders decided not to terminate the Committee when war relief was over, and so they started domestic relief operations in the coal fields of Pennsylvania and West Virginia, where families of striking miners were starving. Friends had never previously intervened in any strike and at first just applied their overseas relief policy that political beliefs should not interfere with giving aid. Miners' families needed to be fed, and later, during their unemployment in the great Depression, they needed to be given tools and help in building their own homes and gardens. Sharecroppers were helped with agricultural methods and enabled to buy their own land. British and American Service Committees' efforts in setting up voluntary work camps exposed students and well-to-do young folk to poverty in rural and urban slums. World War I had led many Philadelphia Quakers to embrace the social gospel. When World War II cut short relief and work-camp programs (though some grew up again afterward), responsibility for Civilian Public Service camps for conscientious objectors made the Committee wrestle with problems arising as it dealt with the army, the government, and men in the camps committed to radically new models for society. Many on the staff of the AFSC since World War II have seen their duty to society as promoting nonviolent social change. Others focused on specific social threats, producing some of the best recent research on the military industrial complex.

FRIENDS COMMITTEE ON NATIONAL LEGISLATION

The Service Committee had meanwhile sought to influence public policy through appeals to legislatures and cultivating of close relationships with government figures, with notable success during both Hoover's and Roosevelt's administrations. During the Depression the government funded certain projects that the AFSC designed. As World War II approached the working alliance between the government and Friends showed strains. The AFSC's status as a tax-exempt charitable institution hindered using it for public advocacy. A group of Friends founded a permanent registered lobby in Washington, the Friends Committee on National Legislation (FCNL), a pioneer for other churches' work in Congress. To be its executive secretary, E. Raymond Wilson moved from the Peace Section of the AFSC.

The FCNL's small staff uses intellectual persuasion rather than an ability to sway many voters. It works by personal visits to local and Yearly Meetings and a monthly newsletter to inform Quakers across the country about issues of national significance and to learn the concerns of individual Meetings. Representatives of the FCNL testify at congressional hearings, hold formal and informal discussion with government leaders, and present facts for the use of those who are sympathetic with Quaker perspectives on topics like the Defense budget, compulsory military training, Indian rights, and civil rights.[8]

The FCNL and AFSC continue to try to engage the whole community of Friends in their projects. They draw their largely Quaker boards from many Yearly Meetings. Staff members report to Yearly Meetings, issue pamphlets, provide speakers, sponsor conferences, and try to formulate policies in accordance with views held by Friends. Yet the listening and teaching roles of these committees are hard to combine. The diversity of political and religious beliefs held by Quakers complicates the work of both organizations. (A poll of opinions of all Indiana Friends by their state Friends Committee on Legislation found only one issue on which there was clear consensus: no liquor should be sold on

Sundays.) Many critics come from Meetings that do not accept pacifism or disarmament or who interpret the Peace Testimony as requiring withdrawal from politics. Evangelical critics of the AFSC are troubled by its religious as well as political values; they disapprove of separating missionary and evangelistic activities from relief and social reconstruction. With limited resources, they say, Quakers should concentrate upon the need for the Gospel. In 1954 the Kansas Yearly Meeting withdrew its support of the AFSC, and in 1964 the California Yearly Meeting decided as a protest not to nominate representatives for the AFSC's Board.[9]

The AFSC has found it hard to decide between professional expertise and openness to service by religiously dedicated individuals. Before World War II most staff and volunteers were Quakers. In the aftermath of that war and particularly after the war in Vietnam, many pacifists who were not Quakers began working for the AFSC. Domestic programs are oriented to the city poor and minorities like black Americans and Hispanics, who are seldom Quakers and whose outlooks are strange to rural and suburban Friends. Programs for them will be less effective if created and implemented by a staff overwhelmingly white and middle class. Now that the generation of leaders who shared in the Civilian Public Service camps is retiring, Quakers consist of only 18 to 20 percent of the AFSC's employees. Since 1917, most AFSC funding has come from non-Friends.

QUAKERS AND BLACKS

Racial issues challenge Friends Meetings themselves as well as their Service Committees. At their 1920 World Conference Friends stated their belief that racism was a cause of war. Both the Hicksite and Orthodox Philadelphia Yearly Meetings and many of those in the Northeast and Midwest had standing committees on racial affairs, which supported antilynching laws and New Deal efforts for relief for blacks. The AFSC in the 1920s hired blacks and created a race relations institute. Henry Cadbury researched and lectured on the reasons that there were so few black Friends.[10] Yet nearly a century after Oberlin College accepted black students, no black students were in any white Quaker school or college: Friends educated blacks in separate schools. Bryn Mawr admitted its first black student in 1927; Oakwood School in Poughkeepsie, New York, in 1933; Media Friends in 1937; Haverford by 1926; and Swarthmore College in 1943 (it was a navy unit that integrated Swarthmore). After World War II Friends became active to break down segregation in the North as well as the South and opened their own institutions to members of minorities. Yearly Meetings endorsed the civil rights movement; some Friends took part in "sit-ins." Quaker institutions did not thereby escape the anger of blacks in the 1960s, who insisted on kinds of integration that did not threaten black cultural identity or self-determination. In 1969 a group of blacks seized the floor during Philadelphia Yearly Meeting to demand funds as "reparation" for past injustices. Although resisting the demand for unconditional funding, the Yearly Meeting created the Economic Development Fund to underwrite businesses controlled by black and other minority communities. The only mainly black Meeting now active is the Chicago Fellowship of Friends, which grew from a young people's recreation program of Steve and Marlene Pedigo.

COMMUNES AND NONVIOLENT REVOLUTION

The black power movement forced Friends to rethink the implications of liberal theology. Quakers who turned to "liberation theology" charged that liberal professors were white, middle-class, male intellectuals who talked about the fatherhood of God and brotherhood of man without realizing that they saw Christianity in paternalist and class terms. Abstract theology, ethics, and mysticism seemed to reflect the interests of the bourgeoisie and capitalism. Radical Friends wanted to merge Marxism and Christianity to mobilize the oppressed in a nonviolent revolution. Friends appropriated the insights of liberation theology without the rhetoric of violence. They identified with suffering in Africa and Central America and refused to define the Peace Testimony in ways that merely reinforced the status quo: a nonviolent social revolution would serve compassion and social justice better than any war. Yet at the same time Friends struggled with the dilemma that it was easier to be a pacifist in America than in Nicaragua and that only a culturally blind person could claim that Quakers fully imitated Christ.

As women began to see their own situation in terms of oppression and liberation, some Friends became sensitive to the need for a transformed sexless religious language, and they identified Friends' long tradition of female leadership with women's emancipation.

In the 1960s when racial crises and the Vietnam War had prepared many liberals to call for total reorganization of society, Hugh Barbour and T. Canby Jones revived for young Friends James Nayler's symbol of "the Lamb's War," calling humans to enroll in God's struggle against evil simultaneously in their own hearts and in society. In those years lively Quaker groups exchanged ideas with both Christian and Marxist radicals. They created their own organizations without an official endorsement by their Meeting or formed in effect new Meetings by their own lives. The Brandywine Alternative Fund found ways to avoid paying war taxes, and many Friends took part in campaigns for a Peace Tax Fund. In general, the Quaker radicals embraced voluntary poverty, engaged in civil disobedience, and hoped to mobilize the poor. Philadelphia Yearly Meeting in 1967 obtained a "sense of the Meeting" not just to oppose the Vietnam War effort but to engage in sending medical supplies across the border to Canada, whence they were sent to North Vietnam, despite an American government ban on such trade.[11] Earl and Barbara Reynolds sailed their yacht *Golden Rule* into the nuclear test zones in the South Pacific and then the *Phoenix* with medical supplies to Haiphong. The Cambridge, Massachusetts, Meeting and several others offered sanctuary to draft resisters. A Quaker Action Group (AQAG), under Lawrence Scott, picketed month by month the germ warfare base at Fort Dietrich. Quaker groups around New York, Pittsburgh, and Media, Pennsylvania, were drawn by the racial violence of the 1960s into working with the police to teach mediating methods and restrain police brutality; they went on to take concern for the whole prison system and for alternative ways of housing and supervising delinquents.

Other groups explored new ways to interpret Quaker ethics. Thomas Kelly had warned that "we have plenty of Quakers to follow God the first half of the way, [but] there is a degree of holy and complete obedience and of joyful self-renunciation . . . that is breathtaking."[12] The New Foundations Fellowship grew out of Lewis Benson's personal call for Christ-centered commitment to an ethic as radical as Anabaptism. A dozen British Quaker psychiatrists and counsellors published in 1963 *Towards a Quaker View of Sex*, which opened the way for a widening but increasingly bitter dialogue about homosexuality and "gay" Friends across the whole spectrum of Quakers until the present. Some homosexual pairs have asked their Meetings to bless their "marriages."

In the 1960s quite different groups of young people committed themselves to living together in new models of a society based on Quaker ideals. New Swarthmoor was one such commune near Ithaca, New York. Later some of its members took part in George Lakey's "Movement for a New Society," whose New Life Centers and books encouraged a nonviolent social revolution.

The largest single Quaker concern in American society from 1945 to the present has been nuclear weapons. For their actions, more Friends have been in jail than in any era since Fox's to protest rearmament. Since the Vietnam War, civil disobedience and providing "sanctuary" for Salvadoran refugees have shown that individual Quakers and whole Meetings now take for granted that they are right to obey their own consciences rather than laws of the state. Although fewer Quakers now than in 1968 give their lives to alternative or radical styles of community life, their sharing of ideals with other believers in social change has hidden from Friends' awareness how far they have moved back beyond the social outlooks of all intermediate Quaker generations to the apocalyptic views of the first Friends. American conservatism in the 1970s and 1980s has taken the confidence of victory from many workers for a new society. It is harder to be sure what overall meaning for social justice Friends in future decades will draw from their tradition, in working out their Testimonies to racial justice, economic opportunity, and social equality.

NOTES

1. See Philip S. Benjamin, *Philadelphia Quakers* (Philadelphia: 1976), Chs. 4, 7.

2. Charles Hopkins, *Rise of the Social Gospel in American Protestantism* (New Haven: 1942); Ronald White and Charles Hopkins, *The Social Gospel: Religion and*

Reform in Changing America (Philadelphia: 1976); Robert Handy, *The Social Gospel in America* (New York: 1966).

3. Benjamin, *Philadelphia Quakers*, 180–91; Charles De Benedetti, *Origins of the Modern American Peace Movement, 1915–1929* (Millwood, N.Y.: 1978).

4. The first All Friends Conference, convened in 1920 as soon as the war ended, included seven commissions of English and American Friends, whose reports are quoted at length in E. W. Orr, *The Quakers in Peace and War* (Eastbourne, Sussex, Eng: 1974), 23–70.

5. Margaret Hope Bacon, *Let This Life Speak: The Legacy of Henry Joel Cadbury* (Philadelphia: 1987).

6. Thomas Kelly, *A Testament of Devotion* (New York: 1941), 69.

7. Ibid, 29, 47.

8. E. Raymond Wilson, *Uphill for Peace: Quaker Impact on Congress* (Richmond, Ind.: 1975), is a general history of the FCNL. See also William J. Weston, "Between the Spheres: A Weberian Study of the Friends Committee on National Legislation" (B.A. thesis, Swarthmore College, 1982).

9. California Yearly Meeting of Friends Church, Official Minutes, 1964, 12.

10. Henry J. Cadbury, "Negro Membership in the Society of Friends," *Journal of Negro History* (1936): 151–213; his lecture was "The Negro Problem—a Study in Whites" (see Margaret Bacon, *Let This Life Speak*, 87, 120).

11. *Proceedings of Philadelphia Yearly Meeting* (Philadelphia: 1969), 21.

12. Kelly, *Testament*, 53.

21
NEW FORMS OF QUAKER INTERACTION, 1960–1987

Quaker pacifism and concern for social service and social change, which grew amid social crises in 1930–45, came to fruition in 1945–50 after World War II in overseas relief, mental hospital reform, and new programs in Quaker colleges. The Korean War and conservatism of the 1950s brought these stands under attack, but in the Kennedy era of the 1960s liberal Friends and much of the nation interacted in new ways with blacks seeking civil rights and with Catholics and "counterculture" activists working for peace. Among Friends, East Africa, Jamaica, and Cuba Yearly Meetings became equal members of the Friends United Meeting, the new name of the Five Years Meeting after its session in 1960, as its structure was simplified and it began meeting every three years.

The relation of American and Third World cultures changed in other ways also. Mystical Quakers had long been cordial to mystics in other faiths. By 1930 E. A. Burtt and other Friends had become expert in Buddhist literature. Douglas Steere and Howard and Anna Brinton studied Buddhism in Japan, as did Tom Kelly in Hawaii. In 1960 Pendle Hill, which was soon to be caught up in peace and social justice issues, focused its program on the relation of Quakerism to other faiths.[1] Many Friends practiced the discipline of Zen meditation. Zen masters taught at Pendle Hill and at American Quaker colleges. Many Friends kept meditation journals. Friends and others who explored the psychology of Carl Jung led the Council on Religion and Psychology's annual conferences and issued a thoughtful journal, *Inward Light*. Friends in the 1960s also responded to Martin Buber's existentialist presentation of Hasidic Judaism and "the life of dialogue." A "working party" of a dozen Quaker writers and social scientists met thrice a year in the 1960s to search for new Quaker symbol–words but agreed only that human sharing of diverse experiences already reflects the undergirding Spirit. Liberal Friends often believed that they could share a common mystical experience that was the essence of all faiths and transcended history and cultures.

In England a recent group of Universalist Quakers formed around a similar understanding of the Inner Light.

MUTUAL LEARNING BY AMERICAN AND THIRD WORLD FRIENDS

The full history of Quaker Yearly Meetings in Europe, Africa, and Hispanic America cannot be covered in this book, but their changing relationship to American Friends reflected their emerging cultural identities. When the 1984 Friends United Meeting (FUM) session took note that the one East African Yearly Meeting had divided into three, it accepted the autonomy of tribal groups. The transfer of the ministry and control from most Western missionaries to local Christians and their national Churches had come already in the 1930s in India, China, and Japan, but it came more slowly in Africa and Spanish America, where a Christian's former culture was more deeply rooted in local languages and life-styles than in nationwide patterns. After World War II, however, national independence movements everywhere rejected missionaries' paternalism.

In the thickly settled rural hills of western Kenya where the Malones' Cleveland Bible College began the Friends African Industrial Mission in 1902, the local tribes—the Marigoli, Tiriki, and Bakusu—were not politically or militarily strong.[2] Missionaries such as "Bwana" Jefferson Ford, who began the Friends Bible Institute, were paternal figures to their converts. The early missionary families—Chilsons, Blackburns, Bonds, Hoyts, and Kellums—stayed a generation and learned the tribal Lurigoli, into which Emory Rees, with Joeli Litu and other Africans, translated the Bible, hymns, and school books. Kenyan village worship still unites everyone in mass singing and Bible study. By 1935 there were 261 village Meetings attended by 19,000 Africans and 289 Quaker elementary schools with 15,000 children, many taught by women. Teachers and pastors, usually with only basic education themselves, had to depend on local support, often in farm produce. Most of them continue tilling their own small farms. In 1921 and 1923 the Friends Mission began girls' and boys' boarding schools. In 1949 they moved the Bible Institute from Lugulu to Kaimosi where in 1953 they opened the Teachers' and Nurses' Training Colleges at the secondary-school level. The mission staff was centralized in Kaimosi, leaving the village work in African hands. After World War II the Kenyan government funded most schools but let churches staff them, including 211 primary and 48 secondary out of 285 Quaker schools. The Kaimosi and Lugulu hospitals, and after 1962 the Friends College at Chavakali, remained partially funded and staffed from Europe and America, but teachers, doctors, and nurses now come for shorter terms, some without training in Bible or African languages.[3] Resisting such trends, Kansas Friends in 1934 had set up a more traditional Evangelical Friends Church of Burundi across Lake Victoria.

The East Africa Yearly Meeting was set up in 1946 as a self-governing body with Benjamin Ngaira as Field Secretary. When he went on to head the Kenyan

Civil Service, Thomas Lung' aho became the powerful executive of the Yearly Meeting. A 1953 report by Charles Lampman and Errol Elliott urged American Friends also to devolve the title deeds of institutions upon the East Africa Yearly Meeting, which was done with due ceremony as Kenyan independence in 1963 drew near. Creative longer-term aid came through David Scull whose Partnership for Productivity helped Kenyan farmers learn "appropriate technology" such as canning and bookkeeping. Major crises still lay ahead for Kenyan Friends. Personal and tribal differences made many Bukusu want an independent Elgon Yearly Meeting, already proclaimed in 1973 despite efforts by the FUM staff to maintain unity and the central institutions at Kaimosi (among the Tiriki). By 1979 southern Marigoli Friends had also decided to form an East Africa Yearly Meeting, South. Later the more scattered Meetings outside Western Province became Nairobi Yearly Meeting. A new East Africa Yearly Meeting, North, centered at Kitale, has been seeking recognition. The more than 130,000 Kenyan Quakers worked together to welcome Friends from all continents to the fifth Friends World Committee for Consultation (FWCC) World Conference at Kaimosi in 1982. As Elgon and East African Yearly Meeting South were welcomed into the FUM in 1984, Thomas Lung'aho embraced their new leaders as brothers.

American missionaries went through similar interactions with new Friends Meetings on other continents. The Meetings and schools at Brumanna, Lebanon (now closed), and Ramallah, Palestine, begun by Sybil and Eli Jones* in 1867–69, remain the only ones in the Near East Yearly Meeting. At Ramallah the Friends Girls School, begun in 1889, and the Friends Boys School, 1901, trained three generations of Arab Christians from the whole Near East. Katie Gabriel, Khalil Totah, and later Fuad and Jean Zaru were Arab leaders at the schools, but 137 teachers and principals have come from America, funded by New England and by FUM Mission Boards. They taught in English, as few teachers learned enough Arabic to teach or preach in it. Since 1948, Jordanian exams set the norms. Maintaining a Quaker witness for nonviolence in the cultural capital of the Palestinian West Bank has not been easy.[4]

Friends churches began in Guatemala in 1902, when Clark Buckley and Thomas J. Kelly, evangelists from California Yearly Meeting, began a mission and schools around Chiquimula. Converts have mostly been Spanish-speaking "Ladino" farmers rather than Indians. The Americans concentrated their work in key towns; village churches were increasingly led by native evangelists, 24 (under 11 Yankees) in 1919, and 66 (with 13 Anglos) by 1929, who carried their work over the borders into Honduras and El Salvador. The Friends Church thrived when American-backed governments were in power. Membership in Guatemala increased most strongly in 1915–21 and again in 1950–60 after Castillo Armas's coup against the liberal Arbenz government. The maximum of about 8,000 Quakers there fell to 4,738 in 1969 and about 3,500 at present. There were grass-roots revivals in 1918, 1930, and 1952, but 60 percent of those converted fell away.[5] From 1921 Guatemalan pastors studied at their own Berea Bible Institute. In 1970 an independent Central American Yearly Meeting was set up. By 1985 the 1,000 Quakers in Honduras had their own Yearly Meeting led by Andres Carranza.

In Mexico Friends arose in four separate areas as the result of various missions, beginning with Samuel Purdie's pioneer work with a church and press in Ciudad Victoria; AFSC made Mexico City a center for village projects. Mexican Friends tend to be cosmopolitan rather than purely traditional in culture.

Bolivian Friends, by contrast, have largely been Aymara Indians of the high central plateau, first reached in 1920 by Juan Ayllon, who returned to La Paz after training at the Berea Bible school in Guatemala. In 1930 Oregon Yearly Meeting took over the field. Outside the capital most Aymaras, though from an older culture than the Incas, had been illiterate peasants and tin miners. After twelve years a staff of six had drawn an average of only 370 attenders in five churches. A farm and Patmos Bible School were started in 1947, but the farm was nationalized and the Bible School moved to La Paz after the social revolution and land reform of 1952. The Bolivians were eager to control their own churches but invited the Americans back; fifteen mission workers stayed on. The Quaker Iglesia Nacional Evangelical Los Amigos was incorporated in 1956 but only recognized by the Oregon Friends in 1974. It now estimates membership at 12,000, the second largest Protestant Church (after Seventh Day Adventists) among the 1.8 million Aymaras. Two Oregon couples moved north from Bolivia into Peru in 1961; there are now thirty-six Meetings and 1,500 members of their own Friends' Iglesia Nacional among the 360,000 Peruvian Aymaras.[6]

Jamaica's culture after the Spanish had been driven out by Admiral Penn, and after slavery was ended in 1833, became a stable self-respecting blend of its British and African roots. The economy, based on sugar and later bauxite, created poverty and illiteracy, which was 50 percent in 1943. The Quakers who followed Evi Sharpless of Iowa into northeastern Jamaica after 1881 stayed to teach for decades: Alma Swift continued in Jamaica until 1935. The Lyndale Girls' school at Highgate and Happy Grove for boys at Seaside always needed more staff than either American or Jamaican Friends could provide, leaving the 450 members in fifteen Quaker churches in north coast villages understaffed. In Kingston several Jamaican Friends have led in teaching and government; others went to pioneer in community work in Zimbabwe and Belize.[7]

Friends in Cuba find their present national government allowing worship in the (state-owned) churches but likely to set up programs for youth in deliberate rivalry to those of Christians. Cuban Quaker congregations were begun in 1902, immediately after the Spanish–American War completed the Cuban revolution for independence but brought an American army to Cuba. With it came the United Fruit Company, one of whose founders pointed out to Zenas Martin in 1907 the Banes area where he would set up a big plantation. Martin wisely chose instead the old inland city of Holguin and the port of Gibara as centers for the work of seven Spanish-speaking Midwest Quakers. The twenty-six missionaries before 1914 averaged fifteen years each in the same north coast Oriente Province and prepared local leaders such as Maulio Ajo and Juan Sierra, later head of the Cuban Quaker congregation in Miami. By 1929 Friends had built schools and a Collegio Los Amigos: a pupil, Sergeant Batista, overthrew the dictator Machado but became dictator himself. When Castro overthrew Batista in 1959 all school buildings and teaching were taken over by the government. Quaker membership has fallen from 600 to 330 since 1960, but faithful Cuban pastors remain.[8]

Alaska Yearly Meeting was another example of cultural interaction. The first converts were Indians among the mountainous Pacific islands next to Canada. The murder of Charles Edward by liquor sellers in 1892, and earlier work by the Weesners and Moons and the local Tlingit Jimmy Coffin at Douglas, inspired Oregon and Kansas Quakers to open schools and missions. In 1912 Sheldon Jackson the Presbyterian persuaded Charles and May Replogle and Perry and Martha Hadley to transfer the Quaker work to the Innuit (Eskimos) of Kotzebue Sound in the Far Northwest. An Innuit prophet, Maniilaq, had already taught ideas making Quakers seem familiar to them. The austere sisters Anna and Martha Hunnicutt and the Eskimo Christian Uyaguq began work in 1897. Within a year the region was inundated by gold prospectors from the Klondike. Friends kept open the churches and schools in the quieter times that followed. World War II and the oil boom of the 1970s brought back Yankee culture, with motorboats, snow tractors, and the dancing and liquor against which Quakers preached. Hindsight suggests that the missionaries' ethic of Holiness, different from both Innuit and secular American cultures, had given the 3,000 Kotzebue Quakers a pattern better able than either culture to protect them from being overrun by outsiders.[9] The next challenge will be handling wealth, as the tribal corporation invests funds from oil rights.

The work Esther Baird began at Bundelkhand in India was so firmly dominated by her for forty years that five younger staff members who wanted to replace her schools and orphanages by a mass movement of evangelism to the "untouchables" resigned in protest in 1934. Ohio evangelical Quakers sent out an experienced Cleveland pastor, Everett Cattell*, and his mission-born wife, Catherine, to head a new phase.[10] In China the Communist revolution closed American work around Nanking. The Evangelical Friends Church, Eastern Region, worked instead at Chiayi on Taiwan. Taiwan Yearly Meeting, set up in 1977, has 2,500 members in twenty-seven churches but few contacts with Quaker tradition.

The first nucleus of Japan Yearly Meeting was the Friends Girls School in Tokyo begun by Philadelphia Friends in 1885, later led by Gilbert Bowles* and Herbert Nicholson, who returned to America to aid Japanese–Americans in Relocation Camps during World War II.[11] Inazo Nitobe's work for peace through the League of Nations in the 1920s gained prestige for Friends in Japan beyond their numbers. The challenge of living as Friends in alien cultures has brought Quakerism back to radical ethical questions like those faced by George Fox* and John Woolman.*

UNITY AMONG QUAKERS

The year 1960 saw also the opening of the Earlham School of Religion (ESR), the first center for advanced Quaker study to be steadily, if not officially, supported by all branches of American Friends. Wilmer Cooper, with help from Elton Trueblood, criss-crossed the country to enlist support for a seminary. Alexander Purdy from Hartford Seminary joined the new faculty. By 1978 they had made ESR a self-sustaining center for Friends from all four major Quaker branches and a setting for dialogue, study, mutual support, and worship, giving Master of Ministry and Master of Arts degrees and professional training for all forms of ministry, especially those unique to Friends.[12] Although some evangelical Quaker churches have been slow to accept graduates from ESR, even silent Meetings have hired them for key roles.

Similar in breadth, but deliberately independent, was the Quaker Theological Discussion Group, founded at a 1957 Conference of Quakers in the Americas in Wilmington, Ohio. It has met annually in the Midwest. Its quarterly *Quaker Religious Thought* has created dialogues on key issues. Since the 1970s it has focused on classic Christian doctrines, in contrast to the more personal witnessing in the series of more than 270 Pendle Hill Pamphlets, better known among non-Friends.

In 1960–85 Friends took part also in more traditional arenas of interaction with other Christians, including the National and World Councils of Churches, in which Francis Brown, Kara Cole, Jean Zaru of Ramallah, and many English Friends took major parts, often challenging other Christian groups regarding nonviolence or silent worship. Some evangelical Friends called these councils too weak in doctrine and too gentle on communism; Rocky Mountain Yearly Meeting split from Nebraska over this.

Unity among Quaker Meetings was the most constant issue. Out of the Friends Fellowship Council, an AFSC-sponsored All Friends Conference in 1929, and the Friends World Conferences in England in 1920, at Swarthmore and Haverford in 1937, and Oxford in 1952, grew the *Friends World Committee for Consultation*, formalized in 1958. It meets triennially all over the Quaker world. The Fourth Friends World Conference under FWCC at Guilford College, North Carolina, in 1967, showed again the ability of American and British Friends to appreciate together the varied kinds of Quaker worship despite doctrinal differences. In the 1960s there developed also FWCC regions and offices, currently those for the Americas, Europe, Africa, and Asia and the Western Pacific. As an international "nongovernmental organization" the FWCC sponsors the Quaker United Nations Office. Between meetings the FWCC staff members travel and help other Friends to travel and share.[13] American Quakers learn humility from Friends who live maturely under pressure in South Africa or East Germany.

The reunions of New England conservative and Orthodox Friends in 1945, and of the Orthodox and Hicksite Yearly Meetings of Philadelphia, New York, and Canada (where conservatives also joined) in 1955, were followed by partial union in Baltimore in 1968. These reunited Yearly Meetings and the joining of the Friends General Conference (FGC) by the midwestern "college Meetings" made the FGC less centered on Philadelphia.

A 1947 gathering in Colorado Springs led to eight triennal meetings of the Association of Evangelical Friends, begun by Edward Mott of Oregon and Homer Cox of Ohio at Cheyenne in 1927. The series included evangelicals from the FUM. But Evangelical Friends Alliance (EFA) was set up as a parallel organization to the FUM in 1963–64 to centralize youth, Sunday schools, and mission work for Kansas, Oregon, Ohio, and Rocky Mountain Friends. The earlier outreach of the EFA led to an important recent movement to unify Friends. When leaders from the EFA and FUM met at the national Conference on Evangelism in 1969, a planning committee was persuaded by Everett Cattell of Malone College to call all American Friends, including the Hicksites, to meet in St. Louis in October 1970. Arthur Roberts noted "the tension between two possible courses of action: . . . The development of the Evangelical Friends Alliance marked a step towards a separate national Friends Church, whereas the St. Louis Conference . . . marked a movement toward a larger but yet undefined [unity]."[14] Addresses at St. Louis were later printed as *What Future for Friends?* but the conference's outcome was in doubt until on the last day an experience of unity in the Spirit brought agreement to continue the dialogue.

Continuing programs were sponsored by the American Section of Friends World Committee: the Faith and Life Movement held regional gatherings for Quakers of all branches. The Faith and Life panel of representative thinkers such as Wilmer Cooper and T. Canby Jones produced volumes of contrasting essays on topics vital for Quaker doctrine. *The Quaker Understanding of Christ and Authority* was prepared for the next national meeting in Indianapolis in 1973. This was the first event at which every American Yearly Meeting—Conservative, Evangelical, from the FGC, and from the FUM—sent official representatives who listened to each other. The follow-up Conference of Friends in the Americas at Wichita in 1977 with delegates from Bolivia, Mexico, and Guatemala was for the first time bilingual. The first World Gathering of Young Friends met at Guilford College, North Carolina in 1985. The Young Friends Conference of North America, although set up as an independent body across the divisions of official Quakerism, had increasingly been led by silent Meeting Quakers. At Guilford mature young delegates from Africa and the North and South American evangelical and "unprogrammed" Yearly Meetings led the new generation to face the same dividing issues and sense of community in the Spirit as their elders.

Meanwhile the New Call to Peacemaking, sparked by Norval Hadley of Oregon, moved out in 1975 from the Faith and Life movement into a series of special conferences that included the other historic peace Churches: the Mennonites and Church of the Brethren. Hoping to integrate the witness of isolated pacifist leaders and war resisters with the quieter peacemaking of local churches, it, too, produced joint volumes of essays and set up a dozen major regional conferences for members from the "grass roots" before three national gatherings in 1978, 1980, and 1982. At national events like a march of 700,000 through the New York streets for the United Nations' Session on Disarmament in June 1983, "peace Church" members again walked together with overseas Friends. Quaker unity is never guaranteed. An effort to hold jointly the biennial or triennial national gatherings of the EFA, FUM, and FGC aroused hesitations in all three groups. The 1987 centennial of the Richmond Declaration of faith reminded Friends that theological differences remain. Those professionally Quaker also interact. The Superintendents of the FGC Yearly Meetings now meet annually with those from EFA and the FUM for a week in October. Pastors from Evangelical and FUM Meetings have held three national conferences. The FWCC called a series of Conferences on Quaker Mission and Service in London and Maryland to bring together evangelists from Quaker mission fields and Friends Service Committees' staff whose work had seemed more secular.

Meanwhile, most American Quaker institutions have been adapted to fit into American culture. Friends began early to set up centers for old people and invalids. There are more than thirty of them today. Stapeley Hall, Philadelphia, and Barclay Home in West Chester, Pennsylvania, have eighty years of tradition. Eight centers are communities of families individually owning homes, following pioneers such as Tanguy and Bryn Gweled in Pennsylvania. The Friends Community in Massachusetts, Quality Quaker Apartments in Wilmington, Ohio, and Friends Homes in Greensboro, North Carolina, are mainly retirement apartments. Kendal and Crosslands, Medford Leas, Cadbury, and Foulkeways near Philadelphia; Richmond, Indiana's, Friends Fellowship Community, Friendsview Manor in Oregon; and Quaker Gardens in California are sophisticated communities providing all degrees of health care.[15] Yet similar patterns are found in retirement communities of every major denomination: the special character of each reflects their residents.

Each major Yearly Meeting invests money and staff to own and run a young people's summer camp: Quaker Lake (Indiana and North Carolina), Quaker Knoll (Ohio), Quaker Hill (Oregon), Quaker Heights (Iowa), and China Lake (Maine). Yet evangelism, Bible study, singing, and group recreation remain the basic programs at most of them; they aim to make Quaker youth more committed Christians rather than better Friends. Central-office Sunday school lessons and the interaction of parents and pastors in the Yearly Meeting Christian Education Committees have not filled Friends' need for better trained teachers or satisfied Quaker churches strict in doctrine.

Quaker primary and secondary schools indeed carry Quaker values into American culture and thrive on non-Quaker students. Incomplete lists include sixty-one schools in 1982 and sixty-nine for 1984; thirty are within thirty miles of Philadelphia and six in the New York area.[16] Yet exciting experiments occur. Germantown Friends School, in an area turning black, has become a creative meeting-place for racial cultures. Argenta in British Columbia, the Meeting School in New Hampshire, and the John Woolman School in California became often breathtaking adventures in deciding by Quaker methods of agreement all aspects of the life of school communities whose teenage members include only a minority from Quaker homes. Meetings of the Friends Council on Education, and more lately of the Friends Association on Higher Education, have been arenas for teachers to discuss new methods. Non-Quaker scholars, such as Michael J. Sheeran, have begun to study the voteless decision process of Quaker Meetings.[17]

Friends' vital ways of interacting are not defined by creeds and institutions. If Friends want to serve as "the conscience of the nation," their consciences and faith need to be reunified not by authority even from the Bible but by sharing Truth among individuals and Meetings. Quakers include a full range of old and young, rich and poor, politically conservative and socialist, American, European, and Third World. Their diversity in doctrine and experience is both stark and creative. Quakerism is not an end in itself. Each Friend must keep loyal to her or his experience and form of commitment to Truth, to the Spirit within, God or Christ. Yet all Friends share a tradition calling each to oppose the evils in themselves and their own culture more than to criticize each other. Quaker history shows that in every land and era Friends have been shaped more than they knew by the cultures where they have been at home. The nuclear age has taught them to be less moved by their own culture and even by its rebels and to learn more from women and aliens, the young and fearful, the old and dying, the quiet in spirit and those who under oppression create new life.

NOTES

1. Eleanore Price Mather, *Pendle Hill* (Wallingford, Pa.: 1980), Chs. 8, 9, describes the vitality, crises, and changes of staff at Pendle Hill during and after the Vietnam War, in Howard and Anna Brinton's retirement years, when Dan Wilson, Bob Scholz, and Ed Sanders were directors.

2. On the growth of East African Quakerism see Levinus Painter, *Hill of Vision* (Kaimosi, Kenya: 1966), and autobiographical works by Alta Hoyt, Helen Ford, Emory Rees, and Edna Chilson. See also Stafford Kay, "The Southern Abaluyia: The Friends Africa Mission and the Development of Education in Western Kenya" (Ph.D. thesis, University of Wisconsin, 1975), and the M.A. theses for Earlham School of Religion by Rose Adede on Emory Rees (1986) and by Ann W. Webster, "East Africa Yearly Meeting: An Evaluation of its Growth" (1963).

3. This information and the paragraph following are largely drawn from manuscript "Climbing the Mountain," condensed as Harold Smuck, *Friends in East Africa* (Richmond, Ind.: 1987). Elgon Friends kept closer to the evangelicalism of the early mission. Audrey Wipper, *Rural Rebels* (Nairobi: 1977), claimed that Bakusu Friends are more tolerant of polygamy. Ford blamed this laxity on doubts cast on the inerrancy of the Genesis creation story. (Helen Ford, *The Steps of a Good Man* [Pearl River, N.Y.: 1976], 74).

4. See Christina Jones, *Friends in Palestine* (Richmond, Ind.: 1981); and Wilma Wilcox, *Quaker Volunteer: An Experience in Palestine* (Richmond, Ind.: 1977).

5. All data are from Paul Enyart, *Friends in Central America* (South Pasadena, Calif.: 1970), based on his doctoral thesis for Fuller Theological Seminary.

6. See Phyllis Cammack, *Missionary Moments* (Newberg, Oreg.: 1966); and Quentin Nordyke, *Animistic Aymaras and Church Growth* (Newberg, Oreg.: 1972).

7. See Ellen Davis, *Friends in Jamaica* (Richmond, Ind.: [1943]); Gilbert L. Farr,

Friends Mission in Jamaica (Richmond, Ind.: 1912); and Mary Langford's "History of Jamaican Friends," forthcoming.

8. Hiram H. Hilty, *Friends in Cuba* (Richmond, Ind.: 1977).

9. See Arthur O. Roberts, *Tomorrow Is Growing Old* (Newberg, Oreg.: 1978).

10. See G. Edwin Robison, "History of the Policy of the American Friends Mission in Central India, 1890–1957" (M.A. thesis, Earlham School of Religion, 1972).

11. See biography of Gilbert Bowles in Part II, and Herbert Nicholson, *Treasure in Earthen Vessels* (Whittier, Calif.: 1974). By other former teachers: Edith Sharpless, *Quakerism in Japan* (Philadelphia: 1944); Gurney Binford, *As I Remember It: Forty-three Years in Japan* (n.p.: 1950). See also Inazo Nitobe, *A Japanese View of Quakerism* (London: 1927).

12. Wilmer Cooper, *The ESR Story: A Quaker Dream Come True* (Richmond, Ind.: 1985. See also *The Three M's of Quakerism* (Richmond, Ind.: 1971).

13. See FWCC's *Finding Friends around the World*, (London: 1982), and their journal *Friends World News*. Herbert Hadley's history of the FWCC is forthcoming.

14. Arthur O. Roberts, *The Association of Evangelical Friends: A Story of Quaker Renewal* (Newberg, Oreg.: 1975), 2, 29.

15. See Janet B. Teeple, "Friends Provision of Housing and Care for the Elderly" (Paper prepared for Earlham School of Religion, 1983). She ignored some smaller units like Plainfield, Indiana, and family communes.

16. From the Friends World Committee for Consultation, *Finding Friends*, 107–10; idem, *FWCC, 1983–84, Friends Directory* (Philadelphia: 1983), 101–4. The former also names 43 of the 455 Quaker schools overseas, of which, besides the 10 in England and 4 in Ireland, the most notable may be Friends Girl's School in Tokyo; Friends School in Hobart, Tasmania; Hanna-Skolen in Copenhagen; and the adult folk-school Viittakivi in Finland founded by the Quaker Elvi Saari.

17. Michael J. Sheeran, *Beyond Majority Rule* (Philadelphia: 1983): See also books in his bibliography, both those by non-Friends and Quaker classics such as Howard Brinton, *Guide to Quaker Practice* (Wallingford, Pa.: 1946); idem, *Reaching Decisions*, Pendle Hill Pamphlet no. 65 (Wallingford, Pa.: 1952); and Cecil W. Sharman, *Servant of the Meeting: Quaker Business Meetings and their Clerks* (London: 1983).

Part Two

A BIOGRAPHICAL DICTIONARY OF FORMER QUAKER LEADERS IN AMERICA

ABBREVIATIONS FOR STANDARD SOURCES AND QUAKER ORGANIZATIONS

SOURCES

BBQ	William C. Braithwaite, *The Beginnings of Quakerism*, ed. H. C. Cadbury (London: 1912; Cambridge: 1955).
BFHA	*Bulletin of the Friends Historical Society* (Philadelphia).
BSP	William C. Braithwaite, *The Second Period of Quakerism* (London: 1919; Cambridge, Eng.: 1961).
DAB	*Dictionary of American Biography*, ed. Allen Johnson and Dumas Malone (New York: 1928–37).
DNB	*Dictionary of National Biography*, ed. Sir Leslie Stephen and Sir Sidney Lee (London: 1937ff.)
DQB	"Dictionary of Quaker Biography," Haverford College and London Friends House Libraries.
Elliott, *Profiles*	Errol T. Elliott, *Quaker Profiles from the American West* (Richmond, Ind.: 1972).
Elliott, *QAE*	Errol Elliott, *Quakers on the American Frontier* (Richmond, Ind.: 1969).
EQW	*Early Quaker Writings*, ed. Hugh Barbour and Arthur O. Roberts (Grand Rapids, Mich.: 1973).
Fox, *Camb. Jnl.*	Endnotes in *The Journal of George Fox*, edited from the MSS by Norman Penney (Cambridge: 1911).
Hamm, *TAQ*	Thomas Hamm, *The Transformation of American Quakerism* (Bloomington, Ind.: 1988).
Hinshaw, Carolina	Seth B. Hinshaw, *The Carolina Quaker Experience* (Greensboro, N.C.: 1982).
JLP	Rufus M. Jones, *The Later Periods of Quakerism* (London: 1921; Westport, Conn.: 1970).

JQAC	Rufus M. Jones, Amelia M. Gummere, and Isaac Sharpless, *Quakers in the American Colonies* (London: 1911; New York: 1966).
JFHS	*Journal of the Friends Historical Society* (London).
PMHB	*Pennsylvania Magazine of History and Biography* (Philadelphia).
QH	*Quaker History* (formerly *BFHA*, renamed in 1962).
QRT	*Quaker Religious Thought* (Alburtis, Pa.).

ABBREVIATIONS FOR QUAKER ORGANIZATIONS

AFSC	American Friends Service Committee (Philadelphia and regions)
ESR	Earlham School of Religion (Richmond, Ind.)
FCNL	Friends Committee on National Legislation (Washington, D.C.)
FWCC	Friends World Committee for Consultation (London and regions)

A

ARCHDALE, John. (1642–1717). *Education*: Self-educated or tutors. *Career*: Colonial governor; English politician.

Archdale had been administrator in Maine for his brother-in-law Sir Ferdinando Gorges, 1664–66, and returned to England before George Fox* convinced him as a Friend; in 1678 he bought in his son's name Lord Berkeley's share as a Proprietor of Carolina and in 1683 settled there; he was asked to act as governor for 1685–86 and returned in 1695–96 with special powers from the Proprietors as landgrave over the 2,000 scattered settlers. He slowly eased the way of Huguenot refugees in Charleston, protected Quakers from oaths or bearing arms, divided the administrations of North and South Carolina, and made peace with and among the Indians and between Friends and Moderated and Low-Church Anglican parties in the Assembly. Returning to England, he was elected to Parliament in 1698 but could not take his seat because an oath was required.

Bibliography

A: *Description of the Carolina Colony* (1789).
B: *BFHA* III, IV, V; *BSP; DAB; DNB*; DQB; *JQAC*; Hinshaw, *Carolina*; *JFHS* II; *QAC*; Wilmer A. Cooper, "Ethical Implications of Quaker Participation in Politics" (M.A. thesis, Haverford College, 1948); William S. Powell, *The Proprietors of Carolina* (Raleigh, N.C.: 1965); Henry G. Hood, Jr., *The Public Career of John Archdale* (Greensboro, N.C.: 1976).

B

BALCH, EMILY GREENE (8 January 1867, Jamaica Plain near Boston, MA—9 January, 1961, Cambridge, MA). *Education*: B.A., Bryn Mawr College, 1889; advanced study, Sorbonne, Harvard Annex, University of Chicago, Berlin. *Career*: Educator; social reformer; Professor Department of Economics and Sociology, Wellesley College, 1897–1918; writer, *The Nation*, 1918–20; secretary–treasurer, cochairman, president, honorary international president, Women's International League for Peace and Freedom (WILPF), 1919–61.

Emily Greene Balch was reared in a patrician Boston Unitarian family. After graduating from college and pursuing advanced study in modern history, economics, and sociology, she became interested in social work and in 1892 helped found the Denison House in Boston. In 1897 she joined the faculty of Wellesley, where she introduced into the department of economics classes on poverty, immigration, sociology, and field work. A strong advocate of the social gospel and for a time a self-proclaimed socialist, Balch helped found the Women's Trade Union League in 1903 and served on the Massachusetts Minimum Wage Commission. Her first book, based upon extensive research in the Balkans and immigrant communities in America, positively evaluated Slavic culture and contributions to America.

Emily Balch's personal involvement in the peace movement came through the American Union against Militarism and the Women's Peace Party. She served as a delegate to the International Congress of Women and visited the leaders of neutral and warring nations in 1915 to see whether continuous mediation without a truce was acceptable. She opposed American preparedness and entrance into World War I. Her pacifism and association with radicals prompted the trustees of Wellesley in 1918 not to renew her contract in spite of twenty years of teaching, service as department chairman, and support from the college president and most of the faculty.

She continued her peace work, becoming one of the founders and international secretary of the Women's International League for Peace and Freedom. Work for that organization occupied the rest of her life. While living in Geneva in 1921, she joined the Society of Friends as a member of the London Yearly Meeting because she wished to avoid becoming either Hicksite or Orthodox. She found in Quakerism a noncredal religion based upon an inward Truth and a social ethic devoted to peace and social justice. Between the wars she worked for disarmament, arbitration, support for the League of Nations, and aid to the victims of tyranny. She had never been an absolute pacifist and in World War II she reluctantly supported American participation in the war but opposed the demand for unconditional surrender and the dropping of the atomic bomb. In 1946 she received the Nobel Peace Prize for her work with WILPF.

Bibliography

A: *Our Slavic Fellow Citizens* (New York: 1910); with Jane Addams and Alice Hamilton, *Women at the Hague* (New York: 1915); *Approaches to the Great Settlement* (New York: 1918); editor, *Pax et Libertas* 1, no. 1 (1920); editor, *Occupied Haiti* (New York: 1927); *A Venture to Internationalism* (Geneva: 1938); *Refugees as Assets* (Washington, D.C.: 1939); *The Miracle of Living* (New York: 1941); *Beyond Nationalism: The Social Thought of Emily Greene Balch*, ed. Mercedes Randall, (New York: 1972).

B: Mercedes Randall, *Improper Bostonian* (New York: 1964); Olga S. Opfell, *The Lady Laureates* (Metuchen, N.J.: 1978); Sam Bass Warner, *Province of Reason* (Cambridge, Mass.: 1984); *Notable American Women*, (Cambridge, Mass.: 1980), IV, 41–44.

BARCLAY, ROBERT (23 December 1648, Gordonstoun, Scotland—3 December 1690, Ury, Scotland). *Education*: Scots College, Paris; University of Aberdeen. *Career*: Laird; theologian; traveling minister in Germany; nonresident governor of East Jersey.

Barclay was tutored as heir of Colonel David Barclay's estates at Gordonstoun and Ury on the Scottish East Coast. Exposure to Catholic doctrine under his uncle in Paris, and to Calvinism at Aberdeen, made him along with Isaac Penington and George Keith* the outstanding theologian of early Friends, whom he joined along with his father in 1666–67, marrying a Quaker, Christian Molleson, in 1669. At the University of Aberdeen he debated with fellow students and in 1673 felt led to walk through the streets in sackcloth. He was jailed in 1672 and 1676. At Ury he evolved a series of systematic summaries of Quaker beliefs and shared in the debate over Meetings' authority over their members. In 1677 he traveled with George Fox*, George Keith, and William Penn* in Holland and Germany, beginning a long friendship with Princess Elizabeth of the Palatinate and in England with Anne Viscountess Conway. Through Penn he became the organizer of the Scottish group who bought East New Jersey from Sir George Carteret; Barclay served as governor to administer the settlement, which was from the start overwhelmingly settled by New Englanders and Scottish non-Quakers. His *Apology* became the normative statement of Quaker beliefs from the 1690s to the present. On his ideas, see Chapter 6.

Bibliography

A: *A Catechism and Confession of Faith* (1673); *The Anarchy of the Ranters* (1674); *Theses Theologicae* (1674); *An Apology for the True Christian Divinity* (Latin, 1675; English, 1678); *Universal Love Considered* (1677); "Robert Barclay's Answers to His Uncle Charles Gordon" (manuscript, 1678); *The Apology Vindicated* (1679); *The Possibility and Necessity of Immediate Inward Revelation* (1682); *Truth Triumphant* (Works, 1692).

B: *BSP; DNB; DQB; EQW*; London Friends Institute, *Biographical Catalogue: Reliquiae Barclaianae* (London: 1870); J. Philip Wragge, *The Faith of Robert Barclay* (? 1948); D. Elton Trueblood, *Robert Barclay* (New York: 1968); Geraldina van Dalfsen, *Het Inwaartsch Licht Bij De Quakers* (published Ph.D. thesis, University of Leyden, 1948); Maurice Creasey, "The Theology of Robert Barclay with special reference to his *Apology*" (B.D. thesis, University of Leeds, 1951); Leif Eeg-Olofson, *The Conception of the Inner Light in Robert Barclay's Theology* (published Ph.D. thesis, University of Lund, 1954); Dorland Bales, "The Theology of Robert Barclay" (Ph.D. thesis, University of Chicago, 1982).

BARNARD, HANNAH JENKINS (1754, Nantucket, MA?—c. 1825, Hudson, NY). *Education*: None. *Career*: Minister.

Hannah Jenkins, born a Baptist, appears to have received no formal education because she did not learn to read until maturity. In 1772 she became a Quaker. She married Peter Barnard, a carter, who moved from Nantucket to Hudson, New York, after the American Revolution. He became an elder. She was recognized as a minister before 1793; in that year she began traveling in New York and later in New England. She seems to have been an eloquent speaker. In 1798 Hannah Barnard traveled to England and Ireland. In Ireland she associated with the so-called New Light, or rationalistic, Friends, sympathetic to the French Revolution, who confirmed her doubts about the moral authority of those portions of the Old Testament dealing with war.

After receiving a certificate from Irish Friends, she returned to London and requested permission to preach on the Continent. After an Irish minister accused her of heresy, the London Yearly Meeting advised her to return home. She appealed the decision and several prolonged hearings on her views were conducted in various London Meetings. Her presentations showed great intelligence and spiritual sensitivity, but her democratic ideals and ideas on the virgin birth, miracle stories, and Israel's Holy Wars infuriated English evangelical Quakers. Her prosecution showed the rise of an evangelical party in the London Yearly Meeting, and their triumph led several Friends to withdraw from membership.

Hannah Barnard returned to America where the Hudson Monthly Meeting disowned her, but not her husband, in 1802. Her positions in 1800 requiring inward revelations to confirm Scripture and downplaying of outward miracles

resemble the preaching of Elias Hicks*. In 1819 she acknowledged their similarities.

Bibliography

B. Thomas Foster, *An Appeal to the Society of Friends, on the Primitive Simplicity of Their Christian Principles and Discipline* (London: 1801); idem, *A Narrative of the Proceedings in the Case of Hannah Barnard* (London: 1809); James Jenkins, *Records and Recollections* (New York: 1984), 339–380; Rufus Jones, *The Later Periods of Quakerism* (London: 1921), I, 299–305; *Notable American Women* (Cambridge, Mass: 1971), I, 88–90.

BARTRAM, JOHN (23 May 1699, Darby, PA—22 September 1777, Darby).
Education: May have attended Darby Friends Meeting school. *Career*: Farmer;
botanist.

John Bartram became famous as a botanist but he considered all nature as his
study and made contributions in ecology, ornithology, and zoology. Largely
self-taught and helped by patrons like James Logan*, after 1729 Bartram turned
part of his farm into a botanic garden and created the finest collection of native
plants in America. In 1733 he began a thirty-five-year correspondence with the
English Quaker naturalist Peter Collinson. Through Collinson, Bartram supplied
seeds and plants used in many English gardens. He conducted experiments in
plant reproduction and carried on an extensive correspondence with many of the
most eminent botanists, including Linnaeus, who named a species in his honor.

Bartram's gift was for close observation of plants and animals rather than for
theory. He traveled extensively in search of new species in the American wilderness going as far north as Lake Ontario, west to Pittsburgh, and south to the
Carolinas and Florida. His son William accompanied Bartram on several journeys
and later became an important American botanist and illustrator. In 1765 John
Bartram was named the King's Botanist in North America. He is thought to
have suggested in 1744 to his friend Benjamin Franklin the idea for an institution
that later became the American Philosophical Society.

Bartram was a birthright Quaker, but his religious ideas were a mixture of
rationalism plus a mystical feeling for God in nature. He was anticlerical, not
a strict pacifist, and freed his own slaves before 1765. In 1758 the Darby Monthly
Meeting disowned him for disbelief in the divinity of Christ, but Bartram continued to attend the meeting for worship and was buried in the Meeting's graveyard.

Bibliography

A: *Observations on the Inhabitants, Climate, Soil, Rivers, Productions, Animals . . . Travels from Pennsylvania to Onondaga* (London: 1751); *An Account of East Florida, with a Journal Kept by John Bartram of Philadelphia* (London: 1767); *Diary of a Journey through the Carolinas, Georgia, and Florida, 1765–66* (Philadelphia: 1942).
B: William Darlington, *Memorials of John Bartram and Humphrey Marshall* (Philadel-
phia: 1849); Ernest Earnest, *John and William Bartram, Botanists and Explorers*

(Philadelphia: 1940); Edmund Berkeley, *The Life and Travels of John Bartram* (Tallahassee, Fla.: 1982)

BATES, ELISHA 10 July 1781, Scimino, VA—5 August 1861, Mt. Pleasant, OH). *Education*: Unknown. *Career*: Publisher; theologian.

Bates was a seventh-generation tidewater Virginia Friend who married Sarah Harrison in 1803 and moved with his in-laws in 1816 to Mount Pleasant, Ohio, where he settled for thirty-five years as a printer. Later he sent silkworms to start there the first midwestern silk industry. He bought there in 1818 an anti-slavery newspaper, *The Philanthropist*, from his friend Charles Osborn. He made it more conservative, rejecting boycotts of slave-grown produce. He broadened its concerns to include war, dueling, capital punishment, prisons, and temperance and in 1822 started a new paper, *The Moral Advocate*, to deal with such issues. He was clerk of Ohio Yearly Meeting for five years before and after the Hicksite split and carried the same crusading spirit into theological debate. For his ideas see Chapter 15. By 1828, Ohio's year of decision, he was a stern advocate of disowning Deists and "infidels." He visited England in 1832–34 and 1836 during the "Beaconite" controversy, staying with Isaac and Anna Braithwaite, who as strict evangelicals had polarized Ohio in 1828. Bates published his letters home in support of the English "Beaconite" evangelical Quakers. In 1836 he was baptized and left the Friends. Ignored by Methodists, he again attended Friends Meetings in his later years.

Bibliography

A: *The Retrospect* (Mt. Pleasant, Ohio: 1821); *Doctrines of Friends* (Mt. Pleasant, Ohio: 1825); *Extracts from the Writings of . . . the Society of Friends* (Mt. Pleasant Ohio: 1825); *Sermons* (London: 1836); ten tracts; journals: *The Philanthropist* (1818–22); *The Moral Advocate* (1821–24); *Miscellaneous Repository* (1827–36).
B: DQB; Robert J. Leach, "Elisha Bates, 1817–1827: Influence . . . upon Social Reform" (M.A. thesis, Ohio State University, 1939); Donald G. Good, "Elisha Bates" (Ph.D. thesis, University of Iowa, 1967), idem, "Elisha Bates and the Beaconite Controversy," QH 73 (Spring 1984): 34–47.

BEAN, JOEL (16 December 1825, Alton, NH—11 January 1914, HI). *Education*: District school, NH; Friends Boarding School, Providence, RI. *Career*: Teacher; Quaker minister.

BEAN, HANNAH ELLIOTT [born SHIPLEY] (12 April 1830, Philadelphia—31 January 1909, San Jose, CA). *Education*: Westtown School, Westtown, PA. *Career*: Quaker minister.

Joel and Hannah Bean were prominent Quaker ministers whose attachment to older Quaker forms of worship brought opposition from Friends who favored pastors and revivals. Both Beans were reared in families that supported conservative Quakerism. They attended Quaker secondary schools and became teachers. Joel Bean moved in 1853 from New England to Iowa, where he met Hannah Shipley, the daughter of a prominent and wealthy Philadelphia Quaker family. After marriage in 1859, they settled in Iowa but spent much time traveling in the ministry. In 1861 they visited Hawaii, introducing Quakerism to the islands but with no intention of becoming missionaries. In 1872 they journeyed to the British Isles. In 1875–77 they lived in Providence while Joel Bean taught in the Quaker school his daughters attended.

The Beans returned to Iowa in 1877, and Joel again became clerk of the Yearly Meeting. Iowa Friends were dividing over evangelical revivals, paid pastors, and a deemphasis on the Inward Light. Joel Bean opposed separations, but— like his friend John G. Whittier*—he preferred traditional Quaker practices. The Beans moved to San Jose, California, but left their membership in the Iowa Yearly Meeting.

When the Beans gathered a worship group in their home and asked Iowa Friends to create a Monthly Meeting in College Park, California, the controversy spread to California. Iowa evangelicals denied the request, refused to recognize the Beans as ministers, and dropped them from membership. More than 400 English Friends protested the Iowa evangelicals' actions. The New England Yearly Meeting received the Beans as members and ministers. The desire to preserve Quaker tradition and to resist the emphases of Ohio and Iowa Friends caused English Friends to participate in the Richmond Conference and Declaration of Faith.

In 1889 the Beans helped found the College Park Association of Friends. In its unprogrammed worship, receptivity to new patterns of thought, and deemphasis upon Discipline, College Park became the prototype of many new Meetings.

Bibliography

A: *The Issue* in the *British Friend* (March 1881), with comments from the *London Friend* (April 1881); *Why I Am a Friend* (San Jose, Calif.: 1894); Bean MSS, Friends Historical Library, Swarthmore College.

B: DQB, *Annual Monitor* (1915), 12; Errol T. Elliott, *Quaker Profiles from the American West* (Richmond, Ind.: 1972), 23–46; Catherine E. B. Cox, *Quaker Biographies*, vol. 3 of Series 2 (Philadelphia: n.d.), 211.

BENEZET, ANTHONY (31 January 1713, St. Quentin, France—3 May 1784, Philadelphia). *Career*: Schoolteacher. (See Chapter 12.)

Anthony Benezet's parents were French Huguenots who left France in 1715 to escape persecution, moving first to Rotterdam and later to London in 1715 and then to Philadelphia in 1731. He joined the Friends in America. He married Joyce Marriot in 1736; she was a minister, and he became an elder. In 1739 after an unsuccessful attempt at manufacturing in Wilmington, Delaware, Benezet became a schoolteacher first at Germantown and later in the English school of the Friends Public School in Philadelphia. He later taught in the girls' school and conducted classes for blacks in his home. Benezet became an influential member of the Philadelphia Meeting for Sufferings and leader in many reform movements: Indian rights, aid to Acadians, temperance, antislavery, pacifism, and education. He republished, as devotional reading, works by French quietists and joined John Churchman* and John Woolman* in attempting to purify the Society of Friends.

Bibliography

A: *Observations on the Inslaving, Importing, and Purchasing of Negroes* (Germantown, Pa.: 1759); *A Short Account of That Part of Africa Inhabited by the Negroes* (Philadelphia: 1762); *A Caution and Warning to Great Britain and Her Colonies* (Philadelphia: 1766); *Some Historical Account of Guinea* (Philadelphia: 1771); *A Collection of Religious Tracts* (Philadelphia: 1773); *The Mighty Destroyer Displayed . . . by Mistaken Use . . . of Distilled Spirituous Liquors* (Philadelphia: 1774); *Thoughts on the Nature of War* (Philadelphia: 1776); *The Pennsylvania Spelling-Book* (Philadelphia: 1779); *A Short Account of the People Called Quakers* (Philadelphia: 1780).
B: George Brookes, *Friend Anthony Benezet* (Philadelphia: 1937); Mary Slocum Hornick, "Anthony Benezet: Eighteenth-Century Social Critic, Educator, and Abolitionist" (Ph.D. diss., University of Maryland, 1974).

BENSON, LEWIS (15 August 1906, Sea Girt, NJ—23, August 1986, Moorestown, NJ). *Education*: Public schools; informal study Woodbrooke, Pendle Hill. *Career*: Prophetic writer.

As a boy, Lewis Benson lived in Weehawken and worked as messenger on Hoboken freight piers. He lost his job in the Depression. After a fling with the philosophy of Gurdjieff, he was turned by a job sorting the library of his Manasquan, New Jersey, Meeting to a lifelong study of George Fox's* writings, which he later read exhaustively during eighteen months at Woodbrooke and the London Friends House Library. In 1936–40 he was librarian at Pendle Hill under Howard Brinton*, and in 1937 he married Sarah Potts. In 1940–43 he was secretary of the Evanston, Illinois, Meeting and then curator of John Woolman's* house in Mt. Holly, New Jersey. He trained himself as a printer, but was deafened by the machines. He refused Alternative Service in wartime but visited many Civilian Public Service (CPS) Camps. In 1943 he wrote *Prophetic Quakerism*, the first of a lifetime series of essays and lectures demanding uncompromising obedience to the teachings of Christ as a Friend's living prophet, priest, and king. Lewis and Sarah became members of a series of groups and "intentional communities" in the Anabaptist tradition: the Woolman Settlement Committee (1943–46), the "Wyck Group" and its *Call* (1954–59), Baring Street Philadelphia (1958–60), and the "Publishers of Truth." From a speaking trip in England in 1974 grew a larger, looser, but more permanent group of disciples and associates, the New Foundation Fellowship.

Bibliography

A: *Prophetic Quakerism* (1944); *The Christian Universalism of George Fox* (Wallingford
   Pa.: 1959); *Catholic Quakerism* (Gloucester, Eng.: 1966); New Foundation Publi-
   cations nos. 1,2,4,5; many mimeographed lecture series; articles in *QRT*.
B: *QRT* 65 (22, no. 3) (Summer 1987).

BILLING [ALSO BYLLINGE, BYLLYNGE, ETC.], EDWARD (c. 1623–86). *Education*: Oxford? *Career*: Brewer; chief founder of New Jersey.

Edward Billing, a cousin of the Quaker Hambly family in Cornwall, first
appeared among Friends while a cavalry officer in Monck's Cromwellian garrison
in Scotland. At Leith in 1657, George Fox* resolved a quarrel between Billing
and his (Scottish?) wife, Lillias. After moving to London, where he spent most
of 1660–61 in jail as a Quaker, and where Billing lived as a brewer, her love
of luxury as well as the Conventicle Act fines may have caused Billing's bankruptcy, involving debts to Friends and their responsibility to non-Quakers. William Penn* had a hand in their mutual friend Lord Berkeley's agreement to sell
Billing his claim on West Jersey. The cash for this real estate venture was put
up by a Quaker fellow officer under Monck, John Fenwick, with Penn as one
of three trustees. But Billing had written in 1659 a tract advocating political
reforms paralleling the Leveller manifestoes, and in 1676 he could put in practice
many of the same ideals when he wrote with Penn ''The Concessions and
Agreements,'' signed by all of the original West Jersey settlers as a constitution,
the forerunner of Penn's ''Frame of Government'' for Pennsylvania.

Bibliography

A: *A Mite of Affection Manifested in 31 Proposals* (London: 1659); ''Concessions and
   Agreements of the Proprietors, Freeholders . . . of West-New-Jersey'' (1676), a man-
   uscript at Council of Proprietors' office, Burlington, N.J. reprinted in W. A. White-
   head, ed., *New Jersey Archives*, 1st ser. (Newark: 1888ff), I, 241ff.
B: *EQW*; Papers by Violet Holdsworth and John L. Nickalls in Howard H. Brinton, ed.,
   Children of Light (1938), 85–133; John E. Pomfret, *Province of West New Jersey,
   1609–1702* (Princeton, N.J.: 1956); Hugh Barbour, ''From the Lamb's War to the
   Quaker Magistrate,'' *QH 55*, no. 1 (1966): 3–23.

BOWLES, GILBERT (1869, Stuart, IA—9 October 1960, Honolulu, HI). *Education*: North Branch Friends Academy, IA; B.A. and M.A., Penn College; Ph.D. in anthropology, University of Chicago. *Career*: Taught briefly in Kansas Public Schools, Tunesassa Friends Indian School, and Penn College and Friends School, Tokyo, Japan, 1901–41.

Iowa and Kansas farms, the covered wagon journey between them, sod homes
or meeting-houses, local Friends Academies and the college that became William
Penn* all shaped the lives of Gilbert Bowles, Errol Elliott, Alexander Purdy*,
and Clarence Pickett*, key leaders in Quaker world service. Bowles' marriage
to Minnie Pickett took him to join her in missionary teaching in Japan under

Philadelphia Yearly Meeting. There he influenced and became close friends with leading Japanese Christian peacemaking diplomats *Nitobe* Inazo and *Sawada* Setzuko; with them and other statesmen, he founded the Japan Peace Society and tried to halt the militarization of Japan in the 1930s. With other Christians he visited Korea and China on missions of international understanding linked to Japan's wars with Russia and China in 1905 and after 1931. The Bowles left Japan in 1941 and settled in Hawaii, where he worked on social and political needs of Japanese–Americans, revisiting Japan twice after World War II.

Bibliography

A: *The Peace Movement in Japan* (Philadelphia: 1944); *Letters on a Visit to Japan* (1947 manuscript in Swathmore College archives).

B: Errol Elliott, *Quaker Profiles*, 47–90; *Friend* (Philadelphia: 1920), 238, 337; see also Chapter 21, footnote 11.

BRAITHWAITE, JOSEPH BEVAN (21 June 1818, Kendal, Westminster, England—15 May 1905, London). *Education*: Kendal Friends school; (law apprenticeships.) *Career*: Lawyer; theologian; Bible Society agent.

"Joe Bev's" parents, Isaac and Anna Lloyd Braithwaite of Kendal, visited American Quakers three times in 1823–29, preaching atonement through Christ and attacking Elias Hicks*. They encouraged Isaac Crewdson in his "Beacon" controversy against London Yearly Meeting and Elisha Bates* on both continents. After his law studies moved him to London, Braithwaite, though bookish and stammering, began to question in print and speech the orthodoxy of George Fox* and early Friends, as he judged by an extensive knowledge of the Bible in Hebrew and the early Greek and Latin Church Fathers. At a crucial point in 1840, although a sister and two brothers had left the Quakers (one to become a pastor), he was moved by the worship at the London Yearly Meeting to reaffirm his Quaker heritage.

Marrying in 1851, he and his young wife, Martha Gillett from Oxfordshire, visited Meetings all over England; he led a London Yearly Meeting committee that "eldered" David Duncan and other Manchester Friends for too liberal views of Christ and the Bible. He went to America in 1865, 1876, and 1878, going to Kansas, and in 1884 went to Canada. He was present and said nothing when Ohio Yearly Meeting concluded that the phrase "Inward Light" is unorthodox. Two of his daughters married Americans and lived in Baltimore; a son and another daughter raised their families in Japan. He also traveled to Ireland, France, Athens, and twice to the Near East, as a committee member and agent for the British and Foreign Bible Society. He was legal agent for his close friend David Livingstone for whose family he found a London home and Quaker schools during Livingstone's last lonely journeys through central Africa.

When Indiana Friends called the Richmond Conference of 1887 to seek consensus on the changes in worship and doctrine that revivals had brought in America, Braithwaite was one of six sent by London Yearly Meeting. Once the need for a common statement of faith was affirmed, he led in drafting the "Richmond Declaration," drawing on post-1828 statements by London and other Yearly Meetings he had brought with him: see Chapter 16. On returning he could not persuade Philadelphia, New York, New England, Ohio, Baltimore, or English or Irish Friends to adopt so credal a document. His last two decades were spent with grandchildren and English Friends.

Bibliography

A: *Extracts from the Writings of Early Friends*, nos. 1–6 (London: 1836); *Memoirs of Joseph John Gurnly* (Philadelphia: 1845) *Thoughts on Books and Reading* (London: 1848); *Paul the Apostle* (poem, 1885); *On the Origin and History of the Society of Friends* (London: 1893); *Memoirs of Anna Braithwaite* (London: 1905)
B: DQB; *Proceedings . . . of the General Conference of Friends, Held in Richmond* (1887); Anna B. Thomas, *J. Bevan Braithwaite: A Friend of the 19th Century* (London: 1909); *Autobiography of Allen Jay* (Philadelphia: 1910); Mark Minear; *Richmond, 1887* (Richmond, Ind.: 1987).

BRIGHT, JOHN (16 November 1811, Rochdale, Lancashire, England—27 March 1889, Rochdale, Lancashire). *Education*: Quaker Schools—Ackworth; Bootham; Newton-in-Bowland. *Career*: Millowner; statesman; orator; member of Parliament.

John Bright's father, Jacob, rose from bookkeeper to own a spinning mill that John, after trying to run away from school to America and making a tour to Turkey, was happy to continue. The death of his wife, Elizabeth Priestman, brought Richard Cobden, inviting him to throw his energy into the campaign of the Corn Law League to end grain tariffs; victory in 1846 found Bright already representing Durham, as only the second Quaker in Parliament; he later sat for Manchester (which gave a nickname to the Free Trade "school" in economics); after a traumatic defeat due to his opposing England's entering the Crimean War, he sat for Birmingham. He twice resigned from Liberal cabinets to oppose English acts of war. He had led the Peace Society against rearmament and spoke for autonomy and cotton growing for India and tenants' rights and disestablishment of the Anglican Church for Ireland, but he opposed acts regulating factory labor. For Americans his key role was in preventing England from breaking by force the Union blockade of Confederate ports during the Civil War in the name of "neutrality." Bright ensured the end of slavery in America, even though the mills and workers of Lancashire, including his own, were out of work due to the blockade.

Bibliography

A: *Speeches on the Public Affairs of the last 20 years* (London: 1869); *Selected Speeches of John Bright* (New York: 1907).
B: *DNB*; George M. Trevelyan, *The Life of John Bright* (London: 1925); Herman Ausubel, *John Bright: Victorian Reformer* (New York: 1966); Keith Robins, *John Bright* (London: 1979).

BRINTON, HOWARD HAINES (24 July 1884, West Chester, PA—9 April 1973, Wallingford, PA). *Education*: B.A., Haverford College, 1904; A.M., Haverford College, 1905; A.M., Harvard University, 1909; Ph.D., University of California, 1925. *Career*: Educator, Friends schools in Philadelphia and Barnesville, Ohio, and Pickering College, Newmarket, Ontario, 1905–17?; acting president and dean; Guilford College, 1917–19; secretary and director of publicity, American Friends Service Committee (AFSC), 1919–20; worked for AFSC in Germany and Upper Silesia, Poland, 1920–21; professor of physics, Earlham College, 1921–28; professor of Philosophy, Mills College, 1928–36; director of studies, Pendle Hill, 1936–54.

BRINTON, ANNA SHIPLEY COX (17 October 1887, San Jose, CA—28 October 1969, Wallingford, PA). *Education*: Westtown School; A.B., 1909; M.A., 1913; and Ph.D., 1917, Stanford University; American Academy in Rome, 1913–14. *Career*: Educator, College of Pacific, 1909–12; Stanford University, 1912–13; Mills College; 1916–22; member, student relief group, AFSC in Germany, 1920; teacher of classics, Earlham College, 1922–28; professor of archeology, 1928–36, and dean of faculty, 1933–36, Mills College, associate director, Pendle Hill, 1938–49.

Howard Brinton was raised in a Quaker family whose ancestors helped settle Chester County at the time of William Penn*. At Haverford College and Harvard, Brinton's primary interest was science, although he worked as a research assistant to Rufus Jones* on the mystics in 1904. He initially taught science at Friends' schools. He met and became engaged to Anna Shipley Cox while both were working on relief activities in Europe for the AFSC, and they were married July 23, 1921.

Anna Cox's grandparents were Joel and Hannah Bean*, and she was reared in a Quaker home before attending Westtown School. At Westtown she became fascinated with Latin. She continued her study of classics at Stanford, and her Ph.D. was in classics and archaeology, the latter subject allowing her to pursue scholarship in the fine arts.

The Brintons began teaching at Earlham College, where Howard taught physics and later religion, while Anna taught Latin. They had three children while at Earlham (a fourth while at Mills) and were early examples of both husband and wife combining academic careers and child rearing. Howard Brinton dropped science in favor of philosophy and religion, and his first book, based on his dissertation, was a study of Jacob Boehme. At Mills College Anna was professor of archaeology, and Howard was professor of philosophy. They spent a year studying at Woodbrooke, England.

In 1938 the Brintons went to Pendle Hill with Howard becoming director of studies and Anna director of administration. Both Brintons recruited students, raised money, taught classes, and helped define the mission of Pendle Hill as a school that offered neither grades nor diplomas but a religious community and retreat center for the study of Quaker mysticism. Pendle Hill provided a setting where the American Friends Service Committee trained its workers and where Orthodox and Hicksite Friends might work together. The Brintons helped create the Pendle Hill Pamphlets, a series of tracts that combined scholarship and religious devotion. Anna wrote three, Howard fifteen; together they edited more than one hundred. Most of Howard Brinton's books originated as Pendle Hill Pamphlets. In content, his writings resemble those of Rufus Jones. Both men's books combined Quaker traditions, insights from psychology, idealistic philosophy, historical research, and their own religious experiences.

After retiring from the directorships, the Brintons served as AFSC representatives in Japan, 1952–55. They then returned to residence in Pendle Hill where Anna served as vice-chairman of the AFSC board and as the Philadelphia Yearly Meeting's representatives to the World Council of Churches, 1962–69. Howard Brinton continued to teach at Pendle Hill and to write.

Bibliography

A: Howard Brinton: *The Mystic Will* (New York: 1930); *Creative Worship* (London: 1931); *Quaker Education in Theory and Practice* (Wallingford, Pa.: 1940); *Friends for 300 Years* (New York: 1952); *Religious Philosophy of Quakerism* (Wallingford, Pa.: 1973); editor, *Children of Light* (New York: 1938); *Byways in Quaker History* (Wallingford, PA: 1944).

Anna Cox Brinton: *Maphaeus Vegius and the Thirteenth Book of the Aeneid* (Stanford, Calif.: 1930); *Fourteen Woodcuts* (Stanford, Calif.: 1934); *A Pre-Raphaelite Aeneid* (1934); editor, *Then and Now* (Philadelphia: 1962).

B: The Brinton Papers will soon be deposited at Haverford College, Haverford, Pa. Eleanore Price Mather, *Anna Brinton*, Pendle Hill Pamphlet no. 176 (Wallingford, Pa.: 1971); idem., *Pendle Hill, A Quaker Experiment in Education and Community* (Wallingford, Pa.: 1980); Dan Wilson, "Howard and Anna Brinton," in *Living in the Light*, ed. Leonard Kenworthy (Kennett Square, Pa.: 1984), I, 41–59.

BROWN, MOSES (12 September, 1738, Providence, RI—6 September 1836, Providence). *Education*: Unknown. *Career*: Merchant; social reformer.

Moses Brown, born into a prominent prosperous Baptist family, served an apprenticeship with his uncle Obadiah Brown in order to learn mercantile practices. Later he joined with his three elder brothers in Nicholas Brown and Co., a firm engaged in iron manufacture, the West Indies trade, the manufacture and sale of spermaceti candles, and—on one occasion—the slave trade. Moses, who married his first cousin Anna, daughter of Obadiah Brown, became wealthy. In the 1760s he became active in civic improvements, politics, agricultural reform, and education—notably the creation of the College of Rhode Island. The death of Anna in 1773 caused Moses Brown to reconsider his priorities, and he began studying Quaker books and attending Meetings. He attempted (unsuccessfully) to withdraw from business, traveled with itinerant Quaker ministers in New England, freed his own slaves, and became an ardent abolitionist and defender of free blacks. In 1774 he requested membership in the Smithfield Monthly Meeting. He soon became a leader of the Rhode Island Friends, serving as elder from 1783 to 1836 and treasurer of the Meeting for Sufferings after 1776.

Before the Revolution, Brown attempted to broaden the antislavery campaign beyond Friends. In 1776 he organized a Quaker relief effort to help those New Englanders suffering the effects of the British blockade. He opposed independence and sought for a neutral course during the war. He had misgivings about the official Quaker stance of not using paper money and not paying mixed taxes. Concerned with what he saw as a lack of educational opportunity for Friends, Brown helped organize a Yearly Meeting school that lasted from 1784 to 1788; twenty years later in Providence he revived this boarding school, which today is called the Moses Brown School.

Brown's charitable and humanistic activities continued after the peace. He led the effort of Friends and other Rhode Islanders to end the slave trade and abolish slavery. Brown worked with non-Quakers in supporting the College of Rhode Island, the American Bible Society, and the Rhode Island Peace Society. Although his lack of formal education left him reticent about publishing, he read widely and corresponded on medical and scientific subjects.

Seeing the distress in Rhode Island after the Revolution, Brown sought to increase economic opportunity by helping to found and serve as a director of the first bank in Rhode Island. His initial qualms about the United States Constitution were overcome by the Bill of Rights, and he mobilized Quakers to support Rhode Island's ratification. He became an expert on cloth manufacture and sponsored Samuel Slater's activities in developing the American textile industry.

Bibliography

B: *DAB*; James B. Hedges, *The Browns of Providence Plantations*, 2 vols (Cambridge, Mass.: 1952–68); Robert M. Hazelton, *Let Freedom Ring* (New York: 1957); Mack Thompson, *Moses Brown, Reluctant Reformer* (Chapel Hill, N.C.: 1962); Moses Brown MSS, John Carter Brown Library, Providence.

BUTLER, ESTHER (10 May 1850, Damascus, OH—1921, Nanking, China). *Education*: Damascus Academy; Lucy R. Myers Missionary Training School. *Career*: Mission founder and field superintendent, thirty-four years.

Esther Butler, a Friend with "Holiness" experience, was teaching school in Damascus, Ohio, when she wrote of her call to work as a missionary nurse to the women Friends Foreign Missionary Society of Ohio (Gurneyite) Yearly Meeting. Her letter came the same day in 1885 that they received a plea from a Methodist doctor, Robert Beede of Nanking; she began nursing training at once and arrived there in 1887. After working under Beebe, in 1890 she founded an independent Friends China Mission, with a "Quakerage" for children, a training school for Bible women, and in 1895 a hospital, to which was added another in 1898 at Luho a few miles north, despite interruptions by the riots of 1891 and the Boxer Rebellion. She died in China as did fellow missioner Dr.

Lucy Gaynor and Dr. George DeVol, who had come to join her. The work was continued by his sons and daughter.

Bibliography

B: DQB; Christina Jones, *American Friends in World Missions* (Elgin, Ill.: 1946); Walter R. Williams, *Rich Heritage of Quakerism* (Grand Rapids: 1962); Ohio Friends Mission Board papers at Malone College Library, Canton, Ohio.

C

CADBURY, HENRY JOEL (1 December 1883, Philadelphia—7 October 1974, Bryn Mawr). *Education*: B.A. Haverford College, 1903; M.A., 1904, Ph.D., 1914, Harvard College. *Career*: Educator; teacher, University Latin School, Chicago, 1904; Westtown, 1905–8; Haverford College, 1910–18; Andover Theological Seminary, 1919–26; Bryn Mawr College, 1926–34; Hollis professor of divinity, Harvard College, 1934–54; chairman, American Friends Service Committee (AFSC), 1928–34, 1944–60; Revised Standard Version of the Bible Committee, 1929–52. (See Chapter 20.)

Henry Cadbury worked for peace, attempted to unite Friends, wrote Quaker history, and participated in the international academic community. He was born into an Orthodox Quaker family and attended Penn Charter School before going on to Haverford where he specialized in Greek and philosophy. The Ph.D. he received from Harvard was in philology. In 1910 Cadbury joined the Haverford College faculty. As a member of Twelfth Street Meeting in Philadelphia, he participated in the Young Friends Movement and in the peace conferences held by the Five Years Meeting. During World War I he became a founder of the AFSC and an effective organizer and publicist on its behalf. After Haverford College suspended him for writing a letter about peace to the *Public Ledger* in 1918, Cadbury accepted a position at Andover Theological Seminary in 1919. In 1923 he introduced to Americans the insights of Martin Dibelius and Rudolf Bultmann and the new technique of form criticism, and in *The Making of Luke—Acts* (1927) he analyzed the writing style and major theses developed by Luke. In 1926 he became a professor of biblical literature at Bryn Mawr but in 1934 returned to Harvard. There he became a leader in the Cambridge Monthly Meeting and was instrumental in its affiliation with both the Five Years' Meeting and Friends General Conference. Throughout his life Cadbury lectured or wrote on peace issues and worked for the American Friends Service Committee. After retirement from Harvard in 1954, he returned to Haverford to teach and lectured at Pendle Hill but continued to write about the New Testament and pursue what he termed his avocation, Quaker history. As both bible scholar and Quaker historian Cadbury was a detective of facts, searching obscure manuscripts in an effort to recreate meticulously individual happenings.

Bibliography

A: Major publications: *National Ideals in the New Testament* (New York: 1920); *The Making of Luke—Acts* (New York: 1927); with Kirsopp Lake, *The Beginnings of Christianity: The Acts of the Apostles*, vols. 4, 5 (London: 1936); ''Negro Membership in the Society of Friends,'' *Journal of Negro History* (21 April 1936): 151–253; *Peril of Modernizing Jesus* (New York: 1937); *Jesus, What Manner of Man* (New York: 1947); with F. G. Grant and C. T. Craig, *Gospel Parallels* (New York: 1949); *The Book of Acts in History* (New York: 1953); *John Woolman in England* (London: 1971); *Friendly Heritage* (Norwalk, Conn.: 1972). Editor: *Annual Catalogue of George Fox's Papers, Compiled in 1694–1697* (London: 1939); *Swarthmoor Documents in America* (London: 1940); *George Fox's Book of Miracles* (Cambridge: 1948); *Narrative Papers of George Fox* (Richmond, Ind.: 1972).

B: Anna Brinton, ed., *Then and Now* (Philadelphia: 1960); S. Garlin Hall, ''The Contribution of Henry J. Cadbury to the Study of the Historical Jesus'' (Ph.D. diss., Boston University, 1961). Margaret Hope Bacon, *Let This Life Speak: The Legacy of Henry Joel Cadbury* (Philadelphia: 1987); Cadbury MSS, Quaker Collection, Haverford College.

CATTELL, EVERETT (16 September 1905, Kensington, OH—2 March 1981, Columbus, OH). *Education*: Alliance High school, Mt. Union and Marion Colleges. *Career*: Pastor, Columbus, Springfield, and Cleveland, OH; mission head, India; superintendent, Ohio Yearly Meeting (Gurneyite); president, Malone College.

Son of an architect, Cattell trained as a carpenter, but his love for oratory and church work sent him to train for the ministry. His fiancée, Catherine DeVol, from a family of missionaries in China, was hard to dissuade from plans to return. From the pastorate of First Friends Church in Cleveland (1931–36), however, they were called both inwardly and outwardly to take over Friends Missionary work in Bundelkhand, India, during its crisis (see Chapter 21), from which eleven of the forty-five American staff in the field between 1896 and 1957 resigned or were fired, mostly from conflicts with Esther Baird and her school-centered work. The Cattells worked instead with the Evangelical Fellowship of India and its Yeotmal Bible School, closing the Quaker schools as the national school system developed. (The membership in Bundelkhand Yearly Meeting in 1982 was 321, in eleven village churches.) Cattell was recalled to be Superintendent of Ohio Yearly Meeting, which later became Evangelical Friends Church, Eastern Region, and kept the Evangelical Friends Alliance from narrowness as it opened contacts with other Friends (see Chapter 21). From 1960 to 1972 as president of Malone College he raised, at the same time, its academic standards and its ties with both the Canton, Ohio, community and the Yearly Meeting. His generosity of spirit was loved by people in all branches of Quakerism.

Bibliography

A: *The Spirit of Holiness* (Grand Rapids, Mich.: 1963); *Christian Mission: A Matter of Life* (Richmond, Ind.: 1981); many mission reports and articles on Quaker unity.
B: G. Edwin Robison, "History of . . . American Friends Mission in Central India" (ESR, M.A. thesis, 1972); Leonard S. Kenworthy, ed., *Living in the Light: Some Quaker Pioneers of the 20th Century* vol. 1 (Kennett Square, Pa.: 1984).

CHALKLEY, THOMAS (3 May 1675, Southwick, England—4 September 1741, Tortola). *Education*: Richard Scoyer's school, London. *Career*: Merchant; planter; sea captain. (See Chapter 9.)

Bibliography

A: *A Collection of the Works of Thomas Chalkley* (Philadelphia: 1749).
B: Eleanor Beiswenger, "Thomas Chalkley: Pious Quaker Businessman" (Ph.D. diss., University of Michigan, 1969).

CHILSON, ARTHUR B. (16 June 1872, Marshalltown, IA—1939, Kiwimbi, Congo). *Education*: Cleveland Bible Institute. *Career*: Pioneer mechanic missionary, Kenya.

Son of a tinner and hardware merchant, Chilson responded to former Africa inland missionary Willis Hotchkiss's call to form a Friends Africa Industrial Mission in 1901, supported by Ohio Gurneyites, notably the Malones. The two men and Edgar Hole in 1902 went to look over the Kavirondo area north of the railroad's end on Lake Victoria. While Hole and Hotchkiss were abed with malaria Chilson climbed a hilltop and found the slope where the Friends center at Kaimosi was located and the stream where Chilson built a sawmill. A small hospital, with American doctors, grew alongside the manual training school and Bible Institute.

On a furlough home in 1906, Chilson married Edna Hill and in 1907 returned with her to Africa where they reared two daughters. He lived in a grass hut while teaching brick-making. After setting up a church for the Tiriki at Kaimosi, Chilson moved to build a home and church at Malava (1919). He returned to America to become superintendent of the Kansas Yearly Meeting, 1928–33, after which he began, with his family, a new mission for Kansas Friends on the same model at Kiwimbi, Congo (now Burundi), where he died.

Bibliography

B: DQB; Christina Jones, *American Friends in World Missions* (Elgin: 1946); Levinus Painter, *The Hill of Vision: Chilson, Ambassador of the King* (Wichita: 1943).

CHURCHMAN, JOHN (4 August 1705, Nottingham, PA—24 July 1775, Nottingham). *Career*: Farmer; surveyor; Quaker minister.

John Churchman became a leading Quaker reformer. Recorded as a minister in 1735, he served for twenty years as clerk of the Nottingham Monthly Meeting. During his stay in the British Isles and Holland from 1750 to 1754, Churchman traveled 9,000 miles and attended an average of five meetings per week. He visited families, urged a guarded Quaker education for children, and advocated a strict enforcement of the Discipline. He helped persuade English Friends to create a Yearly Meeting for Ministers and Elders in 1754 but failed in efforts to establish a Women's Yearly Meeting in London.

Churchman long had reservations about what he saw as the growing worldliness and involvement in politics of Pennsylvania Quakers. He appeared before the Pennsylvania Assembly in 1748 to caution against preparation for war and declined being made a justice of the peace. In the turmoil accompanying the French and Indian War, Churchman refused to pay any war taxes, advocated Quaker withdrawal from the Assembly, and became a strong antislavery advocate. Like his close friend John Woolman, Churchman visited Friends to persuade them to free their slaves, and he became an opponent of the drinking of alcoholic beverages.

Bibliography

A: *An Account of the Gospel Labours and Christian Experiences of . . . John Churchman* (Philadelphia: 1779).

B: DQB; Jack Marietta, *The Reformation of American Quakerism* (Philadelphia: 1984), 32–39.

CLARK, DOUGAN (17 May 1828, Randolph Co., NC—10 October 1896, Richmond, IN). *Education*: New Garden Boarding School, NC; Providence Friends School; Haverford College; Medical Schools of the Universities of Maryland and Pennsylvania (1861). *Career*: Professor of Latin, Greek, later Bible, Earlham; doctor; Holiness theologian.

Although reared in rural Carolina and married to Sarah Bates of Hanover County, Virginia, Clark's intellectual brilliance took him early into many other fields and places. In 1869 he both earned his medical degree and was "recorded" by Friends as a minister but he preached mainly in 1876–79 and practiced in the interim of 1869–88 between his times of teaching at Earlham. "No minister ever went from his classes with the poison of destructive [biblical] criticsm," said Esther Tuttle Pritchard. In 1876 he visited England, France, and Ireland with his lifelong friend David B. Updegraff*, with whom he shared the Holiness experience that shaped his theological writings and at whose memorial service during the 1894 Gurneyite Ohio Yearly Meeting Clark himself felt led to take on water baptism. This step led to his being disbarred from ministerial standing by the Whitewater Quarterly Meeting and eased out of his post at Earlham.

Bibliography

A: *Christ Our Sanctification* (New Vienna, Ohio: 1875,); *Offices of the Holy Spirit* (Philadelphia: 1878, 1879, 1880, 1945); *Instructions to Christian Converts* (Chicago:

1889); *The Holy Ghost Dispensation* (Chicago: 1891); *Theology of Holiness* (Boston: 1893); *The Inner and Outer Life of Holiness* (Portland: 1945).
B: DQB; *Friend* (Philadelphia) 36 (1896): 730; *Memorial Service of Dr. Dougan Clark* (Richmond, Ind.: 1896).

COFFIN, CHARLES F. (3 April 1823, Guilford Co. NC—9 September 1916, Chicago, IL). *Education*: Night school; bank. *Career*: Banker; Yearly Meeting clerk.

COFFIN, RHODA M. JOHNSON (1 February 1826, Paintersville, OH—28 September 1909, Chicago). *Education*: Evan Harris's district school. *Career*: Recorded minister; mission boards.

Among Friends, the Coffins achieved more together than either did alone. As son of Elijah Coffin*, Charles came to Indiana when a year old, moved to Milton, Indiana, and then to Cincinnati and in 1835 moved to Richmond, Indiana, where he began work at once in his father's branch of the State Bank of Indiana. In 1841 he was clerk of the Association of Young Friends to Promote Subscription of the Boarding School (later Earlham College); in 1844 he traveled to visit East Coast Friends (and President Tyler) and in 1847 married Rhoda Johnson, whose farmer father had moved to Waynesville, Ohio, and who had come to Richmond in 1845 to study under Barnabas Hobbs. Both did interchurch Sabbath School work; Charles, as Monthly Meeting clerk, helped heal without formality the breach with the Indiana Yearly Meeting of Anti-Slavery Friends (see Chapter 15), and in 1858 he succeeded his father as clerk of the Indiana Yearly Meeting. But Rhoda was the key figure in the special Young Friends session during the 1860 Yearly Meeting that began the revival movement among Indiana Friends. A link was a weekly Sunday night prayer meeting in the Coffins' home for seven years.

Charles and Rhoda visited prisons with Elizabeth Comstock* and helped set up in 1870 Indiana's House of Refuge for Juvenile Offenders. Charles went to Washington to plead for Quaker conscientious objectors during the Civil War and for the Indians afterward and was proud to have known the Gurneys, Braithwaites, and eight U.S. presidents. His national roles distracted his moral judgment: after the collapse of his bank in a national panic in 1884, to avoid civil suits for misappropriating trust funds and making unsecured loans to his sons, he moved to Chicago for his final thirty years.

Bibliography

A: Rhoda's addresses in Earlham college archive, Richmond, Ind.
B: *Rhoda M. Coffin: Her Reminiscences, Addresses, Papers and Ancestry*, ed. Mary Coffin Johnson, (New York: 1910); Ibid. and Percival Brooks Coffin, *Charles E. Coffin, A Quaker Pioneer* (Richmond, Ind.: 1923); Coffin family archives in libraries of Earlham College, Richmond, Indiana, and Swarthmore College, Swarthmore, Pennsylvania.

COFFIN, ELIJAH (17 November 1798, Guilford Co., NC—22 January 1862, Richmond, IN). *Education*: Jeremiah Hubbard's schools at Deep River and New Garden, NC. *Career*: Banker; Indiana Yearly Meeting clerk.

Tristram Coffin moved to Boston from Devonshire in 1642. The clan lived in Nantucket from 1660. Elijah's grandfather had sailed as a whaler before bringing his family to farm at New Garden, North Carolina, in 1773. Bethuel moved from his own to his parents' farm in 1810; Elijah, the youngest of his nine children, taught school there and married his lifelong "intimate," Naomi Hiatt. In 1818 he scouted for the clan new homesteads at Milford, Indiana, but had been made North Carolina Yearly Meeting clerk and visited Friends north through New England before they moved west in 1824. From 1827 through 1857 he was clerk of the Indiana Yearly Meeting. He became a banker in Cincinnati, 1833–35, and thereafter head of the Richmond branch of the Indiana State Bank. He headed committees to build a boarding school (later Earlham College) and for an aborted asylum and led the "Orthodox," Trinitarian majority in 1828 during the Hicksite separation. He visited many Monthly Meetings promoting Sunday schools and Bible societies. He was host to Joseph John Gurney* in 1837 and invited Henry Clay to the Yearly Meeting in 1842. A Whig seeking compromise, he clashed with his cousin Levi and other abolitionists in 1842–57 (see Chapter 15).

Bibliography

A: *Brief Remarks on the Marriage State; Spiritual Exercises* on Genesis, the Old Testament, and the four Gospels (Cincinnati: 1852–62); *The Mother's Catechism of Christian Doctrine* (Richmond Ind.: 1859); memoirs in Mary C. Johnson, *Life of Elijah Coffin* (Cincinnati: 1863), idem, *Charles E. Coffin* (Richmond, Ind.: 1923).
B: *BFHA* 2, no. 1; DQB; Elliott, *QAF*; *Friends Review* 15 (1862): 357; Coffin family archives in libraries of Earlham and Swarthmore Colleges.

COFFIN, LEVI (Guilford Co., NC, 1798—16 September 1877, Cincinnati, OH). *Education*: Local NC Friends schools. *Career*: Schoolteacher; storekeeper for Free Labor Produce; worker for slaves and freedman.

COFFIN, CATHERINE WHITE (Guilford Co., NC, d. 28 September 1909, Cincinnati, OH). *Education*: Local Quaker Schools. *Career*: Innkeeper for Underground Railroad.

The names of Elijah and Naomi and Charles and Rhoda Coffin are carved on gates of the Earlham Cemetery they founded next the college; their cousin Levi's is as fitly linked to the "Underground Railroad": he was called its "president." Like them, his parents moved from Nantucket to farm in the Piedmont. As a boy he helped a free black kidnapped into slavery and started a black Sunday school, taught school in North Carolina before and after a 1822 trip to visit Indiana cousins, and married Catherine White at New Garden. Together they moved in 1827 to Newport (now Fountain City), Indiana, where their home sheltered overnight 2,000 escaped slaves traveling to Canada (supposed to be the models for the Hallidays in *Uncle Tom's Cabin*. On visits to the South he organized other "stations" and free-labor sources of cotton and sugar. To provide a central store for these items he moved to Cincinnati in 1849. Interchurch antislavery groups met in his meeting-house. When the Indiana Yearly Meeting removed the abolitionists from all committee posts, they formed at Newport the Indiana Yearly Meeting of Anti-Slavery Friends (see Chapter 15), which rejoined the main Yearly Meeting in 1857. Levi Coffin found places at Oberlin for black children of southern white planters. During and after the Civil War he traveled to Arkansas to oversee work with freedmen and to England to raise $100,000 to support it.

Bibliography

A: *Reminiscences of Levi Coffin* (Cincinnati: 1876).

B: DAB; all literature on Underground Railroad; Ruth Ketring Nuermberger, *The Free Produce Movement* (Durham, N.C.: 1942); Bernhard Knollenberg, *Pioneer Sketches of the Upper Whitewater Valley* (Indianapolis: 1945).

COMLY, JOHN (19 November 1773, Byberry, PA—20 August 1850, Byberry). *Education*: Byberry Friends School and Latin School, c. 1780–94. *Career*: Teacher; farmer. (See Chapter 14.)

John Comly was the leader of the so-called Hicksite Friends before and after the separation in 1827. Comly was a country Friend, attending the local Quaker school and then the boarding school of a Baptist minister, where he learned Latin and Greek, and working on the family farm. He served as master of Byberry Friends School from 1794 to 1801 and then taught at Westtown Friends School. In 1804 he and his wife, Rebecca, who also was a Westtown teacher, opened the Pleasant Hill Boarding School for girls. In 1810, perceiving the need of boys for a more advanced education than Westtown offered, he changed his boarding school into an institution for them. Comly, acknowledged a minister in 1813, resigned his school in 1815 to devote his time to travel in the ministry and farming. During the rest of his life his ministry frequently took him to New England, New York, and the South, but he never went to England and visited Ohio only in 1834.

Comly's *Journal* shows the influence of John Woolman's* ideas on simplicity, education, slavery, and silent worship. Comly, like Elias Hicks*, distrusted the rage for internal improvements, reform societies, banks, and commercial activities. He refused to vote or to read newspapers as activities distracting the mind from religious purity. Comly was a quietist who stressed the indwelling Christ and distrusted doctrinal formulations about vicarious atonement and original sin. He was not a rationalist. He saw the Orthodox faction as unfaithful to early Quakerism, interested in power, and destroying freedom within the Meeting. Comly became distressed as controversy grew in the 1820s in Philadelphia. In early 1827 he began meeting with like-minded Friends on the need for a peaceful temporary separation. The events of the Yearly Meeting in 1827 convinced Comly that a withdrawal was necessary. He never envisaged the division as permanent and sought to work out an agreement to divide the property. Still, he sought to strengthen the Hicksites and served as clerk of the Men's Yearly Meeting while his wife served as clerk for the Hicksite Women's Yearly Meeting.

Comly wrote several popular school texts, edited the writings of John Woolman* and Job Scott*, and, with his brother, edited the twelve-volume *Friends Miscellany*, which provided for Hicksites the writings of early Quakers.

Bibliography

A: *English Grammar, Made Easy to the Teacher and Pupil* (Philadelphia: 1803); *Friends Miscellany* (Philadelphia: 1831–39); *Comly's Spelling and Reading Book* (Philadelphia: 1842); *Journal of the Life and Religious Labours of John Comly* (Philadelphia: 1853).

COMSTOCK, ELIZABETH L. ROUS WRIGHT (30 October 1815, Maidenhead, England—3 August 1891, Union Springs, NY). *Education*: Friends Schools, Islington and Croydon. *Career*: Teacher at Croydon and Ackworth schools; farmer's wife; Quaker traveling minister.

"The American Elizabeth Fry" may have visited more sickbeds (115,000) and prisoners (75,000) than any other Quaker; she was descended from Margaret Fell, and lived more simply than either. Student rebel and then beloved teacher at Quaker schools, she married, in 1847, Leslie Wright, market gardener in Essex who died two years later. Her religious experience then was a source of her later ministry. After four years in business in Derbyshire she sailed in 1854 with a sister and small daughter to settle on a farm at Belleville, Ontario, where Canadian Friends recorded her as a minister.

In 1858 she married John T. Comstock, a Quaker farmer of Rollin, south of Lansing, Michigan. Her stories about their home as an Underground Railroad center rival Levi Coffin's*. She visited the Lansing men's prison and those at Michigan City and Sing-Sing; then the American Civil War hospitals around Washington, New York, and Cincinnati; and later those in war zones in Virginia and Tennessee. She spoke with Lincoln, led worship for his wife and cabinet members, and attended his "lying in state." She traveled to visit national Sunday school conventions and most of the American Yearly Meetings and revivalist General Meetings, rebuked Holiness theology, and spoke often from the Chicago pulpit of her friend Dwight L. Moody. She visited Indians beyond Green Bay, Wisconsin, and raised $60,000 for freedmen in Kansas after the Civil War. A tee-totaller, she spoke for temperance and women's equality among Friends on visits to England in 1873–75 and 1883–84. After her husband's painful death in 1884 she moved to Union Springs, New York, for her final years.

Bibliography

B: Caroline Hare, *Life and Letters of Elizabeth L. Comstock* (London: 1895); Errol Elliott, *Quaker Profiles*, 91–120.

CUFFEE, (also CUFFE, COFFEE), PAUL (1759, Cuttyhunk, MA—1817).
Education: Self-taught. *Career*: Shipowner; captain.

Cuffee was the son of a freed slave and an Indian mother, a sailor when aged
sixteen and prisoner of the British at eighteen during the Revolution. Then he
returned home to farm, raise a family with his Indian wife, and study navigation.
His first three merchant ventures with his brother in home-built boats were lost
to pirates, but whaling off Newfoundland gave him capital enough to buy a
schooner and then a brig, crewed by eight blacks and sailing out of New Bedford,
Massachusetts, to Europe, the West Indies, and Africa. He was member and
occasional speaker at the Westport Meeting and visited British Friends on a
return voyage from Sierra Leone, which he encouraged William Allen and Edward Pease to use for a center for returning freed slaves and for schools. He
then became a founder of the American Manumission and Colonization Society
for returning freed blacks to Liberia, carried shiploads there himself, and on one
occasion personally presuaded President Madison to release his cargo and crew
from Norfolk, Virginia. He protested taxation of freed blacks without representation until they were granted voting rights in Massachusetts.

Bibliography

A: Manuscript diary at New Bedford, Massachusetts.
B: DQB; London Friends Institute, *Biographical Catalogue* (London: 1888). Anna Brin-
    ton, *Quaker Profiles* (Wallingford, Pa.: 1964).

D

DOUGLAS, JOHN HENRY (27 November 1832, Fairfield, ME—24 November 1911, Whittier, CA). *Education*: Friends Boarding School, Providence, RI. *Career*: Itinerant revivalist; later pastor; first Iowa Yearly Meeting superintendent.

DOUGLAS, ROBERT WALTER November 1834, Fairfield, ME—18 February 1919, Versailles, OH). *Education*: Friends Boarding School, Providence, RI. *Career*: Itinerant revivalist; later pastor; banker.

In 1850 John Henry Douglas was converted during a storm at sea and moved from Maine to southwestern Ohio in 1853, followed by his parents (who had been on Providence Friends School staff) and his brother Robert, who kept a store and became a banker. Both brothers married Ohio women, were "recorded ministers," and became itinerant evangelists in 1860 in Ohio, reporting through Daniel Hill's *Christian Worker*, John Henry notably among Iowa Friends. His zeal impressed Walter Robson. In 1867 he was the first general secretary of the Peace Association of Friends in America and later helped in founding Wilmington College. He was inspired by Sheldon Jackson to evangelism in Oregon where he clashed with immigrant Friend William Hobson* in forming new congregations, which became Oregon (now Northwest) Yearly Meeting. In 1876 he was called as superintendent—the first among Friends—by Iowa Yearly Meeting, which he led in the calling of permanent pastors for most Meetings, and union revivals with other denominations. Poor health led to his early retirement to Whittier, California.

Robert Douglas in 1878 visited Friends in Hobart, Tasmania, and other settlements in Australia and New Zealand and returned to a pastorate at Wilmington, Ohio (see Chapter 16).

Bibliography

A: John Henry Douglas, *An Address to Parents on the Importance of Sabbath Schools*; many articles in *The Christian Worker*.

B: Dougan Clark and Joseph H. Smith, *David B. Updegraff and His Work* (Cincinnati: 1895); Nathan T. Frame and Esther G. Frame, *Reminiscences of Nathan T. Frame and Esther G. Frame* (Cleveland: 1907); Louis T. Jones, *The Quakers in Iowa* (Iowa City: 1914); *Pacific Friend* 26 (1919): 11; Lawrence E. Barker "The Development of the Pastoral System in Indiana Yearly Meeting of the Religious Society of Friends" (M.A. thesis, ESR:1963); Ralph K. Beebe, *A Garden of the Lord: A History of Oregon Yearly Meeting of Friends Church* (Newberg, Ore.:1968); *An English View of American Quakerism: The Journal of Walter Robson*, ed. Edwin B. Bronner (Philadelphia: 1970); Elliott, *QAF*; Paul Minear, *Richmond, 1887* (Richmond, Ind.:1987); Hamm *TAQ*; DQB.

DYER, MARY BARRET (c. 1615, London—2 June 1660, Boston). *Education*: Unknown. *Career*: prophet-martyr.

Dyer came from a Quendon, Essex, family but was reared in London, served at Court, and in 1633 married William Dyer of Somerset who settled as a milliner in Boston, Mass. There he became a friend of Roger Williams and she of Anne Hutchinson, on whose antinomianism Governor John Winthrop and the Puritans blamed Mary's deformed still-born "monster" baby. The Dyers went together with their friends to Rhode Island in 1638, settling at Aquidneck. To help in the dispute between William Coddington and Williams they returned to England in 1651. William Dyer returned after two years, Mary in 1656. By then she had become a Quaker and perhaps hosted Marmaduke Stephenson and the Friends who sailed on the *Woodhouse* in 1657 to confront the Boston authorities.

In 1659 she went to visit the Friends in Boston jail. Her son William went to Boston to ask clemency, and to take custody of her. Released, she went instead to Long Island and then felt called back to Boston to face the death penalty enacted against Quakers who returned to Massachusetts after banishment. She was sentenced by Governor Endicott along with Stephenson and William Robinson and reprieved when already on the gallows. She returned in 1660 to face another sentence to hanging, this time carried through on Boston Common where "she did hang as a flag." The statue of her by Sylvia Shaw Judson now stands there.

Bibliography

A: Mary Dyer's court hearing is in Edward Burrough, *A Declaration of the Sad and Great Persecution* [1660–61]; earlier visits and letters by Stephenson and Robinson in Peter Pearson, John Whitehead, and others, *A Call from Death to Life* (1660); George Bishop, *New England Judged* (1661); and Joseph Besse, *A Collection of the Sufferings of the People Called Quakers* (London: 1753).

B: James Bowden, *History of the Society of Friends in America* (Boston: 1850); *EQW; JQAC*; DQB. See also chapter 5.

E

EDMONDSON, WILLIAM (1627, Little Musgrave, Westmorland, England—1712, Rosenallis, Ireland). *Education*: Apprenticed as carpenter–joiner. *Career*: Ironside; merchant; farmer; Quaker itinerant "Apostle of Ireland."

Orphaned at eight, youngest of six children, William Edmondson was reared by a harsh uncle until at thirteen he became an apprentice in York. Already Puritan in soul searching, he served in the Puritan army most of 1645–52, fighting at Worcester. Then he married Margaret Stanford, whom he met while on garrison duty in Derbyshire. He was persuaded by a trooper brother to move to Ireland. While a merchant at Antrim he revisited Westmorland in 1653 and became a Friend. In 1654 he moved his family to a shop and farm in Lurgan, Ulster, where he founded the first Irish Meeting. In 1655 he hunted with George Fox on a Leicestershire trip, went with Richard Clayton to preach in Londonderry, and was jailed in Armagh. He moved to a farm at Cavan, where he again gathered a Meeting and was jailed in 1656. Finally, he moved to Rosenellis near Mountmellick. For Irish Friends imprisoned in the 1660s he interceded successfully with the governor, but his home was burned down over their heads in the "Orange" War of 1688–90. His wife died of illness in 1691.

Having felt called to carry Quakerism to America, he sailed with Fox's group in 1671, visiting Antigua, Nevis, Barbados, and Jamaica and traveling through Virginia and the Carolinas. Later he debated with Roger Williams who called him "a stout portly man, given to much speaking." Edmondson returned to the West Indies and all the mainland colonies in 1675–77, worked to convert Negro slaves, and helped Rhode Island Friends amid "King Philip's War." In 1683 he revisited the West Indies and, in his last years, Meetings all over Ireland and England. In 1697 he married Mary Strangman; children included Hindrance and Tryal.

Bibliography

A: 5 tracts (1 survives); Geoffrey Nuttall, *Early Quaker Letters* (London: 1952); *Journal*
    (1715; abridged, ed. Caroline Jacob, Philadelphia: 1968); Swarthmore MSS.
B: *BBQ; DNB*; DQB; Fox, *Camb. Jnl.; JQAC*; Frank Edmondson in *BFHA* 42 (1953).

F

FISHER, MARY [later BAYLY and CROSS] (1623?, Selby?, Yorkshire—1698, Charleston, SC). *Education*: Unknown. *Career*: Pioneer missionary.

First recorded as a servant in Richard Tomlinson's household at Pontefract and convinced with them on George Fox's* Yorkshire trip in 1651, Fisher was imprisoned in York Castle with Thomas Aldam. In 1653 she went to challenge students at Cambridge University, where by the mayor's order she was stripped to the waist and whipped. In 1656 she and Ann Austin were the first Friends to sail via Barbados to Boston, were jailed, and had one hundred Quaker books they had brought burned by the hangman. In 1657 she was in the West Indies again. In 1657–58, with John Perrot and four others, she undertook a mission to the Near East. Sailing via Leghorn and Zante to Smyrna, and turned back, Mary Fisher and Beatrice Buckley jumped ship at Zante. Fisher reached the camp of Sultan Mohammed IV at Adrianople; delivered a message "from the great God," which was heard with courtesy; and returned safely to England. In 1662 she married William Bayly, sea captain of Poole, Dorset. They had three children. After his death at sea in 1675, she married John Cross of London in 1678, with whom she and her children sailed before 1685 to South Carolina. She and her grand-daughter Sophia Hume provided for a century the only leadership for a Meeting in Charleston and entertained shipwrecked Quaker travelers. Her will included a black slave.

Bibliography

A: *The First New Persecution* (1654); Swarthmore MSS 4:193 at London Friends House Library.

B: *BBQ; DNB*; DQB; Fox, *Camb. Jnl.; JQAC*; Gerard Croese, *Historia Quakeriana* (Latin ed'n., 1695; English, 1696) and Willem Sewel *History of the [Rise, Increase and Progress of the Christian People called] Quakers* (English ed'n., 1722). Joseph Besse, *Collection of the Sufferings [of the people called Quakers]* (London: 1753);

James Bowden *History of the Society [of Friends] in America]* (Boston:1850); William Medlin, *Quaker Families of South Carolina & Georgia* (Columbia, S.C.: 1982); JoAnne McCormick, "The Quakers of South Carolina, 1670–1807" (Ph.D. thesis, University of South Carolina: 1984); Susan Williams, *Quaker Biographies* Series 2, Vol. 1 (Philadelphia: 1917).

FOX, GEORGE (July 1624, Fenny Drayton, Leicestershire, England—13, January 1690–91, London). *Education*: Village school; apprenticed at Mancetter as cobbler and shepherd. *Career*: Chief founder, early leader, preacher, and writer of Quakerism. (See Chapters 3, 5.)

In 1640–43 Fox visited local Puritan pastors and in 1643–47 separatist groups in London and throughout central England, seeking answers to despair and temptations. He found darkness and the Light of God or Christ within himself and began to preach among separatists in Nottinghamshire and Leicestershire. Jailed at Derby in 1650–51, he renounced outward weapons. Released, he began a religious "Awakening" in Yorkshire moorlands in 1651 and throughout northwest England, in 1652–53 spreading from a base at Judge Thomas and Margaret Fell's home, Swarthmoor Hall. Jailed in 1653 at Carlisle for blasphemy, he was freed by Cromwell's Nominated Parliament. In 1654 he preached in Durham and organized his coworkers for a mission to London and Southern England. Arrested in Leicestershire and brought to London in 1654, Fox met and was freed by Cromwell and then worked through 1655 mainly in the South. Imprisonment in Launceston in 1655–56 led to conflict of Fox with James Nayler's disciples. In 1657 his longer trips into Wales and Scotland "convinced" fewer; he returned to London to write and organize traveling "ministers." The fall of the Commonwealth in 1659 caused him deep heart searching.

Fearful Royalists again in power threw him and Margaret Fell into Lancaster Castle in 1660 and again in 1663–65. Scarborough Castle in 1665–66 was his coldest jail. Between and after these imprisonments he traveled to organize Friends into self-sustaining local Monthly and Women's Meetings. In 1669, besides traveling in Ireland, he arranged at Bristol to marry Margaret Fell, whose first husband had died a decade earlier. After further itinerating in southern England he sailed in 1671 with twelve other Friends to the American colonies by way of Barbados and Jamaica, convinced and gathered Friends around Chesapeake Bay, visiting among Indians on his group's way northward to a first Yearly Meeting in Rhode Island, where the group debated with Roger Williams. After more work in Maryland and trips south through Virginia and the Carolina sounds, they sailed to England in 1673. Fox's return to Swarthmoor was interrupted by a long jailing at Worcester, where, though ill, he began to dictate his journal to Thomas Lower. In 1677 he traveled with William Penn*, George Keith*, and Robert Barclay* to visit Friends in Holland and Germany. His last years were mainly spent around London, staying at the home of William and Sarah Fell Meade. He died three days after speaking at Gracechurch Street Meeting and was buried in Bunhill Fields.

Bibliography

A: More than 266 tracts he dictated survive, including 20 first published in Dutch and 5 in German, besides 13 Dutch, 13 Latin, and 5 French translations in his lifetime. *The Great Mistery of the Great Whore Unfolded* (1659), a *Catechism* (1657), and *A Battle-Door for Teachers and Professors to Learn Singular and Plural* (1660) were the fullest. Many short works were reprinted in *Gospel Truth Demonstrated*, later called "Fox's *Doctrinals*" (1706), which was edited by Thomas Ellwood, who also edited Fox's *Journal* (1694; Thomas Lower's original manuscript and attached documents were edited in 1911 as the *"Cambridge Journal"*). With the *Epistles* and *Great Mistery* they were reprinted as *The Works of George Fox*, 8 vols. Philadelphia: 1831), recently photoreprinted. Some Fox manuscripts and notebooks were reconstructed and published by Henry J. Cadbury as the *Annual Catalogue of George Fox's Papers* (Philadelphia and London: 1939), *George Fox's Book of Miracles* (Cambridge: 1948), and *Narrative Papers of George Fox* (Richmond, Ind.: 1972).

B: Detailed notes by Norman Penney in Fox, *Camb. Jnl*, and John Nickalls in the 1952 edition of the *Journal*. Biographies of Fox were written by Samuel N. Janney (Philadelphia: 1853); A. Neave Brayshaw (London: 1918); Rachel Knight (London: (1923); Rufus Jones (New York: 1930); Paul Held (Basel: 1949); W. Vernon Noble (New York: 1952); Arthur Roberts (Portland: 1959); Harry E. Wildes (1965); Hanna D. Monaghan (Philadelphia: 1970), and others, but none is definitive. On Fox's teachings see notes to Chapters 4 and 6; Lewis Benson, *Catholic Quakerism* (1968); Douglas Gwyn, *Apocalypse of the Word* (1984).

FRAME, ESTHER GORDON (10 August 1840, Wayne County, IN—6 November 1920, Texas). *Education*: Thorntown IN, Friends and Methodist Academies; Blue River, IN, Seminary: *Career*: Itinerant evangelist; Quaker minister.

"My Grandfather Gordon preached until he was ninety years of age; . . . Grandfather McGray preached until he was ninety years old, and I want to preach until I am one hundred." Converted in a Thorntown revival, Esther married a Methodist preacher's son who was converted in her parents' parlor after they moved to Salem, Iowa; Nathan and Esther moved to that town several times between stays in Indiana. When the Methodist Church refused her a preaching license, she applied for Friends membership and was hesitantly accepted, since she rejected plain dress.

Feeling a call—"Preach my Gospel"—she moved with Nathan and children to Chester, Indiana, teaching school, holding revivals, notably in Richmond and Walnut Ridge, and meetings in jails. Revivals near Chillicothe, Ohio, led the Frames to move to New Vienna, Ohio, from where they traveled to revivals she began at Brooklyn and Glens Falls, New York; and Centerville, London, Xenia, and Hillsboro, Ohio (where she suffered temporary paralysis), in 1871–77. She was identified as a Friend but preached in churches of all denominations. Her revivals continued throughout Ohio and Indiana in the 1880s. She visited prisons in Ohio, Iowa, and Minnesota and in 1888–92 made four trips to Alabama and Tennessee and then two in 1893–94 to Kansas, Texas, and New Mexico. An 1898 visit to Penn College, Iowa, made President Rosenberger her permanent supporter. In 1901–2 the Frames held revivals among Friends in Oregon and California and from then on were often in the Southwest.

Bibliography

A: *Reminiscences of Nathan T. Frame and Esther G. Frame* (Cleveland: 1907).
B: DQB; Elliott, *QAF*; Hamm, *TAQ*.

FRY, ELIZABETH GURNEY (21 May 1780, Norwich, England—12 October 1845, Ramsgate, England). *Education*: Probably educated at home by her mother and tutors. *Career*: Quaker minister; social reformer. (See Chapter 13.)

Elizabeth Fry was born into one of the wealthiest families in England, whose fortune rested upon the textile trade and banking. Her early life was one of parties and studies with her brothers, sisters, and cousins in the Norwich area. At age eighteen, after hearing a sermon by William Savery, she recorded in her diary: "Today I have felt there is a God." Influenced also by Deborah Darby, she gradually began to renounce dancing, fashionable dress, and recreations of the world and became a plain Quaker. She founded a school for poor children, whom she taught in the Earlham Hall laundry. At nineteen she wedded Joseph Fry, a banker and a son of another prominent Quaker family. Her early years of married life were taken up with domestic responsibilities, including bearing eleven children. Like her brother, Joseph John Gurney*, she moved easily in evangelical circles and, at age twenty-nine, at her father's funeral, spoke for the first time in a Meeting.

Elizabeth Fry in 1813 visited Newgate prison, and witnessing poverty, filth, overcrowding, and moral degradation, she felt moved to reform the institution. She began by visiting and talking with the women, bringing food and clothing, and reading the Bible. Soon she decided that a complete reordering of the women's section was necessary. So with the permission of the warden, she founded a school to teach reading to prisoners and their children and persuaded the women to adopt a strict evangelical code of behavior—no swearing, no drinking, no fighting, a regular schedule—and instituted a program of sewing to occupy their time and to earn money. In 1817 she organized the Association for the Improvement of Female Prisoners, which did volunteer work in the prisons and obtained support from London aldermen and the home secretary for reform. The association's goals and methods became a model for many other voluntary service organizations of evangelicals in England and America.

Socially prominent Victorians, impressed that a wealthy woman would devote herself to the care of the underclass, flocked to Newgate to watch Fry read the Bible to the fallen women. In 1818 she became the first woman to testify before Parliament, using the opportunity to describe conditions and to advocate strict separation of the sexes, with women to care for women prisoners. Elizabeth Fry wrote pamphlets, organized an order of nursing sisters, exposed abuses in the system of transporting convicts to Australia, conducted a tour of prisons in Europe, and presented her ideas of reform to Europe's monarchs. She mainly ignored the women's suffrage and women's rights movements. She joined committees against slavery, but at the World Antislavery Convention in 1840 she refused to welcome Lucretia Mott*, who as a Hicksite was supposedly a Unitarian.

In 1835, in the wake of the great Reform bill that followed the Chartist tumults and European revolutions, Elizabeth Fry's prison efforts became part of a national concern for a centralized and reformed prison system, less dominated by greedy wardens but also less open to volunteer humanitarians.

She had considerable success in focusing attention upon prison life. Some of her ideas, like using women wardens, were accepted. But society did not accept her insights that a prison could not be a place for both punishment and reformation; that solitary confinement, healthy at night, was too harsh by day; and that capital punishment neither deterred crime nor changed the criminal.

Bibliography

A: *Observations on . . . Female Prisoners* (London: 1827); *Report Addressed to Marquess Wellesley . . .* (London: 1827); Preface to John Venn, *Sermon on the Gradual Progress of Evil* (London: 1830); *Texts for Every Day in the Year* (London: 1831).
B: *DNB*; DQB; Janet Whitney, *Elizabeth Fry, Quaker Heroine* (Boston: 1936); *Memoir of the Life of Elizabeth Fry, with Extracts from Her Journal* (London: 1847); James Kent, *Elizabeth Fry (London: 1962);* June Rose, *Elizabeth Fry* (London: 1980).

G

GARRETT, THOMAS (21 August 1789, Upper Darby, PA—25 January, 1871, Wilmington, DE). *Education*: Unknown. *Career*: Iron and hardware storekeeper.

Thomas Garrett was an abolitionist who became a leading figure in the Underground Railroad. A lifelong Quaker, Garrett's first involvement with slavery came in 1813 when he rescued a household servant who had been kidnapped. In 1818 he joined the Pennsylvania Abolitionist Society and later became a supporter of William Lloyd Garrison.

In 1822 Garrett moved to Wilmington, where he became a wealthy merchant and made no secret of his antislavery views and activities. He became a Hicksite after 1827 and associated with Lucretia Mott*. While not encouraging slaves to run away, he believed that aiding them was a Christian duty and claimed in 1863 to have helped 2,322, of whom only 3 were recaptured. Garrett provided financial aid to Harriet Tubman, ventured into slave states to help kidnapped free blacks, and helped support two schools for blacks in Wilmington. In 1848, after suffering disastrous business reverses that cost him his fortune, he was arrested, tried, and convicted for aiding fugitive slaves. In spite of paying a $1,500 fine, Garrett announced that he would continue to help blacks. He rebuilt his business and became prosperous again and continued to help fugitive slaves. A nonresistant who refused to vote, he decided that the Civil War was the only possible means of freeing all slaves.

Bibliography

B: James A. McGowan, *Station Master on the Underground Railroad: The Life and Letters of Thomas Garrett* (Moylan, Pa.: 1977).

GRELLET, STEPHEN [ETIENNE DE GRELLET DU MABILLIER] (2 November 1773, Limoges, France—16 November 1855, Burlington, NJ). *Education*: Military College of Lyon, France. *Career*: Quaker minister; prison reformer.

Stephen Grellet, the son of a wealthy Catholic porcelain manufacturer whose estate was confiscated during the French revolution, joined Royalist forces in 1791. Captured, he escaped to Holland and went to Demerara, Dutch Guiana, where he spent two years in business with his brother. Migrating to the United States in 1795, he learned to speak English and, with the aid of a dictionary, read the Bible and Penn's *No Cross, No Crown*, and began attending meetings. Moved by Deborah Darby, he joined Friends in 1796 and was recognized as a minister in 1798. During the Philadelphia yellow fever epidemic, Grellet helped care for the victims of that contagious disease. In 1800 he moved to New York where he became a merchant with his brother and, after 1815, formed the firm of Pearsall and Grellet. His marriage to Rebecca Collins made him a relative of many prominent Quakers.

Grellet traveled widely as a minister in the United States and Europe. He traveled to Haiti to see how a nation of freed slaves fared and whether American freedmen should be sent there. He returned to Europe for four major journeys, preaching and visiting prisons, hospitals, asylums. He managed to present his findings of conditions in their prisons to the czar, the pope, the sultan, and kings of Spain, Prussia, Norway, and Sweden.

A conservative politically (he welcomed the restoration of the French king in 1814), Grellet was also a social reformer. In 1813 he showed Elizabeth Fry* how prisoners in Newgate were treated, helping to launch her career as a prison reformer.

Grellet was an effective preacher, a combination of mystic and evangelical. Perhaps because he was an ex-Catholic, he was able to communicate his religious feelings to members of other churches. He first attempted to convince Elias Hicks* of errors in 1808; in the 1820s he publicly preached against him. In the aftermath of the separation in Philadelphia Yearly Meeting in 1827, Grellet traveled to Meetings in New York, New England, the South, and the Midwest, denouncing the Hicksites.

Bibliography

A: *Memoirs of the Life and Gospel Labours of Stephen Grellet*, ed. Benjamin Seebohm (London: 1860).
B: DQB; William Wistar Comfort, *Stephen Grellet* (New York: 1942).

GRIMKE, SARAH MOORE (26 November, 1792, Charleston SC—23 December, 1873 Hyde Park, Boston). *Education*: At home with lawyer brother Thomas: *Career*: Abolitionist.

GRIMKE, ANGELINA [later WELD] (20 February 1805, Charleston, SC—26 October 1879, Hyde Park, Boston). *Education*: Charleston Seminary, *Career*: Abolitionist.

The Grimke sisters were the sixth and fourteenth of the children of Judge John Faucheraud Grimke, plantation owner from an old Huguenot family. Sarah was Angelina's godmother but learned from her the injustice of slavery: Sarah's conversion at eighteen led her to spend most of 1819 nursing her dying father in Philadelphia and Long Branch, New Jersey. Returning, she was convinced of Quakerism by John Woolman's* *Journal*, lent her on the ship by Israel Morris, who invited her to live in Philadelphia with his sister Catherine, 1821–28, after his wife's death but whom she refused to marry. She joined Arch Street Meeting.

Angelina, converted by Presbyterians in 1826, joined Charleston Meeting for its antislavery stand. Tried before the Presbyterian Session in 1829, she moved to Philadelphia, refused an offer to teach under Catherine Beecher and became involved in the abolition movement in 1834–35 as a Southern witness to violence against slaves by her published letter to Garrison. With Sarah she trained among Theodore Weld's seventy "Antislavery Apostles" and addressed women's meetings in New York and the Female Anti-Slavery Convention of 1837. In New England she spoke seventy-nine times in five months to crowds averaging 500 despite angry mobs and protests by Weld, Catherine Beecher, and the New York Anti-Slavery leaders over "promiscuous" audiences of mixed race and sex. Her tour climaxed in addresses to the Massachusetts legislature and a series at the Odeon Theater, February–March 1838. Angelina married Weld on May 14, 1838, in Philadelphia and was disowned by Friends, as was Sarah for attending; Angelina spoke at the Anti-Slavery Convention of American Women in Pennsylvania Hall, May 15, and saw it burned by a mob on May 17.

In the 1840s Sarah lived with the Welds at a farm in Belleville, New Jersey, and at a Raritan Bay commune, mothering their three children. In the 1850s both sisters returned to abolition lecturing. After 1868 they adopted three sons of brother Henry Grimke and his female slave.

Bibliography

A: Angelina Grimke: *Appeal to the Christian Women of the South* (New York: 1836); *Appeal to the Women of the Nominally Free States* (Boston: 1837); *Letters to Catherine Beecher* (Boston: 1838). Sarah Grimke: *Epistle to the Clergy of the Southern States* (1836); *Letters on the Equality of the Sexes* (Boston: 1838); with Theodore Weld, *American Slavery as It Is* (New York: 1839). *Letters of Theodore Dwight Weld, Angelina Grimke Weld, and Sarah Grimke, 1822–1844,* ed. Gilbert H. Barnes and Dwight L. Dumond, 2 vols. (New York: 1934); Archives at Oberlin, Boston Public Library, University of Michigan.

B: Gerda Lerner, *The Grimke Sisters from South Carolina* (Boston: 1967), Katharine duPre Lumpkin, *The Emancipation of Angelina Grimke* (Chapel Hill, N.C.: 1974).

GURNEY, JOSEPH JOHN (2 August 1788, Earlham Hall, Norwich, England—4 January 1847, Earlham Hall, Norwich). *Education*: Tutors at Earlham Hall; Anglican boarding schools at Norwich and Hingham; tutor John Rogers at Oxford. *Career*: Banker; philanthropist; biblicist; theologian. (See Chapter 15.)

The Gurneys had raised sheep on their manors near Norwich for six generations when the first John Gurney was jailed as a Quaker in 1682–85. His son John of Norwich was called "the weavers' friend" for organizing them during a depression. His nephew, a third John, became a banker by advancing money to weavers and leased Earlham Hall. He was a father of eleven, including Joseph John and Elizabeth Gurney Fry.* The Gurneys intermarried with the Barclays and Hoares, owned a London bank, and were "gay Friends." In Joseph John's and his children's generations many joined their social peers and in-laws in the Church of England. "Betsy" and Joseph John danced or were schooled with princes or gentry and shared the concerns of Anglican evangelicals for theology, slavery, prisons, and the poor but bravely reaffirmed their Quaker heritage. As a "plain Friend" Joseph John wore his hat as he joined the bishop of Norwich at a dinner but enjoyed Church music more than silence and helped found the Norwich Bible Society. As he headed the Board of Ackworth School "he walked like a prince."

After the death of his first wife, Jane Birkbeck, he wrote the *Evidences of Christianity* and *The Peculiarities of Friends* in 1824 and 1825, giving strength to the Quaker evangelicals during the Hicksite controversy. He headed a London Yearly Meeting Committee to reconcile to Quakerism Isaac Crewdson's *Beacon* circle and was criticized for his sympathy with their strong atonement doctrines. Only after sharp debate did the London Yearly Meeting endorse Joseph John's minute approving his plans to visit American Friends after the death of his second wife, Mary Fowler.

Landing in Philadelphia in 1837, Gurney drove west to the Ohio and Indiana Yearly Meetings, where 3,000 came to hear him. He encouraged the building of the school that became Earlham College and a never-funded plan for an asylum. He drove a carriage over the Appalachians to North Carolina, where slaves could not be freed, and chartered a brig to visit the British West Indies, where blacks had been freed in 1833 and were found to work better and cheaper than slaves. He visited President Van Buren and leaders of Congress, leading them in prayer. He traveled among Friends in New England, New York, and Canada to urge Bible study and Sunday schools. The quietist John Wilbur* followed him to protest splitting "Orthodox Friends" into "Wilburites" and "Gurneyites." After returning to England, Gurney with his third wife, American Eliza Kirkbride, and his sister Elizabeth Fry traveled through Europe, visiting schools and prisons and urging the kings and queens of Denmark, Holland, and France to free slaves in their West Indian colonies. His son ornithologist John Henry Gurney married out of Meeting. His daughter Anna married a Friend, John Backhouse. Joseph John died after a fall from his horse.

Bibliography

A: *Observations on the Religious Peculiarities of the Society of Friends* (London and Norwich, England; Edinburgh, Scotland: 1824; 1829; 1834; reprinted 1979 as *A Peculiar People); Essays on the Evidences, Doctrines, and Practical Operation of Christianity* (London: 1825); *Guide to the Instruction of Young Persons in the Holy Scriptures* (London: 1827); *Essay on the Habitual Exercise of Love of God* (London, Norwich: 1834); *A Winter in the West Indies . . . to Henry Clay* (London: 1840; photoreprinted); *A Journey in North America* (Norwich: 1841); Memoirs of William Wilberforce and Thomas Fowell Buxton and his own *Memoirs*, ed. Joseph Bevan

Braithwaite; (London and Philadelphia: 1854) fifteen sets of printed sermons or addresses; ten printed "open letters"; sixteen other printed essays and tracts.

B: David E. Swift, *Joseph John Gurney: Banker, Reformer, and Quaker* (Middletown,
Conn.: 1962); Verily Anderson, *Friends and Relations* (London: 1980).

H

HANCOCK, CORNELIA (8 February 1840, Hancock Bridge, NJ—31 December 1927, Atlantic City, NJ). *Education*: Salem, NJ, Adademy. *Career*: Nurse; teacher; social worker.

Cornelia Hancock was raised in a Hicksite Quaker family of pronounced antislavery sentiments. During the Civil War her two brothers joined the Union Army. After Gettysburg her brother-in-law, who had volunteered as an emergency surgeon, encouraged Cornelia to help him. Rejected as an army nurse because of her good looks and youth, she went to Gettysburg untrained and on her own and began serving. In three weeks she had charge of eight tents of amputees. Later she worked with the Contraband Negroes in Washington and, holding a permanent pass from the secretary of war, nursed the wounded in the Wilderness Campaign.

In January 1866 the Friends Association for the Aid and Elevation of the Freedman sent her to South Carolina. She began teaching black children in Mt. Pleasant, South Carolina. With financial aid from Friends and the Freedmen's Bureau, she created a school and remained as principal of the Laing School for ten years.

On a trip to England she learned how Londoners dealt with the urban poor. In Philadelphia in 1878 she helped found the Society for Organizing Charity (now the Family Society of Philadelphia) and served as one of the first workers. In 1883 she joined in the establishment of the Children's Aid Society and served as a secretary and board member. In the 1880s she attempted to show in the Wrightsville slum of Philadelphia how benevolent ownership could help tenants. In the name of "housing reform" Wrightsville obtained better sanitation, libraries, a savings bank, recreation areas, and an improved school system. She continued living in Wrightsville until 1914 by which time the tenants had become homeowners.

Bibliography

A: *South after Gettysburg: Letters of Cornelia Hancock, 1863–1868*, ed. Henrietta S. Jacquette (New York: 1956).
B: *Notable American Women* (Cambridge, Mass: 1971), II, 127–129.

HICKS, EDWARD (4 April 1780 Attleborough, PA—23 August 1849, Newtown, PA). *Education*: Apprentice to a carriage maker. *Career*: painter; farmer.

Edward Hicks, whose mother died young and whose father was exiled as a Tory during the Revolution, was reared by Elizabeth and David Twining, prosperous Bucks County Friends who treated him as an adopted child. Because he did not excel at either book learning or farming, Hicks at thirteen was apprenticed to a carriage maker. After attending several religious societies, Hicks became a Quaker in 1803, began speaking as a minister in 1810, and first traveled in the ministry in 1813.

Unsuccessful at farming, Hicks moved in 1811 to Newtown where he supported himself as a coach and sign painter, an occupation that he had qualms about because of Friends' suspicions of art. Hicks approved of farmers, mechanics, temperance, and apolitical abolition; he disliked banks, lawyers, clergymen, speculation, voluntary associations, boarding schools, and higher education. His major heroes were William Penn* and George Washington, and he was intensely patriotic and equally opposed to the materialism in American life. Hicks was a quietist who opposed the evangelicals and became a strong supporter of his relative Elias Hicks*. He blamed the schism on a wealthy aristocracy seeking to impose a creed. After the separation, Hicks reacted against the Unitarian, liberal, and antiscriptural tendencies within the Hicksites.

Today Hicks is esteemed as a major American primitive artist. He painted more than sixty versions of ''The Peaceable Kingdom'' in which the prophecy in Isaiah 9 about the lion and the lamb is juxtaposed to either William Penn's treaty with the Indians or an assemblage of Quakers. Scholars see the Peaceable Kingdom works as psychological landscapes reflecting the tensions of the 1827 separation and Hicks's struggle for inward tranquility. His journal, which was not submitted to Friends before publication, contains an unusually candid portrait of Hicks and his contemporaries.

Bibliography

A: *Memoirs of the Life and Religious Labors of Edward Hicks* (Philadelphia: 1851).
B: Eleanore Price Mather, *Edward Hicks, Primitive Quaker: His Religion in Relation to His Art* (Wallingford, Pa.: 1970); idem, *Edward Hicks: His Peaceable Kingdoms and Other Paintings* (New York: 1983); Alice Ford, *Edward Hicks: His Life and Art* (New York: 1985).

HICKS, ELIAS (19 March 1748, Hempstead, Long Island, NY—27 February, 1830, Jericho, Long Island). *Education*: Friends School at Hempstead; apprenticed to a carpenter; knowledge of surveying. *Career*: Farmer; partner in a tannery; Quaker minister. (See Chapter 14.)

Elias Hicks at age thirteen went to live with his older brother and departed from his strict Quaker upbringing and learned to enjoy attending horse races, dancing, and playing cards. During his apprenticeship, he repudiated such practices. After his marriage in 1771 to Jemima Seaman, daughter of a farmer and tanner, Elias became more religious, speaking in meetings in 1775 and being recognized as a minister in 1779. During the next fifty years, Hicks made sixty-three journeys as a ministering Friend, visiting Meetings throughout America but never going abroad. His quietism forbade preparation before speaking, but Hicks's preaching was so eloquent he was compared with Daniel Webster. Hicks was a prosperous, simple-living farmer with a quiet dignity and courtly manners. In addition to studying the Bible, Hicks read accounts of Quakers by Joseph Besse, John Gough, and Thomas Clarkson and was influenced by the rational, skeptical, and historical writings of David Hume, Charles Rollins, Joseph Priestley, and Johann Mosheim.

Hicks remained a traditional Quaker. He supported a guarded education, taught at intervals in the local Quaker school, and sent his children to the New York Yearly Meeting's Nine Partners Boarding School, where he served as a trustee. He opposed the creation of common schools as an infringement upon parents' rights to determine the religious upbringing of their children. Hicks did not like cities, speculation for wealth, railroads, or canals. He opposed hireling ministers, higher education, formal theology, secret societies, and Bible and tract societies. He was a fierce proponent of the immediate freeing of slaves and insisted that using the fruits of slave labor was a sin. He pitched his own hay. To Hicks, as to Job Scott*, the emergent evangelical emphasis upon the authority of Scripture, the Trinity, and the atonement seemed to be putting intellectual notions above surrendering self-will to the inward Christ. Heaven, hell, and the atonement expressed spiritual Truths and could be used to elucidate the inward journey of a true Christian. Hicks believed in the historic Christ, accepted the virgin birth (though recognizing that some accounts in the gospels and Paul made the doctrine suspect), the Trinity, and the authority of Scripture. But Hicks insisted that such outward manifestations were of little significance.

Despite efforts by evangelical London and Philadelphia Quakers to stop his itinerant preaching, Hicks, aged seventy in 1820, had no intention of ceasing to travel in the ministry. He received support in New York, Philadelphia, and Maryland. His sermons were first published by opponents who contrasted them with biblical texts and supporters who paralleled them with writings of George Fox* and William Penn*. Hicks encouraged his followers to resist what he viewed as attempts to change the beliefs of Friends and to erect a hierarchy of elders but took no role in the maneuverings in the Philadelphia Yearly Meeting before 1827. When the split occurred, Hicks sought to make sure that if a similar separation occurred in the New York Yearly Meeting, the minority party of Orthodox would withdraw. He later traveled to Philadelphia, Maryland, Ohio, and Indiana in an attempt to mobilize his followers and to repudiate the evangelical emphasis of ministers such as Thomas Shillitoe, David Sands, and Elisha

Bates*. Hicks saw himself as presenting traditional Quakerism. Opponents labeled his followers Hicksites, a term he and they resisted.

Hicks's intellectual development is difficult to trace because he published no theological works or sermons until late in his career. Hicks's *Journal*, based upon travel diaries, was printed after the separation and after his death.

Bibliography

A: *Observations on the Slavery of the Africans and Their Descendants* (New York: 1810); *A Series of Extemporary Discourses* (Philadelphia: 1825); *The Substance of Two Discourses, Delivered in New York, 17 Dec. 1824, by Elias Hicks* (New York: 1825); *The Quaker: A series of Sermons* (Philadelphia: 1827); *Journal of the Life and Religious Labors of Elias Hicks, written by himself* (New York: 1832).
B: Bliss Forbush, *Elias Hicks: Quaker Liberal* (New York: 1956).

HOBBS, BARNABAS COFFIN (4 October, 1815 Salem, Washington Co., IN—22 June, 1892, Bloomingdale, IN). *Education*: "The old log school-house" of Monthly Meeting; county seminary; Cincinnati College (Greek and Latin). *Career*: Teacher; educational administrator.

Hobbs went directly from college to teaching school in 1833. He married Rebecca Tatum in 1843. In 1839 he had been called as principal of the Friends Boarding School, Mt. Pleasant, Ohio, and, for fifteen years after 1851, of the Friends Academy of Bloomingdale, Indiana, where he later retired. Responding to Friends' discontent with secular textbooks, he prepared a series of "select readers" titled *School Friend*. In 1847–49 and following 1866, he headed the Boarding School at Richmond, turning it into Earlham College in 1867, training Allen Jay*, Joseph Moore*, and other future Quaker leaders. But as an Earlham board member (1880–92) he led a committee that fired Professor William Pinkham and ex-President Joseph Moore. In 1868–71 Hobbs was Indiana's first superintendent of public instruction and advocated and secured the establishment of a state Reform School for juvenile offenders. He received an honorary M.A. (Wabash) in 1858 and an LL.D. from Indiana University in 1870.

Hobbs was also active in Quaker Meetings and was clerk of the Western Yearly Meeting in 1877, hoping in vain to prevent Conservative Friends from walking out of the increasingly revivalist Yearly Meeting. In 1878 he felt led to visit the czar of Russia, carrying an appeal from the London Meeting for Sufferings against the persecution of Mennonites; he lectured in Europe and America on international peace and arbitration.

Bibliography

A: *Baptism* (Glasgow: 1879); *The Paschal Supper* (Columbus, Ohio: 1880); *Earlham Lectures* (1895); articles and textbooks.
B: Elliott, *QAF*; JLP; Jas. H. Smart, ed., *The Schools of Indiana* (1876); Ethel Hittle McDaniel, *Contribution of the Society of Friends to Education in Indiana* (Indianapolis: 1939); Elbert Russell, *History of Quakerism* (New York: 1942); Opal Thornburg, *Earlham* (Richmond, Ind.: 1963); Richard Ratliff, *Our Special Heritage* (New Castle, Ind.: 1970).

HOBSON, WILLIAM (4 February 1820, Yadkin Valley, NC—25, June 1891, Willamette Valley, OR). *Education*: Non-Quaker village school; Meeting Library in family home; New Garden, NC, Boarding School. *Career*: Farmer; itinerant "minister"; migration pioneer.

Hobson's family had founded Fairfax Quarterly Meeting in Virginia in 1730s, moving into the North Carolina mountains in 1787. At school he was active in Free Labor Produce movement. He married classmate Sarah Tulburt in 1844; moved with two children to Westfield, Indiana, in 1847, following her brother; and then moved to Pleasant Plain, Iowa, later that year. In 1851 he bought a farm and orchard and became a "recorded minister" at Honey Creek, Iowa. His brother stayed in North Carolina and died in the Confederate Army. Hobson traveled widely in ministry in Iowa and Kansas, encouraging Bible study but opposing hymn singing, revivals, and hireling pastors, in opposition to John Henry Douglas* there and after both moved to Oregon.

In 1870 and 1875 he traveled to Northern California and Oregon to visit scattered Quaker settlers and seek a site for a central Quaker settlement. He chose Chehalem (later Newberg) in the Willamette Valley, where a Monthly Meeting began in his home in 1878 from settlers he had gathered in Iowa. In 1885 he and Jesse Edwards founded the Friends Pacific Academy, later George Fox College. In 1890 the Pastoral and Evangelistic Committee supported Douglas's revival meetings there against Hobson's conservative stand. The Oregon Yearly Meeting was "set off" two years after his death.

Bibliography

A: MS Letters at Conrad and New Providence, Iowa; diaries and manuscript "Journal of the Life of William Hobson" at Newberg, Oregon; letters in Friends Historical Library, Swarthmore College.
B: The primary source is Myron D. Goldsmith, "William Hobson and the Founding of Quakerism in the Pacific Northwest" (Ph.D. thesis, Boston University, 1962). See also Ralph K. Beebe, *A Garden of the Lord: A History of Oregon Yearly Meeting of Friends Church* (Newberg, Ore.: 1968); Elliott: *Profiles*.

HOOTON, ELIZABETH (c. 1600, Ollerton, Nottinghamshire—(?) February 1671–72, Port Royal, Jamaica): *Education*: Unknown: *Career*: Mother; Quaker itinerant.

Hooton can be called the first Quaker, since the separatist group she led out of a Baptist congregation at Mansfield had called themselves Friends before George Fox* joined them in 1646; later writers called her his first disciple. During 1633–36 she and her husband, Oliver, moved from Ollerton to Skegby near Mansfield. Fox and Friends met at her home in 1649. The first woman Quaker to travel preaching, she was arrested along with Fox at Derby in 1651; her letter to "Mayor" Bullock of Derby and Fox's more legible copy survive. Imprisonment again at York in 1652–53 inspired her letter to Cromwell and a tract written jointly with other Friends. She was jailed at Lincoln in 1654 and 1655, about six months each, for further prophetic warnings to pastors.

In 1661 she traveled with Joan Brocksopp to Boston via Barbados and Virginia to protest persecutions under the "Cart & Whip Act." After visits to Charles II she felt led to Boston again in 1663–65, entering repeatedly from Rhode Island. For preaching warnings at Boston, at Cambridge, and at Endicott's funeral she was whipped through each town back to the border. In 1671 she sailed with Fox's party to America and died in Jamaica in the presence of James Lancaster. Her son Oliver also became a Friend and wrote her biography, now lost.

Bibliography

A: A. R. Barclay MS 14 and 16, Swarthmore MS 2:43; Thomas Aldam, Elizabeth Hooton, et al., *False Prophets and False Teachers* (York: 1653); manuscript in Manners (below).

B: *BBQ; BSP; DNB;* DQB; Fox, *Camb. Jnl.; EQW*; Joseph Bessem, *A Collection of the Sufferings* (London: 1753); Emily Manners, *Elizabeth Hooton, First Quaker Woman Preacher* in JFHS, Supplement 12 (London: 1914).

HOOVER, HERBERT CLARK (10 August, 1874, West Branch, IA—20, October 1964, New York). *Education*: Friends Boarding School, Newberg, OR; Stanford University, 1891–95: *Career*: Mining engineer; international relief administrator; secretary of commerce; president of the United States.

As an orphan aged nine in Iowa, his guardian was Laurie Tatum, but he was sent to stay with uncle John Minthorn, missionary and Quaker school head at Newberg, Oregon. He supported himself at Stanford by day labor in the Mayflower Mine; by 1899 he had become chief engineer in the Chinese government Department of Mines. In 1900, in Tientsin, he organized aid for fellow "Westerners" trapped by the Boxer Rebellion. In 1914 in England Hoover arranged the return of 120,000 Americans trapped in Europe as World War I broke out; and thereafter for the transport of food through the Allied blockade to 7.5 million Belgians and 2.5 million French. In 1919–21 he was administrator of massive American food relief in Germany and then worked with the Red Cross and the American Friends Service Committee (AFSC) for Russian famine relief. Both Democrats and Republicans (with whom he joined) nominated him for president in 1920, but he gained few convention votes. From 1921 to 1928 he was Secretary of Commerce in Presidents Harding and Coolidge's cabinets, where he was noted for his "drive and diffidence" though skilled in publicity. He headed commissions that planned the St. Lawrence Waterway and what became the Hoover Dam on the Colorado.

As president from 1928 he supported Prohibition; helped farmers by the Agricultural Marketing Act, Federal Farm Board, and Hawley-Smoot Tariff; and sought international peace by the London Naval Conference of 1930. His liberal trust in human nature and progress clashed with his economic conservatism. After the 1929 crash he faced the Depression but let the government intervene only cautiously by the Reconstruction Finance Corporation and Federal Land Bank. Because he opposed public poor relief he was blamed for the "Bonus March" of World War I Veterans and its break-up by Federal troops under General Douglas MacArthur.

As a person he was called "abnormally sensitive, . . . with an impassioned pride in his personal integrity" (Lloyd, 4); he attended the Florida Avenue Meeting while president but never openly discussed his religious faith.

Bibliography

A: *Principles of Mining* (1909); with Lou Henry Hoover, trans. and ed., *Agricola De Re Metallica* (London: 1912); *American Individualism* (1922); *The Challenge to Liberty* (1934); *Addresses upon the American Road*, speeches in 5 vols. (New York: 1938, 1945, 1949; Stanford, Calif.: 1955; Caldwell, Idaho: 1961); *America's First Crusade* (1941); with Hugh Gibson, *The Basis of a Lasting Peace* (1943); *Memoirs* (1951–62); *The Ordeal of Woodrow Wilson* (1958); *An American Epic: Relief of Belgium and Northern France*, 3 Vols. (Chicago: 1959). Papers at Stanford University and Hoover Library, West Branch, Iowa.

B: *Collier's Encyclopedia; Encyclopedia Americana*; DQB; D. S. Hinshaw, *Herbert Hoover, American Quaker* (New York: 1950); Harris S. Warren, *Herbert Hoover and the Great Depression* (New York: 1959); Louis P. Lochner, *Herbert Hoover and Germany* (New York: 1960); Richard Norton Smith, *Herbert Hoover and Germany* (New York: 1960); John Forbes, *The Quaker Star under Seven Flags, 1917–1927* (Philadelphia: 1962); Craig Lloyd, *Aggressive Introvert* (Columbus, Ohio: 1972); David Butner, *Herbert Hoover: A Public Life* (New York: 1979); Robert Bolt, "Herbert Hoover: A Quaker President Misunderstood" (Canton, Ohio: 1986).

HOPPER, ISAAC (3 December 1771, Deptford Township, NJ—7 May 1852, New York City). *Education*: Apprentice. *Career*: Tailor, bookstore keeper.

Isaac Hopper, whose father was a Quaker and mother a Presbyterian, joined the Society of Friends at age twenty-two after being influenced by the minister William Savery*. Hopper became convinced of the evil of slavery during childhood and, while still an apprentice in Philadelphia, helped a fugitive slave. As an adult he joined the Pennsylvania Abolition Society and became an overseer of the Quaker school for black children. Viewing any holding of slaves as unjust, he relied upon common sense, courage in the face of danger, the intricacies of the law, subterfuge, and defiance as tactics to help runaways and kidnapped freed blacks. His success as a voluntary advocate for blacks in court made him famous.

Hopper was a humanitarian willing to risk his life to aid victims of the Philadelphia yellow fever epidemic, and committed to prison reform and good care of the insane. When the separation occurred, Hopper supported the Hicksites even though many of his customers were Orthodox. His business reverses in 1829 prompted him to move to New York, where he opened a bookstore. His support of Garrison and the American Anti-Slavery Society distressed Hicksites opposed to mingling in reform organizations using tactics they opposed. Hopper's role as book agent, treasurer of the Anti-Slavery Society, and editor of the *National Anti-Slavery Standard* marked him, and in 1841 the New York Monthly Meeting disowned him over an article that he did not write or see previous to publication but that criticized a prominent quietist Quaker minister. Both the Quarterly and Yearly Meetings sustained the decision. Hicksite reformers in Philadelphia and elsewhere were outraged. Hopper's disownment showed how inward looking and lukewarm in the antislavery cause many Meetings had become. Hopper continued to wear Quaker garb and to attend the meeting for worship.

From 1845 to 1852 Hopper served as agent for the New York Prison Society, lobbying for the incorporation of the organization, visiting prisons, and helping inmates adjust to life after their incarceration. He did not cease his outspoken opposition to slavery, defending the runaway slaves who defended themselves in the Christiana (Pennsylvania) affair of 1851 and defying the fugitive slave law of 1850.

Bibliography

B: *Narrative of the Proceedings of the Monthly Meeting of New York, and Their Subsequent Confirmation by the Quarterly and Yearly Meetings, in the case of Isaac T. Hopper* (New York: 1843); Lydia Maria Child, *Isaac T. Hopper: A True Life* (Boston: 1853).

HOWLAND, EMILY (20 November 1827, Sherwood, NY—29 June 1929, Sherwood, NY). *Education*: Attended several boarding schools, 1835–57. *Career*: Teacher; philanthropist.

Emily Howland was raised in an Orthodox Quaker family. Her father, who supported Garrisonian abolitionism, sent his daughter to a variety of Quaker boarding schools in New York and later, for brief periods, to the schools of Mary Grew and Mary Robinson in Philadelphia. All of her teachers were abolitionists, and her Philadelphia instructors were also early feminists. Emily Howland became friends with a group of single women who were reformers and feminists.

Unhappy at being confined to domestic duties in her home in Sherwood, in 1857 she went to Washington, D.C., to teach black children. She also supported John Brown's militant abolitionism. In 1862 she began working in a "contraband" camp for newly freed blacks in Virginia. During the next eight years she worked as a teacher and later as a founder of a black farming community called Arcadia. She worked with the Freedmen's Bureau and received help from the Friends Freedmen's Association. The school she founded and supported at Arcadia survived until incorporation into the Virginia public school system in the twentieth century.

Called home in 1870 to attend to her elderly parents, Emily Howland again chafed at domestic responsibility and carried on an extensive correspondence with friends involved in social reform and suffrage agitation, including Quakers

Cornelia Hancock and Susan B. Anthony. Emily Howland had long been critical of the narrowness of Friends, and during the twelve-year period of caring for her father, she stopped attending Meetings. In 1883 Emily Howland created and supported a high school in Sherwood in which she taught. Having inherited wealth, she proved to be a shrewd businesswoman and became the first woman bank director in New York. She continued to work for women's and black's rights and supported several schools in the South until her death.

Bibliography

A. The Howland MSS are at Cornell University and Friends Historical Library, Swarthmore College, Swarthmore, Pa.
B: Judith C. Breault, *The World of Emily Howland* (Millbrae, Calif.: 1976).

HULL, WILLIAM ISAAC (19 November 1868, Baltimore—14 November 1939, Philadelphia). *Education*: B.A., 1889, Ph.D., 1892, Johns Hopkins University, study in Berlin, Leiden, Paris. *Career*: Educator, professor of history and economics, political science, international relations, 1892–1929, professor of Quaker History, 1929–39, Swarthmore College; librarian, Friends Historical Library, 1936–39.

HULL, HANNAH CLOTHIER (21 July 1872, Wynnewood, PA—4 July 1958, Swarthmore, Pa.). *Education*: B.A., Swarthmore College, 1891. *Career*: Peace activist; Women's International League for Peace and Freedom (WILPF): chairman, 1924–28; chairman, board of directors, 1929–33; president, 1934–38; honorary president, 1938–58; vice-chairman of board, American Friends Service Committee, 1928–47.

William I. and Hannah Clothier Hull shared an interest in Quakerism, in working for international peace, and in education. Before 1914 he had published a book on the Hague conferences and pamphlets opposing preparedness. In 1914 they helped organize the Church Peace Union. Both continued to defend pacifism during the war and took active roles in the organization of the American Friends Service Committee. Hannah Hull associated with Jane Addams in creating the Women's Peace Party and the Women's International League for Peace and Freedom. She was also active in the women's suffrage movement. At the end of the war William Hull had several meetings with his former mentor, President Wilson, about the League of Nations and disarmament. Hull supported the League and the World Court but opposed Article 10, which called for collective security. The Hulls remained active in peace causes in the interwar period. He published extensively on arbitration, international affairs, and disarmament and testified before Congress. Hannah Hull helped organize the 1932 Peace Caravan in California and the People's Mandate to Government, efforts aimed at persuading people to petition their governments for disarmament. William I. Hull, who served on the board of virtually every American peace society, wrote in 1926 the Draft Treaty on Disarmament. After 1929 his appointment as Jenkins Professor of Quaker History and Research allowed him leisure to write, and he produced six monographs that remain the authoritative sources on early Dutch Quakerism.

Bibliography

A: William I. Hull: with Charles Haskins, *A History of Higher Education in Pennsylvania* (Washington, D.C: 1902); *The Two Hague Conferences* (Boston: 1908); *The New Peace Movement* (Swarthmore, Pa.: 1909); *Preparedness* (New York: 1916); *American Experiments in Disarmament* (Philadelphia: 1927, 1930, 1932); *The War Method and the Peace Method* (New York: 1929); *Willem Sewel of Amsterdam* (Swarthmore, Pa.: 1933); *William Penn and Dutch Quaker Migration to Pennsylvania* (Swarthmore, Pa.: 1935); *Eight First Biographies of William Penn* (Swarthmore, Pa.: 1936, London: 1937); *The Rise of Quakerism in Amsterdam* (Swarthmore, Pa.: 1938); *Benjamin Furly and Quakerism in Rotterdam* (Swarthmore, Pa.: 1941).

B: Janet Whitney, ''William I. Hull, A Biographical Sketch,'' in *Byways in Quaker History*, ed. Howard Brinton (Wallingford Pa.: 1944), 1–18; Frederick B. Tolles, ''Partners for Peace: William I. Hull and Hannah Clothier Hull,'' *Swarthmore College Bulletin*, December 1958, 3, 44, 46; William I. Hull Papers, 1892–1941, Friends Historical Library of Swarthmore College, Swarthmore, Pa.; Hannah Clothier Hull Papers, 1889–1958, Swarthmore College Peace Collection, Swarthmore, Pa.

J

JANNEY, SAMUEL MCPHERSON (11 January 1801 Goose Creek, VA—
30 April 1880, Lincoln, VA). *Education*: Local schools; independent reading;
merchant apprentice. *Career*: Merchant; educator; historian; Indian Service superintendent.

Samuel Janney, a child of Quakers, received his primary education in school
but obtained most of his knowledge of literature by reading. He refused for
religious reasons to study Latin and the classics. At fourteen he was apprenticed
to his uncle, a commission merchant and iron importer. Janney worked briefly
as a clerk and merchant and in 1828 helped found a cotton factory in Occoquan,
Virginia. Its failure left him a debt of $ 14,000 which he labored twenty years
to pay off. In 1839 he opened a boarding school in Springdale, Virginia, where
he taught and served as principal. His later life was spent in writing and traveling
in the ministry.

As a child Janney had been religiously sensitive, but in 1824 he had a mystical
experience. When the separation occurred, Janney sympathized with the Orthodox Quakers' theology but not their methods, and so he became a Hicksite. He
insisted that early Friends had not believed in the vicarious atonement or the
infallibility of the Bible, but he deplored the division that obscured an essential
unity among all branches of the Society of Friends. In 1852 he suggested that
the Baltimore (Maryland) Yearly Meeting initiate a more equitable division of
property with the Orthodox, a proposal the Hicksites approved in 1864. In 1857
he attempted to reopen formal communication with the London Yearly Meeting.
During his travels he conversed with Orthodox ministers, worshipped on occasion
with the Orthodox, and welcomed them to his meetings.

In the 1820s Janney began antislavery activities. He was willing to consider
colonization, but his primary effort was to help free Negroes gain legal rights
and education, and he founded a school for them in Alexandria. As a Southerner

he managed to publish essays on antislavery in local newspapers. In 1850 he was arrested for an antislavery article but managed to win acquittal with a defense grounding antislavery in religious freedom. Janney never joined an abolition society or an antislavery political party. In Ohio and Indiana in the mid-1840s he sought to heal a breach between the Progressive Friends and the Hicksite Meetings. During the Civil War Janney crossed battle lines to attend Yearly Meetings, nursed the wounded of both sides, and negotiated the release of hostages.

In the 1840s Janney was a leader in the movement in Virginia to create a system of common schools. In his efforts to promote unity among Friends Janney became a historian, and he was gratified at the positive reception of his books on Penn and Fox by both Orthodox and Hicksites. Janney became a leading interpreter of the principles of Friends and his account of the separation and four-volume *History of the Society of Friends* remain notable for their ironic tone, balance, and accuracy.

Under President Grant's "Peace Policy," with the Indians, Friends took responsibility for Indian affairs, and Samuel Janney, at age sixty-seven, became superintendent for the Northern District and responsible for the tribes in Nebraska. Janney viewed Indians much as he had seen blacks; they were victims of their environment and should be encouraged to adopt the major features of white civilization—schools, private property, and Christianity. During his service with the Indians Janney had to contend with hostile whites, inadequate funding from Washington, and Indian opposition. His somewhat heavy-handed paternalism did not lead to major successes, and he retired in 1871. He continued to travel in the ministry, write, and lecture on Indian affairs.

Bibliography

A: *Conversation on Religious Subjects* (Philadelphia: 1853); *The Life of William Penn*(Philadelphia; 1852); *The Life of George Fox* (Philadelphia: 1853); *History of the Religious Society of Friends from its Rise to the Year 1828* (Philadelphia: 1859–67); *An Examination of the Causes Which Led to the Separation of the Religious Society of Friends in America, in 1827–28* (Philadelphia: 1868); *Memoirs of Samuel M. Janney* (Philadelphia: 1881).

B: Gail Brooks Gerlach, "Samuel McPherson Janney: Quaker Reformer" (M.A. thesis, University of Utah, 1977).

JAY, ALLEN (11 October 1831, Miami Co., OH—8 May 1910, Richmond, IN). *Education*: Local Friends schools; Richmond Friends Boarding School (later Earlham), 1851; Farmer's Institute Academy, 1852; Antioch College, 1854. *Career*: Teacher; farmer; postwar rebuilder of Carolina and Indiana Quakerism. (See Chapter 16.)

The Jay family and that of Allen's mother, Rhoda Cooper, had moved from Pennsylvania to Virginia and the Carolinas and settled on farms around Dayton, Ohio, in 1803. He was converted at age thirteen at West Branch Meeting. In the 1850s his parents moved by covered wagon to Marion, Indiana. In 1854 Allen married Martha Sleeper and taught school near Marion and then bought a farm near her family home at Farmer's Institute near Lafayette. Two of their five children died. He began visiting Indiana Quaker families: 3,000–4,000 in three years. Despite a cleft palate, he began traveling in ministry. He was "recorded" as elder in 1860, as a minister 1864. The governor prevented the sale of his livestock for refusing the war draft.

After an 1866 visit to the Baltimore Yearly Meeting and Peace Conference, he was called in 1868 by Francis King and the Baltimore Association to succeed Joseph Moore* in rebuilding schools and Meetings in thirteen North Carolina counties. He organized Bible schools, Meeting schools, and brief Normal Schools and later Guilford College to prepare teachers; he encouraged revivals and began a model farm. Northern Friends sent $138 million in aid.

In 1875 he spent six months in Ireland, England, and Norway visiting Meetings and becoming a friend of John Bright* and Joseph Bevan Braithwaite* for whom he was host at Richmond in 1887. During 1877–81 Jay was treasurer of Moses Brown School, Providence, Rhode Island; in 1881–87 he was superintendent and in 1881–90 treasurer at Earlham; he was clerk of the Indiana Yearly Meeting, 1892–95, and played a key role in setting up the Friends Board of Missions and Five Years Meeting.

Bibliography

A: *Autobiography of Allen Jay* (Philadelphia: 1910); "Letters to Martha Jay during His Visit to Ireland, England and Norway," transcribed in 1949 for the North Carolina Friends Historical Society by Dorothy Gilbert. His papers are in the Earlham Archives, Richmond, Ind.
B: Hamm *TAQ*: Hinshaw, *Carolina; Quaker Biographies*, Series 2, vol. 3, by Votaw (Philadelphia: 1926).

JONES, RUFUS MATTHEW (25 January 1863, South China, ME—16 June 1948, Haverford, PA). *Education*: B.A., M.A., Haverford College, 1882–86; M.A., Harvard University, 1901. *Career*: Educator, Haverford College, 1893–1933; chairman, American Friends Service Committee (AFSC), 1917–28, 1935–44. (See Chapter 17.)

Bibliography

A: *Finding the Trail of Life* (New York; 1926); *The Trail of Life in College* (New York: 1929); *The Trail of Life in the Middle Years* (New York: 1934); *A Small Town Boy* (autobiography, New York: 1941). A good anthology is *Rufus Jones Speaks to Our Time*, ed. Harry Emerson Fosdick (New York: 1951). See also *A Bibliography of the Published Writings of Rufus M. Jones*, compiled by Nixon O. Rush (Waterville Maine: 1944).
B: *DAB*; David Hinshaw, *Rufus Jones: Master Quaker* (New York: 1951); Elizabeth Gray Vining, *Friend of Life: The Biography of Rufus M. Jones* (New York: 1958).

JONES, SYBIL (28 February 1808, Brunswick, ME—4 December 1873, China Lake, ME). *Education*: Local schools, Augusta, ME. Friends Boarding School, Providence, RI, 1824–27. *Career*: Teaching; farming; itinerant Quaker ministry.

JONES, ELI (1807, China Lake, ME—4 February 1899, China Lake). *Education*: Local schools, China Lake, ME; Friends Boarding School, Providence, RI, 1824–27. *Career*: Teaching; farming; itinerant Quaker ministry.

From two Jones clans they met at school: Sybil was daughter of Ephraim and Susannah Dudley Jones; she taught and he farmed until they were married in 1833. She had rebeled against strict Quaker garb but was converted among Methodists and in 1840 began traveling in ministry in Nova Scotia and New Brunswick; he often later traveled as her companion. On the Bay of Fundy "I was not very seasick; he . . . holdeth the waters in His hand." In 1845–46 they visited Yearly and local Meetings west to Indiana and south to Carolina. She felt called in 1851 to visit recolonized black freedmen in Liberia, leaving five children in boarding school or friends' homes. They were both ill most of the voyage but made many ports, visited President Roberts at Monrovia, and gave "god palaver" to unconverted tribes; on return, they spent the winter of 1851–52 preaching in St. Thomas, West Indies. In 1852–53 they traveled, visiting Meetings and speaking for total abstinence from alcohol, in England, Ireland, Norway, Denmark, Germany, and the south of France.

Eli was elected state legislator in 1854–57; his colleagues as a joke elected him major general of militia. His "acceptance speech" ordering all ranks to ground their arms made him famous. He reopened Oak Grove Academy, raised money for it, and served a year as its president. She took part in young people's revival at Earlham in 1860. Their son James Parnell enlisted and was killed in the Civil War; Eli and Sybil spent the war years visiting military hospitals. In 1867–69 they traveled in Lebanon and Palestine, with an interlude to raise support in England; they opened Brummana and Ramallah schools and enlisted Theophilus Waldmeier as the head. Sybil ministered in harems. In 1876 and 1882, after her death, Eli revisited the schools.

Bibliography

B: DQB: Elliott, *QAF*; Rufus Jones, *Eli and Sybil Jones* (Philadelphia: 1889); Christina Jones, *Friends in Palestine* (Richmond, Ind.: 1981).

JONES, THOMAS ELSA (22 March, 1888, Fairmount, IN—5 August 1973, Richmond, IN). *Education*: Grant School; Fairmount (Friends) Academy; A.B. Earlham, 1912); B. D., Hartford Theological Seminary, 1915; Ph.D., Columbia University (economics and political science), 1916; honorary degrees. *Career*: Young Friends traveling secretary; missionary in Japan; president, Fisk University, Earlham College; consultant on college administration.

A big man, farm raised, Jones worked his way through college and the seminary, serving half-time as the first staff member of the National Young Friends, which he helped found and whose conferences he led. In 1914–17 he traveled 30,000 miles, visiting 200 Meetings. He spent a summer at Woodbrooke and biked to English Meetings and work camps; then he brought the English Young Friends to visit across America. He fell in love with another of the fifteen Quaker students then at Hartford Seminary, Esther Balderston. Since she was already committed to mission work in Japan, he joined her there after their marriage in 1917, working with Gilbert Bowles* at the Friends Girls School in Tokyo and teaching at Keio University. He spent a year in American Friends Service Committee (AFSC) work with fugitives from the Russian Revolution in Vladivostock and did relief work after the Tokyo earthquake of 1923. He did research on value attitudes in rural villages, which became his Ph.D. thesis for Columbia. He continued his hobby of mountain climbing in Japan.

Jones was called to be president of Fisk University in 1926. He brought there Charles S. Johnson and other key black scholars and led two multimillion dollar fund drives with help from John D. Rockefeller, Jr., and black alumni. In 1940–41 he set up the Civilian Public Service Camps for conscientious objectors, thereafter run by the AFSC and the U.S. Army. In 1938 he had taken another leave to travel in southern Africa, after which he persuaded the British government not to turn over Botswana and other small protectorates to South African domination. Jones was then made president of Earlham College, 1946–58, providing ten new buildings in ten years and rebuilding a postwar faculty around former Civilian Public Service (CPS) camp men, Quaker scientists, and Elton Trueblood. As at Fisk, he drew a nationwide student body, with paternal care. He encouraged Foreign Study and Community Dynamics programs to give students direct experience. He founded the Associated Colleges of Indiana. After his retirement he raised support for Richmond's black Townsend Community Center and the new Earlham School of Religion.

Bibliography

A: "Mountain Folk of Japan" (Ph.D. thesis, Columbia University: 1926); *Close Proving of All* (Plainfield, Ind.: 1958); *Letters to a College President* (Englewood: 1964); *Light on the Horizon* (autobiography, Richmond, Ind.: 1973).
B: DQB; Opal Thornburg, *Earlham: The Story of the College* (Richmond, Ind.: 1963).

K

KEITH, GEORGE (1638, Peterhead, in Aberdeenshire, Scotland—27 March 1716, Edburton, England). *Education*: M.A., Marischall College, Aberdeen, 1654–58. *Career*: Surveyor; schoolteacher; Anglican clergyman. (See Chapter 7.)

George Keith, raised a Presbyterian, received a good education becoming learned in philosophy, theology, languages, and mathematics. He converted to Quakerism in 1663 and soon became a leader, first in Scotland and later in England, and suffered imprisonment in 1664, 1667, and 1675. Influenced by Descartes, the Cambridge Platonists, and Protestant mystics on the Continent, Keith early proved receptive to new intellectual currents and was willing to consider the theological implications of Quaker beliefs. Along with his good friend Robert Barclay*, Keith in debates and numerous tracts provided a systematic defense of Friends' ideas. After moving to London in 1670 Keith became a close associate of leading English Quakers and, along with George Fox*, William Penn*, and Barclay, journeyed to the Continent in 1677. Ostensibly, Keith was a surveyor and schoolteacher, but he spent much of his time writing and in the traveling ministry.

In 1684 Keith migrated to East Jersey, where he obtained extensive property, drew the boundary between East and West New Jersey, and served as surveyor-general. He journeyed to New England to defend Rhode Island Quakers against the Puritans. In 1689 he moved to Philadelphia and became master of the Quaker school. By 1691 he had decided to return to England when an elderly Quaker minister accused him of the heresy of preaching two Christs, an inward and spiritual Christ versus an outward and historical Jesus.

Keith, who had a forceful personality, demanded vindication and the resulting impasse eventually created a major division, with Keith charging many of the leading members of the Philadelphia Yearly Meeting with holding unsound beliefs. The authorities in Pennsylvania, several of whom had both political and religious power, used the institutions of the Meeting and then of the government in an attempt to silence him. Keith responded with a series of tracts. Keith organized his followers, termed Christian Quakers, into a separate body before returning to London in 1693. The London Yearly Meeting first attempted to mediate the dispute, rebuking both sides. Keith refused to be silent or to repudiate his tracts, and in 1695 he was disowned.

In England Keith attempted to engage Friends in debates, wrote numerous tracts accusing them of not being Orthodox Christians, and held his own services at Turner's Hall in London. In 1700 he took communion in the Church of England and became a priest in 1702. The Society for Propagation of the Gospel sent him to America between 1702 and 1704 to convert dissenters, particularly his former followers and Quakers. Keith attempted to debate with Friends and caused considerable controversy, but he had more successes in strengthening the Church of England in the Middle Colonies than in weakening the Friends. Upon his return to England, he became rector of Edburton in 1705 and served there until his death.

Bibliography

A: Among his most significant writing are *Immediate Relevation . . . Not Ceased* (Amsterdam: 1665); *The Benefit, Advantage, and Glory of Silent Meetings* (London: 1670); *The Way to the City of God Described* (London: 1678); *The Presbyterian and Independent Visible Churches of New England and Elsewhere Brought to the Test* (Philadelphia: 1689); *The Standard of the Quakers Examined or an Answer to the Apology of Robert Barclay* (London: 1702); *The Keithian Controversy in Early Pennsylvania*, ed. J. William Frost (Norwood, Pa.: 1980).
B: Ethyn Williams Kirby, *George Keith* (New York: 1942); Jon Butler, " 'Gospel Order Improved,'' the Keithian Schism and the Exercise of Quaker Ministerial Authority in Pennsylvania,'' *William and Mary Quarterly*, 3d ser. 31 (July 1974): 431–52.

KELLY, THOMAS RAYMOND (4 June 1893, near Londonderry, OH—17 January 1941, Haverford, PA). *Education*: B.S., Wilmington College, 1913; Haverford College 1913–14; B.D., 1919, Ph.D., 1924, Hartford Theological Seminary; Harvard College, 1930–32. *Career*: educator, Pickering College, Ontario, 1914–16; teaching Bible, Wilmington College, 1919–21; Friends International Centre in Berlin, Germany, 1924–25; professor: Earlham College, 1925–30, 1932–35; University of Hawaii, 1935–36; Haverford College, 1936–41. (See Chapter 20.)

Thomas Kelly, reared in an evangelical home, majored in science at Wilmington College. At Haverford, influenced by Rufus Jones*, Kelly's interest began to shift to philosophy and religion. He took an active role in the Young Friends Movement; worked for the American Friends Service Committee (AFSC) during World War I, caring for German prisoners of war in England; and headed the food relief program of the AFSC in Germany, 1924–25; in between he returned to Hartford Theological Seminary determined to become a philosopher.

Kelly's quest for excellence resulted in his achieving a Ph.D. at Hartford and, after a period of teaching, to attempt to obtain a second Ph.D. from Harvard. At Earlham and the University of Hawaii, Kelly taught religion and philosophy and became interested in Eastern thought.

Kelly's major impact upon Friends came during the last three years of his life while teaching at Haverford. He failed to pass the oral examinations at Harvard and in his depression experienced a religious reorientation. His concern for philosophical rigor in his early writing was replaced by a sensitivity to mystical experience. Kelly's new approach combined traditional evangelical language with distinctive Quaker emphases. A visit to Germany under Nazi rule in 1938 deepened his awareness of tragedy. The *Testament of Devotion*, a collection of Kelly's writings published after his death at age forty-one of a heart attack, rapidly became a popular devotional manual.

Bibliography

A: *Explanations and Reality in the Philosophy of Emile Meyerson* (London: 1937); *A Testament of Devotion* (New York: 1941); *Reality of the Spiritual World* (Wallingford, Pa.: 1942); *The Eternal Promise* (New York: 1966).
B: DQB; Douglas Steere, "Biographical Memoir," in Thomas Kelly, *A Testament of Devotion*; (New York: 1941) Richard M. Kelly, *Thomas Kelly: A Biography* (New York: 1966); T. Canby Jones, "Thomas R. Kelly: His Life as a Miracle," in *Living in the Light*, ed. Leonard Kenworthy (Philadelphia: 1984), 146–61.

KIRKBRIDE, THOMAS STORY (31 July, Bucks County, PA—16 December 1883, Philadelphia, PA). *Education*: Four years classical education with Jared D. Taylor in Trenton; one year studying mathematics with John Gummere of Burlington; apprenticeship to Dr. Nicholas Belleville; M.D., University of Pennsylvania, 1828–32. *Career*: Medical reformer of treatment of the insane; resident physician: Friends' Asylum for the Insane, 1832–33; Pennsylvania Hospital, 1833–35; general practice, 1835–39; physician in chief and superintendent, Pennsylvania Hospital for the Insane, 1840–83.

Kirkbride served as superintendent of the Pennsylvania Hospital for the Insane for forty-three years, beginning with that asylum's opening in 1841. Serving as head of both the therapeutic and administrative programs, he instituted a modified form of the moral treatment.

The Pennsylvania Hospital for the Insane was a private nonsectarian institution, though both Kirkbride and the members of the Board of Managers were Friends. The hospital served all classes and all religions and was financed by patron fees—the wealthy subsidized the poor—and private subscriptions. Kirkbride appeared to his patients and their families as a Christian doctor, a moralist whose treatments combined science and personal responsibility. He used drugs in treatment but was most interested in creating a harmonious family environment in which the curable and seemingly hopeless cases would be treated with equal compassion. Kirkbride sought to have patients physically comfortable, intellectually stimulated, and aesthetically satisfied. So he insisted on beautiful grounds, moderate exercise, a regular but not rigid schedule, entertainments in the evening, and well-designed buildings. Kirkbride viewed mental illness as curable and approached patients and their families in a nonjudgmental, caring way. The success rate in the hospital—patients well enough to leave or significantly improved—was about the same as in mental institutions today.

Kirkbride's ideas in patient treatment had immense impact on the care of the insane and the design of asylums in America before the Civil War. His skills as a doctor, ability to raise money, and decision to limit the size of the hospital were hard to emulate. After the 1870s doctors who wanted to be more scientific than Kirkbride and state legislatures governed by frugality repudiated his practices.

Bibliography

A: *Code of Rules and Regulations . . . of Pennsylvania Hospital for the Insane* (Philadelphia: 1841); *Remarks on the Construction and Arrangements of Hospitals for the Insane* (Philadelphia: 1847); *On the Construction, Organization, and General Arrangements of Hospitals for the Insane* (Philadelphia: 1851); Reports of Pennsylvania Hospital for the Insane.

B: *DAB;* Earl Bond, *Dr. Kirkbride and His Mental Hospital* (Philadelphia: 1947); Nancy Tomes, *A Generous Confidence: Thomas Story Kirkbride and the Art of Asylum Keeping, 1840–1883* (New York: 1984).

L

LLOYD, DAVID (1656, Wales—6 April 1731, Chester, PA). *Education*: Studied law. *Career*: Lawyer; land speculator; farmer; attorney general of Pennsylvania, 1686–1700; chief justice of Pennsylvania, 1717–31; member of Assembly intermittently, often speaker, 1694–1726.

David Lloyd was a poor Welshman who gained a good legal education and became acquainted with William Penn* through working in a law office in London dealing with Pennsylvania from 1683 to 1686. He migrated to Pennsylvania in 1686 and became the colony's attorney general. He allied himself with his kinsman, Thomas Lloyd, president of the council, against Penn's deputy governor, John Blackwell, in 1688. Lloyd later opposed the attempts of Benjamin Fletcher, the royal governor, to gain a militia and war tax. Lloyd continued his defiance of both the royal and proprietary prerogatives, and in 1700 Penn rebuked him and removed him as attorney general. Lloyd continued to be an inveterate opponent of Penn.

Soon after he moved to Pennsylvania, Lloyd became a Quaker. He consistently opposed appropriations for defense and favored using the affirmation in court cases. He became an overseer in Chester Monthly Meeting and participated in the 1729 revision of the Discipline. His political opponents —James Logan*, Penn, and the deputy governors —thought Lloyd able but unscrupulous. The Philadelphia Yearly Meeting twice publicly intervened in politics against him and on each occasion he was defeated.

As leader of the popular party in the assembly, Lloyd sought to divide Pennsylvania from Delaware, to reduce the power of the Proprietor over the courts and lands, to make the Council a purely advisory body, and to strengthen the power of the Assembly. As speaker of the Assembly and one of the few lawyers in early Pennsylvania, he played an important role in shaping the colony's laws.

In later years he mellowed, working with Logan against Governor Keith, and signed a laudatory memorial to William Penn.

Bibliography

A: *A Vindication of the Legislative Power* . . . (Philadelphia: 1725); *A Defense of the Legislative Constitution of the Province of Pennsylvania* (Philadelphia: 1728).
B: Roy Lokken, *David Lloyd, Colonial Lawmaker* (Seattle, Wash.: 1959).

LOGAN, JAMES (20 October 1674, Lurgan, County Armagh, Ireland —31 October 1751, Germantown, PA). *Education*: Learned Greek, Latin, and Hebrew in his father's school in Bristol, England. *Career*: Merchant: farmer; secretary of province of Pennsylvania and clerk of Provincial Council, 1701–17; commissioner of property and receiver general of Pennsylvania, member of Provincial Council, 1702–47; chief justice of Supreme Court, 1731–39; mayor of Philadelphia, 1722.

James Logan, the son of an Anglican minister who turned Quaker, received an excellent classical education. After an apprenticeship and brief attempt to become a linen merchant, he became William Penn's secretary and accompanied him to Pennsylvania in 1699. Logan for fifty years protected Penn's financial interests in selling lands, attempted to collect quitrents, and represented the Proprietor, his widow, and his sons' political purposes as a member of the Council, negotiator with the Indians, and adviser to the deputy governors. Conservative in political philosophy, Logan feared the rabble, opposed democratic and leveling tendencies, and sought to preserve a hierarchical society in which the able ruled and the people obeyed. His primary political opponent was the Quaker David Lloyd*.

While serving the Penn family, Logan at the same time created his own fortune through land speculation, trade with Indians, and importing and exporting goods. As a businessman he was shrewd and occasionally unscrupulous, and his smuggling and fraudulent treatment of the Indians would have outraged most Friends. Logan was the most brilliant Quaker in eighteenth-century Pennsylvania: the first American Quaker scientist of note, engaging in experiments to prove the sexuality of plants and corresponding with European naturalists; a classical linguist producing translations of Cicero and Cato; and a collector creating one of the finest libraries in the colonies. Logan built an elegant mansion on the outskirts of Philadelphia, showing that for him Quaker plainness did not require cheapness. Logan was a sporadically devout Quaker, serving on the committee on oversight of the press but advocating the legitimacy of defensive war and the expansion of the British empire. After he retired from active involvement in politics in 1747, Logan devoted his time to the study of natural science corresponding with Europeans and befriending Benjamin Franklin and John Bartram*.

Bibliography

A: *The Charge Delivered From the Bench* . . . Philadelphia: 1723); *Correspondence between William Penn and James Logan, . . . 1700–1750*, ed. Edward Armstrong, in

Memoirs of the Historical Society of Pennsylvania, 2 vols. (Philadelphia: 1870–72); *The Correspondence of James Logan and Thomas Story*, ed. Norman Penney (Philadelphia: 1927); *The Scientific Papers of James Logan*, ed. Roy N. Lokken (Philadelphia: 1972); Logan Papers, Historical Society of Pennsylvania, Philadelphia, Pa.
B: Frederick Tolles, *James Logan and the Culture of Provincial America* (Boston: 1957); Edwin Wolf, 2nd., *The Library of James Logan of Philadelphia, 1674–1751* (Philadelphia: 1974).

LUNDY, BENJAMIN (4 January 1789, Sussex (Warren) Co., NJ—22 August, 1839, McNabb, IL). *Education*: Mt. Pleasant Friends Academy. *Career*: Abolitionist; journalist; Free Labor produce storekeeper.

At the age of nineteen, with Lundy's health hindering his work on the family farm, he apprenticed and then worked as a saddler in Wheeling, West Virginia. In 1815 he married Esther Lewis (d. 1826), raising five children at St. Clairsville, Ohio; but in 1816 he saw a chain gang of slaves and organized a Humane Society. He began to publish *The Genius of Universal Emancipation* in 1820 and in 1821–24 he moved that journal and his family to Tennessee. In 1825 he visited the Carolinas and Haiti, whither he had sent eleven freed slaves and now arranged regular resettlement for freedmen. In 1826 he opened a Free Labor produce store in Baltimore and visited New England and William Lloyd Garrison Lundy soon moved to Philadelphia, making more visits to Haiti and three lengthy trips through Texas and northern Mexico in 1833–35 as war fever there grew, visiting General Santa Ana and provincial governors in hopes to settle freedmen's colonies there; but he found "slavery is worse in Mexico than in the United States." He lobbied fiercely against the United States' annexation of Texas as a slave state. He was involved in the Anti-Slavery Conventions in Philadelphia, siding with gradualists against Garrison. He lost all of his books and clothes in the Pennsylvania Hall arson of 1838. He then moved to join his children in the Hicksite community of Clear Creek, Illinois, dying soon after. Lundy was small, slender, gentle, and deaf.

Bibliography

A: *The Life, Travels, and Opinions of Benjamin Lundy* (Philadelphia: 1847); *The Genius of Universal Emancipation* (reports on Haiti, 1820–26).
B: *DAB*; DQB; William C. Armstrong, *The Lundy Family* (New Brunswick, N.J.: 1902); Carleton Mabee, *Black Freedom: The Non-Violent Abolitionists from 1830 through the Civil War* (New York and London: 1970); Jane H. Pease and William H. Pease, *Bound with Them in Chains: A Biographical History of the Anti-Slavery Movement* (Westport, Conn.: 1972).

M

MALONE, J. WALTER (11 August, 1857, Clermont Co., OH—30 December, 1935, Cleveland, OH). *Education*: New Vienna, OH, school; Earlham, 1873–75; B.A., Chickering Institute, Cincinnati, 1877. *Career*: Co-founder, Cleveland Bible Institute, and of Ohio Yearly Meeting mission work.

MALONE, EMMA BROWN (30 January, 1859, Pickering, Ontario, Canada—10 May, 1924, Cleveland, OH). *Education*: Cleveland, OH, public schools. *Career*: Co-founder, Cleveland Bible Institute, and of Ohio Yearly Meeting mission work. (See Chapter 16.)

In 1880 Walter Malone moved to join a brother in his stone-quarrying business in Cleveland leaving his boyhood home, New Vienna, Ohio, a town that John Henry Douglas* and Esther Frame* had made into the center of Ohio Quaker revivalism. Malone was chosen at once to direct the Sunday school of the little First Friends Church of Cleveland. Emma Brown, converted under Dwight L. Moody in 1877, was already attending, and there both Malones experienced sudden Holiness under the ministry of Dougan Clark. They were married in 1886. In 1892 they felt called to open a training school for church workers and home missionaries, where the Bible would be taught without "higher criticism." A building was erected in 1897; William P. Pinkham came as Bible professor; in 1899 the Cleveland Bible Institute was incorporated. Their program slowly grew from one year's training to three; two more buildings were added. Enrollment averaged one-hundred. By 1902 the school could list twenty-one alumni serving as foreign missionaries; eighty graduates would go abroad in the first sixty years, including Esther Baird in India and Arthur Chilson*, Jefferson Ford, Willis Hotchkiss, Edgar Hole, and Emory Rees in Kenya, where the Malones had persuaded the Ohio Yearly Meeting's committees to support missions. Most of the remaining graduates became pastors or evangelists. Among the well-known faculty were Everett Cattell* and Walter R. Williams. The school's theology emphasized Holiness, but Walter Malone had worked with Rufus Jones* in 1894 to unite the Quaker journals *Christian Worker* and *Friends Review* into the new *American Friend*. In 1957, after the Malones' death, their son-in-law President Byron L. Osborne led the college and the Yearly Meeting to the decision to move from Cleveland and reopen under the name Malone College in Canton, Ohio, so as to serve a thousand local students as well as the Yearly Meeting.

Bibliography

A: The Malone papers are in family hands or at the Malone College Library, Canton, Ohio.

B: Byron L. Osborne, *The Malone Story* (Newton, Kans.: 1970); Elliott, *Profiles*; T. Hamm, *TAQ*.

MENDENHALL, NEREUS (14 August, 1819, Jamestown, NC—29 October, 1893, Jamestown). *Education*: Schools in home and village; Haverford College, 1837–39; M.D., Jefferson Medical College, Philadelphia, 1845. *Career*: Printer; teacher; principal; doctor; civil engineer; state legislator; Yearly Meeting clerk.

Mendenhall worked as printer for four years to earn money for Haverford College; he fell in love with teaching while principal at New Garden, North Carolina, returning to it after a few years in medicine and as a railway builder. In 1851 he married Orianna Wilson. For her sake he packed their belongings in 1860 to join many antislavery Carolina Friends in Indiana but at the New Garden railroad station felt led by God to stay. He served as Yearly Meeting clerk during and after the Civil War, 1860–71, protecting conscientious objectors and maintaining the New Garden School until its postwar rebuilding as Guilford College. He provided the local support for the work of the Baltimore Association in reopening schools and Meetings. He was asked to help draft the postwar Constitution for North Carolina and set up the state's mental hospital. His moves to teach at Penn Charter School, 1876–8, and Haverford College, 1878–80, may have reflected unease with the growth of Carolina revivalism.

Bibliography

A: His papers are at Guilford College Library, New Garden, N.C.

B: DQB: Elliott, *QAF*; *Autobiography of Allen Jay*. (Philadelphia: 1910); *Quaker Biographies*, Series 2, vol. 5, by Mary Mendenhall Hobbs (Philadelphia: 1926): 245–305; Elliott, *Profiles*, 1–21.

MOORE, JOSEPH (29 February 1832, Salem, IN—9 July 1905, Richmond, IN). *Education*: Blue River (Friends) Academy; Friends Boarding School, Richmond, IN; Harvard. *Career*: Biologist; pioneer teacher of science and evolution.

Moore's family was from Perquimans County in the Carolina tidewater, homesteading in a southern Indiana log cabin. Weak health and eager interest led him to teach locally after leaving school and again after finishing at the academy that became Earlham College. There Barnabas Hobbs* sent him to train to teach science. At Harvard, 1859–61, Moore was an intimate as well as a student of

Louis Agassiz, learning to observe animals and plants and to teach with specimens and chalk diagrams. Returning to Earlham with a double degree in comparative anatomy and biology, his gentle teaching of evolution aroused disputes. In 1862 he married a classmate, Deborah Stanton, who died of typhoid in 1864. His second wife, Mary Thorne, and their families had to deal with his tuberculosis.

In 1865, after being recorded as a minister, he visited Friends Meetings in Iowa, Minnesota, and Michigan. From December 1865 to mid-1869 he was the Baltimore Association's appointee to rebuild the Quaker schools in North Carolina. This work he left to Allen Jay* when he was called to be president of Earlham, 1869–74. Health again required him to leave teaching for a trip to Hawaii, and he stopped on the way to study gold and silver smelting in Nevada. In Hawaii he sketched the lava flows of Mauna Loa and Kilauea, early Hawaiian monuments, and new mission schools. Multiple crates of specimens that he sent to Earlham became the nucleus of the present Joseph Moore Museum. In 1883–88 he left the presidency to become principal of Guilford College. He also resigned from Earlham to protest the firing of veteran professors Calvin Pearson and Alpheus McTaggart by Charles Coffin and the board, but he returned to his museum and geology teaching in 1888–94.

Bibliography

A: "Description of a New Species of Gigantic Beaverlike Rodent" and other published papers on Castorides Ohioensis; manuscript journals of his youth and Hawiian voyage; letters and MSS in Earlham archives, Richmond, Ind.
B: Stephen Anshutz, "The Life and Times of Joseph Moore" (MS, Earlham); See article by Anna Moore Cadbury in *Quaker Biographies*, Series 2, vol. 4, (Philadelphia: 1926); Opal Thornburg, *Earlham* (Richmond, Ind.: 1963).

MOTT, LUCRETIA COFFIN (3 January 1793, Nantucket, MA—11 November 1880, Philadelphia). *Education*: Nine Partners Boarding School. *Career*: Quaker minister; social reformer.

Lucretia Coffin Mott helped to break down the influence of sectarian and quietist influences among Hicksite Quakers while becoming a major figure in two important reform movements, antislavery and women's rights.

Born the daughter of Thomas and Anna Coffin, Lucretia Coffin Mott cherished and emulated her Nantucket heritage of coping since she had a happy marriage, successfully managed a large household, raised a family, helped her neighbors, served her Meeting, and pioneered social reforms. She went to school on the island until she was eleven, then moved to Boston, and finally completed her formal education at the new Nine Partners Boarding School in Dutchess County, New York. There she obtained what nineteenth-century Friends regarded as an excellent education for a girl, served for an interval as an assistant teacher, learned about discrimination against women through the differential in wages paid to men and women teachers, and met James Mott, a teacher and son of the principal.

The Coffins moved to Philadelphia, and her father opened a nail factory. James Mott married Lucretia, who was eighteen, in 1811 and went to work in the family firm. Lucretia Mott's description of an ideal marriage in 1849 applies to her own: "In the true marriage relationship the independence of the husband and wife is equal, their dependence mutual, and their obligations reciprocal." James Mott was a merchant's clerk for a while but eventually became a cotton trader until in 1830 he switched into the wool trade because he refused to sell products of slave labor when the profits went only to the owners.

During the first sixteen years of her marriage, Lucretia Mott devoted her primary attention to raising her six children. After the death of her first son, she began reading religious books and eventually spoke a few words in a Meeting. In 1821 at age twenty-eight she was recorded a minister. She had heard Elias Hicks* preach as a child, entertained him in Philadelphia as an adult, and sympathized with his advocacy of the free produce movement. The Motts became Hicksites, and Lucretia served as clerk of the Women's Yearly Meeting and traveled widely in the ministry.

Lucretia Mott had long questioned the stringency of the Discipline, but in the aftermath of the schism, quietists defeated her attempts to ease marriage regulations and to increase the power of women within the Meeting. As she became more active in antislavery agitation and women's rights and more liberal theologically, some Hicksites tried to persuade her to resign from membership or to disown her. But she stayed within the Meeting as a powerful voice for change.

Lucretia Mott had become convinced of the evils of slavery while still a child. In 1830 the Motts met William Lloyd Garrison, became his friends, and remained his supporters for many years. James participated in the formation of the American Antislavery Society in 1833; Lucretia was allowed in as an observer but could not become a member. Along with other Quakers and free blacks, she created the Philadelphia Female Antislavery Society. The society raised money for abolition causes through annual fairs and provided relief for blacks; its slogan "Am I Not a Woman and a Sister?" served as a poignant reminder that half of the slaves were women. She walked through the streets in the 1830s arm-in-arm with black women, entertained blacks at her home, supported charities for blacks, preached at black churches, and agitated against the discriminatory treatment of blacks in the North.

The Motts welcomed William Lloyd Garrison's attempt to include women in the American Antislavery Society and supported him after the splintering of the American Antislavery Society. James and Lucretia went to England as delegates to the first World Antislavery Convention, but women were not seated as delegates. The battle over women's credentials and Lucretia Mott's prominence made her a celebrity first in London and later in America. In London Lucretia Mott became friends with Elizabeth Cady Stanton, and both resolved to work for the equality of women.

In 1848 while Lucretia Mott traveled in the ministry, she and Elizabeth Stanton announced a conference on women's rights to be held at Seneca Falls, New

York. The conference demanded an end to legal discrimination against women. The Seneca Falls Declaration was the effective beginning of the women's suffrage movement in America.

Lucretia Mott was one of the most influential speakers for women's freedom. Her feminism did not accept the supposed moral superiority of women to men. Rather, it rested upon the God-given equality of the sexes. She wanted a woman to have her right to define her own sphere—to progress as far as she was capable without society imposing restraints. She should have an equal right to an education, a right to vote, a right to property.

Lucretia Mott believed in progress and freedom. She disliked a rationalism that exalted mind over the Inward Light; she opposed theology and creeds as substituting the words of men for the experience of God. She often quoted Unitarians and approved of transcendentalists like Ralph Waldo Emerson because they appealed for vindication to a source of God within. She preached against the doctrines of original sin and the atonement as cruel and arbitrary doctrines unfair to the nature of God and nobility of humankind. Mott read the Bible and could quote it at length, but she refused to idolize it. The Bible, reason, nature, humanity, were to be confirmed by the Inner Light. The term *Inner Light*, or inward monitor, was used by Lucretia Mott and other Hicksites to show that God was within people and not some external, alien, supernatural being. By her preaching and example, Lucretia Mott exemplified the unity she sought between reason and belief, worship and action. She refused to be confined within the narrowness of sectarian Quakers or to leave the Meeting.

Certain that education was the best way of opposing superstition and fostering moral reform, Lucretia Mott chaired a committee of Philadelphia Yearly Meeting (Hicksite), advocating better schools. Her agitation for an advanced school bore fruit with the founding of Swarthmore College. In 1859 she and James Mott had supported the establishment of the nation's first medical school for women, the Female Medical College of Pennsylvania, and, showing the easing of her prejudices against fine arts, approved the School of Design for Women, now Moore College of Art.

Bibliography

A. *Discourse on Woman* (Philadelphia: 1850); *Slavery and the Woman Question, ed.* Frederick B. Tolles *(Haverford, PA. 1952); Lucretia Mott: Her Complete Speeches and Sermons*, ed. Dana Greene (New York: 1980).

B. *DAB*; DQB; Otelia Cromwell, *Lucretia Mott* (Cambridge, Mass: 1958); Margaret Hope Bacon, *Valiant Friend: The Life of Lucretia Mott* (New York: 1980); Anna Davis Hallowell, *James and Lucretia Mott* (New York: 1984).

P

PEMBERTON, ISRAEL, JR. (19 May 1715, Philadelphia—22 April 1779, Philadelphia). *Education*: Penn Charter School, Philadelphia. *Career*: Merchant.

Israel Pemberton, Jr., was a most important religious–political leader of Pennsylvania Friends from the late 1740s until the time of the American Revolution. His father, Israel Pemberton, Sr., was a wealthy merchant, prominent politician, and devout Quaker whose three sons—Israel, Jr., James (1723–1809), and John (1727–1795) shared their father's abilities in business, serving in politics, and being strict Quakers. The Pembertons became the wealthiest family in Pennsylvania, making money in trade, farming, and land speculation. Israel, Jr., served as clerk of Philadelphia Yearly Meeting from 1750 to 1759; James for eighteen years between 1761 and 1789; John became a minister in 1751.

Israel engaged in a wide range of philanthropic activities. He was a founder of the Pennsylvania Hospital, a fire company, a fire insurance company, a society to aid distressed blacks, and the American Philosophical Association. He also was clerk of the committee of Penn Charter School and promoted Quaker education. Israel and John Pemberton became early supporters of the revival of Discipline, strict pacifism, and antislavery. James served several terms in the Assembly and, after the Revolution, became a founder and then president of the Pennsylvania Abolition Society.

Israel Pemberton in 1739 opposed the Pennsylvania governor's request for funds for defense. He tried in 1744 to select more consistent Quakers than those proposed by Speaker John Kinsey to be Philadelphia's assemblymen. Israel was outraged when the Assembly in 1755 voted £60,000 for war, and he supported those who refused to pay the tax. He blamed the Proprietors for mistreating the Indians, opposed Pennsylvania's declaration of war against the Delawares, served as an observer at the negotiations at Easton in 1756, and became a leader in the Friendly Association for Regaining and Preserving Peace with the Indians. Israel

Pemberton's support of Indian rights earned him the enmity of the Paxton boys. He did not favor Franklin's plan to make Pennsylvania a royal colony.

In the struggle preceding the American Revolution, Israel, James, and John Pemberton opposed English taxation and sought to conciliate differences. They saw the continuation of Quaker rights as dependent upon the Charter granted to Penn. The Pembertons were influential members of the Meeting for Sufferings, whose declarations of opposition to independence and neutrality among contending parties seemed pro-British. So when the English army approached Philadelphia in 1777, the revolutionary government exiled Israel, James, and John Pemberton to Virginia. Israel died soon after his return to Philadelphia.

Bibliography

A: The Pemberton MSS are at the Historical Society of Pennsylvania, Philadelphia, Pa.
B: *DAB*, DQB; Theodore Thayer, *Israel Pemberton, King of the Quakers* (Philadelphia: 1943); Judy Di Stefano, "A Concept of the Family in Colonial America: The Pembertons of Philadelphia" (Ph.D. diss., Ohio State University, 1970).

PENN, WILLIAM (14 October 1644, London—30 August 1718, Ruscombe, Berkshire, Eng.). *Education*: Chigwell School (Essex), 1648–56; Christ Church College, Oxford, 1660–62; Saumur Protestant Academy, 1663–64; Lincoln's Inn, 1664–66. *Career*: Gentleman; writer and debater for Quakerism; founder of Pennsylvania. (See Chapters 2, 6, and 7 for Quaker events and Penn's ideas.)

From their Tower Hill home in London, Will Penn was sent by his father, Admiral Sir William Penn, to learn classics and court manners in the finest schools while England went through the Restoration, the Plague, and two Dutch Wars. Yet on the family's estate in Ireland in 1666–67 he found a new identity in joining the persecuted Quakers. His father briefly disowned him. Penn's tracts and debates against Anglican, Presbyterian, and Baptist pastors were interrupted by imprisonment in the Tower of London (1668–69) and also twice in Newgate prison, after the "Penn-Mead trial" and his father's death in 1670 and 1671. He wrote *No Cross, No Crown*, and *The Great Case of Liberty of Conscience* in jail. In 1672 he married Gulielma Springett, daughter of Mary Penington, whose husband Isaac's library in Bucks guided his theological writing. He visited Dutch and German Friends and Princess Elizabeth of the Palatinate in 1671 and with George Fox*, Robert Barclay*, and George Keith* in 1677.

In 1675, as a trustee for Edward Billing, Penn helped to plan the West New Jersey settlement. He plunged into parliamentary politics in 1678–80, supporting Whigs for toleration in England, but in 1680–82 he turned to statecraft when Charles II chartered Pennsylvania. For it, Penn drew up many drafts of a Frame of Government, bought the land from the Delaware Indians, and campaigned to bring Mennonites and German sectarians to his colony. Despite providing for estates there for himself, his children, and friends, Penn could only live there in 1682–84 and 1699–1701, due to a long court case in England against Lord Baltimore over Pennsylvania's Maryland boundary. Penn was involved in the toleration policy and then the fall of his friend King James II. His enforced retirement allowed Penn time to write *Fruits of Solitude* and speak in English Meetings. After Gulielma's death in 1694 he married Hannah Callowhill of Bristol, but costs of his colony and his financial imprudence led to his imprisonment for debt in 1705. He had protected the Quaker colonists by a new Charter of Privileges in 1701, but was still wrestling to maintain his solvency and Pennsylvania's autonomy under the Crown when a stroke inactivated him from 1712 until his death.

Bibliography

A: Penn's 109 works in English, plus five Dutch, one German, and two Latin originals and six translations in his lifetime make him, with Fox, the most prolific early Friend. Many of these works and some letters were reprinted in Joseph Besse's two-folio edition of Penn's *Works* (1726). In the centennial years of Pennsylvania, *No Cross, No Crown; Rise and Progress of the ... Quakers;* and *Some Fruits* were reprinted; AMS photoreprinted Besse's *Works*. Letters to and from Penn are in print in four volumes of *The Papers of William Penn* (Philadelphia: 1981ff.) edited by Mary Maples Dunn, Richard Dunn, and associates, with a fifth volume, a definitive bibliography of Penn imprints, by Edwin Bronner and David Fraser. Hugh Barbour's edition is *Penn on Religion and Ethics* (New York: 1989)

B: The best biographies remain William I. Hull, *William Penn: A Topical Biography* (London: 1937), and Catherine Peare, *William Penn* (Ann Arbor: 1956, 1966). On his theology see Melvin B. Endy, Jr., *William Penn and Early Quakerism* (Princeton: 1973). On his political and social ethics see Edwin C. O. Beatty, *William Penn as Social Philosopher* (New York: 1939); Edwin Bronner, *William Penn's "Holy Experiment"* (New York: 1962); and Mary Dunn, *William Penn: Politics and Conscience* (Princeton: 1967).

PENNINGTON, LEVI T. (29 August 1875, Amo, IN—15 March 1975, Newberg, OR). *Education*: Coffield ungraded school and Traverse City school and high school, MI, 1894; Earlham, 1908–10. *Career*: College president.

The moves of his pastor father made insecure Penington's early home and funds for schooling. Between high school and college he taught four years, was a journalist for two papers and preacher in two Hoosier Meetings, and married Bertha May Waters. They had two girls before she died in 1903. In 1904 he married Rebecca Kidd. At college he studied Bible, starred in oratory and debate, and was famous as a storyteller. Before he graduated he was invited to become president of Pacific (later George Fox) College, though he continued for a year as pastor of the South 8th Street Friends Church in Richmond before moving to Oregon in 1911. Four Pacific College presidents in the previous decade had struggled to raise money and buildings. Pennington faced the same needs and those for state accreditation; both demanded many journeys east. Enrollment fell from forty-one to twenty-seven as World War I drew students away.

In 1919–20 he was given leave to be "minister at large" for the Friends Forward Movement for Five Years Meeting, recruiting Quaker pastors and teachers as well as finances and thereafter students for Pacific College. He traveled among English and Irish Friends in 1930–31 and opposed the Oregon Yearly Meeting's withdrawal from the Five Years Meeting in 1926. Both he in 1941 and his successor Emmett Gulley in 1947 left the presidency after clashes in World War II with nonpacifist Edward Mott, superintendent of the Oregon Yearly Meeting.

Bibliography

A: *Rambling Recollections of Ninety Happy Years* (Portland, Oreg.: 1967); printed sermons and addresses; papers at George Fox College.

B: Ralph Beebe, *A Garden of the Lord: Oregon* (Newberg, Ore.: 1968); Donald McNichols, *Portrait of a Quaker: Levi T. Penington* (Newberg, Oreg.: 1980).

PICKETT, CLARENCE EVAN (19 October 1884, Cisna Park, IL—15 March 1965, Boise, ID). *Education*: High school, Glen Elder, KS; B.A., Penn College, 1910; B.D., Hartford Theological Seminary, 1913; Harvard University, 1922–23. *Career*: Minister: Toronto, Canada, 1913–17; Oskaloosa, IA, 1917–19; executive secretary, Young Friends Movement, 1919–22; professor of biblical literature, Earlham College, 1923–29; executive secretary, American Friends Service Committee (AFSC), 1929–50.

Clarence Evan Pickett was raised in a farming community of Iowa Gurneyite Quakers. While attending William Penn College he resolved to become a minister and, along with his lifelong friend Alexander Purdy*, attended Hartford Theological Seminary. After brief pastorates complicated by Pickett's pacifist stance in World War I, he became secretary to the Young Friends, a group interested in peace, social reconstruction, and unity among Quakers. After a year in graduate study at Harvard, he taught at Earlham College. From 1929 until his death, he played a crucial role in the work of the AFSC, first as executive secretary and, after his retirement in 1950, as honorary executive secretary.

In his years with the AFSC, Pickett supervised programs relieving families of textile strikers in North Carolina, settled coal miners in homestead communities, provided relief in Europe after 1935, worked in numerous peace campaigns, helped Japanese–Americans interned during World War II, and mediated between Jews and Arabs in Palestine. He consulted with President Hoover on relief to coal miners, ran a New Deal subsistence homestead program and advised Franklin and Eleanor Roosevelt about aid programs, and talked with President Truman about civil rights and with John Kennedy about the Peace Corps. Pickett helped develop the Quaker program at the United Nations, served as cochairman of the Committee for a Sane Nuclear Policy (SANE), and sought at the height of the Cold War to improve relations between the two superpowers.

In 1950 he published an autobiographical account of his twenty-two years with the Service Committee, which provides a clear statement of how the Quaker Peace Testimony influenced his work.

Bibliography

A: *For More Than Bread: An Autobiographical Account of Twenty-two Years' Work with the American Friends Service Committee* (Boston: 1950).
B: DQB; *Clarence Pickett: A Memoir*, ed. Walter Kahoe, (1966).

PURDY, ALEXANDER C. (1890, West Laurens, NY—10 April 1976, Swarthmore, PA). *Education*: B.A., Penn College, 1910; B.D., 1913, Ph.D., 1916, Hartford Theological Seminary, D.D., 1960, Penn College; LL.D., 1964, Swarthmore College. *Career*: New Testament scholar.

As the son of pastor Ellison Purdy, Alexander had many boyhood homes and, being too shy to teach, channeled his Quaker faith and integrity into his scholarship. After learning textual and historical disciplines at Hartford, he taught Bible and church history at Earlham from 1916 to 1923, although he was released in 1919–20 for Quaker relief work in Germany. He had been brought in to help and then to replace Elbert Russell*, but Purdy, too, met the conservatives' growing fear of "higher criticism." He tried to lead students through biblical text skills to more solid knowledge of Christ. A Yearly Meeting "Committee on Earlham," meeting on neutral ground at the First Friends Church under Edgar Nicholson, cleared him and the college of unsoundness but left Purdy willing to accept in 1923 Hartford's call to teach the New Testament. There he continued as Hosmer Professor from 1933 and as dean from 1954 until his retirement in 1960. A dozen per year of the best minds among future Quaker pastors and teachers had taken his biblical seminars. From 1960 until his second retirement in 1965, he added his weight and grace to the new Earlham School of Religion. He retired to Swarthmore and Buck Hill Falls, Pennsylvania, where for decades he had remained a director of the Fox Howe Association in the Poconos.

Bibliography

A: *The Way of Christ* (New York: 1918); *Pathways to God* (New York: 1922); *Jesus' Way with People* (New York: 1926); with G. H. C. MacGregor, *Jew and Greek, Tutors unto Christ* (New York: 1936); *Commentary on Hebrews for the Interpreters Bible*; many published addresses, study guides, and so on.
B: *Quaker Life*, June 1976; Opal Thornburg, *Earlham* (Richmond, Ind.: 1963).

R

RUSSELL, ELBERT. (29 August, 1871, Friendsville, TN—21 September, 1951, St. Petersburg, FL). *Education*: Friendsville, TN, school; West Newton, IN, school and high school, 1879–90; B. A. (German), Earlham, 1890–95; Ph.D. (New Testament), University of Chicago, 1901–3. *Career*: Bible professor; seminary dean.

Russell's mother and his father, a poet, sawmiller, and schoolteacher, died when he was eight; he was raised on a hoosier grandfather's farm. At college he studied the German and Gothic languages. His vacations at college were sawmilling and biking in the Tennessee hills. He was already clerk of his Preparative Meeting at eighteen. He had married his high school friend Lieuetta Cox when suddenly President J. J. Mills asked him to stay on to teach at Earlham. The next year, 1896, he was asked to replace Dougan Clark* as Professor of Bible and was sent to Moody Bible Institute and Chautauqua to learn Hebrew. He used historical and language skills to seek personalities within the Bible. After five years of teaching he insisted on full graduate work at Chicago. He returned to Earlham a liberal in theology and concerned for social ministry as well as missions. William Pinkham accused Russell of not believing in the devil. In 1909 the Russells and their two children visited English and Irish Friends and lectured. In 1914 he ran for Congress for Roosevelt's Progressive Party.

His concerns to liberalize Quakerism and keep Earlham Quaker led him and the West Richmond Meeting to propose building a large meeting-house on campus to serve also for Yearly Meeting session and for students, of whom he was chaplain. When this idea was rejected in 1915, both by President Kelly and by Indiana Friends through the Earlham Board, Russell resigned, going to teach and study at Johns Hopkins and in 1917 to direct the Woolman School, predecessor to Pendle Hill, in Swarthmore, Pennsylvania. In 1924–5 the Russells spent fifteen months in England, Germany, and Palestine, working for Woodbrooke College and the American Friends Service Committee (AFSC); he attended a Peace Congress in Berlin and a Life and Work movement interchurch conference at Stockholm. In 1926 he was invited to the new Duke University Divinity School and in 1928 to become its dean, in which post he remained until his retirement in 1951. He built up a personal library of Quaker works and began to write Quaker history. The Russells traveled throughout Asia in 1933–34 and took part in the Friends World Conference and the World Churches' Faith and Order and Life and Work conferences in 1937. The Russells retired to Florida, but he continued to teach and lecture until his death.

Bibliography

A: *Jesus of Nazareth in the Light of Today* (Philadelphia: 1909); *The Parables of Jesus* (New York: 1909); ''Paranomasia and Kindred Phenomena in the New Testament'' (Ph.D. thesis, University of Chicago, 1920); *The Beatitudes* (New York: 1929); *The Message of the Fourth Gospel* (Nashville: 1931); *Chapel Talks*, 2 vols. (Nashville: 1935, 1938); *History of Quakerism* (New York: 1942); *Elbert Russell, Quaker: An Autobiography* (Jackson, Tenn.: 1956).
B: Opal Thornburg, *Earlham* (Richmond, Ind.: 1963).

S

SAVERY, WILLIAM (14 September 1750—19 June 1804, Philadelphia). *Education*: Unknown. *Career*: Tanner; Quaker minister.

William Savery became one of the most famous Quaker ministers of the late eighteenth century. His father, also named William (1722–87), was a cabinet-maker whose furniture is now esteemed as among the finest produced in colonial America. There is no record of where young William Savery attended school, but in later life he supported education and appears to have been well read. From 1761 to 1771 he served an apprenticeship to a tanner and had sufficient capital to buy a tannery in 1778. Savery's *Journal* describes how he repudiated worldliness to become a strict Friend, began speaking in Meetings in 1779, and gained recognition as a minister in 1781. He traveled frequently in the ministry, but his absences did not result in business difficulties.

Savery's longest trip as a minister was in Europe from 1796 to 1798. In England most of his preaching was directed at non-Quakers, and thousands came to hear him speak. Several collections of his sermons, taken in shorthand without his permission, became popular reading. He influenced Elizabeth Gurney (later Fry*) in 1798 to become a plain Friend. When Abraham Shackleton of Ireland sought guidance over doubts about the divine inspiration of the wars in the Old Testament, Savery showed little sympathy with what he saw as nascent deism. Savery's preaching represents a synthesis of late eighteenth-century Quakerism—quietist inspiration, moderately evangelical in doctrine, traditional in the emphasis upon separation from the world, and inclusive in his vision of the potential spiritual unity among all Christians.

Bibliography

A: *Discourses Delivered by William Savery* . . . (London: 1806); *Seven Sermons and a Prayer* . . . (Philadelphia: 1808); *A Journal of the Life, Travels, and Religious Labours* . . . (London: 1844).
B: Francis Taylor, *Life of William Savery* (New York: 1925).

SCOTT, JOB (18 October 1751, Providence, RI—22 November 1793, Bali-
tore, Ireland). *Education*: Unknown. *Career*: Schoolteacher; doctor; Quaker
minister.

Job Scott was the most creative Quaker theologian in eighteenth-century America. His mother, who died when he was ten, was a Quaker who took him to
Meetings, but his father was irreligious. As a youth Scott attended Baptist
services, but his mystical experiences, which began in childhood, convinced
him that the only true baptism was inward and spiritual. In 1771 Scott joined
the Friends and first spoke in 1774. He conducted schools in Providence in 1774
and at Smithfield in 1778; he moved in 1783 to Gloucester, where he may have
practiced medicine. As a minister Scott frequently visited families, supported
the strengthening of the Discipline, and refused to pay war taxes or use paper
money during the Revolution. He visited friends in three extended journeys: in
1784 to Vermont and the Hudson River Valley, in 1786 to Pennsylvania and
New Jersey, and in 1793 to Europe. While traveling in Ireland, he contracted
smallpox and died.

Scott was a quietist who saw all outward means—including the Bible, reason,
learning—as either irrelevant or a hindrance to salvation. Crucial for him was
the experience of the inward Christ who was born anew in purity in every
Christian. Christ's new birth and sufferings within each person recapitulated
events in the life of Jesus. Scott refused to use the term *Trinity* as creating three
gods, denigrated the historic atonement, and denied any distinction between
justification and sanctification. Creeds stood in the way of God. Like Elias
Hicks*, Scott made the Inward Light the entire substance of faith. During his
lifetime there was no opposition to Scott's beliefs, but his frank statements in
his *Journal* (1797) brought opposition from evangelicals.

Bibliography

A: *Journal of the Life, Travels, and Gospel Labours of Job Scott* and *The Works of . . .
    Job Scott* (Philadelphia: 1831), in two volumes.
B: *DAB*; DQB; Henry W. Wilbur, *Job Scott an Eighteenth Century Friend* (Philadelphia:
    1911); Rufus Jones, *Later Periods of Quakerism* (London: 1921).

SHARPLESS, ISAAC (16 December 1848, Birmingham, PA—16 January
1920, Haverford, PA). *Education*: Westtown School; B.S., Harvard, 1873;
Sc.D., University of Pennsylvania, 1883. *Career*: Teacher of science, Westtown
School, 1867–68, 1873–75; instructor and then professor of mathematics and
astronomy, 1875–84; dean, 1884–87; and president, 1887–1917, Haverford College.

Isaac Sharpless was an early leader of the liberal movement in the Philadelphia
Yearly Meeting (Orthodox). He was reared in an Orthodox Quaker family and
went directly from student to teacher at Westtown School. His first publications
were textbooks in geometry (1879), astronomy (1882), and natural philosophy
(1900). At Haverford College he became almost a second founder—recruiting

an able faculty, revolutionizing the treatment of students, tightening entrance standards, raising money, and improving the facilities. Under his leadership Haverford became a modern college. Sharpless edited and wrote for the first Quaker periodical devoted to educational reform, and he spent 1891–92 in Britain studying English educational methods. His histories of colonial Pennsylvania contained much valuable information and showed the contrast between early Friends and their nineteenth-century descendants. Sharpless helped found and served as president of the Friends Historical Association.

Although raised as an evangelical, Sharpless as an adult came to accept the liberal positions of using biblical criticism, advocating involvement in politics and broadening the peace Testimony. He worked with the Hicksites in the interest of Quaker unity. As a minister as well as a college president, Sharpless used his influence to persuade the Philadelphia Yearly Meeting (Orthodox) to endorse minicipal reform, international arbitration, and the social gospel.

Bibliography

A: *A Quaker Experiment in Government* (Philadelphia: 1898); *The Quakers in the Revolution* (Philadelphia: 1899); *Two Centuries of Pennsylvania History* (Philadelphia: 1900); *Quakerism and Politics* (Philadelphia: 1905); *A Quaker Boy on the Farm and at School* (Philadelphia: 1908); "Quakers in Pennsylvania," in *Quakers in the American Colonies*, by Rufus Jones, (London: 1911); *The American College* (New York: 1915); *The Story of a Small College* (Philadelphia: 1918); *Political Leaders of Provincial Pennsylvania* (New York: 1919).

B: "Isaac Sharpless," *Bulletin of Friends Historical Society* 9 (May 1920): 90–99, contains a complete bibliography. See also *DAB*; DQB; Rufus Jones, *Haverford College* (New York: 1933), 60–93; Philip Benjamin, *Philadelphia Quakers in the Industrial Age* (Philadelphia: 1976).

SMITH, HANNAH WHITALL (7 February 1832, Philadelphia—1 May 1911, London). *Education*: Philadelphia Friends schools. *Career*: Religious writer.

Hannah Whitall's father, a strict Orthodox Friend, pioneered in a glass-blowing industry that grew to provide support for an extended family and a vocation for two decades for her handsome young husband, Robert Piersall Smith, descended from James Logan*. They lived thirteen years in Germantown and Philadelphia, began to raise a boy and a girl (the girl and later three more children died), and left Friends in 1859 following conversion experiences. At Millville, New Jersey, where they lived in 1864–69 to direct a glass works, they accepted the doctrine of instant total Holiness from Methodist workers; Hannah also began to believe in "restitution," the universal offering of salvation in this life or the next, and that "a happy life" depended on the will, not the emotions. Robert, intensely emotional in both religion and family life, went through two severe times of depression. His "rest trip" to England in 1873 suddenly drew them both into two years of leading evangelical meetings at Broadlands House, in Oxford, and in Brighton (he also drew elite crowds in Berlin and Switzerland), which ended just as abruptly after his involvement with a woman disciple. Meanwhile, Hannah's articles for Robert's journal, printed as *The Christian's Secret of a Happy Life*, became a religious classic. After she spent a decade preaching, writing, and speaking for temperance, the family moved permanently to England, where her son Logan Piersall Smith found fame as a writer, and her two daughters, Mary and Alys, married Frank Costelloe, Bernhard Berenson, and Bertrand Russell, and the family became friends with Walt Whitman, Henry and William James, and George Bernard Shaw. She continued to write religious books.

Bibliography

A: *The Christian's Secret of a Happy Life* (New York: 1875); *Everyday Religion, or the Common-Sense Teaching of the Bible*, (New York: 1893); *Child Culture* (New York: 1894); *John M. Whitall* (biography, 1879); *The Unselfishness of God* (autobiography, New York: 1903); *God of All Comfort* (New York: 1906); *Religious Fanaticism* (London: 1928).

B: Logan Pearsall Smith, *Unforgotten Years* (Boston: 1939); idem, ed., *Philadelphia Quaker: The Letters of Hannah Whitall Smith* (New York: 1950); Robert Allerton Parker, *The Transatlantic Smiths* (New York: 1959); Barbara Strachey, *Remarkable Relations* (London: 1981); B: Marie Henry, *The Secret Life of Hannah Whitall Smith* (Grand Rapids, Mich.: 1984)

T

TRUEBLOOD, BENJAMIN FRANKLIN (25 November 1847, Salem, IN—28 October 1916, Newton Highlands, MA. *Education*: Friends Blue River Academy, IN; A.B., Earlham, 1869. *Career*: President, Wilmington and Penn Colleges; general secretary, American Peace Society.

Trueblood came from the same southern Indiana Quaker farm village as Joseph Moore*. An expert in French and German, he taught Greek and Latin at Penn College, Iowa, 1870–74; married Sarah Terrell; and was called to be president of Wilmington College, Ohio, 1874–79, and of Penn College, Iowa, 1879–90, being the key person in building academically these just-opened Quaker colleges. While in Iowa, he wrote on "Ministers' Wages" for *The Christian Worker*, in support of John Henry Douglas's* program of paying pastors from a central fund. He took part in the Richmond Conference of 1887, supporting paid pastorates against Joseph Beuan Braithwaite.

After a year traveling and speaking in Europe on international arbitration, 1890–91, he served as general secretary of the American Peace Society, 1892–1915, living mostly near Boston but attending annually national peace congresses and speaking widely. He pioneered the methods of rational, persuasive, long-term lobbying in Washington later used by the American Friends Service Committee (AFSC) and the Friends Committee on National Legislation (FCNL).

Bibliography

A: *William Penn's Holy Experiment* (Boston: 1895); *The Federation of the World* (Boston: 1899; many editions); *The Historic Development of the Peace Idea* (pamphlet, Boston: 1906, many editions): *International Arbitration at the Opening of the Twentieth Century* (Boston: 1909). Trueblood's papers: those of his daughter and secretary, Lydia T. Wolkins; and those of the American Peace Society are in the Swarthmore College Peace Collection, Swarthmore, Pa.

B: George Selleck, *Quakers in Boston, 1656–1964* (Cambridge, Mass.: 1976); Paul Minear, *Richmond, 1887: A Quaker Drama Unfolds* (Richmond, Ind.: 1987).

U

UPDEGRAFF, DAVID BRAINERD (1830, Mt. Pleasant, OH—23 May 1894, Mt. Pleasant). *Education*: Local Ohio schools; Haverford College; *Career*: Preacher of instantaneous, entire Holiness. (For his experiences see Chapter 16.)

David's father's family, who came as Mennonites to Germantown, Pennsylvania, with Pastorius, carried the first protest against slavery to Monthly and Quarterly Meetings and settled as millers in Mt. Pleasant; his mother, Rebecca, friend of revivalist Charles G. Finney, named David after the missionary Brainerd, converted in the Great Awakening. David's first wife, also Rebecca, was present at his conversion in a Methodist revival in 1860. The Wilburites disowned him in 1865. His second wife, Eliza, a Presbyterian minister's daughter, asked for a Church wedding, for which David was briefly disowned by the Gurneyites, too, in 1867.

Updegraff was still a farmer and businessman, dissatisfied with his own lukewarmness, when he came to know John S. Inskip, preacher of Holiness. After Updegraff's own experience of sudden, entire sanctification by the Spirit in 1869, he became an intense preacher at Inskip's summer camp Meetings in eastern Holiness centers. Thereafter he went wherever Quaker revivals broke out, especially in Iowa and Ohio, often splitting Meetings over Holiness doctrines. He also became a biblical literalist, persuading the Ohio Yearly Meeting that the doctrine of "the Inner Light" would mean that every person had the Spirit. He was baptized by a Baptist pastor in 1882. Updegraff's baptizing and urging baptism on other Friends led to intense conflict within the Ohio Yearly Meeting, which in 1885 refused to condemn him. Other Yearly Meetings called the 1887 Richmond Conference to unite against "Ordinances." Updegraff's last years were spent editing the *Friends' Expositor* to defend his doctrines and ensuring their toleration in the Ohio Yearly Meeting.

Bibliography

A: *The Ordinances, and the Position of Friends* (Columbus, Ohio: 1885); *Old Corn, or Sermons and Addresses* (Boston: 1892).

B: Dougan Clark and Joseph H. Smith, *David B. Updegraff and His Work* (Cincinnati: 1895); J. Brent Bill, *David B. Updegraff: Ohio Holiness Preacher* (Richmond, Ind.: 1983); Paul Minear, *Richmond, 1887* (Richmond, Ind: 1987).

V

VAUX, ROBERTS (21 January 1786, Philadelphia—7 January 1836, Philadelphia). *Education*: Friends Academy, Philadelphia. *Career*: Social reformer.

Son of a prominent Philadelphia Quaker family, Roberts Vaux at age twenty-six, possessing a substantial inherited fortune, left business and devoted himself to a wide variety of philanthropic endeavors. Best remembered for his work in fostering private charity and creating the free public education system in Philadelphia, Vaux saw in educational institutions a method of ending illiteracy and promoting virtue among the poor. Vaux wanted to provide free education, and he at first worked to encourage the use of English Quaker Joseph Lancaster's monitorial system; he became increasingly convinced of the need for public tax support. From 1818 to 1831 Vaux served as the first president of the Board of Controllers of the school system.

As a member of the Quaker-dominated Prison Reform Society, Vaux took an active role in their efforts to change prisons into penitentiaries—institutions where criminals would learn to be sorry for their misdeeds and change their way of living. Reformation would be fostered by a program of manual labor, solitude, and regular visitation of inmates by members of the Prison Society and other respectable people. Vaux lobbied the state legislature to build a model penitentiary, the Eastern State Prison, which opened in 1830. Vaux also persuaded the state to build a juvenile reformatory to separate children from adult criminals.

Convinced that the upper classes needed to be reminded of the simple moral living of their ancestors, Vaux wrote biographies of earlier antislavery reformers and helped found the Historical Society of Pennsylvania, the Philadelphia Athenaeum, and the Academy of Natural Sciences. He supported the Pennsylvania Abolition Society, wrote many articles on improving farming methods, served on the boards of the Pennsylvania Hospital and Friends Asylum at Frankfort, and helped create the Apprentice's Library and the Philadelphia Savings Fund

Society. Increasingly fearful that pamphlets, voluntary organizations, and good works were ineffective, Vaux turned to politics and scandalized his conservative friends by becoming a supporter of Jacksonian Democrats. In 1832 he declined appointment as commissioner to deal with Indian removals and in 1834 refused to join the Bank of the United States. In 1835 he became associate of the Court of Common Pleas. Vaux, uninterested in theology and alienated from the business orientation of Philadelphia, illustrates the continuing eighteenth-century Quaker concern with social justice.

Bibliography

A: *Memoirs of the Lives of Benjamin Lay and Ralph Sandiford* (Philadelphia: 1815); *Memoirs of the Life of Anthony Benezet* (Philadelphia: 1817); *Memoir of the Locality of the Great Treaty between William Penn and the Indian Natives in 1682* (Philadelphia: 1825); *Notices of the Original and Successive Efforts to Improve the Discipline of the Prison at Philadelphia* (Philadelphia: 1826); *Letter on the Penitentiary System of Pennsylvania* (Philadelphia: 1827); *Reply to Two Letters of William Roscoe . . . on the Penitentiary System of Pennsylvania* (Philadelphia: 1827); *Memoir of Benjamin Lay* (New York: 1842).

B: *DAB*; DQB; Joseph McCadden, *Education in Pennsylvania, 1801–1835, and Its Debt to Roberts Vaux* (Philadelphia; 1937); R. N. Ryon, "Roberts Vaux: A Biography of a Reformer" (Ph.D. diss., Pennsylvania State University, 1966).

W

WHITTIER, JOHN GREENLEAF (17 December 1807, Haverhill, MA—7 September 1892, Hampton Falls, NH). *Education*: Haverhill Academy, 1827–28; LL.D., Harvard, 1881. *Career*: Journalist; poet; editor: *American Manufacturer, Haverhill Gazette, New England Review*, 1829–32; *Pennsylvania Freeman*, 1838–40; *Middlesex Standard*, 1844–45; *National Era*, 1847–60; member, MA legislature, 1835.

John Greenleaf Whittier became the most famous nineteenth-century American Quaker, respected by Orthodox and Hicksites who rejoiced in his celebrity as an advocate of morality and inward spirituality. Whittier was the child of a poor family of Quaker farmers of Haverhill, Massachusetts. At home he immersed himself in the Bible, living the stories of the Old and New Testament in his imagination and absorbing the Bible's language and cadences. He also learned of New England's history and legends and the stories of the early Quaker martyrs. At age fourteen Whittier began writing verses. William Lloyd Garrison published Whittier's first poem in 1826 and persuaded the parents to allow their son to gain a quick classical education by spending two terms at Haverhill Academy.

Strongly influenced by Byron, Burns, and Wordsworth, Whittier began producing a large number of poems—more than eighty were published in local newspapers. During the next few years Whittier entered society and edited several new England newspapers. Fascinated with politics, Whittier became a politician and attempted in 1832 to become a candidate for Congress. Although he later served one term in the Massachusetts legislature, Whittier's great political skill came in the back-room negotiations necessary for success.

In 1833 Whittier set aside his chances for a career in politics by publishing his tract directed at obtaining the immediate and unconditional emancipation of slaves. For the next twelve years Whittier became an effective propagandist for antislavery—writing poems and essays, speaking, and editing leading abolitionist journals. His notoriety was second only to that of William Lloyd Garrison, and in 1835 in Concord, New Hampshire, he was mobbed and stoned. When during a riot in Philadelphia in 1838 a mob wrecked and burned Pennsylvania Hall, a building that served as a headquarters for abolition activities, Whittier disguised himself in order to enter the burning structure to save the galleys of his newspapers.

Whittier and Garrison disagreed upon the necessity of political action. Garrison preached nonresistance and attacked all evils at once. Whittier decided antislavery needed a political vehicle and in 1839 helped found the Liberty Party. He also worked to ensure that Massachusetts' politicians supported antislavery not only at home but in Washington. Whittier helped persuade Charles Sumner to run for the Senate to succeed Webster; he was an advisor to Fremont in his first Republican try for the presidency and was listened to respectfully by Massachusetts' senators during the Civil War and Reconstruction.

After 1840 the ill health that haunted Whittier most of his adult life forced him to retire to a house in Amesbury, Massachusetts. During the 1850s Whitter's poetry celebrated rural life in New England by drawing upon its history and traditions in "Skipper Ireson's Ride" and "The Double-Headed Snake of Newbury." Whitter, like other Quakers during the Civil War, was caught with divided loyalties: hating war, affirming his love of union, and desiring the end of slavery.

In 1866 Whittier published "Snow Bound," a poem recreating winter life in the New England home of his parents. Both it and the "Tent on the Beach" celebrated a nostalgic life before industrialism that appealed to many Americans tired of stresses caused by war and social change. These poems were artistic and financial successes and, in company with Emerson, Lowell, and Longfellow, Whittier was acclaimed a major American poet.

Whittier's religion centered upon experience and not theology; his poems interpreted Quaker quietism, Hicksite universalism, and rationalism, and evangelical reverence for Christ and the Bible. His poems expressed anguish over unjust suffering and the tensions between doubt and faith. He attended Meetings regularly, but he is never known to have spoken in a Meeting, and he disliked much preaching. He remained a member of New England Yearly Meeting (Orthodox) but openly associated with Hicksites, who supported Garrison, and disapproved of the emergence of paid ministers and revivalism among western Friends. Still, he never knowingly attended a Hicksite meeting for worship. Whittier seems to have believed in the Trinity, but he was not much concerned with theories of atonement, creeds, or the inerrancy of Scripture. The Bible was a source of Truth, but it provided confirmation of an inward knowledge rather than being the ground of that experience. Whittier also was not bothered by Charles Darwin and higher or historical criticism of the Bible. Whittier's influence paved the way for the emergence of liberalism among Gurneyite Quakers.

Today critics rank Whittier's poetic gifts below those of Walt Whitman and Emily Dickinson. What modern scholars define as weaknesses—Whittier's sub-

ordination of his art to religious purposes, his moralism, and his sentimentality—
were features that attracted the Victorians.

Bibliography

A: *Songs of Labor* (Boston: 1850); *Home Ballads* (Boston: 1860); *Snow Bound: A Winter
   Idyl* (Boston: 1866); *Tent on the Beach* (Boston: 1867); *Among the Hills* (Boston:
   1869); *Pennsylvania Pilgrim and Other Poems* (Boston: 1872); *The King's Missive
   and Other Poems* (Boston: 1881); *The Writings of John Greenleaf Whittier*, 7 vols.
   (Boston: 1888–89).
B: John B. Pickard, *John Greenleaf Whittier: An Introduction and Interpretation* (New
   York: 1961); Edward Wagenknecht, *John Greenleaf Whittier: A Portrait in Paradox*
   (New York: 1967).

WILBUR, JOHN (17 July 1774, Hopkinton, RI—1 June 1856, Hopkinton).
Education: Unknown. *Career*: Farmer; land surveyor.

John Wilbur's *Journal* describes his parents as devout Quakers and, while
providing no details about his formal education, indicates that at age eighteen
he became a schoolteacher. Wilbur became an Elder in 1802 and a minister in
1812. He saw the supporters of Elias Hicks* as undermining belief in the atonement, the divinity of Jesus, and the necessity of Scriptures. In the aftermath of
the separations beginning in 1827, Wilbur detected in New England and England
a response against the so-called idolatries of Hicks leading to an overemphasis
on the outward and historical forms and a weakening of the experience of the
indwelling of the Holy Spirit.

On a visit to Europe between 1831 and 1833 Wilbur joined English quietists
Thomas Shillitoe, Sarah Grubb, and Ann Jones in opposing the evangelicals.
Wilbur's letters to George Crosfield, published in 1832, provided a summary of
the quietist position that true worship required a slow inward purification and
growth in grace. Wilbur disliked reasoning about religion, foreign missions,
Sunday schools, Bible societies, and cooperation with non-Quakers. He saw
Joseph John Gurney*, Elisha Bates*, and the Beaconites as Satan's emissaries
working to subvert true spiritual religion.

When Gurney visited America in 1838, Wilbur sought unsuccessfully to persuade him to recant and go home. So Wilbur in his traveling ministry publicly
denounced Gurney. The evangelicals in the New England Yearly Meeting, outraged by Wilbur's attacks on a fellow minister, attempted to silence him. After
the South Kingston Monthly Meeting, where Wilbur belonged, refused to discipline him, a committee of the Yearly Meeting persuaded the Quarterly Meeting
to dissolve South Kingston and join its members to Greenwich Meeting. In 1843
Greenwich disowned Wilbur. When the New England Yearly Meeting affirmed
the decision, Wilbur and approximately 500 supporters formed a competing
Yearly Meeting. Wilbur journeyed to England, New York, and Pennsylvania
seeking supporters.

The London Yearly Meeting repudiated Wilbur and supported the evangelicals.
The Philadelphia Yearly Meeting (Orthodox) was so divided that after 1857

organizational unity was maintained only by refusing to recognize officially any other Yearly Meeting. The Ohio Yearly Meeting (Orthodox) in 1854 had a major separation over whether to recognize Gurneyite or Wilburite traveling ministers.

Bibliography

A: *Letters to a Friend, on Some of the Primitive Doctrines of Christianity* (London: 1832); *A Narrative and Exposition of the Late Proceedings of New England Yearly Meeting* (New York: 1845); *A Letter Dated, Manchester, 12 month, 1853* (Manchester NH?: 1853); *A Few Remarks upon the Controversy between Good and Evil* (Boston: 1855); *Journal of the Life of John Wilbur* (Providence, R.I.: 1859).
B: *JLP* Vol. 1, 511–15; William Hodgson, *The Society of Friends in the Nineteenth Century* (Philadelphia. 1875–76).

WILSON, E[DWARD] RAYMOND 20 September 1896, Morning Sun, IA— 27 June 1987, Sandy Spring, MD. *Education*: Country school; Morning Sun High School; Monmouth College, 1915–16; Great Lakes Naval Training Station, 1917–18; B.A. Iowa State College (University), 1921 M.A. religious education, Teachers College, 1925; Ph.D. except thesis, Columbia University, 1925–26 on Lydia Roberts Fellowship; LL.D., Haverford, 1958. *Career*: Executive secretary, Pennsylvania Committee on Militarism in Education, 1927–31; staff of Peace Section, American Friends Service Committee AFSC, 1931–42; executive secretary, Friends Committee on National Legislation (FCNL), after 1962, emeritus.

Wilson became the pioneer religious lobbyist of this century by never losing the style, drawl, and social idealism of a third-generation Iowa farmer, of which he was full time only in 1914–15 and most of 1927–29. He was raised a ''Covenanter'' Presbyterian; a year preparing for Navy service did not change his ideas, but the Student YMCA and Student Volunteer Movement turned him to Christian service and pacifism. While at New York's Teachers College he lived at the International House; for 1926–27 he won the Japanese Brotherhood Scholarship, a response to America's Japanese Exclusion Act, which gave Wilson a year to travel throughout Japan and Formosa and study village cultures. After his father's death and a part-time job trying to restrict militarism in education in compulsory ROTCs, he traveled in Europe in 1930. Wilson returned there with his bride, Miriam Davidson, in 1932 and for Quaker seminars in 1938 and 1940. Throughout the 1930s Wilson built up the Institutes of International Relations program of the AFSC, being dean for eleven of them. The Wilsons were founding members of the Bryan Gweled cooperative community in Bucks Country Pennsylvania, in 1942, but the Draft and World War II called him to Washington to negotiate for alternative service for Conscientious objectors.

In 1943 the constant, growing concerns of a Friends War Problems Committee, and the desire to center AFSC on tax-free service, led to the forming of the Friends Committee on National Legislation on Capitol Hill. Although Wilson was executive secretary over a growing staff, he kept personal contact with hundreds of senators and congressmen, providing detailed information on paper and in person to them and to Quaker constituents throughout America (notably by a monthly Washington newsletter), teaching and drawing together lobbyists from other Church groups as they arose and campaigning for years at a time for ending the Draft, the Korean and Vietnam Wars, and nuclear testing and weapons; guiding and encouraging the formation of Food Relief Programs, the Peace Corps, the Arms Control and Disarmament Agency, and "law of the sea" treaties; and protecting civil liberties and Indian rights. Wilson formally joined the Friends in 1936, becoming a tireless delegate, officer, and resolution writer in the Federal and National Councils of Churches.

Bibliography

A: *Thus Far on My Journey* (Richmond, Ind.: 1976); *Uphill for Peace: Quaker Impact on Congress* [history of FCNL] (Richmond, Ind.: 1985); articles (many unsigned) in FCNL's *Washington Newsletter*.

WOODWARD, WALTER C. (28 November 1878, Mooresville, IN—14 April 1942, Richmond, IN). *Education*: Friends Pacific Academy, Newberg, OR; B.A., Pacific College, 1898; B.LL., Earlham, 1899; M.A. 1908, Ph.D. 1910, University of California. *Career*: Teacher; editor; General Secretary of Five Years Meeting. (See Chapter 18.)

Woodward's family moved to the Chehalem Valley in Oregon when he was two; he grew up, studied, worked on the town newspaper, and taught in that evangelical Quaker community, apart from his years of graduate study in history, until 1910. From 1910 to 1917 he taught history at Earlham, later serving as board chairman. He married in 1912, raising three daughters. In 1917 he was asked to take over as editor of *The American Friend* (which he remained until his death in 1942) and to be general secretary of the Five Years Meeting (until 1928). His life work was the effort to unite Friends of all branches and make worldwide ties to other Churches. He tried in vain to raise a multimillion dollar Friends Forward Movement fund for missions and colleges. He attended the first World Conference of Friends in London in 1920 and took part in planning of the interchurch Faith and Order conferences, revisiting Europe in 1930. At his memorial services in Indiana and Oregon, tributes to his wit, warmth, and Christian dedication came from fellow editor Rufus Jones * and both evangelical and liberal Quaker leaders. Yet his effort to increase the central effectiveness of the Five Years Meeting had met intense resistance from "Holiness" Quakers of Oregon and Kansas Yearly Meetings, who withdrew from that body.

Bibliography

A: Rise and Early History of Political Parties in Oregon, 1843–1863 (Ph.D. diss., University of California, 1910); *The American Friend* (now *Quaker Life*, 1917–42; *Friendly Tales of Foreign Trails* (Richmond, Ind.: 1921); *Timothy Nicholson—Master Quaker* (Richmond, Ind.: 1927). The manuscript of his unpublished history of "sleepers," "Pullman's Progress" (1927), and his papers and letters are in the Earlham archives, Richmond, Ind.

B: *American Friend*, May 7, 1942, 190–210.

WOOLMAN, JOHN (19 October 1720, Burlington Co., NJ—8 October 1772). *Education*: Unknown. *Career*: Farmer; tailor; schoolmaster. (See Chapter 11).

Bibliography

A: *Journal and Major Essays of John Woolman*, ed. Amelia Mott Gummere (New York: 1922); *Journal and Major Essays of John Woolman*, ed. Phillips P. Moulton (New York: 1971).

B: Janet Whitney, *John Woolman, American Quaker* (Boston: 1942); Edwin H. Cady, *John Woolman* (New York: 1965); Paul Rosenblatt, *John Woolman* (New York: 1969); Henry J. Cadbury, *John Woolham in England: A Documentary History*, Supplement 32, *Journal of the Friends Historical Society* (London: 1971).

APPENDIX: CHRONOLOGY

Quaker Events	Dates	American Religious Events
Fox born (Puritans blocked by King Charles I).	1624–25	Virginia and Plymouth colonies founded.
English separatists and baptists emerge.	1630–40	Massachusetts Bay, Connecticut, and Maryland founded.
Fox "seeker" (future Friends in Puritan army in English Civil War beat king).	1642–47	E. Hutchinson, R. Williams in Rhode Island; Dutch in New York and New Jersey.
Fox and Friends in English Midlands.	1647–51	Congregational Platform, Massachusetts.
Quaker "Awakening" in Northwest England.	1652–53	
Quaker Mission throughout England and Ireland.	1654–55	Jesuit mission, Ontario.
Nayler's fall; England turns conservative.	1656–57	Quakers in Boston, New York, and Maryland.
Quakers in Holland, France, Mediterranean.	1658–59	Flushing Remonstrance, New York.
Quaker Act follows Restoration of Charles II.	1660–61	Mary Dyer hanged in Boston.
Quakers jailed under Clarendon Code; most leaders die; Conventicle Act; Penn, Barclay convinced.	1662–67	English capture New York, New Jersey; found Delaware and Carolina.
Organization of Quaker Meetings; Second Conventicle Act.	1667–74	
Quakers found West Jersey; Penn pleads for toleration in England.	1675	

Penn founds Pennsylvania; final English persecution.	1680–82	"Half-Way Covenant," Massachusetts.
"Glorious Revolution" vs. James II: Act of Toleration.	1688–89	Mennonites to Pennsylvania.
Philadelphia Yearly Meeting issues first book of Discipline.	1704	Anglican SPCK mission sends George Keith to America.
Pennsylvania Assembly keeps peace testimony.	1737–42	"Great Awakening."
Woolman and Pennsylvania Quaker reformers forbid slavery.	1754–63	French War: Pennsylvania Quakers resign.
Quakers neutral; migrate to Hudson Valley, Piedmont.	1764–82	Churches back American Revolution.
Quakers migrate to Ohio valley, Great Lakes, Indiana.	1782–1815	Second Awakening; 1812 War.
Hicksite-Evangelical separation: Philadelphia, New York, Ohio, Baltimore.	1827–28	Evangelical missions; Unitarian split.
Gurney, Grellet travel: Wilburite separation, Northeast; "underground railroad" and Indiana Antislavery Yearly Meeting.	1830–45	C. G. Finney's revivalism.
Wilburite-Gurneyite split: Ohio; migration to Iowa.	1845–56	Churches split North vs. South.
Quakers migrate to Kansas; divided on fighting.	1860–65	American Civil War.
Quaker revivals; missions; Indian work for President Grant; Updegraff and Douglas.	1867–79	Darwin; Dwight L. Moody; Holiness camp meetings.
Richmond Conference and Declaration; pastoral system.	1887	Student Volunteer Movement for Foreign Missions.
Oregon and California Yearly Meetings; American Friends Board of Foreign Missions.	1893–95	Holiness churches separated.
Friends General Conference; Five Years Meeting organized.	1900–02	Spanish American War.
Quakers into East Africa, Cuba, Jamaica, Alaska.	1902–14	Fundamentalism.
American Friends Service Committee founded.	1917	World War I; Federal Council of Churches.
All Friends Conferences: London; Swarthmore and Haverford.	1920;1937	World War I and Depression cut missions support.

Friends Committee on National Legislation; college meetings rise.	1943	World War II: Civilian Public Service camps.
Reunions of Philadelphia, New York, Baltimore, Canadian Yearly Meetings.	1955	Civil Rights movement.
Evangelical Friends Alliance; Friends United Meeting; Central America and East Africa Yearly Meetings.	1963	Vietnam War, Martin Luther King.
Faith and Life Movement; New Call to Peacemaking.	1970s	Antinuclear movement.

BIBLIOGRAPHIC ESSAY

The following guide to further research in American Quaker history is not an exhaustive bibliography. Additional citations on periods and regions are found in the chapter notes; biographies are listed in the Biographical Dictionary. Most dissertations are cited only in biographical entries or chapter notes.

GENERAL HISTORIES

The most comprehensive history of Quakers was planned as the "Rowntree Series," which, though now dated, remains the starting place for serious research: William C. Braithwaite, *The Beginnings of Quakerism* (London: Macmillan, 1912); revised by Henry J. Cadbury (Cambridge: Cambridge University Press, 1955), deals with the origins; Braithwaite's *Second Period of Quakerism* (London: Macmillan, 1919); revised by Henry Cadbury (Cambridge: Cambridge University Press, 1961), begins with the Restoration of 1660 and ends in the early eighteenth century. Rufus M. Jones, Amelia M. Gummere, and Isaac Sharpless, *Quakers in the American Colonies* (London: Macmillan, 1911; New York: Norton, 1966), continues the story until the American Revolution. Rufus Jones, *Later Periods of Quakerism*, 2 vols. (London: Macmillan, 1921), deals with events in England and America until World War I.

Among other histories, John Punshon, *Portrait in Grey: A Short History of the Quakers* (London: Quaker Home Service, 1984), is thoughtful and readable but more definitive on England than on America. Thorough and still useful is Elbert Russell, *The History of Quakerism* (New York: Macmillan, 1942; Friends United Press, 1979). Books with a historical overview and expressing a liberal, mystical theological perspective include Howard Brinton, *Friends for 300 Years* (New York: Harper, 1952; Wallingford, Pa.: Pendle Hill, 1965); A. Neave Brayshaw, *The Quakers: Their Story and Message* (London: George Allen & Unwin, 1927); and Elfrida Vipont, *The Story of Quakerism*, 2d ed. (London: Bannisdale, 1960). More evangelical emphases appear in D. Elton Trueblood, *The People Called Quakers* (New York: Harper & Row, 1966), and Walter R. Williams, *The Rich Heritage of Quakerism* (Grand Rapids, Mich.: Eerdmans, 1962; Newberg, Oreg.: Barclay Press, 1987).

BIBLIOGRAPHICAL WORKS

Joseph Smith, *Descriptive Catalogue of Friends' Books* (London: 1859); *Supplement to a Descriptive Catalogue of Friends Books* (London: 1892); and *Bibliotheca Anti-Quakeriana* (London: 1893) list all editions Smith knew of books by or against Friends. A few additional references can be found in Donald Wing's wider and more recent *Short Title Catalogue*, 3 vols. (New York: Columbia University Press, 1951). Smith's work should be supplemented by the *Catalog of the Books and Serials Collection of the Friends Historical Library, Swarthmore College*, 2 vols. (New York: 1982), and by Angela Turner, *A Bibliography of Quaker Literature, 1893–1967* (Ann Arbor, Mich.: Xerox University Microfilms, 1976), a guide to literature written about English Friends or published in Britain. The "Dictionary of Quaker Biography" (DQB), with copies at Friends House, London, and Haverford College, is a constantly growing unpublished compilation of biographies and sources on thousands of Friends. Genealogists and historians of local Meetings have been saved countless hours by the exhaustive tables of personal data from Meeting minutes in *The Encyclopedia of American Quaker Genealogy*, edited by William Wade Hinshaw in six volumes (1936–50), for all surviving nineteenth-century minutes from North Carolina, Ohio, and Virginia (and the oldest from near Philadelphia), continued in the six-volume *Abstracts of the Records of the Society of Friends in Indiana*, edited by Willard Heiss (Indianapolis: Indiana Historical Society, 1962–75).

PRIMARY SOURCES

Virtually complete collections of Quaker writings from all centuries are in the Library of Friends House, Euston Road, London, and the Quaker libraries at Haverford and Swarthmore Colleges. Historical magazines regularly printing early letters and manuscript documents are *The Bulletin of the Friends Historical Association*, now titled *Quaker History*, concentrating on American Friends, and the British *Journal of the Friends Historical Society*. Two excellent introductory collections of primary sources are Jessamyn West, *The Quaker Reader* (New York: Viking Press, 1962), and Douglas V. Steere, *Quaker Spirituality: Selected Writings* (New York: Paulist Press, 1984). Hugh Barbour and Arthur Roberts, eds., *Early Quaker Writings, 1650–1700* (Grand Rapids, Mich.: Eerdmans, 1973), presents journals and tracts parallel to William Penn's* works, George Fox's* *Journal*, and Robert Barclay's* *Apology*. Exhaustive scholarship on the manuscripts underlies *The Papers of William Penn*, vols. 1–4, ed. Mary Maples Dunn and Richard Dunn (Philadelphia: University of Pennsylvania Press, 1981–87); and vol. 5, ed. Edwin B. Bronner and David Fraser, summarizes and identifies editions of *William Penn's Published Writings 1660–1726*. Photoreprint editions are available of early editions of Fox's and Penn's works. The only edition of Robert Barclay's *Apology* in print is a modern-English version by Dean Freiday. *The Journal of George Fox*, ed. John L. Nickalls (Cambridge: Cambridge University Press, 1952), is the best one-volume edition. The scholarly edition of the original manuscript is *The Journal of George Fox*, 2 vols., ed. Norman Penney (Cambridge: Cambridge University Press, 1911). The endnotes in this edition of the *Journal*, the endnotes in Braithwaite's *Beginnings*, and Geoffrey Nuttall's summary and notes in *Early Quaker Letters from the Swarthmore MSS to 1660* are the best sources for minor Quaker personalities and seventeenth-century events.

QUAKERS IN SEVENTEENTH-CENTURY ENGLAND

Rufus Jones, *Spiritual Reformers in the 16th and 17th Centuries* (New York: Macmillan, 1914); idem, *Mysticism and Democracy in the English Commonwealth* (Cambridge, Mass.: Harvard University Press, 1923); and the introduction to *JQAC* trace what Jones saw as the mystical and Anabaptist forebears of Friends. Geoffrey Nuttall, *The Holy Spirit in Puritan Faith and Experience* (Oxford: Blackwell, 1946), emphasizes the similarities between Quakers and Puritans. An extension of this perspective is Hugh Barbour, *The Quakers in Puritan England* (New Haven: Yale University Press, 1964). Christopher Hill, *The World Turned Upside Down: Radical Ideas during the English Revolution* (New York: Viking, 1972); idem, *The Experience of Defeat* (New York: Viking, 1984); and Barry Reay, *The Quakers and the English Revolution* (London: Temple Smith, 1985), emphasize the close links between Quakers and other radical sectarians and the backlash of conservatives. The social class backgrounds of Friends are discussed in Alan Cole, "Quakers and Politics, 1652–1660" (Ph.D. thesis, Cambridge University, 1955), and Richard Vann, *The Social Development of English Quakerism, 1655–1755* (Cambridge, Mass.: Harvard University Press, 1969). Richard Bauman, *Let Your Words Be Few: Symbolism and Silence among Seventeenth-Century Quakers* (Cambridge: Cambridge University Press, 1983), uses linguistics to probe the inner experience of early Friends. For works on Fox, Penn, and Margaret Fell, see the dictionary entries in this volume. Other early Quaker leaders deserve biographies.

COLONIAL AMERICA

Sydney James, *A People among Peoples: Quaker Benevolence in Eighteenth-Century America* (Cambridge, Mass.: Harvard University Press, 1963), is much broader than its title and is the best one-volume study of the Friends in America from the 1650s until 1800. J. William Frost, *The Quaker Family in Colonial America: A Portrait of the Society of Friends* (New York: St. Martin's, 1973) also uses materials from all of the colonies. The account in *JQAC* on New England has been superseded by Arthur Worrall, *Quakers in the Colonial Northeast* (Hanover, N.H.: University Press of New England, 1980). Discussions of persecution and toleration in Massachusetts are in Kai Erikson, *Wayward Puritans* (New York: Wiley, 1966); Jonathan Chu, *Neighbors, Friends, or Madmen: The Puritan Adjustment to Quakerism* (Westport, Conn.: Greenwood Press, 1985); and Mary Hoxie Jones, *The Standard of the Lord Lifted Up: A History of Friends in New England from 1656–1700 . . .* (New England Yearly Meeting of Friends, 1961).

John Pomfret, *The Province of East Jersey, 1609–1702* (Princeton, N.J.: Princeton University Press, 1962), and idem, *The Province of West New Jersey, 1609–1702* (Princeton, N.J.: Princeton University Press, 1956), are the standard works on early New Jersey. Amelia Gummere, ed., *The Journal and Essays of John Woolman* (New York: MacMillan, 1922), contains much information on Friends in New Jersey. Historians generally treat New Jersey and Pennsylvania Friends as equivalent since they were in the same Yearly Meeting. There is no monograph detailing the political activities of Friends in New Jersey. For southern Friends, Kenneth Carroll, *Quakerism on the Eastern Shore* (Baltimore: Maryland Historical Records, 1970), supplements the discussion in Stephen Weeks, *Southern Quakers and Slavery* (Baltimore: Johns Hopkins University Press, 1896).

Literature on Penn in Pennsylvania flourished in the 1980s but his politics are of perennial interest.

Mary Maples Dunn, *William Penn: Politics and Conscience* (Princeton, N.J.: Princeton University Press, 1967), and Joseph Illick, *William Penn the Politician* (Ithaca, N.Y.: Cornell University Press, 1965), provide much information on Penn's efforts for toleration. Melvin Endy, *William Penn and Early Quakerism* (Princeton, N.J.: Princeton University Press, 1973), is an excellent study of Penn's theology. *The World of William Penn*, ed. Richard S. Dunn and Mary Maples Dunn (Philadelphia: University of Pennsylvania Press, 1986), contains a wide range of articles seeking to place Penn in context. Edwin B. Bronner, *William Penn's Holy Experiment* (New York: Temple University Press, 1962), and Gary Nash, *Quakers and Politics: Pennsylvania, 1680–1726* (Princeton, N.J.: Princeton University Press, 1968), are detailed accounts of the political and social developments in early Pennsylvania. *The Keithian Controversy in Early Pennsylvania*, ed. J. William Frost (Norwood, Pa.: Norwood Editions, 1980), reprints the documents of the separation.

Frederick B. Tolles, *Meeting House and Counting House* (Chapel Hill: University of North Carolina Press, 1948); idem, *Quakers and the Atlantic Culture* (New York: MacMillan, 1960); and idem, *James Logan and the Culture of Provincial America* (New York: Little, Brown, 1953), describe the cultural life of Pennsylvania Quakers and the tensions between religious purity and the pursuit of wealth. Alan Tully, *William Penn's Legacy: Politics and Social Structure in Pennsylvania, 1726–1755* (Baltimore: Johns Hopkins University Press, 1977), and Jack Marietta, "The Growth of Quaker Self-Consciousness in Pennsylvania, 1720–1748," in *Seeking the Light: Essays in Quaker History*, ed. J. William Frost and John M. Moore (Wallingford, Pa.: Pendle Hill Publications, 1986), 79–104, offer contrasting views of Quakers and Pennsylvania politics.

The only work discussing Quaker antislavery activities from the 1670s until the Civil War is Thomas Drake, *Quakers and Slavery* (New Haven: Yale University Press, 1950): Jean Soderlund, *Quakers and Slavery: A Divided Spirit* (Princeton, N.J.: Princeton University Press, 1985), shows when Middle Colony Friends began freeing slaves. *Quaker Origins of Antislavery*, ed. J. William Frost (Norwood, Pa.: Norwood Editions, 1980), and *Am I Not a Man and a Brother*, ed. Roger Bruns (New York: Chelsea, 1977), print the most important antislavery documents. J. William Frost, "The Origins of the Quaker Crusade against Slavery: A Review of Recent Literature," *Quaker History* 67 (Spring 1978): 42–58, summarizes existing scholarship. Hiram Hilty, *Toward Freedom for All: North Carolina Quakers and Slavery* (Richmond, Ind.: Friends United Press, 1984), adds information to Week's *Southern Quakers and Slavery* and discusses the entire pre–Civil War period.

The literature on the American Revolution and Pennsylvania is immense. The only books mentioned here focus primarily on Friends. Jack Marietta, *The Reformation of American Quakerism, 1748–1783* (Philadelphia: University of Pennsylvania Press, 1984), is the most comprehensive history but deals mainly with Pennsylvania. A different interpretation is found in Richard Bauman, *For the Reputation of Truth: Politics, Religion, and Conflict among the Pennsylvania Quakers, 1750–1800* (Baltimore: Johns Hopkins University Press, 1971). Arthur Mekeel, *The Relation of Quakers to the American Revolution* (Washington, D.C.: University Press of America, 1979), discusses Quakers in all colonies.

THE NINETEENTH CENTURY

Migration patterns are discussed in several dissertations cited in Chapter 13. Erroll T. Elliott, *Quakers on the American Frontier* (Richmond, Ind.: Friends United Press, 1969), tells the story of formation of new Yearly Meetings in the West. Errol Elliott, *Quaker Profiles from the American West* (Richmond, Ind.: 1972), deals with important Western leaders in the nineteenth and twentieth centuries.

Histories of individual Yearly Meetings include *Friends in the Delaware Valley*, ed. John M. Moore (Haverford, Pa.: Friends Historical Association, 1981); Bliss Forbush, *A History of Baltimore Yearly Meeting of Friends* (Sandy Springs, Md.: Baltimore Yearly Meeting, 1972); Seth B. Hinshaw, *The Carolina Quaker Experience, 1665–1985* (Greensboro, N.C.: North Carolina Friends Historical Society, 1984); William Taber, *Eye of Faith: A History of Ohio Yearly Meeting, Conservative* (Barnesville, Ohio: Representative Meeting of Ohio Yearly Meeting, 1985); Arthur O. Roberts, *The Association of Evangelical Friends: A Story of Quaker Renewal in the Twentieth Century* (Newberg, Oreg.: Barclay Press, 1975); Louis T. Jones, *The Quakers of Iowa* (Iowa City: State Historical Society of Iowa, 1914); John Buys, "Quakers in Indiana in the Nineteenth Century" (Ph.D. diss., University of Florida, 1973); David LeShana, *Quakers in California* (Newberg, Oreg.: Barclay Press, 1969); Ralph Beebe, *A Garden of the Lord: A History of Oregon Yearly Meeting of Friends Church* (Newberg, Oreg.: Barclay Press, 1968); and, on Alaska, Arthur Roberts, *Tomorrow Is Growing Old: Stories of the Quakers in Alaska* (Newberg, Oreg.: Barclay Press, 1978). Philip Benjamin, *Philadelphia Quakers in an Age of Industrialism, 1870–1920* (Philadelphia: Temple University Press, 1976), is a model of the integration of social and religious history.

For Quakers outside the United States there is Arthur Dorland, *The Quakers in Canada* (Toronto: Ryerson Press, 1968); Levinus Painter, *Hill of Vision: The Story of the Quaker Movement in East Africa, 1902–1965* (Nairobi, Kenya: East Africa Yearly Meeting, 1966); and Harold Smuck, *Friends in East Africa* (Richmond, Ind.: 1987) on Kenyan Friends; Hiram H. Hilty, *Friends in Cuba* (Richmond, Ind.: Friends United Press, 1977); and Paul Enyart, *Friends in Central America* (Pasadena, Calif.: 1970). For other missionary-inspired Meetings outside the United States see Chapter 21.

H. Larry Ingle, *Quakers in Conflict: The Hicksite Reformation* (Nashville, Tenn.: University of Tennessee Press, 1986), is the best description of events in the separation. Robert Doherty, *The Hicksite Separation* (New Brunswick, N.J.: Rutgers University Press, 1967), is a sociological analysis. Edwin B. Bronner, *The Other Branch: London Yearly Meeting and the Hicksites* (London: Friends Historical Society, 1975), shows the response of British Friends to the schism. Richard Wood, "Evangelical Quakers in the Mississippi Valley" (Ph.D. diss., University of Minnesota, 1984), recounts the history of the Gurneyites in the Midwest. Thomas Hamm, *The Transformation of American Quakerism: Orthodox Friends, 1800–1907* (Bloomington: Indiana University Press, 1988), is a superb account of the impact of the Holiness movement on Friends. Mark Minear, *The Richmond Conference, 1887: A Quaker Drama Unfolds* (Richmond Ind.: Friends United Press, 1987), presents the personalities behind the adoption of the Richmond Confession of Faith.

Peter Brock, *Pioneers of the Peaceable Kingdom* (Princeton, N.J.: Princeton University Press, 1968), is the standard account of the peace Testimony from the 1650s until 1900.

Raynor Kelsey, *Friends and the Indians, 1655–1917* (Philadelphia: Associated Executive Committee of Friends on Indian Affairs, 1917), is the only general account. Clyde A. Milner II, *With Good Intentions: Quaker Work among the Pawnees, Otoes, and Omahas in the 1870s* (Lincoln: University of Nebraska Press), is the best monograph. Clyde Milner II and Floyd A. O'Neil, *Churchmen and the Western Indians, 1820–1920* (Norman: University of Oklahoma Press, 1985), has a chapter devoted to Albert K. Smiley and the Lake Mohonk conferences.

Margaret Bacon, *Mothers of Feminism: the Story of Quaker Women in America* (San Francisco: Harper & Row, 1986), is the only book devoted to Quaker feminists, but there are several articles and dissertations: Mary Maples Dunn, "Women of Light," in *Women of America: A History*, ed. Carol Ruth Berkin and Mary Beth Norton, (Boston: Houghton Mifflin, 1979), 114–38; Nancy Hewitt, "Feminist Friends: Agrarian Quakers and the Emergence of Women's Rights in America," *Feminist Studies* 12, no. 1 (Spring 1986); 27–50; and idem, *Women's Activism and Social Change* (Ithaca, N.Y.: Cornell University Press, 1984). Carol and John Stoneburner, ed., *Influence of Quaker Women on American History* (Lewiston, N.Y.: Mellen Press, 1986), presents a series of papers on Quaker women from a 1979 conference.

Many Quaker schools and colleges have commissioned histories; see notes to Chapter 18. General interpretations of Quaker education are Helen Hole, *Things Useful and Civil* (Richmond, Ind.: Friends United Press, 1980), and Howard Brinton, *Quaker Education in Theory and Practice* (Wallingford, Pa.: Pendle Hill, 1949). Useful now primarily for factual information are Thomas Woody, *Early Quaker Education in Pennsylvania* (New York: Teacher's College, Columbia University, 1920); idem, *Quaker Education in the Colony and State of New Jersey* (Philadelphia: University of Pennsylvania Press, 1923); Zora Klain, *Educational Activities of New England Quakers* (Philadelphia: Westbrook, 1928); idem, *Quaker Contributions to Education in North Carolina* (Philadelphia, 1924); and William Dunlap, *Quaker Education in Baltimore and Virginia Yearly Meetings* (Lancaster, Pa.: Science Press, 1936).

TWENTIETH-CENTURY QUAKERISM

The historiography of modern American Quakerism has still to be written. The best beginning place for research is in the various Quaker periodicals: *The American Friend, The Friends Intelligencer, The Friends Journal, Quaker Life, The Evangelical Friend, and Pendle Hill Pamphlets*. Each of the Yearly Meetings has a Discipline. Margaret Hirst, *Quakers in Peace and War* (London: Swarthmore Press, 1923), summarized the peace Testimony to the end of World War I. E. W. Orr, *Quakers in Peace and War, 1920–1967* (Sussex, Eng.: W. J. Offord, 1974), continued the story until the Vietnam War. Leonard Kenworthy, ed., *Living in the Light: Some Pioneers of the Twentieth Century, Vol. 1: Quakers in the United States of America* (Kennett Square, Pa.: Friends General Conference and Quaker Publications, 1984), is a series of biographies. John Ormerod Greenwood, *Quaker Encounters*, 3 vols. (York, Eng.: Sessions, 1975–78), is a history of English Quaker foreign activities that shows the connection between missions and relief activities. There is nothing comparable for American missions. The last summary is Christina Jones, *American Friends in World Missions* (Richmond, Ind.: Printed by Brethren Publishing House for the American Friends Board of Missions, 1946). Historical information about Quaker relief can be found in Rufus Jones, *A Service of Love in War Time: American Friends' Relief Work in Europe, 1917–1919* (New York:

MacMillan, 1920); Mary Hoxie Jones, *Swords into Ploughshares: An Account of the American Friends Service Committee, 1917–1939* (New York: Macmillan, 1937); John Forbes, *The Quaker Star under Seven Flags, 1917–1927* (Philadelphia: University of Pennsylvania Press, 1962); and Clarence Pickett, *For More Than Bread* (Boston: Little, Brown, 1953). Clarence H. Yarrow, *The Quaker Experience in International Conciliation* (New Haven: Yale University Press, 1979), discusses work in the Cold War, the Nigerian Civil War, and India and Pakistan. E. Raymond Wilson, *Uphill for Peace: Quaker Impact on Congress* (Richmond, Ind.: Friends United Press, 1975), describes the Friends Committee on National Legislation. The biographies of Rufus Jones and Henry Cadbury, cited in the text, also contain valuable information.

INDEX

Page numbers in **bold face** indicate locations of biographical entries.

About the Authors

HUGH BARBOUR is Professor of Religion at Earlham College and Professor of Church History at Earlham School of Religion. His previous books include *Quakers in Puritan England, Slavery and Theology: Writings of Seven Quaker Reformers*, and *Reading and Understanding the Old Testament*.

J. WILLIAM FROST is Howard M. and Charles F. Jenkins Professor of Quaker History and Research and Director of the Friends Historical Library, Swarthmore College. He is the author of *The Quaker Family in Colonial America* and editor of numerous volumes, including *Quaker Origins of Antislavery* and *The Keithian Controversy in Early Pennsylvania*.